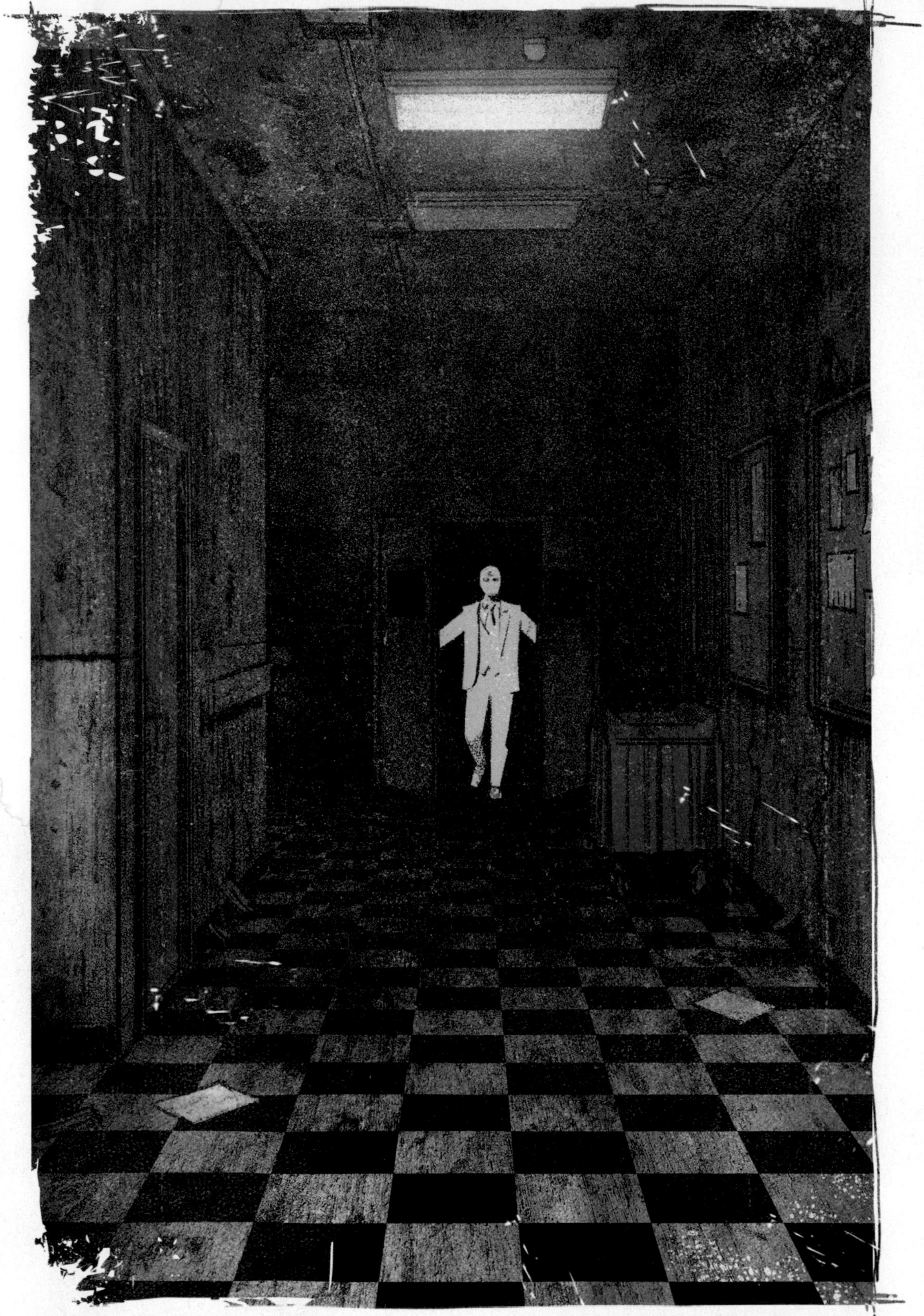

COLLECTION EDITOR: JENNIFER GRÜNWALD
ASSISTANT EDITOR: DANIEL KIRCHHOFFER
ASSISTANT MANAGING EDITOR: MAIA LOY
ASSOCIATE MANAGER, TALENT RELATIONS: LISA MONTALBANO
VP PRODUCTION & SPECIAL PROJECTS: JEFF YOUNGQUIST
SVP PRINT, SALES & MARKETING: DAVID GABRIEL
BOOK DESIGN: JAY BOWEN
EDITOR IN CHIEF: C.B. CEBULSKI

MERCENARY MARC SPECTOR DIED IN EGYPT UNDER A STATUE OF THE MOON GOD KHONSHU. IN
THE SHADOW OF THE ANCIENT DEITY, MARC RETURNED TO LIFE AND TOOK ON KHONSHU'S ASPECT
TO FIGHT CRIME FOR HIS OWN REDEMPTION. HE WENT COMPLETELY INSANE AND DISAPPEARED
FOR A TIME, BUT RETURNED TO PROTECT THOSE WHO TRAVEL BY NIGHT. AT LEAST HE THINKS THAT'S
WHAT HAPPENED...

MOON KNIGHT

THE COMPLETE COLLECTION

WRITER
JEFF LEMIRE

ARTIST
GREG SMALLWOOD

COLOR ARTIST
JORDIE BELLAIRE

STEVEN GRANT ARTISTS, #5-9
WILFREDO TORRES & MICHAEL GARLAND

JAKE LOCKLEY ARTIST, #5-9
FRANCESCO FRANCAVILLA

THE MOON KNIGHT ARTIST, #5-9
JAMES STOKOE

LETTERER
VC's CORY PETIT

COVER ART
GREG SMALLWOOD

ASSISTANT EDITOR
KATHLEEN WISNESKI

EDITOR
JAKE THOMAS

MOON KNIGHT BY LEMIRE & SMALLWOOD: THE COMPLETE COLLECTION. Contains material originally published in magazine form as MOON KNIGHT (2016) #1-14. Third printing 2022. ISBN 978-1-302-93363-0. Published by MARVEL WORLDWIDE, INC., a subsidiary of MARVEL ENTERTAINMENT, LLC. OFFICE OF PUBLICATION: 1290 Avenue of the Americas, New York, NY 10104. © 2021 MARVEL No similarity between any of the names, characters, persons, and/or institutions in this book with those of any living or dead person or institution is intended, and any such similarity which may exist is purely coincidental. **Printed in Canada.** KEVIN FEIGE, Chief Creative Officer; DAN BUCKLEY, President, Marvel Entertainment; DAVID BOGART, Associate Publisher & SVP of Talent Affairs; TOM BREVOORT, VP, Executive Editor; NICK LOWE, Executive Editor, VP of Content, Digital Publishing; DAVID GABRIEL, VP of Print & Digital Publishing; SVEN LARSEN, VP of Licensed Publishing; MARK ANNUNZIATO, VP of Planning & Forecasting; JEFF YOUNGQUIST, VP of Production & Special Projects; ALEX MORALES, Director of Publishing Operations; DAN EDINGTON, Director of Editorial Operations; RICKEY PURDIN, Director of Talent Relations; JENNIFER GRÜNWALD, Director of Production & Special Projects; SUSAN CRESPI, Production Manager; STAN LEE, Chairman Emeritus. For information regarding advertising in Marvel Comics or on Marvel.com, please contact Vit DeBellis, Custom Solutions & Integrated Advertising Manager, at vdebellis@marvel.com. For Marvel subscription inquiries, please call 888-511-5480. **Manufactured between 8/12/2022 and 9/13/2022 by SOLISCO PRINTERS, SCOTT, QC, CANADA.**

10 9 8 7 6 5 4 3

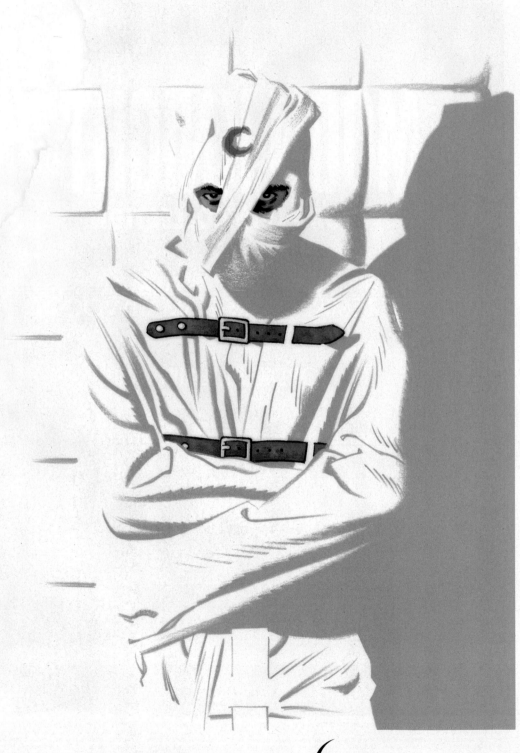

WELCOME TO NEW EGYPT
PART ONE

1

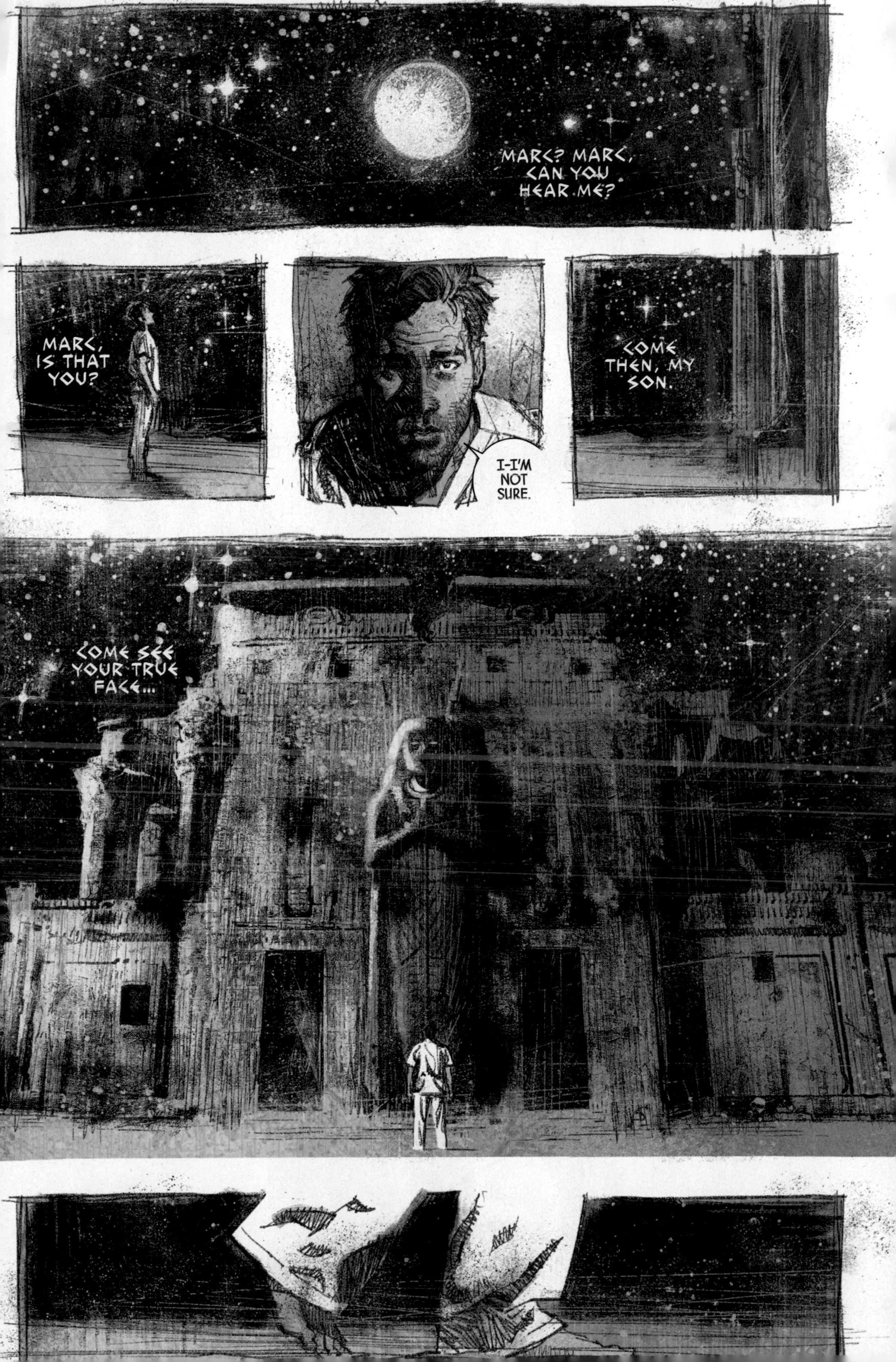
MARC? MARC, CAN YOU HEAR ME?
MARC, IS THAT YOU?
I-I'M NOT SURE.
COME THEN, MY SON.
COME SEE YOUR TRUE FACE...

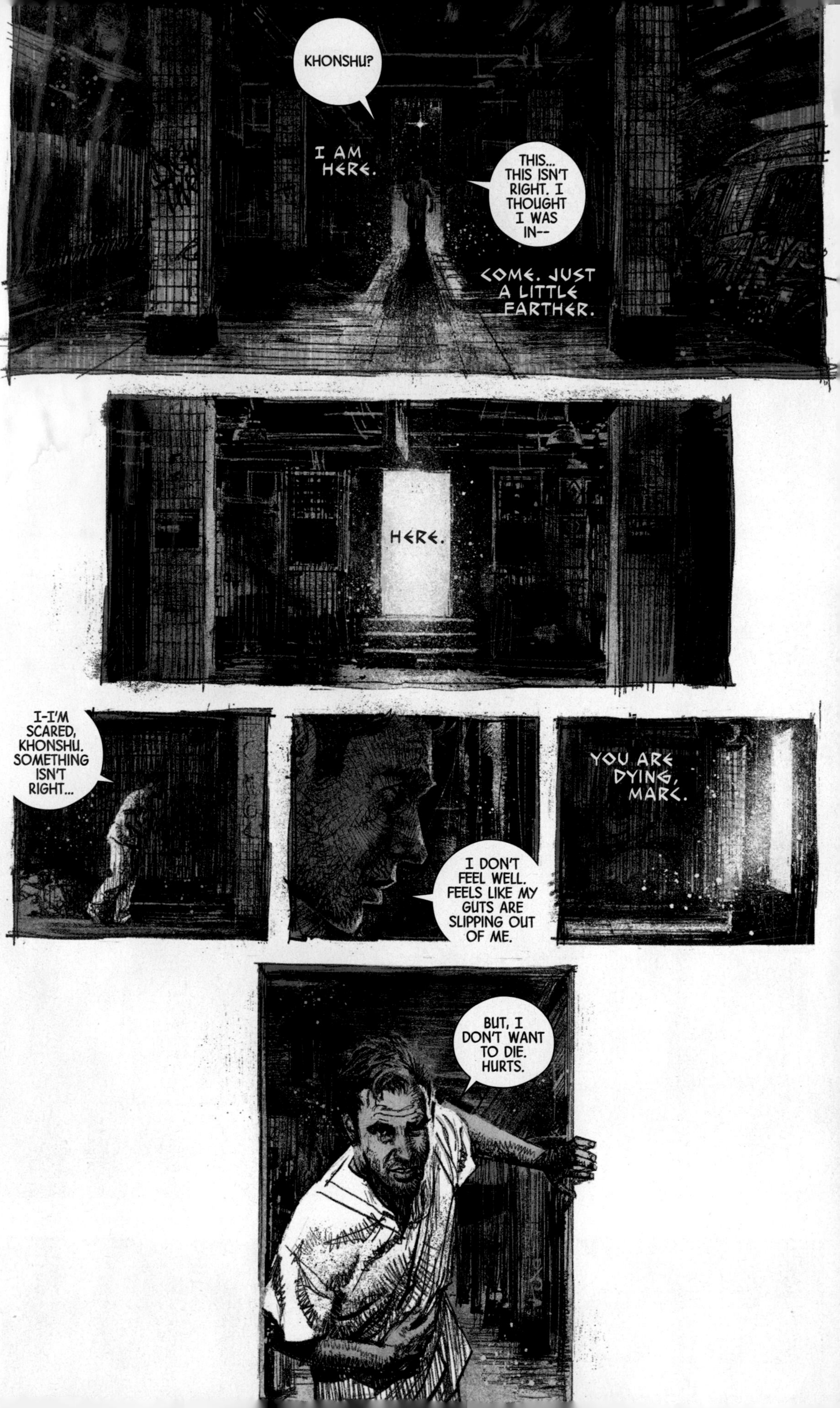
KHONSHU?
I AM HERE.
THIS... THIS ISN'T RIGHT. I THOUGHT I WAS IN--
COME. JUST A LITTLE FARTHER.
HERE.
I-I'M SCARED, KHONSHU. SOMETHING ISN'T RIGHT...
I DON'T FEEL WELL. FEELS LIKE MY GUTS ARE SLIPPING OUT OF ME.
YOU ARE DYING, MARC.
BUT, I DON'T WANT TO DIE. HURTS.

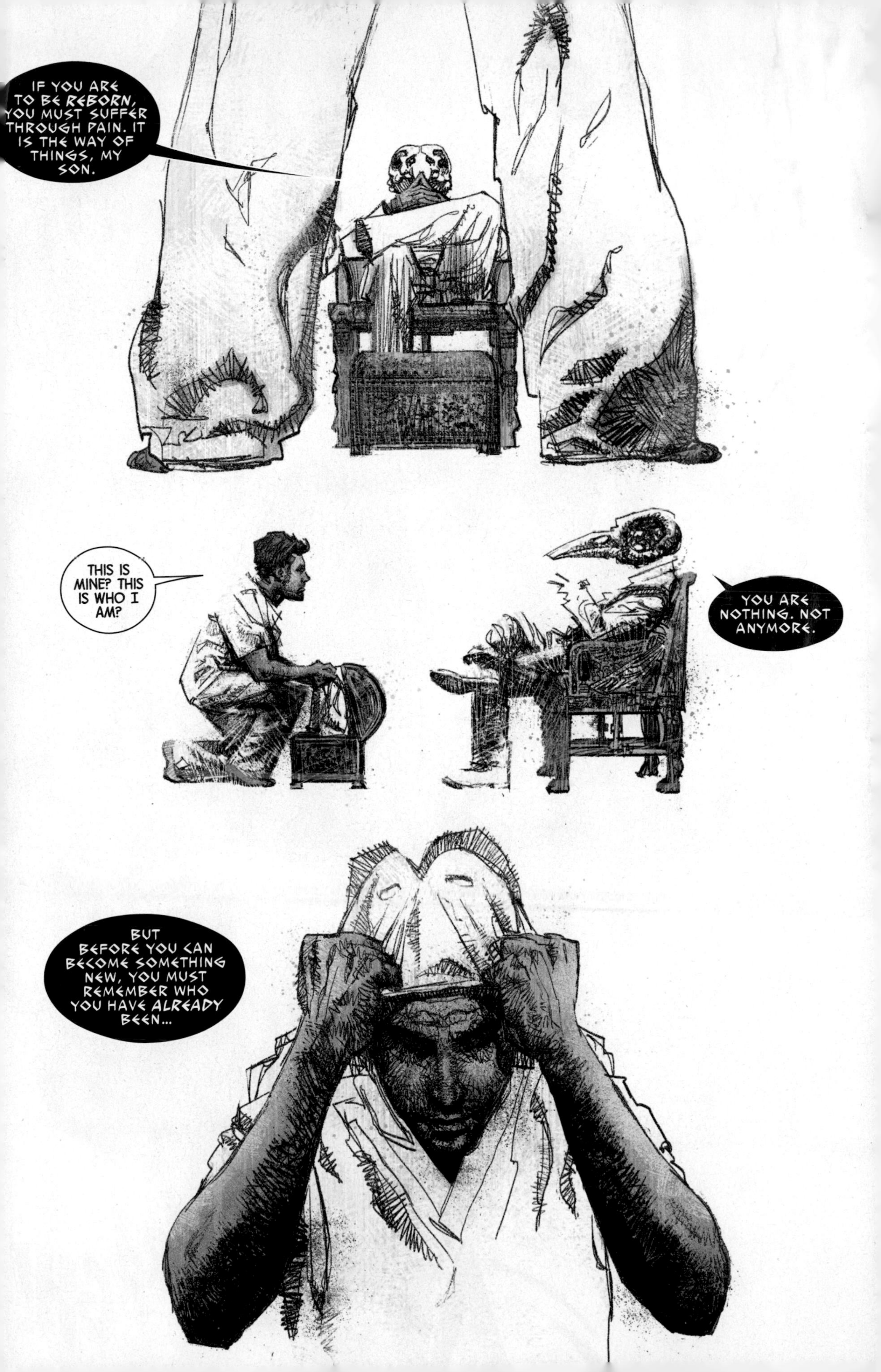
IF YOU ARE TO BE REBORN, YOU MUST SUFFER THROUGH PAIN. IT IS THE WAY OF THINGS, MY SON.
THIS IS MINE? THIS IS WHO I AM?
YOU ARE NOTHING. NOT ANYMORE.
BUT BEFORE YOU CAN BECOME SOMETHING NEW, YOU MUST REMEMBER WHO YOU HAVE ALREADY BEEN...

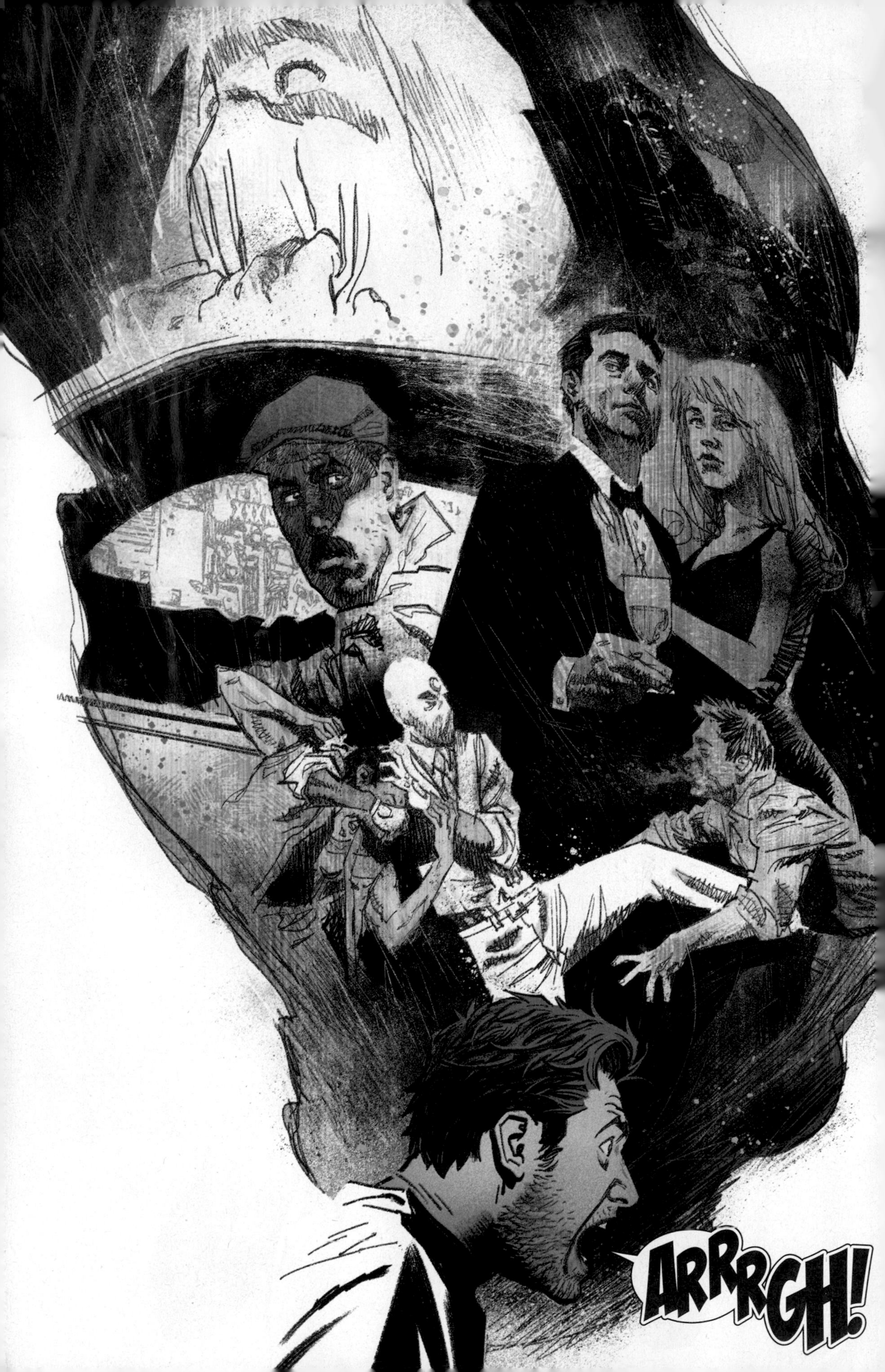
ARRRGH!

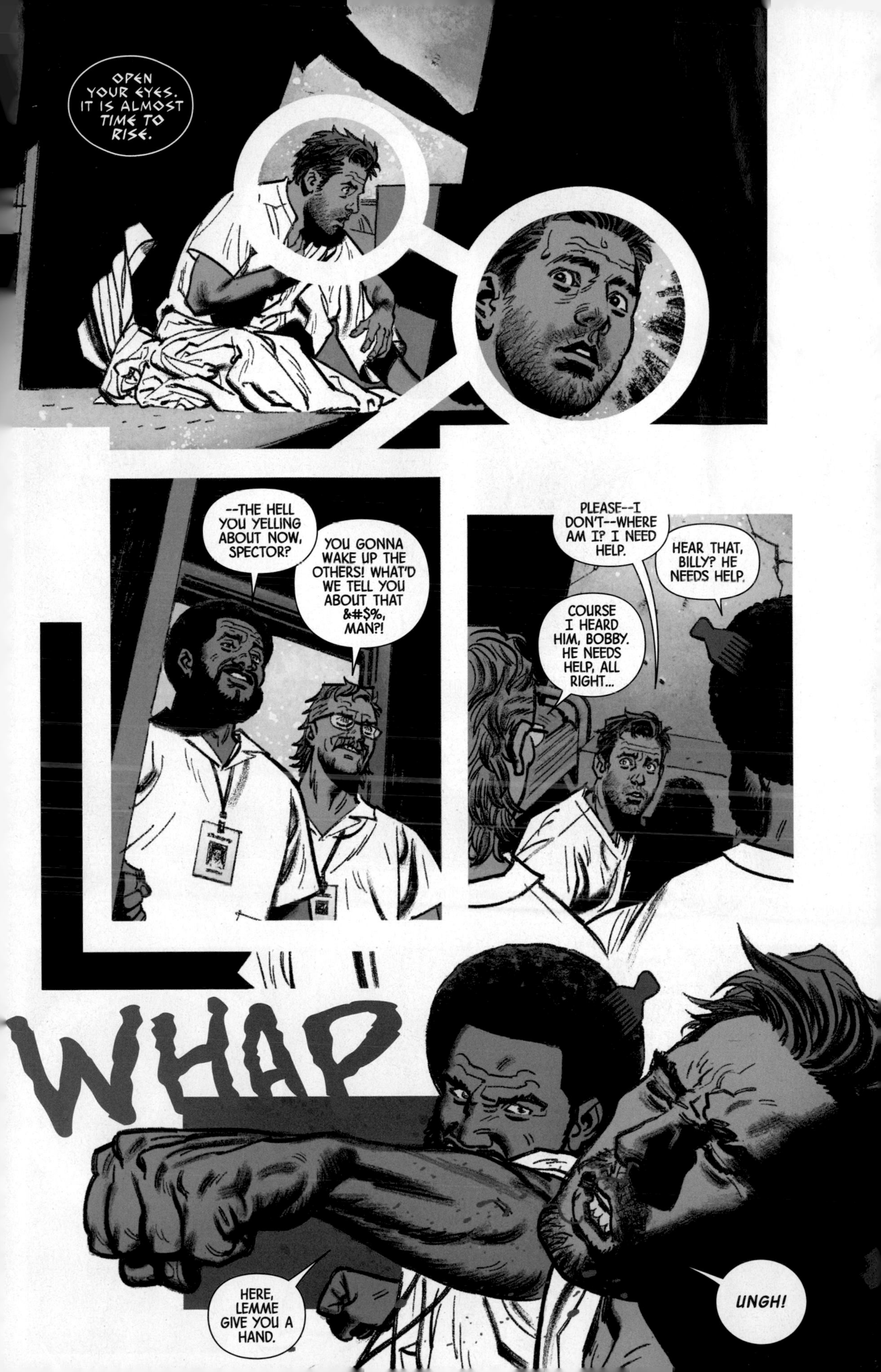
OPEN YOUR EYES. IT IS ALMOST TIME TO RISE.
--THE HELL YOU YELLING ABOUT NOW, SPECTOR?
YOU GONNA WAKE UP THE OTHERS! WHAT'D WE TELL YOU ABOUT THAT &#$%, MAN?!
PLEASE--I DON'T--WHERE AM I? I NEED HELP.
HEAR THAT, BILLY? HE NEEDS HELP.
COURSE I HEARD HIM, BOBBY. HE NEEDS HELP, ALL RIGHT...
WHAP
HERE, LEMME GIVE YOU A HAND.
UNGH!

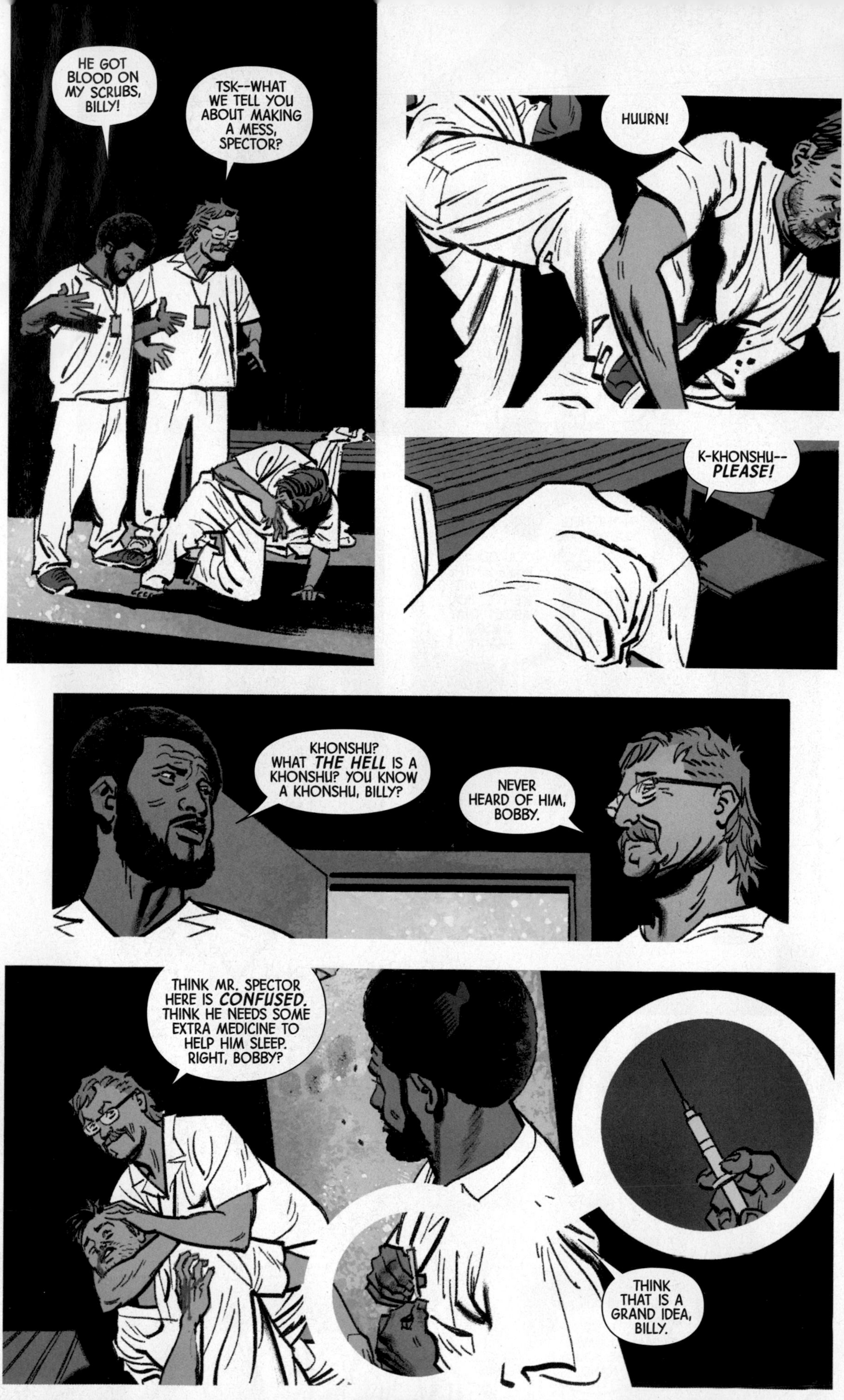
HE GOT BLOOD ON MY SCRUBS, BILLY!
TSK--WHAT WE TELL YOU ABOUT MAKING A MESS, SPECTOR?
HUURN!
K-KHONSHU-- PLEASE!
KHONSHU? WHAT THE HELL IS A KHONSHU? YOU KNOW A KHONSHU, BILLY?
NEVER HEARD OF HIM, BOBBY.
THINK MR. SPECTOR HERE IS CONFUSED. THINK HE NEEDS SOME EXTRA MEDICINE TO HELP HIM SLEEP. RIGHT, BOBBY?
THINK THAT IS A GRAND IDEA, BILLY.

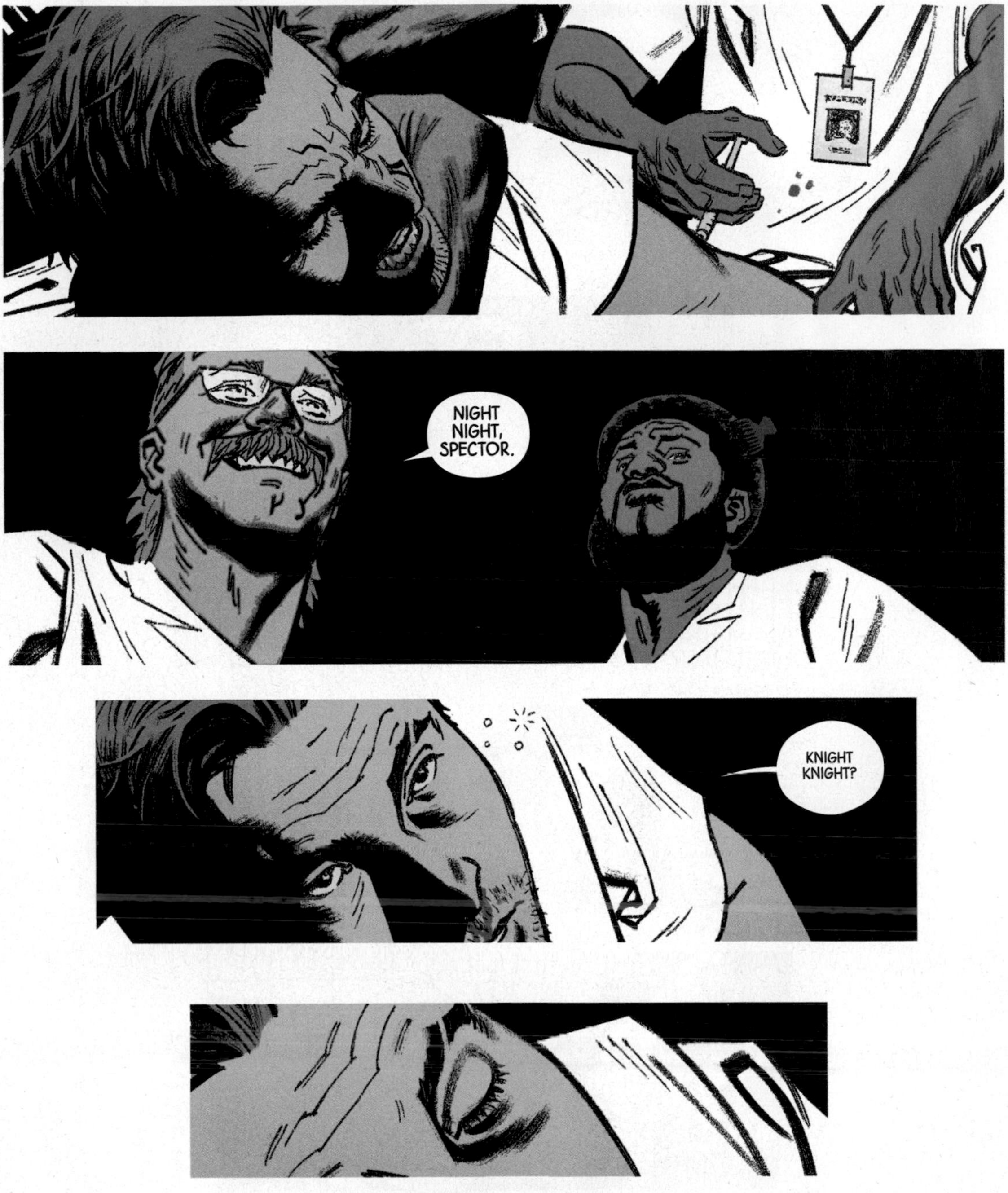
NIGHT NIGHT, SPECTOR.
KNIGHT KNIGHT?

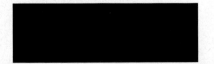

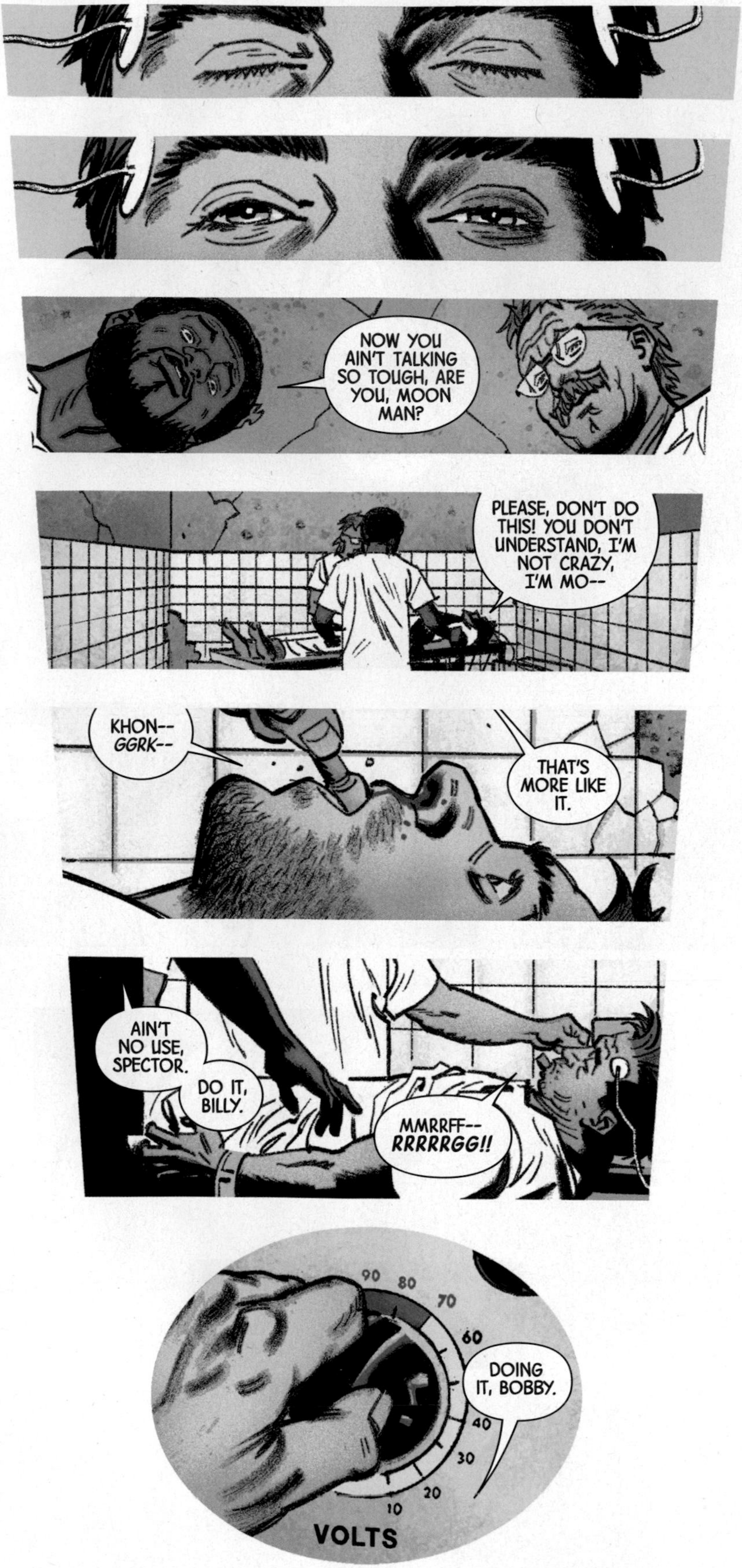
NOW YOU AIN'T TALKING SO TOUGH, ARE YOU, MOON MAN?
PLEASE, DON'T DO THIS! YOU DON'T UNDERSTAND, I'M NOT CRAZY, I'M MO--
KHON-- GGRK--
THAT'S MORE LIKE IT.
AIN'T NO USE, SPECTOR.
DO IT, BILLY.
MMRRFF-- RRRRRGG!!
90 80 70 60 40 30 20 10
VOLTS
DOING IT, BOBBY.

MMRGH!!!
70 60 50 40 30 20 10 200 190 180
MIN
MRRF...
HEH HEH...

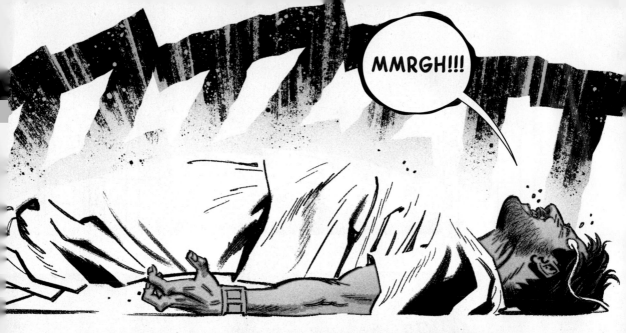

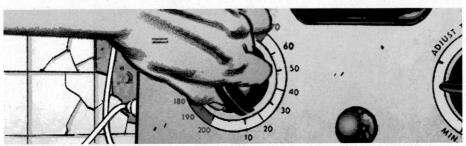

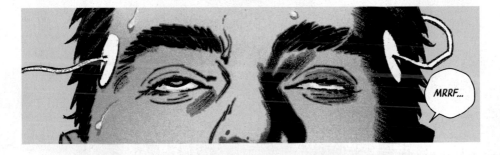

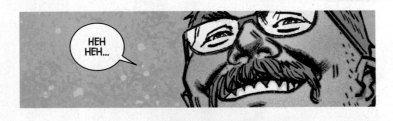

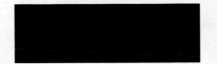

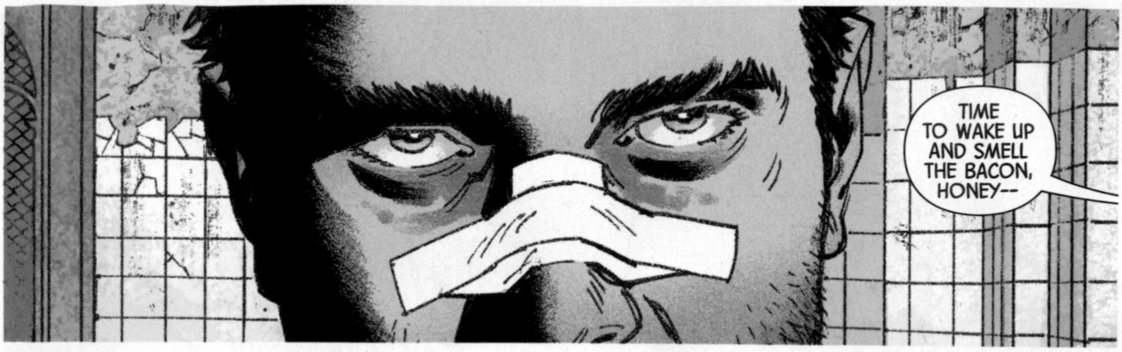
TIME TO WAKE UP AND SMELL THE BACON, HONEY--

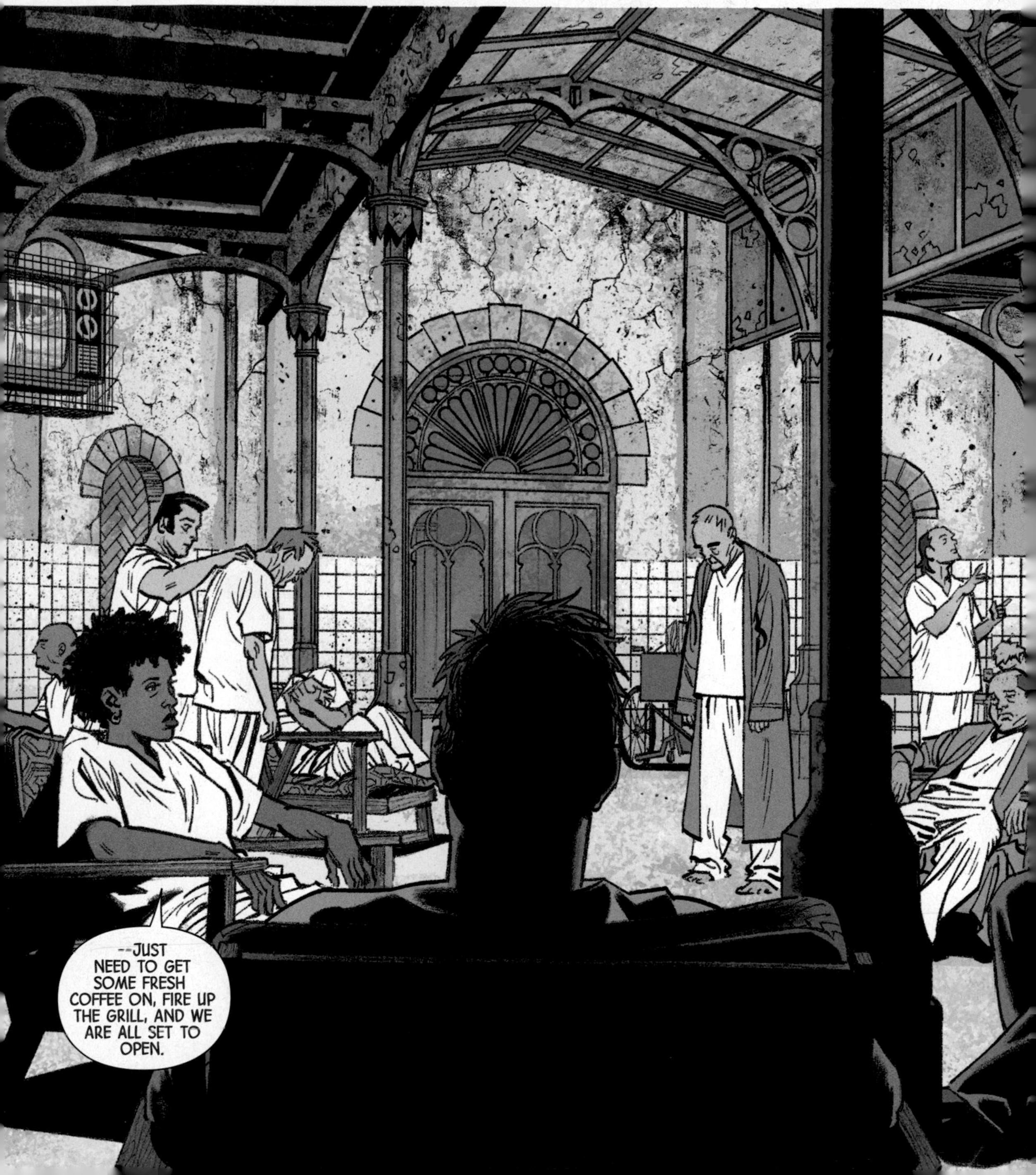
--JUST NEED TO GET SOME FRESH COFFEE ON, FIRE UP THE GRILL, AND WE ARE ALL SET TO OPEN.

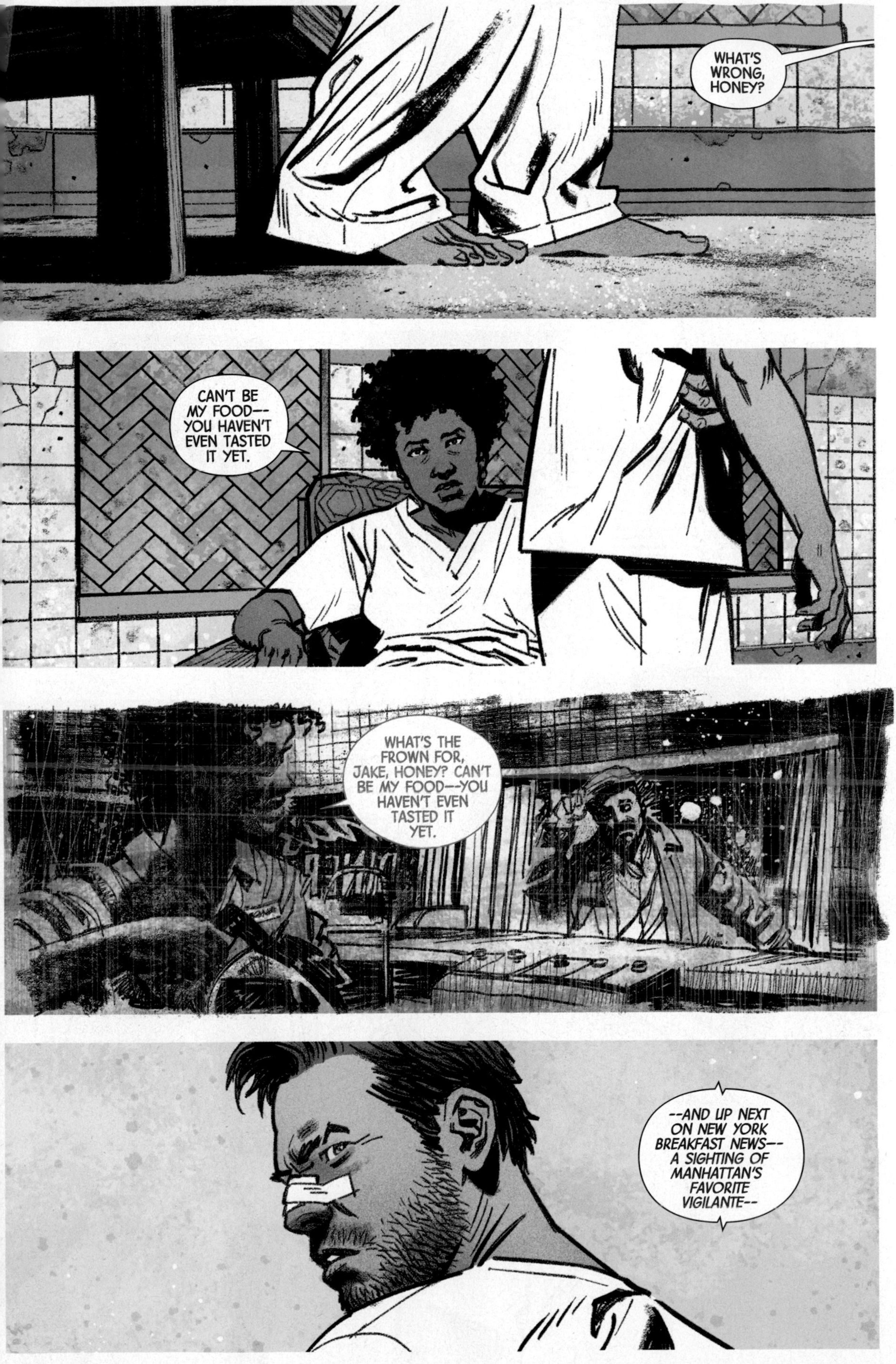
WHAT'S WRONG, HONEY?
CAN'T BE MY FOOD-- YOU HAVEN'T EVEN TASTED IT YET.
WHAT'S THE FROWN FOR, JAKE, HONEY? CAN'T BE MY FOOD--YOU HAVEN'T EVEN TASTED IT YET.
--AND UP NEXT ON NEW YORK BREAKFAST NEWS-- A SIGHTING OF MANHATTAN'S FAVORITE VIGILANTE--

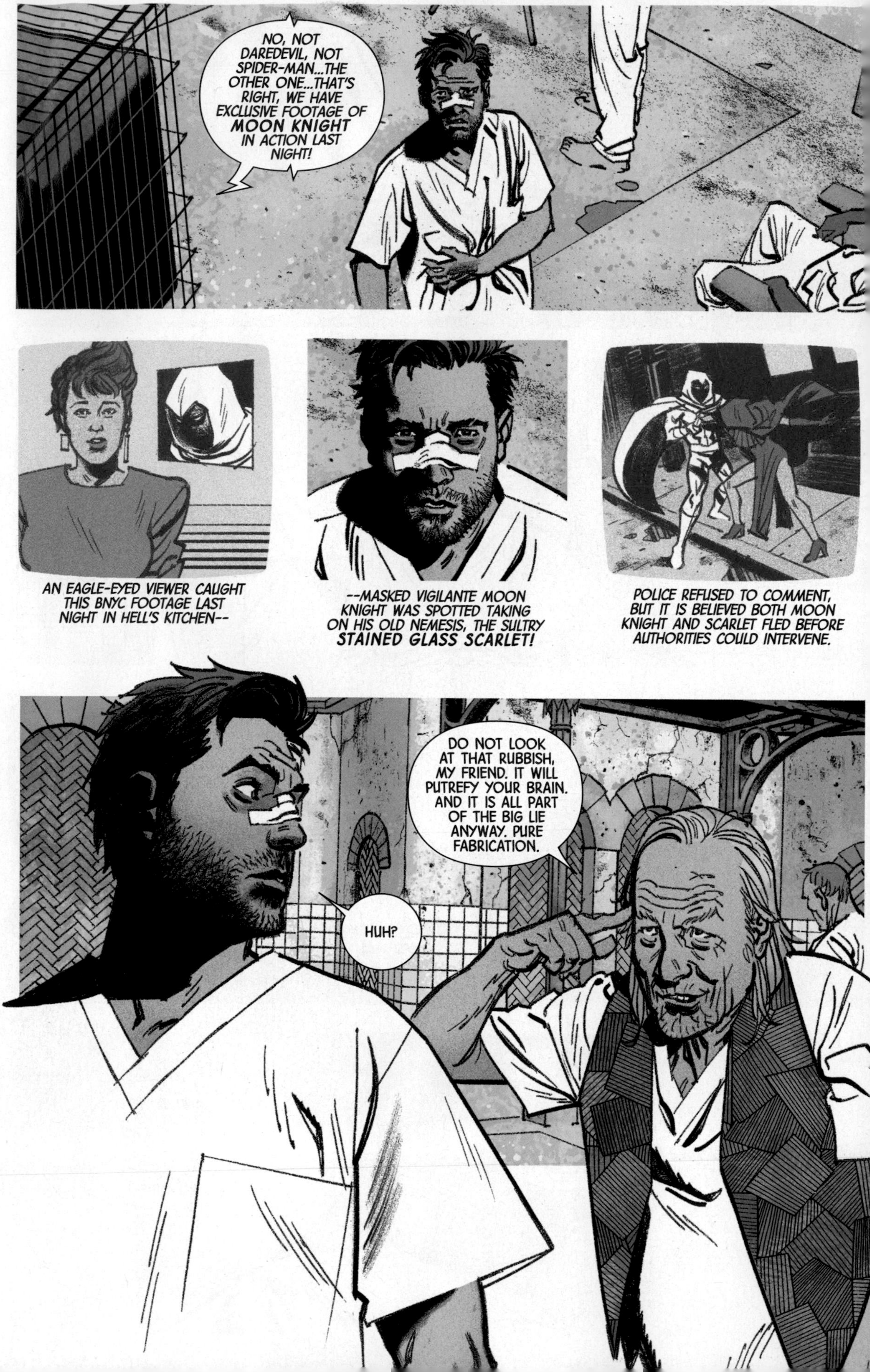

NO, NOT DAREDEVIL, NOT SPIDER-MAN...THE OTHER ONE...THAT'S RIGHT, WE HAVE EXCLUSIVE FOOTAGE OF MOON KNIGHT IN ACTION LAST NIGHT!
AN EAGLE-EYED VIEWER CAUGHT THIS BNYC FOOTAGE LAST NIGHT IN HELL'S KITCHEN--
--MASKED VIGILANTE MOON KNIGHT WAS SPOTTED TAKING ON HIS OLD NEMESIS, THE SULTRY STAINED GLASS SCARLET!
POLICE REFUSED TO COMMENT, BUT IT IS BELIEVED BOTH MOON KNIGHT AND SCARLET FLED BEFORE AUTHORITIES COULD INTERVENE.
DO NOT LOOK AT THAT RUBBISH, MY FRIEND. IT WILL PUTREFY YOUR BRAIN. AND IT IS ALL PART OF THE BIG LIE ANYWAY. PURE FABRICATION.
HUH?

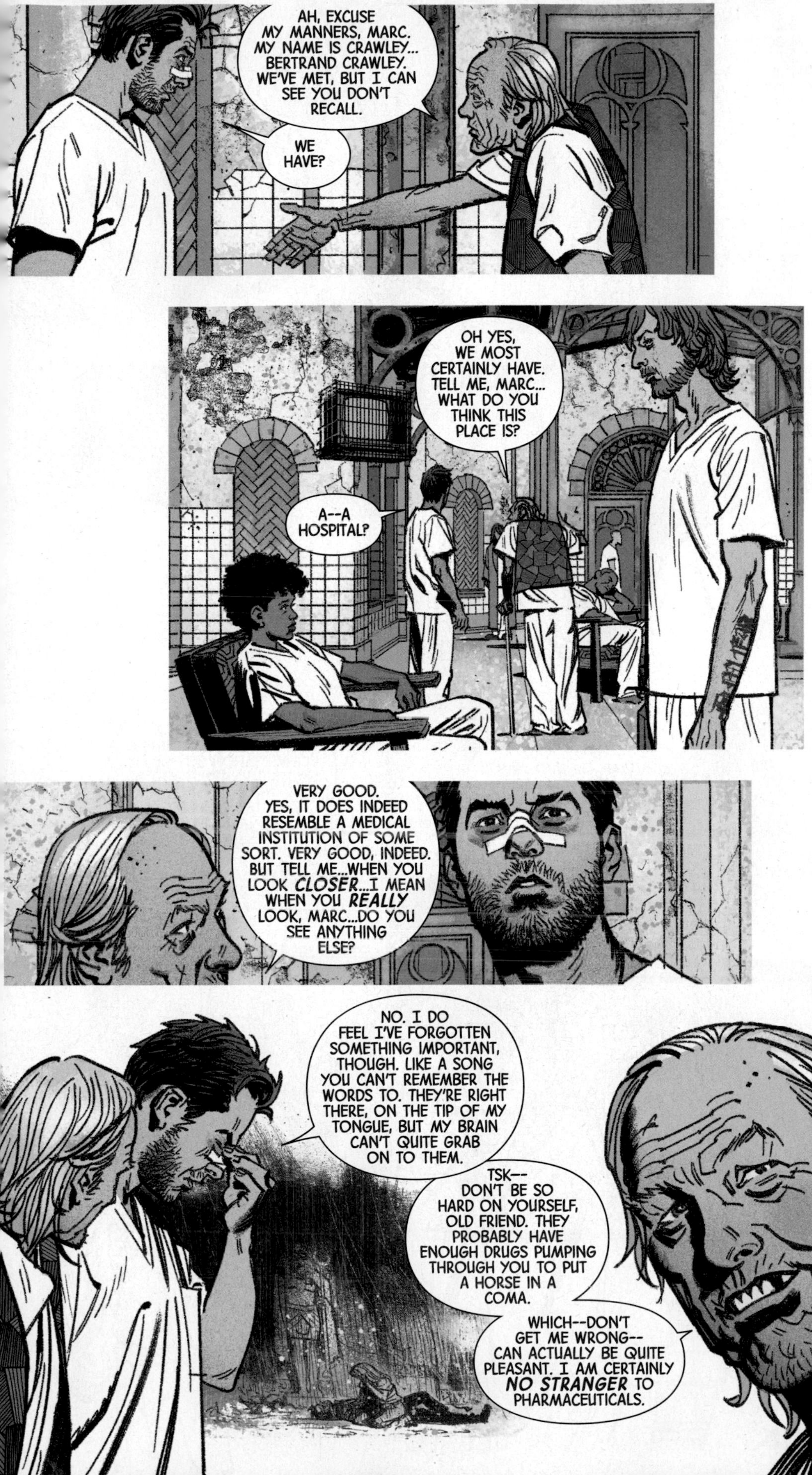
AH, EXCUSE MY MANNERS, MARC. MY NAME IS CRAWLEY... BERTRAND CRAWLEY. WE'VE MET, BUT I CAN SEE YOU DON'T RECALL.
WE HAVE?
OH YES, WE MOST CERTAINLY HAVE. TELL ME, MARC... WHAT DO YOU THINK THIS PLACE IS?
A--A HOSPITAL?
VERY GOOD. YES, IT DOES INDEED RESEMBLE A MEDICAL INSTITUTION OF SOME SORT. VERY GOOD, INDEED. BUT TELL ME...WHEN YOU LOOK CLOSER...I MEAN WHEN YOU REALLY LOOK, MARC...DO YOU SEE ANYTHING ELSE?
NO. I DO FEEL I'VE FORGOTTEN SOMETHING IMPORTANT, THOUGH. LIKE A SONG YOU CAN'T REMEMBER THE WORDS TO. THEY'RE RIGHT THERE, ON THE TIP OF MY TONGUE, BUT MY BRAIN CAN'T QUITE GRAB ON TO THEM.
TSK-- DON'T BE SO HARD ON YOURSELF, OLD FRIEND. THEY PROBABLY HAVE ENOUGH DRUGS PUMPING THROUGH YOU TO PUT A HORSE IN A COMA.
WHICH--DON'T GET ME WRONG--CAN ACTUALLY BE QUITE PLEASANT. I AM CERTAINLY NO STRANGER TO PHARMACEUTICALS.

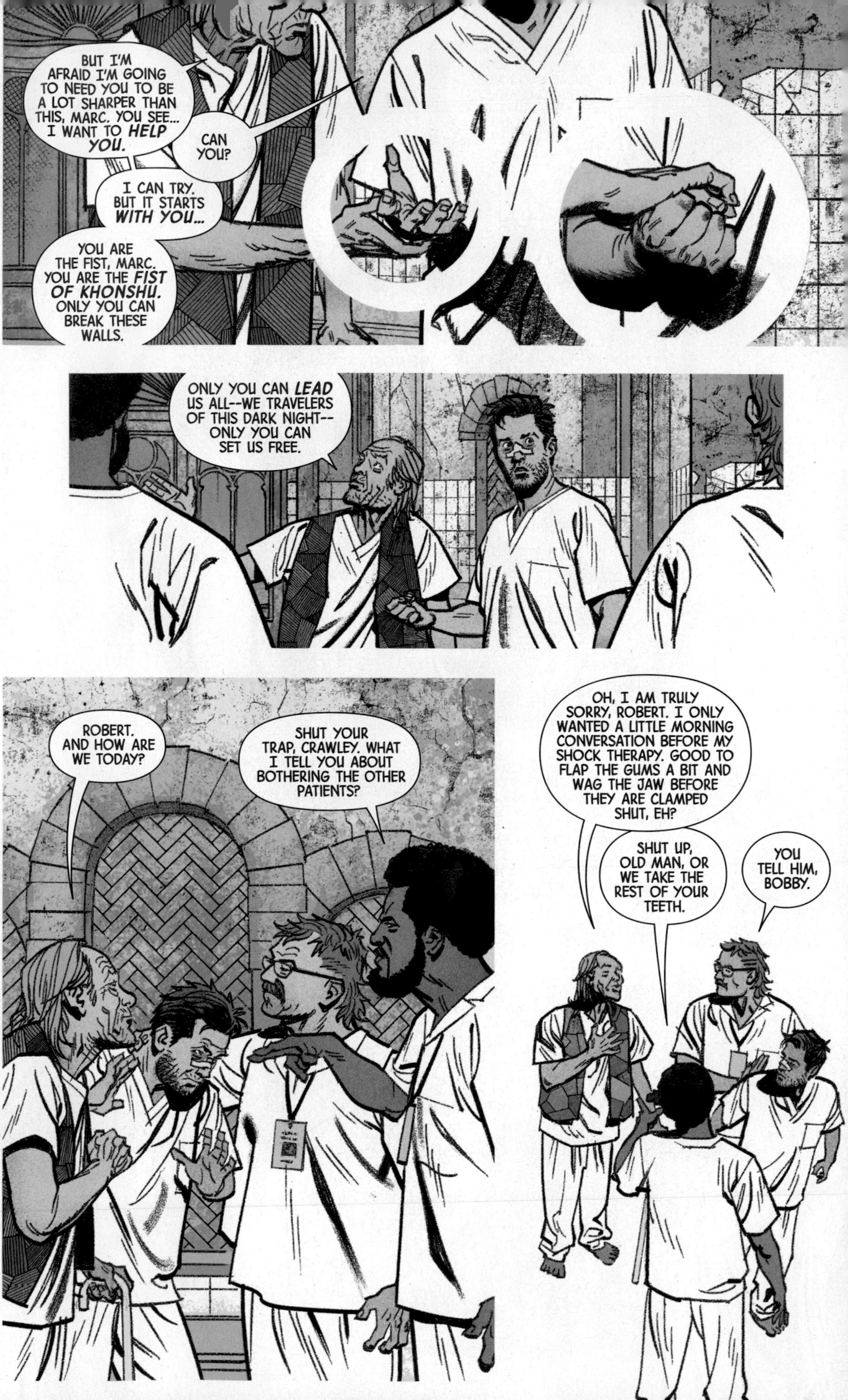
BUT I'M AFRAID I'M GOING TO NEED YOU TO BE A LOT SHARPER THAN THIS, MARC. YOU SEE... I WANT TO HELP YOU.
CAN YOU?
I CAN TRY. BUT IT STARTS WITH YOU...
YOU ARE THE FIST, MARC. YOU ARE THE FIST OF KHONSHU. ONLY YOU CAN BREAK THESE WALLS.
ONLY YOU CAN LEAD US ALL--WE TRAVELERS OF THIS DARK NIGHT--ONLY YOU CAN SET US FREE.
ROBERT. AND HOW ARE WE TODAY?
SHUT YOUR TRAP, CRAWLEY. WHAT I TELL YOU ABOUT BOTHERING THE OTHER PATIENTS?
OH, I AM TRULY SORRY, ROBERT. I ONLY WANTED A LITTLE MORNING CONVERSATION BEFORE MY SHOCK THERAPY. GOOD TO FLAP THE GUMS A BIT AND WAG THE JAW BEFORE THEY ARE CLAMPED SHUT, EH?
SHUT UP, OLD MAN, OR WE TAKE THE REST OF YOUR TEETH.
YOU TELL HIM, BOBBY.

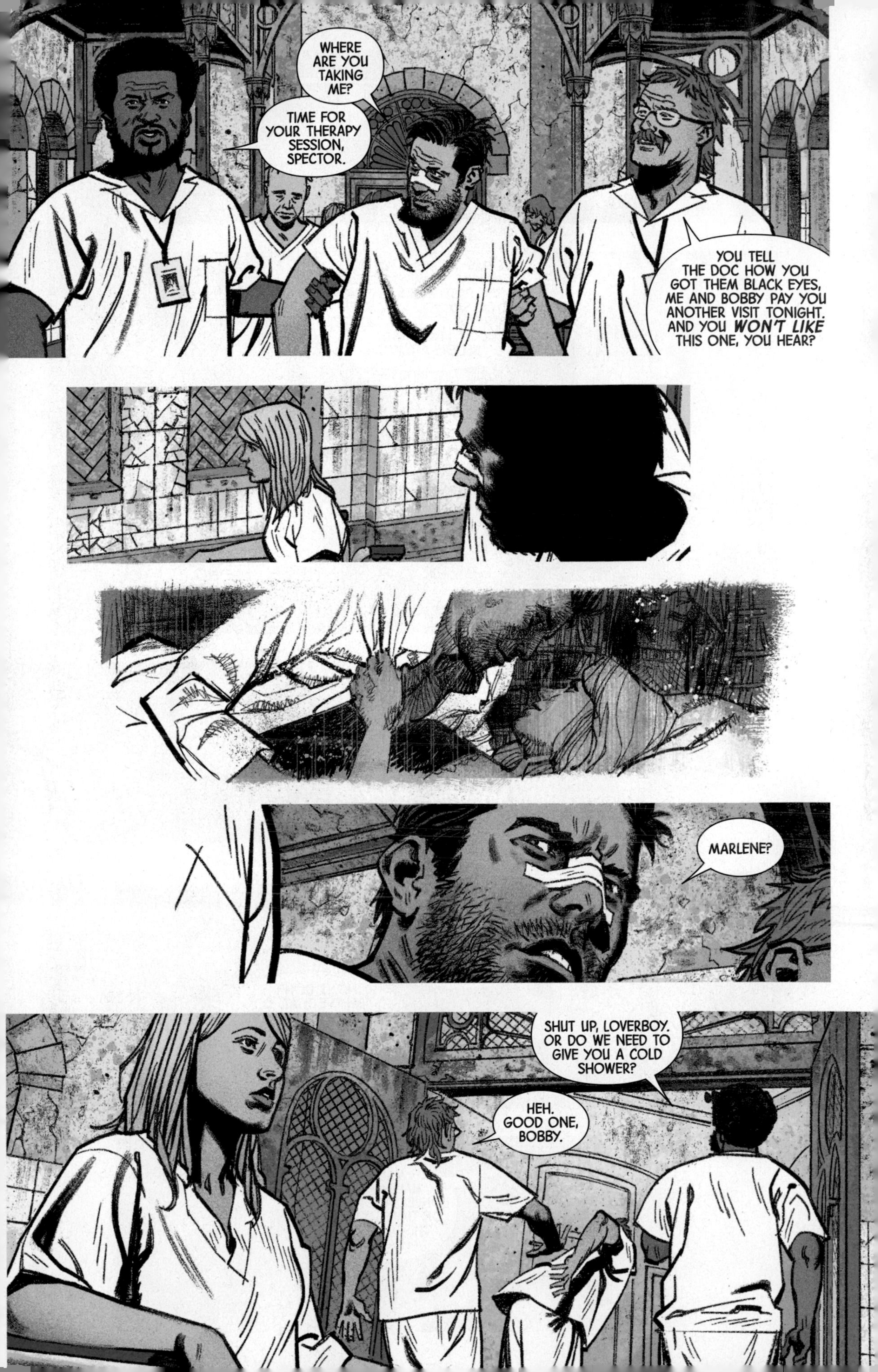
WHERE ARE YOU TAKING ME?
TIME FOR YOUR THERAPY SESSION, SPECTOR.
YOU TELL THE DOC HOW YOU GOT THEM BLACK EYES, ME AND BOBBY PAY YOU ANOTHER VISIT TONIGHT. AND YOU *WON'T LIKE* THIS ONE, YOU HEAR?
MARLENE?
SHUT UP, LOVERBOY. OR DO WE NEED TO GIVE YOU A COLD SHOWER?
HEH. GOOD ONE, BOBBY.

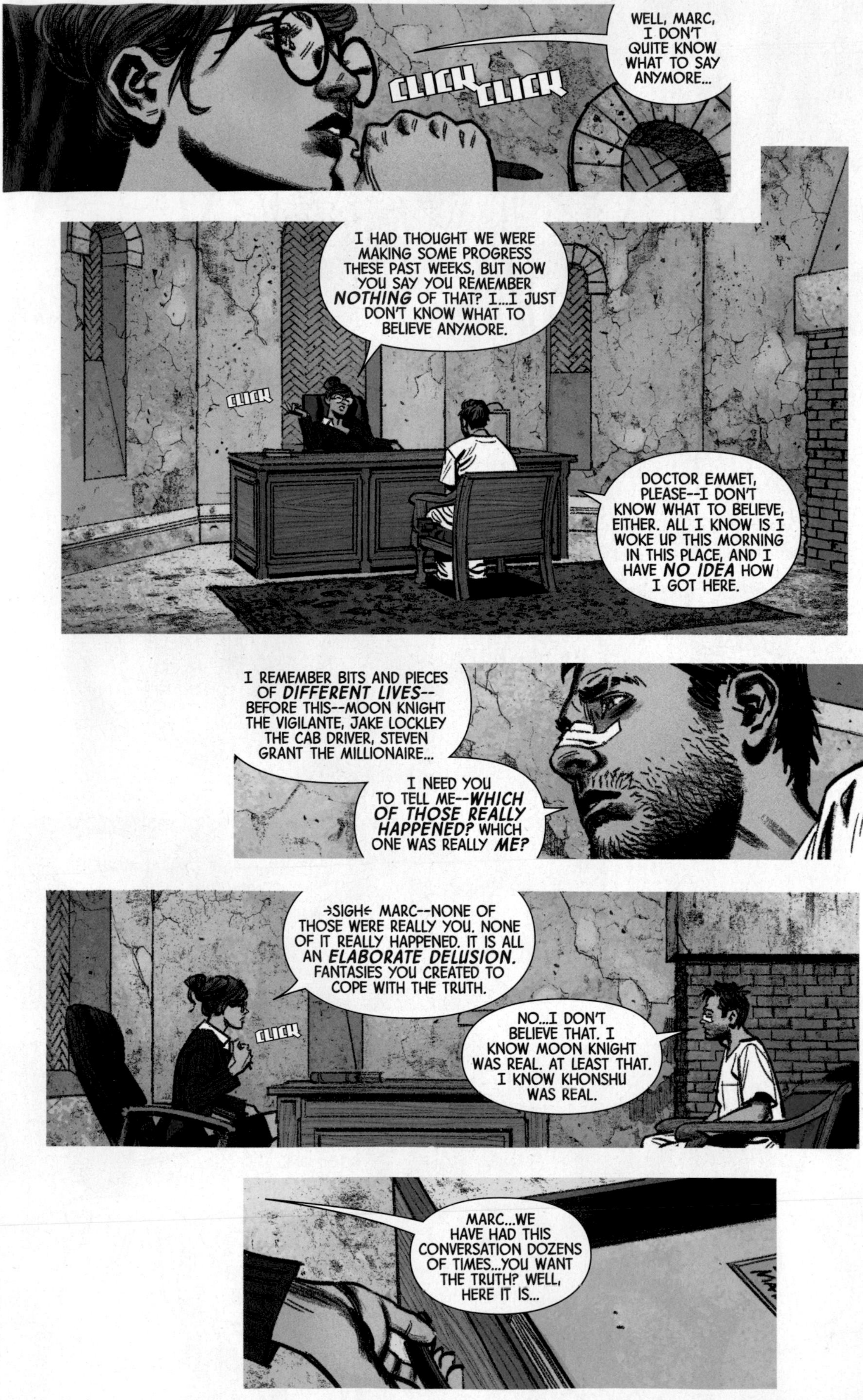
WELL, MARC, I DON'T QUITE KNOW WHAT TO SAY ANYMORE...
CLICK CLICK
I HAD THOUGHT WE WERE MAKING SOME PROGRESS THESE PAST WEEKS, BUT NOW YOU SAY YOU REMEMBER NOTHING OF THAT? I...I JUST DON'T KNOW WHAT TO BELIEVE ANYMORE.
CLICK
DOCTOR EMMET, PLEASE--I DON'T KNOW WHAT TO BELIEVE, EITHER. ALL I KNOW IS I WOKE UP THIS MORNING IN THIS PLACE, AND I HAVE NO IDEA HOW I GOT HERE.
I REMEMBER BITS AND PIECES OF DIFFERENT LIVES-- BEFORE THIS--MOON KNIGHT THE VIGILANTE, JAKE LOCKLEY THE CAB DRIVER, STEVEN GRANT THE MILLIONAIRE...
I NEED YOU TO TELL ME--WHICH OF THOSE REALLY HAPPENED? WHICH ONE WAS REALLY ME?
SIGH MARC--NONE OF THOSE WERE REALLY YOU. NONE OF IT REALLY HAPPENED. IT IS ALL AN ELABORATE DELUSION. FANTASIES YOU CREATED TO COPE WITH THE TRUTH.
CLICK
NO...I DON'T BELIEVE THAT. I KNOW MOON KNIGHT WAS REAL. AT LEAST THAT. I KNOW KHONSHU WAS REAL.
MARC...WE HAVE HAD THIS CONVERSATION DOZENS OF TIMES...YOU WANT THE TRUTH? WELL, HERE IT IS...

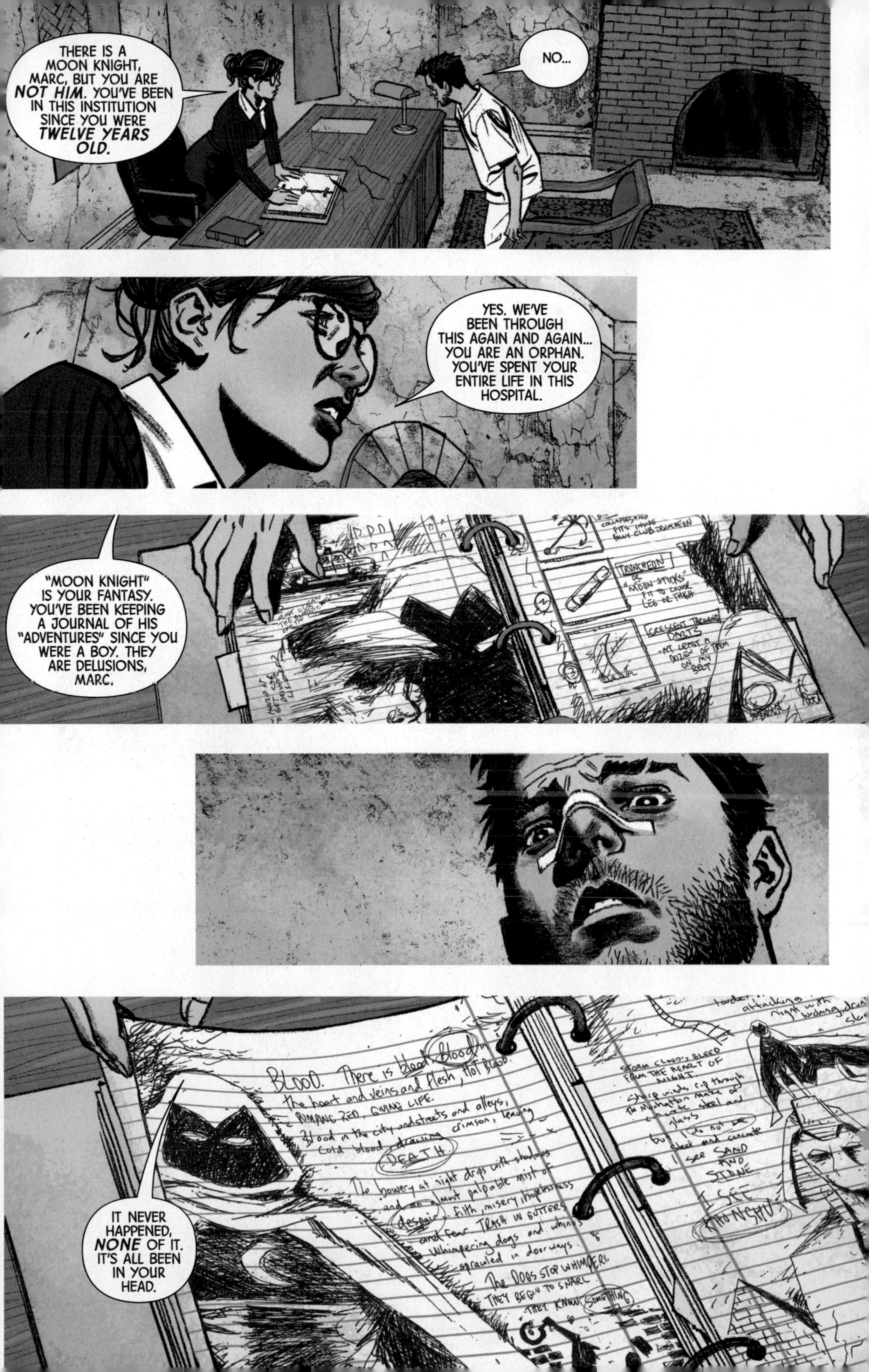
THERE IS A MOON KNIGHT, MARC, BUT YOU ARE NOT HIM. YOU'VE BEEN IN THIS INSTITUTION SINCE YOU WERE TWELVE YEARS OLD.
NO...
YES. WE'VE BEEN THROUGH THIS AGAIN AND AGAIN... YOU ARE AN ORPHAN. YOU'VE SPENT YOUR ENTIRE LIFE IN THIS HOSPITAL.
"MOON KNIGHT" IS YOUR FANTASY. YOU'VE BEEN KEEPING A JOURNAL OF HIS "ADVENTURES" SINCE YOU WERE A BOY. THEY ARE DELUSIONS, MARC.
IT NEVER HAPPENED, NONE OF IT. IT'S ALL BEEN IN YOUR HEAD.

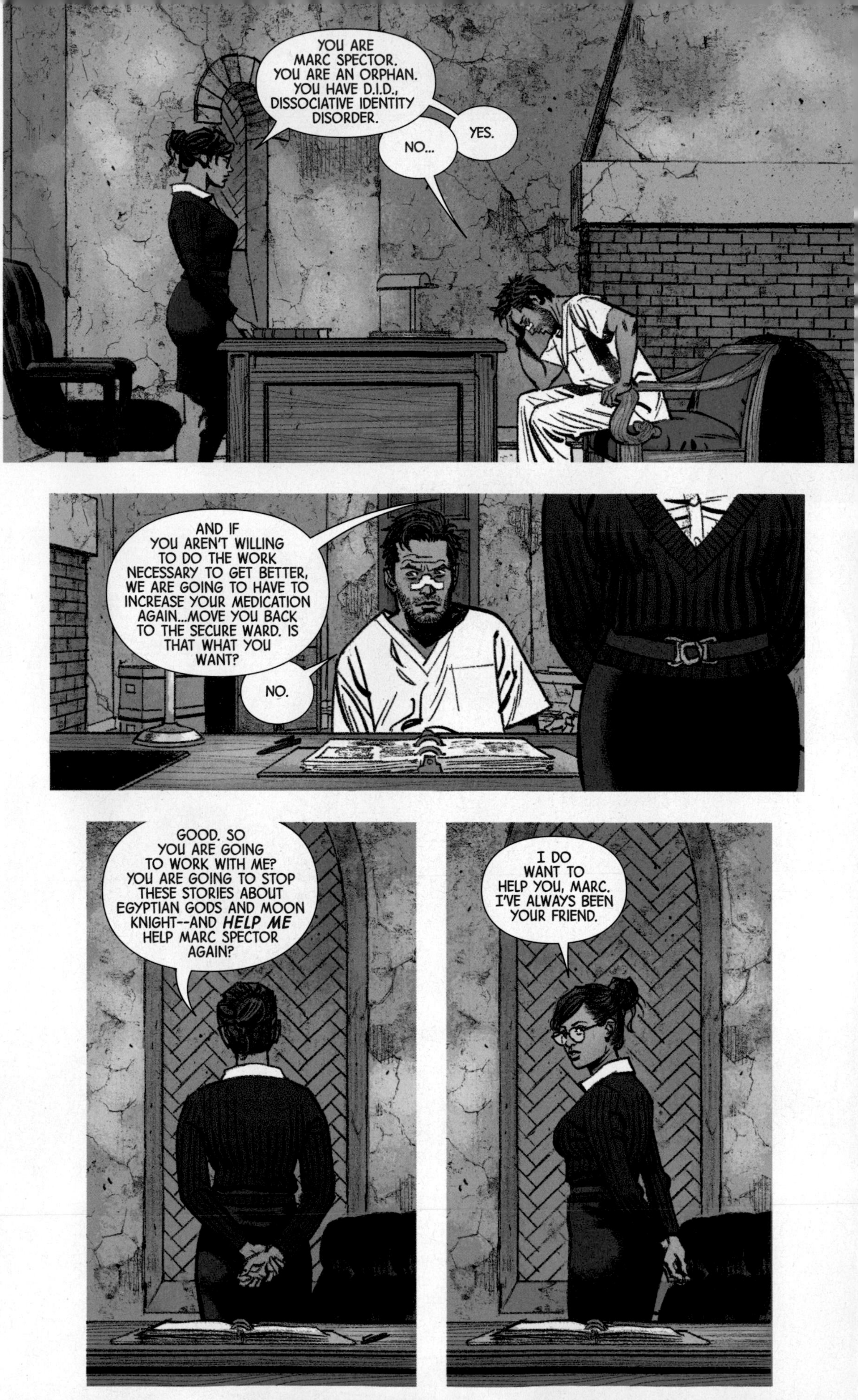
YOU ARE MARC SPECTOR. YOU ARE AN ORPHAN. YOU HAVE D.I.D., DISSOCIATIVE IDENTITY DISORDER.
YES.
NO...
AND IF YOU AREN'T WILLING TO DO THE WORK NECESSARY TO GET BETTER, WE ARE GOING TO HAVE TO INCREASE YOUR MEDICATION AGAIN...MOVE YOU BACK TO THE SECURE WARD. IS THAT WHAT YOU WANT?
NO.
GOOD. SO YOU ARE GOING TO WORK WITH ME? YOU ARE GOING TO STOP THESE STORIES ABOUT EGYPTIAN GODS AND MOON KNIGHT--AND *HELP ME* HELP MARC SPECTOR AGAIN?
I DO WANT TO HELP YOU, MARC. I'VE ALWAYS BEEN YOUR FRIEND.

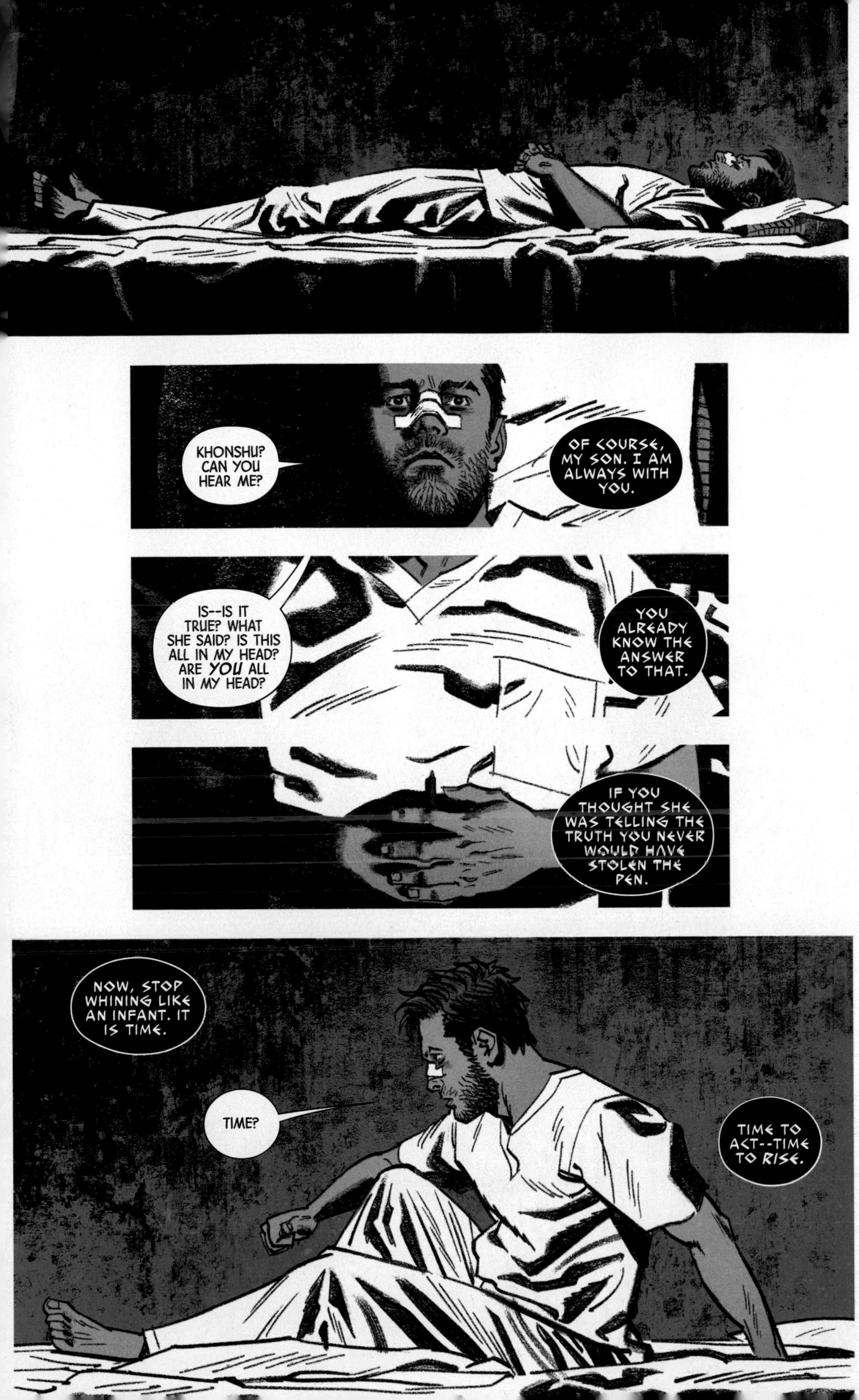
KHONSHU? CAN YOU HEAR ME?
OF COURSE, MY SON. I AM ALWAYS WITH YOU.
IS--IS IT TRUE? WHAT SHE SAID? IS THIS ALL IN MY HEAD? ARE YOU ALL IN MY HEAD?
YOU ALREADY KNOW THE ANSWER TO THAT.
IF YOU THOUGHT SHE WAS TELLING THE TRUTH YOU NEVER WOULD HAVE STOLEN THE PEN.
NOW, STOP WHINING LIKE AN INFANT. IT IS TIME.
TIME?
TIME TO ACT--TIME TO RISE.

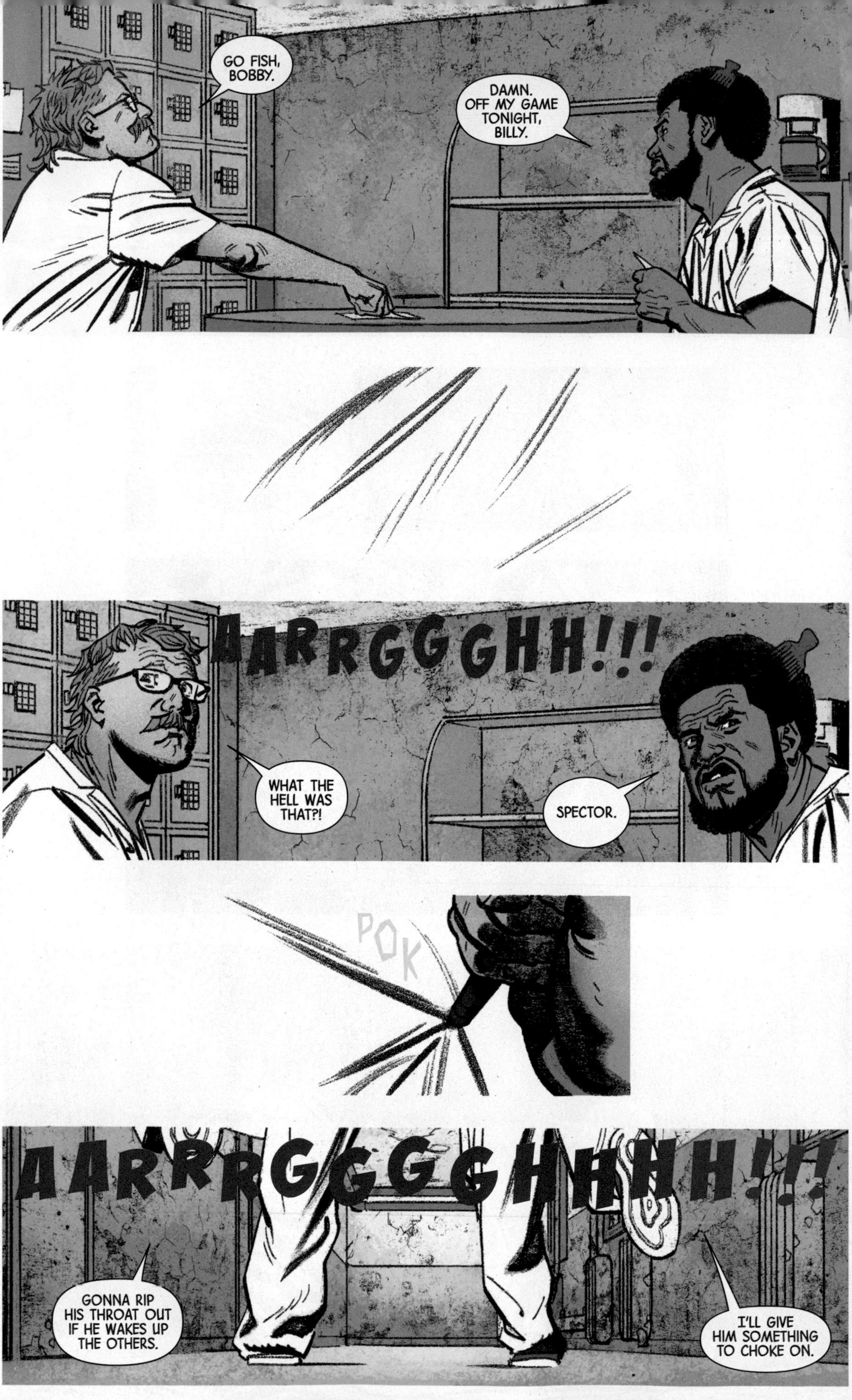
GO FISH, BOBBY.
DAMN. OFF MY GAME TONIGHT, BILLY.
AARRGGGHH!!!
WHAT THE HELL WAS THAT?!
SPECTOR.
POK
AARRRGGGGHHHHH!!!
GONNA RIP HIS THROAT OUT IF HE WAKES UP THE OTHERS.
I'LL GIVE HIM SOMETHING TO CHOKE ON.

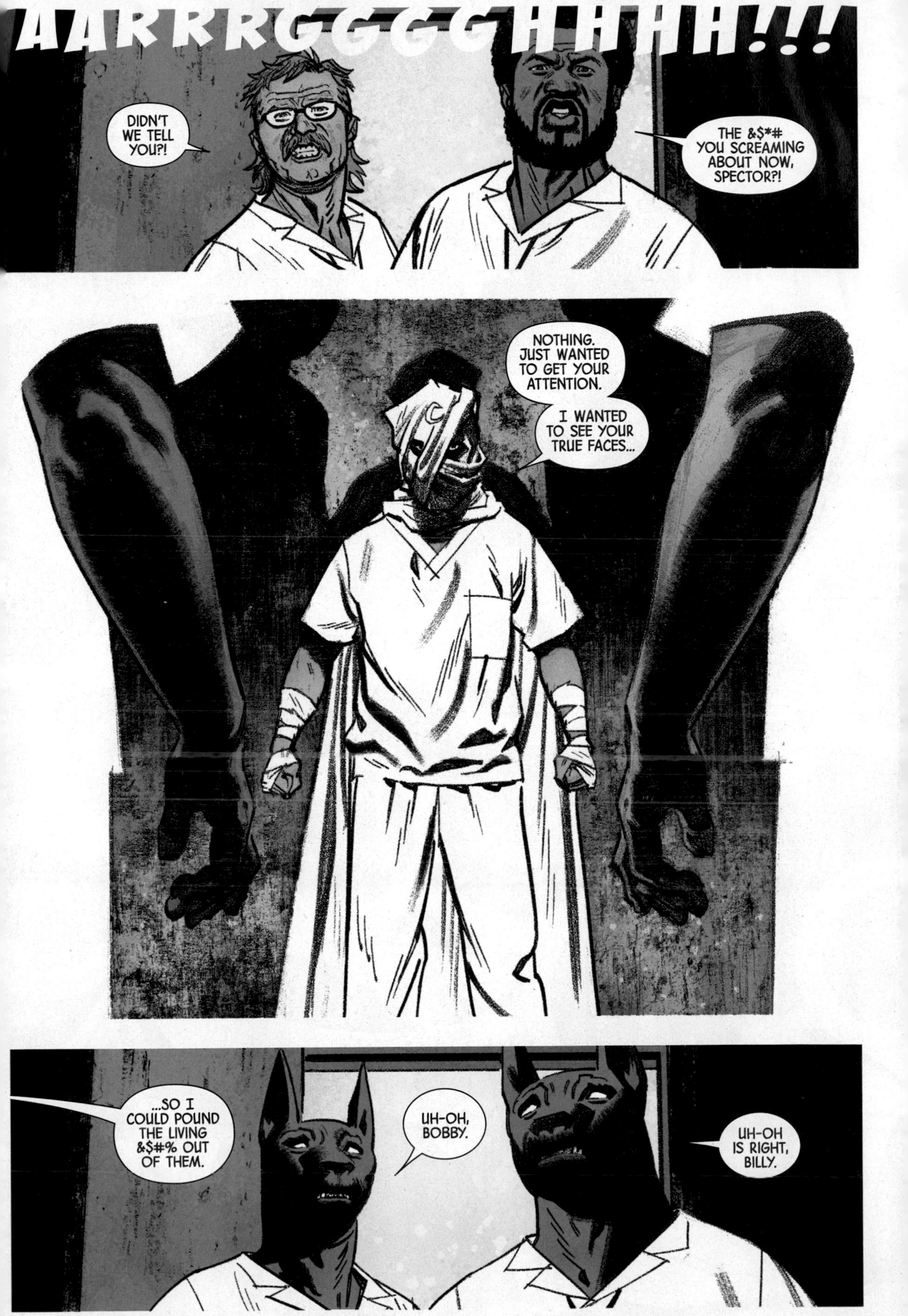
AARRRGGGGGHHHHH!!!
DIDN'T WE TELL YOU?!
THE &$*# YOU SCREAMING ABOUT NOW, SPECTOR?!
NOTHING. JUST WANTED TO GET YOUR ATTENTION.
I WANTED TO SEE YOUR TRUE FACES...
...SO I COULD POUND THE LIVING &$#% OUT OF THEM.
UH-OH, BOBBY.
UH-OH IS RIGHT, BILLY.

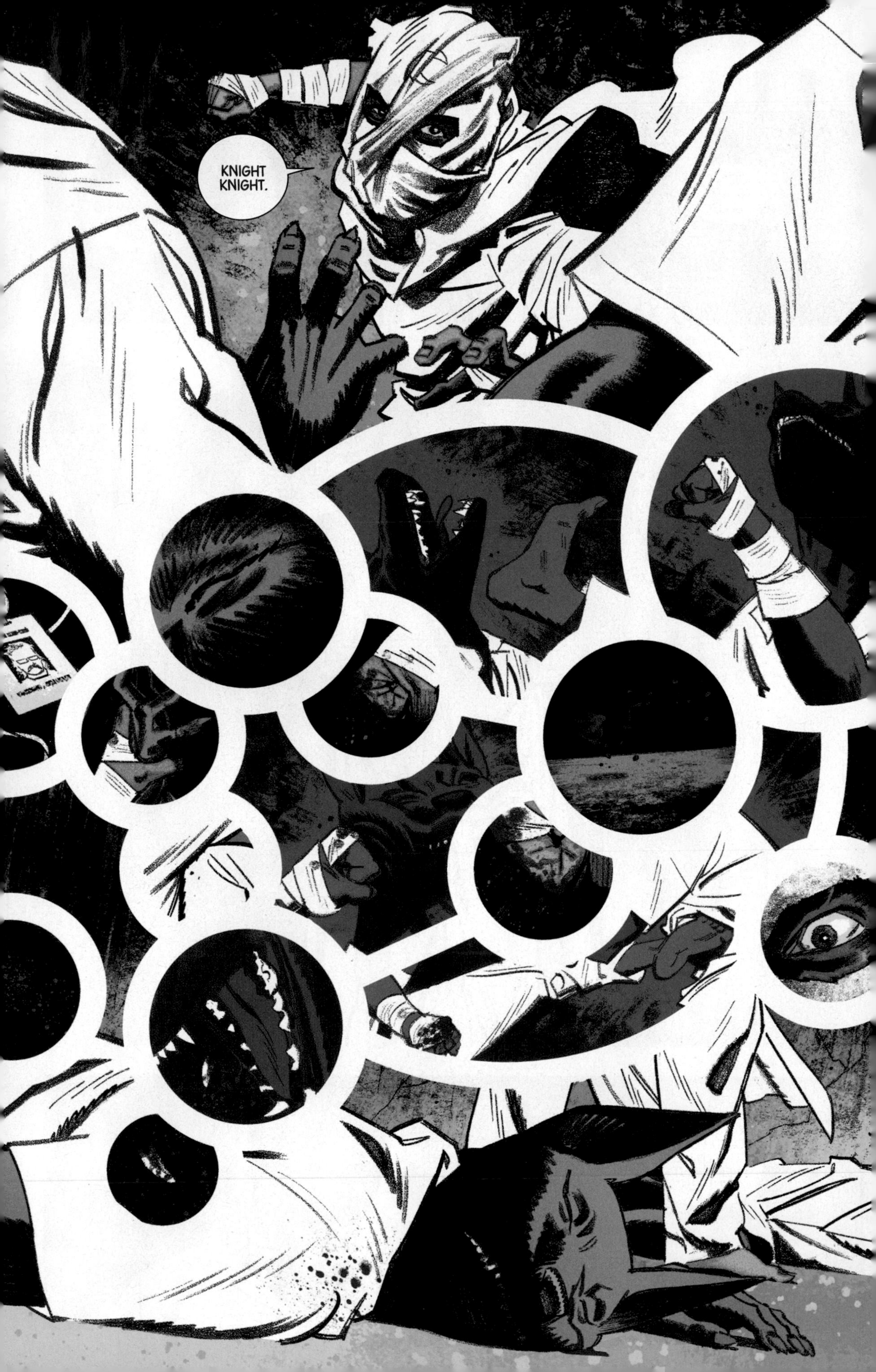
KNIGHT KNIGHT.

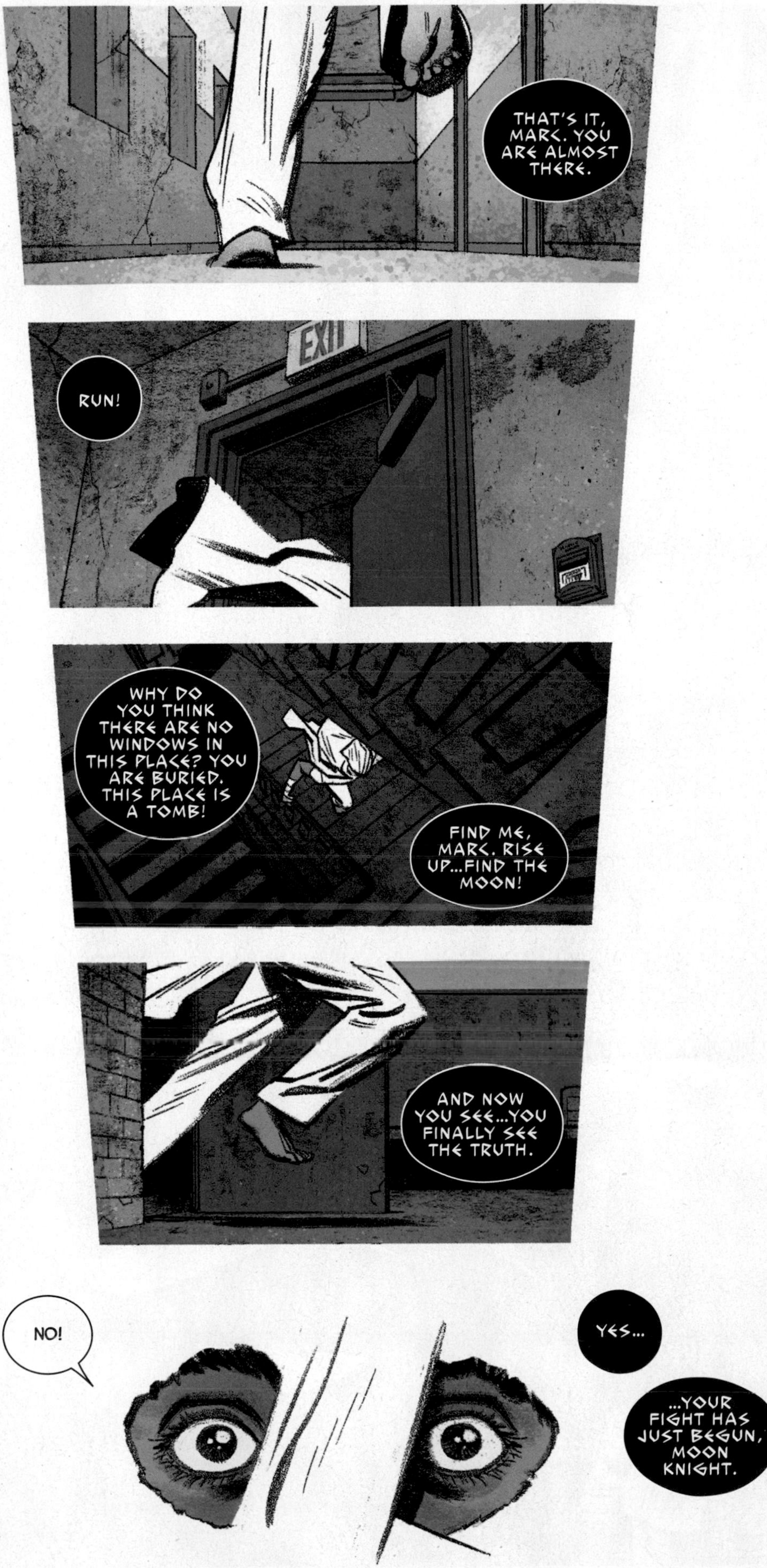
THAT'S IT, MARC. YOU ARE ALMOST THERE.
RUN!
WHY DO YOU THINK THERE ARE NO WINDOWS IN THIS PLACE? YOU ARE BURIED. THIS PLACE IS A TOMB!
FIND ME, MARC. RISE UP...FIND THE MOON!
AND NOW YOU SEE...YOU FINALLY SEE THE TRUTH.
NO!
YES...
...YOUR FIGHT HAS JUST BEGUN, MOON KNIGHT.

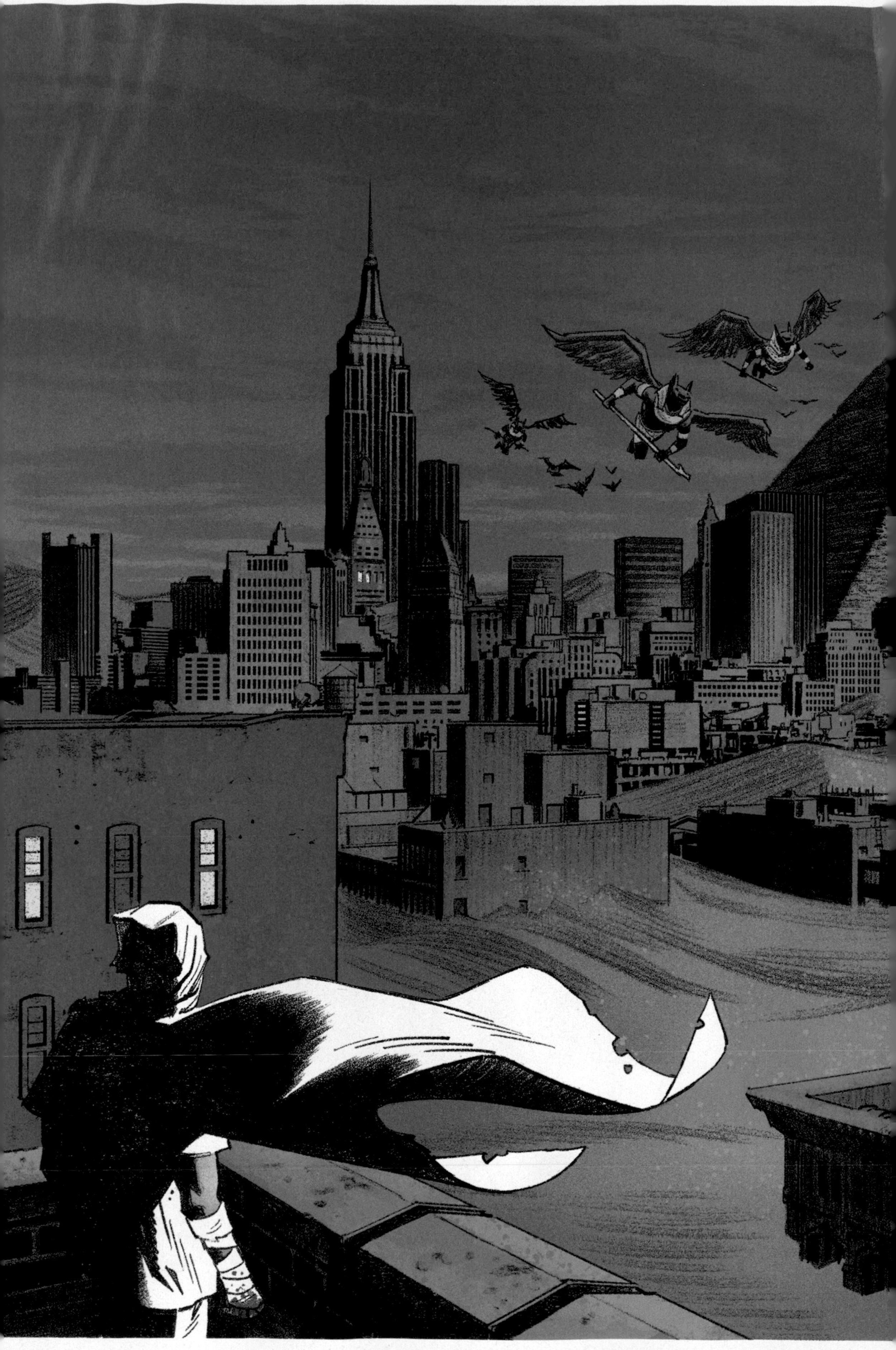

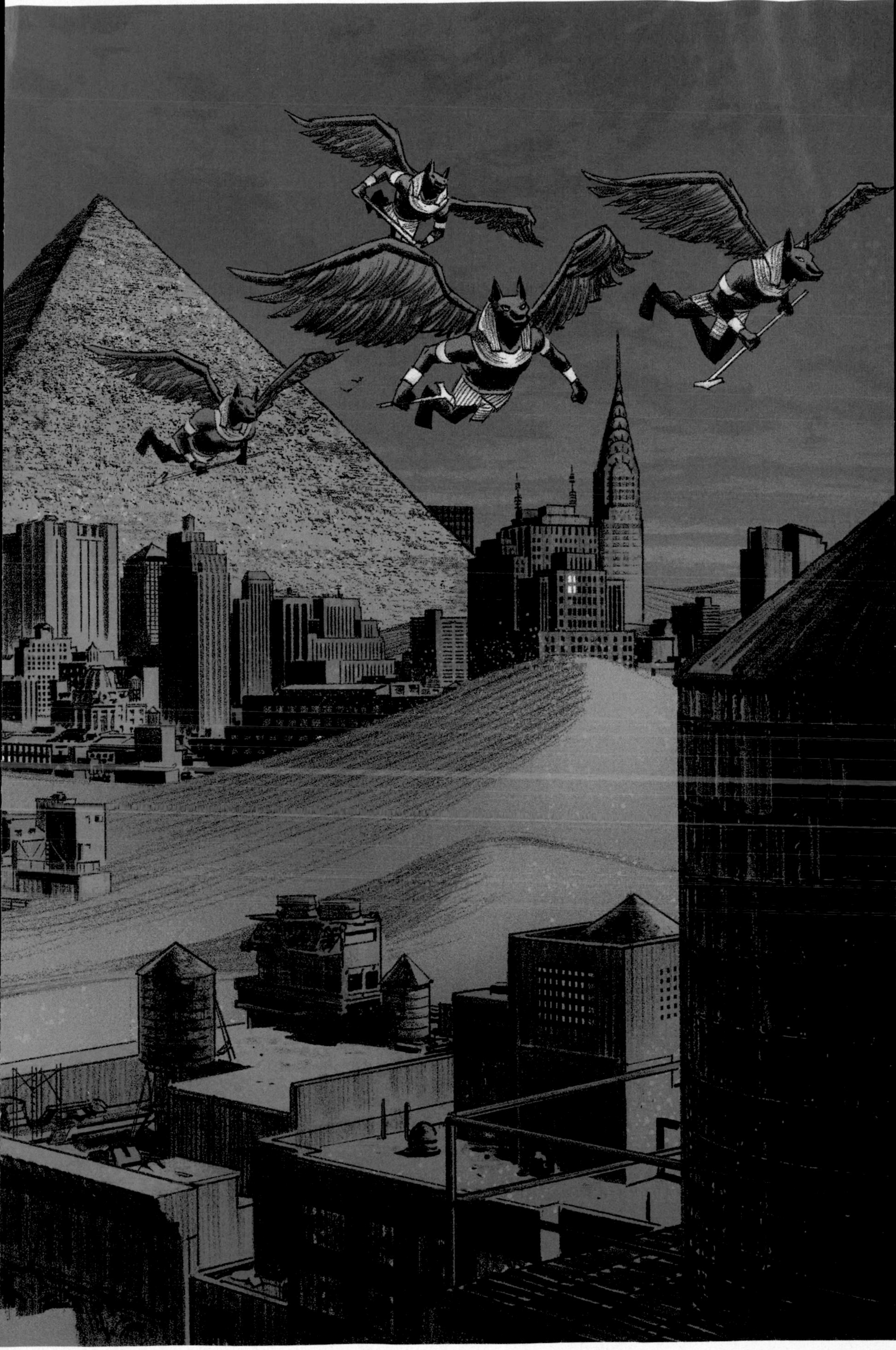

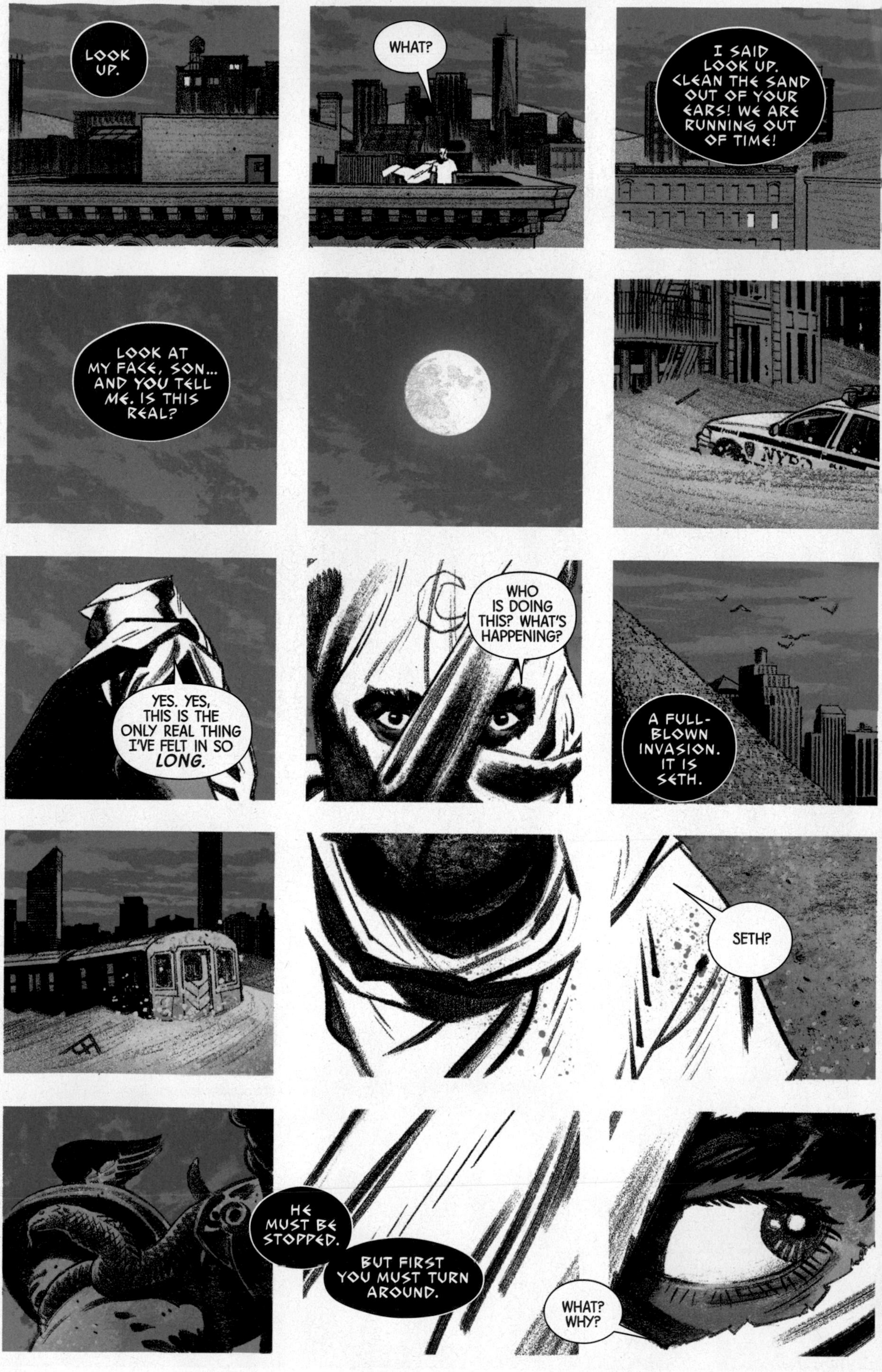
LOOK UP.
WHAT?
I SAID LOOK UP. CLEAN THE SAND OUT OF YOUR EARS! WE ARE RUNNING OUT OF TIME!
LOOK AT MY FACE, SON... AND YOU TELL ME. IS THIS REAL?
NYPD
YES. YES, THIS IS THE ONLY REAL THING I'VE FELT IN SO LONG.
WHO IS DOING THIS? WHAT'S HAPPENING?
A FULL-BLOWN INVASION. IT IS SETH.
SETH?
HE MUST BE STOPPED.
BUT FIRST YOU MUST TURN AROUND.
WHAT? WHY?

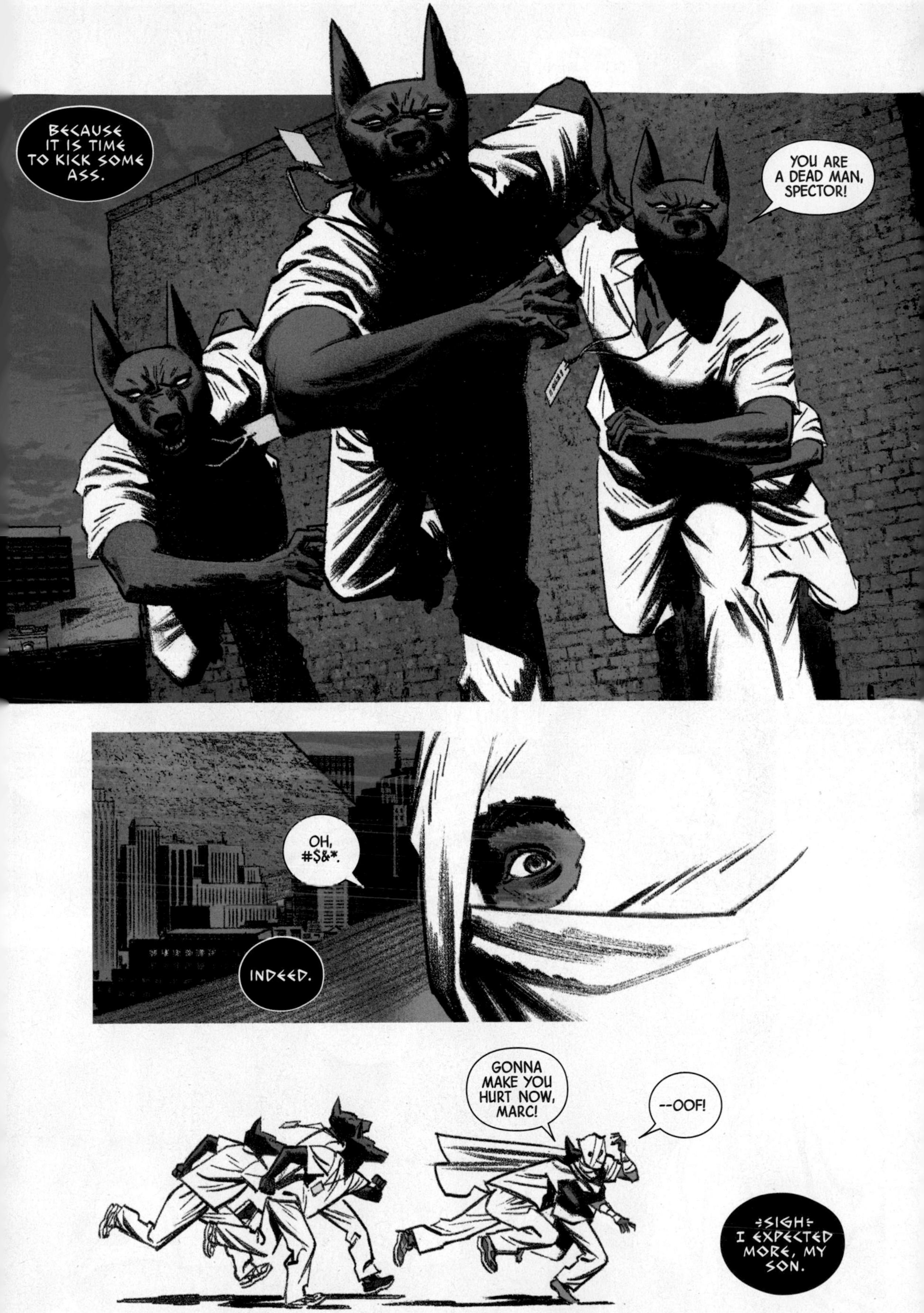
BECAUSE IT IS TIME TO KICK SOME ASS.
YOU ARE A DEAD MAN, SPECTOR!
OH, #$&*.
INDEED.
GONNA MAKE YOU HURT NOW, MARC!
--OOF!
=SIGH= I EXPECTED MORE, MY SON.

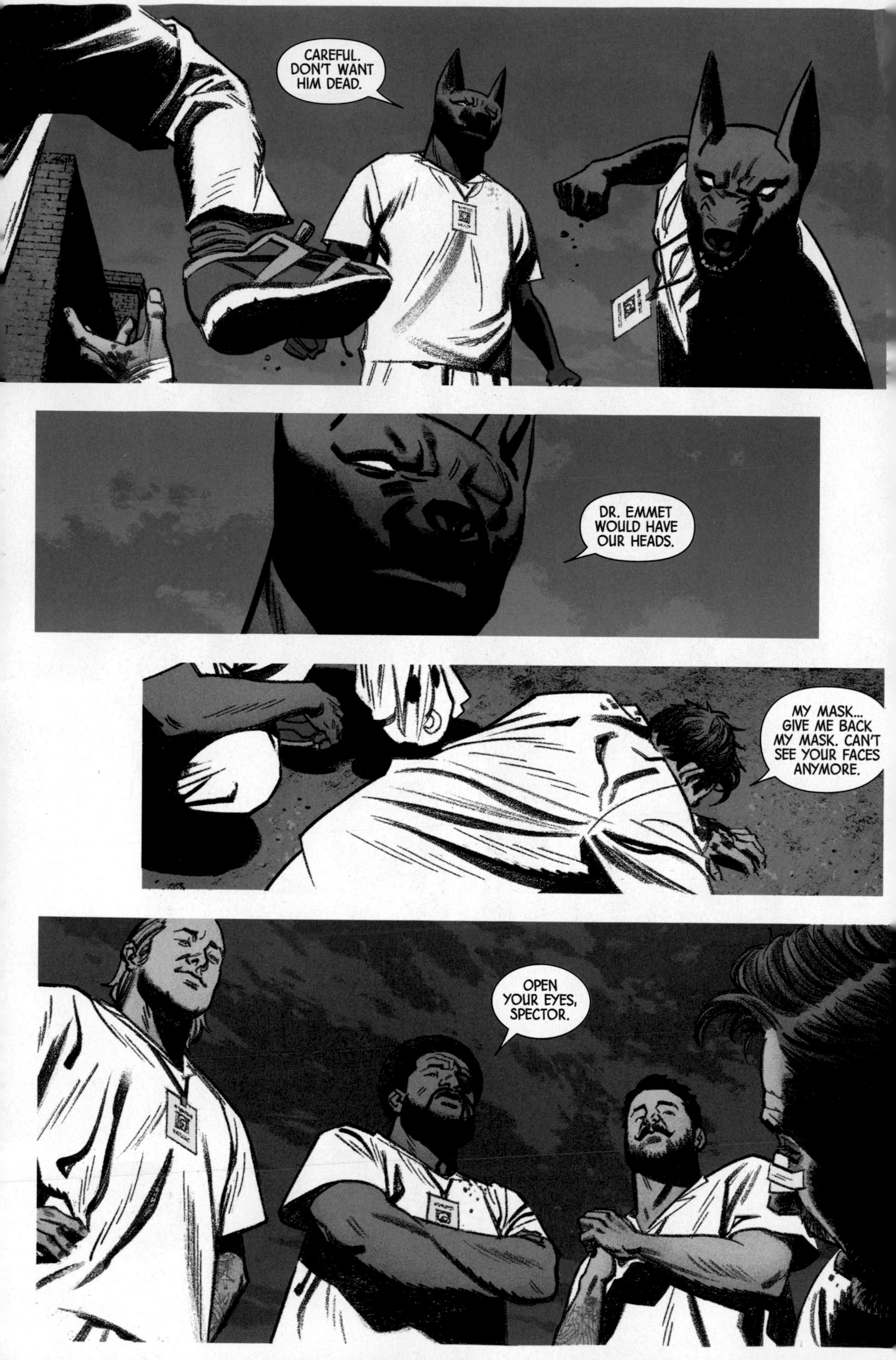
CAREFUL. DON'T WANT HIM DEAD.
DR. EMMET WOULD HAVE OUR HEADS.
MY MASK... GIVE ME BACK MY MASK. CAN'T SEE YOUR FACES ANYMORE.
OPEN YOUR EYES, SPECTOR.

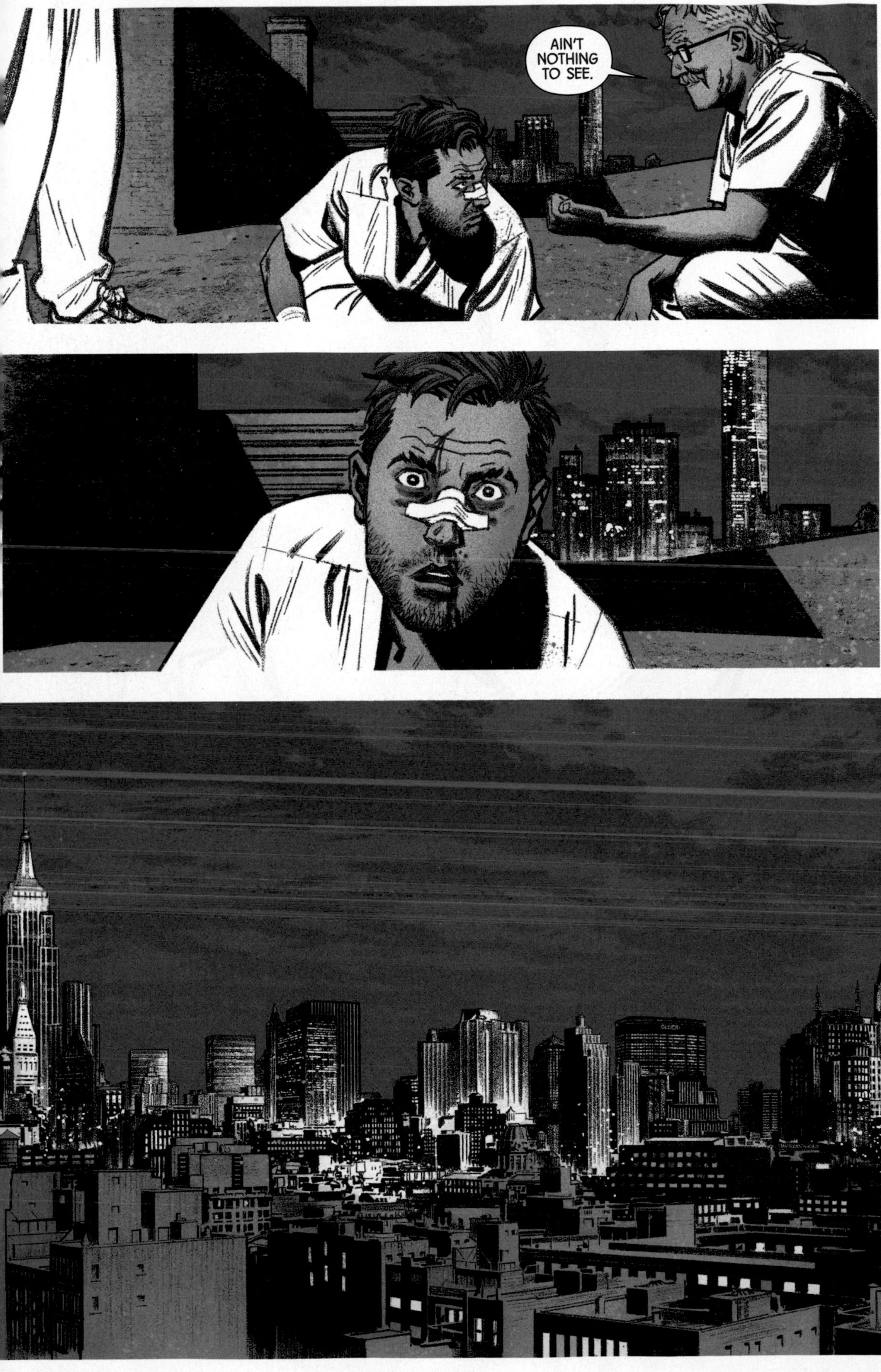
AIN'T NOTHING TO SEE.

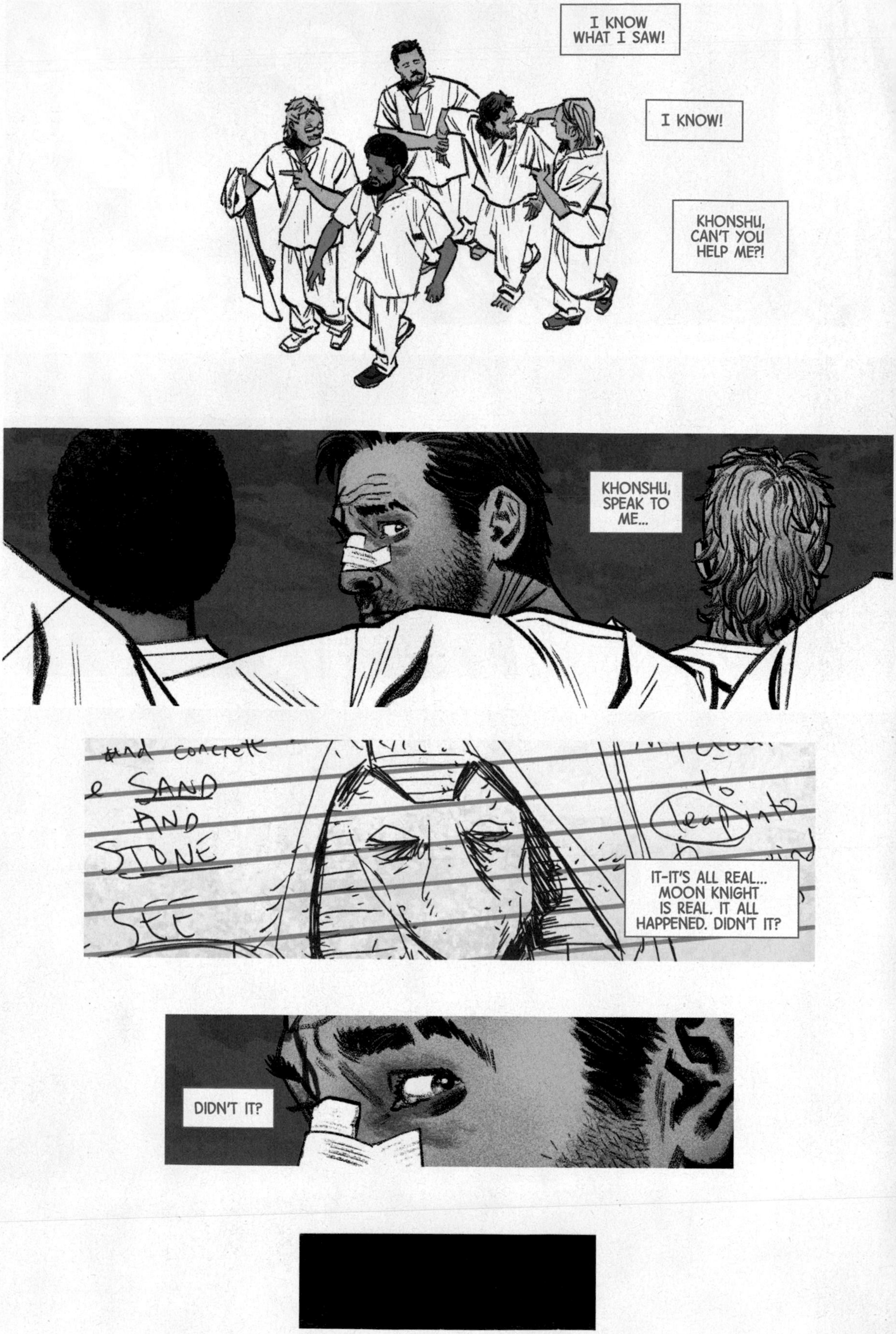
I KNOW WHAT I SAW!
I KNOW!
KHONSHU, CAN'T YOU HELP ME?!
KHONSHU, SPEAK TO ME...
and concrete
SAND AND STONE
SEE
IT-IT'S ALL REAL... MOON KNIGHT IS REAL. IT ALL HAPPENED. DIDN'T IT?
DIDN'T IT?

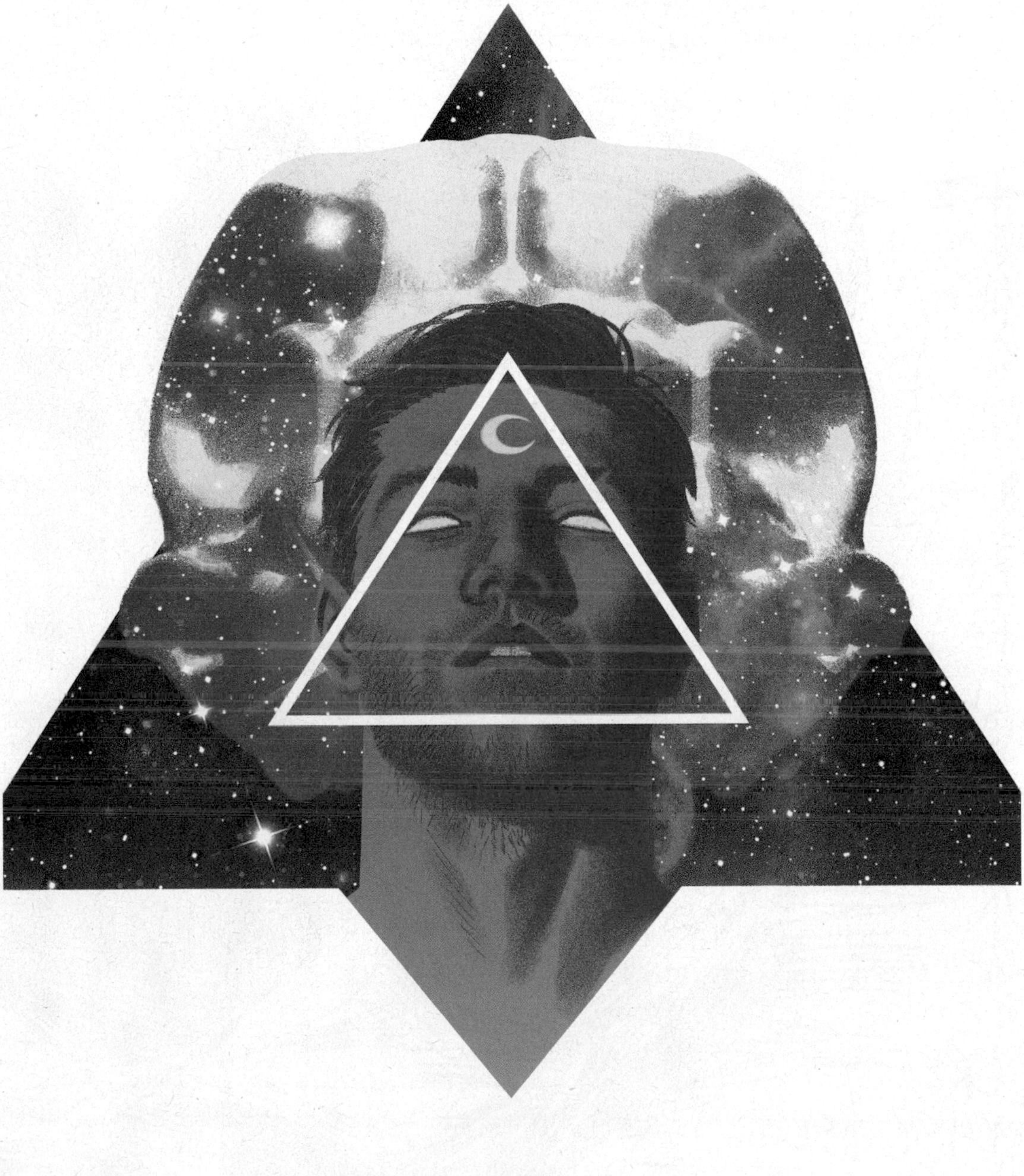

WELCOME TO NEW EGYPT
PART TWO

2

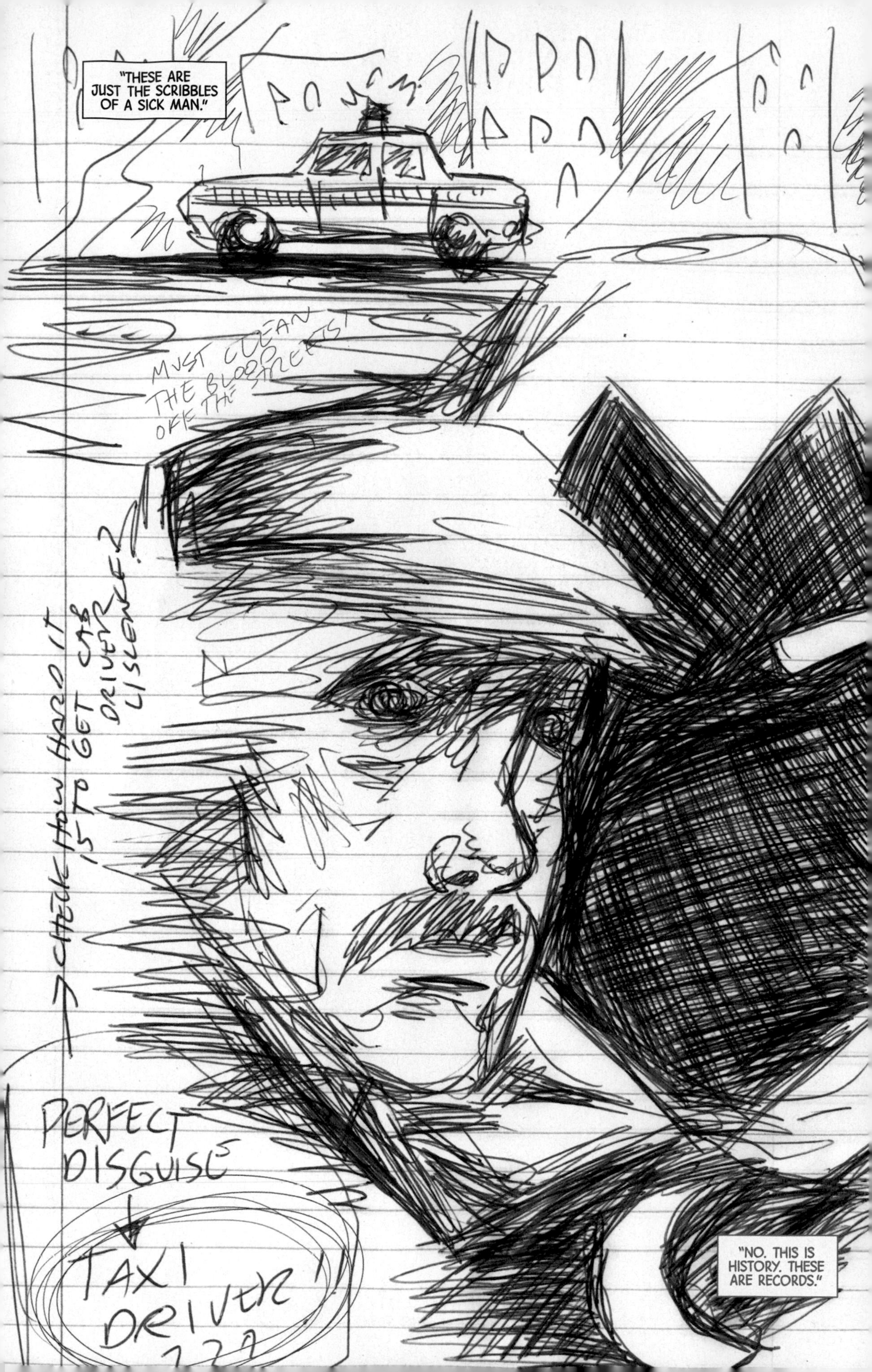
"THESE ARE JUST THE SCRIBBLES OF A SICK MAN."
MUST CLEAN THE BLOOD OFF THE STREETS!
CHECK HOW HARD IT IS TO GET CAB DRIVER LISCENCE?
PERFECT DISGUISE
TAXI DRIVER!!
"NO. THIS IS HISTORY. THESE ARE RECORDS."

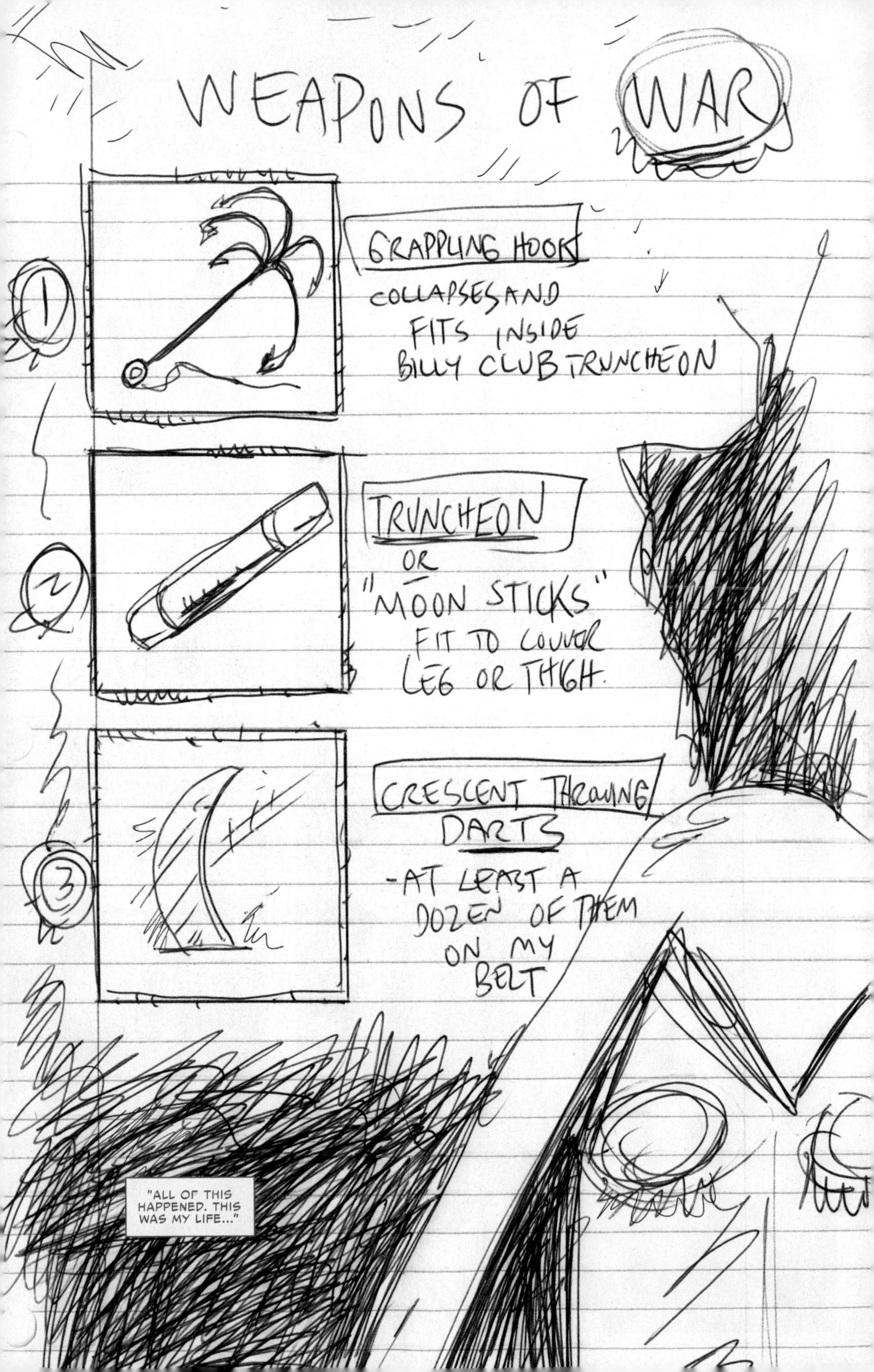
WEAPONS OF WAR
1
GRAPPLING HOOK
COLLAPSES AND FITS INSIDE BILLY CLUB TRUNCHEON
2
TRUNCHEON OR "MOON STICKS"
FIT TO COUVER LEG OR THIGH.
3
CRESCENT THROWING DARTS
-AT LEAST A DOZEN OF THEM ON MY BELT
"ALL OF THIS HAPPENED. THIS WAS MY LIFE..."

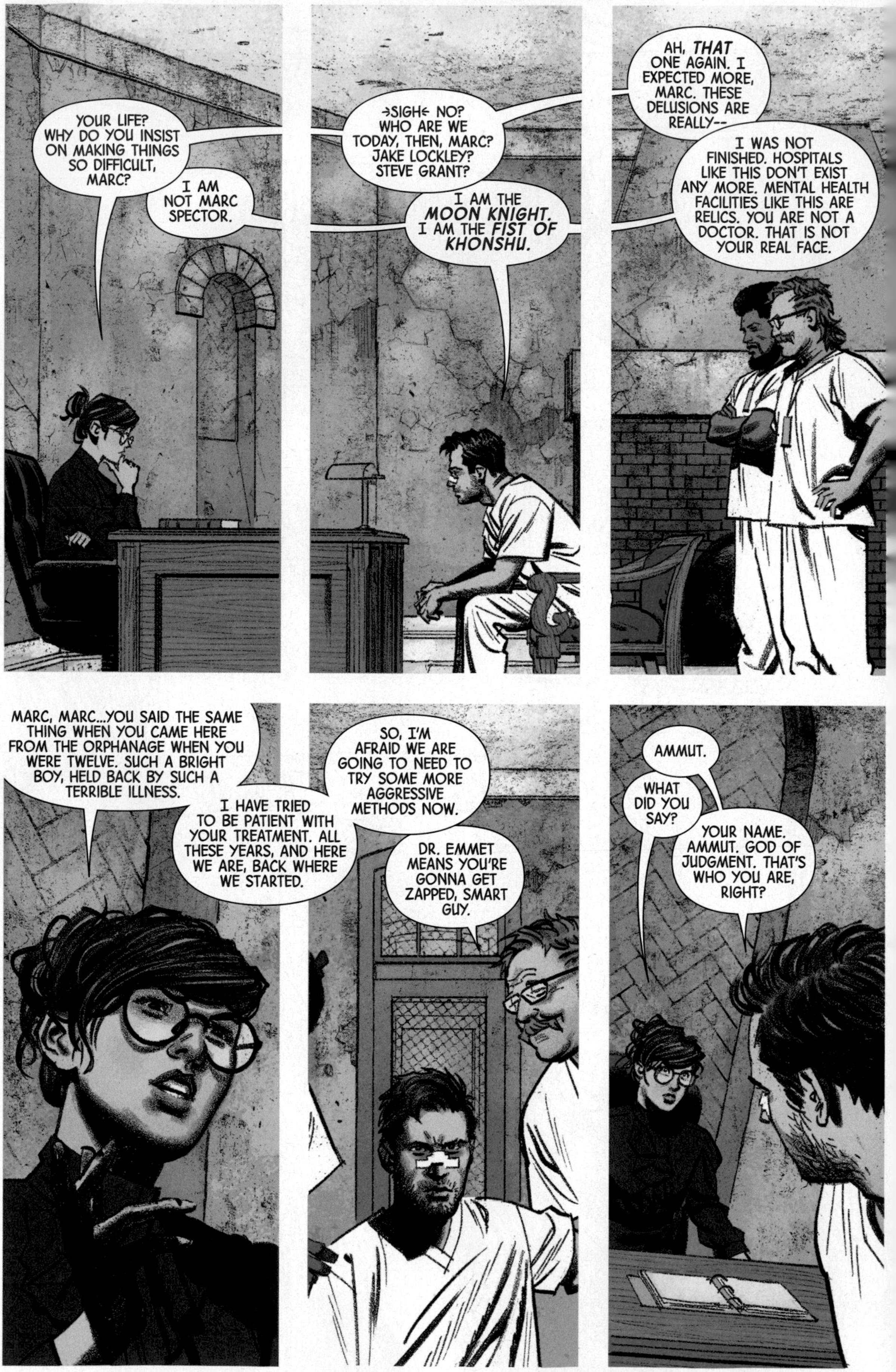
YOUR LIFE? WHY DO YOU INSIST ON MAKING THINGS SO DIFFICULT, MARC?
I AM NOT MARC SPECTOR.
→SIGH← NO? WHO ARE WE TODAY, THEN, MARC? JAKE LOCKLEY? STEVE GRANT?
I AM THE MOON KNIGHT. I AM THE FIST OF KHONSHU.
AH, THAT ONE AGAIN. I EXPECTED MORE, MARC. THESE DELUSIONS ARE REALLY--
I WAS NOT FINISHED. HOSPITALS LIKE THIS DON'T EXIST ANY MORE. MENTAL HEALTH FACILITIES LIKE THIS ARE RELICS. YOU ARE NOT A DOCTOR. THAT IS NOT YOUR REAL FACE.
MARC, MARC...YOU SAID THE SAME THING WHEN YOU CAME HERE FROM THE ORPHANAGE WHEN YOU WERE TWELVE. SUCH A BRIGHT BOY, HELD BACK BY SUCH A TERRIBLE ILLNESS.
I HAVE TRIED TO BE PATIENT WITH YOUR TREATMENT. ALL THESE YEARS, AND HERE WE ARE, BACK WHERE WE STARTED.
SO, I'M AFRAID WE ARE GOING TO NEED TO TRY SOME MORE AGGRESSIVE METHODS NOW.
DR. EMMET MEANS YOU'RE GONNA GET ZAPPED, SMART GUY.
AMMUT.
WHAT DID YOU SAY?
YOUR NAME. AMMUT. GOD OF JUDGMENT. THAT'S WHO YOU ARE, RIGHT?

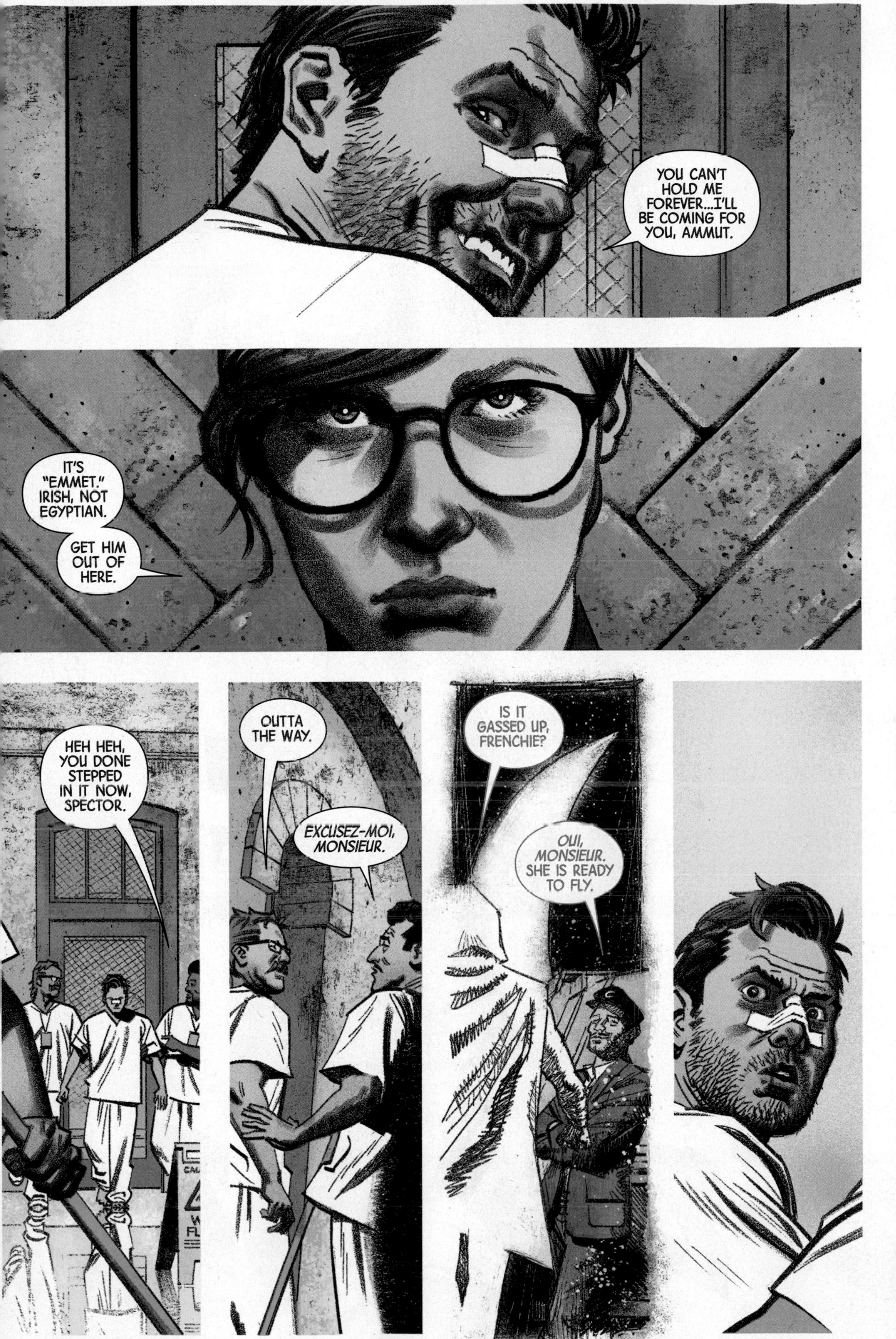
YOU CAN'T HOLD ME FOREVER...I'LL BE COMING FOR YOU, AMMUT.
IT'S "EMMET." IRISH, NOT EGYPTIAN.
GET HIM OUT OF HERE.
HEH HEH, YOU DONE STEPPED IN IT NOW, SPECTOR.
OUTTA THE WAY.
EXCUSEZ-MOI, MONSIEUR.
IS IT GASSED UP, FRENCHIE?
OUI, MONSIEUR. SHE IS READY TO FLY.

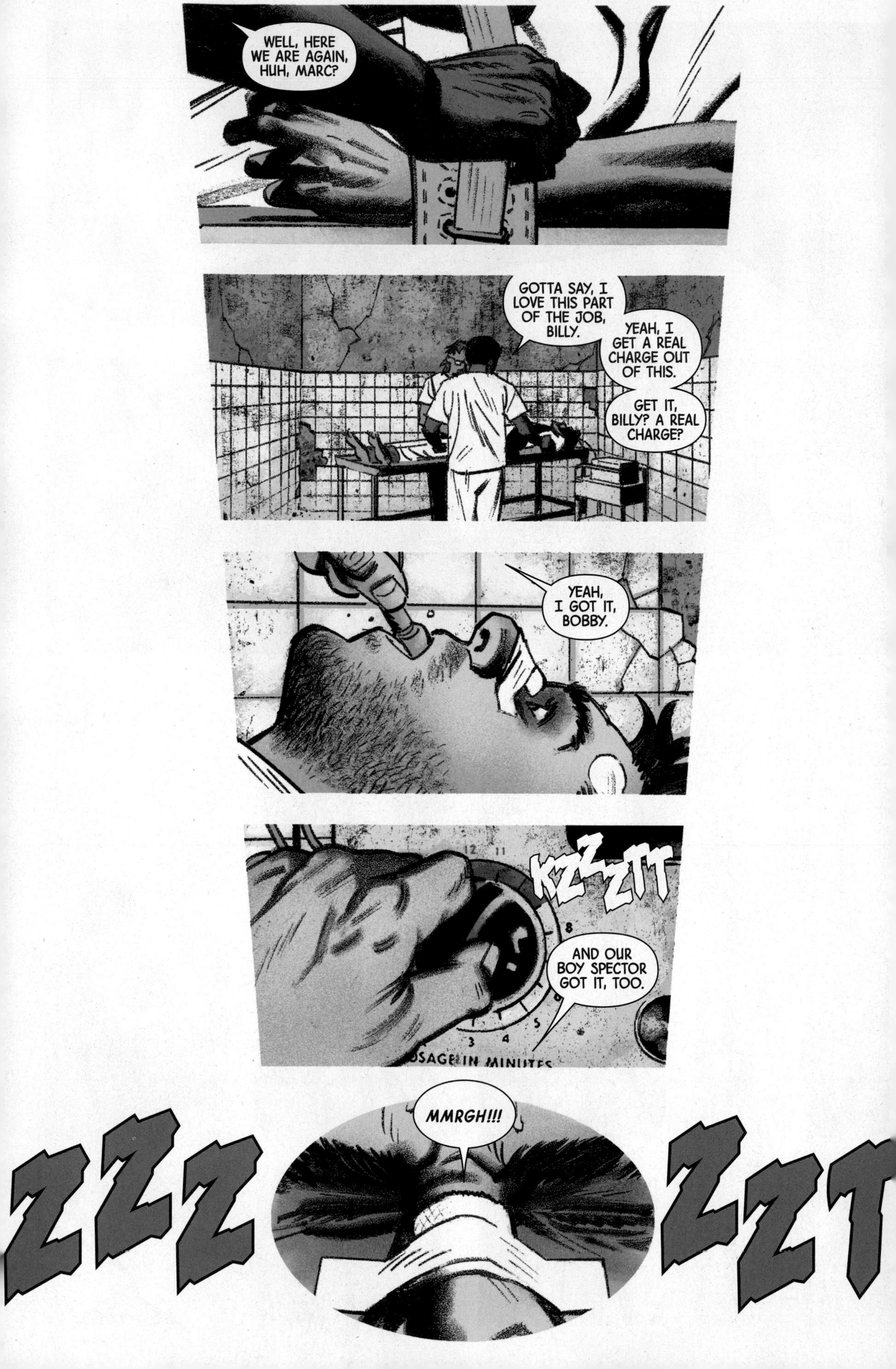
WELL, HERE WE ARE AGAIN, HUH, MARC?
GOTTA SAY, I LOVE THIS PART OF THE JOB, BILLY.
YEAH, I GET A REAL CHARGE OUT OF THIS.
GET IT, BILLY? A REAL CHARGE?
YEAH, I GOT IT, BOBBY.
KZZZZTT
AND OUR BOY SPECTOR GOT IT, TOO.
MMRGH!!!
ZZZZZT

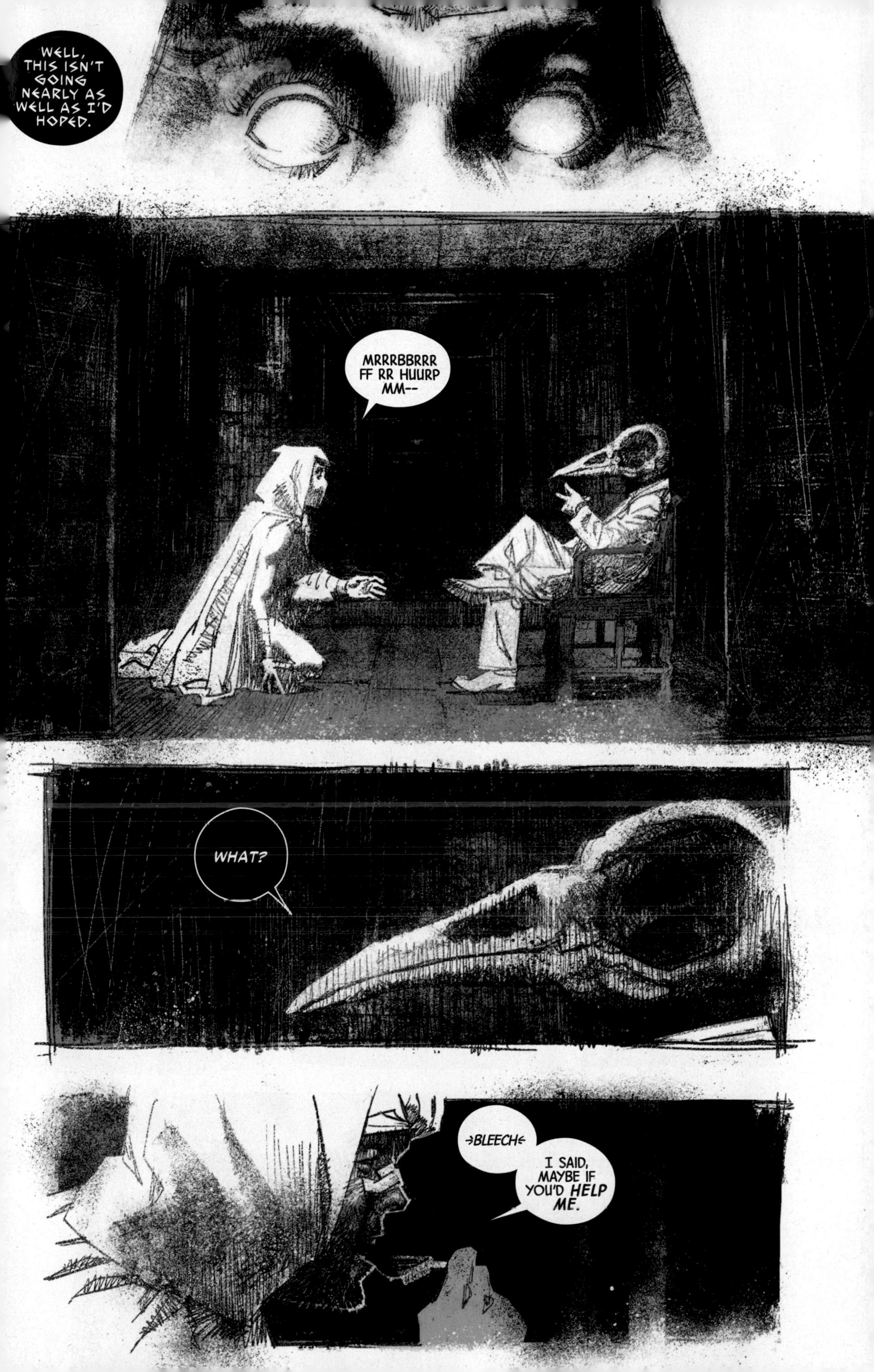
WELL, THIS ISN'T GOING NEARLY AS WELL AS I'D HOPED.
MRRRBBRRR FF RR HUURP MM--
WHAT?
→BLEECH←
I SAID, MAYBE IF YOU'D HELP ME.

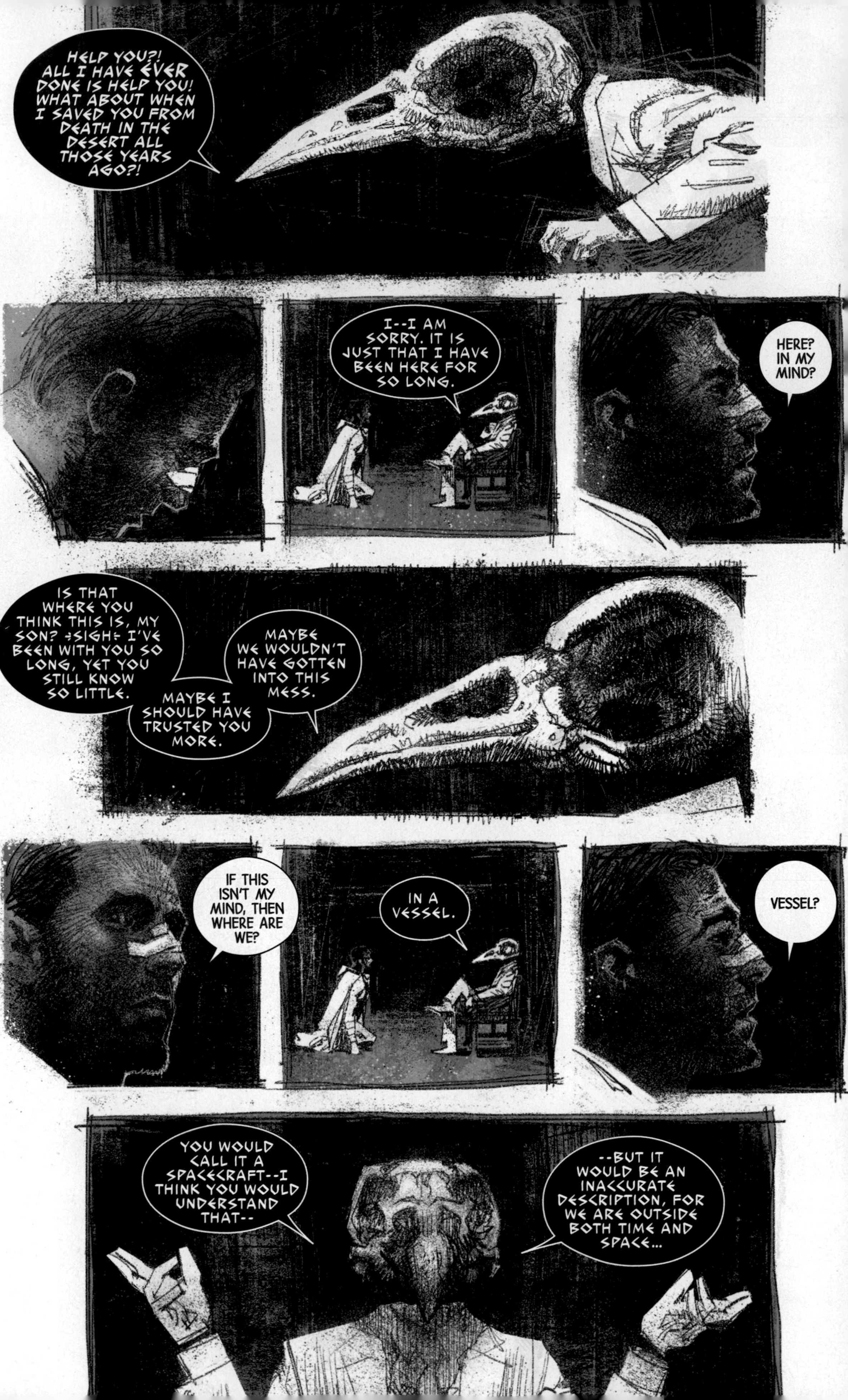
HELP YOU?! ALL I HAVE EVER DONE IS HELP YOU! WHAT ABOUT WHEN I SAVED YOU FROM DEATH IN THE DESERT ALL THOSE YEARS AGO?!
I--I AM SORRY. IT IS JUST THAT I HAVE BEEN HERE FOR SO LONG.
HERE? IN MY MIND?
IS THAT WHERE YOU THINK THIS IS, MY SON? =SIGH= I'VE BEEN WITH YOU SO LONG, YET YOU STILL KNOW SO LITTLE.
MAYBE I SHOULD HAVE TRUSTED YOU MORE.
MAYBE WE WOULDN'T HAVE GOTTEN INTO THIS MESS.
IF THIS ISN'T MY MIND, THEN WHERE ARE WE?
IN A VESSEL.
VESSEL?
YOU WOULD CALL IT A SPACECRAFT--I THINK YOU WOULD UNDERSTAND THAT--
--BUT IT WOULD BE AN INACCURATE DESCRIPTION, FOR WE ARE OUTSIDE BOTH TIME AND SPACE...

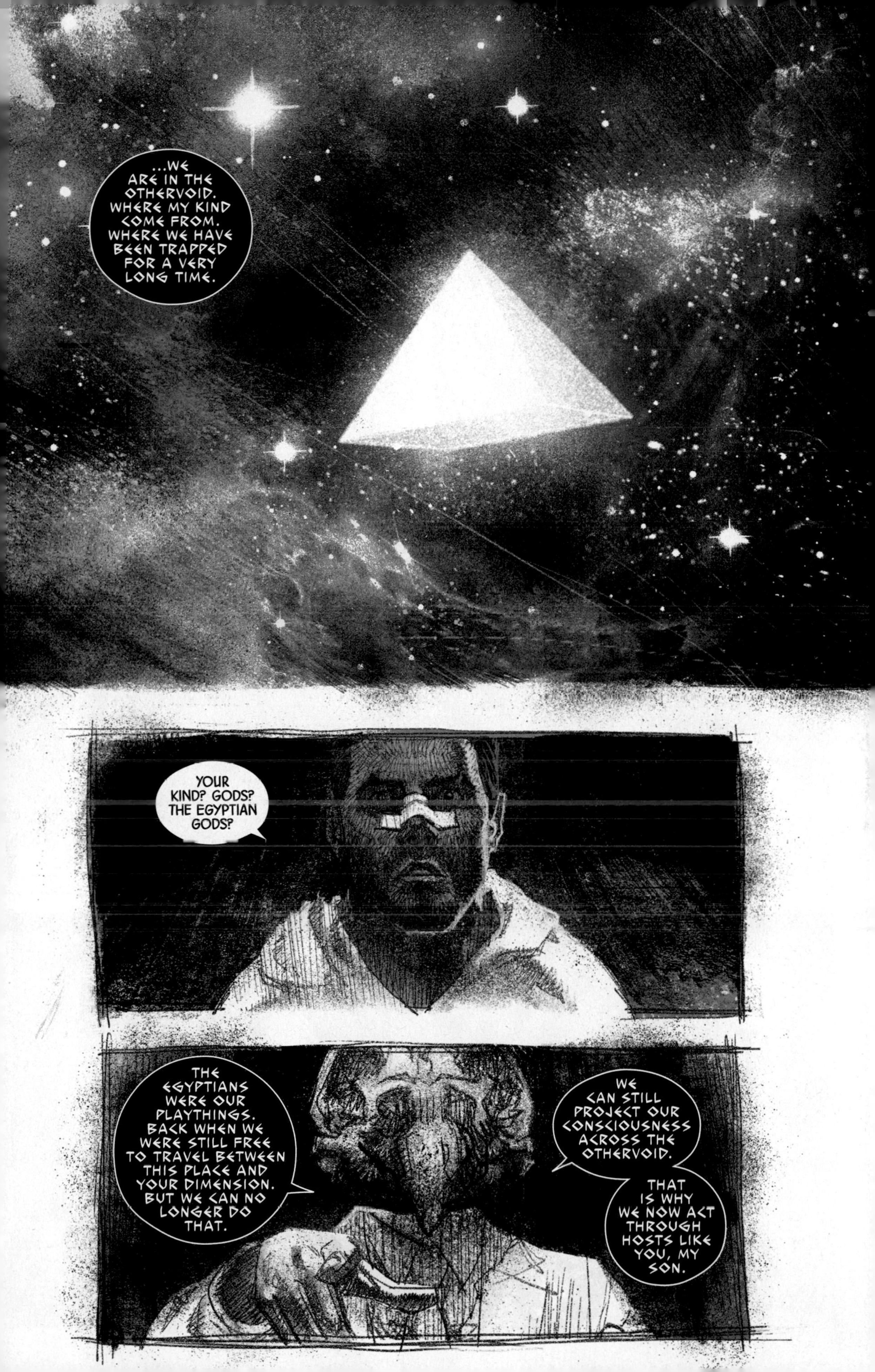
...WE ARE IN THE OTHERVOID. WHERE MY KIND COME FROM. WHERE WE HAVE BEEN TRAPPED FOR A VERY LONG TIME.
YOUR KIND? GODS? THE EGYPTIAN GODS?
THE EGYPTIANS WERE OUR PLAYTHINGS. BACK WHEN WE WERE STILL FREE TO TRAVEL BETWEEN THIS PLACE AND YOUR DIMENSION. BUT WE CAN NO LONGER DO THAT.
WE CAN STILL PROJECT OUR CONSCIOUSNESS ACROSS THE OTHERVOID.
THAT IS WHY WE NOW ACT THROUGH HOSTS LIKE YOU, MY SON.

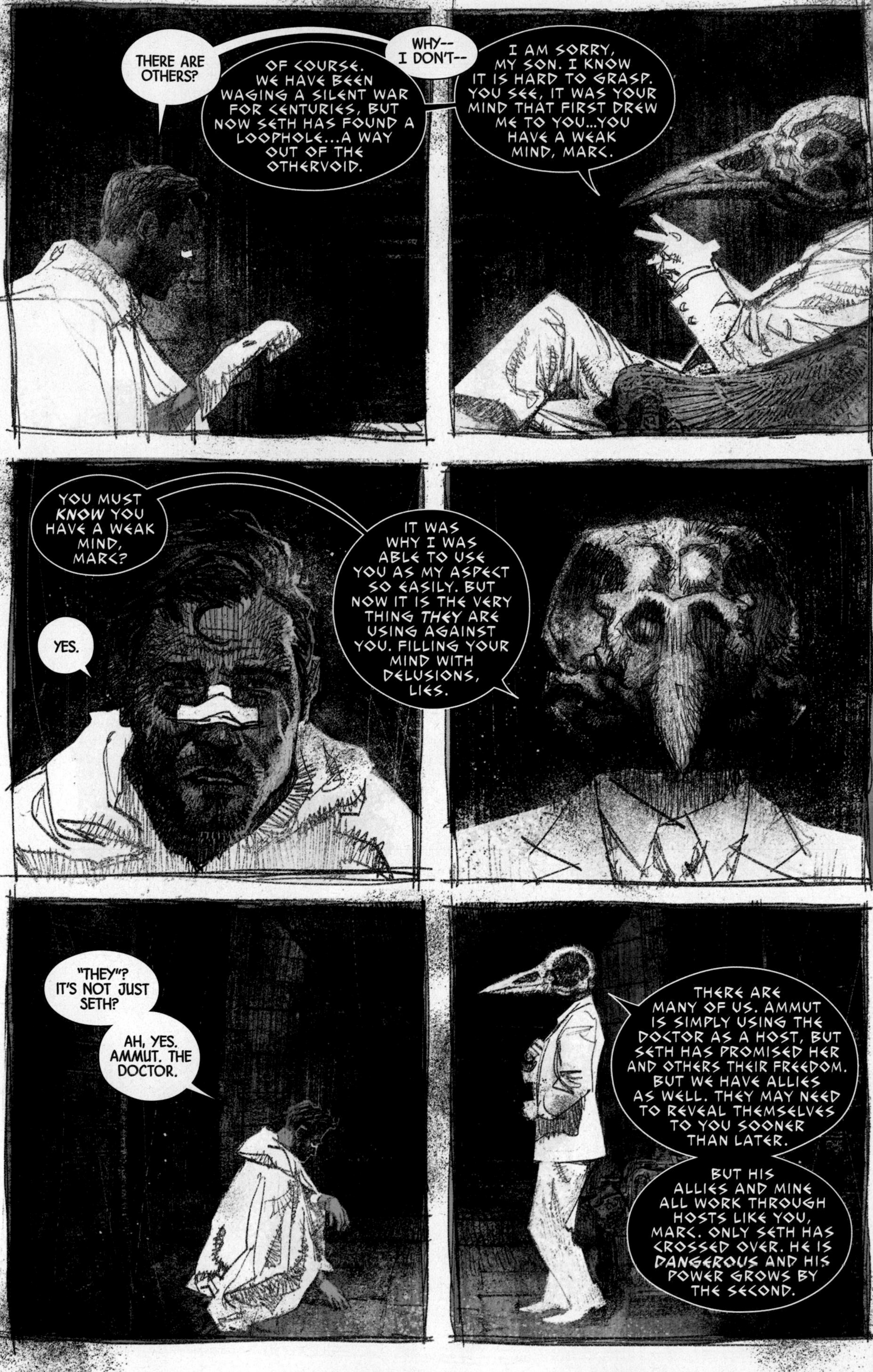
THERE ARE OTHERS?
OF COURSE. WE HAVE BEEN WAGING A SILENT WAR FOR CENTURIES, BUT NOW SETH HAS FOUND A LOOPHOLE...A WAY OUT OF THE OTHERVOID.
WHY-- I DON'T--
I AM SORRY, MY SON. I KNOW IT IS HARD TO GRASP. YOU SEE, IT WAS YOUR MIND THAT FIRST DREW ME TO YOU...YOU HAVE A WEAK MIND, MARC.
YOU MUST KNOW YOU HAVE A WEAK MIND, MARC?
YES.
IT WAS WHY I WAS ABLE TO USE YOU AS MY ASPECT SO EASILY. BUT NOW IT IS THE VERY THING THEY ARE USING AGAINST YOU. FILLING YOUR MIND WITH DELUSIONS, LIES.
"THEY"? IT'S NOT JUST SETH?
AH, YES. AMMUT. THE DOCTOR.
THERE ARE MANY OF US. AMMUT IS SIMPLY USING THE DOCTOR AS A HOST, BUT SETH HAS PROMISED HER AND OTHERS THEIR FREEDOM. BUT WE HAVE ALLIES AS WELL. THEY MAY NEED TO REVEAL THEMSELVES TO YOU SOONER THAN LATER.
BUT HIS ALLIES AND MINE ALL WORK THROUGH HOSTS LIKE YOU, MARC. ONLY SETH HAS CROSSED OVER. HE IS DANGEROUS AND HIS POWER GROWS BY THE SECOND.

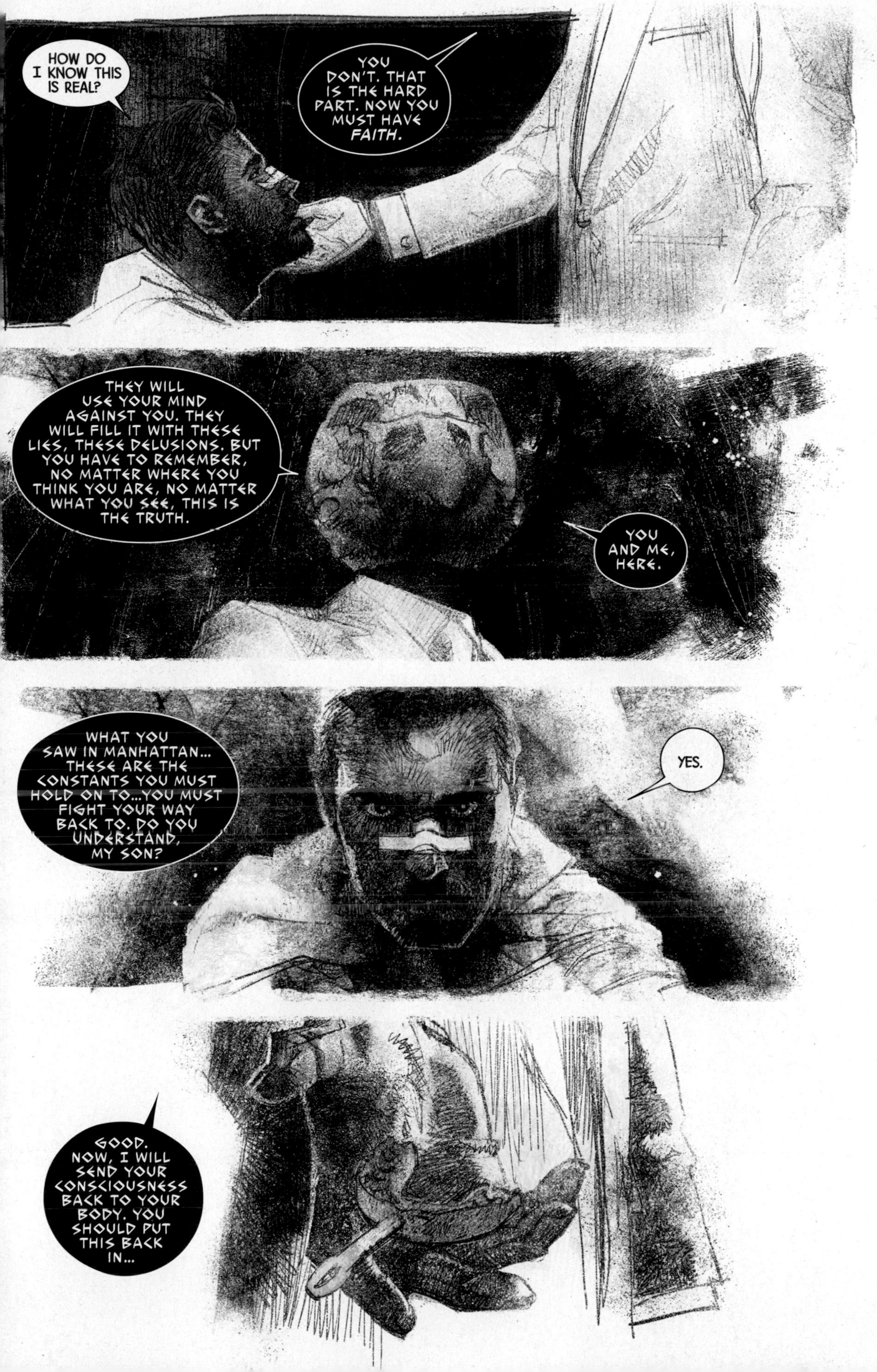

HOW DO I KNOW THIS IS REAL?
YOU DON'T. THAT IS THE HARD PART. NOW YOU MUST HAVE *FAITH*.
THEY WILL USE YOUR MIND AGAINST YOU. THEY WILL FILL IT WITH THESE LIES, THESE DELUSIONS. BUT YOU HAVE TO REMEMBER, NO MATTER WHERE YOU THINK YOU ARE, NO MATTER WHAT YOU SEE, THIS IS THE TRUTH.
YOU AND ME, HERE.
WHAT YOU SAW IN MANHATTAN... THESE ARE THE CONSTANTS YOU MUST HOLD ON TO...YOU MUST FIGHT YOUR WAY BACK TO. DO YOU UNDERSTAND, MY SON?
YES.
GOOD. NOW, I WILL SEND YOUR CONSCIOUSNESS BACK TO YOUR BODY. YOU SHOULD PUT THIS BACK IN...

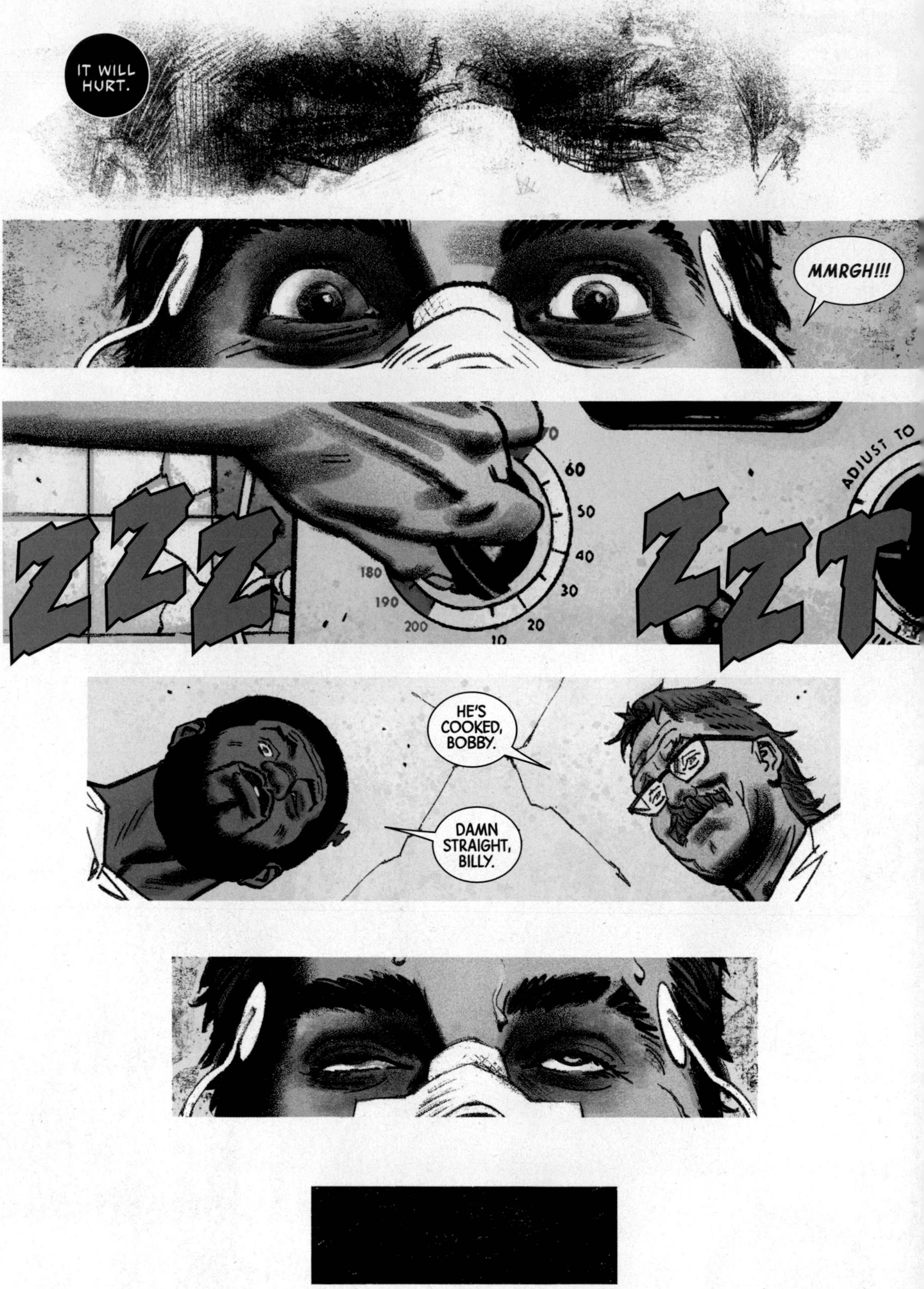
IT WILL HURT.
MMRGH!!!
ZZZ
ADJUST TO
ZZT
HE'S COOKED, BOBBY.
DAMN STRAIGHT, BILLY.

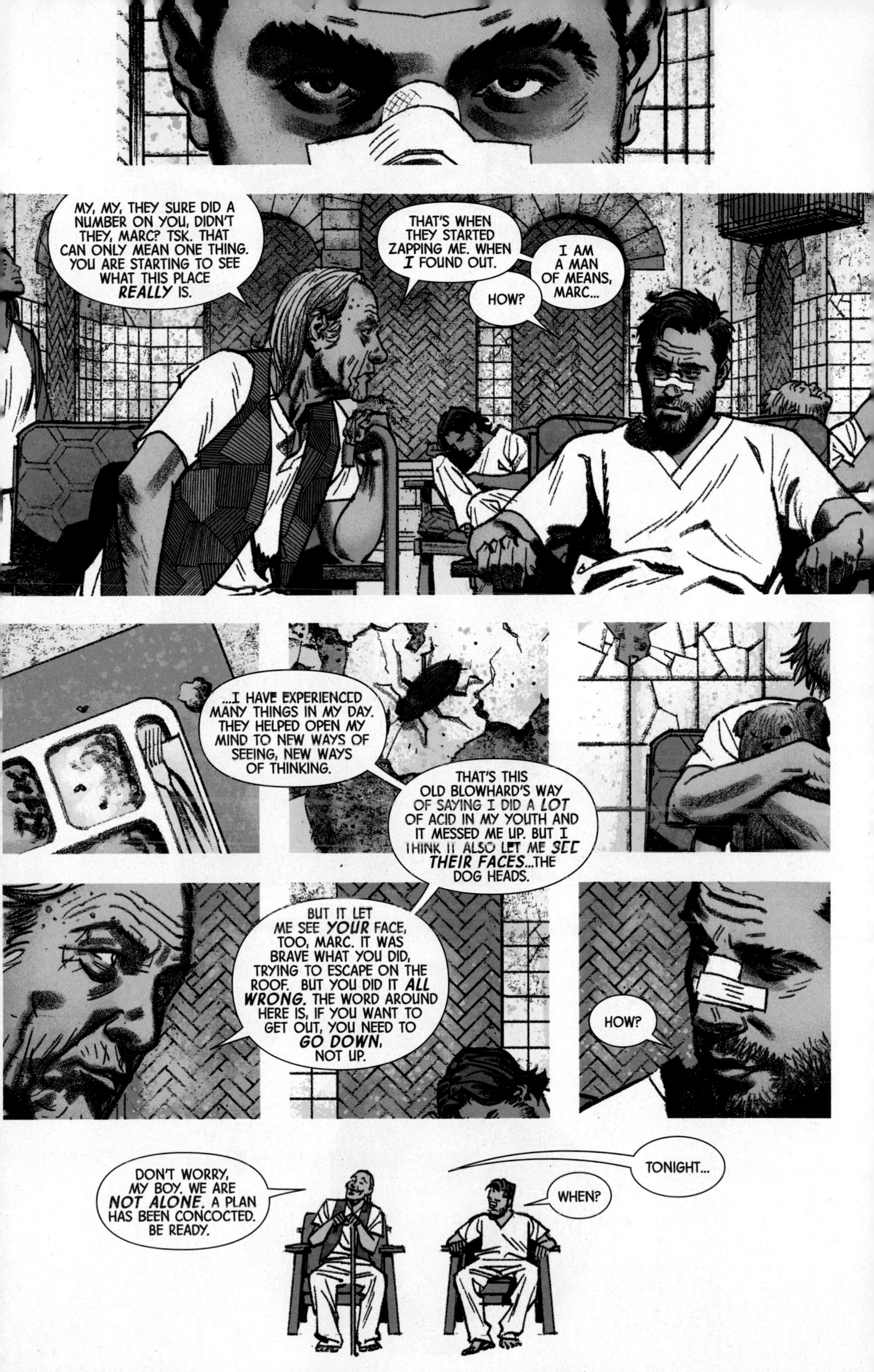

MY, MY, THEY SURE DID A NUMBER ON YOU, DIDN'T THEY, MARC? TSK. THAT CAN ONLY MEAN ONE THING. YOU ARE STARTING TO SEE WHAT THIS PLACE REALLY IS.
THAT'S WHEN THEY STARTED ZAPPING ME. WHEN I FOUND OUT.
HOW?
I AM A MAN OF MEANS, MARC...
...I HAVE EXPERIENCED MANY THINGS IN MY DAY. THEY HELPED OPEN MY MIND TO NEW WAYS OF SEEING, NEW WAYS OF THINKING.
THAT'S THIS OLD BLOWHARD'S WAY OF SAYING I DID A LOT OF ACID IN MY YOUTH AND IT MESSED ME UP. BUT I THINK IT ALSO LET ME SEE THEIR FACES...THE DOG HEADS.
BUT IT LET ME SEE YOUR FACE, TOO, MARC. IT WAS BRAVE WHAT YOU DID, TRYING TO ESCAPE ON THE ROOF. BUT YOU DID IT ALL WRONG. THE WORD AROUND HERE IS, IF YOU WANT TO GET OUT, YOU NEED TO GO DOWN, NOT UP.
HOW?
DON'T WORRY, MY BOY. WE ARE NOT ALONE. A PLAN HAS BEEN CONCOCTED. BE READY.
WHEN?
TONIGHT...

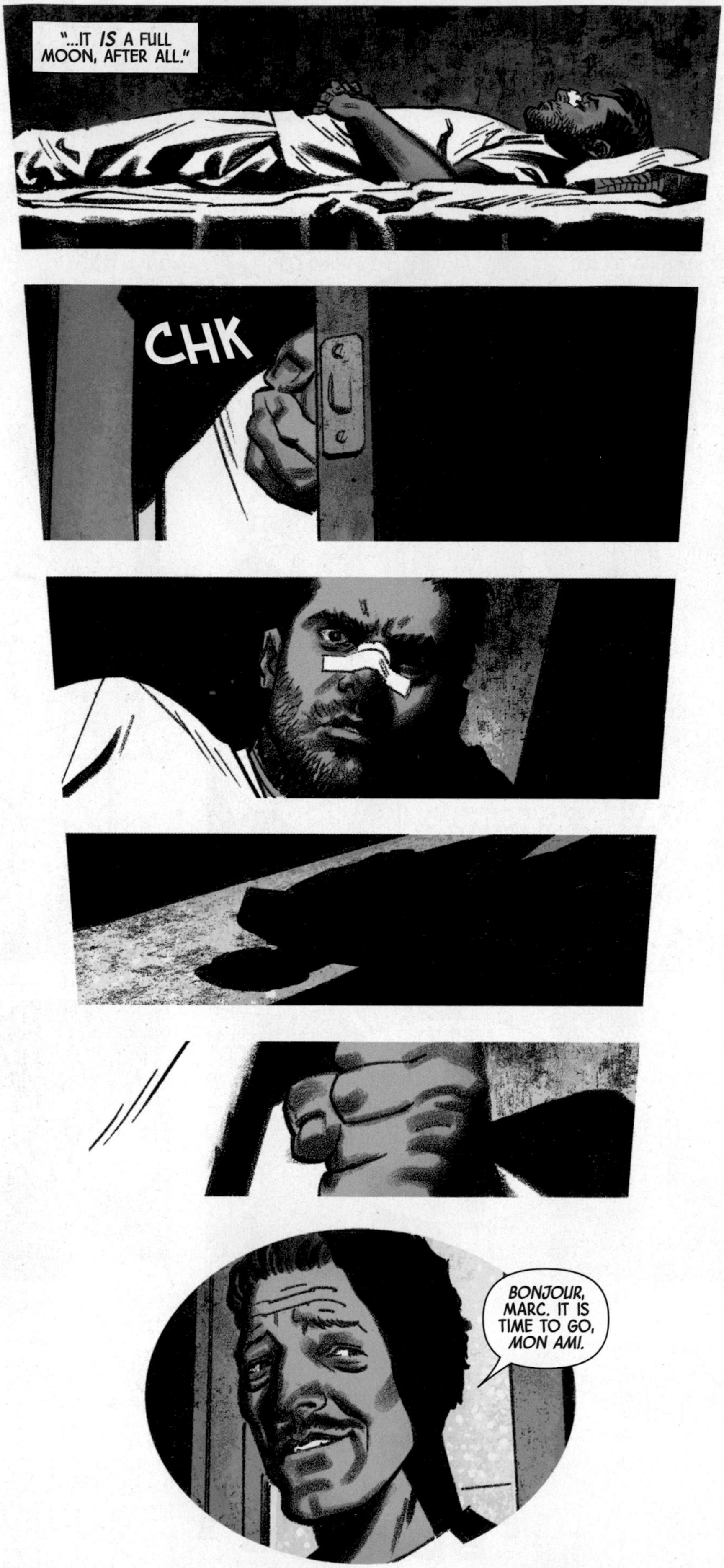
"...IT IS A FULL MOON, AFTER ALL."
CHK
BONJOUR, MARC. IT IS TIME TO GO, MON AMI.

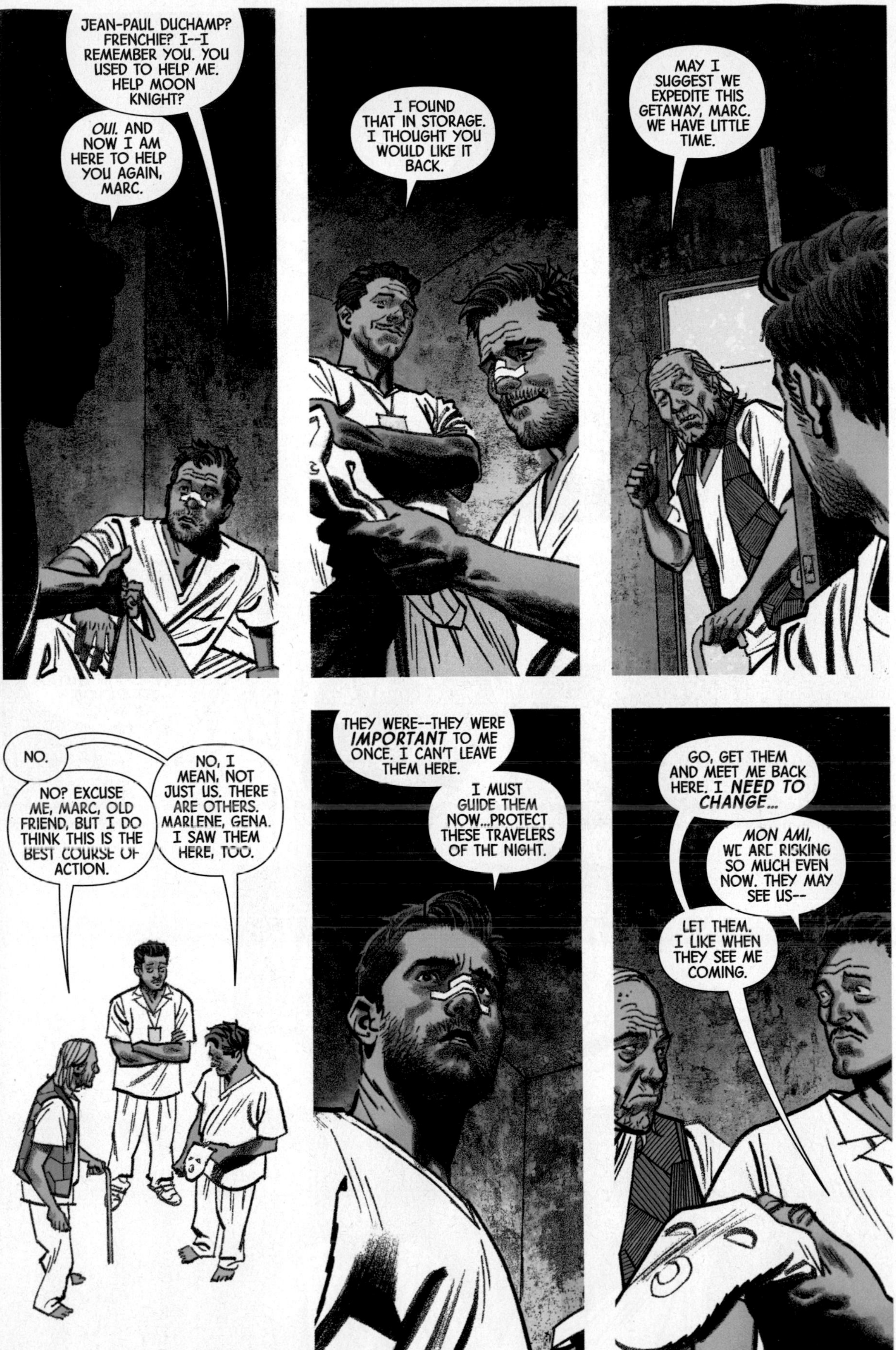
JEAN-PAUL DUCHAMP? FRENCHIE? I--I REMEMBER YOU. YOU USED TO HELP ME. HELP MOON KNIGHT?
OUI. AND NOW I AM HERE TO HELP YOU AGAIN, MARC.
I FOUND THAT IN STORAGE. I THOUGHT YOU WOULD LIKE IT BACK.
MAY I SUGGEST WE EXPEDITE THIS GETAWAY, MARC. WE HAVE LITTLE TIME.
NO.
NO? EXCUSE ME, MARC, OLD FRIEND, BUT I DO THINK THIS IS THE BEST COURSE OF ACTION.
NO, I MEAN, NOT JUST US. THERE ARE OTHERS. MARLENE, GENA. I SAW THEM HERE, TOO.
THEY WERE--THEY WERE IMPORTANT TO ME ONCE. I CAN'T LEAVE THEM HERE.
I MUST GUIDE THEM NOW...PROTECT THESE TRAVELERS OF THE NIGHT.
GO, GET THEM AND MEET ME BACK HERE. I NEED TO CHANGE...
MON AMI, WE ARE RISKING SO MUCH EVEN NOW. THEY MAY SEE US--
LET THEM. I LIKE WHEN THEY SEE ME COMING.

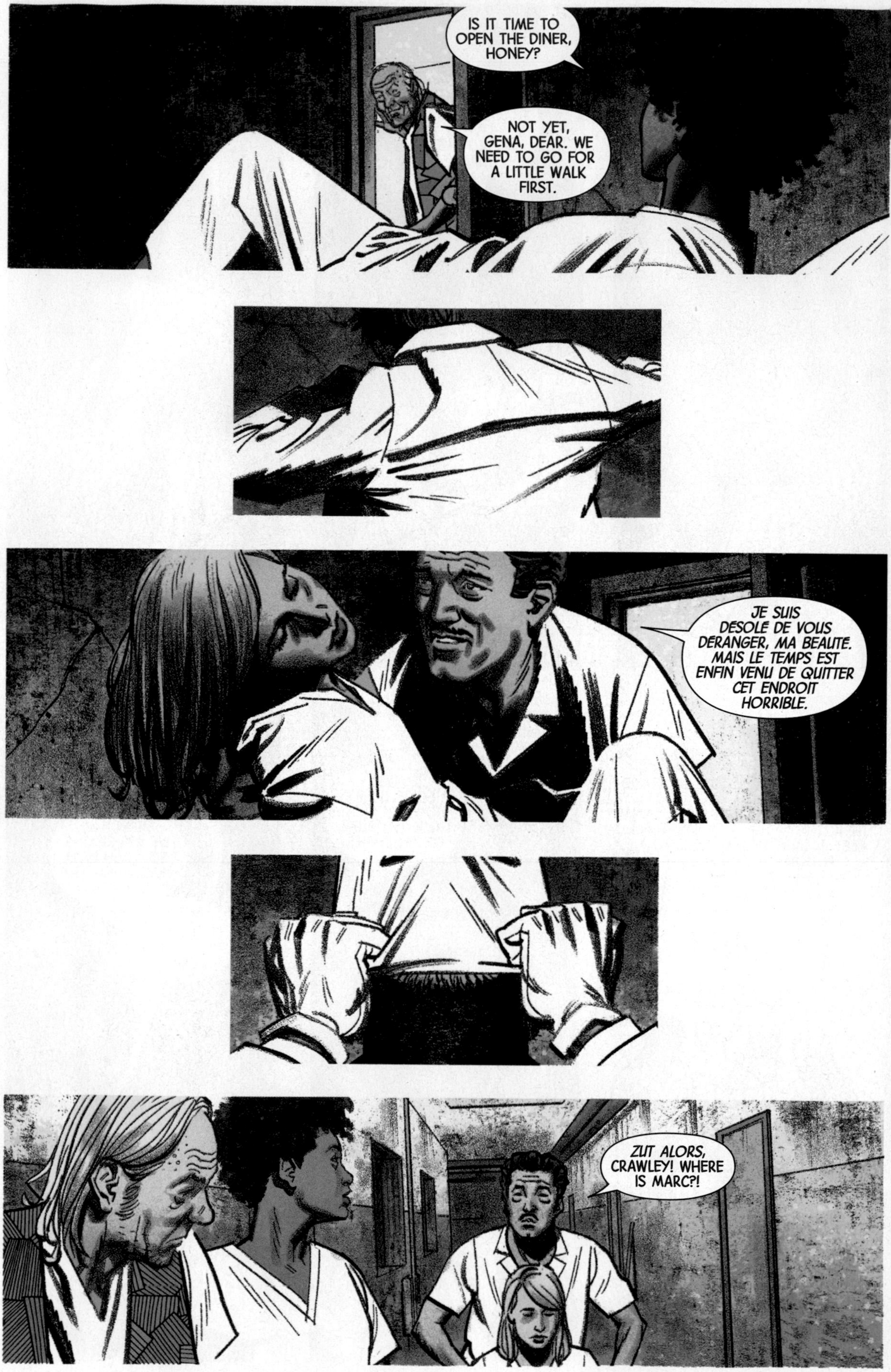
IS IT TIME TO OPEN THE DINER, HONEY?
NOT YET, GENA, DEAR. WE NEED TO GO FOR A LITTLE WALK FIRST.
JE SUIS DESOLE DE VOUS DERANGER, MA BEAUTE. MAIS LE TEMPS EST ENFIN VENU DE QUITTER CET ENDROIT HORRIBLE.
ZUT ALORS, CRAWLEY! WHERE IS MARC?!

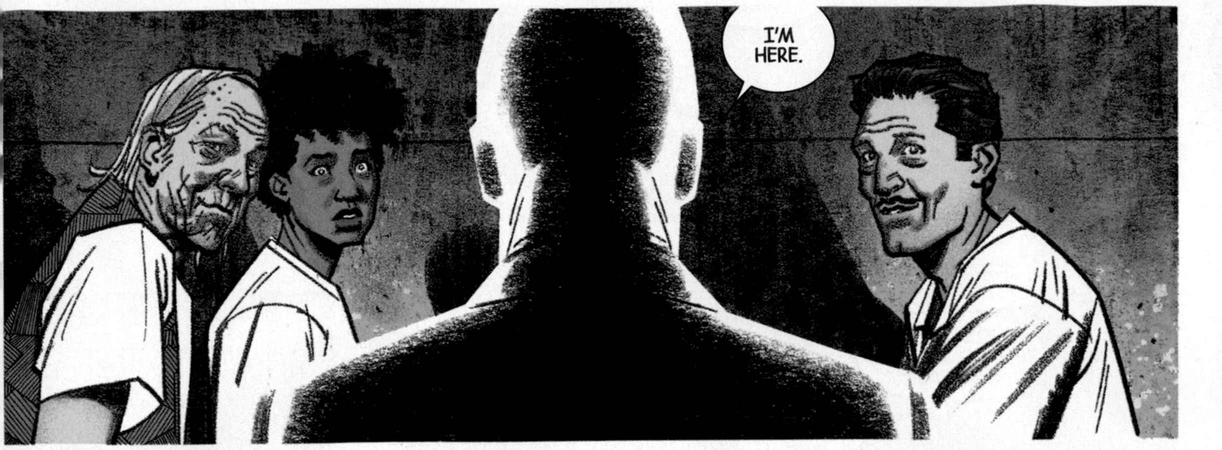
I'M HERE.

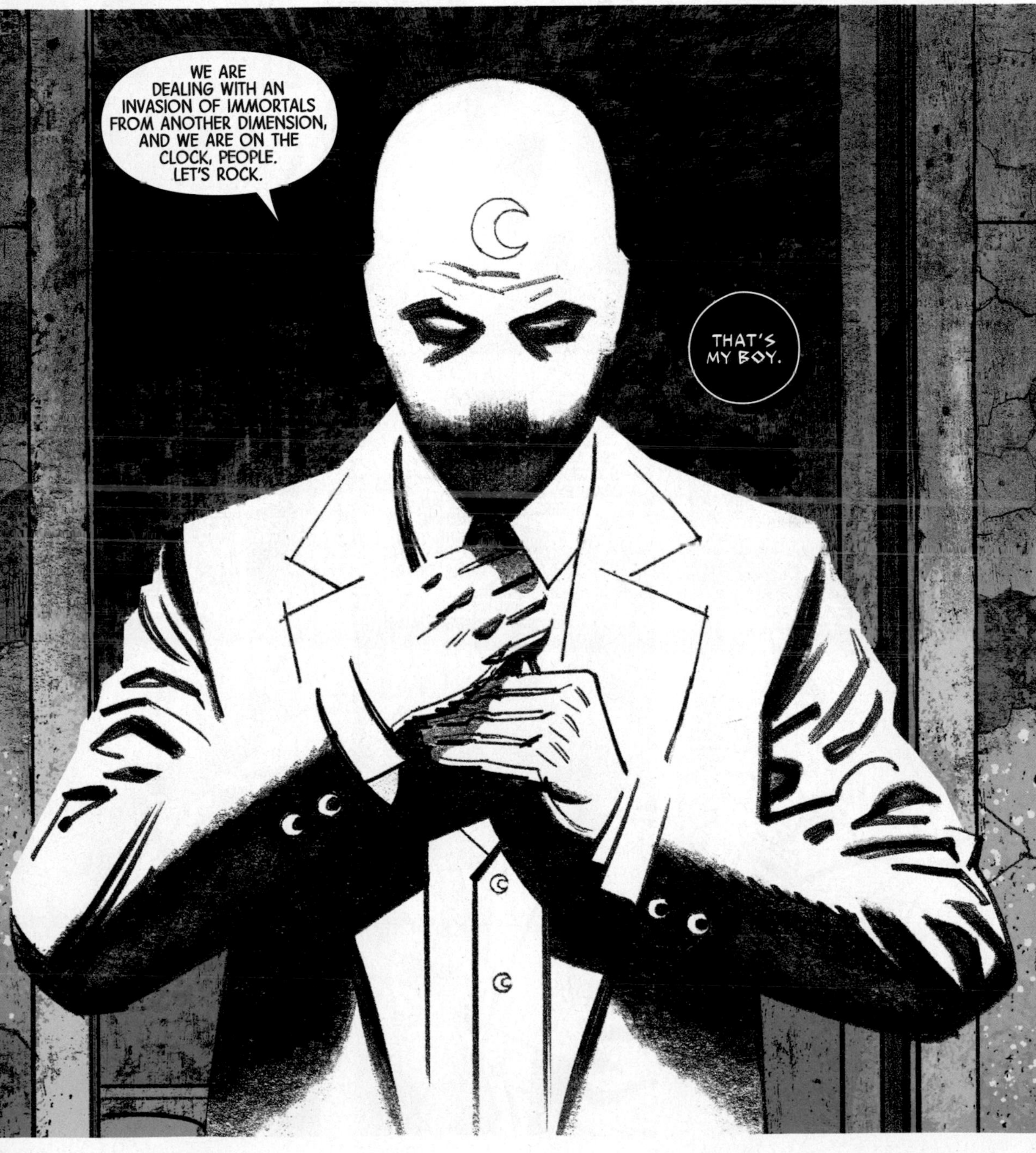
WE ARE DEALING WITH AN INVASION OF IMMORTALS FROM ANOTHER DIMENSION, AND WE ARE ON THE CLOCK, PEOPLE. LET'S ROCK.
THAT'S MY BOY.

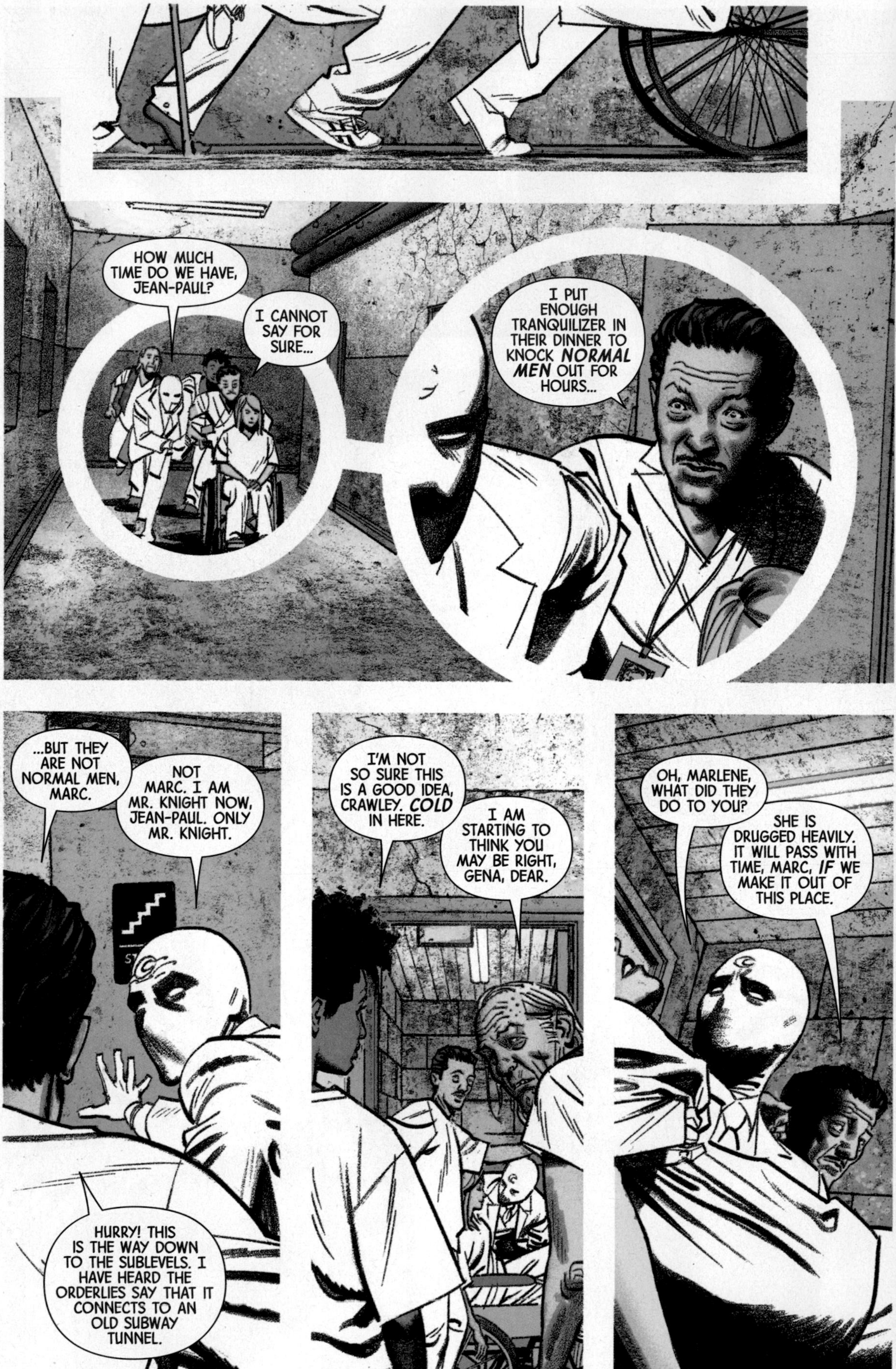
HOW MUCH TIME DO WE HAVE, JEAN-PAUL?
I CANNOT SAY FOR SURE...
I PUT ENOUGH TRANQUILIZER IN THEIR DINNER TO KNOCK NORMAL MEN OUT FOR HOURS...
...BUT THEY ARE NOT NORMAL MEN, MARC.
NOT MARC. I AM MR. KNIGHT NOW, JEAN-PAUL. ONLY MR. KNIGHT.
HURRY! THIS IS THE WAY DOWN TO THE SUBLEVELS. I HAVE HEARD THE ORDERLIES SAY THAT IT CONNECTS TO AN OLD SUBWAY TUNNEL.
I'M NOT SO SURE THIS IS A GOOD IDEA, CRAWLEY. COLD IN HERE.
I AM STARTING TO THINK YOU MAY BE RIGHT, GENA, DEAR.
OH, MARLENE, WHAT DID THEY DO TO YOU?
SHE IS DRUGGED HEAVILY. IT WILL PASS WITH TIME, MARC, IF WE MAKE IT OUT OF THIS PLACE.

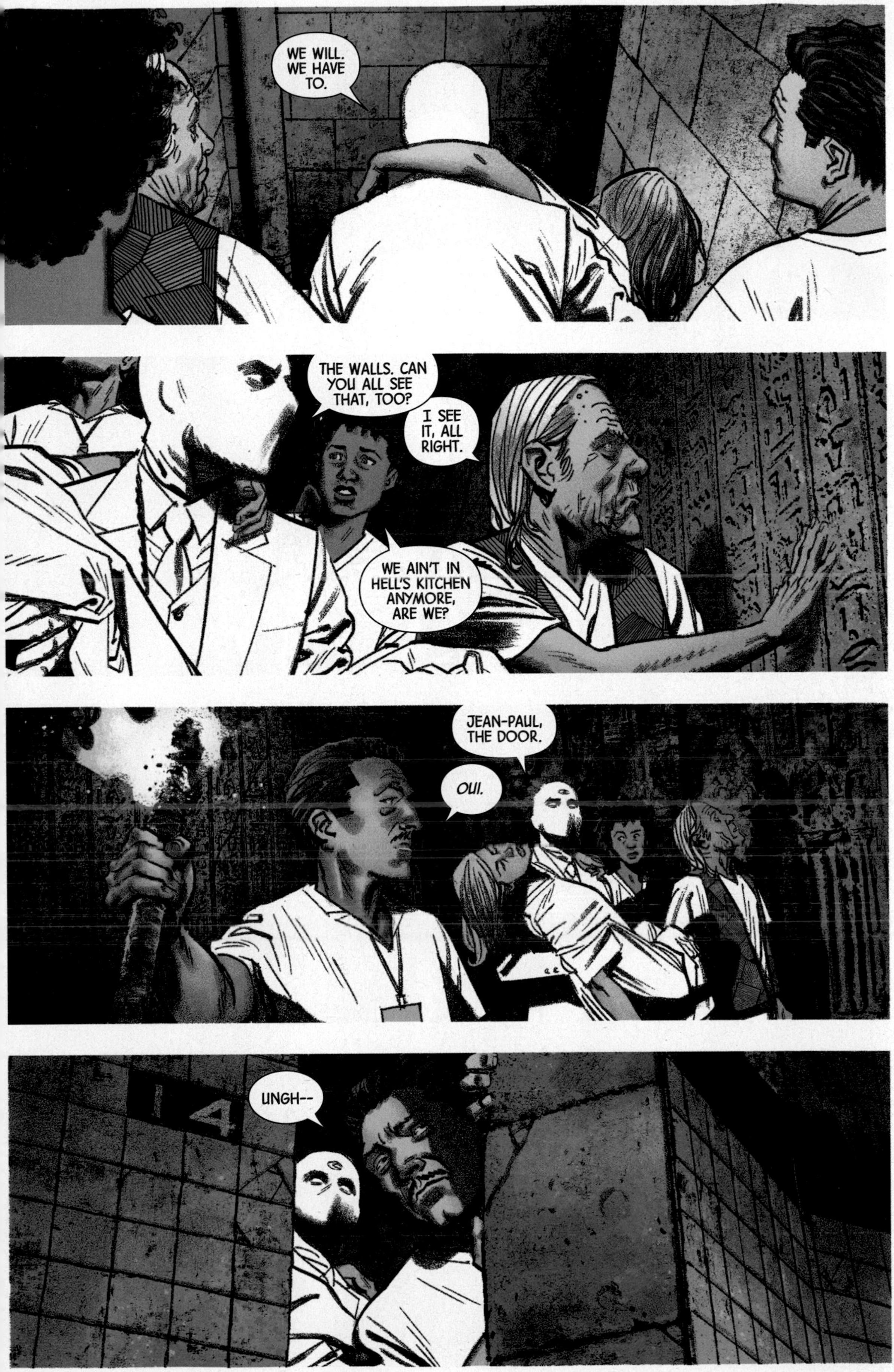
WE WILL. WE HAVE TO.
THE WALLS. CAN YOU ALL SEE THAT, TOO?
I SEE IT, ALL RIGHT.
WE AIN'T IN HELL'S KITCHEN ANYMORE, ARE WE?
JEAN-PAUL, THE DOOR.
OUI.
UNGH--

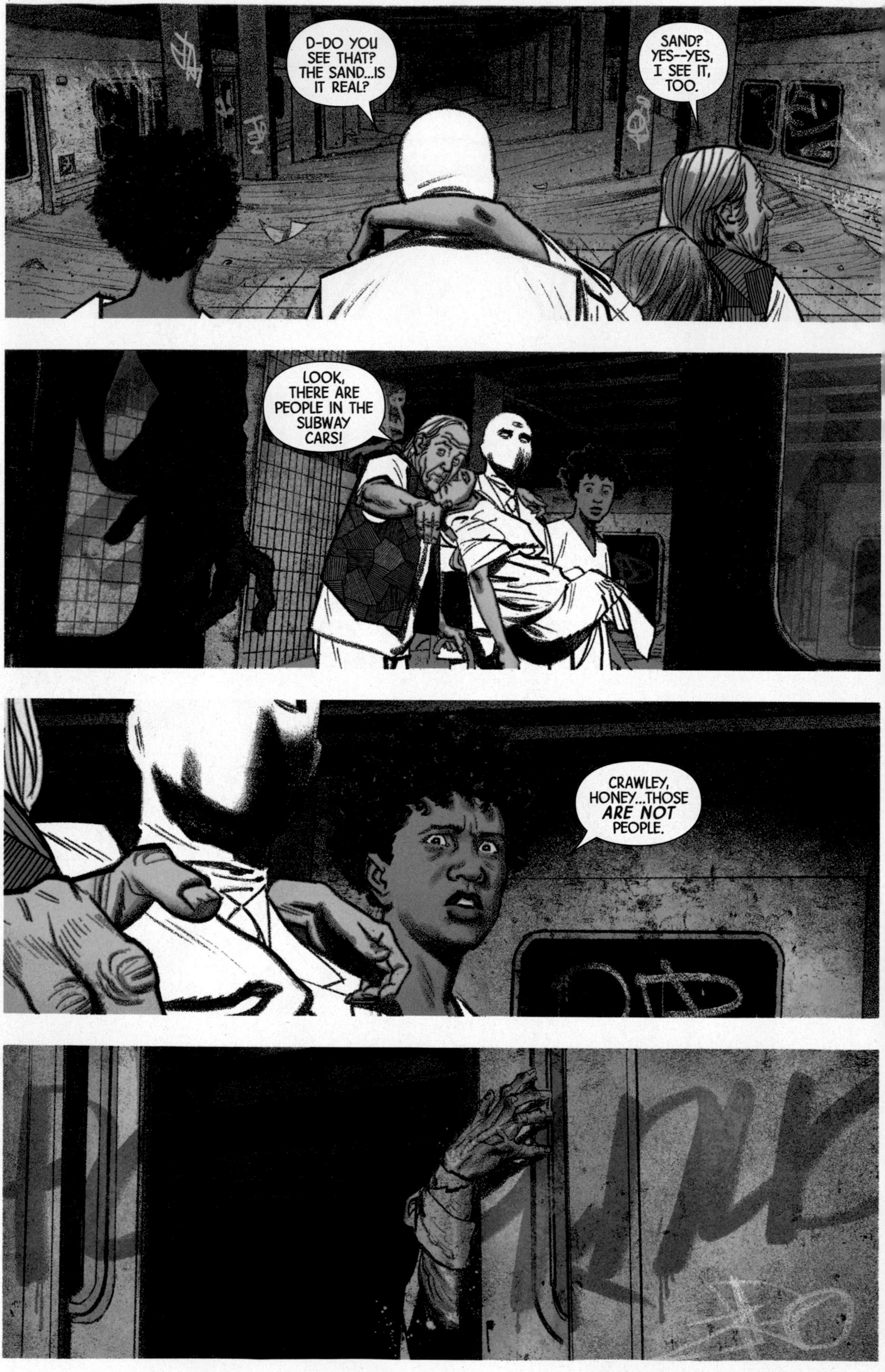
D-DO YOU SEE THAT? THE SAND...IS IT REAL?
SAND? YES--YES, I SEE IT, TOO.
LOOK, THERE ARE PEOPLE IN THE SUBWAY CARS!
CRAWLEY, HONEY...THOSE ***ARE NOT*** PEOPLE.

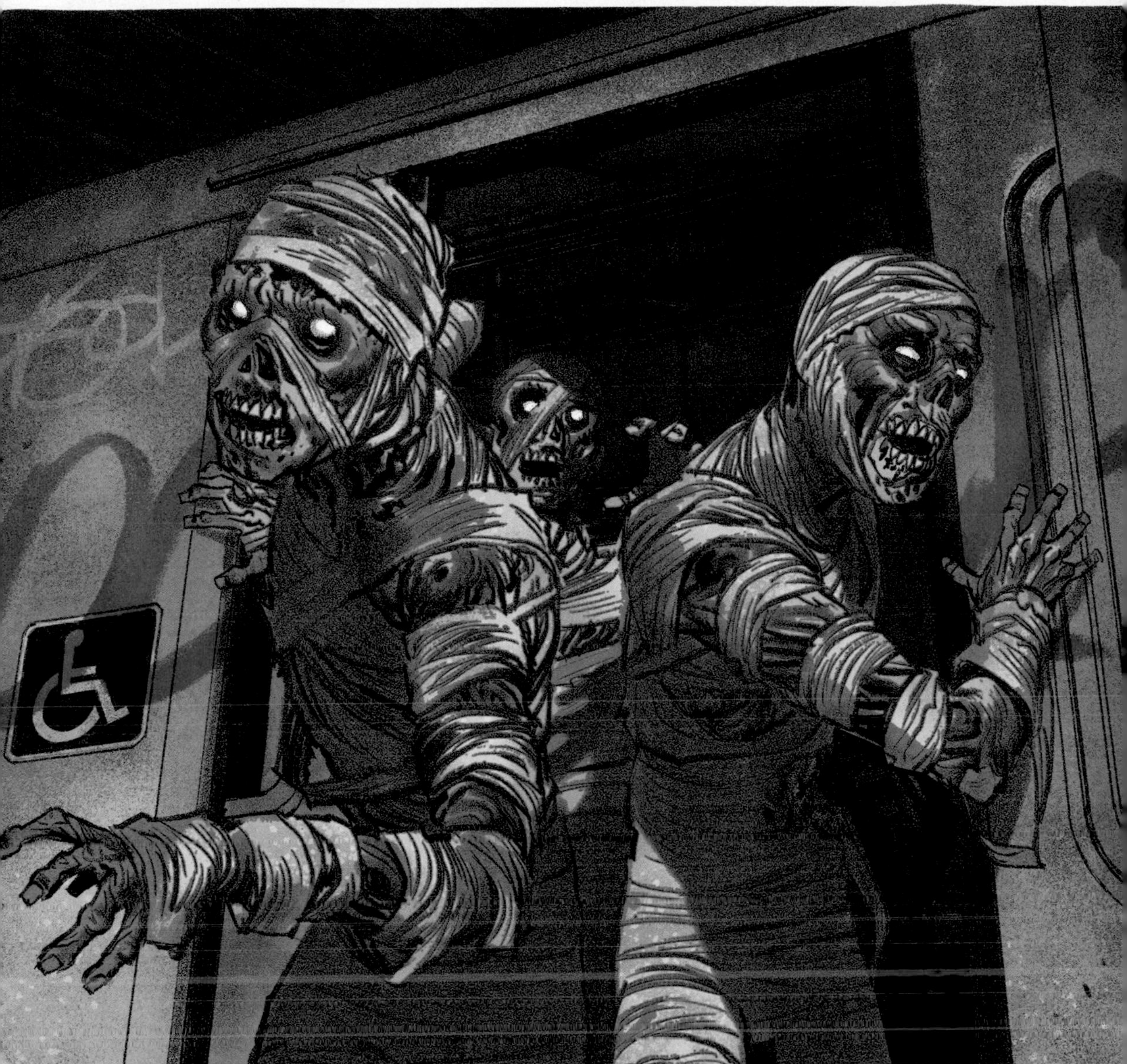

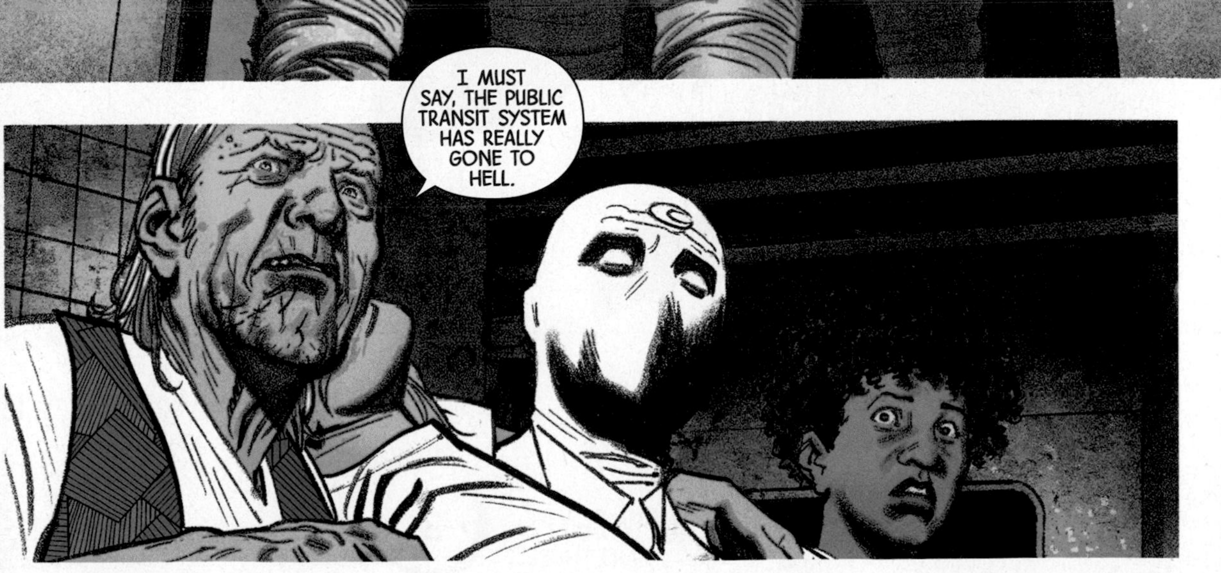
I MUST SAY, THE PUBLIC TRANSIT SYSTEM HAS REALLY GONE TO HELL.

WELCOME TO NEW EGYPT

PART THREE

3

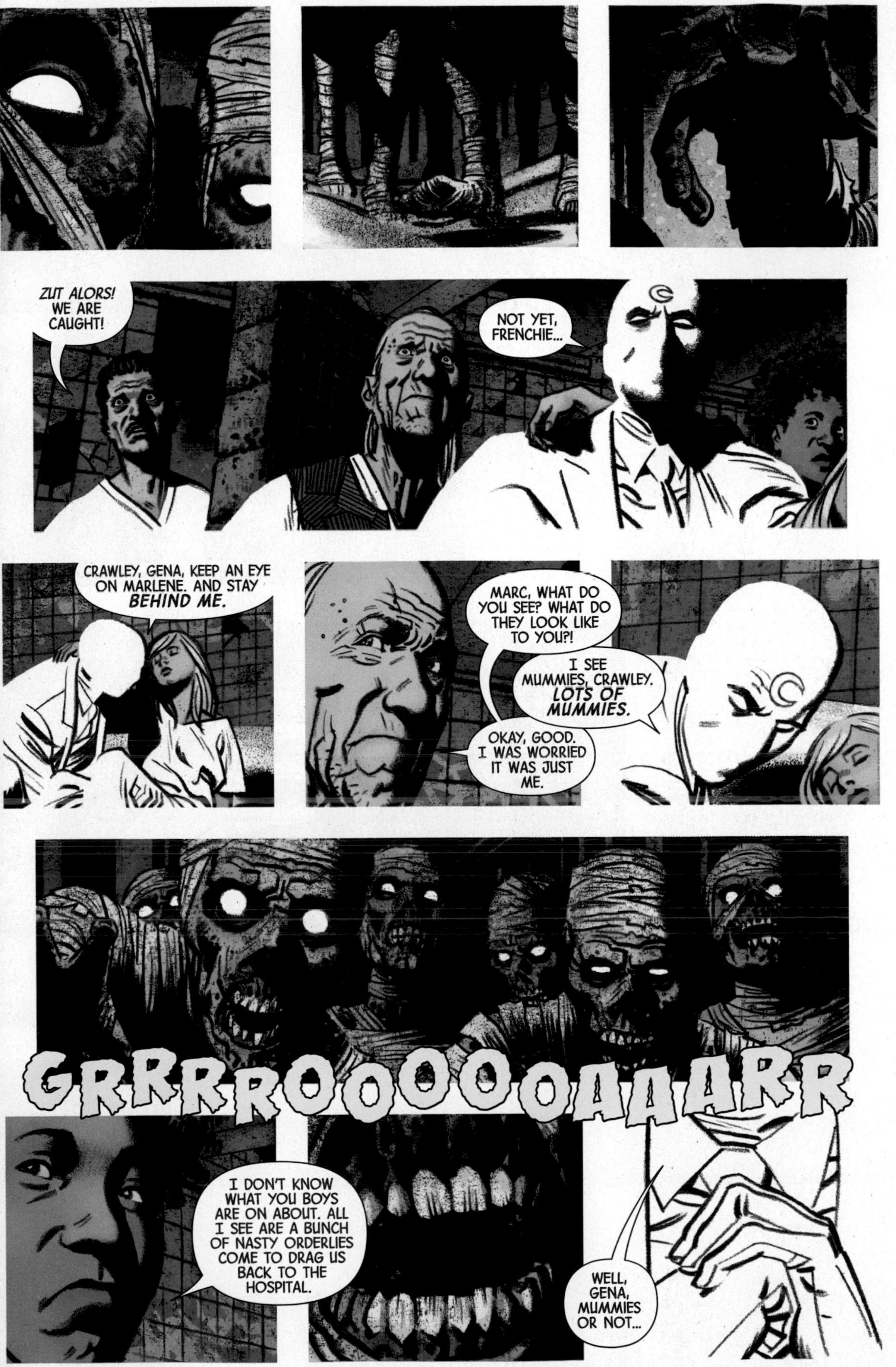
ZUT ALORS! WE ARE CAUGHT!
NOT YET, FRENCHIE...
CRAWLEY, GENA, KEEP AN EYE ON MARLENE. AND STAY *BEHIND ME.*
MARC, WHAT DO YOU SEE? WHAT DO THEY LOOK LIKE TO YOU?!
I SEE MUMMIES, CRAWLEY. *LOTS OF MUMMIES.*
OKAY, GOOD. I WAS WORRIED IT WAS JUST ME.
GRRRROOOOOAAARR
I DON'T KNOW WHAT YOU BOYS ARE ON ABOUT. ALL I SEE ARE A BUNCH OF NASTY ORDERLIES COME TO DRAG US BACK TO THE HOSPITAL.
WELL, GENA, MUMMIES OR NOT...

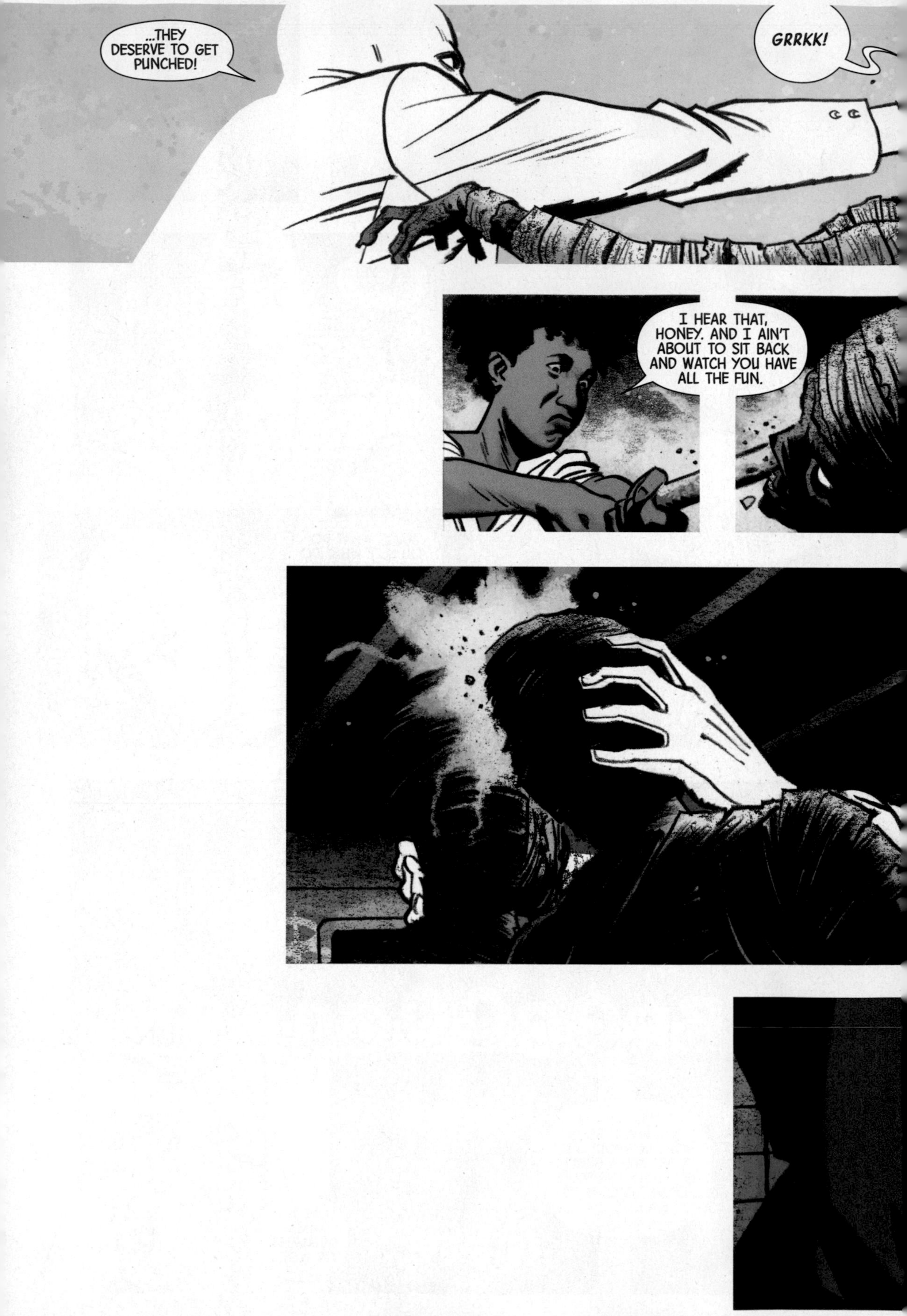
...THEY DESERVE TO GET PUNCHED!
GRRKK!
I HEAR THAT, HONEY. AND I AIN'T ABOUT TO SIT BACK AND WATCH YOU HAVE ALL THE FUN.

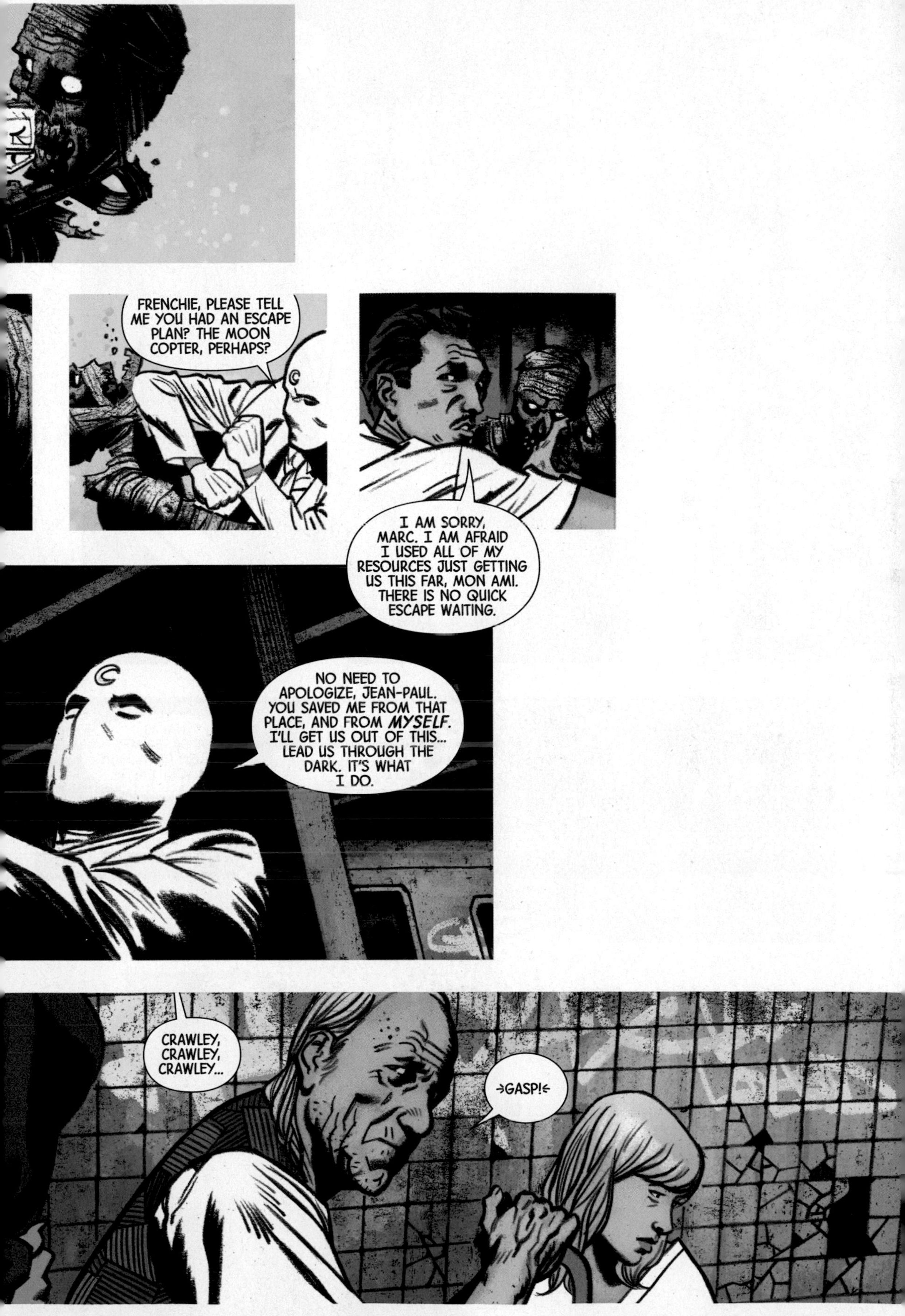
FRENCHIE, PLEASE TELL ME YOU HAD AN ESCAPE PLAN? THE MOON COPTER, PERHAPS?
I AM SORRY, MARC. I AM AFRAID I USED ALL OF MY RESOURCES JUST GETTING US THIS FAR, MON AMI. THERE IS NO QUICK ESCAPE WAITING.
NO NEED TO APOLOGIZE, JEAN-PAUL. YOU SAVED ME FROM THAT PLACE, AND FROM *MYSELF*. I'LL GET US OUT OF THIS... LEAD US THROUGH THE DARK. IT'S WHAT I DO.
CRAWLEY, CRAWLEY, CRAWLEY...
GASP!

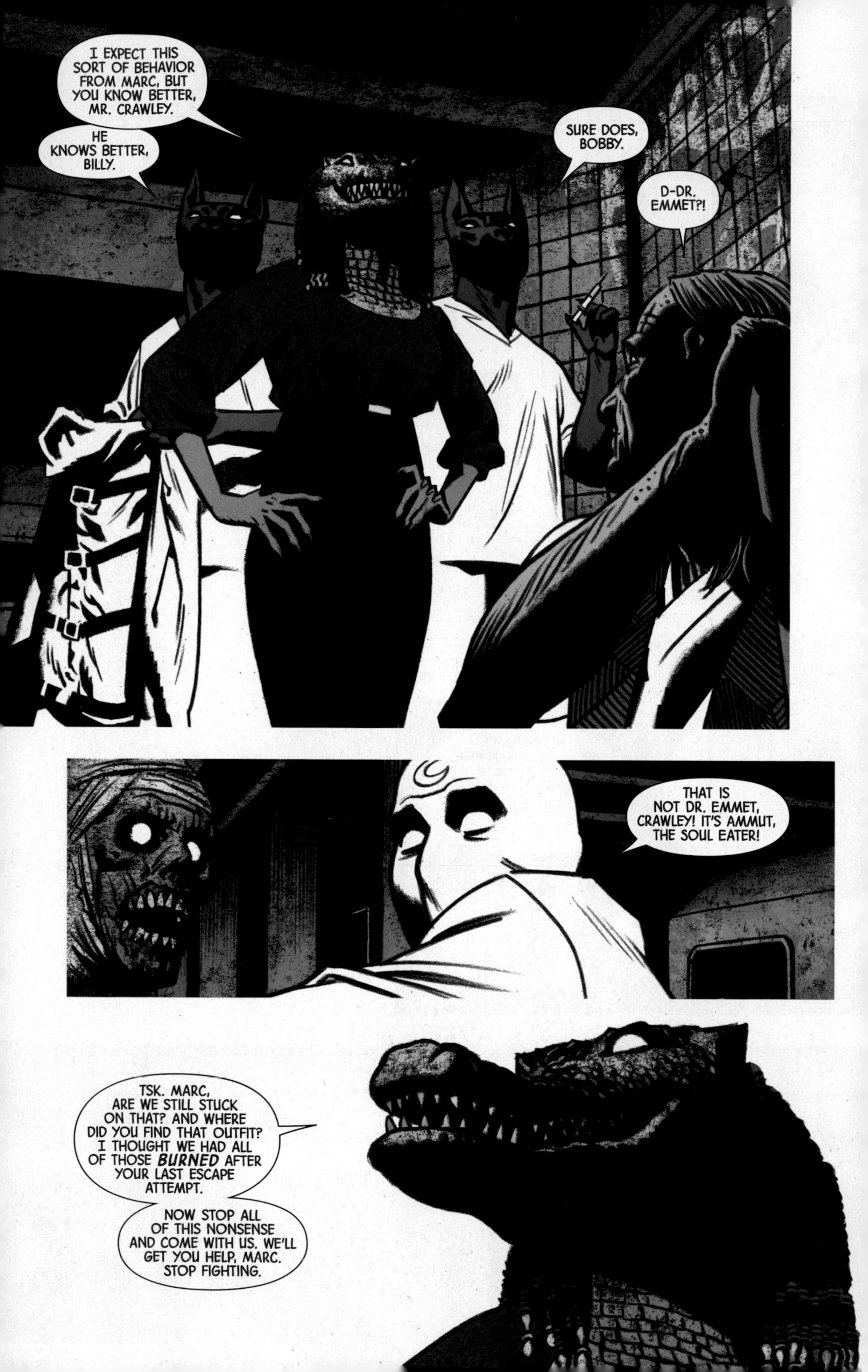
I EXPECT THIS SORT OF BEHAVIOR FROM MARC, BUT YOU KNOW BETTER, MR. CRAWLEY.
HE KNOWS BETTER, BILLY.
SURE DOES, BOBBY.
D-DR. EMMET?!
THAT IS NOT DR. EMMET, CRAWLEY! IT'S AMMUT, THE SOUL EATER!
TSK. MARC, ARE WE STILL STUCK ON THAT? AND WHERE DID YOU FIND THAT OUTFIT? I THOUGHT WE HAD ALL OF THOSE BURNED AFTER YOUR LAST ESCAPE ATTEMPT.
NOW STOP ALL OF THIS NONSENSE AND COME WITH US. WE'LL GET YOU HELP, MARC. STOP FIGHTING.

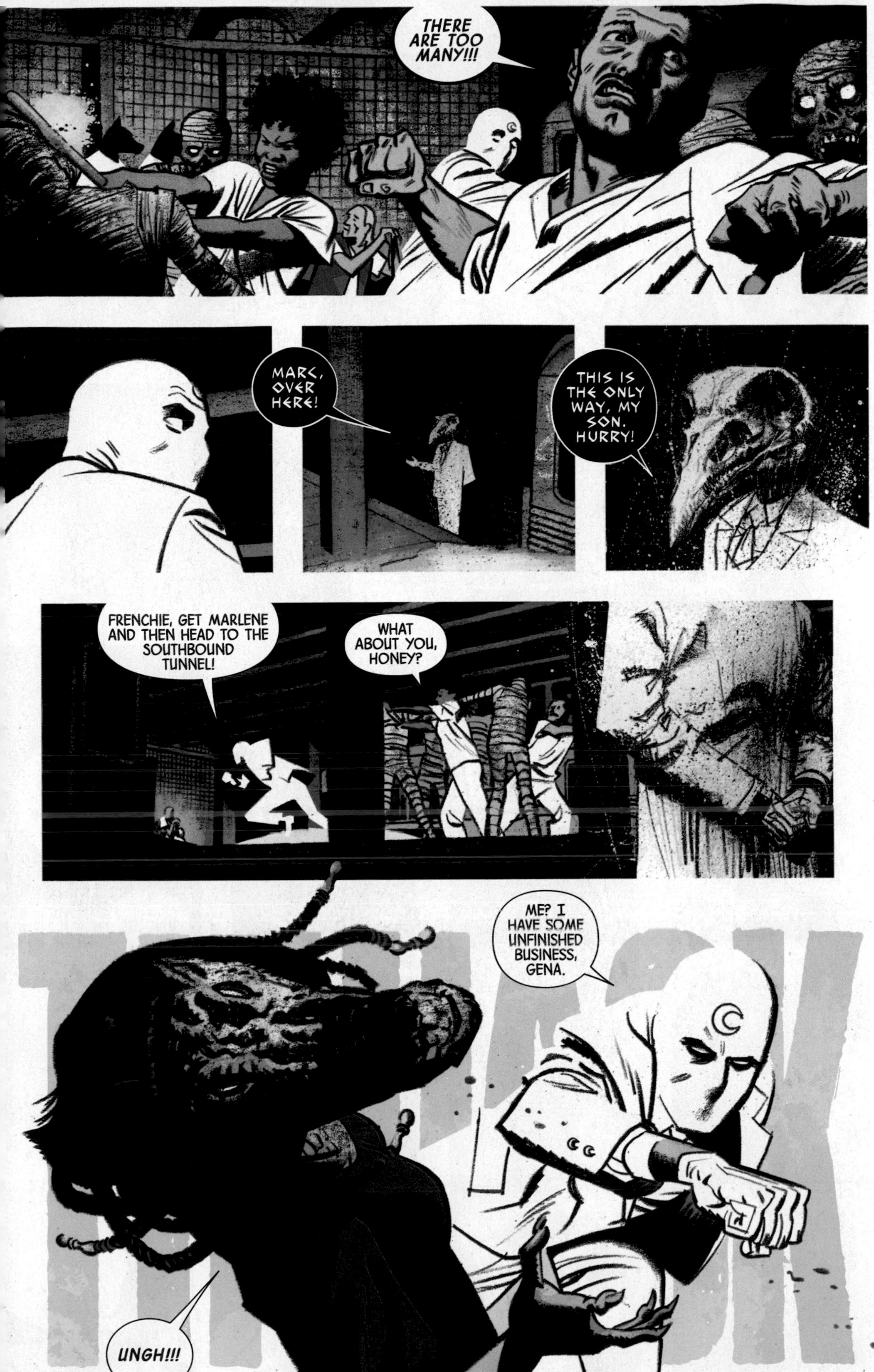
THERE ARE TOO MANY!!!
MARC, OVER HERE!
THIS IS THE ONLY WAY, MY SON. HURRY!
FRENCHIE, GET MARLENE AND THEN HEAD TO THE SOUTHBOUND TUNNEL!
WHAT ABOUT YOU, HONEY?
ME? I HAVE SOME UNFINISHED BUSINESS, GENA.
UNGH!!!

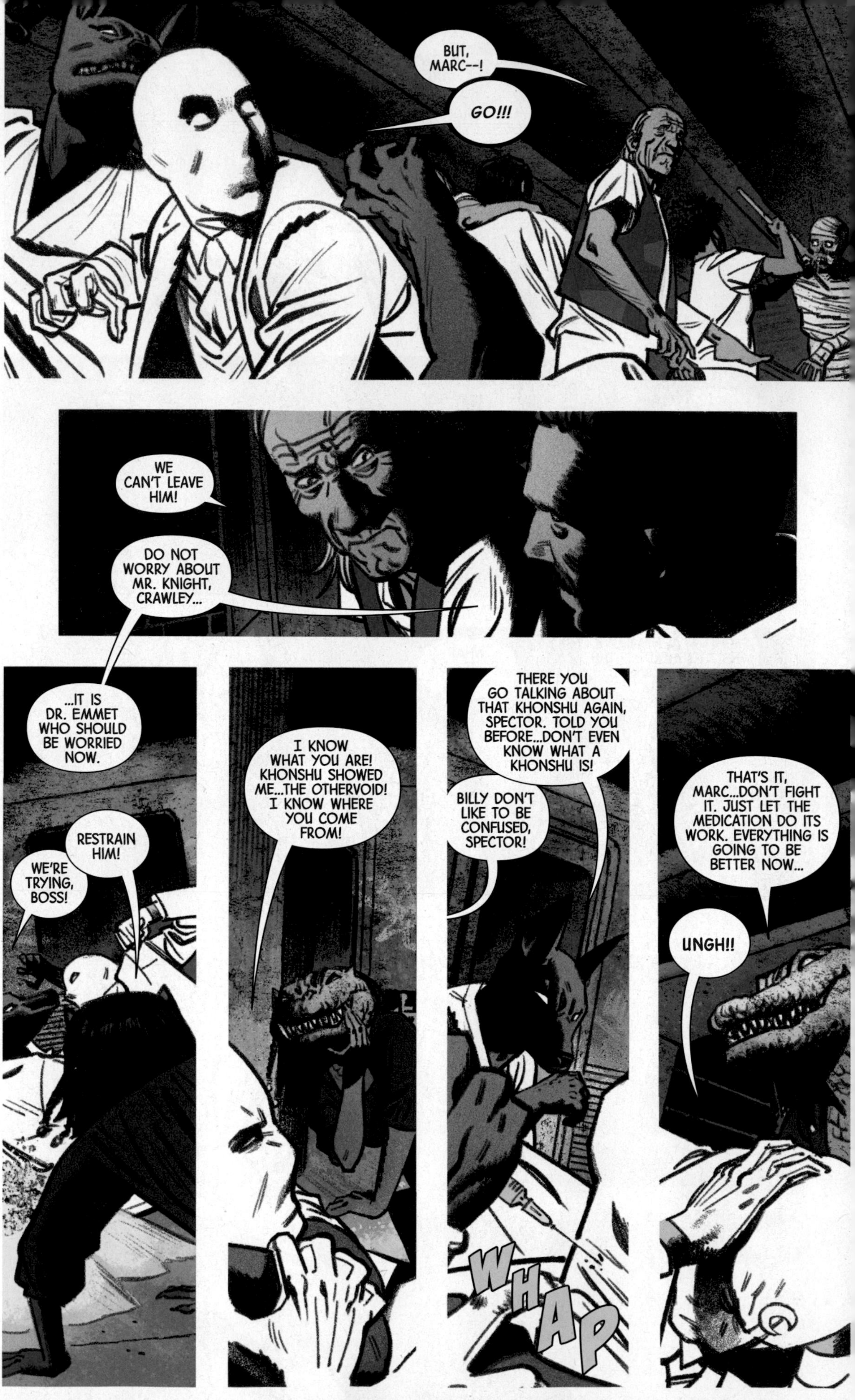

BUT, MARC--!
GO!!!
WE CAN'T LEAVE HIM!
DO NOT WORRY ABOUT MR. KNIGHT, CRAWLEY...
...IT IS DR. EMMET WHO SHOULD BE WORRIED NOW.
RESTRAIN HIM!
WE'RE TRYING, BOSS!
I KNOW WHAT YOU ARE! KHONSHU SHOWED ME...THE OTHERVOID! I KNOW WHERE YOU COME FROM!
THERE YOU GO TALKING ABOUT THAT KHONSHU AGAIN, SPECTOR. TOLD YOU BEFORE...DON'T EVEN KNOW WHAT A KHONSHU IS!
BILLY DON'T LIKE TO BE CONFUSED, SPECTOR!
WHAP
THAT'S IT, MARC...DON'T FIGHT IT. JUST LET THE MEDICATION DO ITS WORK. EVERYTHING IS GOING TO BE BETTER NOW...
UNGH!!

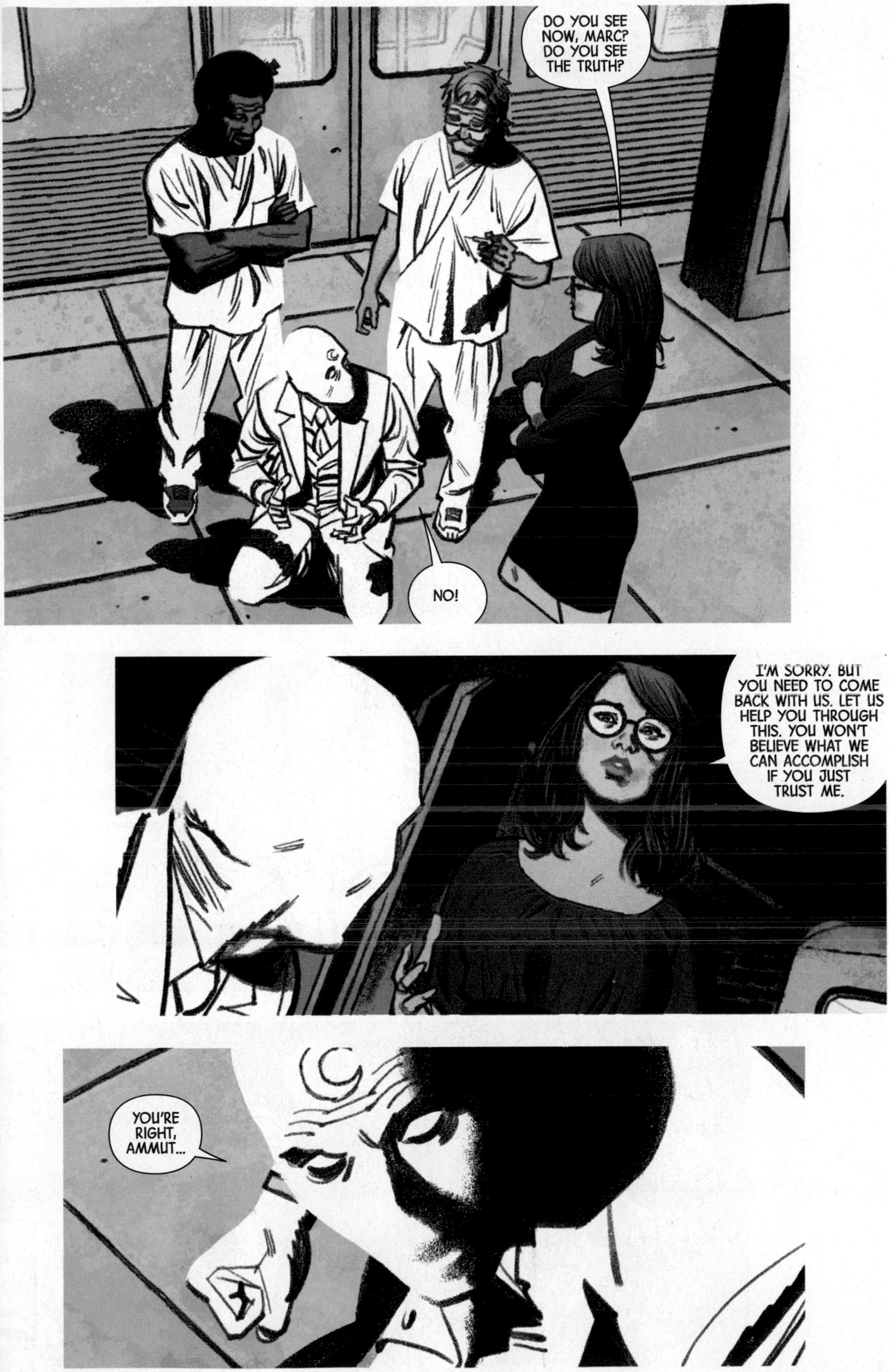
DO YOU SEE NOW, MARC? DO YOU SEE THE TRUTH?
NO!
I'M SORRY. BUT YOU NEED TO COME BACK WITH US. LET US HELP YOU THROUGH THIS. YOU WON'T BELIEVE WHAT WE CAN ACCOMPLISH IF YOU JUST TRUST ME.
YOU'RE RIGHT, AMMUT...

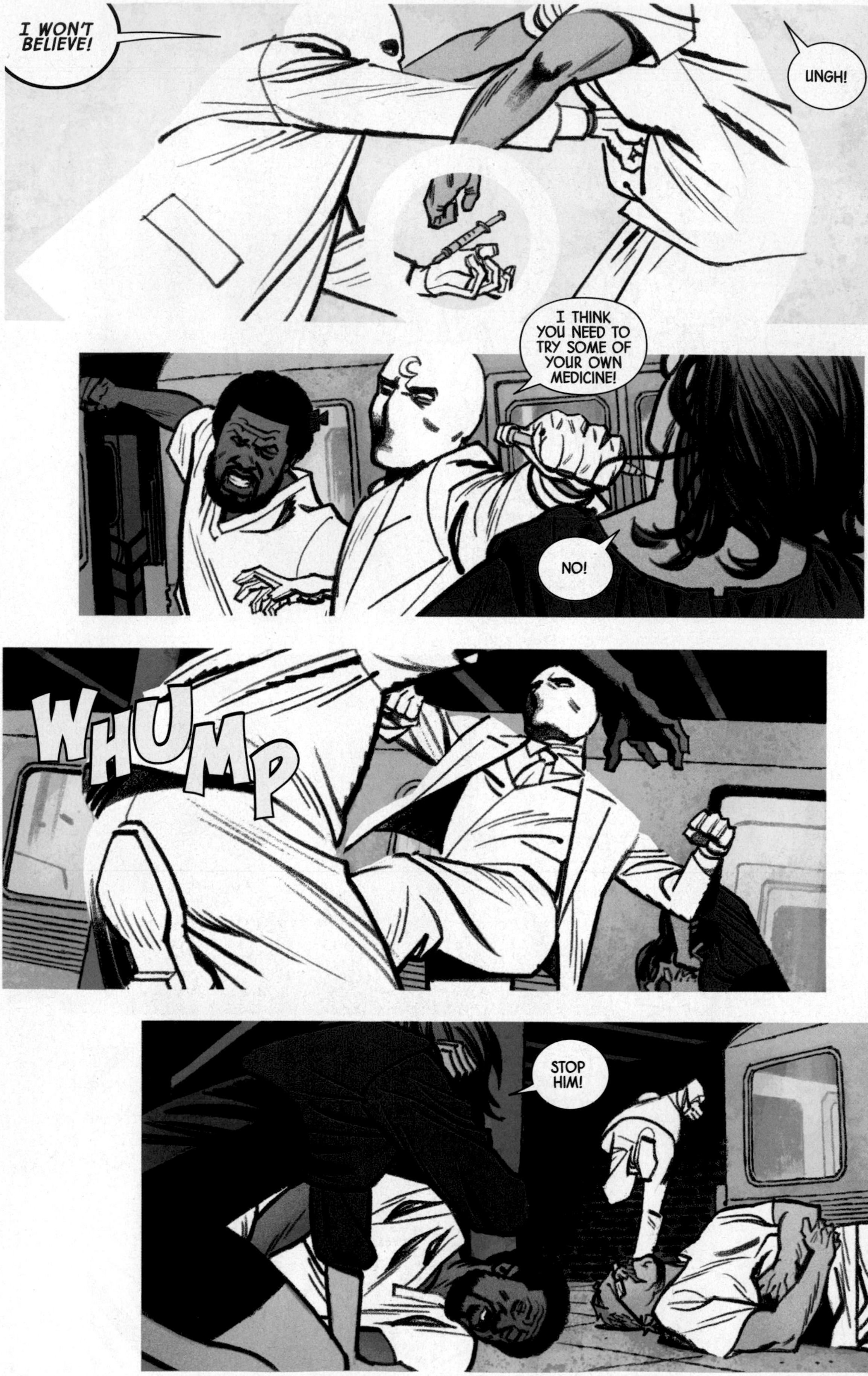
I WON'T BELIEVE!
UNGH!
I THINK YOU NEED TO TRY SOME OF YOUR OWN MEDICINE!
NO!
WHUMP
STOP HIM!

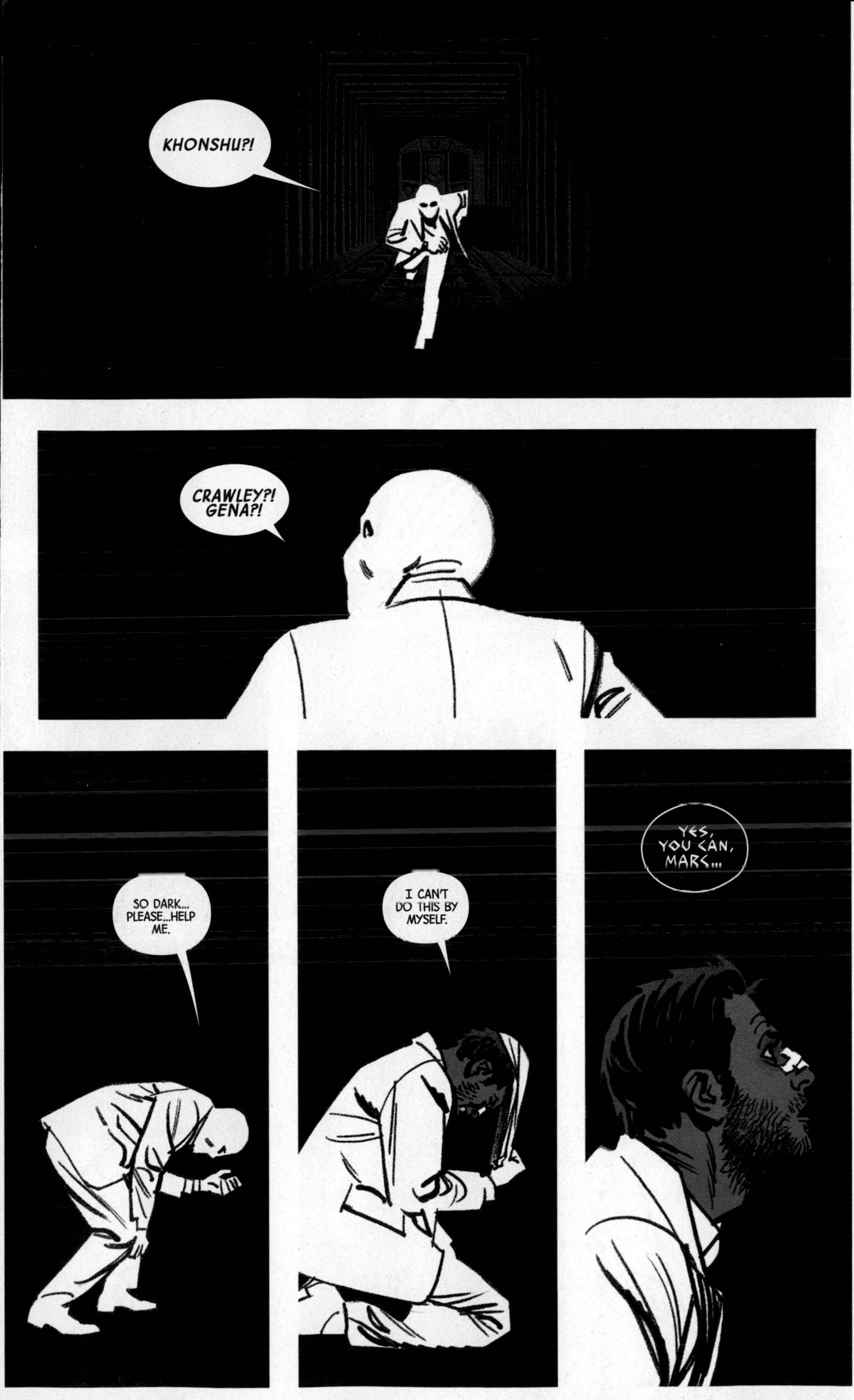
KHONSHU?!
CRAWLEY?! GENA?!
SO DARK... PLEASE...HELP ME.
I CAN'T DO THIS BY MYSELF.
YES, YOU CAN, MARC...

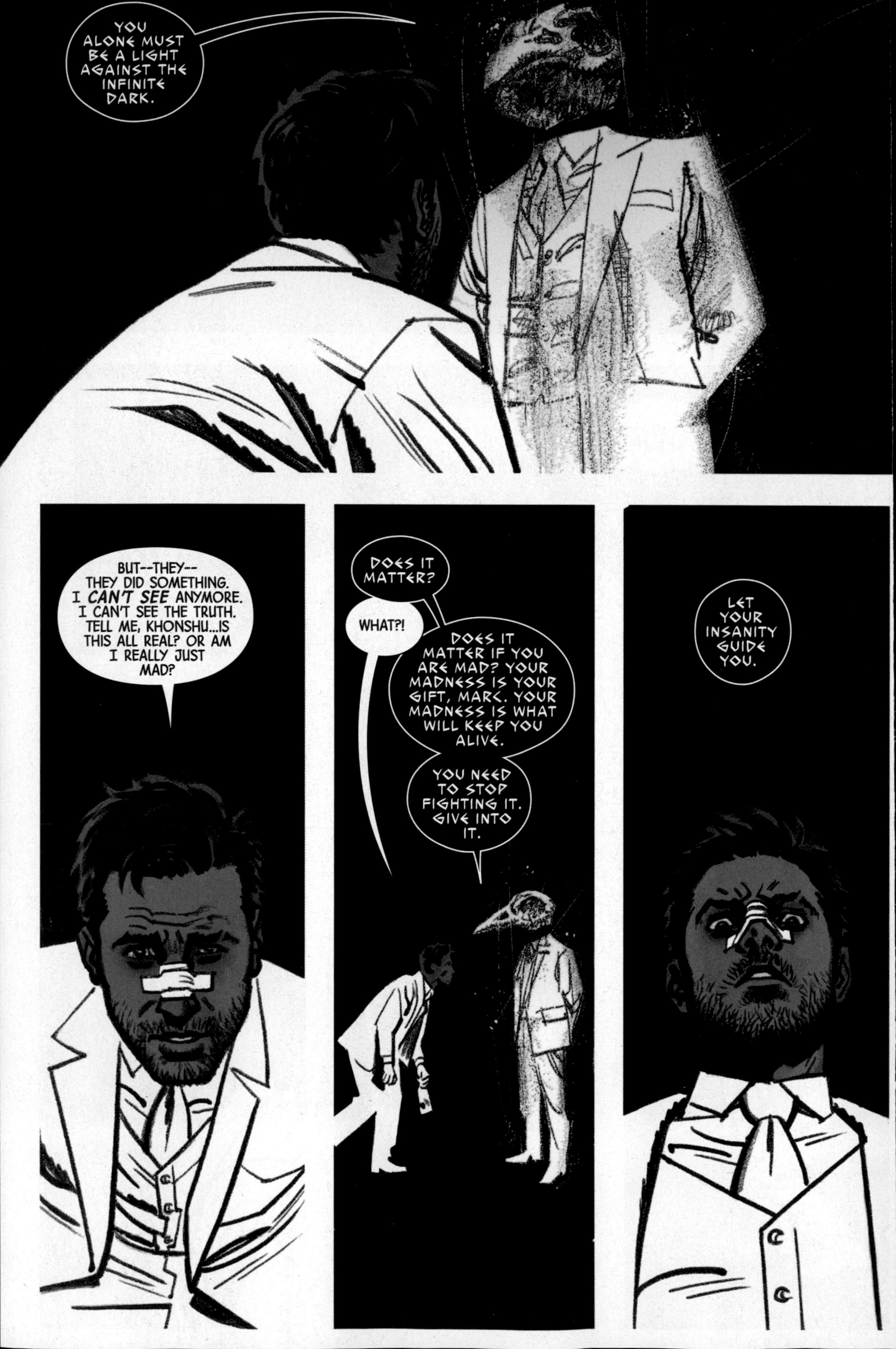
YOU ALONE MUST BE A LIGHT AGAINST THE INFINITE DARK.
BUT--THEY-- THEY DID SOMETHING. I *CAN'T SEE* ANYMORE. I CAN'T SEE THE TRUTH. TELL ME, KHONSHU...IS THIS ALL REAL? OR AM I REALLY JUST MAD?
DOES IT MATTER?
WHAT?!
DOES IT MATTER IF YOU ARE MAD? YOUR MADNESS IS YOUR GIFT, MARC. YOUR MADNESS IS WHAT WILL KEEP YOU ALIVE.
YOU NEED TO STOP FIGHTING IT. GIVE INTO IT.
LET YOUR INSANITY GUIDE YOU.

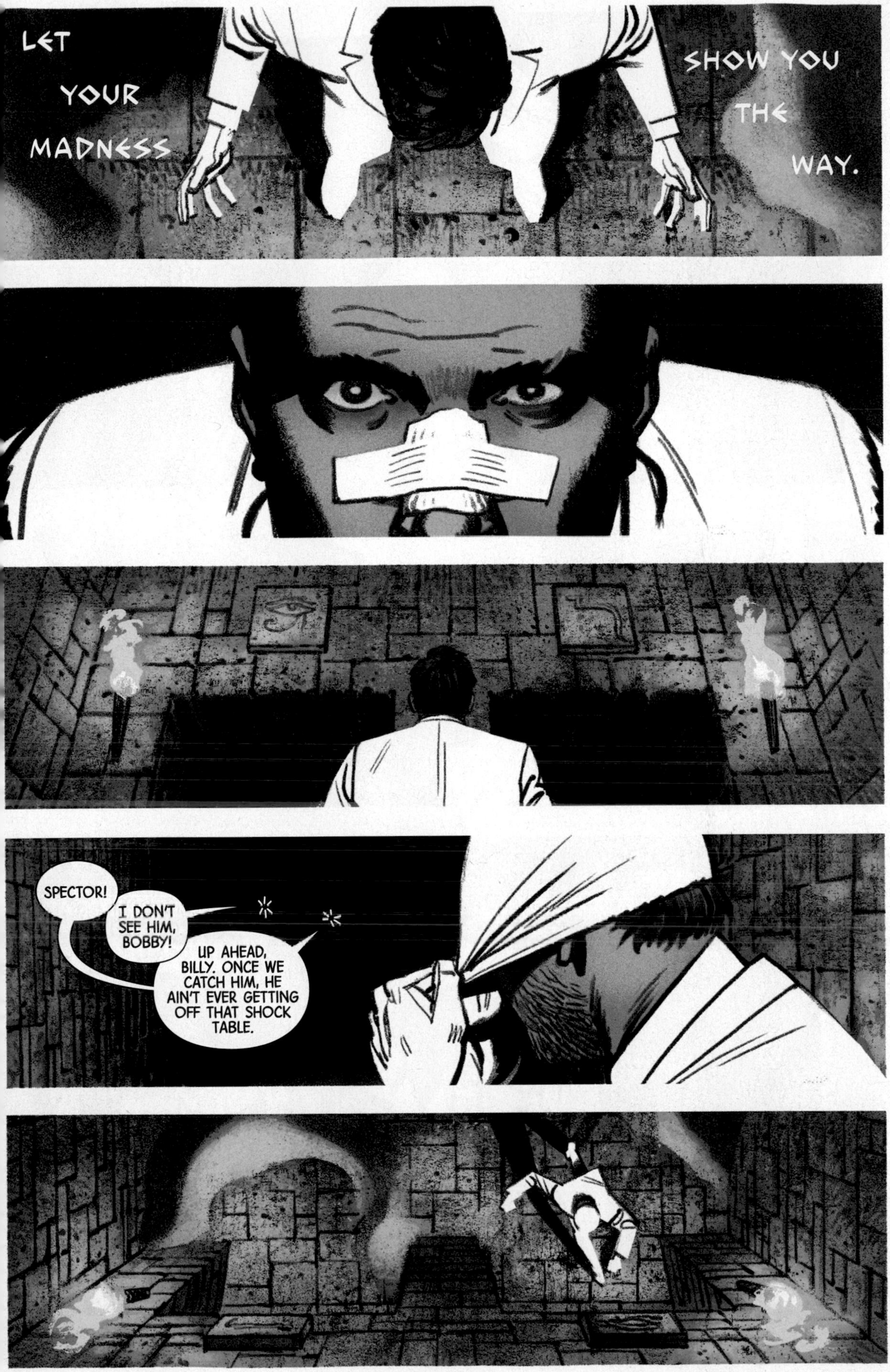
LET YOUR MADNESS
SHOW YOU THE WAY.
SPECTOR!
I DON'T SEE HIM, BOBBY!
UP AHEAD, BILLY. ONCE WE CATCH HIM, HE AIN'T EVER GETTING OFF THAT SHOCK TABLE.

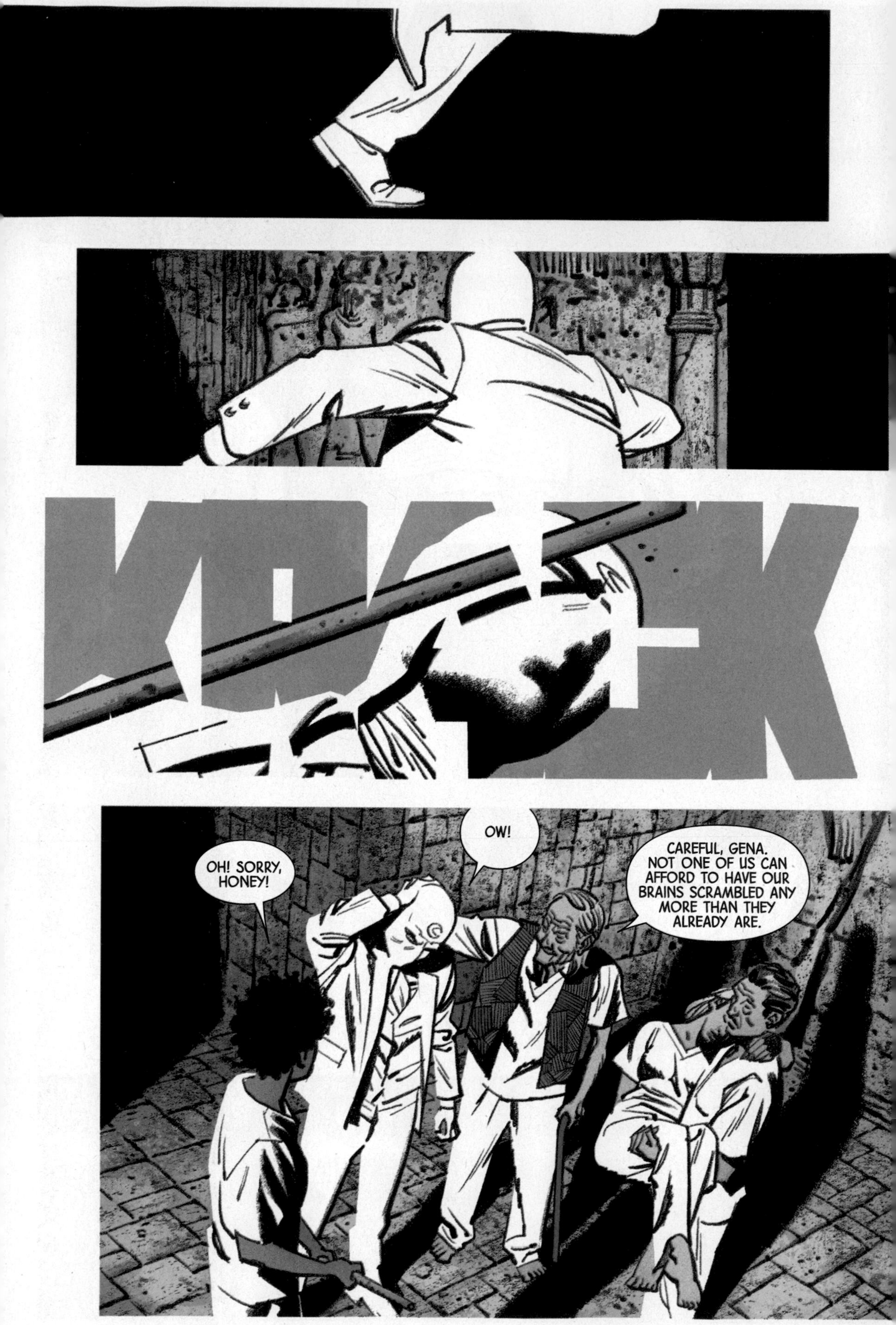

OH! SORRY, HONEY!
OW!
CAREFUL, GENA. NOT ONE OF US CAN AFFORD TO HAVE OUR BRAINS SCRAMBLED ANY MORE THAN THEY ALREADY ARE.

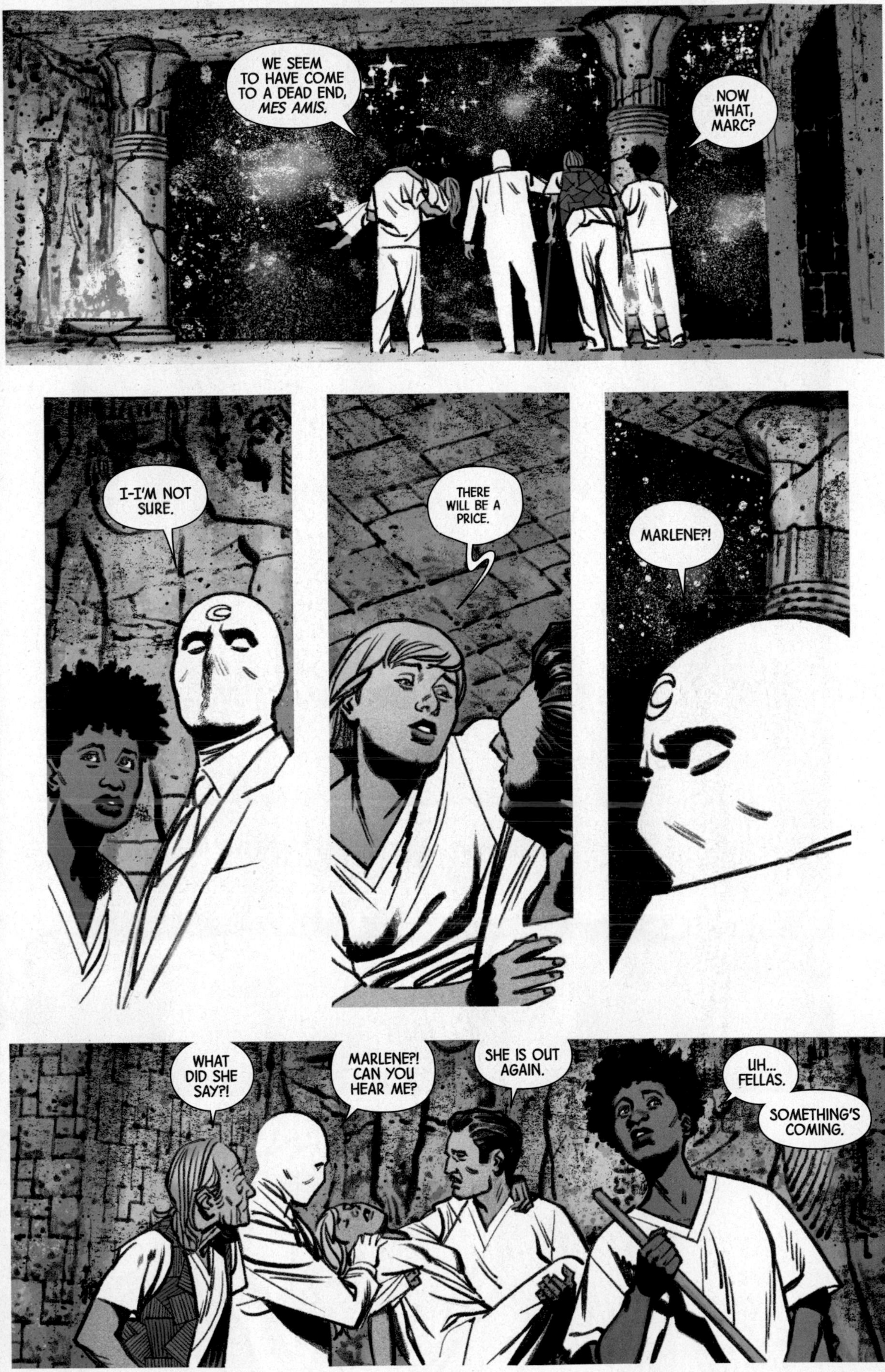
WE SEEM TO HAVE COME TO A DEAD END, *MES AMIS.*
NOW WHAT, MARC?
I-I'M NOT SURE.
THERE WILL BE A PRICE.
MARLENE?!
WHAT DID SHE SAY?!
MARLENE?! CAN YOU HEAR ME?
SHE IS OUT AGAIN.
UH... FELLAS.
SOMETHING'S COMING.

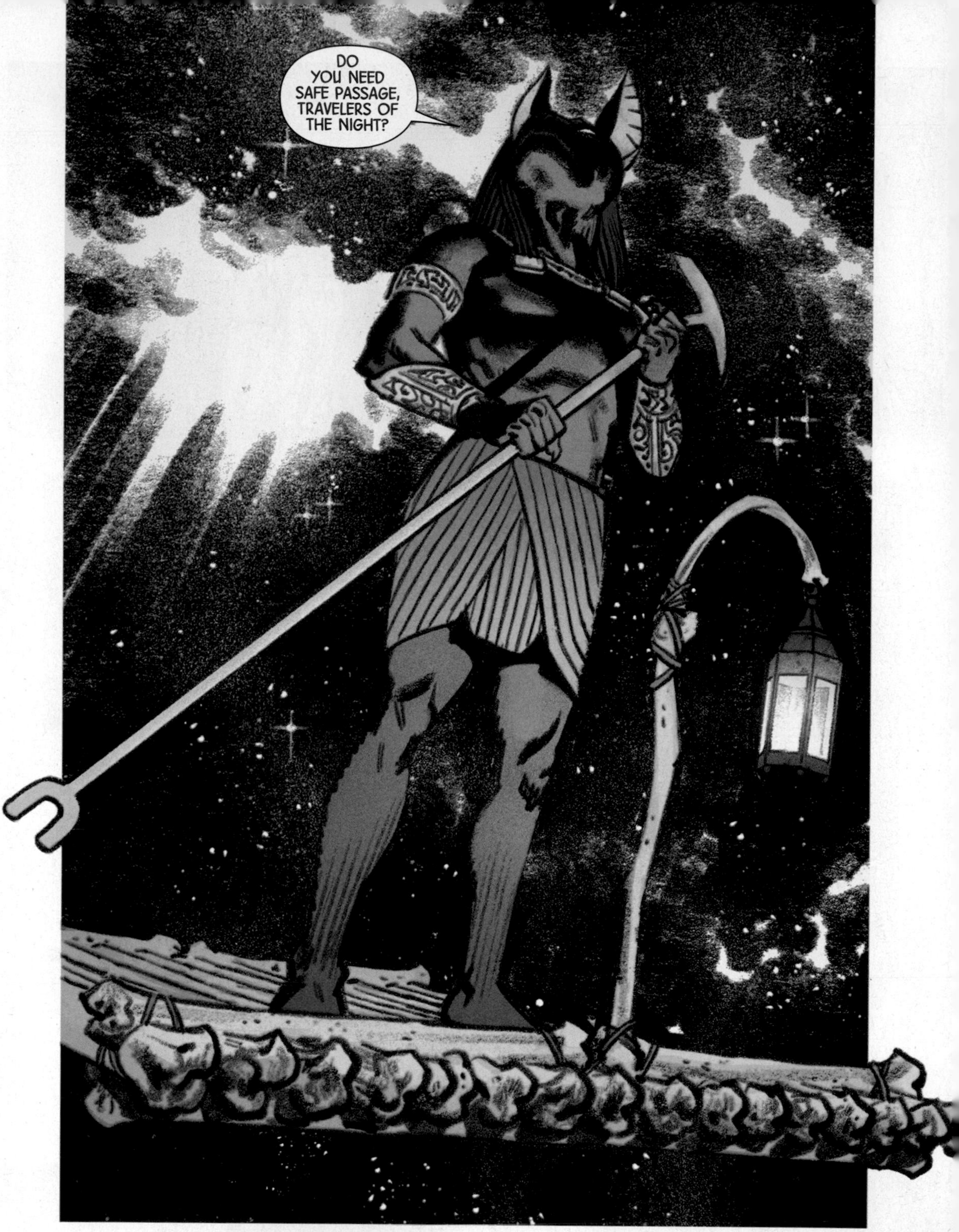
DO YOU NEED SAFE PASSAGE, TRAVELERS OF THE NIGHT?
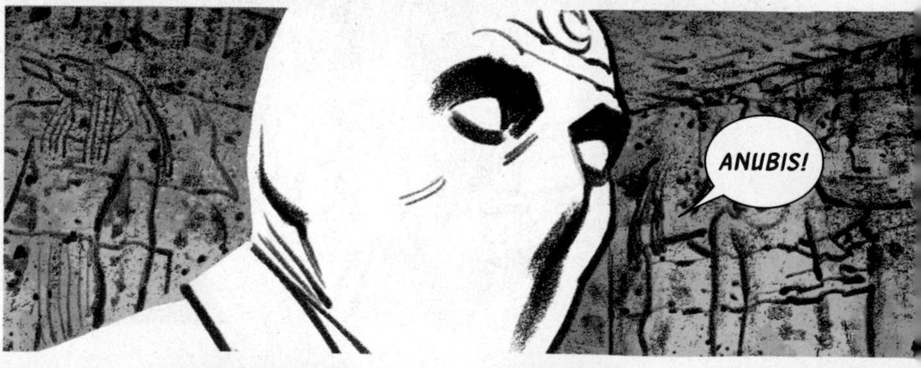
ANUBIS!

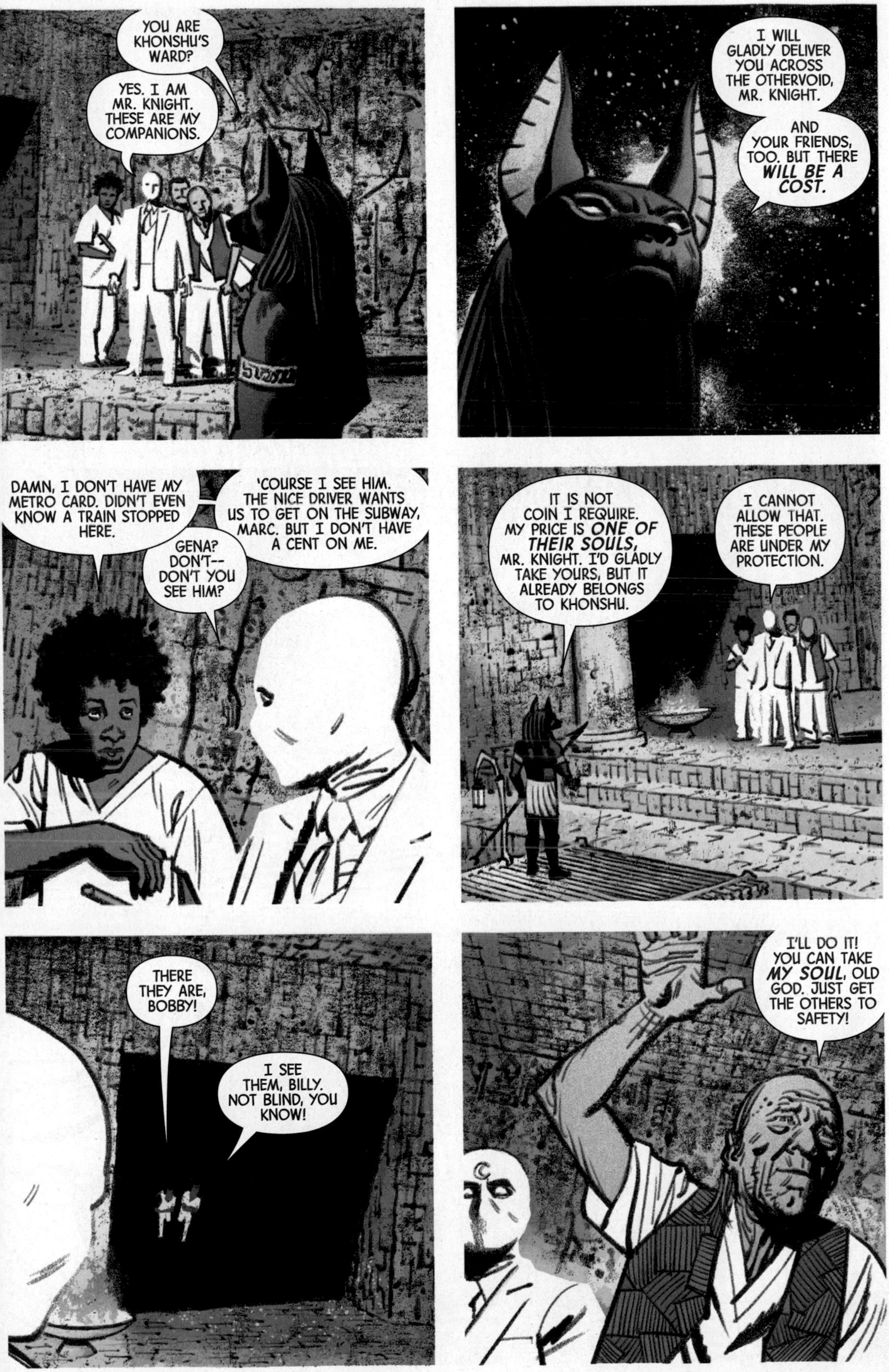
YOU ARE KHONSHU'S WARD?
YES. I AM MR. KNIGHT. THESE ARE MY COMPANIONS.
I WILL GLADLY DELIVER YOU ACROSS THE OTHERVOID, MR. KNIGHT.
AND YOUR FRIENDS, TOO. BUT THERE WILL BE A COST.
DAMN, I DON'T HAVE MY METRO CARD. DIDN'T EVEN KNOW A TRAIN STOPPED HERE.
'COURSE I SEE HIM. THE NICE DRIVER WANTS US TO GET ON THE SUBWAY, MARC. BUT I DON'T HAVE A CENT ON ME.
GENA? DON'T-- DON'T YOU SEE HIM?
IT IS NOT COIN I REQUIRE. MY PRICE IS ONE OF THEIR SOULS, MR. KNIGHT. I'D GLADLY TAKE YOURS, BUT IT ALREADY BELONGS TO KHONSHU.
I CANNOT ALLOW THAT. THESE PEOPLE ARE UNDER MY PROTECTION.
THERE THEY ARE, BOBBY!
I SEE THEM, BILLY. NOT BLIND, YOU KNOW!
I'LL DO IT! YOU CAN TAKE MY SOUL, OLD GOD. JUST GET THE OTHERS TO SAFETY!

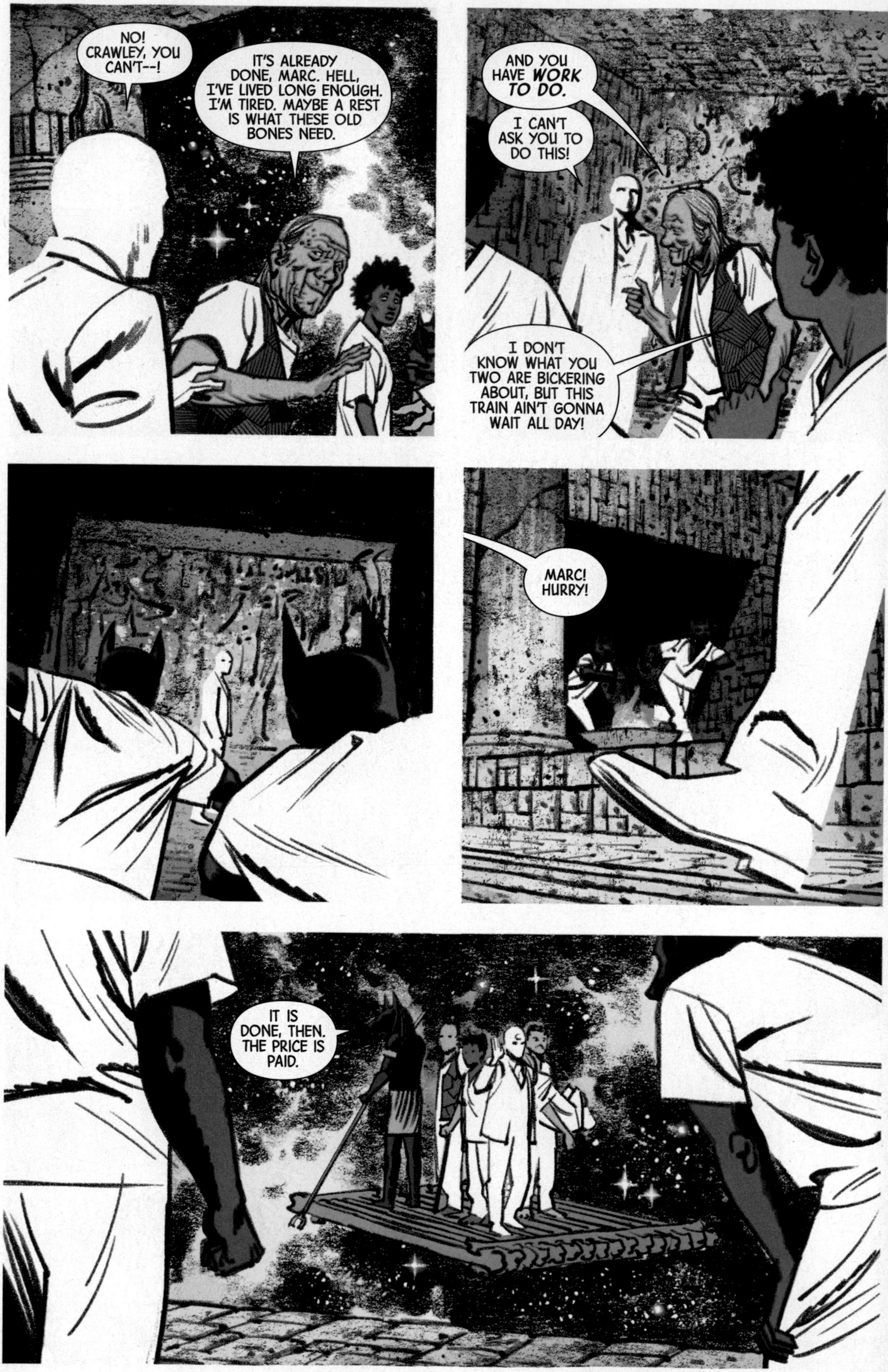
NO! CRAWLEY, YOU CAN'T--!
IT'S ALREADY DONE, MARC. HELL, I'VE LIVED LONG ENOUGH. I'M TIRED. MAYBE A REST IS WHAT THESE OLD BONES NEED.
AND YOU HAVE *WORK TO DO.*
I CAN'T ASK YOU TO DO THIS!
I DON'T KNOW WHAT YOU TWO ARE BICKERING ABOUT, BUT THIS TRAIN AIN'T GONNA WAIT ALL DAY!
MARC! HURRY!
IT IS DONE, THEN. THE PRICE IS PAID.

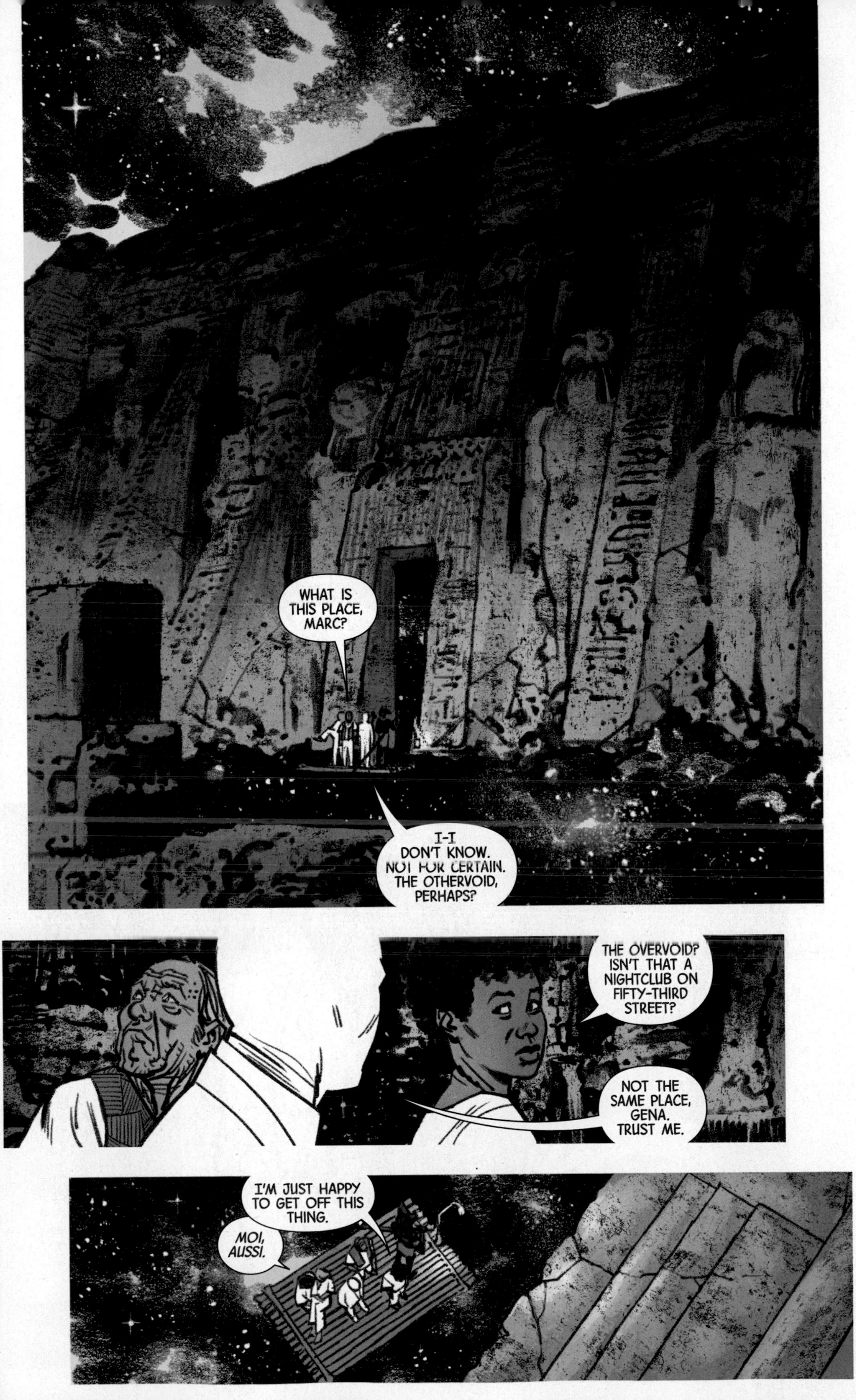
WHAT IS THIS PLACE, MARC?
I-I DON'T KNOW. NOT FOR CERTAIN. THE OTHERVOID, PERHAPS?
THE OVERVOID? ISN'T THAT A NIGHTCLUB ON FIFTY-THIRD STREET?
NOT THE SAME PLACE, GENA. TRUST ME.
I'M JUST HAPPY TO GET OFF THIS THING.
MOI, AUSSI.

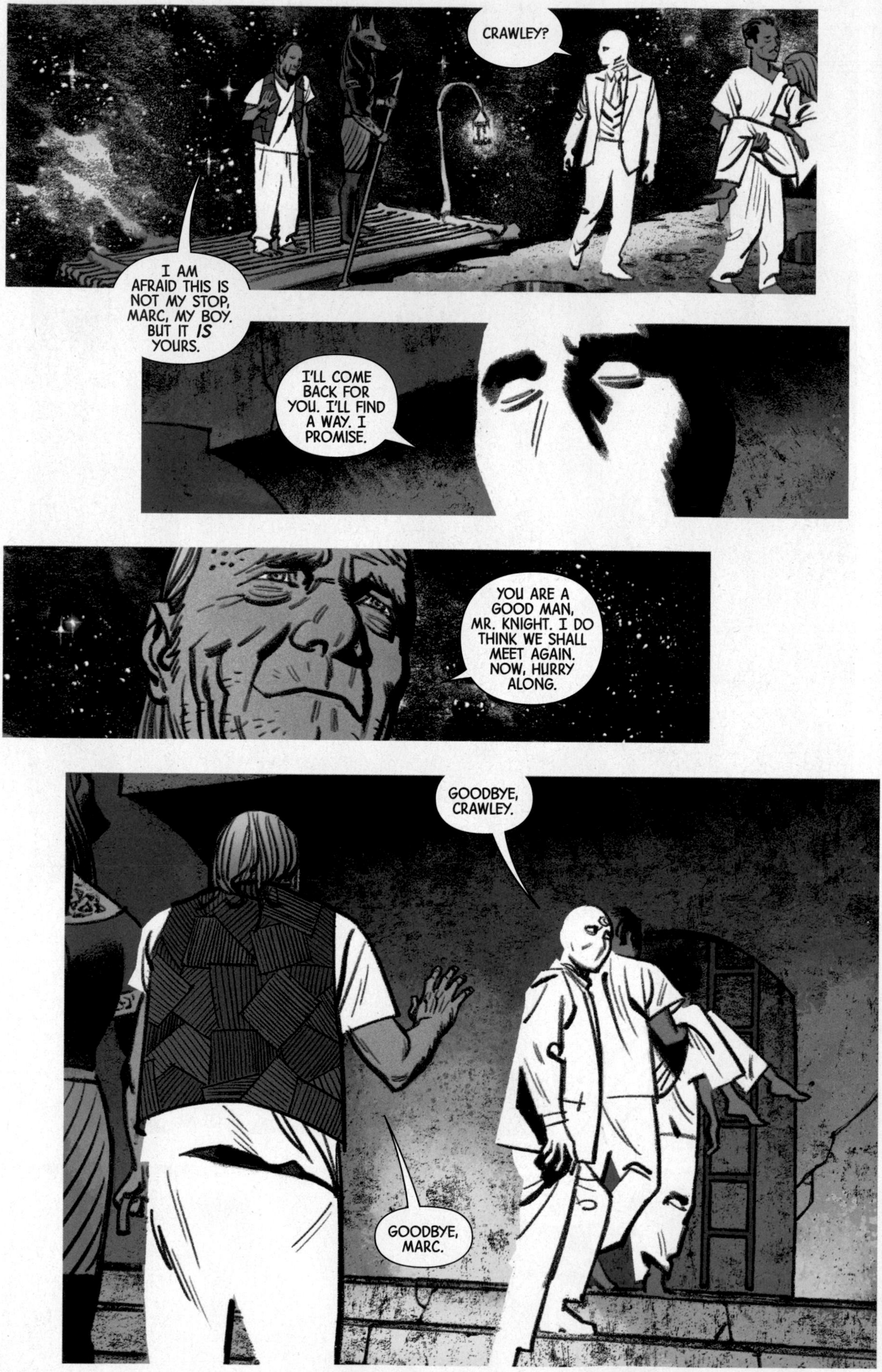
CRAWLEY?
I AM AFRAID THIS IS NOT MY STOP, MARC, MY BOY. BUT IT *IS* YOURS.
I'LL COME BACK FOR YOU. I'LL FIND A WAY. I PROMISE.
YOU ARE A GOOD MAN, MR. KNIGHT. I DO THINK WE SHALL MEET AGAIN. NOW, HURRY ALONG.
GOODBYE, CRAWLEY.
GOODBYE, MARC.

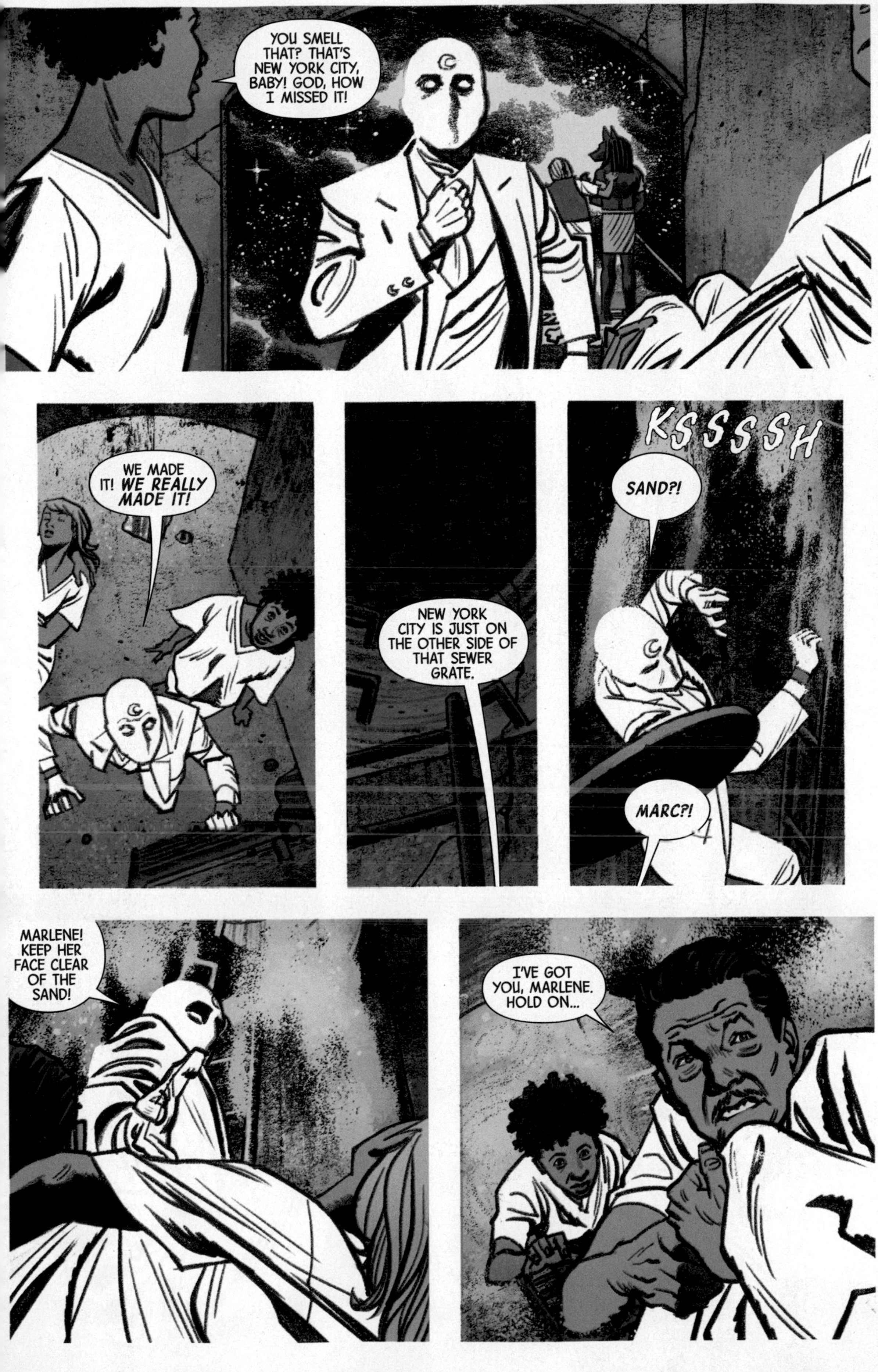
YOU SMELL THAT? THAT'S NEW YORK CITY, BABY! GOD, HOW I MISSED IT!
WE MADE IT! WE REALLY MADE IT!
NEW YORK CITY IS JUST ON THE OTHER SIDE OF THAT SEWER GRATE.
KSSSSH
SAND?!
MARC?!
MARLENE! KEEP HER FACE CLEAR OF THE SAND!
I'VE GOT YOU, MARLENE. HOLD ON...

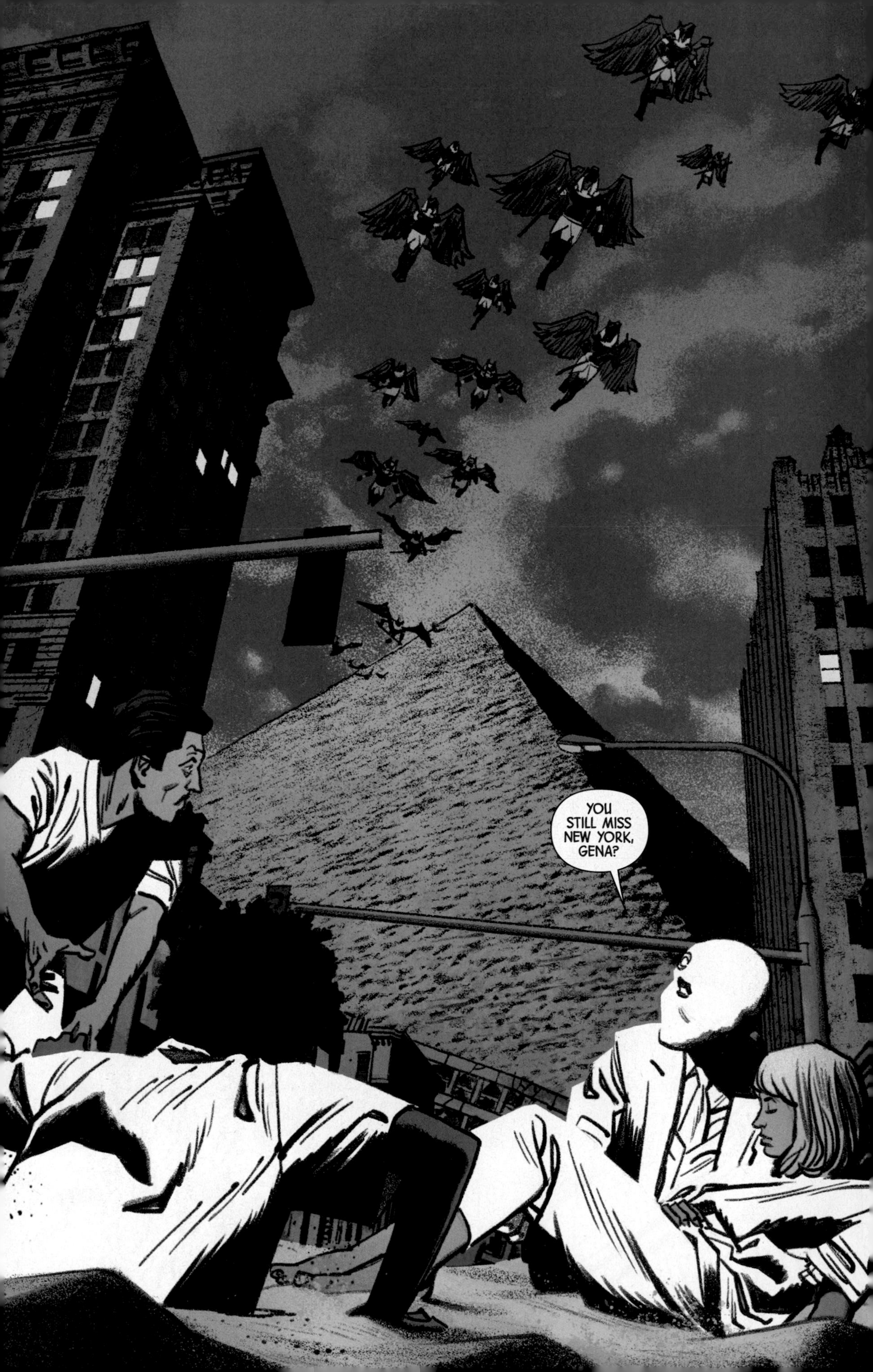
YOU STILL MISS NEW YORK, GENA?

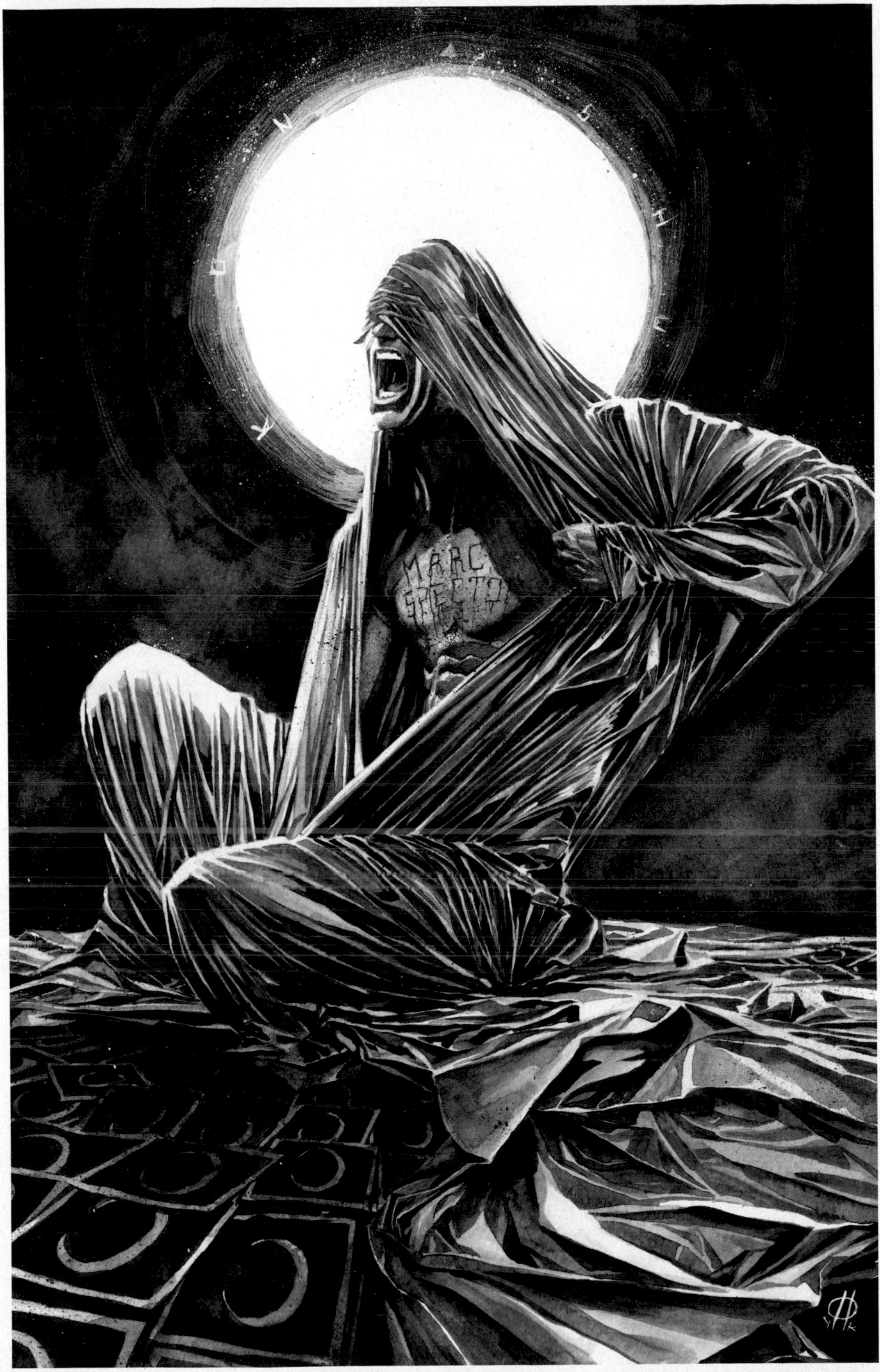
MARC
SPECTO

#1 VARIANT BY MARCO RUDY

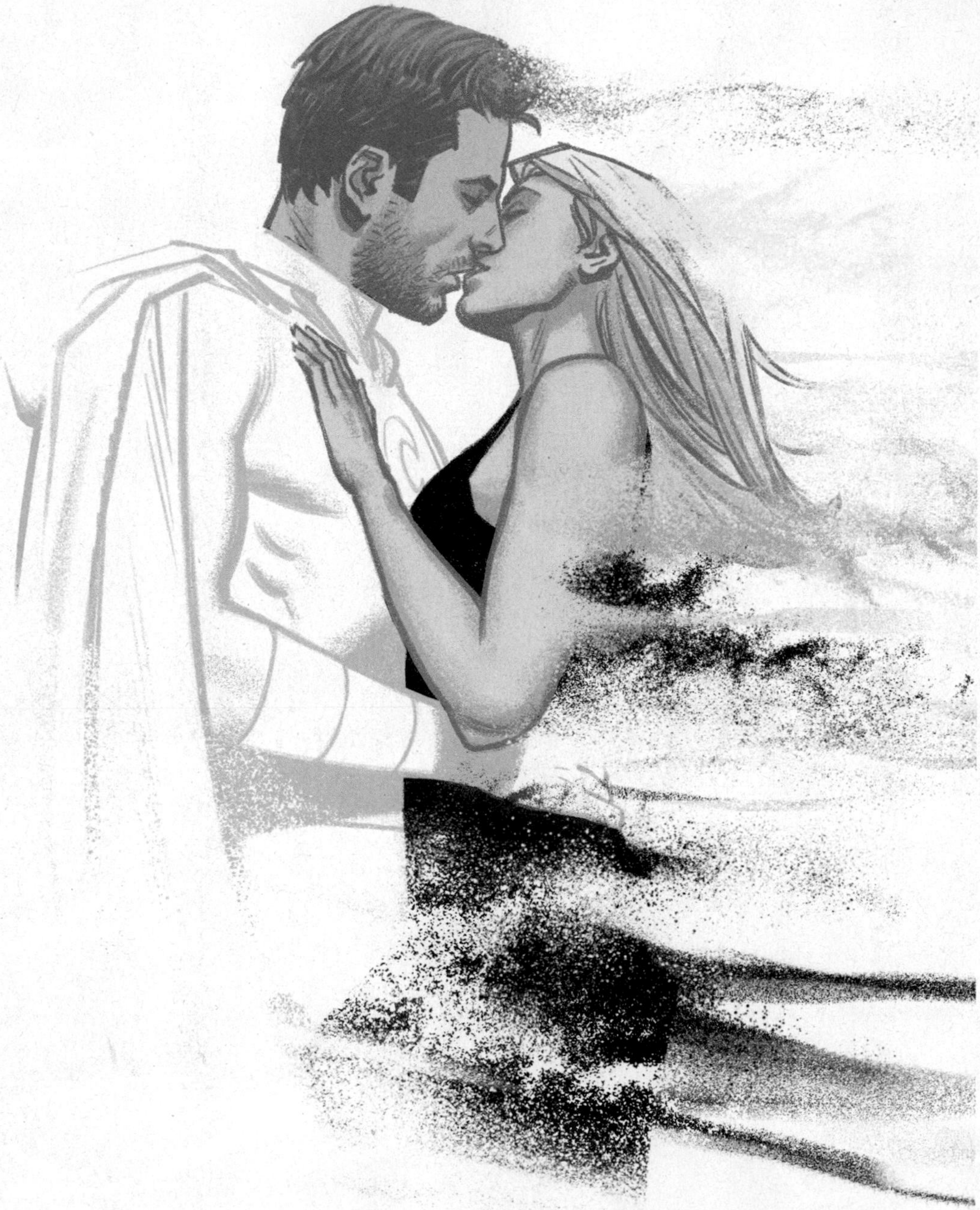

WELCOME TO NEW EGYPT
PART FOUR

4

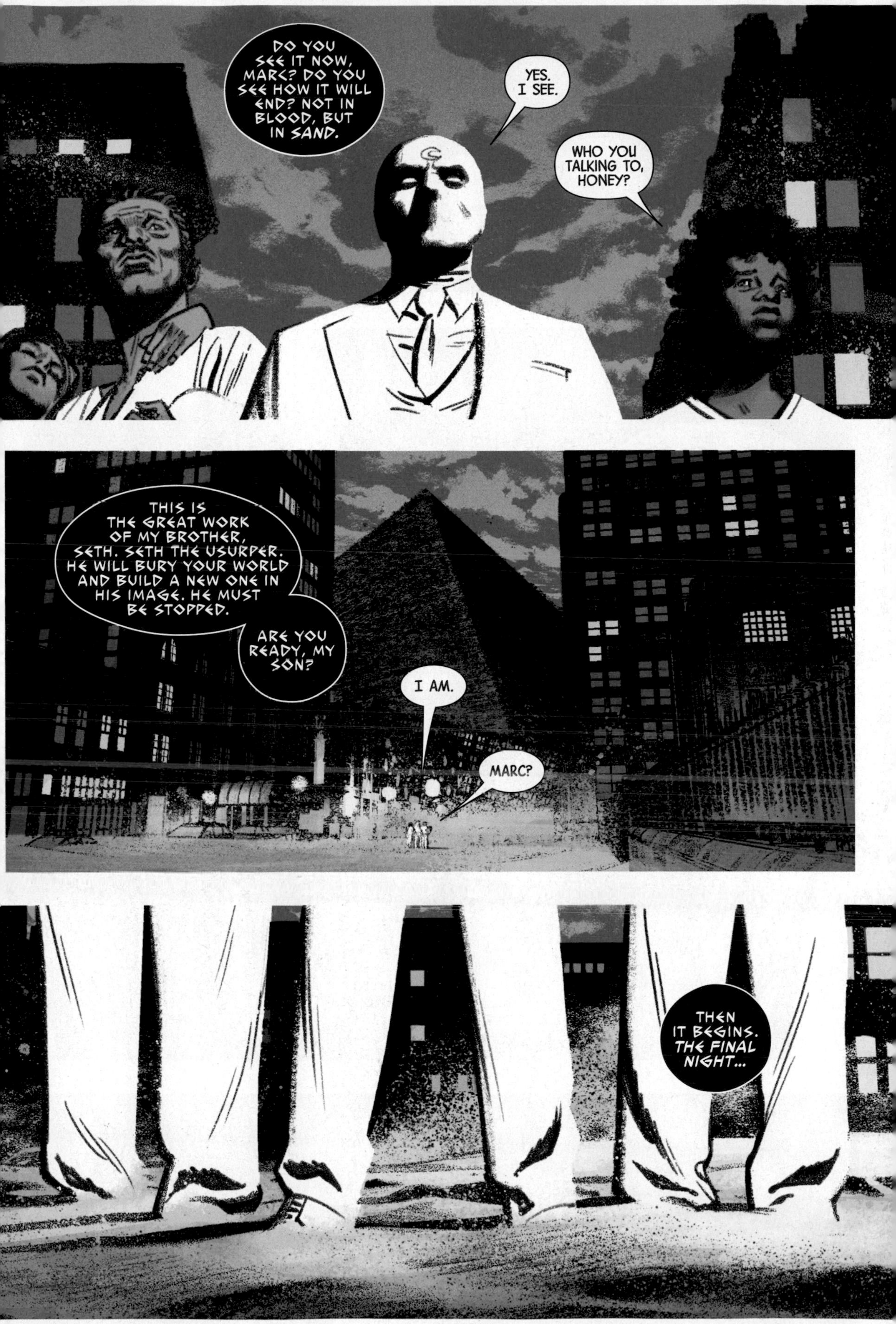
DO YOU SEE IT NOW, MARC? DO YOU SEE HOW IT WILL END? NOT IN BLOOD, BUT IN *SAND.*
YES. I SEE.
WHO YOU TALKING TO, HONEY?
THIS IS THE GREAT WORK OF MY BROTHER, SETH. SETH THE USURPER. HE WILL BURY YOUR WORLD AND BUILD A NEW ONE IN HIS IMAGE. HE MUST BE STOPPED.
ARE YOU READY, MY SON?
I AM.
MARC?
THEN IT BEGINS. *THE FINAL NIGHT...*

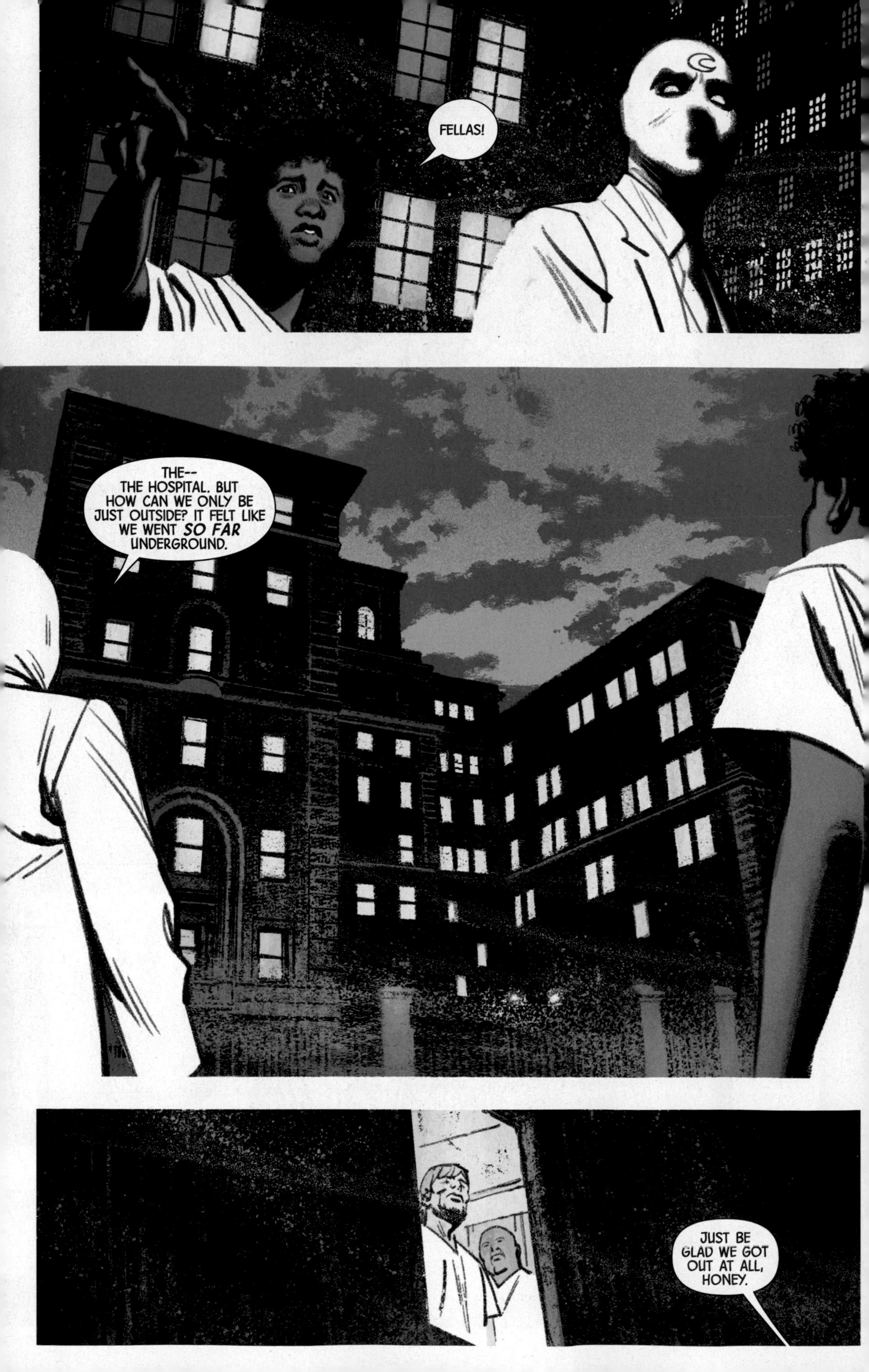
FELLAS!
THE-- THE HOSPITAL. BUT HOW CAN WE ONLY BE JUST OUTSIDE? IT FELT LIKE WE WENT SO FAR UNDERGROUND.
JUST BE GLAD WE GOT OUT AT ALL, HONEY.

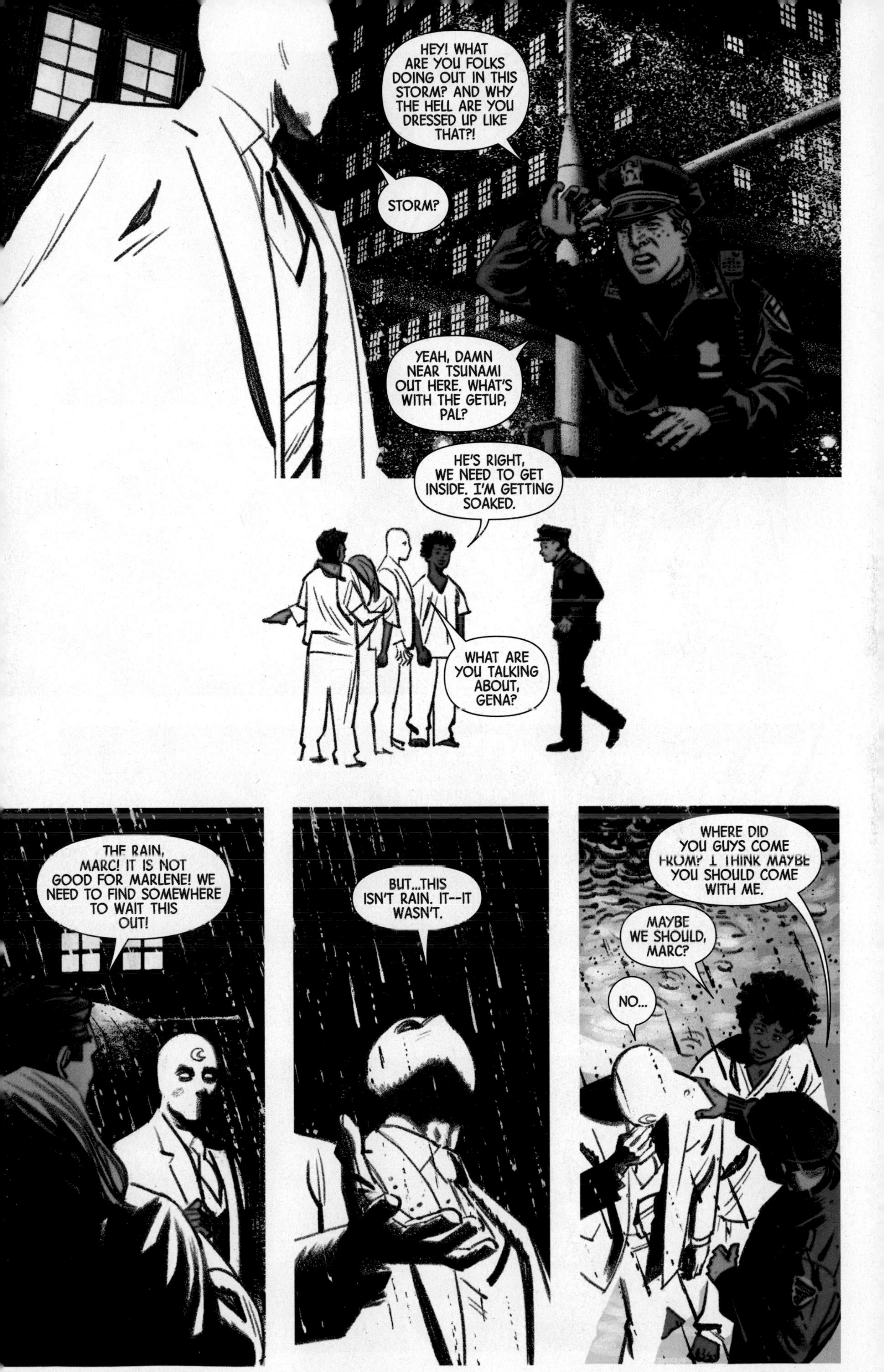
HEY! WHAT ARE YOU FOLKS DOING OUT IN THIS STORM? AND WHY THE HELL ARE YOU DRESSED UP LIKE THAT?!
STORM?
YEAH, DAMN NEAR TSUNAMI OUT HERE. WHAT'S WITH THE GETUP, PAL?
HE'S RIGHT, WE NEED TO GET INSIDE. I'M GETTING SOAKED.
WHAT ARE YOU TALKING ABOUT, GENA?
THE RAIN, MARC! IT IS NOT GOOD FOR MARLENE! WE NEED TO FIND SOMEWHERE TO WAIT THIS OUT!
BUT...THIS ISN'T RAIN. IT--IT WASN'T.
WHERE DID YOU GUYS COME FROM? I THINK MAYBE YOU SHOULD COME WITH ME.
MAYBE WE SHOULD, MARC?
NO...

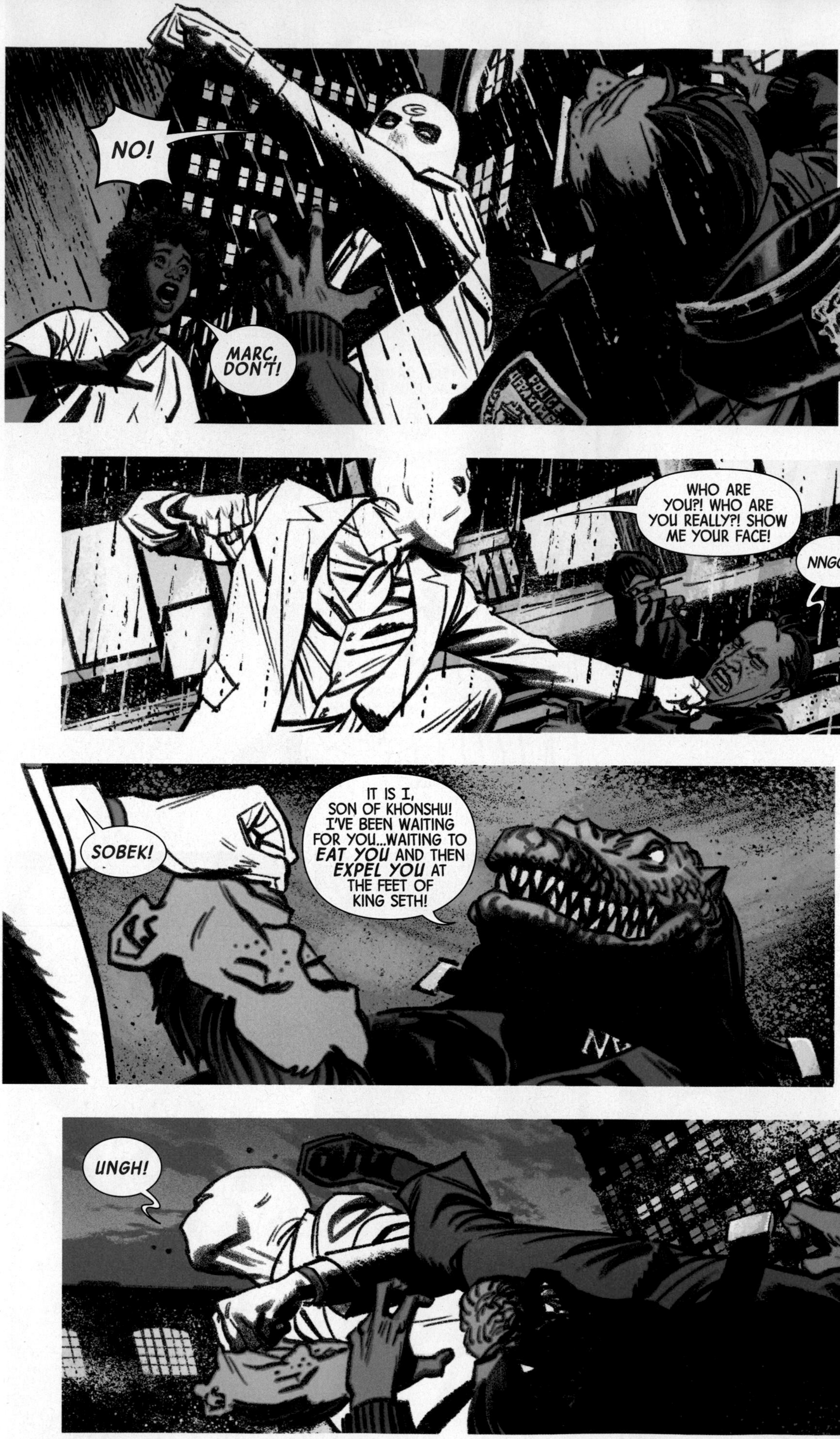
NO!
MARC, DON'T!
WHO ARE YOU?! WHO ARE YOU REALLY?! SHOW ME YOUR FACE!
NNGGH!
SOBEK!
IT IS I, SON OF KHONSHU! I'VE BEEN WAITING FOR YOU...WAITING TO *EAT YOU* AND THEN *EXPEL YOU* AT THE FEET OF KING SETH!
UNGH!

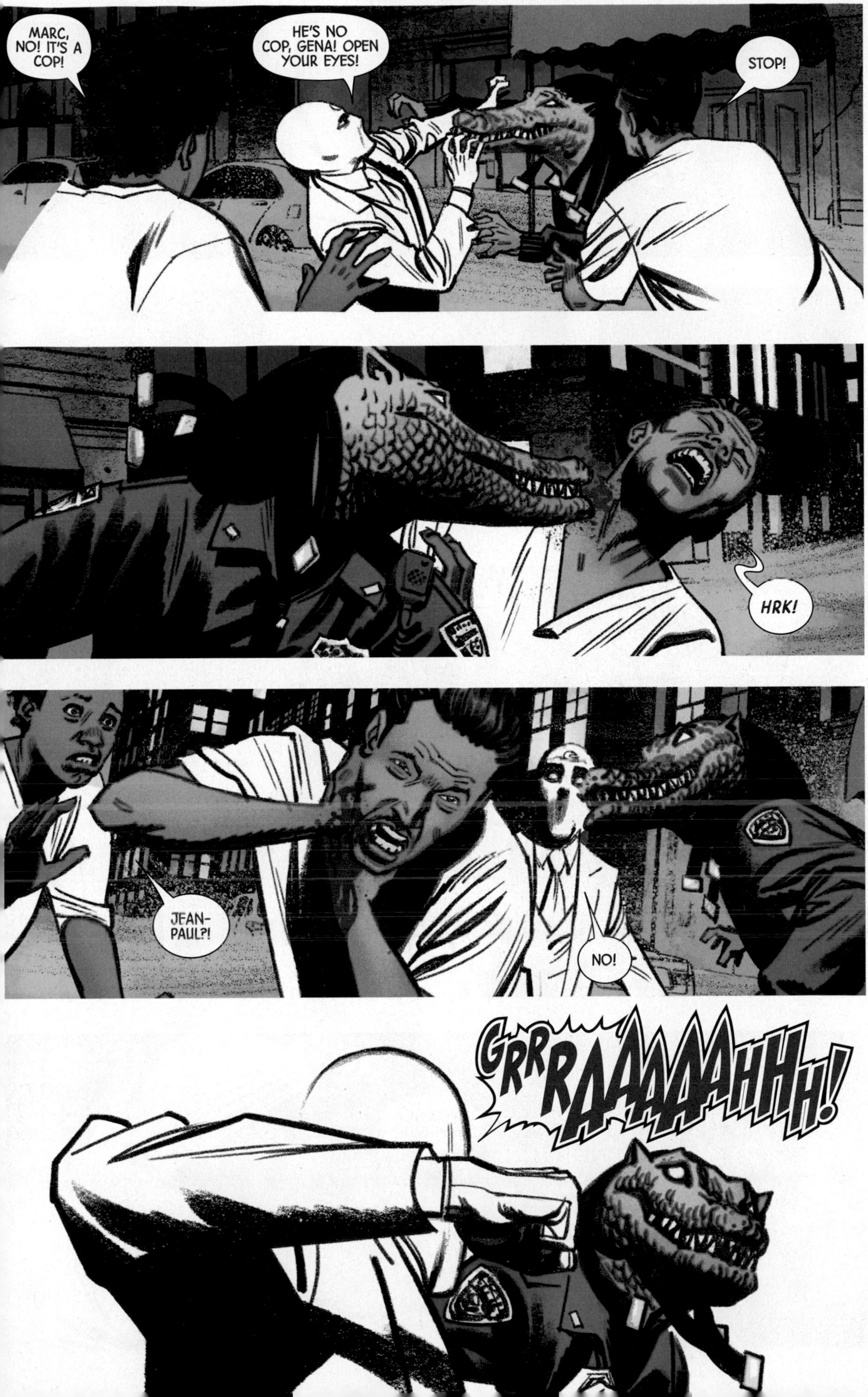
MARC, NO! IT'S A COP!
HE'S NO COP, GENA! OPEN YOUR EYES!
STOP!
HRK!
JEAN-PAUL?!
NO!
GRRRAAAAAHHH!

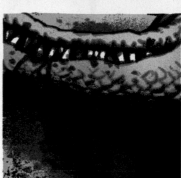

OH, GOD!

FRENCHIE? JEAN-PAUL?

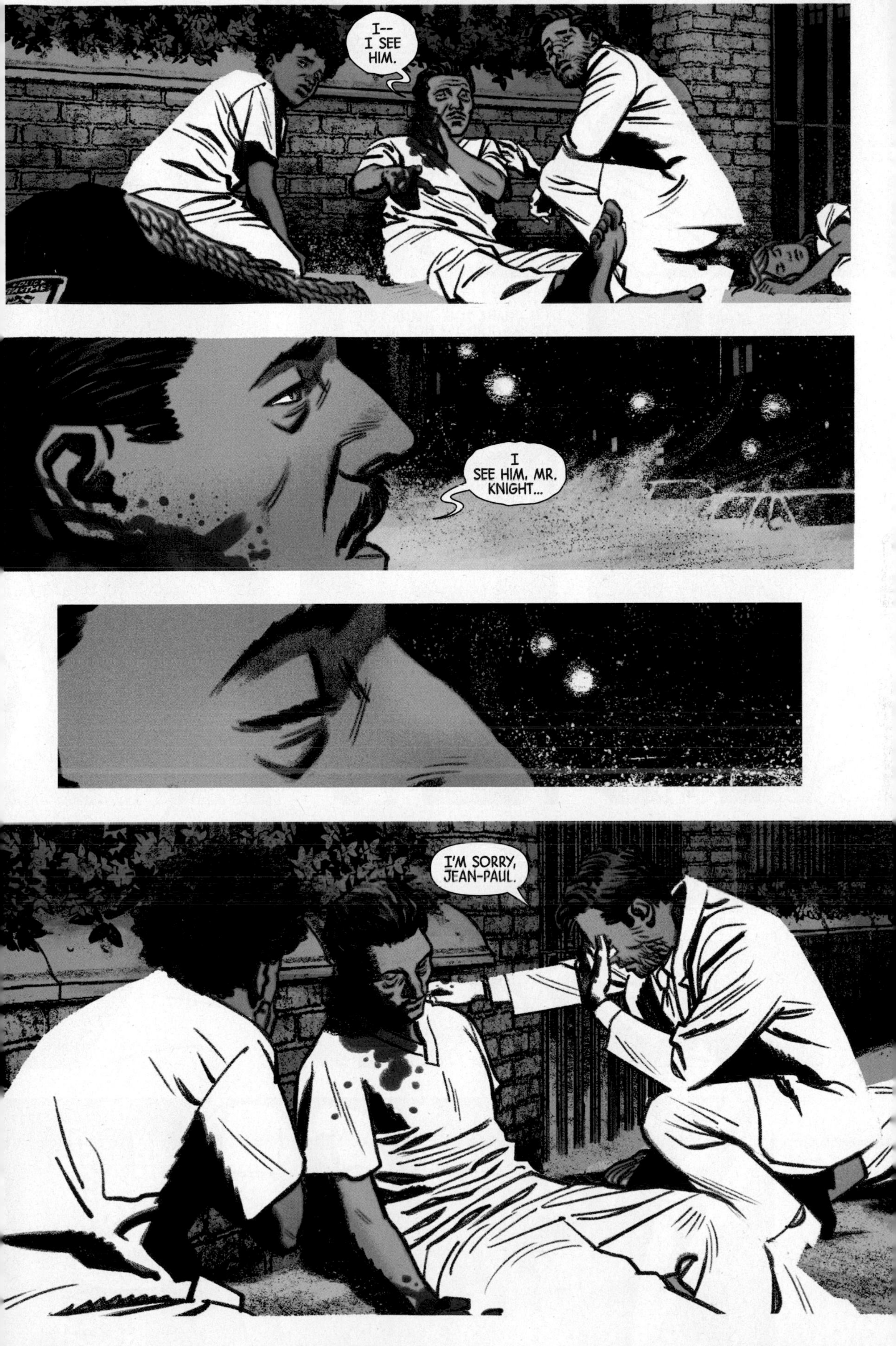
I-- I SEE HIM.
I SEE HIM, MR. KNIGHT...
I'M SORRY, JEAN-PAUL.

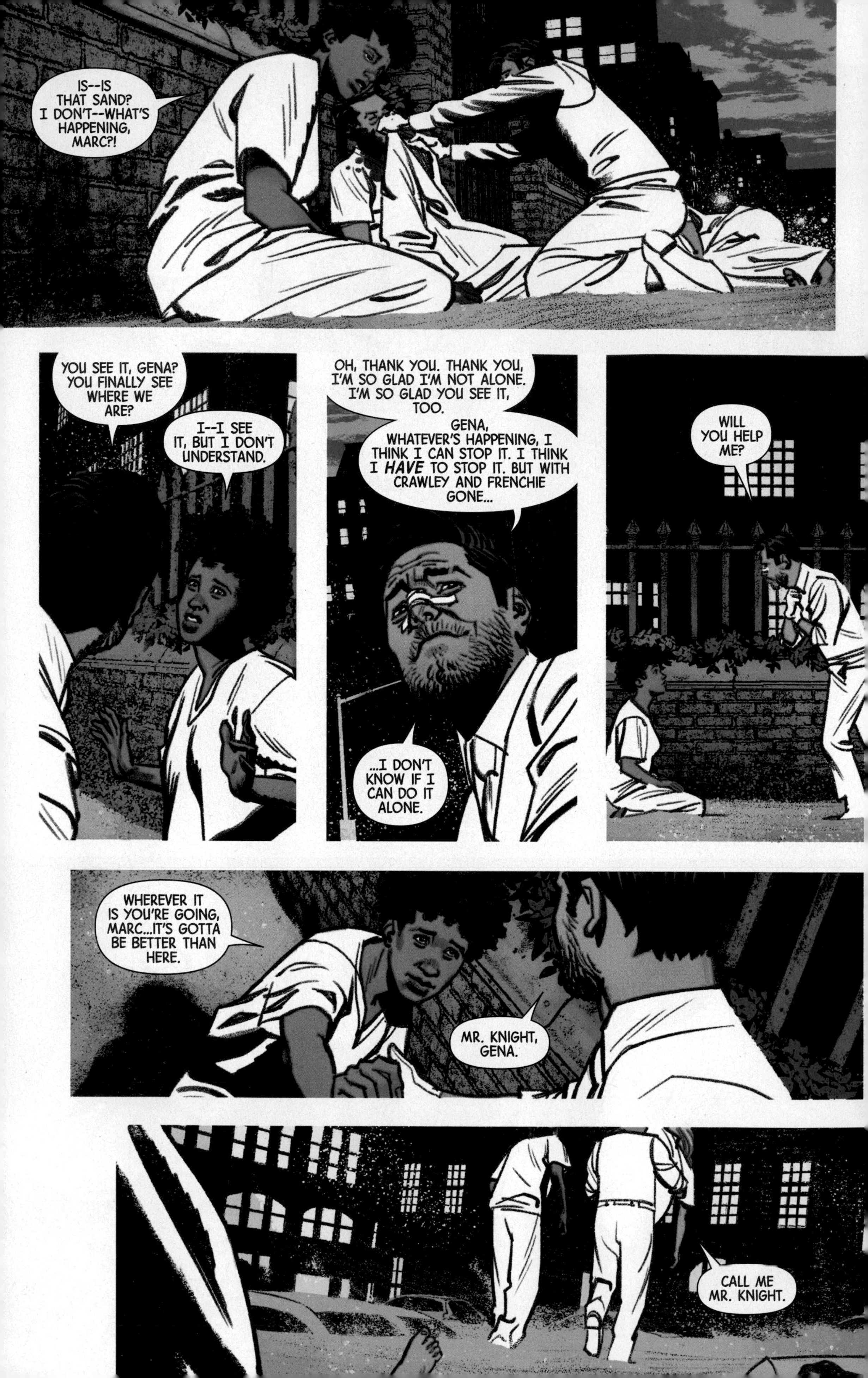
IS--IS THAT SAND? I DON'T--WHAT'S HAPPENING, MARC?!
YOU SEE IT, GENA? YOU FINALLY SEE WHERE WE ARE?
I--I SEE IT, BUT I DON'T UNDERSTAND.
OH, THANK YOU. THANK YOU, I'M SO GLAD I'M NOT ALONE. I'M SO GLAD YOU SEE IT, TOO.
GENA, WHATEVER'S HAPPENING, I THINK I CAN STOP IT. I THINK I *HAVE* TO STOP IT. BUT WITH CRAWLEY AND FRENCHIE GONE...
...I DON'T KNOW IF I CAN DO IT ALONE.
WILL YOU HELP ME?
WHEREVER IT IS YOU'RE GOING, MARC...IT'S GOTTA BE BETTER THAN HERE.
MR. KNIGHT, GENA.
CALL ME MR. KNIGHT.

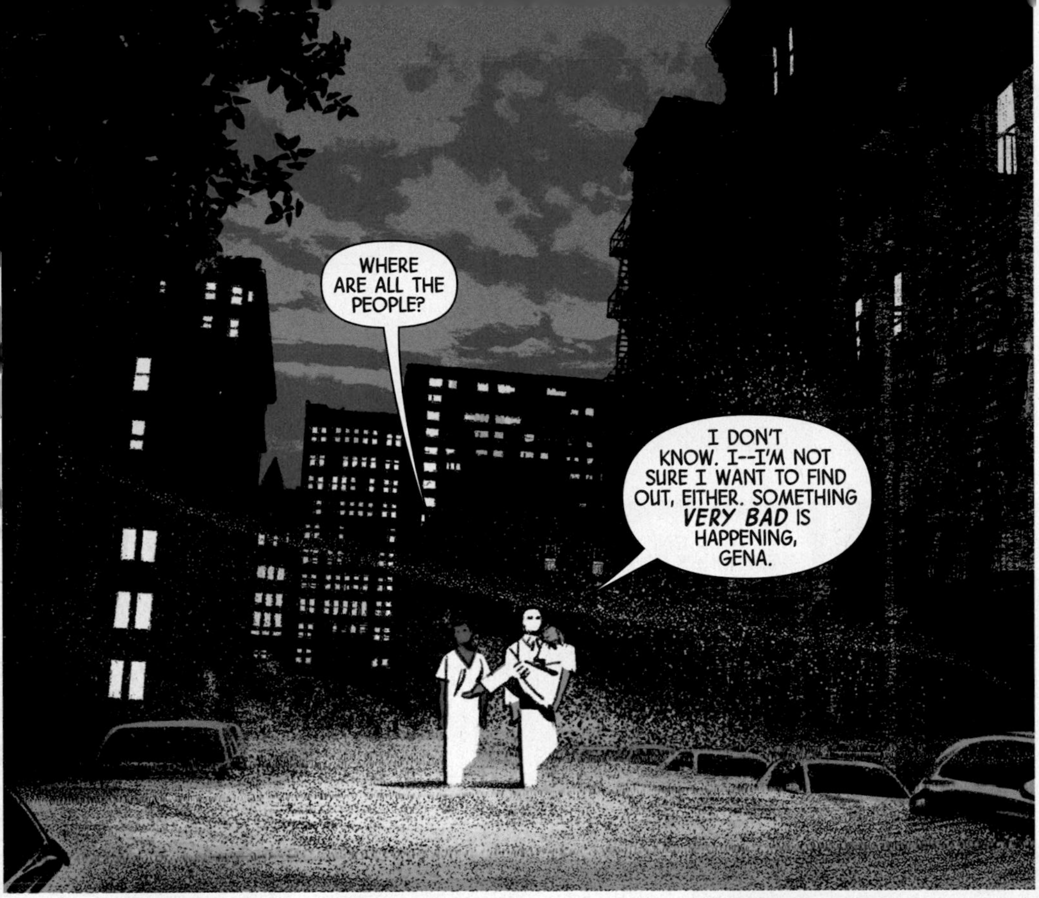
WHERE ARE ALL THE PEOPLE?
I DON'T KNOW. I--I'M NOT SURE I WANT TO FIND OUT, EITHER. SOMETHING *VERY BAD* IS HAPPENING, GENA.

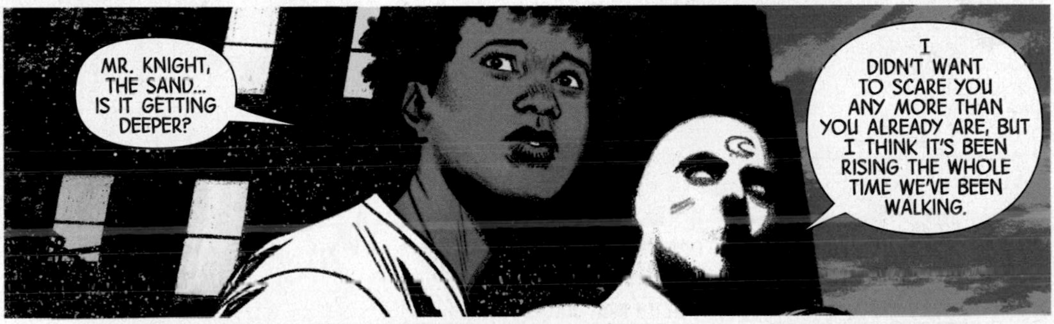
MR. KNIGHT, THE SAND... IS IT GETTING DEEPER?
I DIDN'T WANT TO SCARE YOU ANY MORE THAN YOU ALREADY ARE, BUT I THINK IT'S BEEN RISING THE WHOLE TIME WE'VE BEEN WALKING.

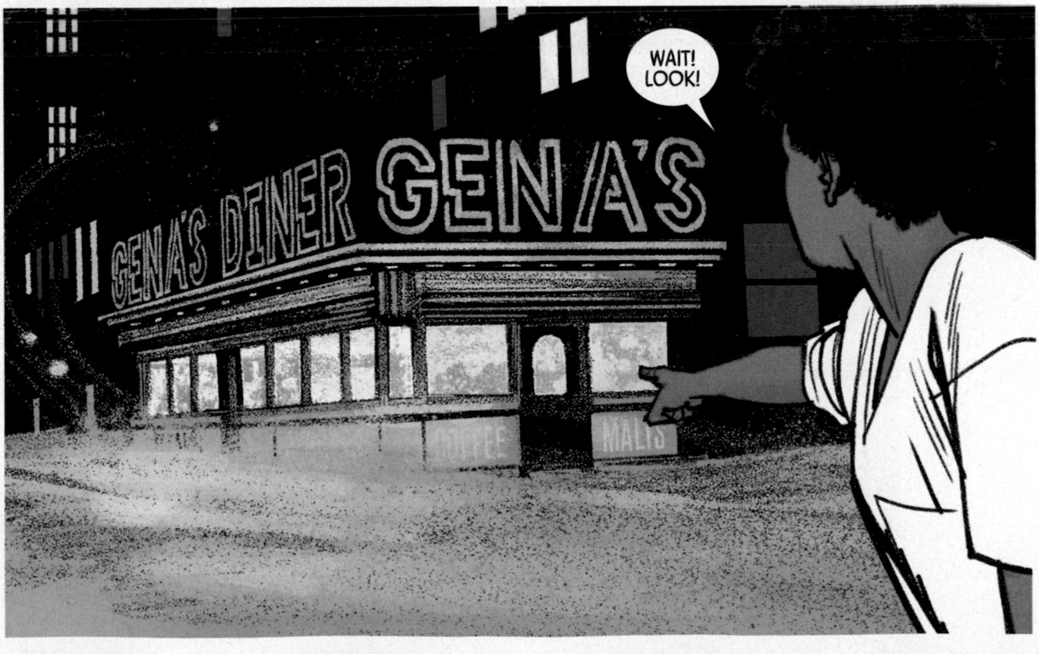
WAIT! LOOK!
GENA'S DINER
GENA'S
COFFEE
MALTS

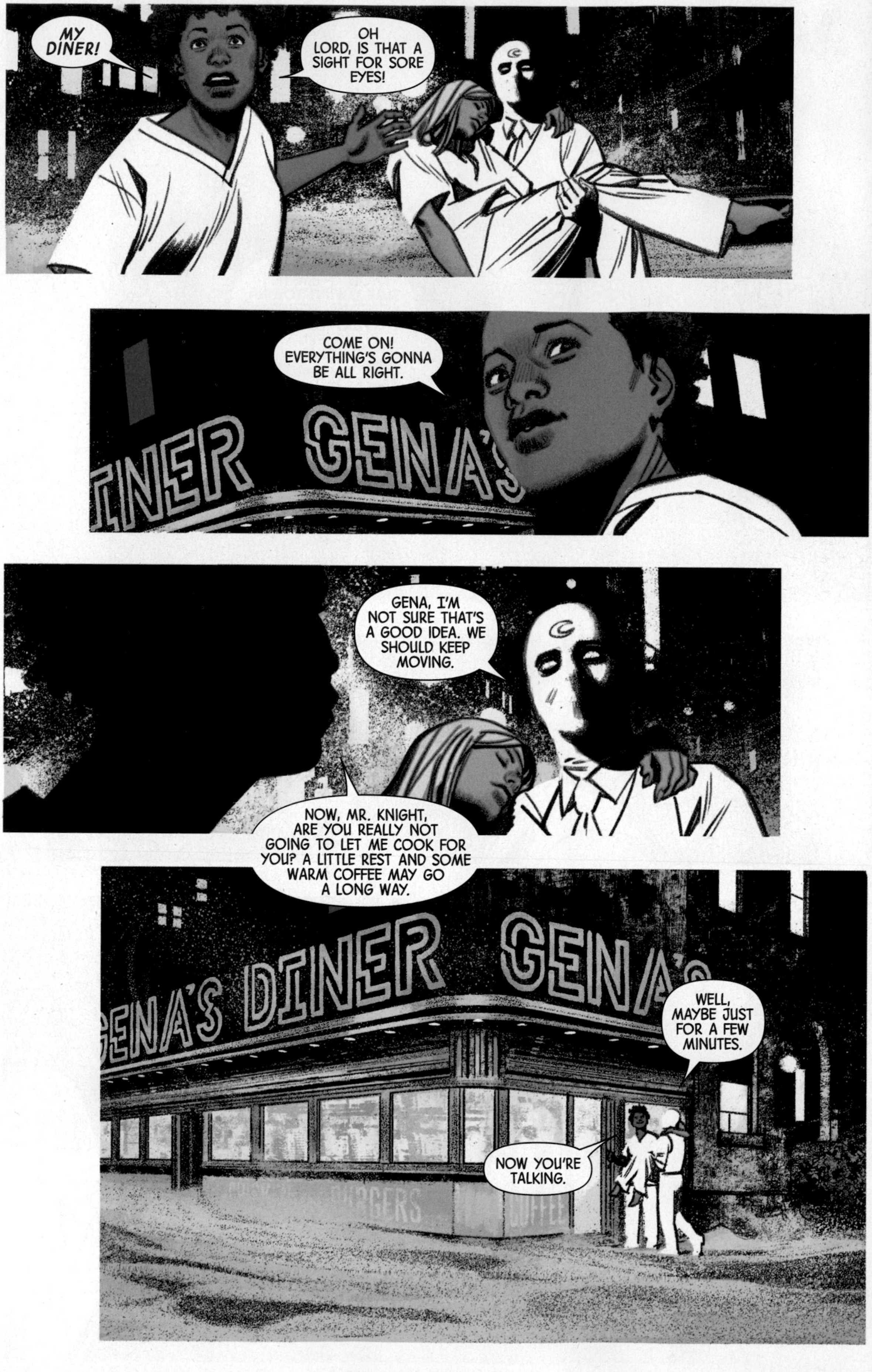
MY DINER!
OH LORD, IS THAT A SIGHT FOR SORE EYES!
COME ON! EVERYTHING'S GONNA BE ALL RIGHT.
DINER GENA'S
GENA, I'M NOT SURE THAT'S A GOOD IDEA. WE SHOULD KEEP MOVING.
NOW, MR. KNIGHT, ARE YOU REALLY NOT GOING TO LET ME COOK FOR YOU? A LITTLE REST AND SOME WARM COFFEE MAY GO A LONG WAY.
GENA'S DINER GENA'S
WELL, MAYBE JUST FOR A FEW MINUTES.
NOW YOU'RE TALKING.

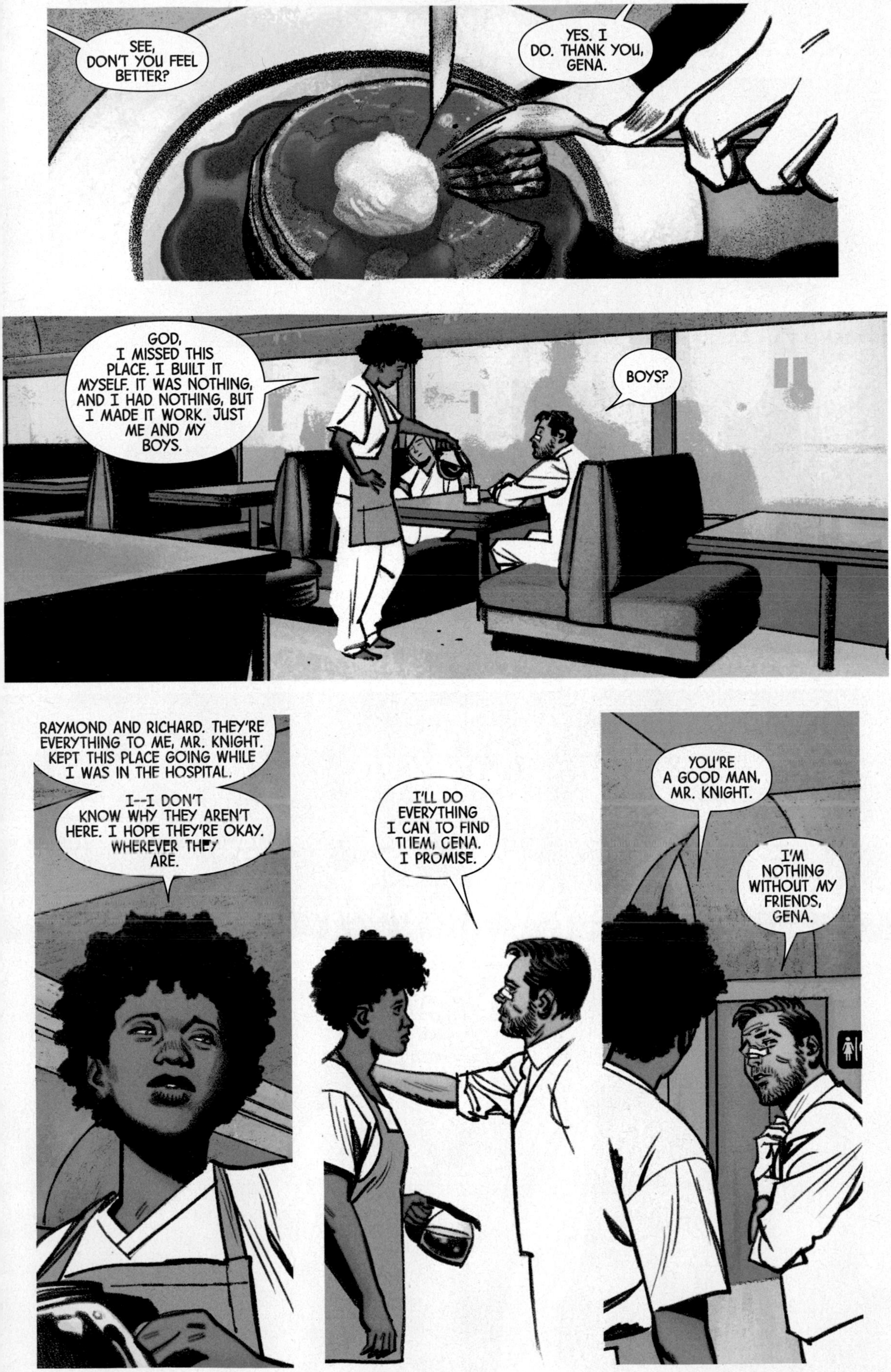
SEE, DON'T YOU FEEL BETTER?
YES. I DO. THANK YOU, GENA.
GOD, I MISSED THIS PLACE. I BUILT IT MYSELF. IT WAS NOTHING, AND I HAD NOTHING, BUT I MADE IT WORK. JUST ME AND MY BOYS.
BOYS?
RAYMOND AND RICHARD. THEY'RE EVERYTHING TO ME, MR. KNIGHT. KEPT THIS PLACE GOING WHILE I WAS IN THE HOSPITAL.
I--I DON'T KNOW WHY THEY AREN'T HERE. I HOPE THEY'RE OKAY. WHEREVER THEY ARE.
I'LL DO EVERYTHING I CAN TO FIND THEM, GENA. I PROMISE.
YOU'RE A GOOD MAN, MR. KNIGHT.
I'M NOTHING WITHOUT MY FRIENDS, GENA.

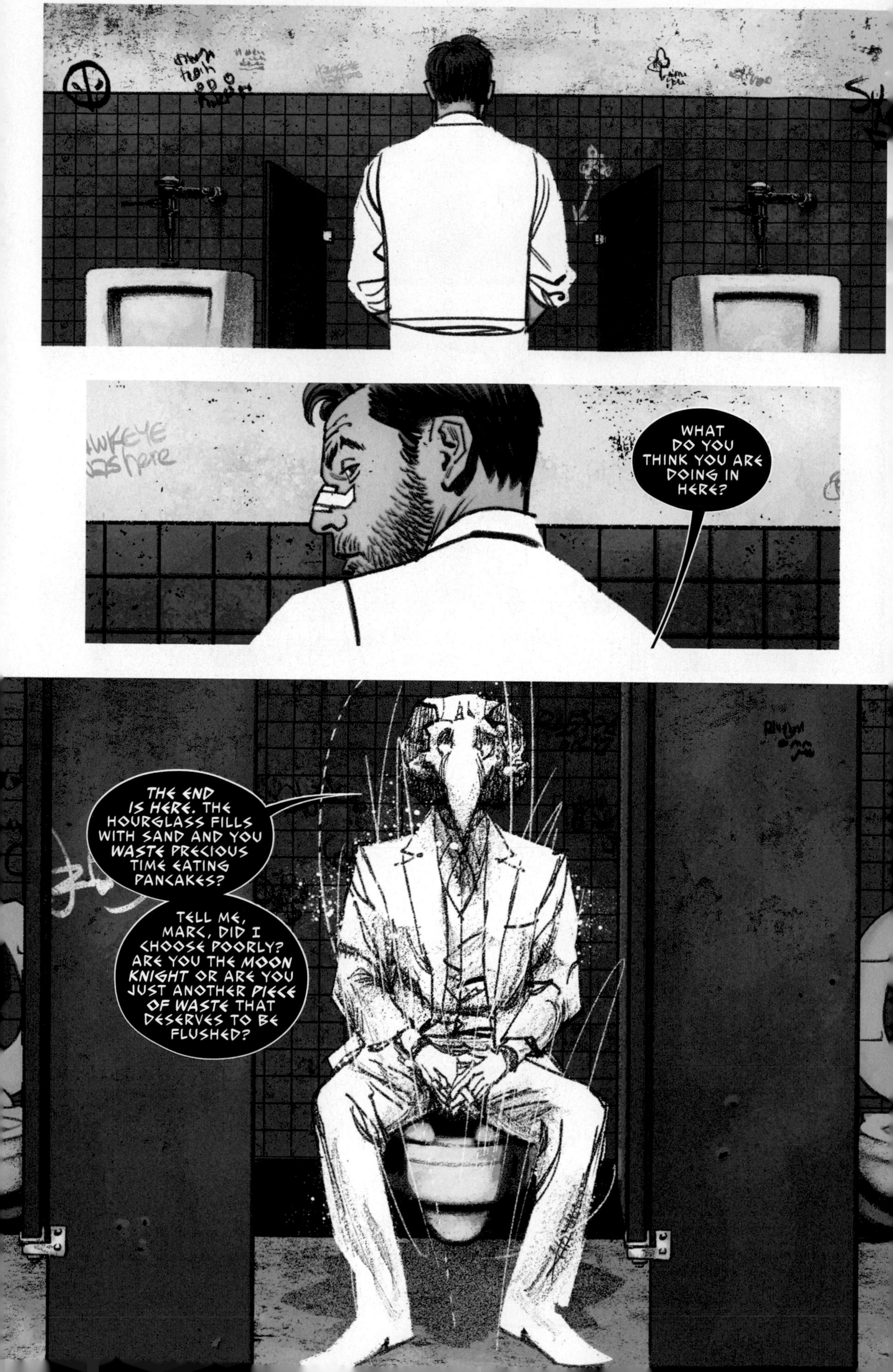
WHAT DO YOU THINK YOU ARE DOING IN HERE?
THE END IS HERE. THE HOURGLASS FILLS WITH SAND AND YOU WASTE PRECIOUS TIME EATING PANCAKES?
TELL ME, MARC, DID I CHOOSE POORLY? ARE YOU THE MOON KNIGHT OR ARE YOU JUST ANOTHER PIECE OF WASTE THAT DESERVES TO BE FLUSHED?

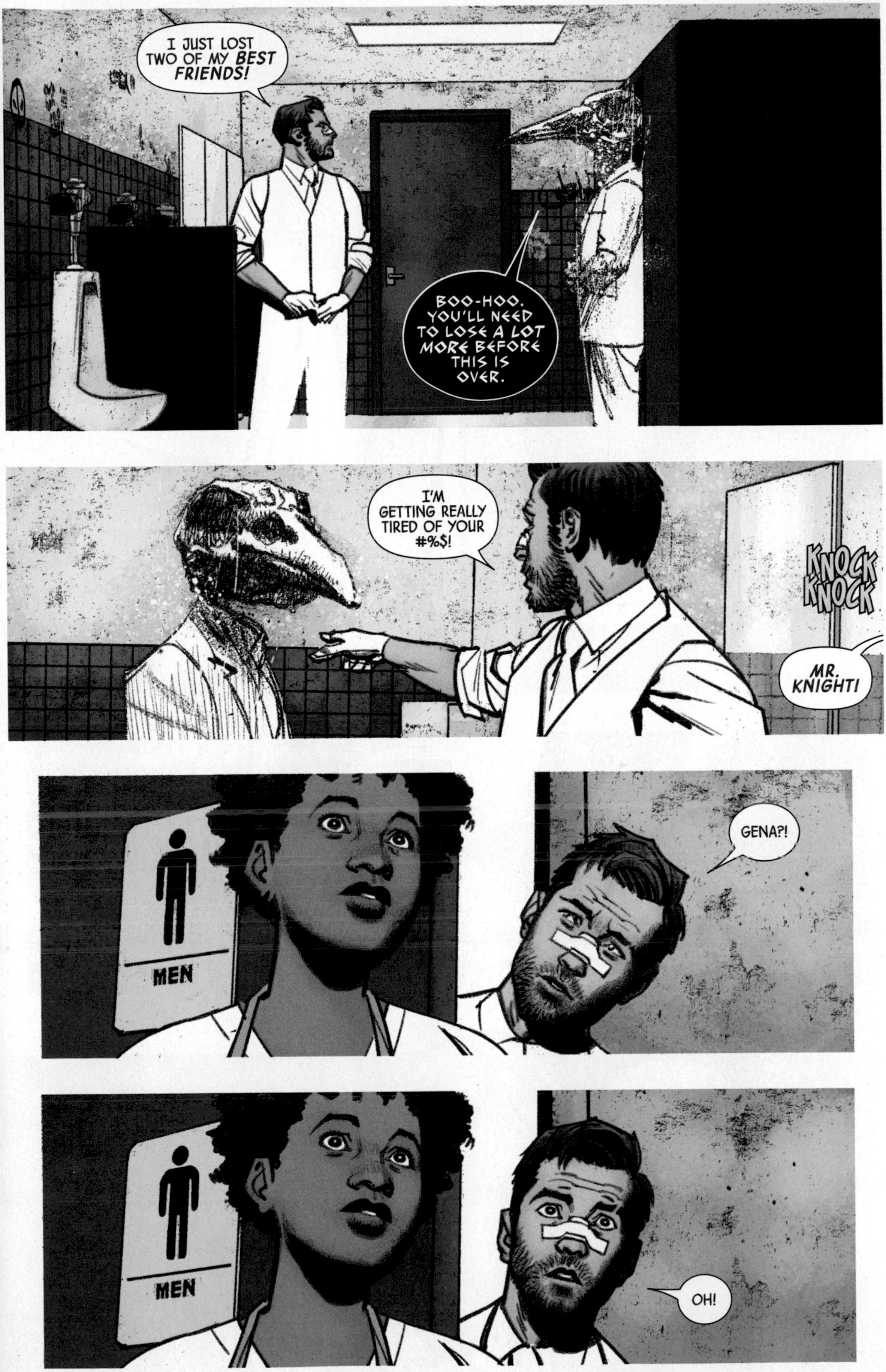
I JUST LOST TWO OF MY BEST FRIENDS!
BOO-HOO. YOU'LL NEED TO LOSE A LOT MORE BEFORE THIS IS OVER.
I'M GETTING REALLY TIRED OF YOUR #%$!
KNOCK KNOCK
MR. KNIGHT!
MEN
GENA?!
MEN
OH!

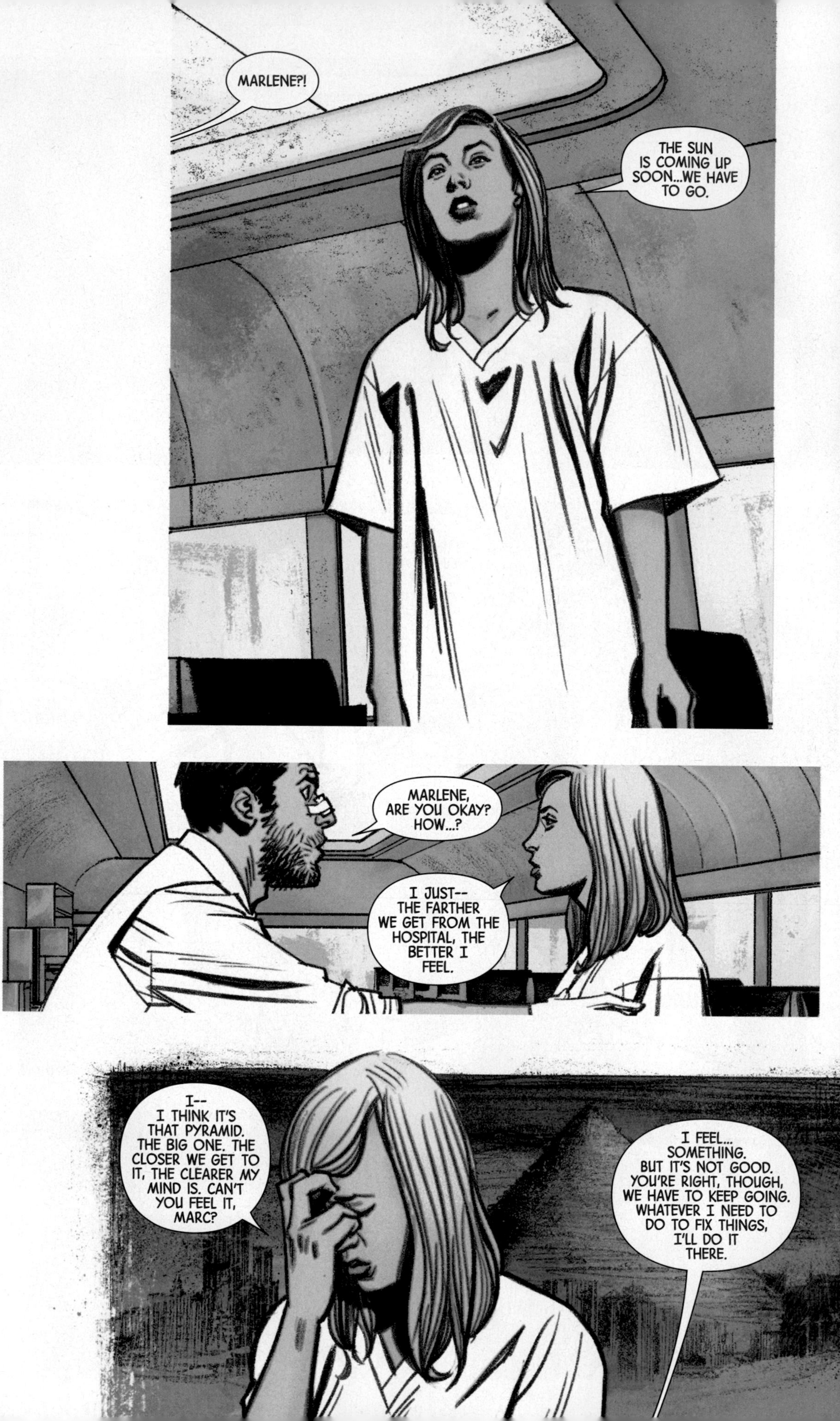
MARLENE?!
THE SUN IS COMING UP SOON...WE HAVE TO GO.
MARLENE, ARE YOU OKAY? HOW...?
I JUST-- THE FARTHER WE GET FROM THE HOSPITAL, THE BETTER I FEEL.
I-- I THINK IT'S THAT PYRAMID. THE BIG ONE. THE CLOSER WE GET TO IT, THE CLEARER MY MIND IS. CAN'T YOU FEEL IT, MARC?
I FEEL... SOMETHING. BUT IT'S NOT GOOD. YOU'RE RIGHT, THOUGH, WE HAVE TO KEEP GOING. WHATEVER I NEED TO DO TO FIX THINGS, I'LL DO IT THERE.

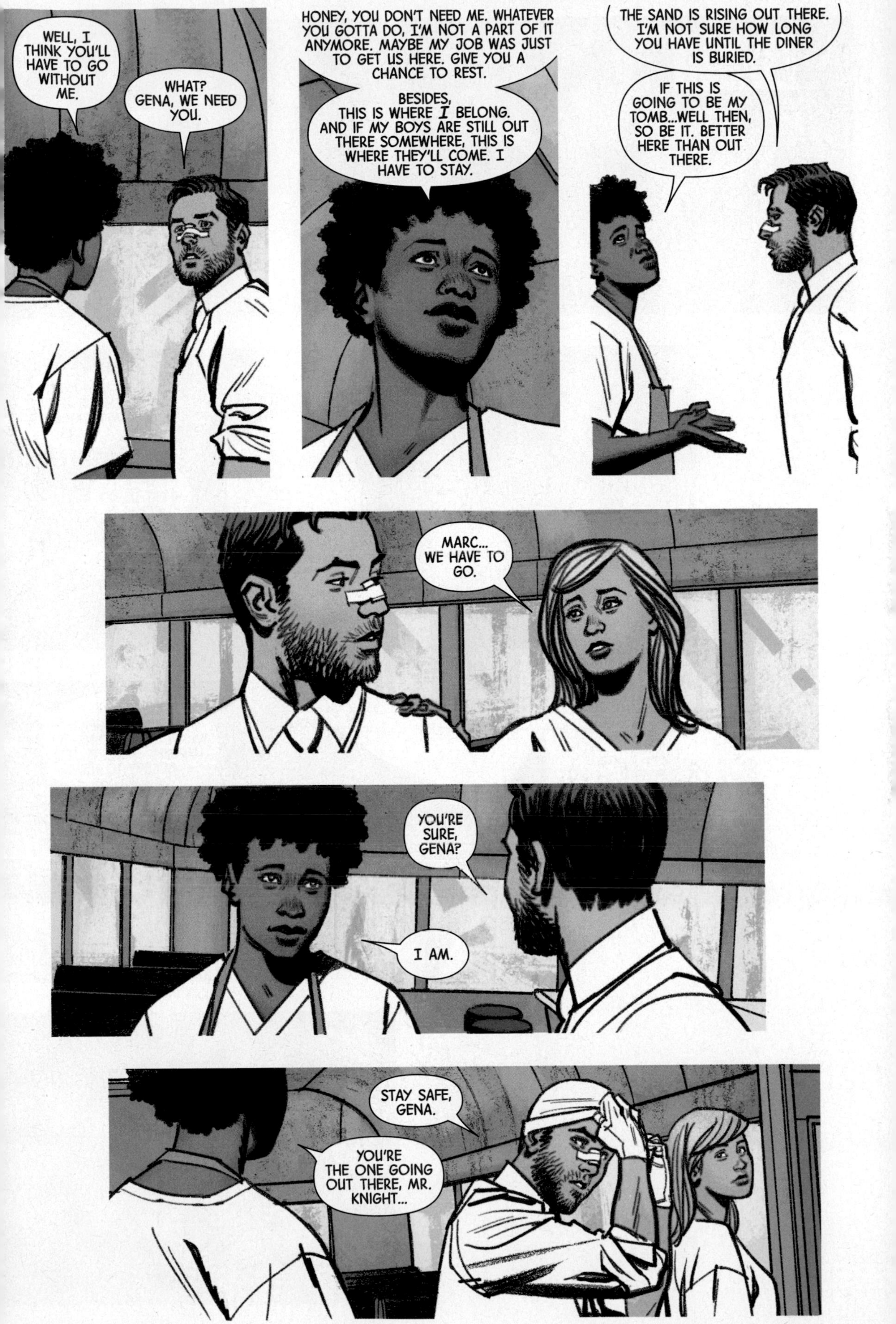
WELL, I THINK YOU'LL HAVE TO GO WITHOUT ME.
WHAT? GENA, WE NEED YOU.
HONEY, YOU DON'T NEED ME. WHATEVER YOU GOTTA DO, I'M NOT A PART OF IT ANYMORE. MAYBE MY JOB WAS JUST TO GET US HERE. GIVE YOU A CHANCE TO REST.
BESIDES, THIS IS WHERE I BELONG. AND IF MY BOYS ARE STILL OUT THERE SOMEWHERE, THIS IS WHERE THEY'LL COME. I HAVE TO STAY.
THE SAND IS RISING OUT THERE. I'M NOT SURE HOW LONG YOU HAVE UNTIL THE DINER IS BURIED.
IF THIS IS GOING TO BE MY TOMB...WELL THEN, SO BE IT. BETTER HERE THAN OUT THERE.
MARC... WE HAVE TO GO.
YOU'RE SURE, GENA?
I AM.
STAY SAFE, GENA.
YOU'RE THE ONE GOING OUT THERE, MR. KNIGHT...

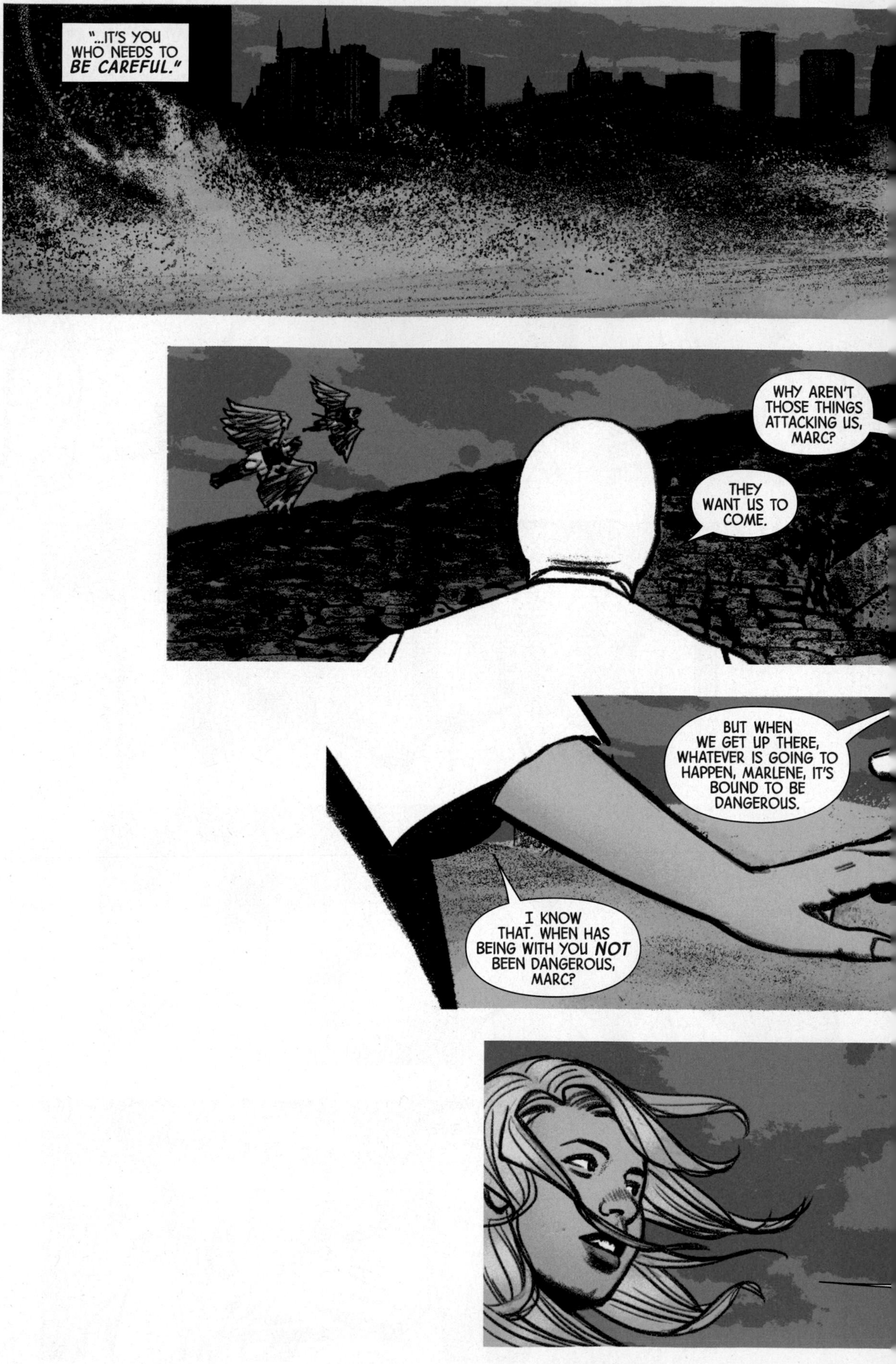
"...IT'S YOU WHO NEEDS TO BE CAREFUL."
WHY AREN'T THOSE THINGS ATTACKING US, MARC?
THEY WANT US TO COME.
BUT WHEN WE GET UP THERE, WHATEVER IS GOING TO HAPPEN, MARLENE, IT'S BOUND TO BE DANGEROUS.
I KNOW THAT. WHEN HAS BEING WITH YOU NOT BEEN DANGEROUS, MARC?

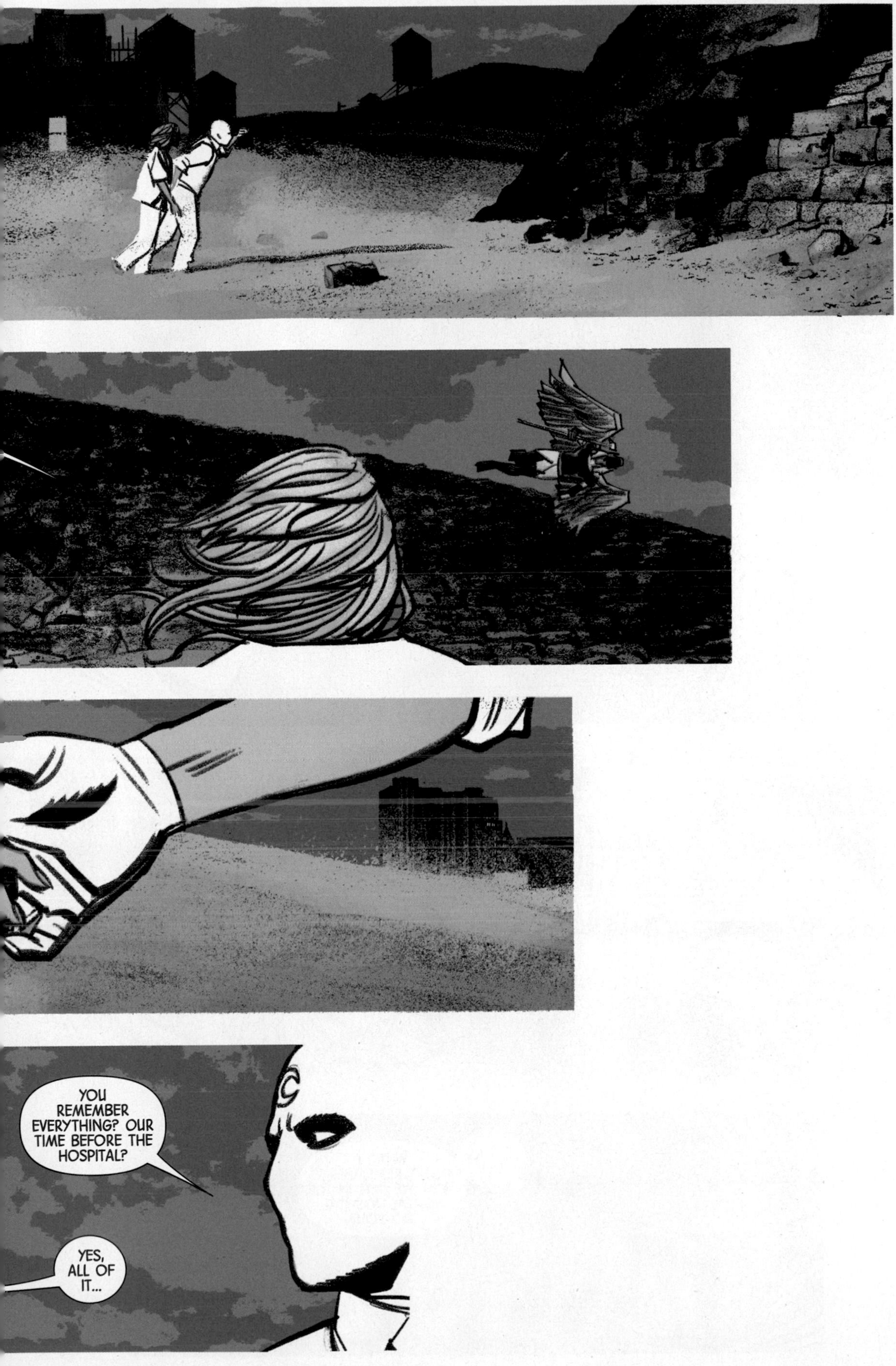
YOU REMEMBER EVERYTHING? OUR TIME BEFORE THE HOSPITAL?
YES, ALL OF IT...

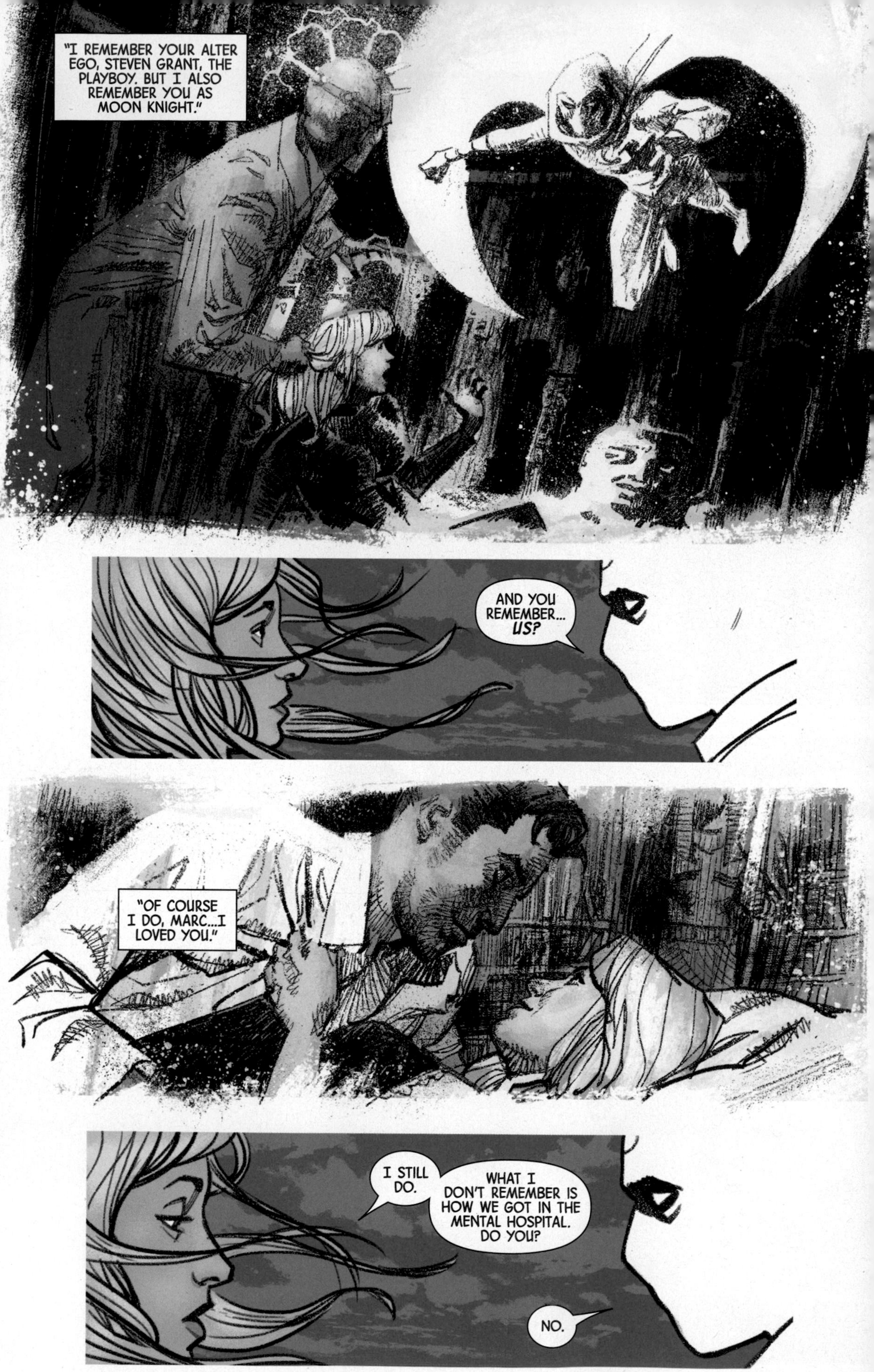
"I REMEMBER YOUR ALTER EGO, STEVEN GRANT, THE PLAYBOY. BUT I ALSO REMEMBER YOU AS MOON KNIGHT."
AND YOU REMEMBER... *US?*
"OF COURSE I DO, MARC...I LOVED YOU."
I STILL DO.
WHAT I DON'T REMEMBER IS HOW WE GOT IN THE MENTAL HOSPITAL. DO YOU?
NO.

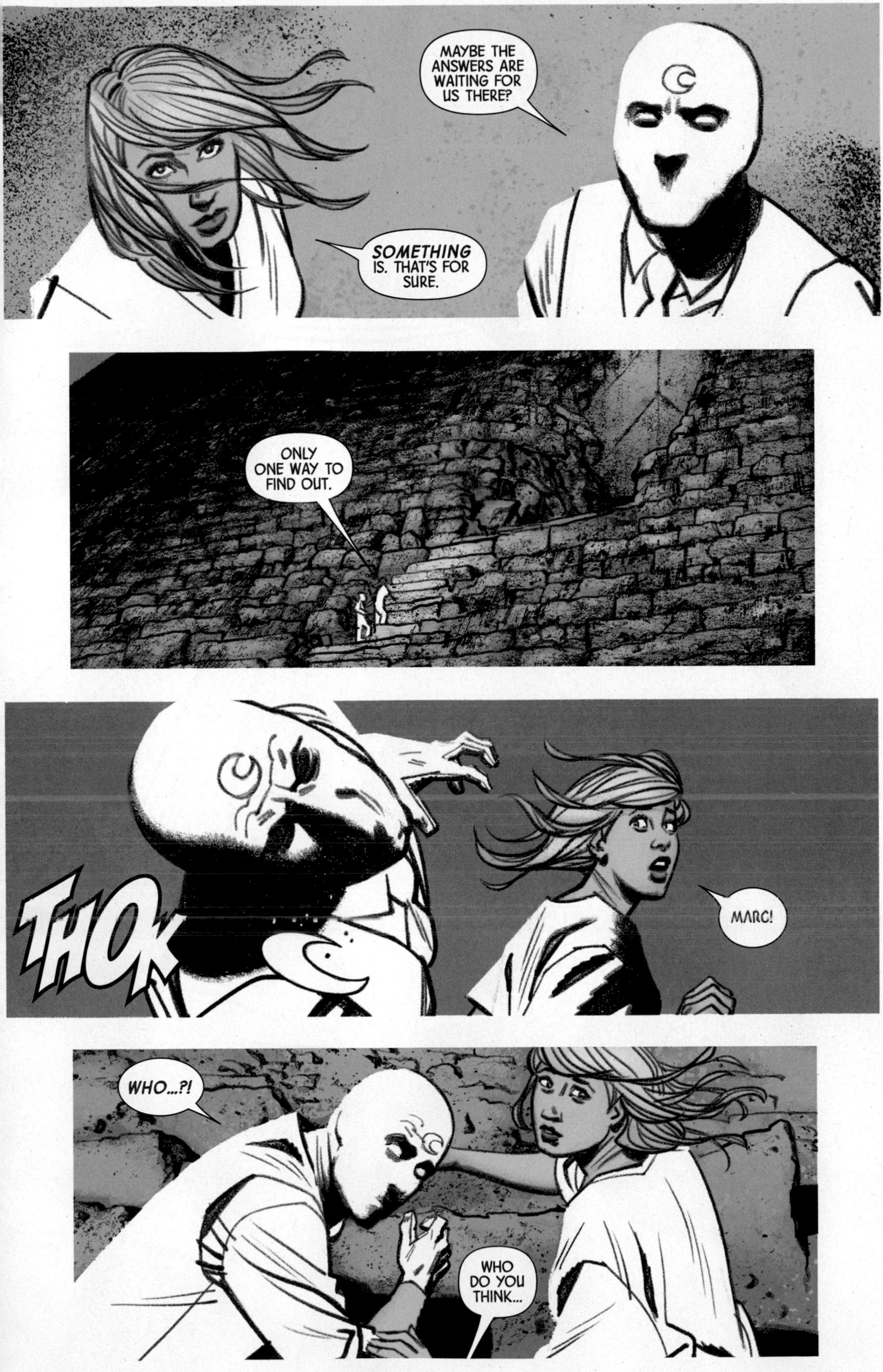
MAYBE THE ANSWERS ARE WAITING FOR US THERE?
SOMETHING IS. THAT'S FOR SURE.
ONLY ONE WAY TO FIND OUT.
THOK
MARC!
WHO...?!
WHO DO YOU THINK...

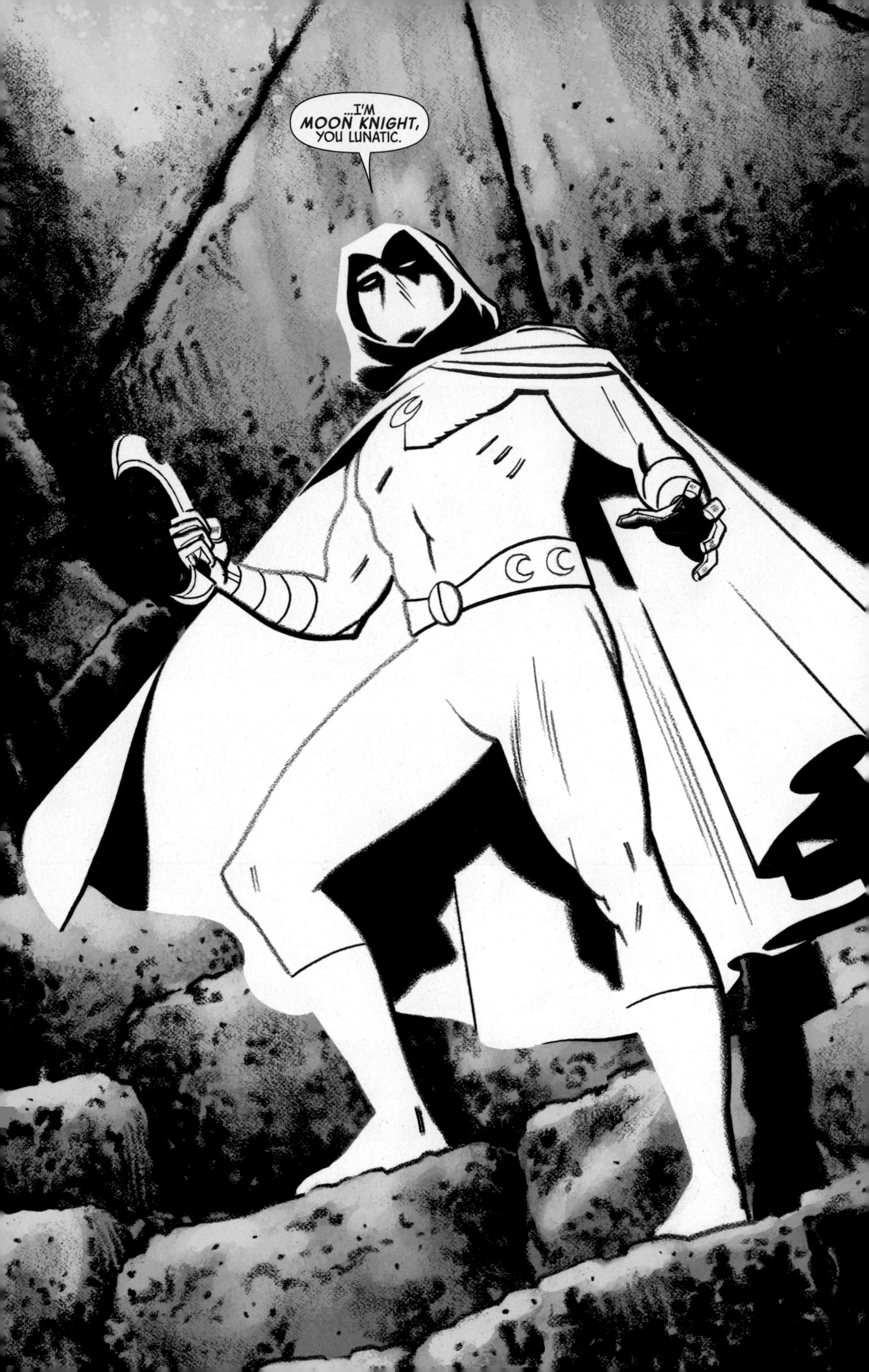
...I'M MOON KNIGHT, YOU LUNATIC.

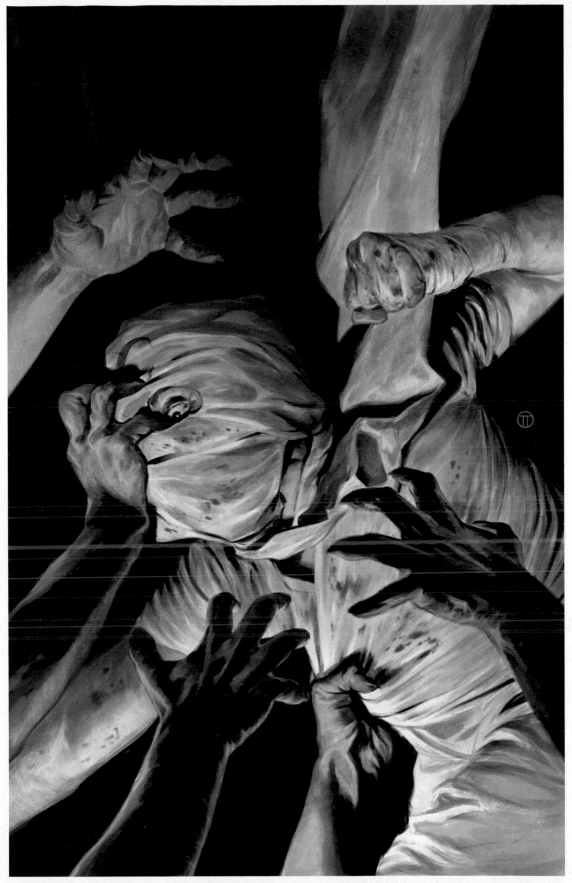

#2 VARIANT BY JULIAN TOTINO TEDESCO

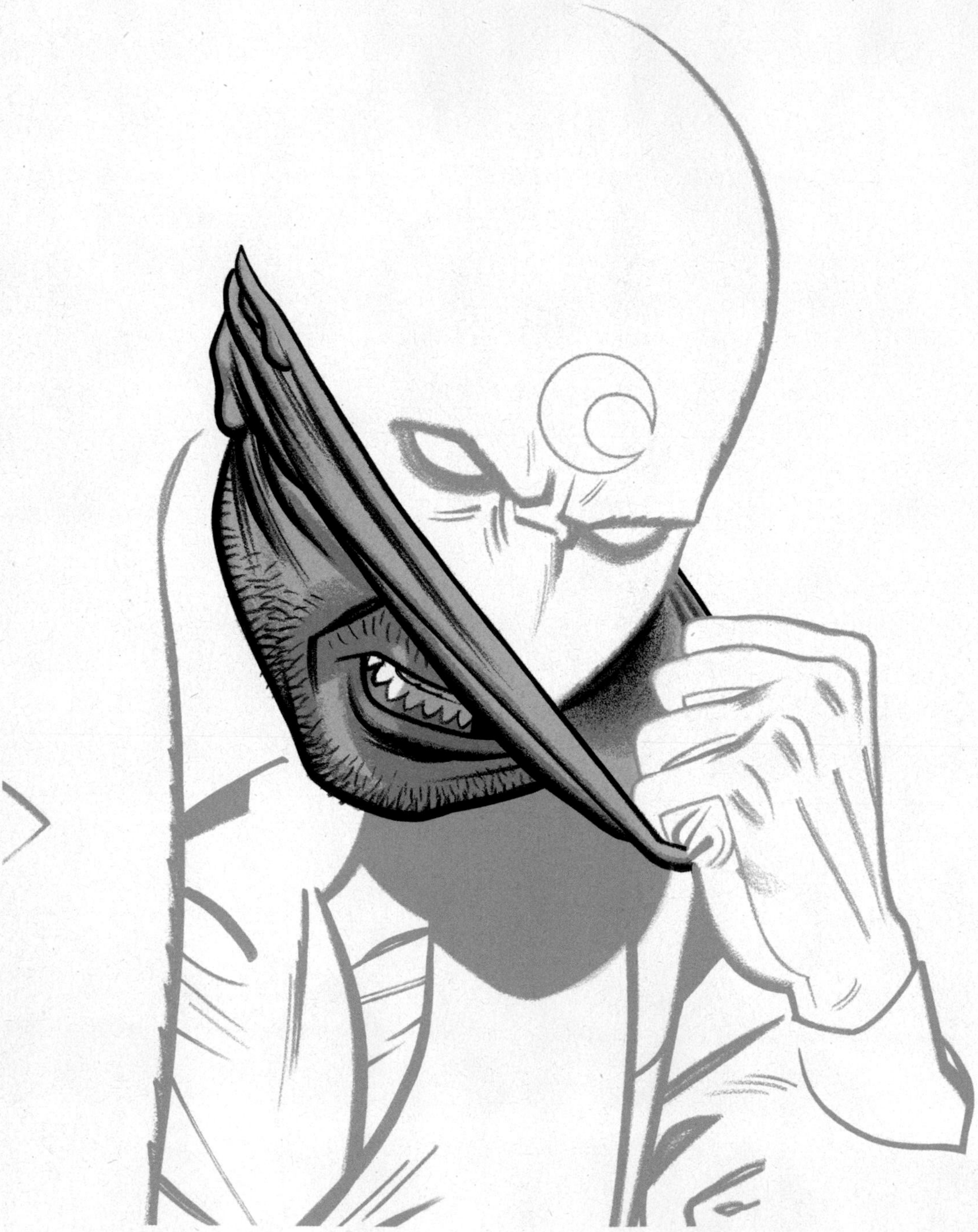

WELCOME TO NEW EGYPT
PART FIVE

5

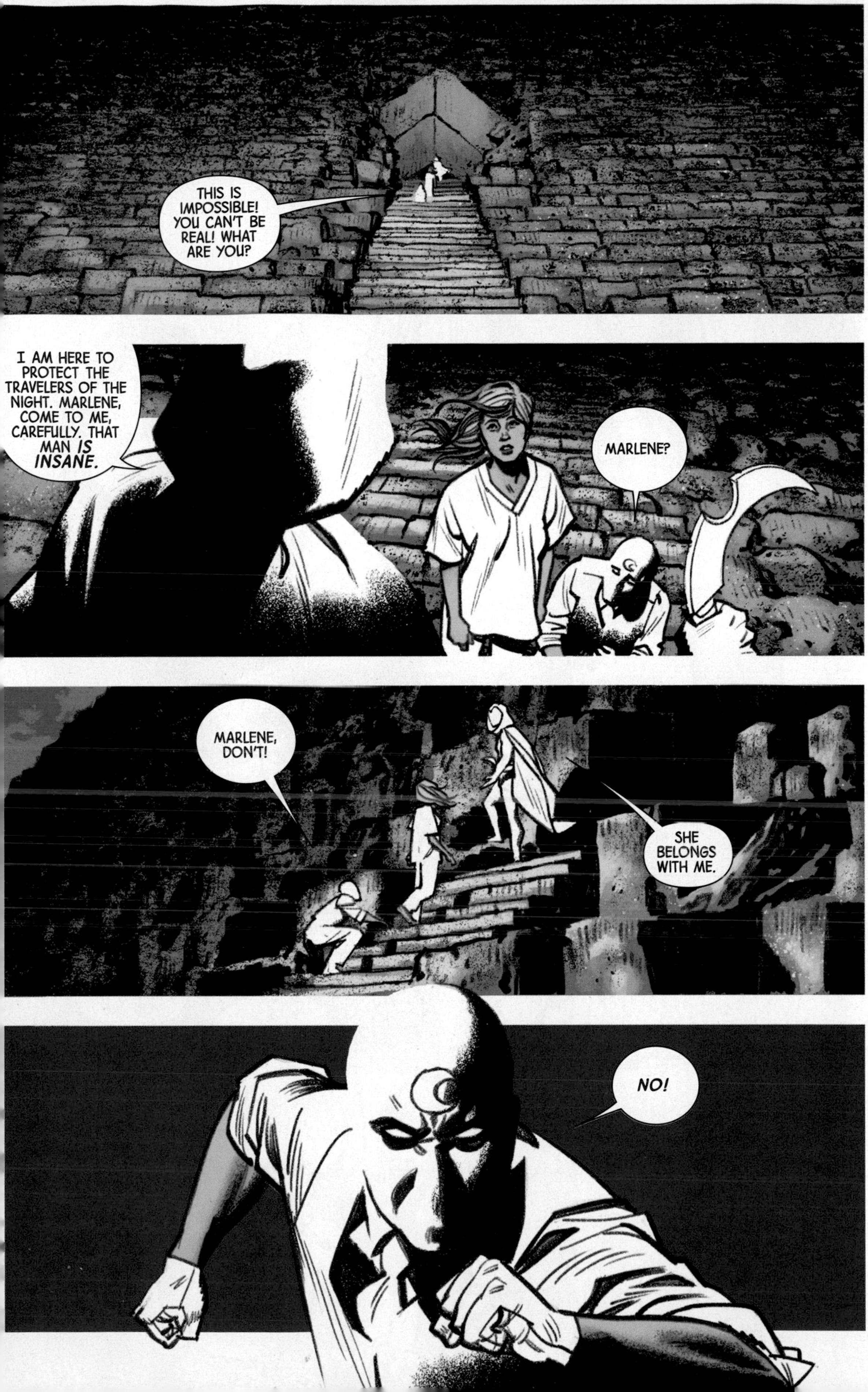
THIS IS IMPOSSIBLE! YOU CAN'T BE REAL! WHAT ARE YOU?
I AM HERE TO PROTECT THE TRAVELERS OF THE NIGHT. MARLENE, COME TO ME, CAREFULLY. THAT MAN *IS INSANE.*
MARLENE?
MARLENE, DON'T!
SHE BELONGS WITH ME.
NO!

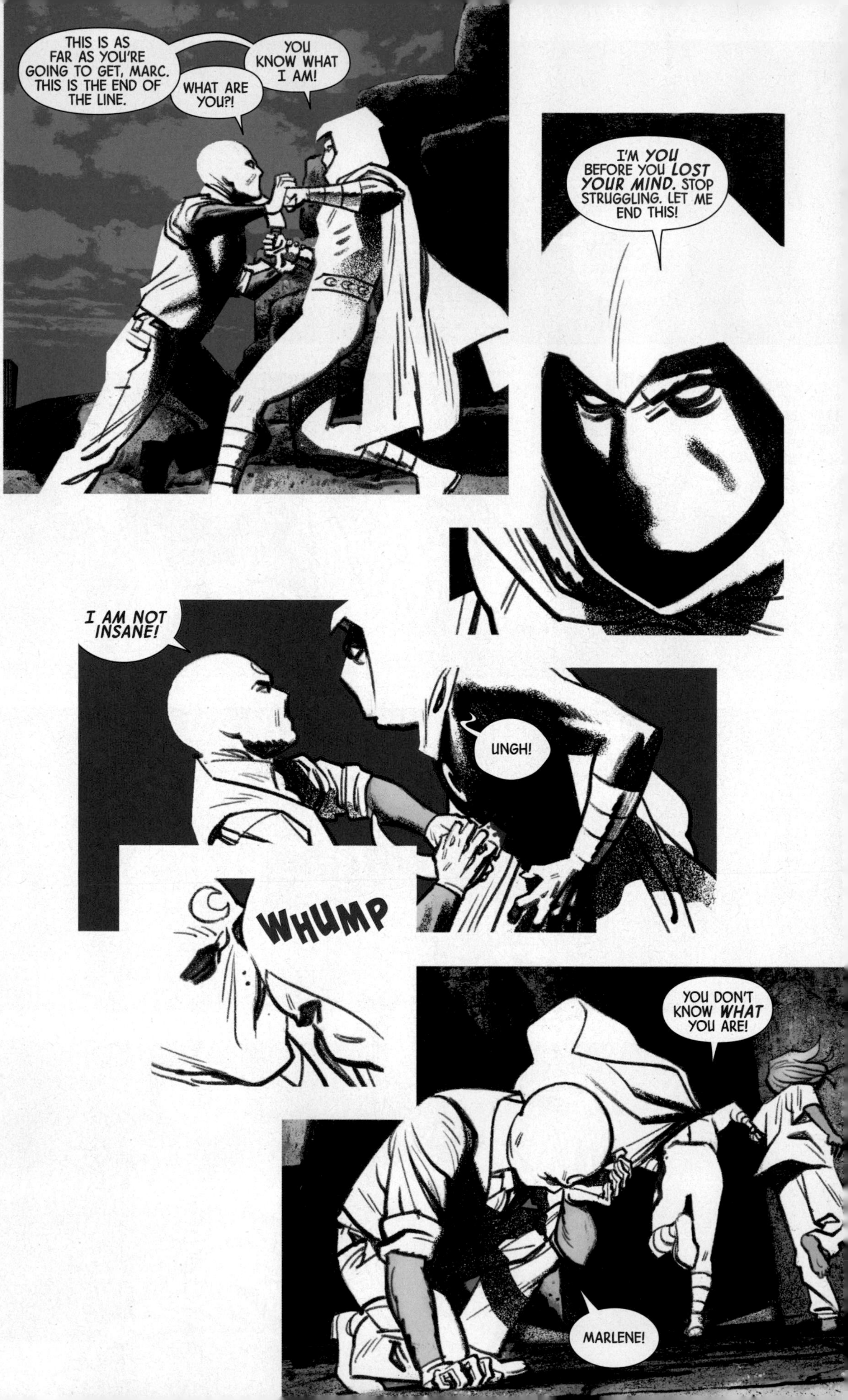
THIS IS AS FAR AS YOU'RE GOING TO GET, MARC. THIS IS THE END OF THE LINE.
WHAT ARE YOU?!
YOU KNOW WHAT I AM!
I'M YOU BEFORE YOU LOST YOUR MIND. STOP STRUGGLING. LET ME END THIS!
I AM NOT INSANE!
UNGH!
WHUMP
YOU DON'T KNOW WHAT YOU ARE!
MARLENE!

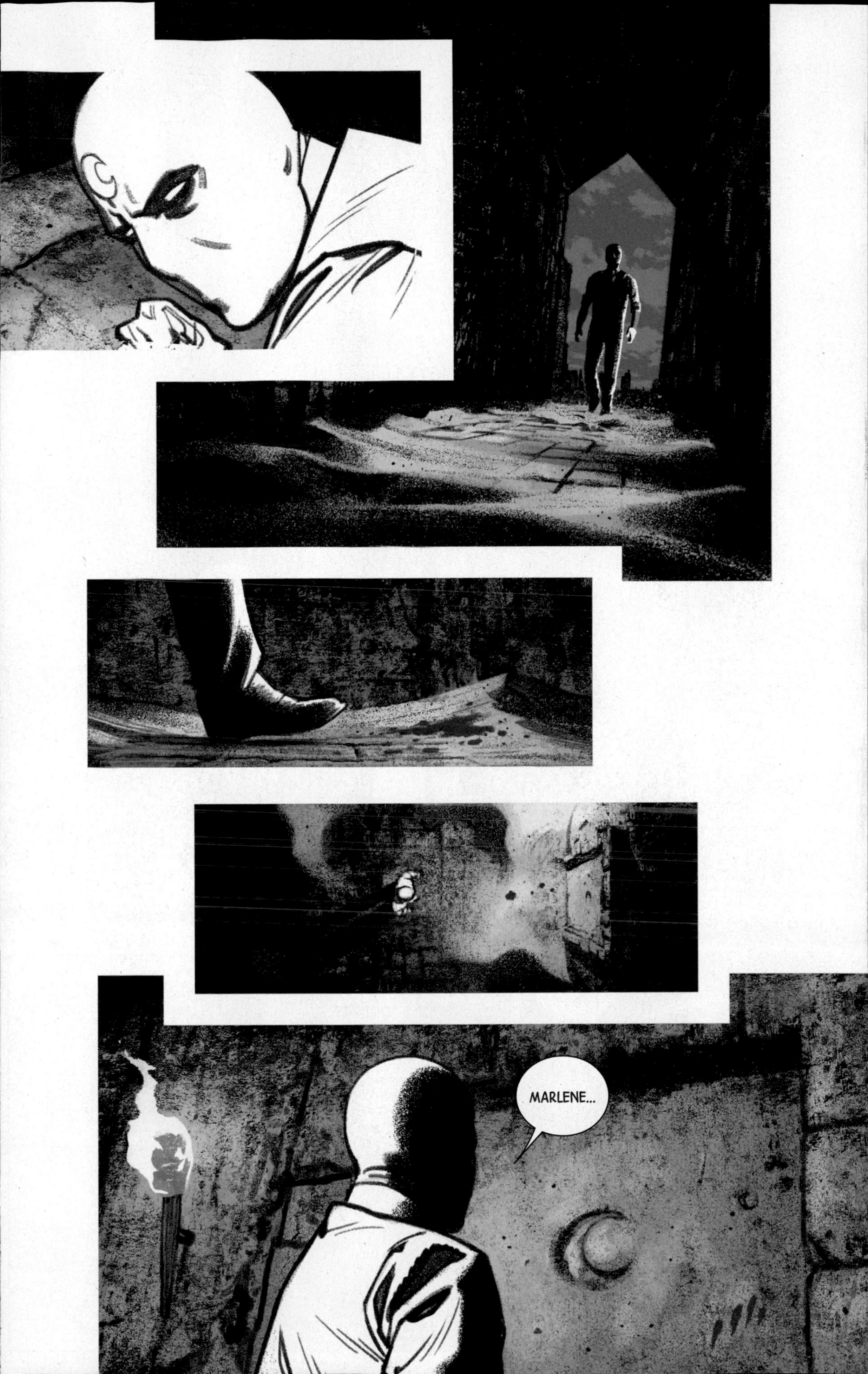
MARLENE...

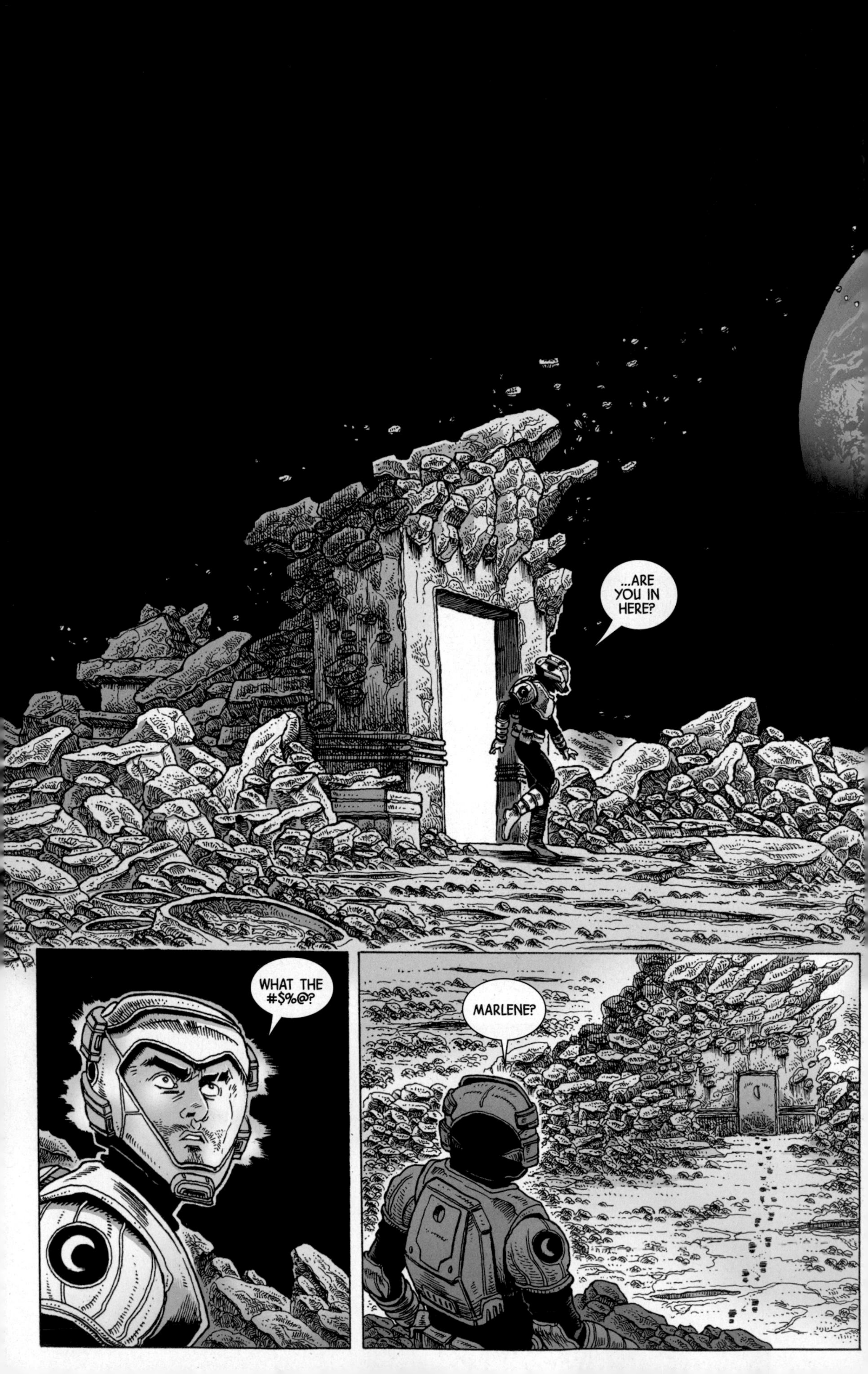
...ARE YOU IN HERE?
WHAT THE #$%@?
MARLENE?

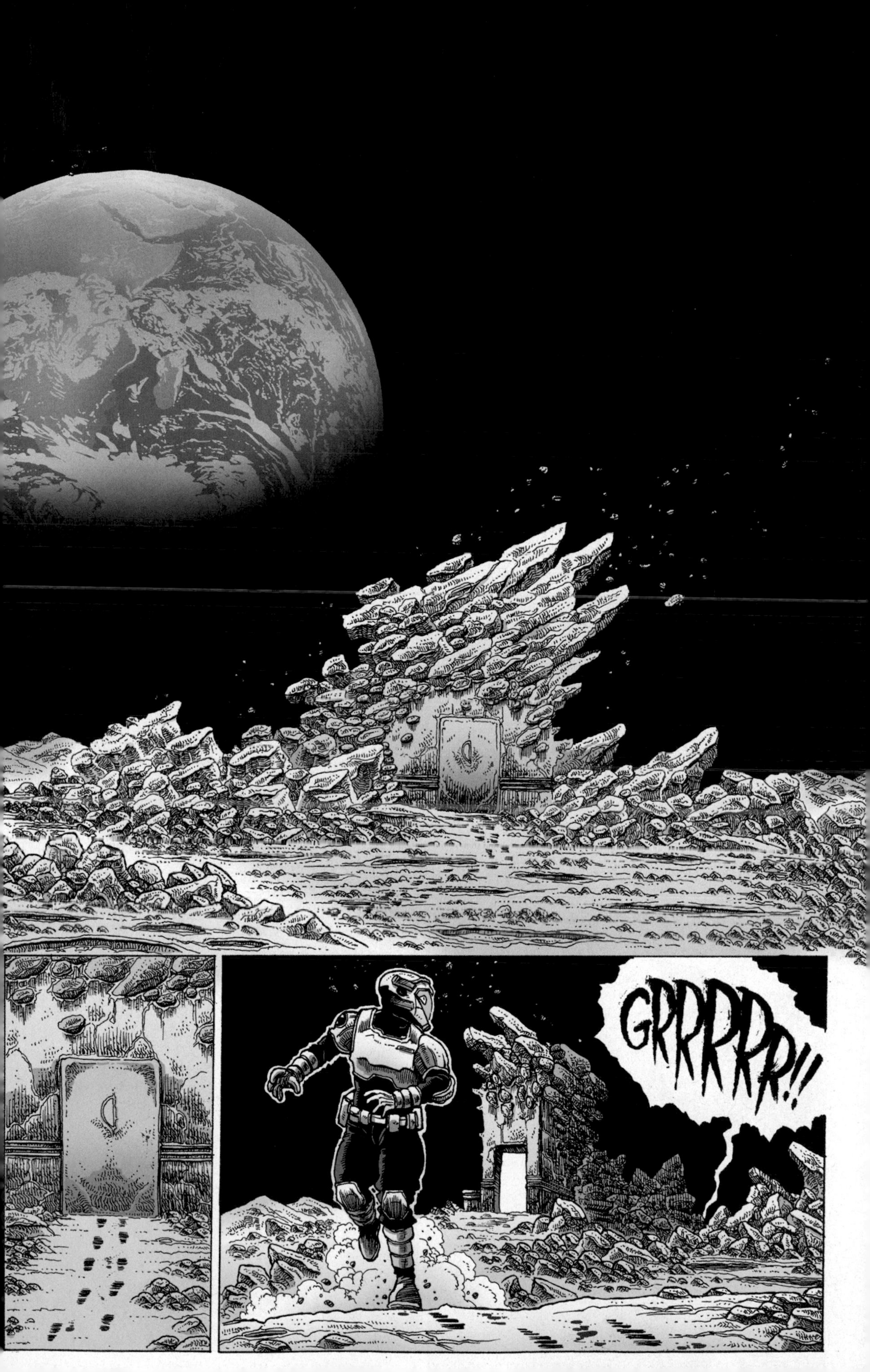
GRRRRR!!

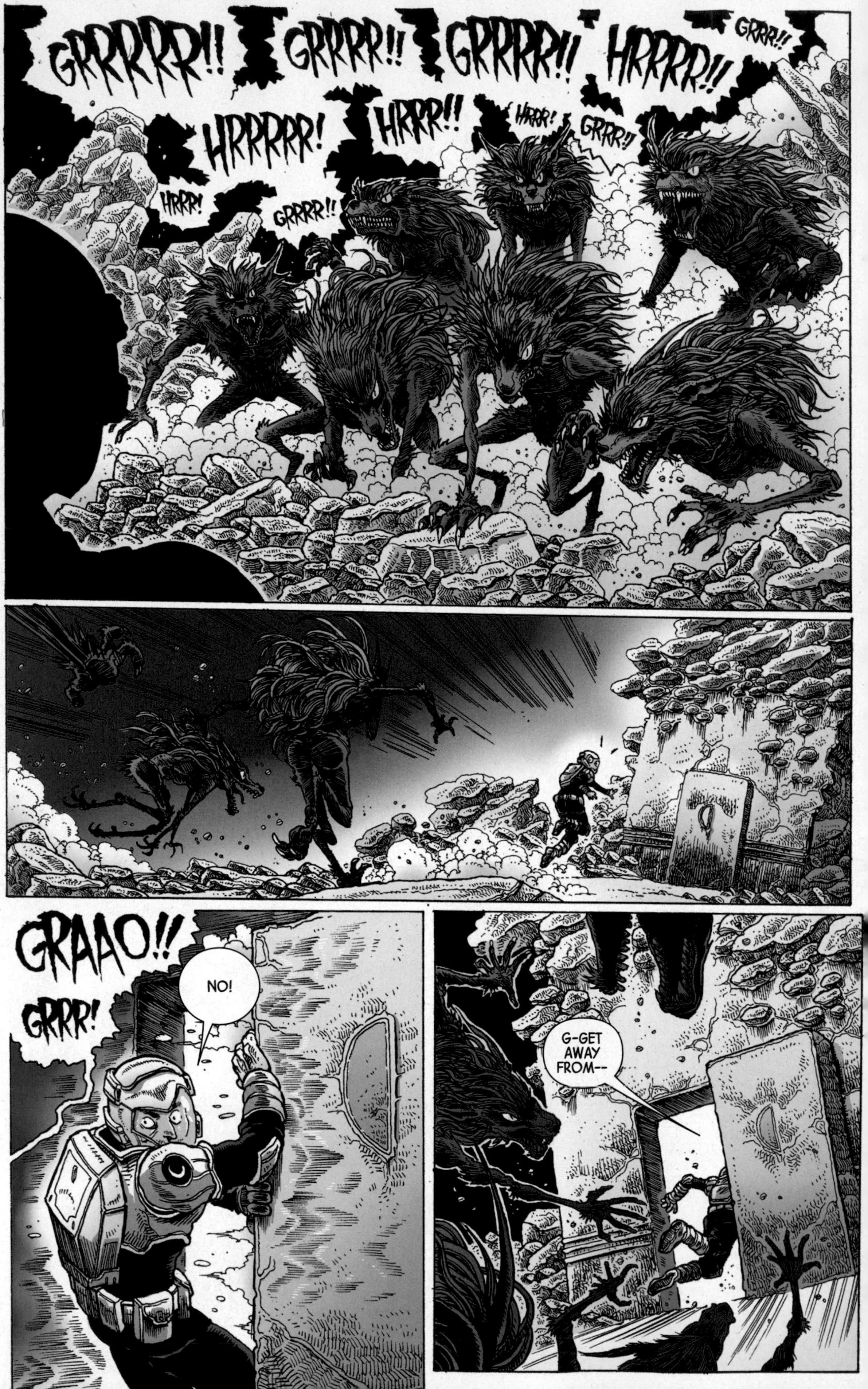
GRRRRR!!
GRRRR!!
GRRRR!!
HRRRR!!
GRRR!!
HRRRRR!
HRRR!!
HRRR!
GRRR!!
HRRR!
GRRRR!!
GRAAO!!
GRRR!
NO!
G-GET AWAY FROM--

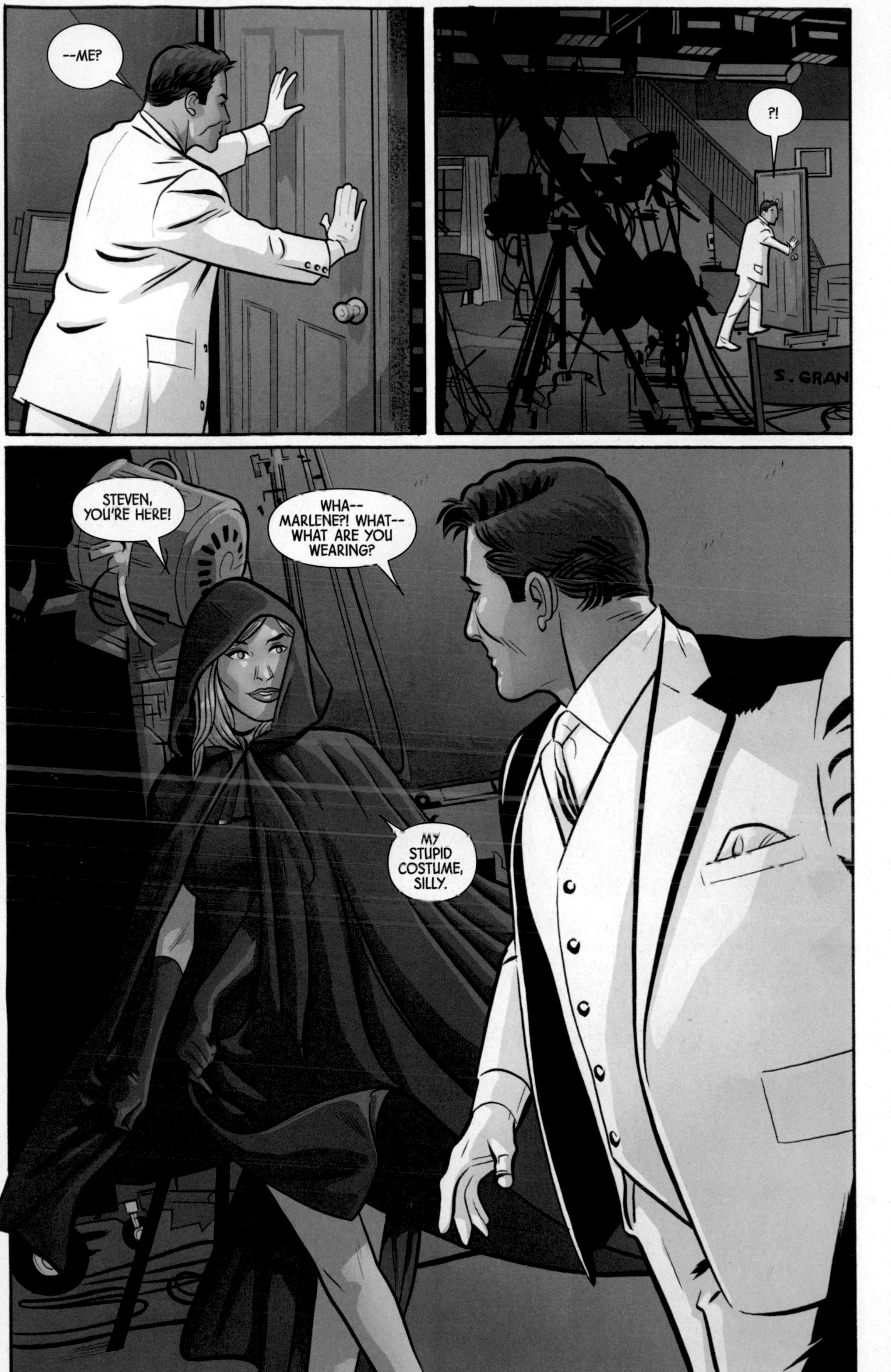
--ME?
?!
S. GRAN
STEVEN, YOU'RE HERE!
WHA-- MARLENE?! WHAT-- WHAT ARE YOU WEARING?
MY STUPID COSTUME, SILLY.

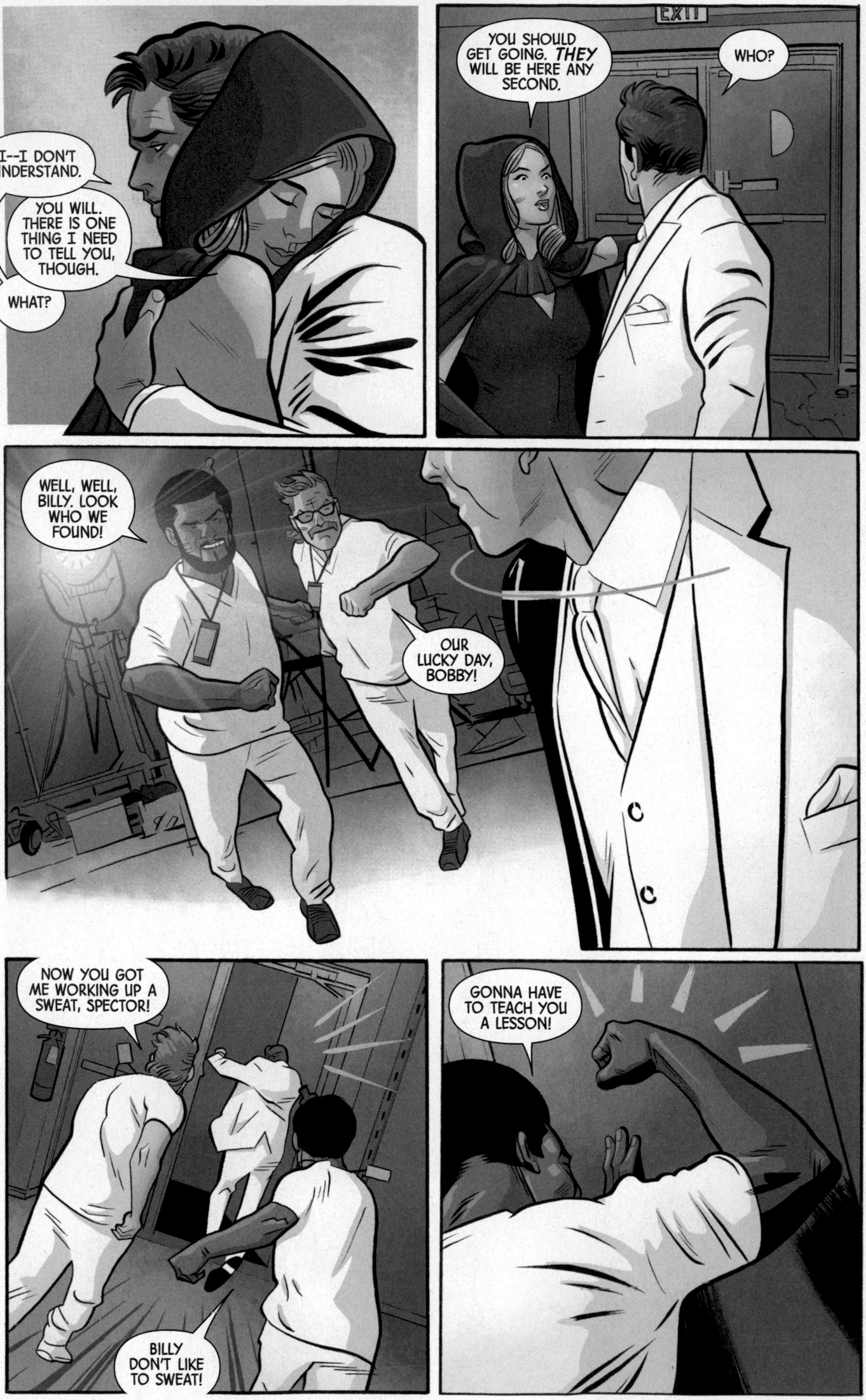
I--I DON'T UNDERSTAND.
YOU WILL. THERE IS ONE THING I NEED TO TELL YOU, THOUGH.
WHAT?
EXIT
YOU SHOULD GET GOING. THEY WILL BE HERE ANY SECOND.
WHO?
WELL, WELL, BILLY. LOOK WHO WE FOUND!
OUR LUCKY DAY, BOBBY!
NOW YOU GOT ME WORKING UP A SWEAT, SPECTOR!
BILLY DON'T LIKE TO SWEAT!
GONNA HAVE TO TEACH YOU A LESSON!

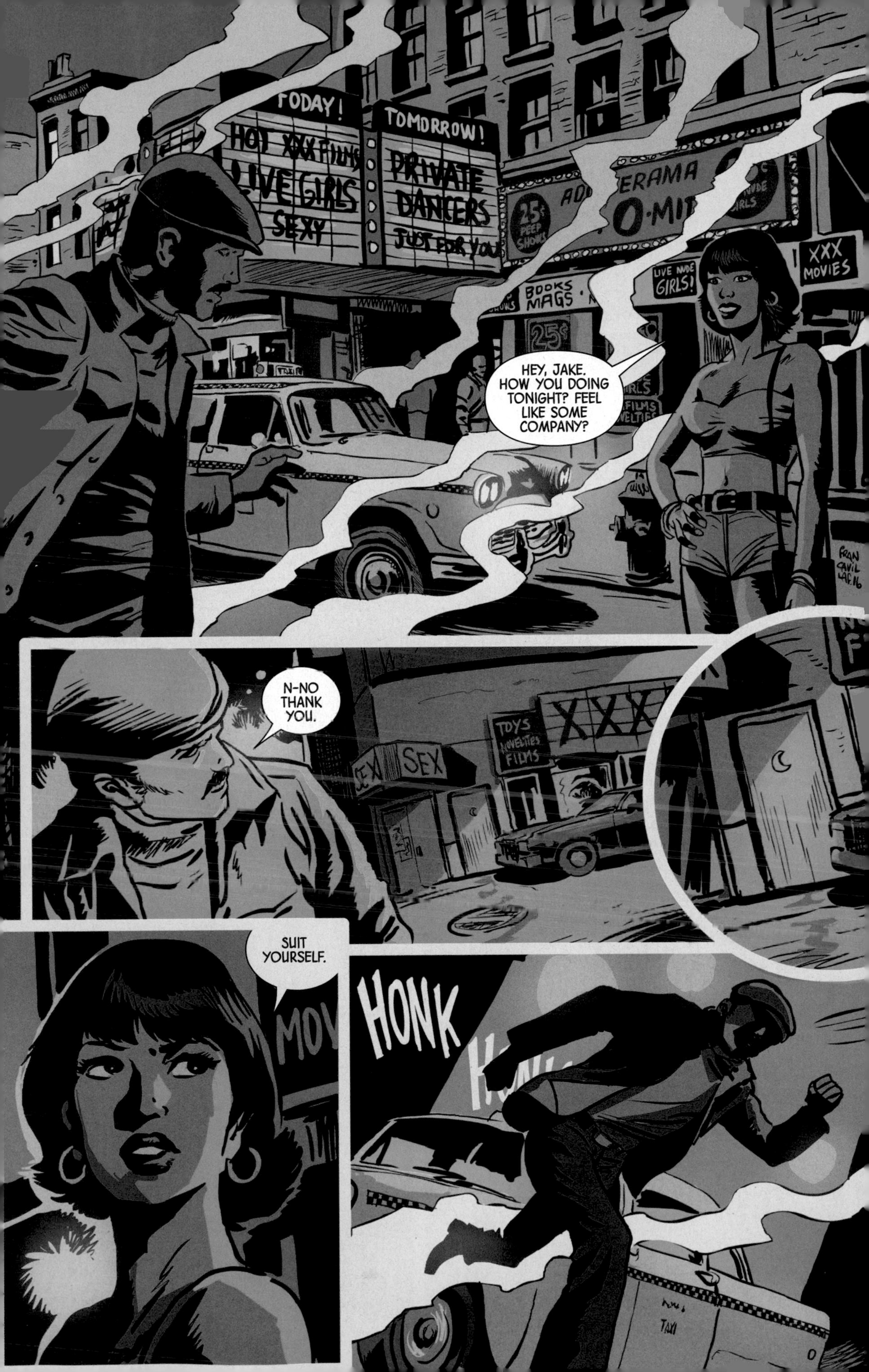
TODAY!
HOT XXX FILMS
LIVE GIRLS
SEXY
TOMORROW!
PRIVATE
DANCERS
JUST FOR YOU
25¢ PEEP SHOWS
BOOKS
MAGS
LIVE NUDE GIRLS!
XXX MOVIES
HEY, JAKE. HOW YOU DOING TONIGHT? FEEL LIKE SOME COMPANY?
N-NO THANK YOU.
TOYS NOVELTIES FILMS
SEX SEX
SUIT YOURSELF.
HONK
TAXI

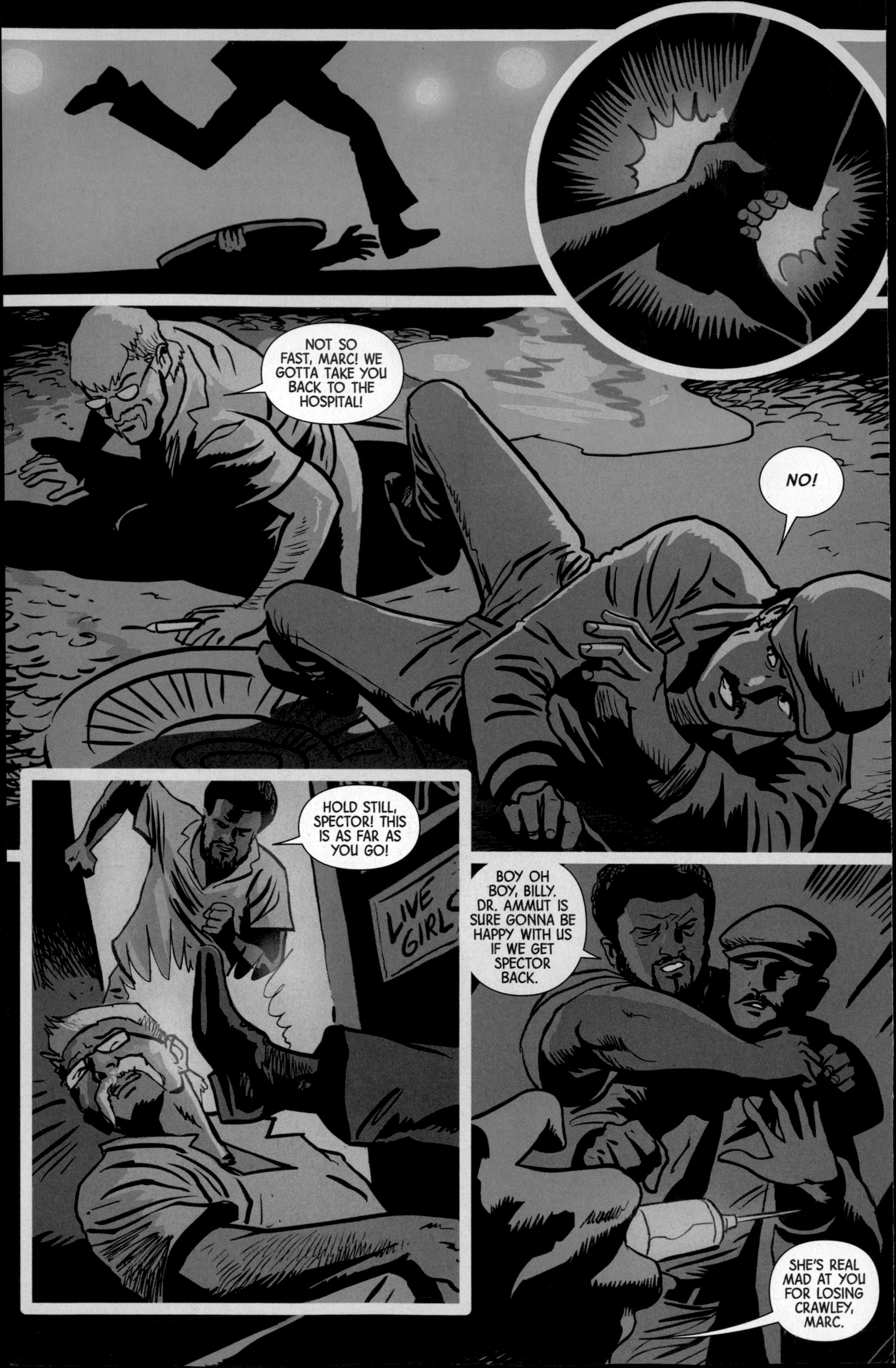
NOT SO FAST, MARC! WE GOTTA TAKE YOU BACK TO THE HOSPITAL!
NO!
HOLD STILL, SPECTOR! THIS IS AS FAR AS YOU GO!
LIVE GIRLS
BOY OH BOY, BILLY. DR. AMMUT IS SURE GONNA BE HAPPY WITH US IF WE GET SPECTOR BACK.
SHE'S REAL MAD AT YOU FOR LOSING CRAWLEY, MARC.

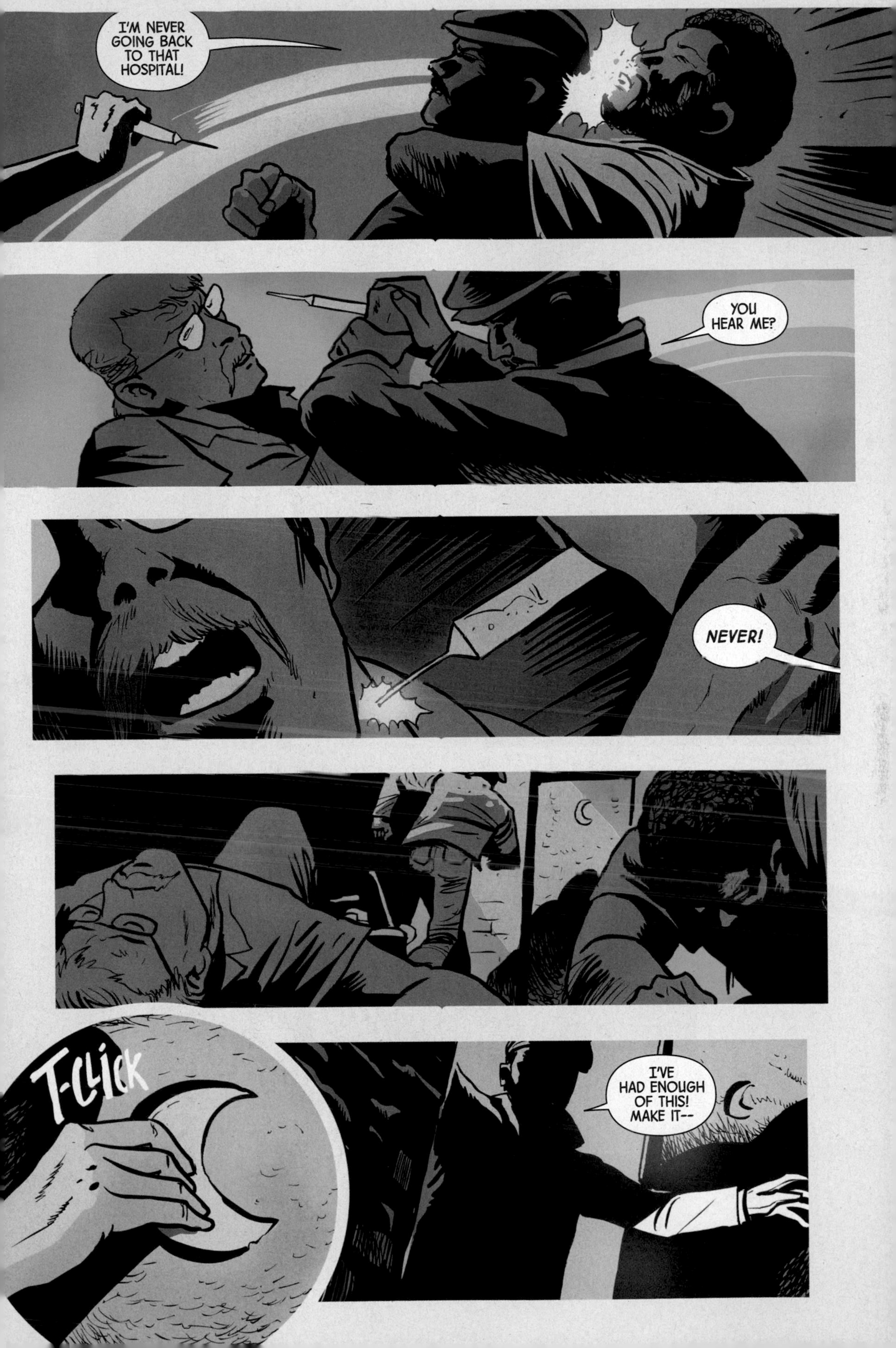
I'M NEVER GOING BACK TO THAT HOSPITAL!
YOU HEAR ME?
NEVER!
T-CLICK
I'VE HAD ENOUGH OF THIS! MAKE IT--

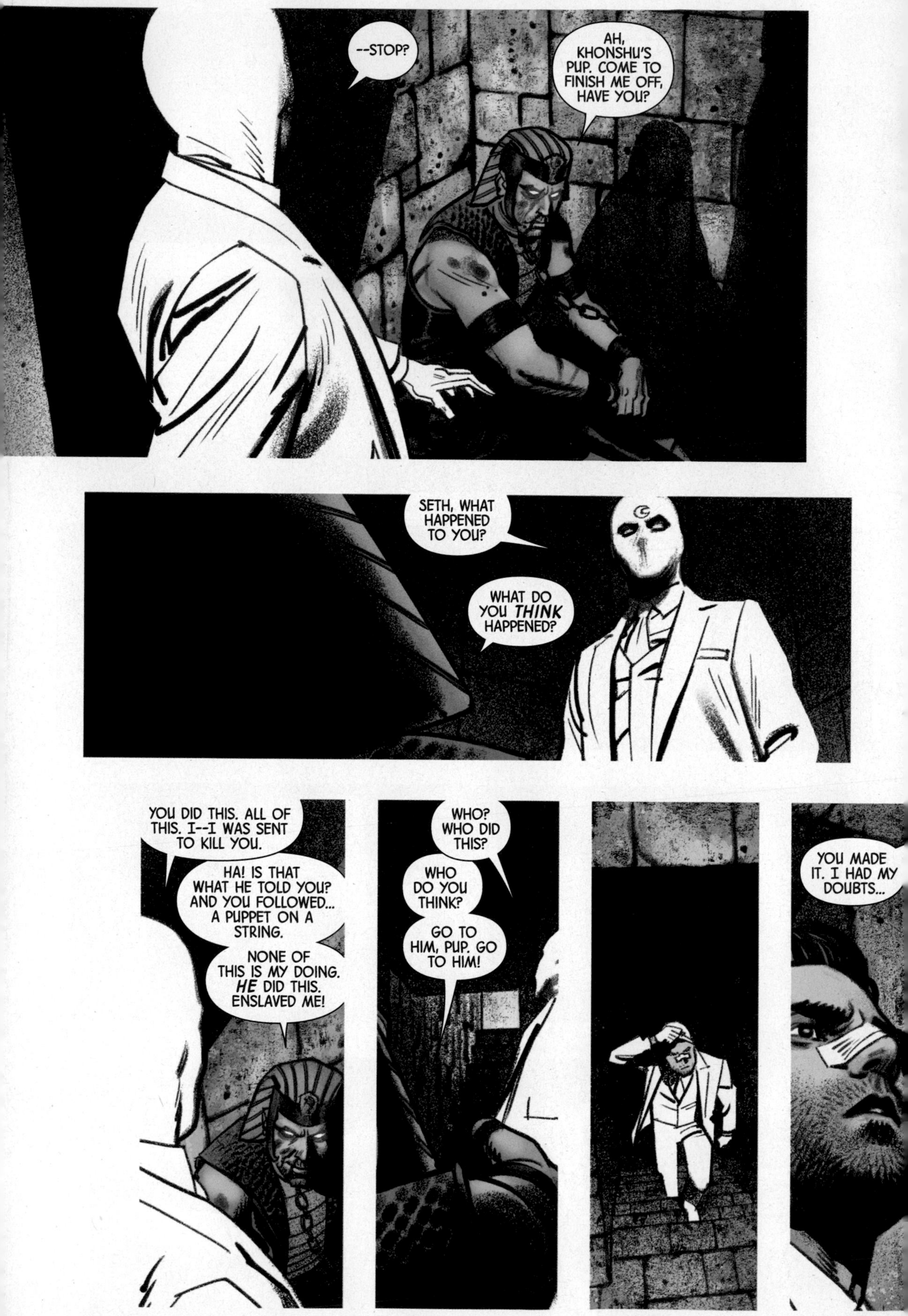
--STOP?
AH, KHONSHU'S PUP. COME TO FINISH ME OFF, HAVE YOU?
SETH, WHAT HAPPENED TO YOU?
WHAT DO YOU *THINK* HAPPENED?
YOU DID THIS. ALL OF THIS. I--I WAS SENT TO KILL YOU.
HA! IS THAT WHAT HE TOLD YOU? AND YOU FOLLOWED... A PUPPET ON A STRING.
NONE OF THIS IS MY DOING. *HE* DID THIS. ENSLAVED ME!
WHO? WHO DID THIS?
WHO DO YOU THINK?
GO TO HIM, PUP. GO TO HIM!
YOU MADE IT. I HAD MY DOUBTS...

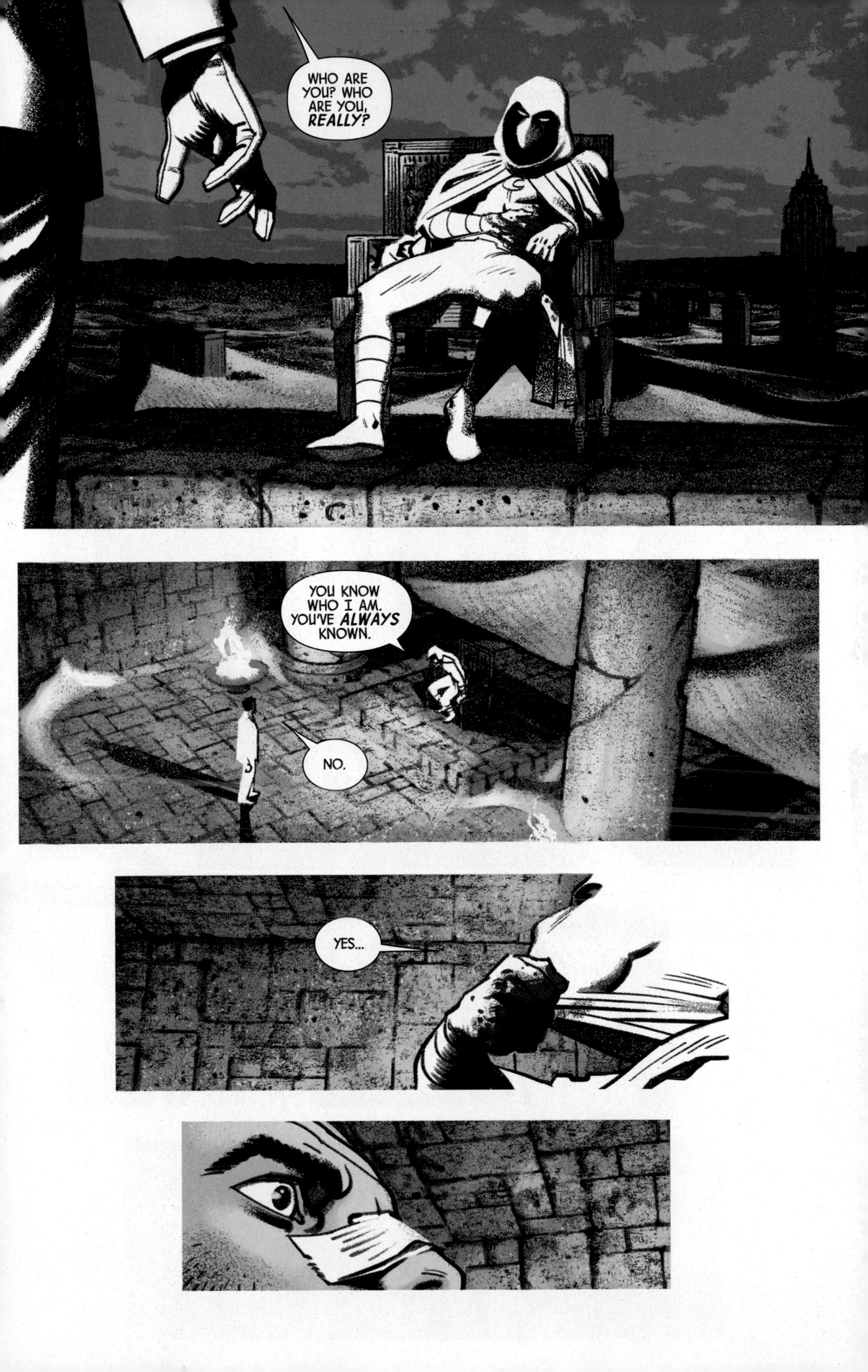
WHO ARE YOU? WHO ARE YOU, *REALLY*?
YOU KNOW WHO I AM. YOU'VE *ALWAYS* KNOWN.
NO.
YES...

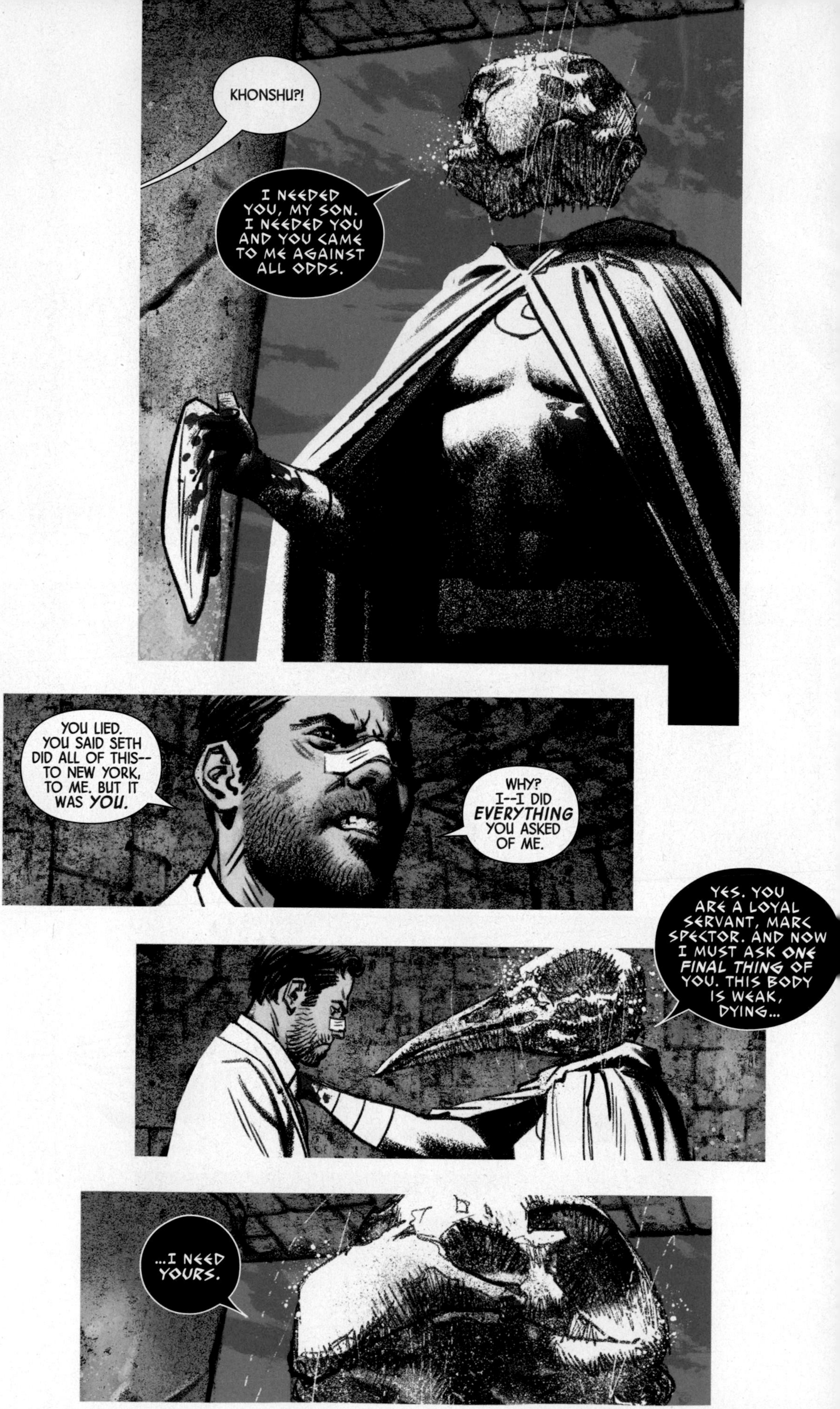
KHONSHU?!
I NEEDED YOU, MY SON. I NEEDED YOU AND YOU CAME TO ME AGAINST ALL ODDS.
YOU LIED. YOU SAID SETH DID ALL OF THIS-- TO NEW YORK, TO ME. BUT IT WAS *YOU.*
WHY? I--I DID *EVERYTHING* YOU ASKED OF ME.
YES. YOU ARE A LOYAL SERVANT, MARC SPECTOR. AND NOW I MUST ASK *ONE FINAL THING* OF YOU. THIS BODY IS WEAK, DYING...
...I NEED YOURS.

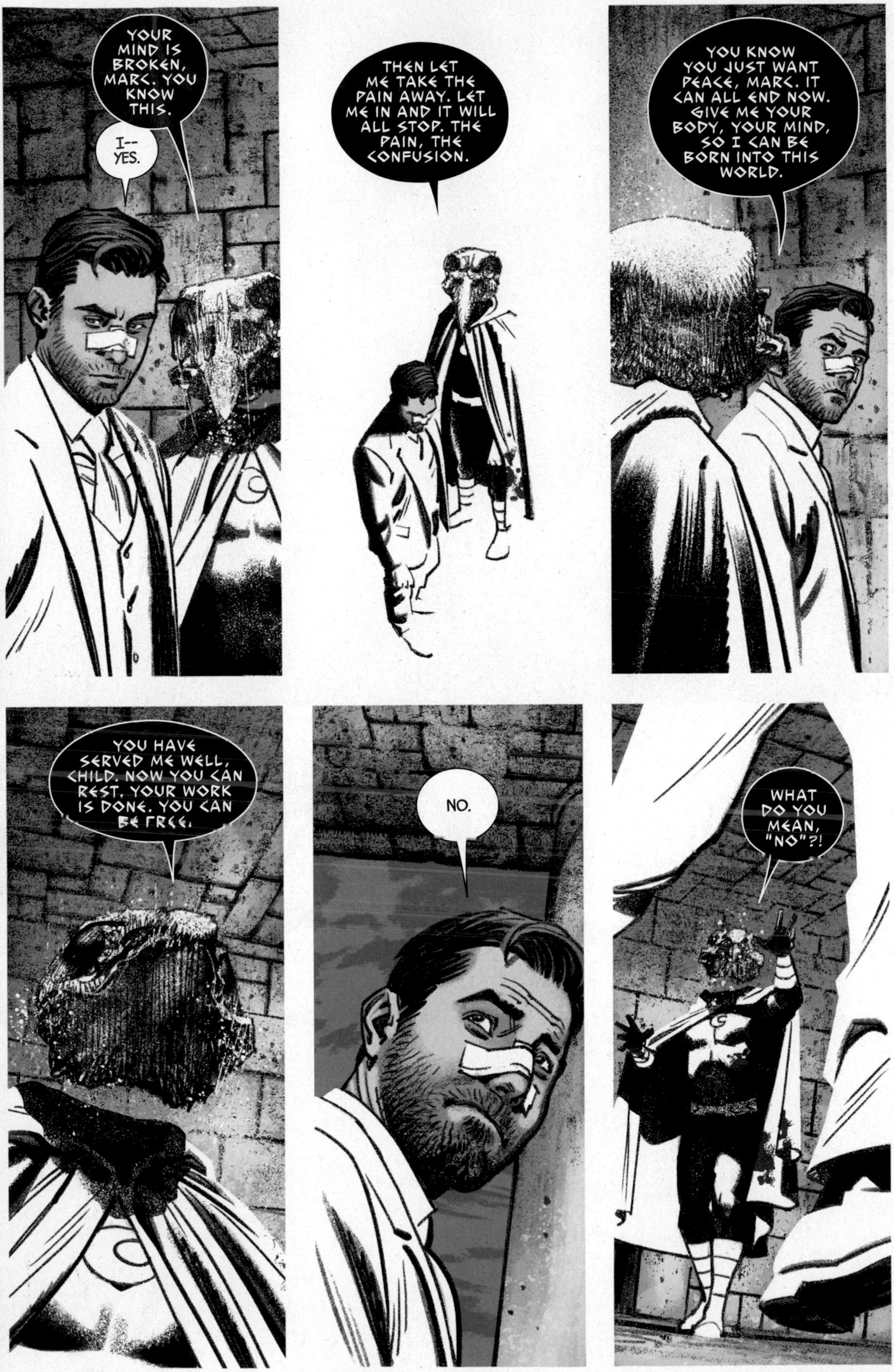
YOUR MIND IS BROKEN, MARC. YOU KNOW THIS.
I-- YES.
THEN LET ME TAKE THE PAIN AWAY. LET ME IN AND IT WILL ALL STOP. THE PAIN, THE CONFUSION.
YOU KNOW YOU JUST WANT PEACE, MARC. IT CAN ALL END NOW. GIVE ME YOUR BODY, YOUR MIND, SO I CAN BE BORN INTO THIS WORLD.
YOU HAVE SERVED ME WELL, CHILD. NOW YOU CAN REST. YOUR WORK IS DONE. YOU CAN BE FREE.
NO.
WHAT DO YOU MEAN, "NO"?!

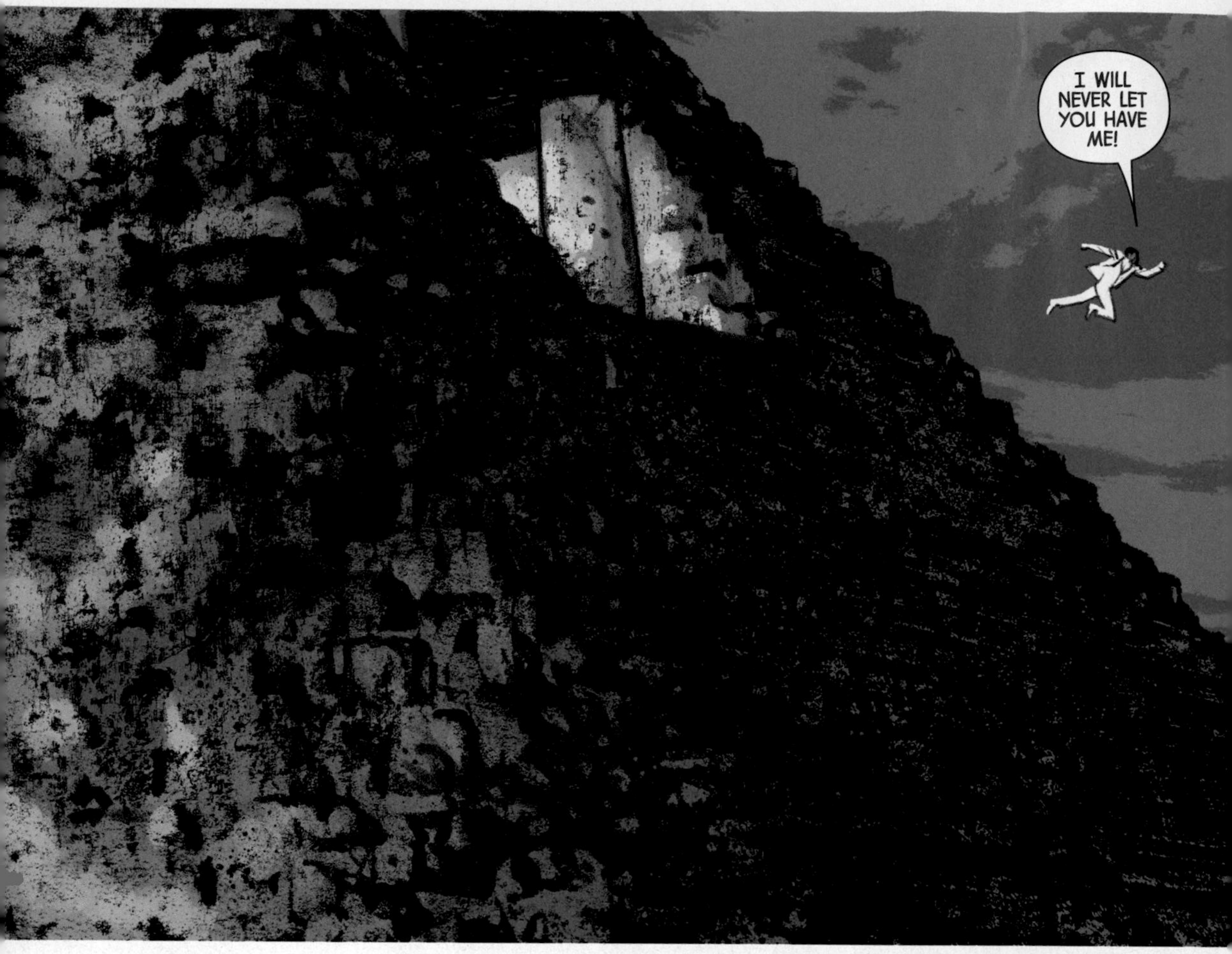
I WILL NEVER LET YOU HAVE ME!

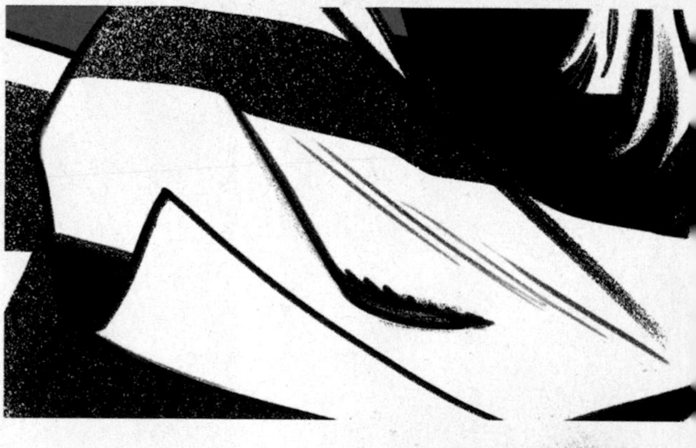

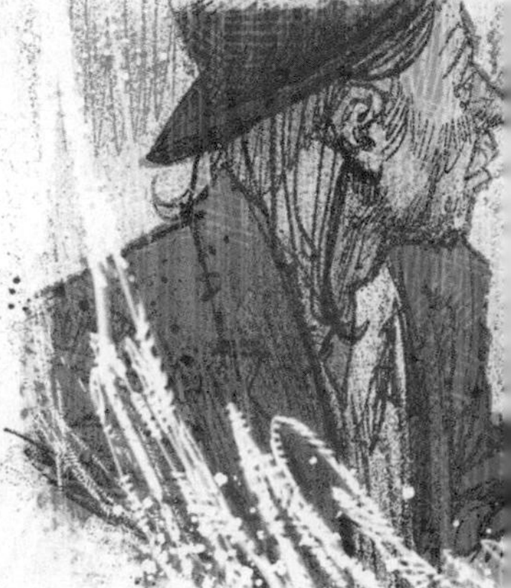

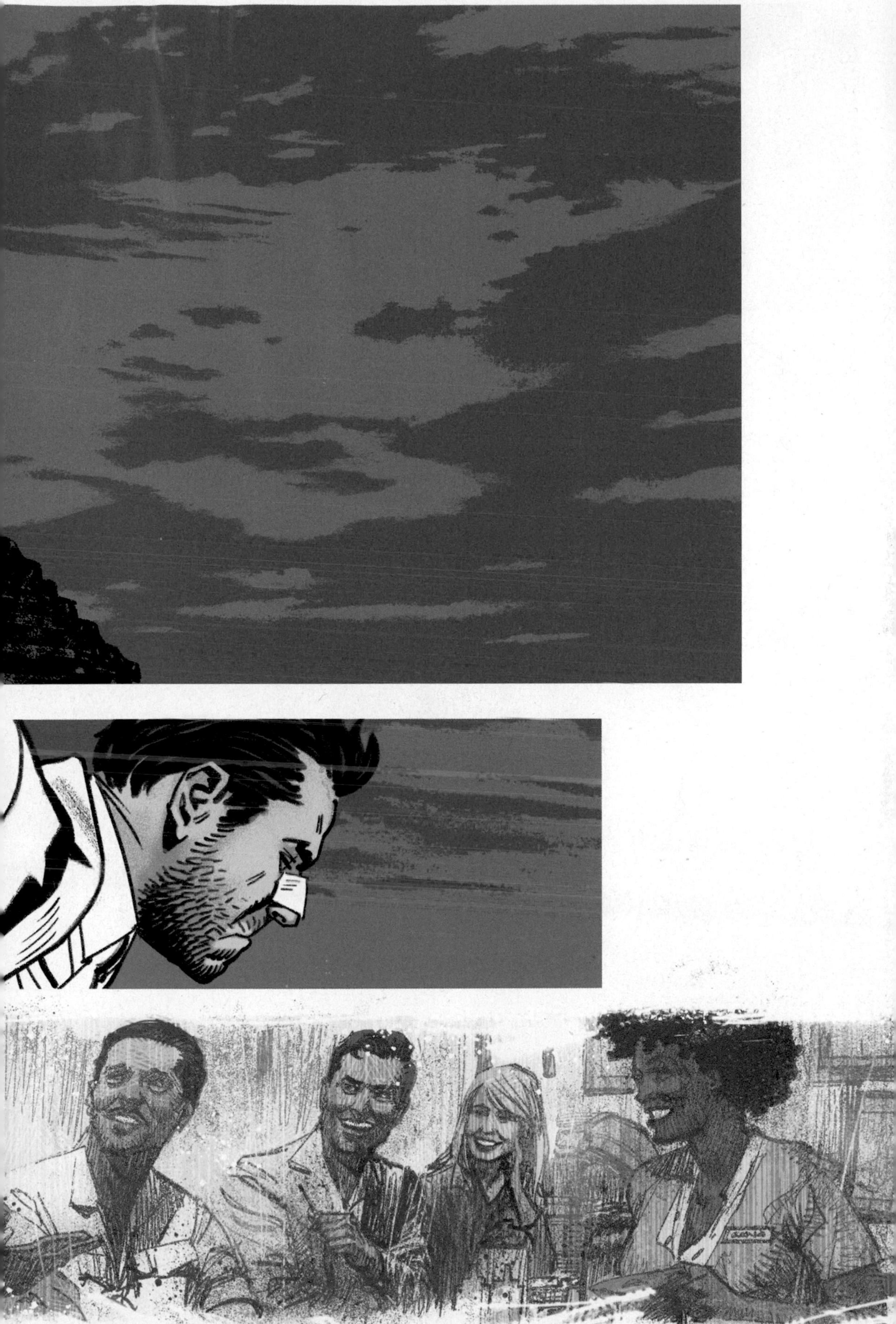

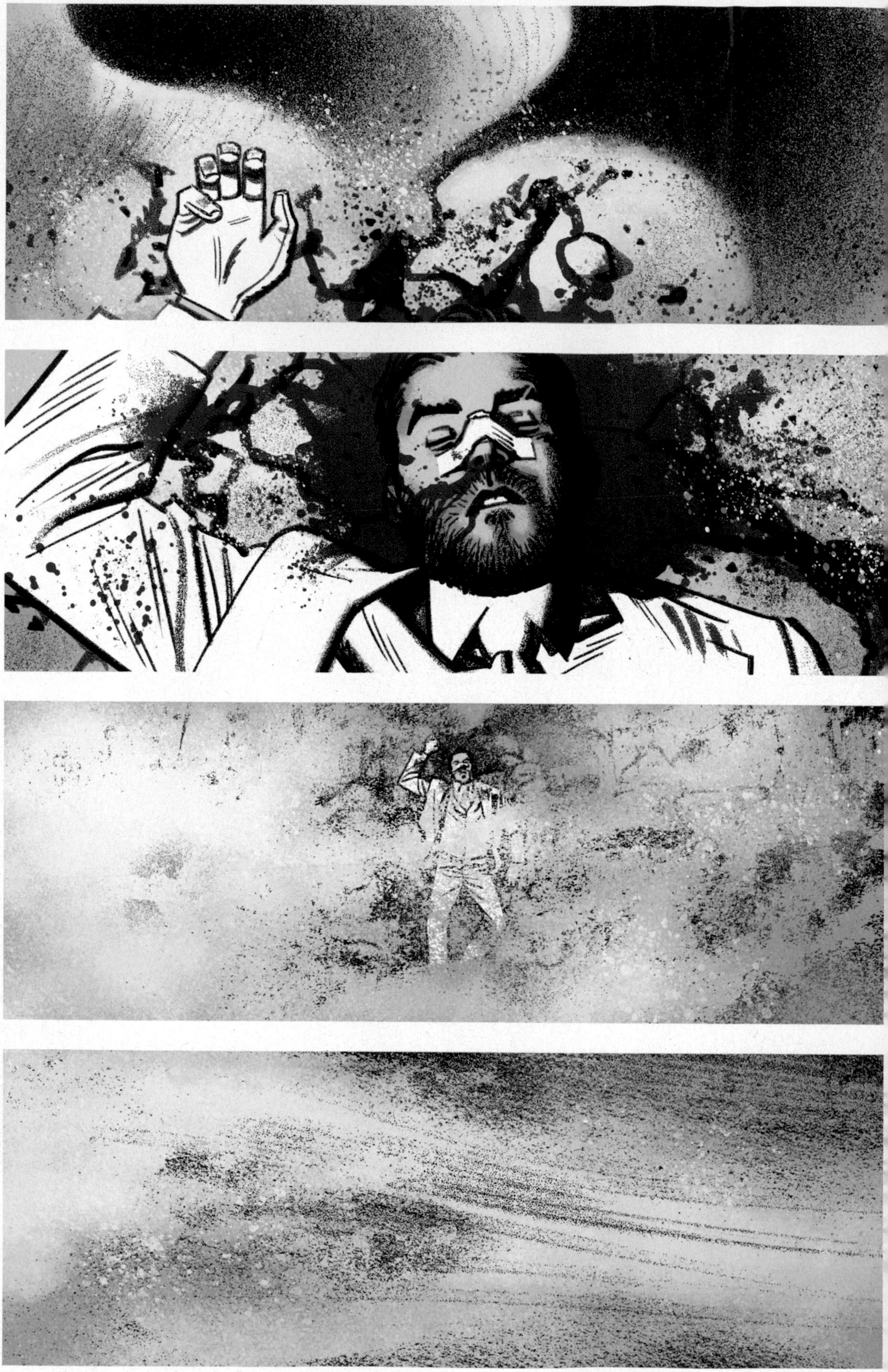

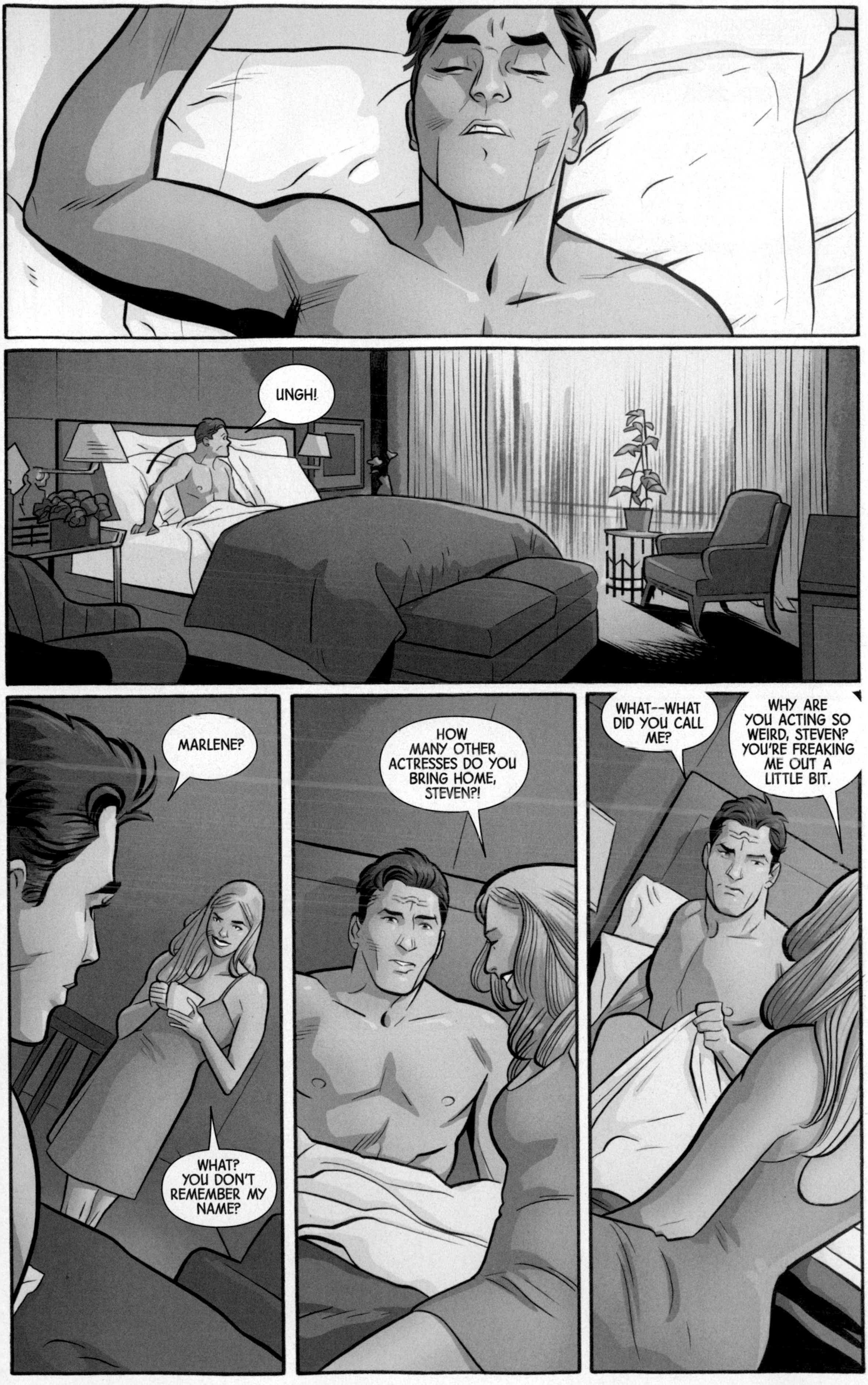
UNGH!
MARLENE?
WHAT? YOU DON'T REMEMBER MY NAME?
HOW MANY OTHER ACTRESSES DO YOU BRING HOME, STEVEN?!
WHAT--WHAT DID YOU CALL ME?
WHY ARE YOU ACTING SO WEIRD, STEVEN? YOU'RE FREAKING ME OUT A LITTLE BIT.

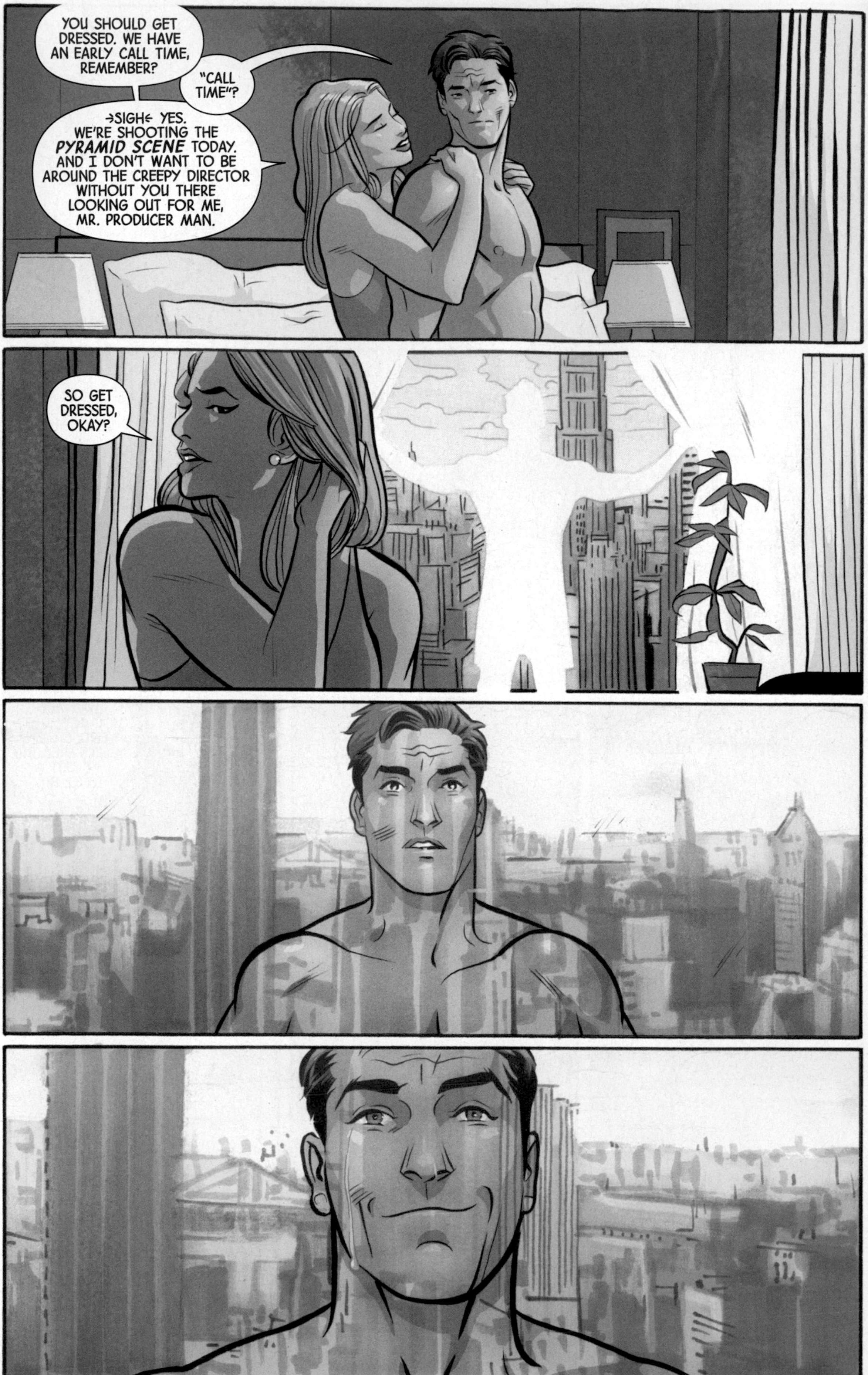
YOU SHOULD GET DRESSED. WE HAVE AN EARLY CALL TIME, REMEMBER?
"CALL TIME"?
→SIGH← YES. WE'RE SHOOTING THE PYRAMID SCENE TODAY. AND I DON'T WANT TO BE AROUND THE CREEPY DIRECTOR WITHOUT YOU THERE LOOKING OUT FOR ME, MR. PRODUCER MAN.
SO GET DRESSED, OKAY?

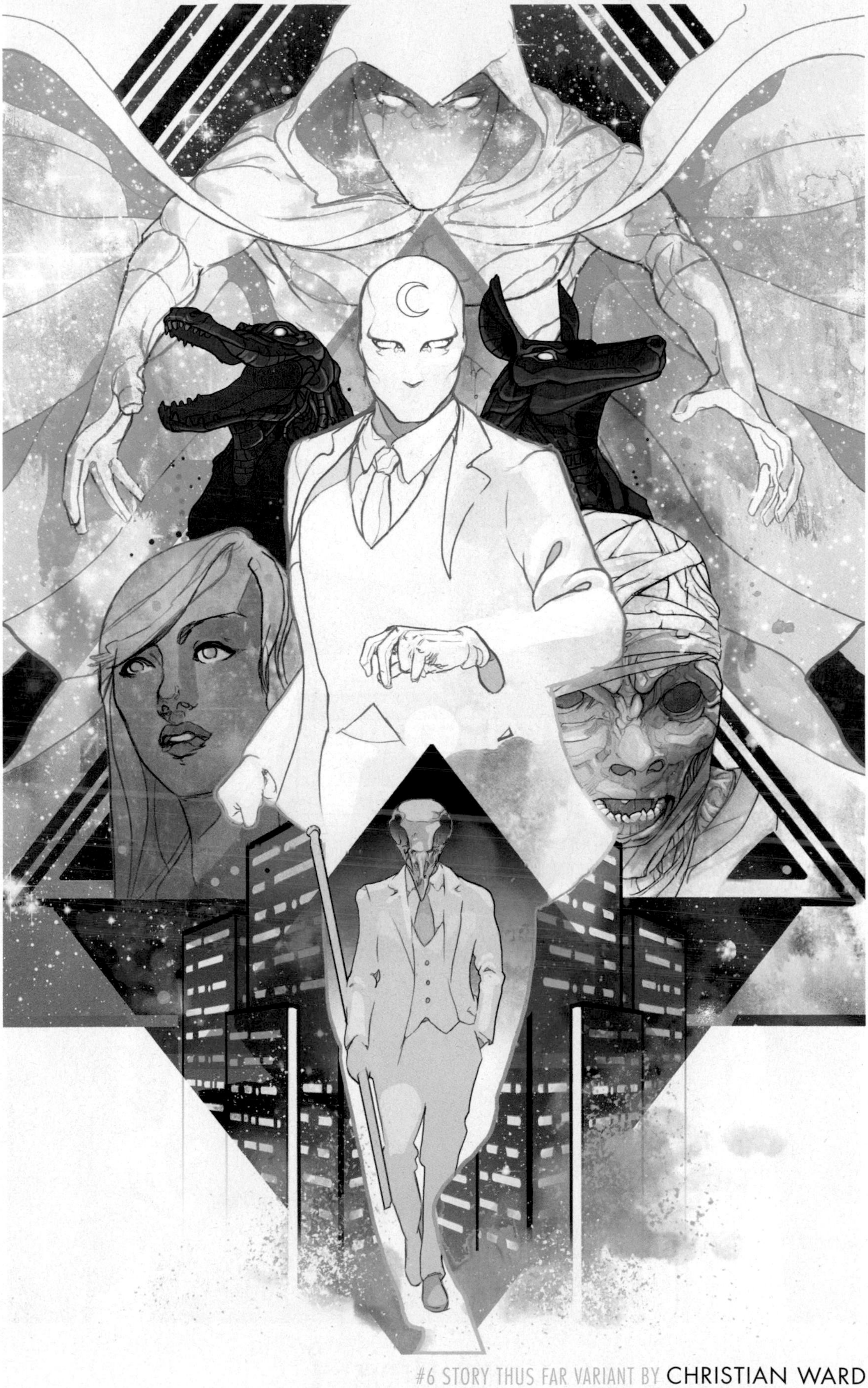

#6 STORY THUS FAR VARIANT BY CHRISTIAN WARD

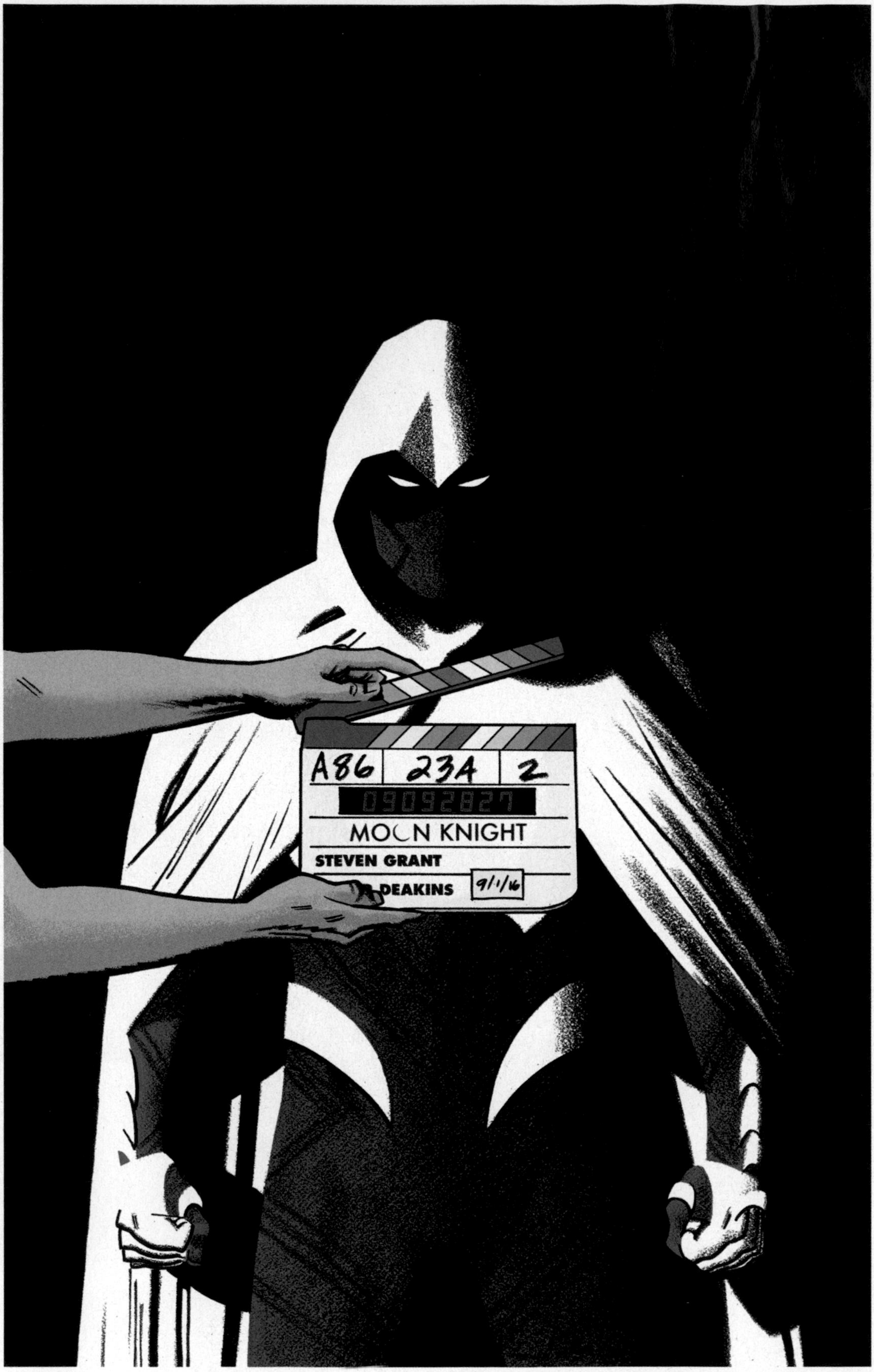
A86
23A
2
09092827
MOON KNIGHT
STEVEN GRANT
DEAKINS
9/1/16

INCARNATIONS
PART ONE

6

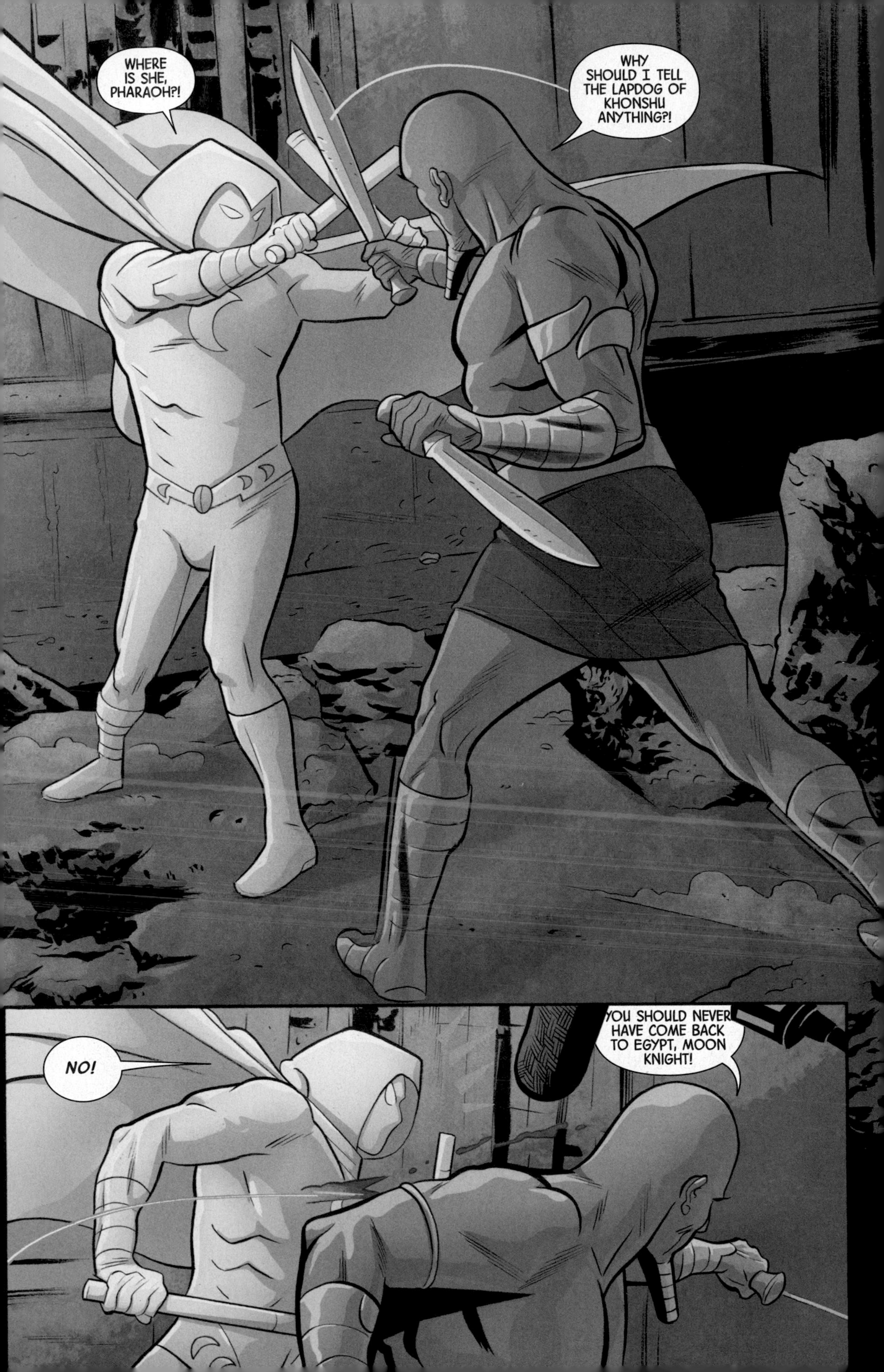
WHERE IS SHE, PHARAOH?!
WHY SHOULD I TELL THE LAPDOG OF KHONSHU ANYTHING?!
NO!
YOU SHOULD NEVER HAVE COME BACK TO EGYPT, MOON KNIGHT!

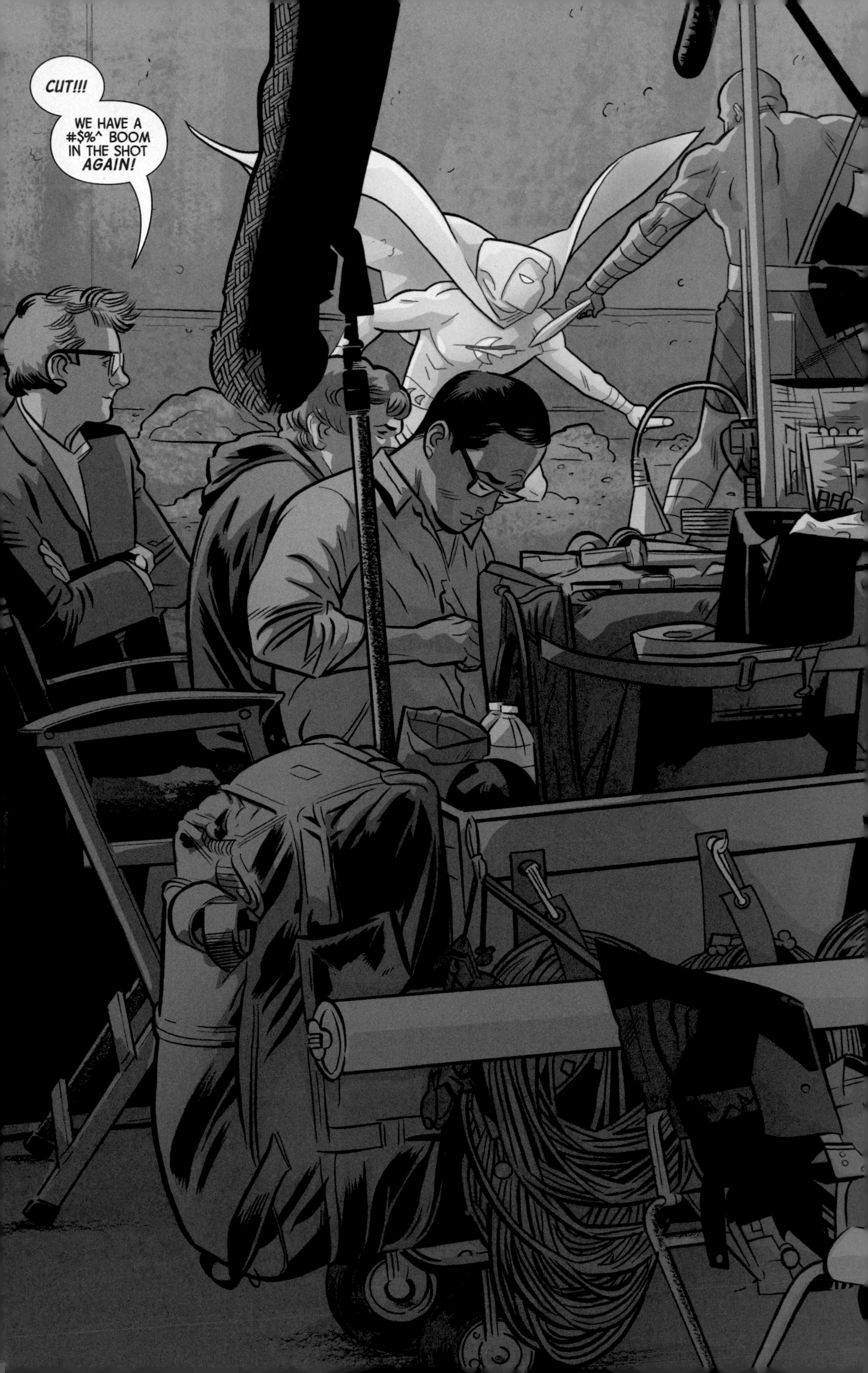
CUT!!!
WE HAVE A #$%^ BOOM IN THE SHOT AGAIN!

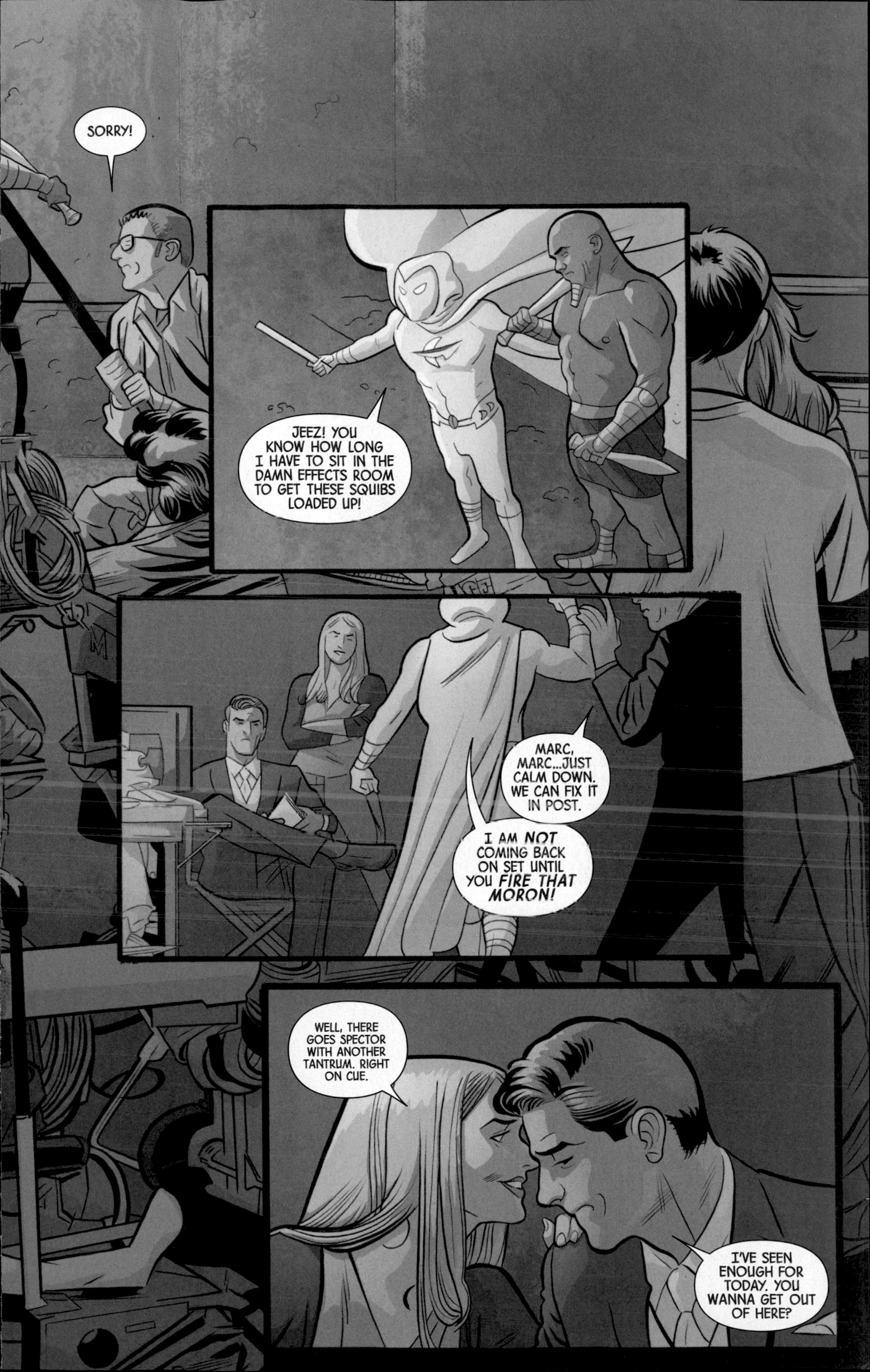
SORRY!
JEEZ! YOU KNOW HOW LONG I HAVE TO SIT IN THE DAMN EFFECTS ROOM TO GET THESE SQUIBS LOADED UP!
MARC, MARC...JUST CALM DOWN. WE CAN FIX IT IN POST.
I AM NOT COMING BACK ON SET UNTIL YOU FIRE THAT MORON!
WELL, THERE GOES SPECTOR WITH ANOTHER TANTRUM. RIGHT ON CUE.
I'VE SEEN ENOUGH FOR TODAY. YOU WANNA GET OUT OF HERE?

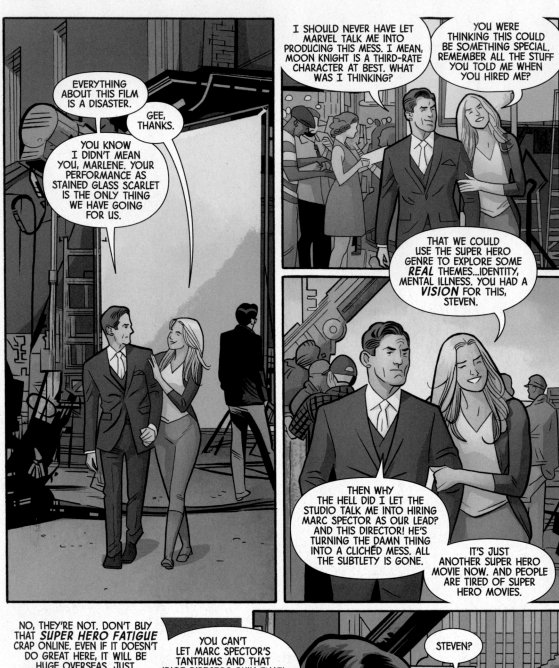

EVERYTHING ABOUT THIS FILM IS A DISASTER.

GEE, THANKS.

YOU KNOW I DIDN'T MEAN YOU, MARLENE. YOUR PERFORMANCE AS STAINED GLASS SCARLET IS THE ONLY THING WE HAVE GOING FOR US.

I SHOULD NEVER HAVE LET MARVEL TALK ME INTO PRODUCING THIS MESS. I MEAN, MOON KNIGHT IS A THIRD-RATE CHARACTER AT BEST. WHAT WAS I THINKING?

YOU WERE THINKING THIS COULD BE SOMETHING SPECIAL. REMEMBER ALL THE STUFF YOU TOLD ME WHEN YOU HIRED ME?

THAT WE COULD USE THE SUPER HERO GENRE TO EXPLORE SOME *REAL* THEMES...IDENTITY, MENTAL ILLNESS. YOU HAD A *VISION* FOR THIS, STEVEN.

THEN WHY THE HELL DID I LET THE STUDIO TALK ME INTO HIRING MARC SPECTOR AS OUR LEAD? AND THIS DIRECTOR! HE'S TURNING THE DAMN THING INTO A CLICHÉD MESS. ALL THE SUBTLETY IS GONE.

IT'S JUST ANOTHER SUPER HERO MOVIE NOW. AND PEOPLE ARE TIRED OF SUPER HERO MOVIES.

NO, THEY'RE NOT. DON'T BUY THAT *SUPER HERO FATIGUE* CRAP ONLINE. EVEN IF IT DOESN'T DO GREAT HERE, IT WILL BE HUGE OVERSEAS. JUST LOOK AT *ANT-MAN.*

YOU CAN'T LET MARC SPECTOR'S TANTRUMS AND THAT IDIOT DIRECTOR RUIN THAT! YOU NEED TO TAKE CONTROL, STEVEN. IT'S LIKE I SAID LAST NIGHT, *YOU* SHOULD TAKE OVER AND DIRECT IT.

STEVEN?

IT'S TOO LATE FOR THAT NOW.

NO, IT'S NOT. YOU'RE STEVEN GRANT. YOU ARE ONE OF THE MOST POWERFUL PRODUCERS IN HOLLYWOOD. YOU CAN DO WHATEVER YOU WANT.

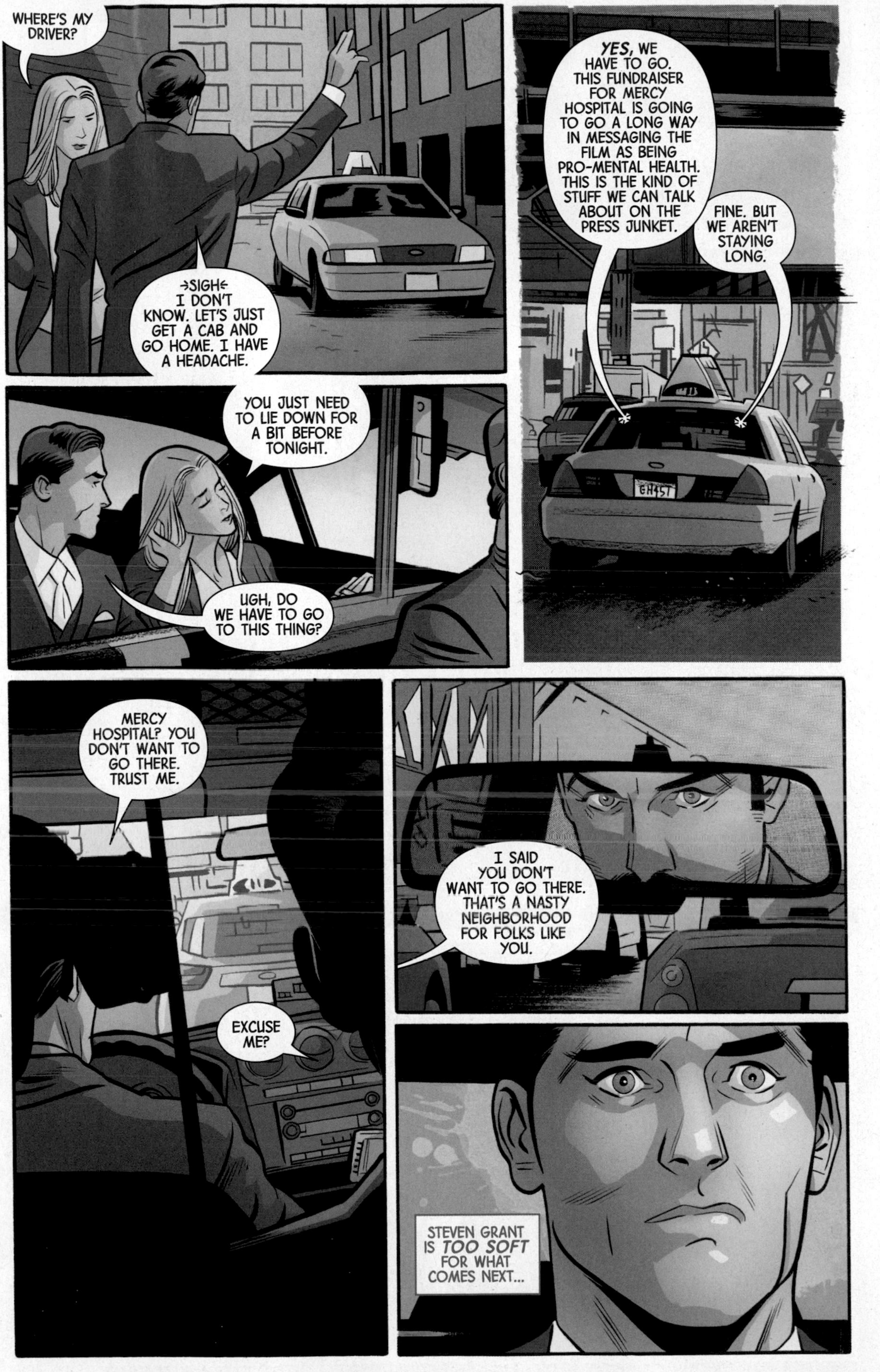
WHERE'S MY DRIVER?
→SIGH← I DON'T KNOW. LET'S JUST GET A CAB AND GO HOME. I HAVE A HEADACHE.
YOU JUST NEED TO LIE DOWN FOR A BIT BEFORE TONIGHT.
UGH, DO WE HAVE TO GO TO THIS THING?
YES, WE HAVE TO GO. THIS FUNDRAISER FOR MERCY HOSPITAL IS GOING TO GO A LONG WAY IN MESSAGING THE FILM AS BEING PRO-MENTAL HEALTH. THIS IS THE KIND OF STUFF WE CAN TALK ABOUT ON THE PRESS JUNKET.
FINE. BUT WE AREN'T STAYING LONG.
GH4ST
MERCY HOSPITAL? YOU DON'T WANT TO GO THERE. TRUST ME.
EXCUSE ME?
I SAID YOU DON'T WANT TO GO THERE. THAT'S A NASTY NEIGHBORHOOD FOR FOLKS LIKE YOU.
STEVEN GRANT IS TOO SOFT FOR WHAT COMES NEXT...

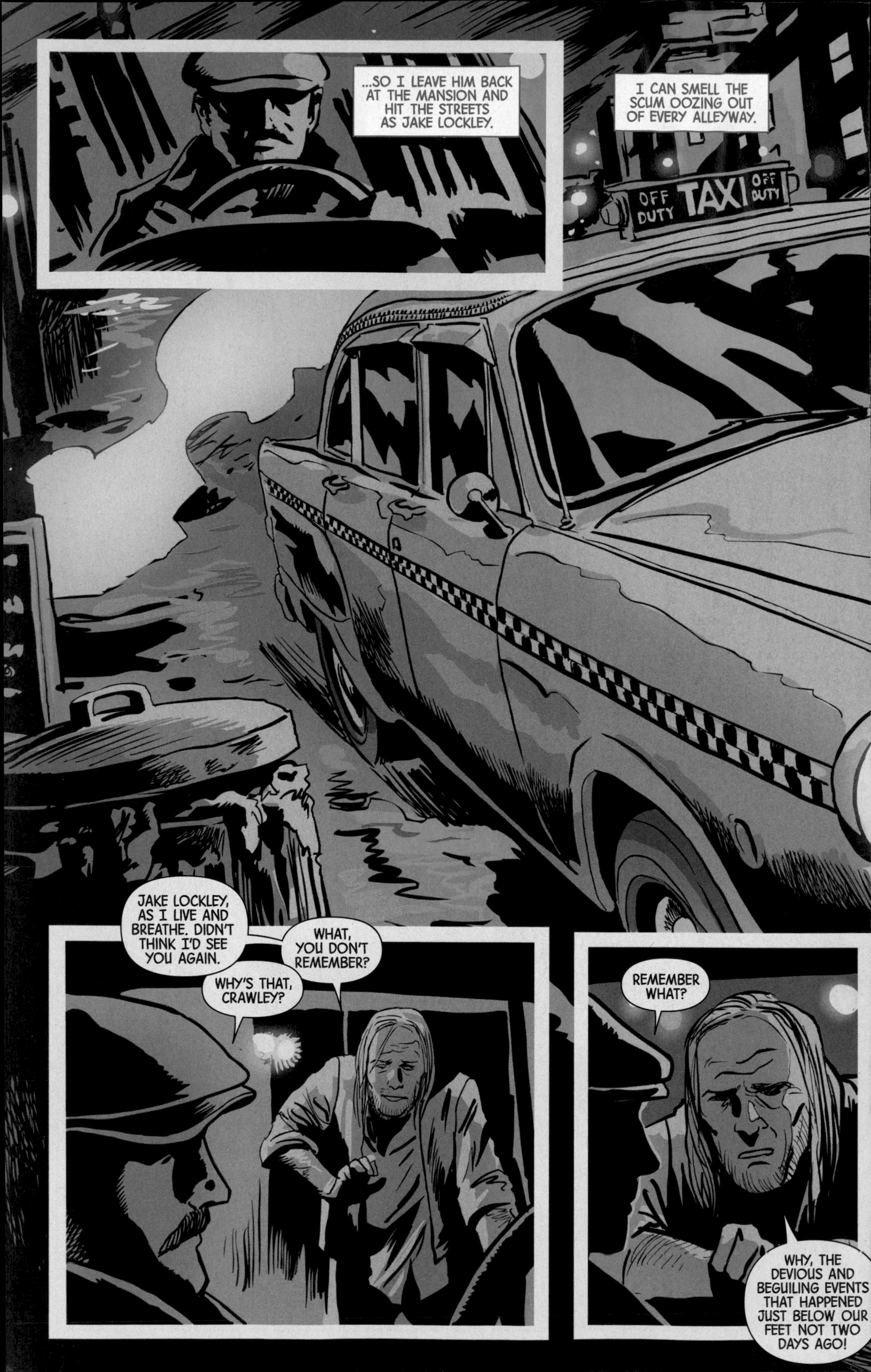
...SO I LEAVE HIM BACK AT THE MANSION AND HIT THE STREETS AS JAKE LOCKLEY.
I CAN SMELL THE SCUM OOZING OUT OF EVERY ALLEYWAY.
OFF DUTY TAXI OFF DUTY
JAKE LOCKLEY, AS I LIVE AND BREATHE. DIDN'T THINK I'D SEE YOU AGAIN.
WHY'S THAT, CRAWLEY?
WHAT, YOU DON'T REMEMBER?
REMEMBER WHAT?
WHY, THE DEVIOUS AND BEGUILING EVENTS THAT HAPPENED JUST BELOW OUR FEET NOT TWO DAYS AGO!

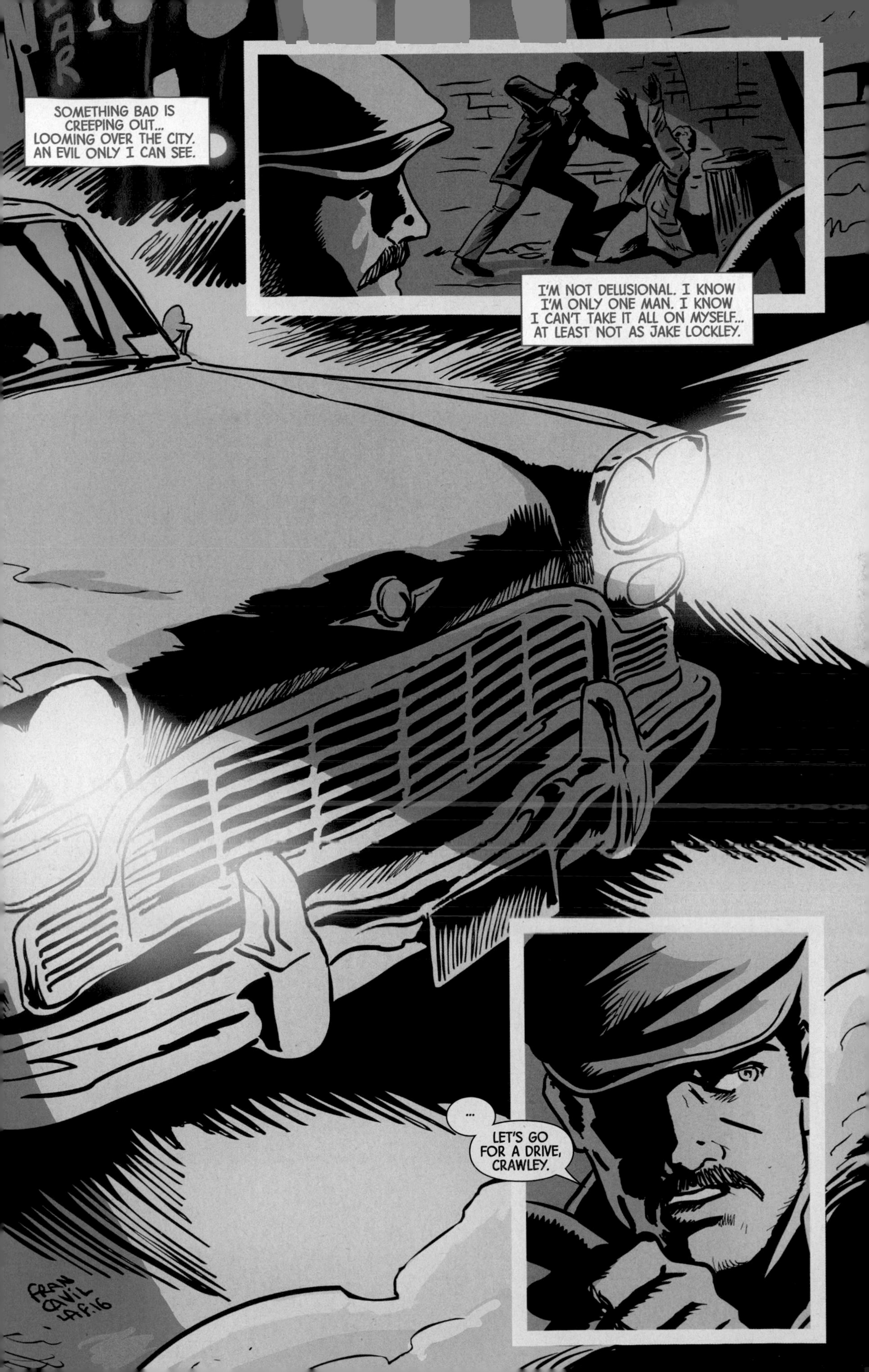
SOMETHING BAD IS CREEPING OUT... LOOMING OVER THE CITY. AN EVIL ONLY I CAN SEE.
I'M NOT DELUSIONAL. I KNOW I'M ONLY ONE MAN. I KNOW I CAN'T TAKE IT ALL ON MYSELF... AT LEAST NOT AS JAKE LOCKLEY.
...
LET'S GO FOR A DRIVE, CRAWLEY.

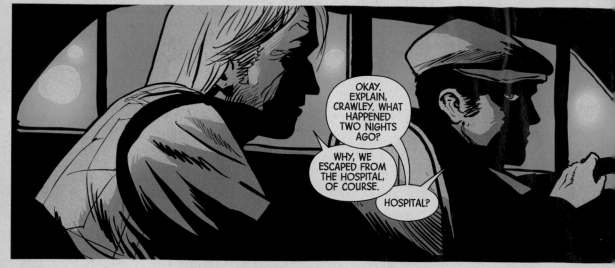

OKAY. EXPLAIN, CRAWLEY. WHAT HAPPENED TWO NIGHTS AGO?

WHY, WE ESCAPED FROM THE HOSPITAL, OF COURSE.

HOSPITAL?

MERCY HOSPITAL FOR THE MENTALLY ILL. YOU, FRENCHIE, MARLENE, GENA, AND I ESCAPED THROUGH THE SUBWAYS.

I DON'T KNOW WHAT THE HELL YOU'RE ON ABOUT.

OH, DEAR. IT'S WORSE THAN I FEARED, THEN. ARE YOU REALLY SAYING YOU DON'T REMEMBER ANY OF IT? THE MUMMIES, ANUBIS?

ANUBIS?!

YES, JAKE. ANUBIS--ANUBIS TOOK MY SOUL. I GAVE IT UP SO YOU COULD ESCAPE.

BUT NOW I SEE YOU FAILED. YOU'RE RIGHT BACK WHERE YOU STARTED, AREN'T YOU? AND MY SOUL...IT'S GONE NOW. I--I'M LOST.

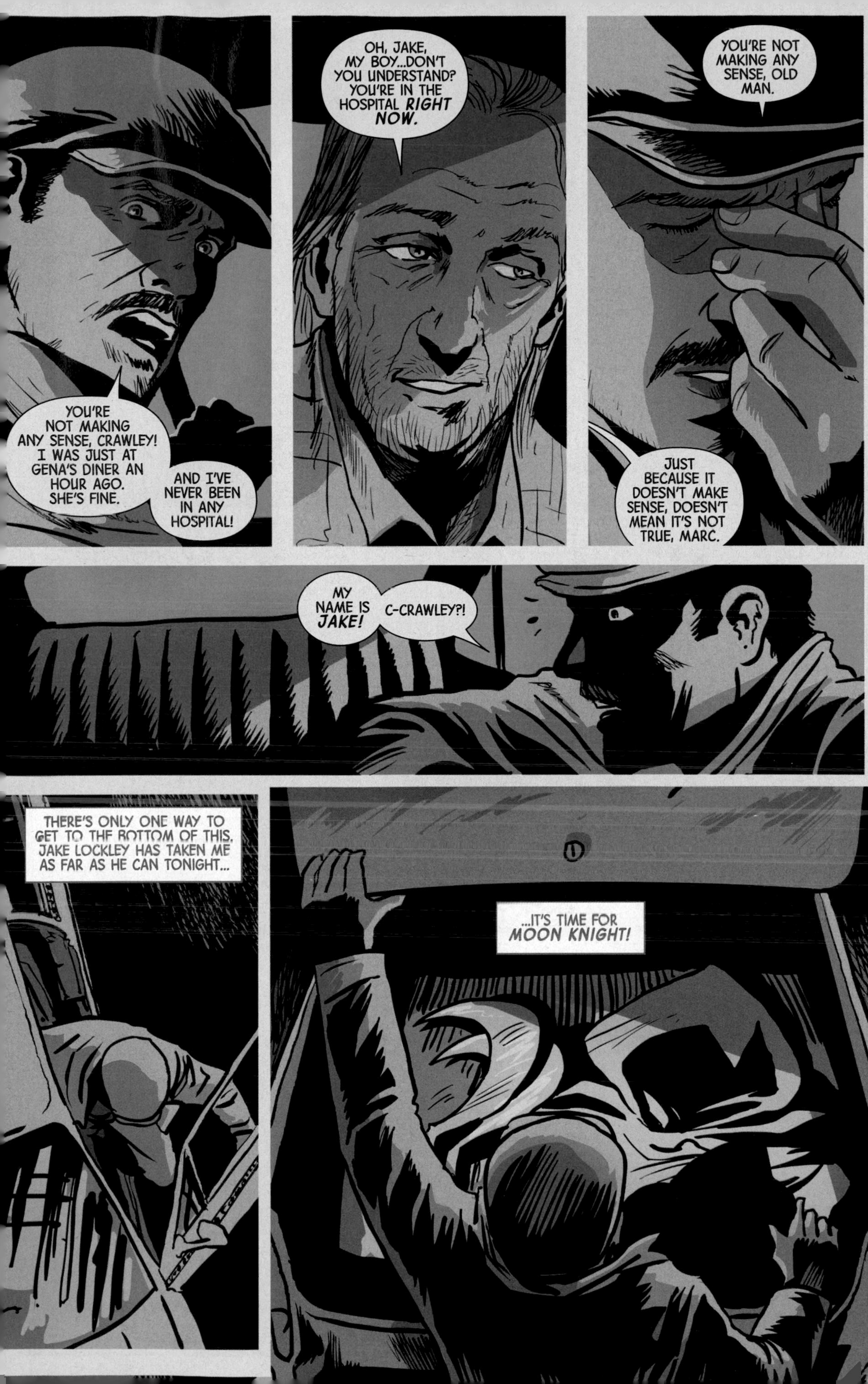
YOU'RE NOT MAKING ANY SENSE, CRAWLEY! I WAS JUST AT GENA'S DINER AN HOUR AGO. SHE'S FINE.
AND I'VE NEVER BEEN IN ANY HOSPITAL!
OH, JAKE, MY BOY...DON'T YOU UNDERSTAND? YOU'RE IN THE HOSPITAL RIGHT NOW.
YOU'RE NOT MAKING ANY SENSE, OLD MAN.
JUST BECAUSE IT DOESN'T MAKE SENSE, DOESN'T MEAN IT'S NOT TRUE, MARC.
MY NAME IS JAKE!
C-CRAWLEY?!
THERE'S ONLY ONE WAY TO GET TO THE BOTTOM OF THIS. JAKE LOCKLEY HAS TAKEN ME AS FAR AS HE CAN TONIGHT...
...IT'S TIME FOR MOON KNIGHT!

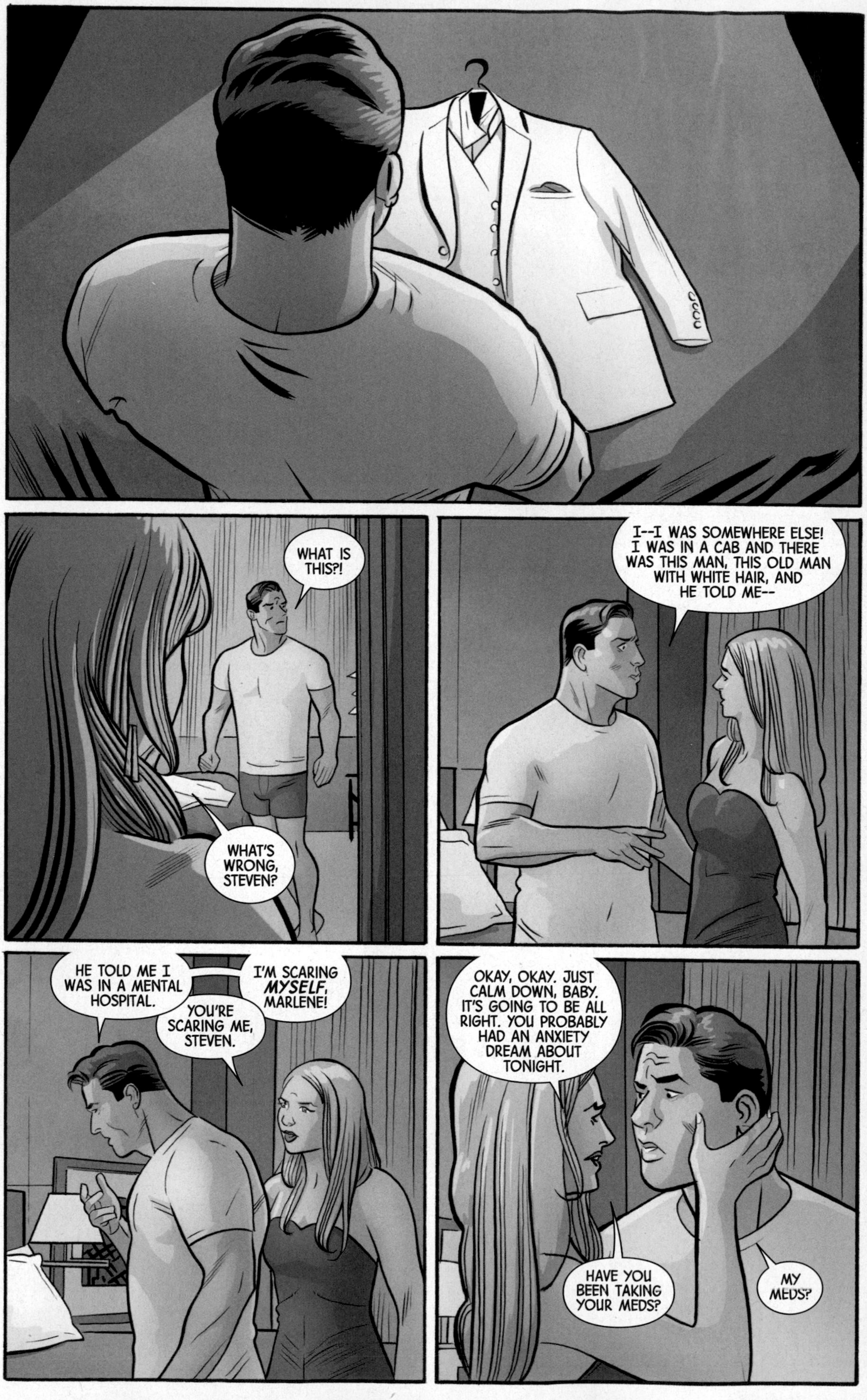
WHAT IS THIS?!
WHAT'S WRONG, STEVEN?
I--I WAS SOMEWHERE ELSE! I WAS IN A CAB AND THERE WAS THIS MAN, THIS OLD MAN WITH WHITE HAIR, AND HE TOLD ME--
HE TOLD ME I WAS IN A MENTAL HOSPITAL.
YOU'RE SCARING ME, STEVEN.
I'M SCARING MYSELF, MARLENE!
OKAY, OKAY. JUST CALM DOWN, BABY. IT'S GOING TO BE ALL RIGHT. YOU PROBABLY HAD AN ANXIETY DREAM ABOUT TONIGHT.
HAVE YOU BEEN TAKING YOUR MEDS?
MY MEDS?

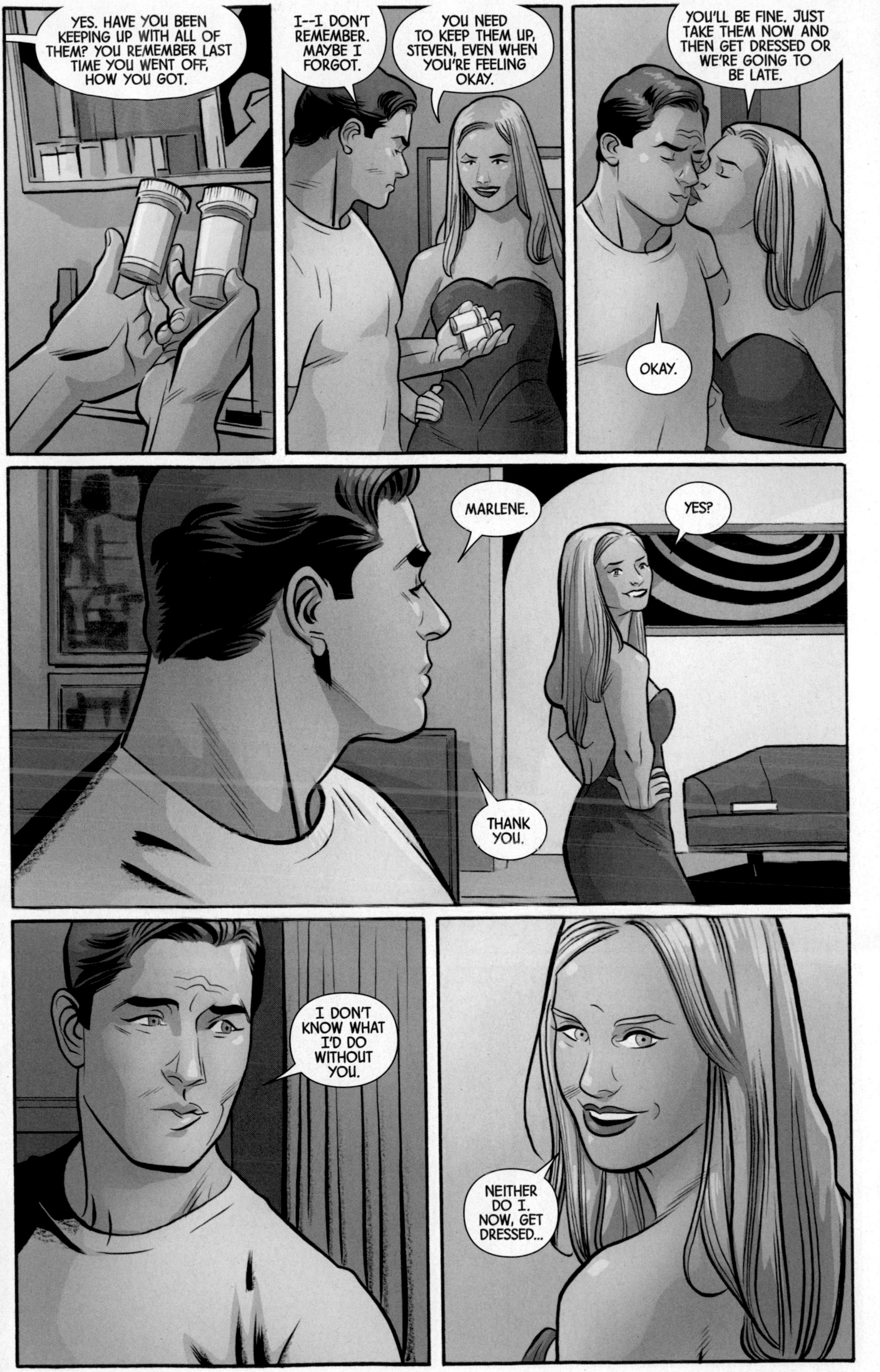
YES. HAVE YOU BEEN KEEPING UP WITH ALL OF THEM? YOU REMEMBER LAST TIME YOU WENT OFF, HOW YOU GOT.
I--I DON'T REMEMBER. MAYBE I FORGOT.
YOU NEED TO KEEP THEM UP, STEVEN, EVEN WHEN YOU'RE FEELING OKAY.
YOU'LL BE FINE. JUST TAKE THEM NOW AND THEN GET DRESSED OR WE'RE GOING TO BE LATE.
OKAY.
MARLENE.
YES?
THANK YOU.
I DON'T KNOW WHAT I'D DO WITHOUT YOU.
NEITHER DO I. NOW, GET DRESSED...

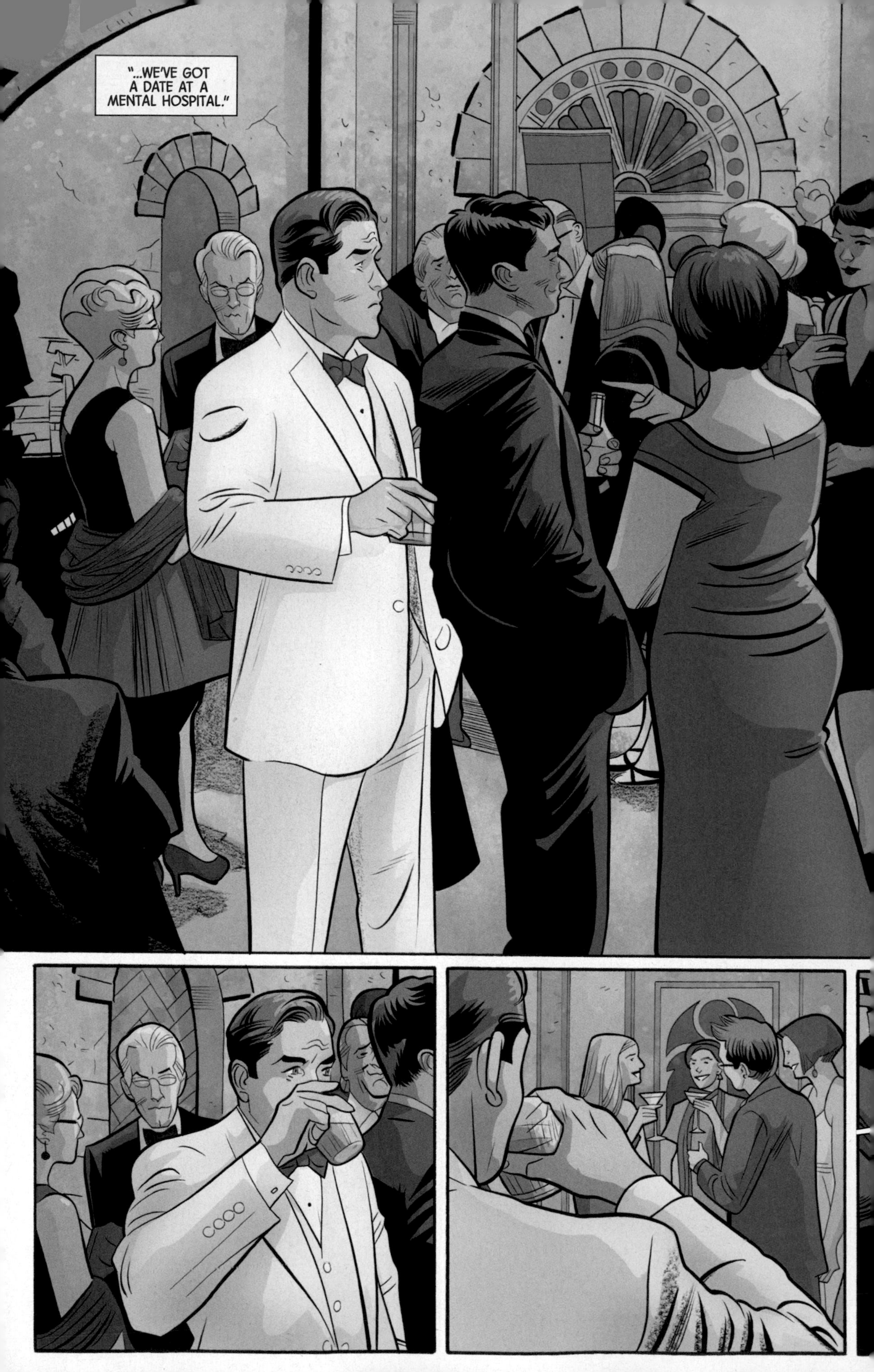
"...WE'VE GOT A DATE AT A MENTAL HOSPITAL."

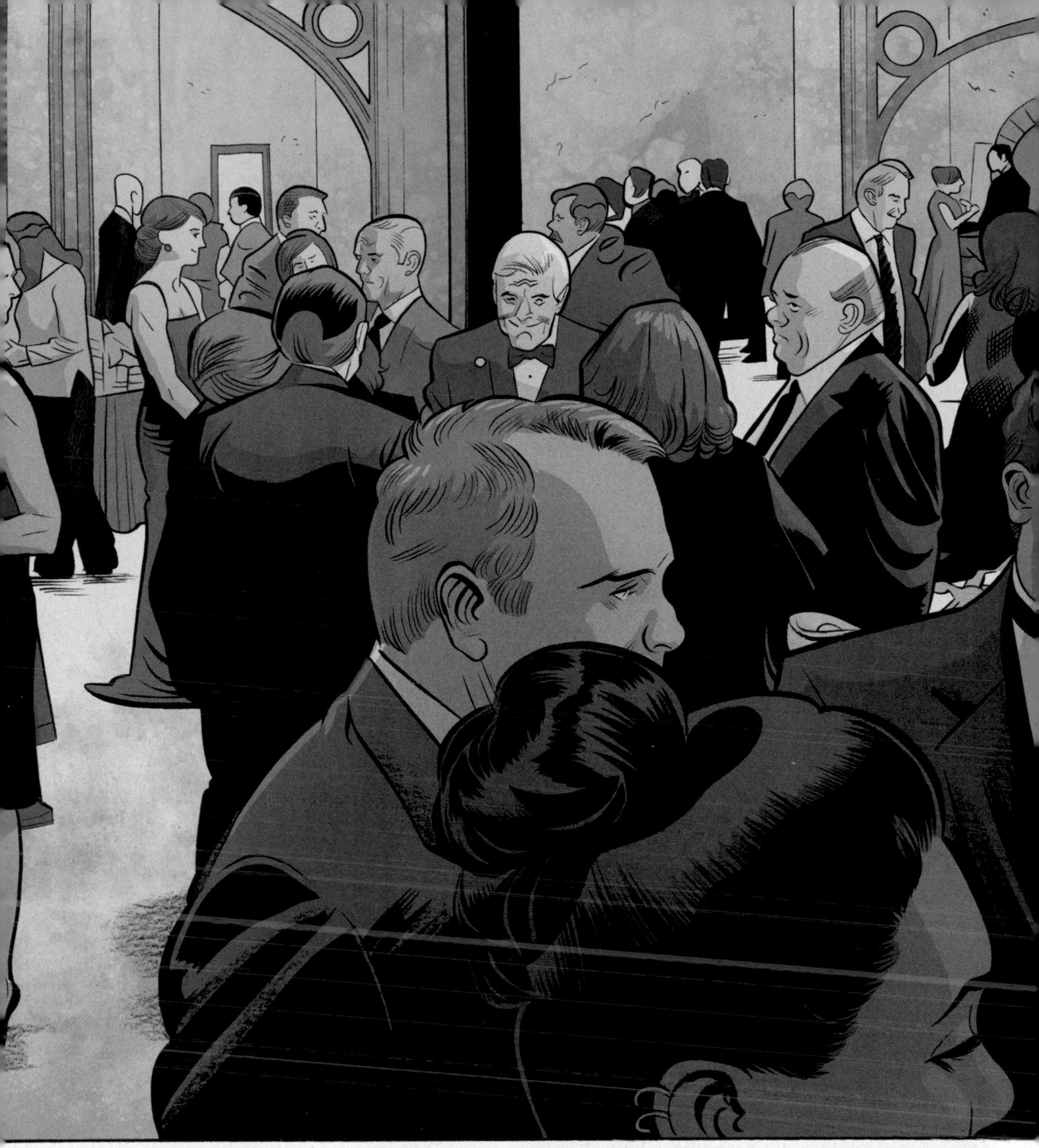

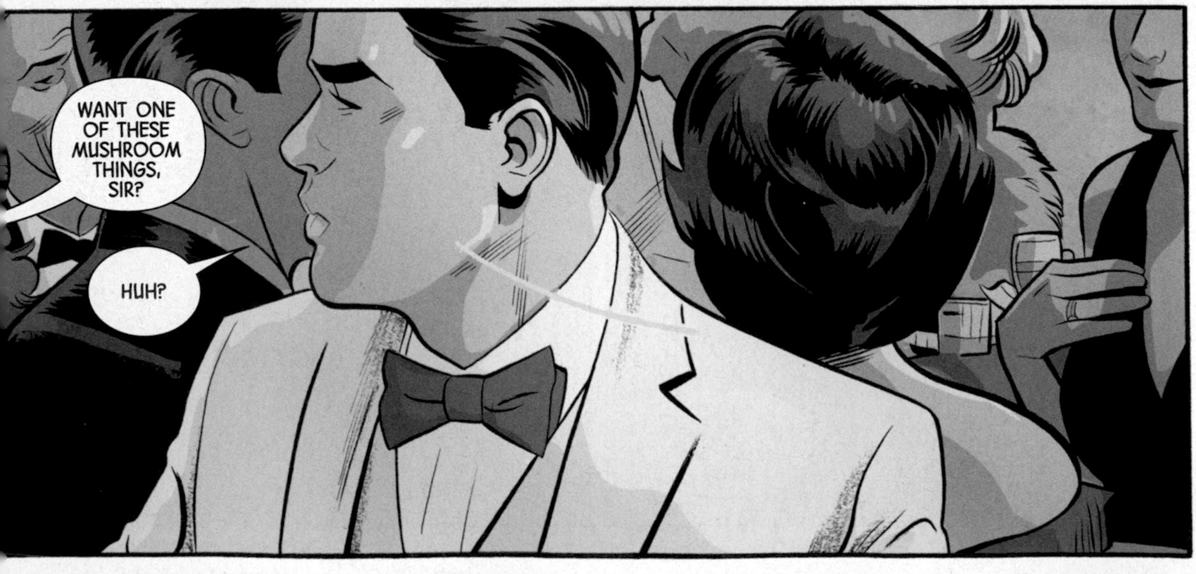
WANT ONE OF THESE MUSHROOM THINGS, SIR?
HUH?

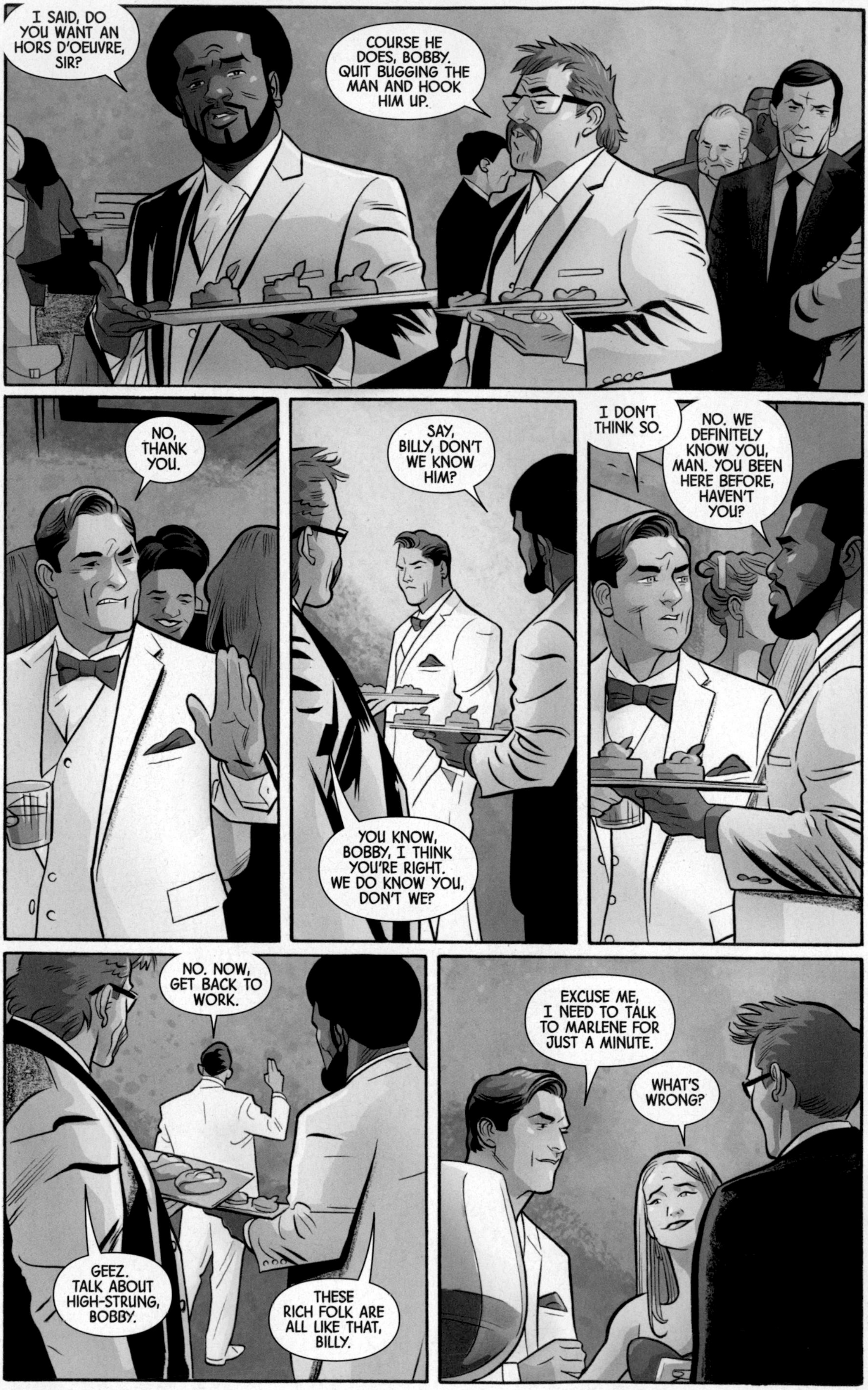
I SAID, DO YOU WANT AN HORS D'OEUVRE, SIR?
COURSE HE DOES, BOBBY. QUIT BUGGING THE MAN AND HOOK HIM UP.
NO, THANK YOU.
SAY, BILLY, DON'T WE KNOW HIM?
YOU KNOW, BOBBY, I THINK YOU'RE RIGHT. WE DO KNOW YOU, DON'T WE?
I DON'T THINK SO.
NO. WE DEFINITELY KNOW YOU, MAN. YOU BEEN HERE BEFORE, HAVEN'T YOU?
NO. NOW, GET BACK TO WORK.
GEEZ. TALK ABOUT HIGH-STRUNG, BOBBY.
THESE RICH FOLK ARE ALL LIKE THAT, BILLY.
EXCUSE ME, I NEED TO TALK TO MARLENE FOR JUST A MINUTE.
WHAT'S WRONG?

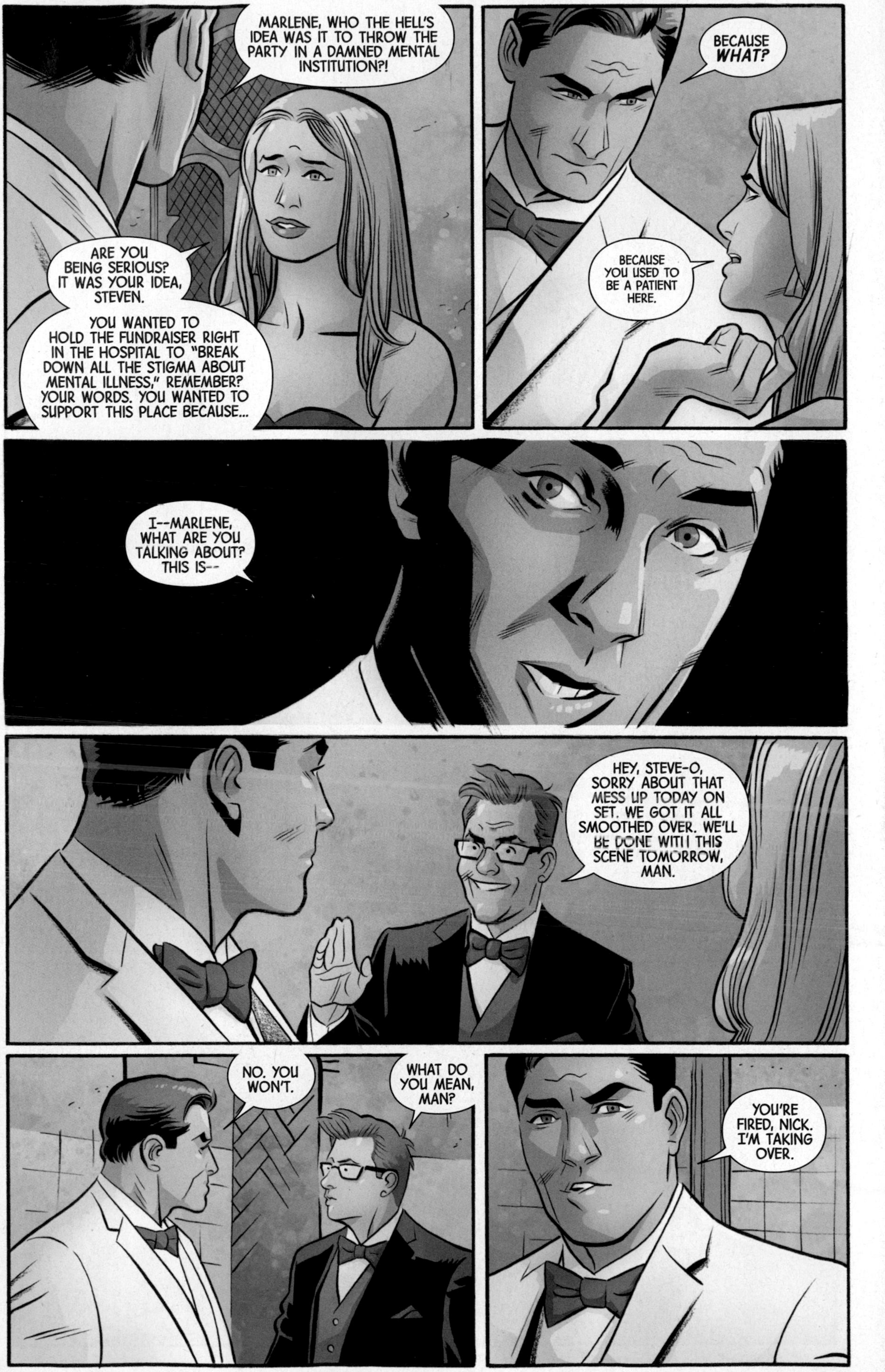
MARLENE, WHO THE HELL'S IDEA WAS IT TO THROW THE PARTY IN A DAMNED MENTAL INSTITUTION?!
ARE YOU BEING SERIOUS? IT WAS YOUR IDEA, STEVEN.
YOU WANTED TO HOLD THE FUNDRAISER RIGHT IN THE HOSPITAL TO "BREAK DOWN ALL THE STIGMA ABOUT MENTAL ILLNESS," REMEMBER? YOUR WORDS. YOU WANTED TO SUPPORT THIS PLACE BECAUSE...
BECAUSE WHAT?
BECAUSE YOU USED TO BE A PATIENT HERE.
I--MARLENE, WHAT ARE YOU TALKING ABOUT? THIS IS--
HEY, STEVE-O, SORRY ABOUT THAT MESS UP TODAY ON SET. WE GOT IT ALL SMOOTHED OVER. WE'LL BE DONE WITH THIS SCENE TOMORROW, MAN.
NO. YOU WON'T.
WHAT DO YOU MEAN, MAN?
YOU'RE FIRED, NICK. I'M TAKING OVER.

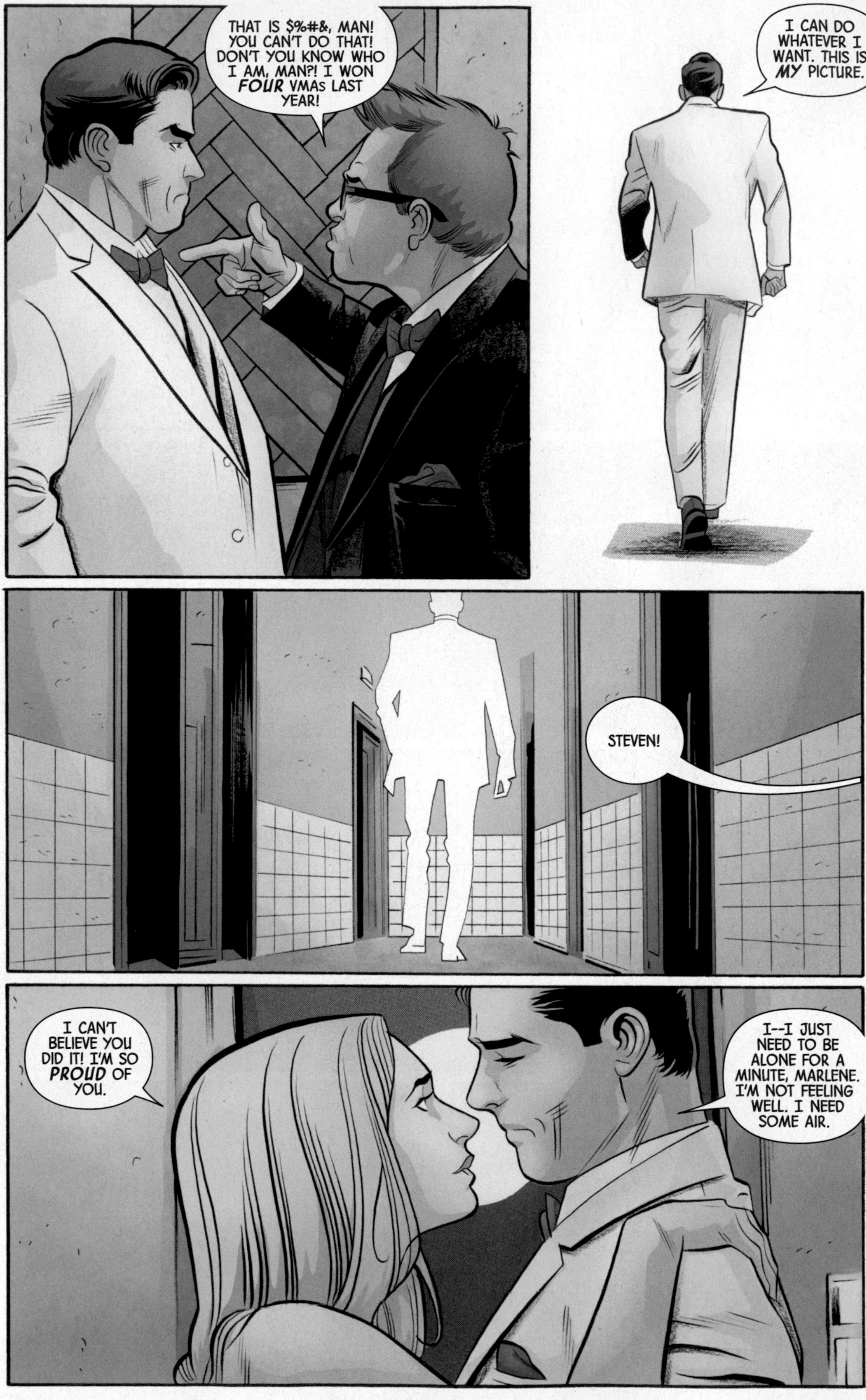
THAT IS $%#&, MAN! YOU CAN'T DO THAT! DON'T YOU KNOW WHO I AM, MAN?! I WON FOUR VMAs LAST YEAR!
I CAN DO WHATEVER I WANT. THIS IS MY PICTURE.
STEVEN!
I CAN'T BELIEVE YOU DID IT! I'M SO PROUD OF YOU.
I--I JUST NEED TO BE ALONE FOR A MINUTE, MARLENE. I'M NOT FEELING WELL. I NEED SOME AIR.

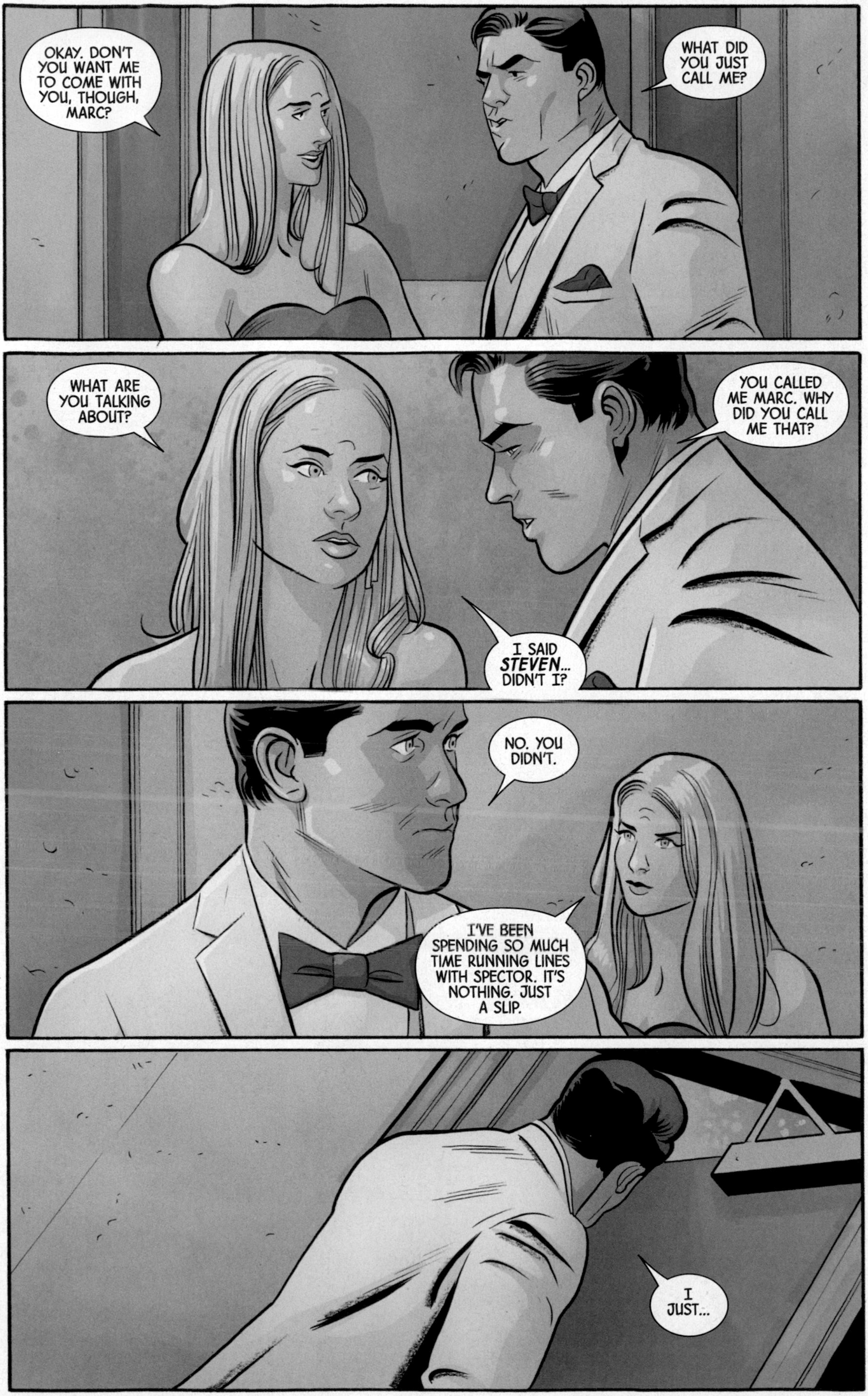
OKAY. DON'T YOU WANT ME TO COME WITH YOU, THOUGH, MARC?
WHAT DID YOU JUST CALL ME?
WHAT ARE YOU TALKING ABOUT?
YOU CALLED ME MARC. WHY DID YOU CALL ME THAT?
I SAID *STEVEN*... DIDN'T I?
NO. YOU DIDN'T.
I'VE BEEN SPENDING SO MUCH TIME RUNNING LINES WITH SPECTOR. IT'S NOTHING. JUST A SLIP.
I JUST...

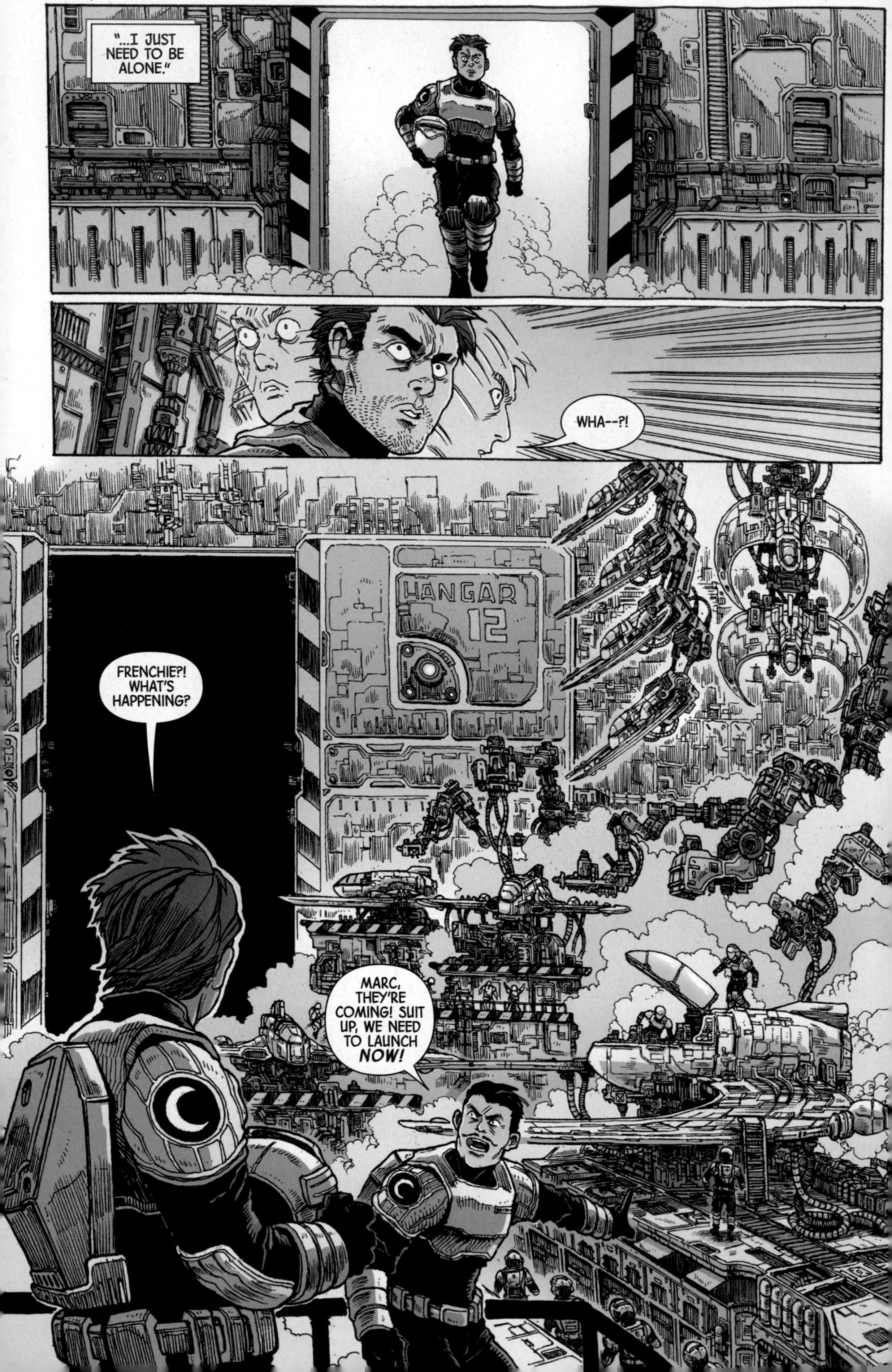
"...I JUST NEED TO BE ALONE."
WHA--?!
HANGAR 12
FRENCHIE?! WHAT'S HAPPENING?
MARC, THEY'RE COMING! SUIT UP, WE NEED TO LAUNCH NOW!

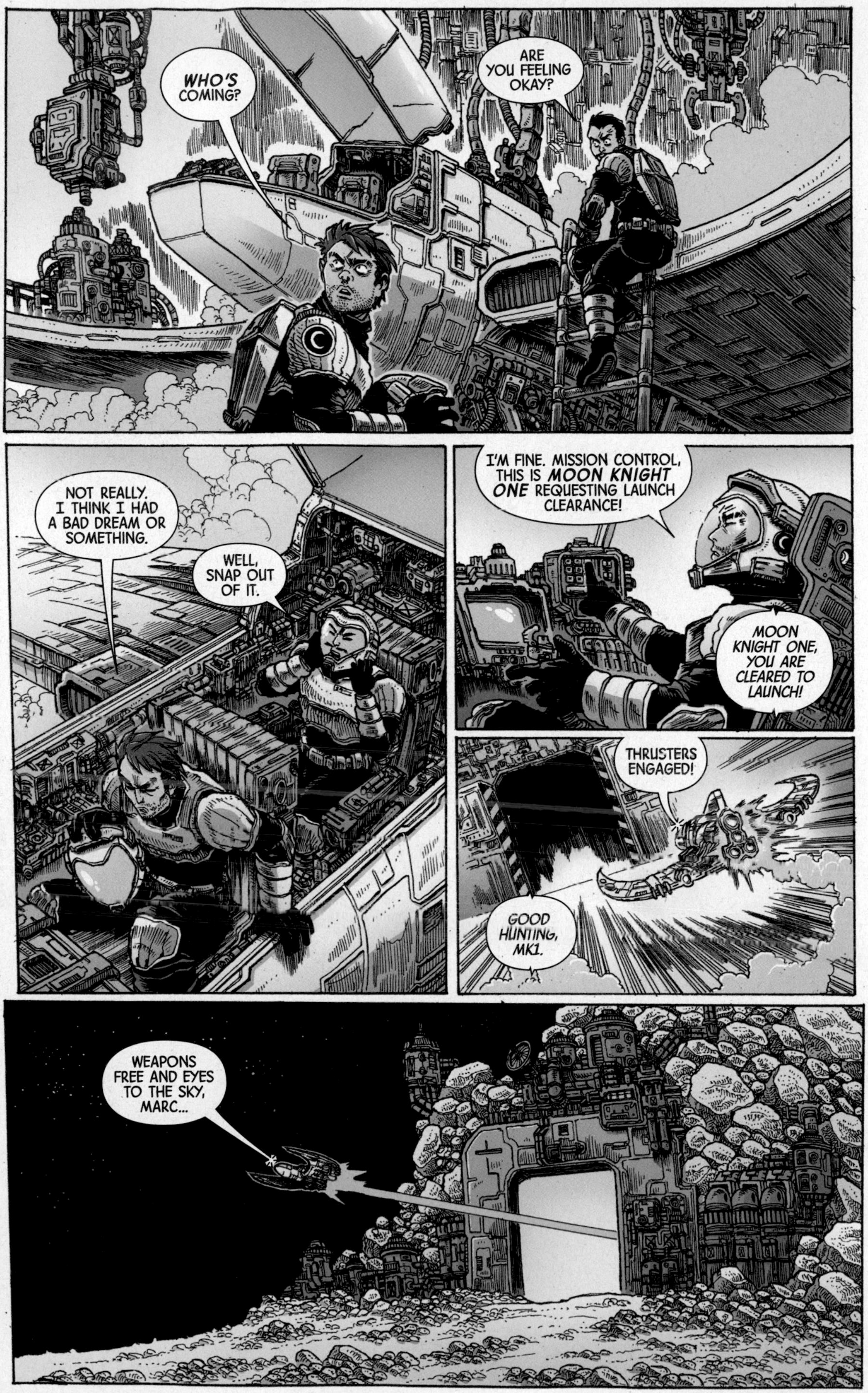
WHO'S COMING?
ARE YOU FEELING OKAY?
NOT REALLY. I THINK I HAD A BAD DREAM OR SOMETHING.
WELL, SNAP OUT OF IT.
I'M FINE. MISSION CONTROL, THIS IS MOON KNIGHT ONE REQUESTING LAUNCH CLEARANCE!
MOON KNIGHT ONE, YOU ARE CLEARED TO LAUNCH!
THRUSTERS ENGAGED!
GOOD HUNTING, MK1.
WEAPONS FREE AND EYES TO THE SKY, MARC...

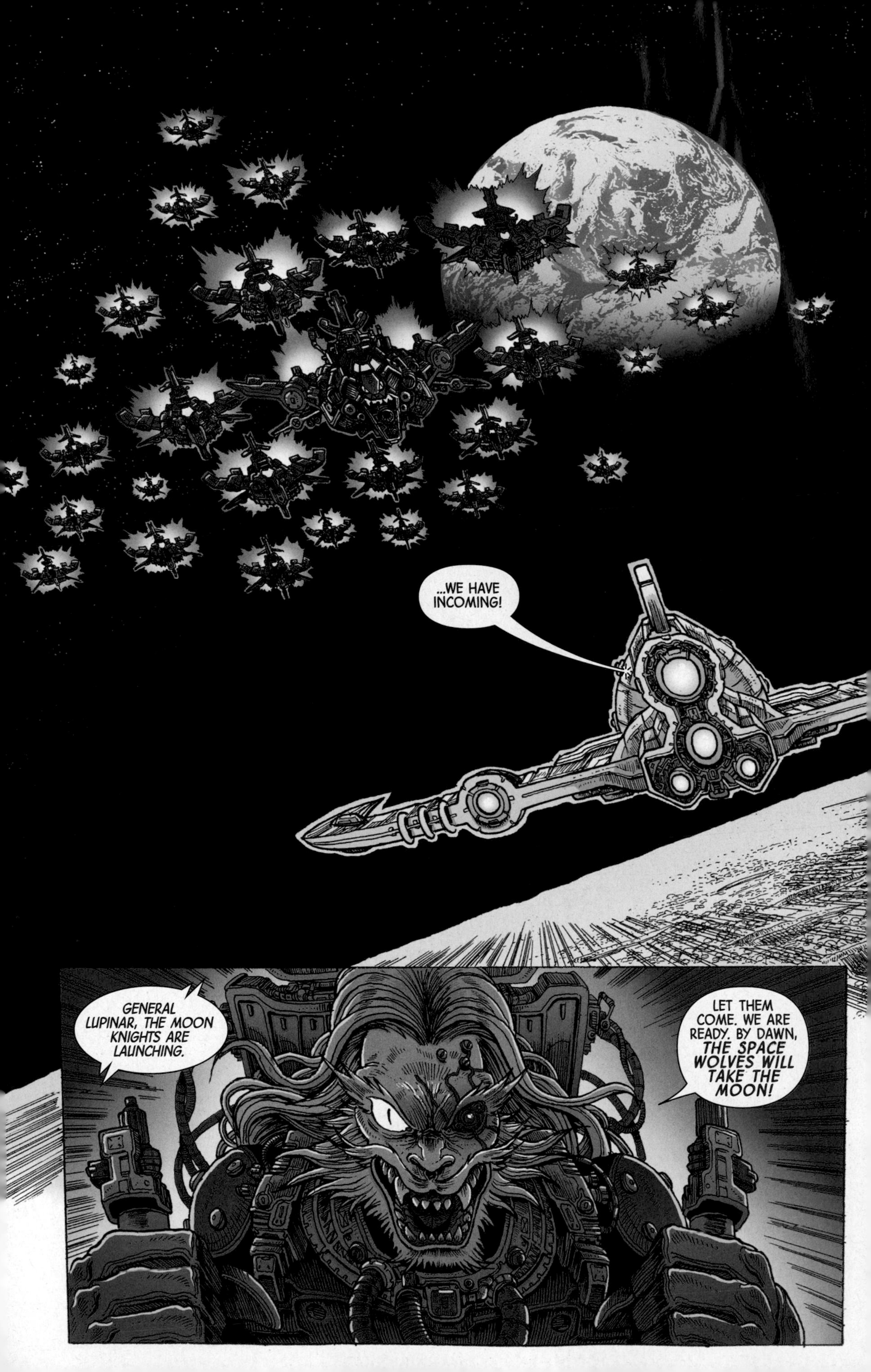
...WE HAVE INCOMING!
GENERAL LUPINAR, THE MOON KNIGHTS ARE LAUNCHING.
LET THEM COME. WE ARE READY. BY DAWN, THE SPACE WOLVES WILL TAKE THE MOON!

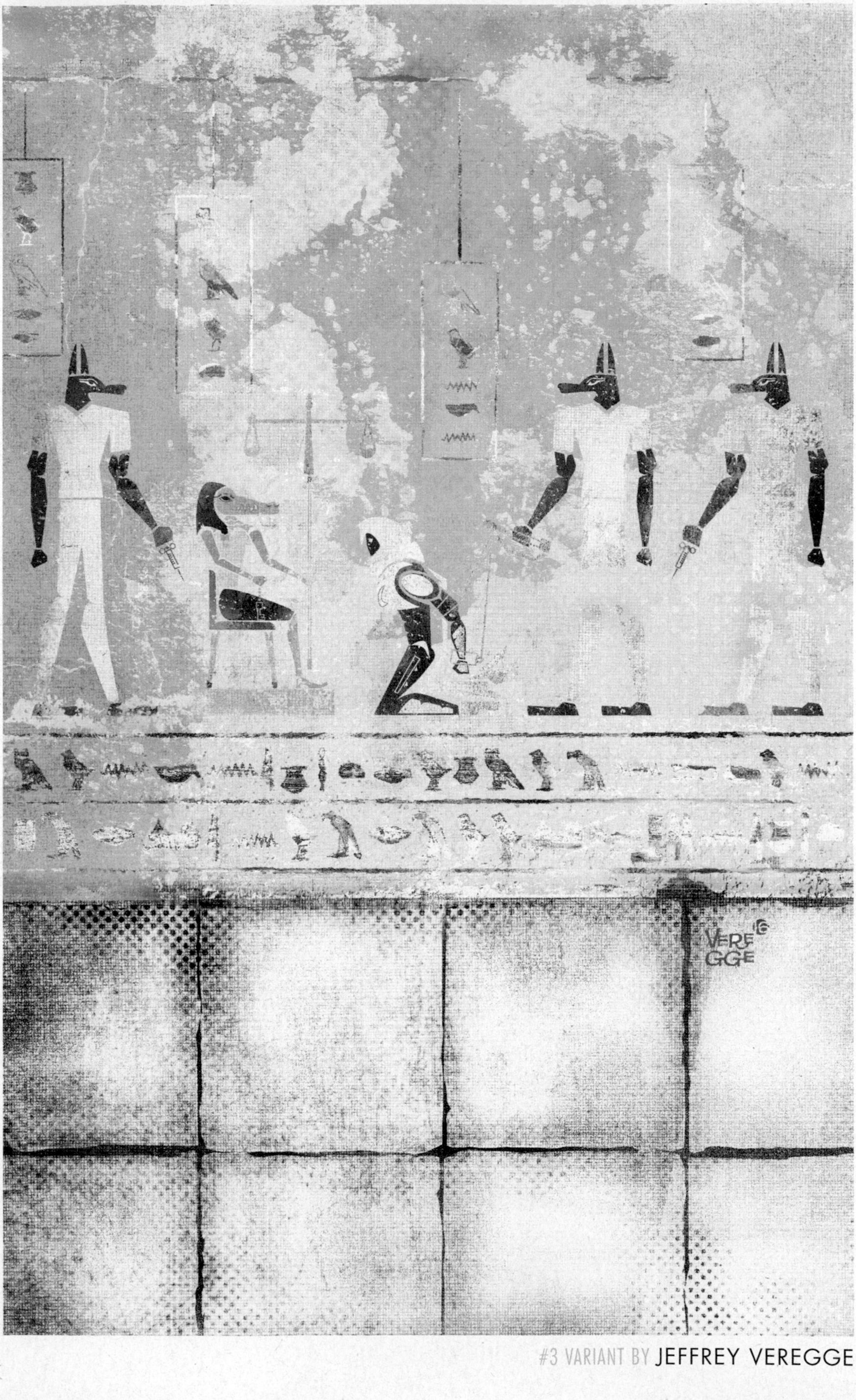
VEREGGE

#3 VARIANT BY JEFFREY VEREGGE

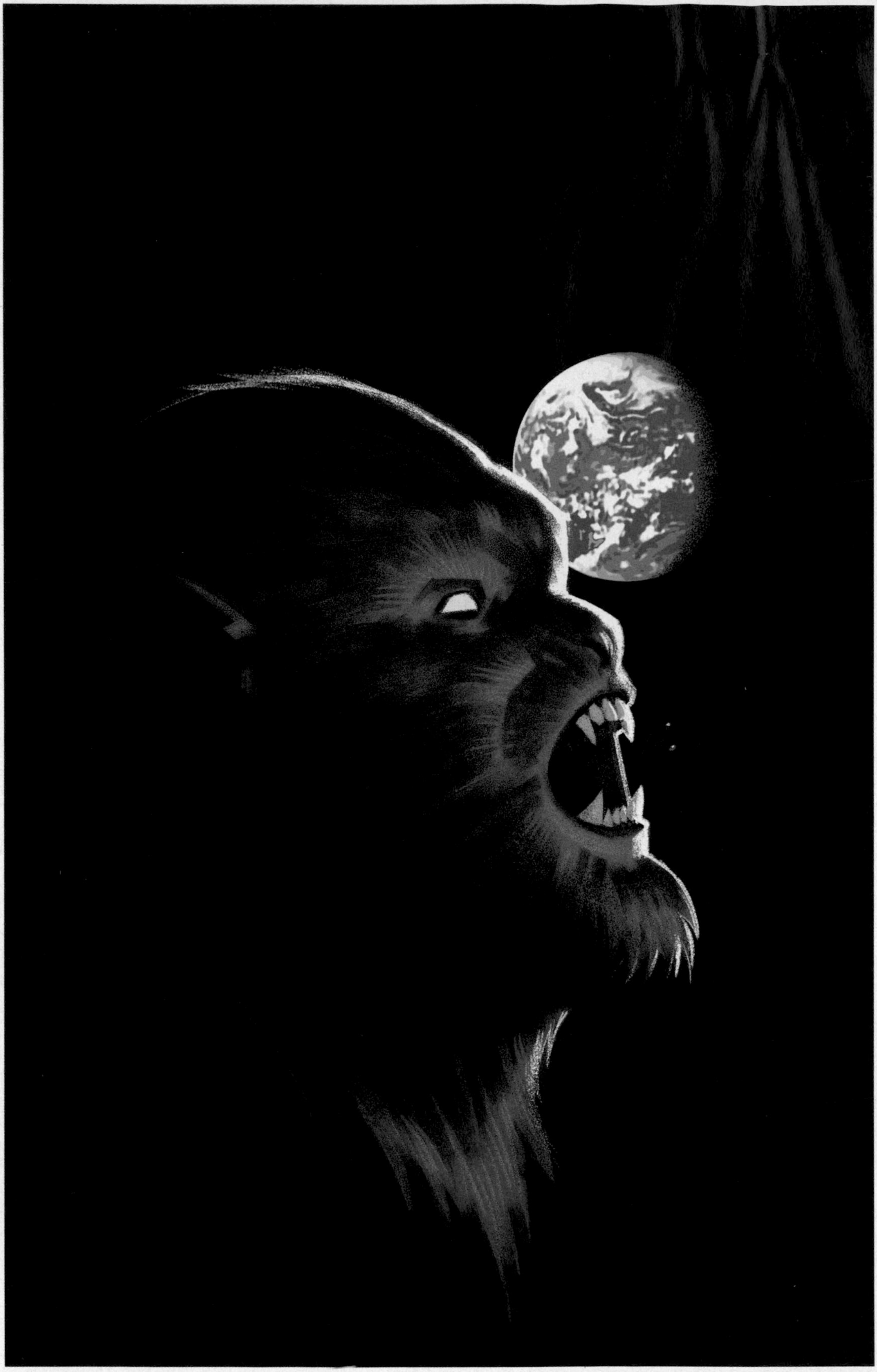

INCARNATIONS
PART TWO

7

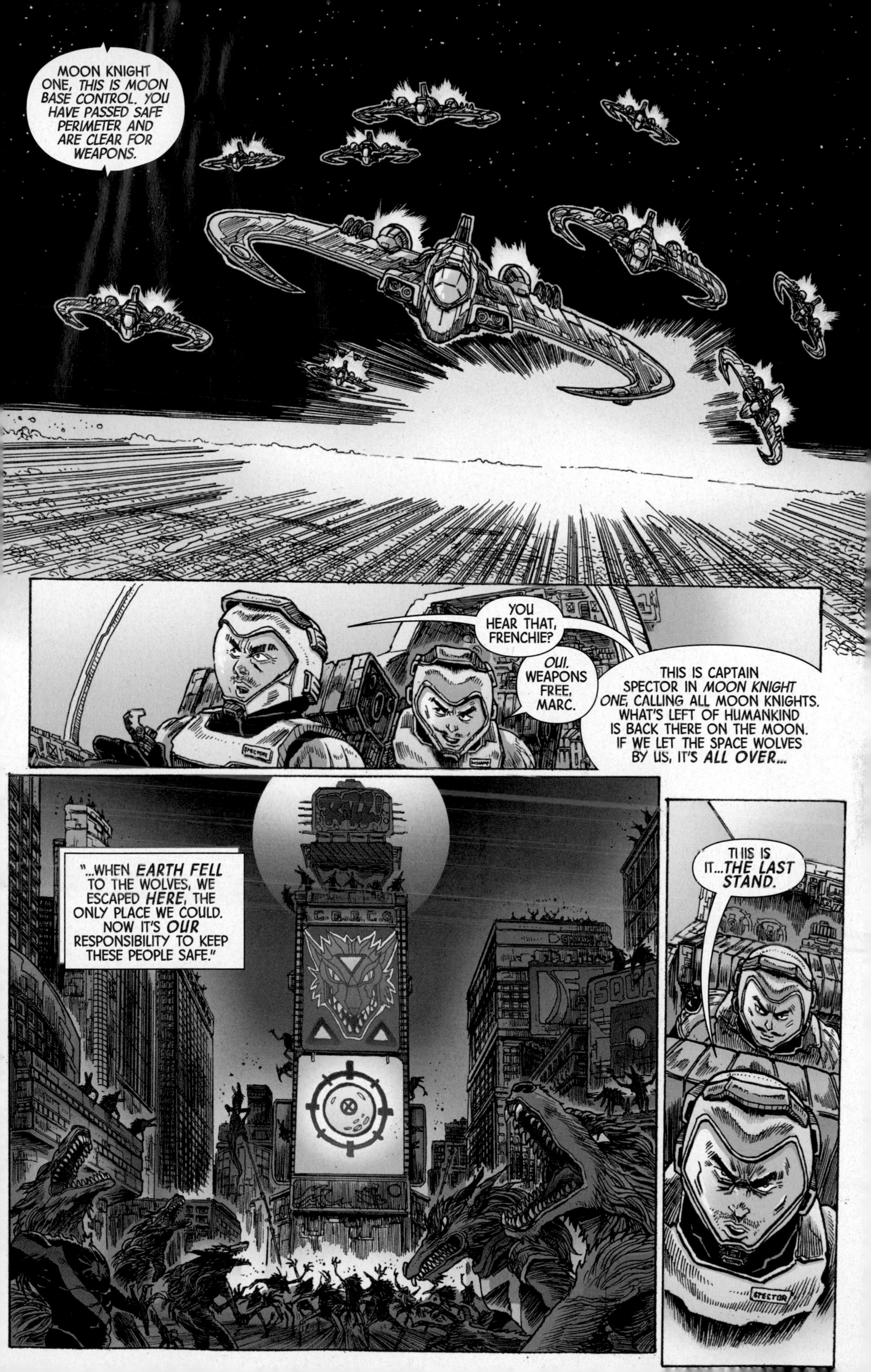
MOON KNIGHT ONE, THIS IS MOON BASE CONTROL. YOU HAVE PASSED SAFE PERIMETER AND ARE CLEAR FOR WEAPONS.
YOU HEAR THAT, FRENCHIE?
OUI. WEAPONS FREE, MARC.
THIS IS CAPTAIN SPECTOR IN MOON KNIGHT ONE, CALLING ALL MOON KNIGHTS. WHAT'S LEFT OF HUMANKIND IS BACK THERE ON THE MOON. IF WE LET THE SPACE WOLVES BY US, IT'S ALL OVER...
"...WHEN EARTH FELL TO THE WOLVES, WE ESCAPED HERE, THE ONLY PLACE WE COULD. NOW IT'S OUR RESPONSIBILITY TO KEEP THESE PEOPLE SAFE."
THIS IS IT...THE LAST STAND.

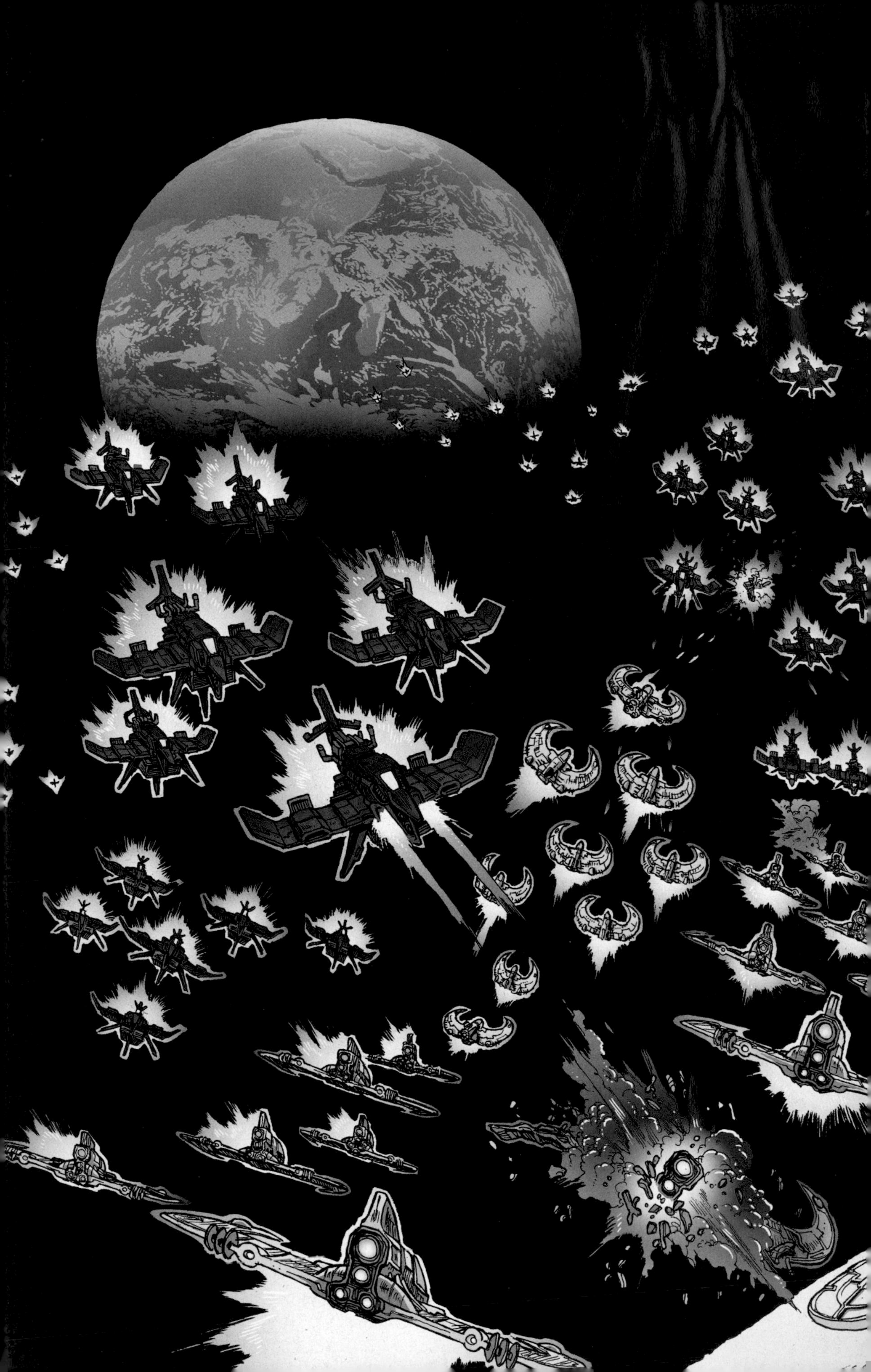

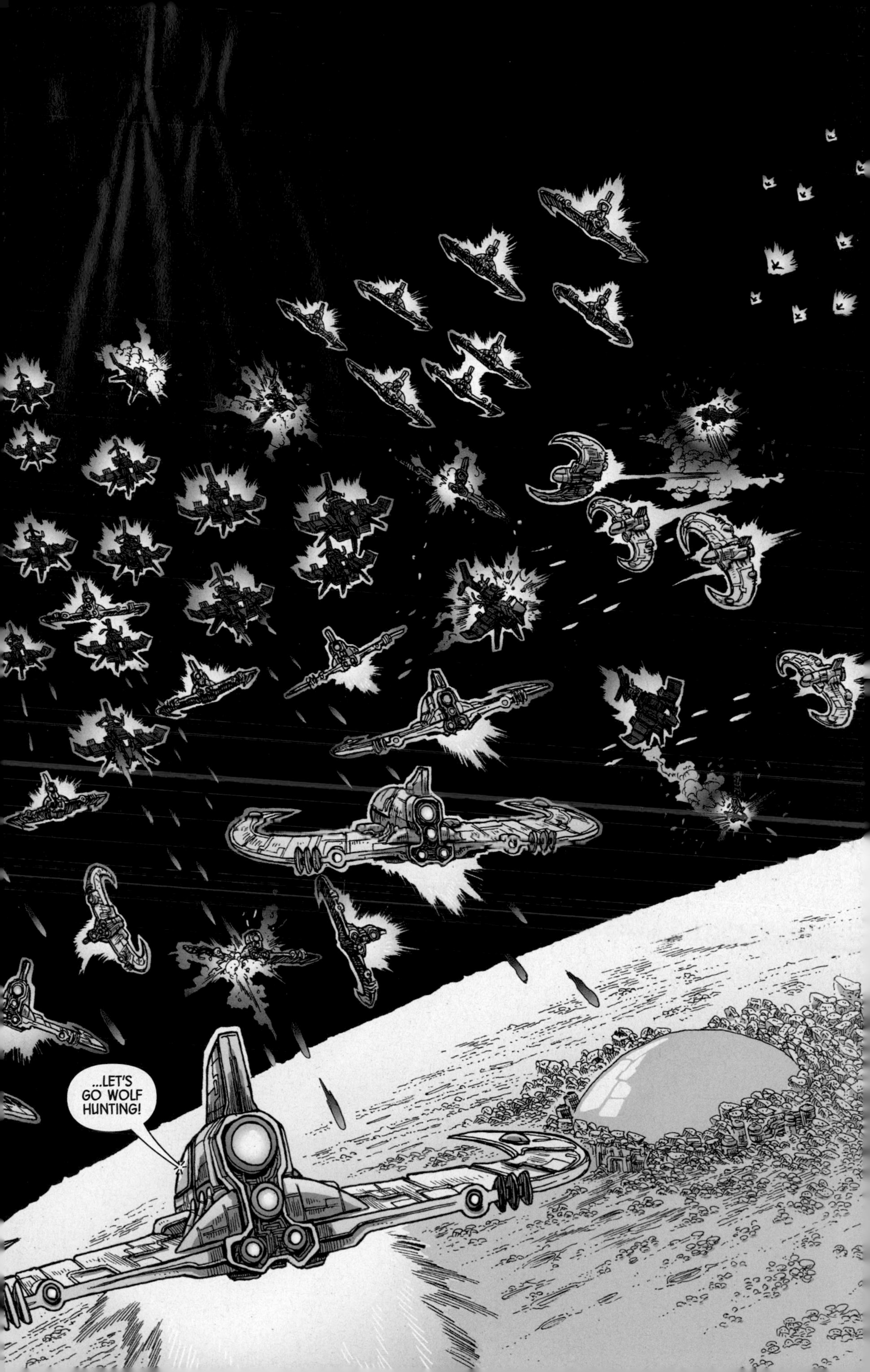
...LET'S GO WOLF HUNTING!

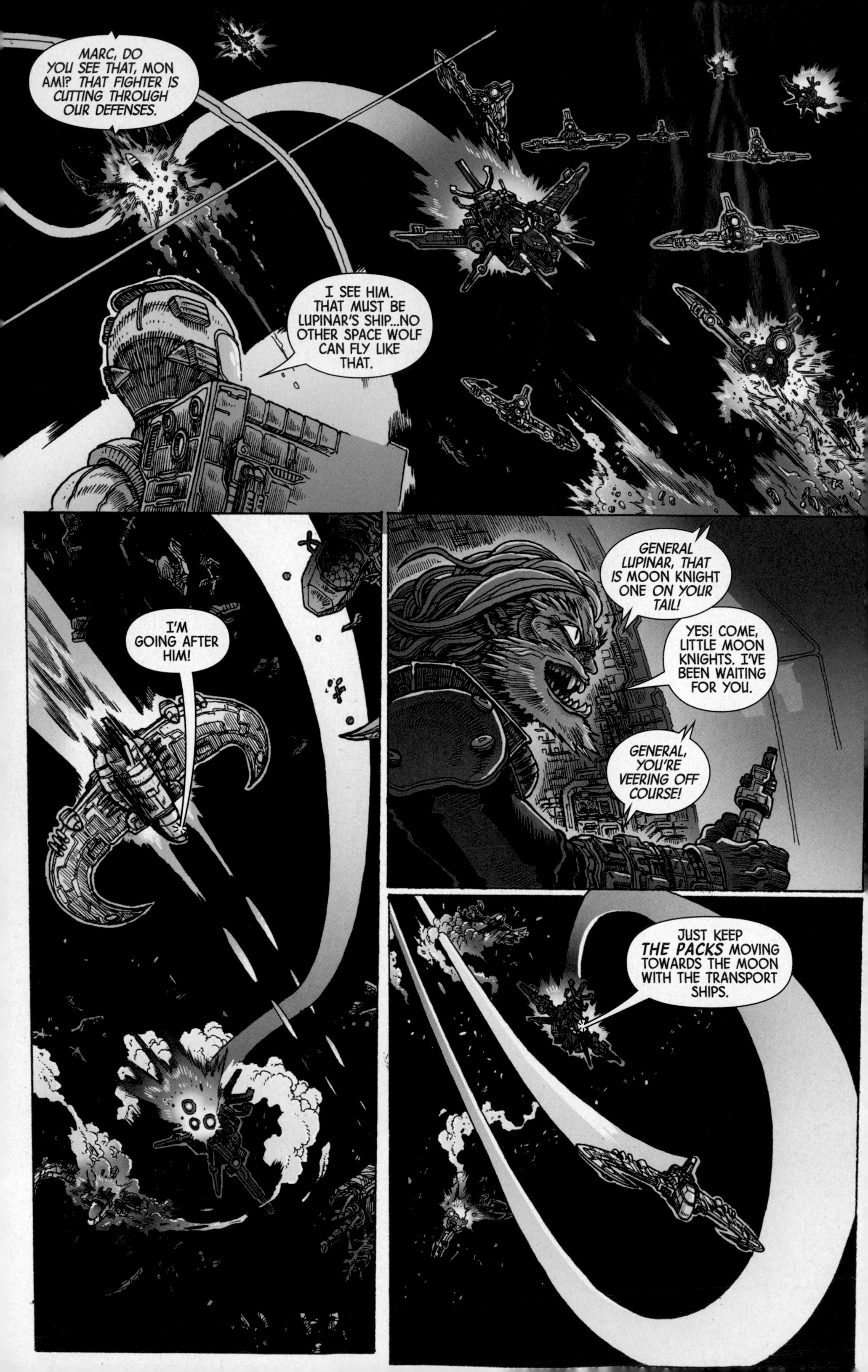
MARC, DO YOU SEE THAT, MON AMI? THAT FIGHTER IS CUTTING THROUGH OUR DEFENSES.
I SEE HIM. THAT MUST BE LUPINAR'S SHIP...NO OTHER SPACE WOLF CAN FLY LIKE THAT.
I'M GOING AFTER HIM!
GENERAL LUPINAR, THAT IS MOON KNIGHT ONE ON YOUR TAIL!
YES! COME, LITTLE MOON KNIGHTS. I'VE BEEN WAITING FOR YOU.
GENERAL, YOU'RE VEERING OFF COURSE!
JUST KEEP THE PACKS MOVING TOWARDS THE MOON WITH THE TRANSPORT SHIPS.

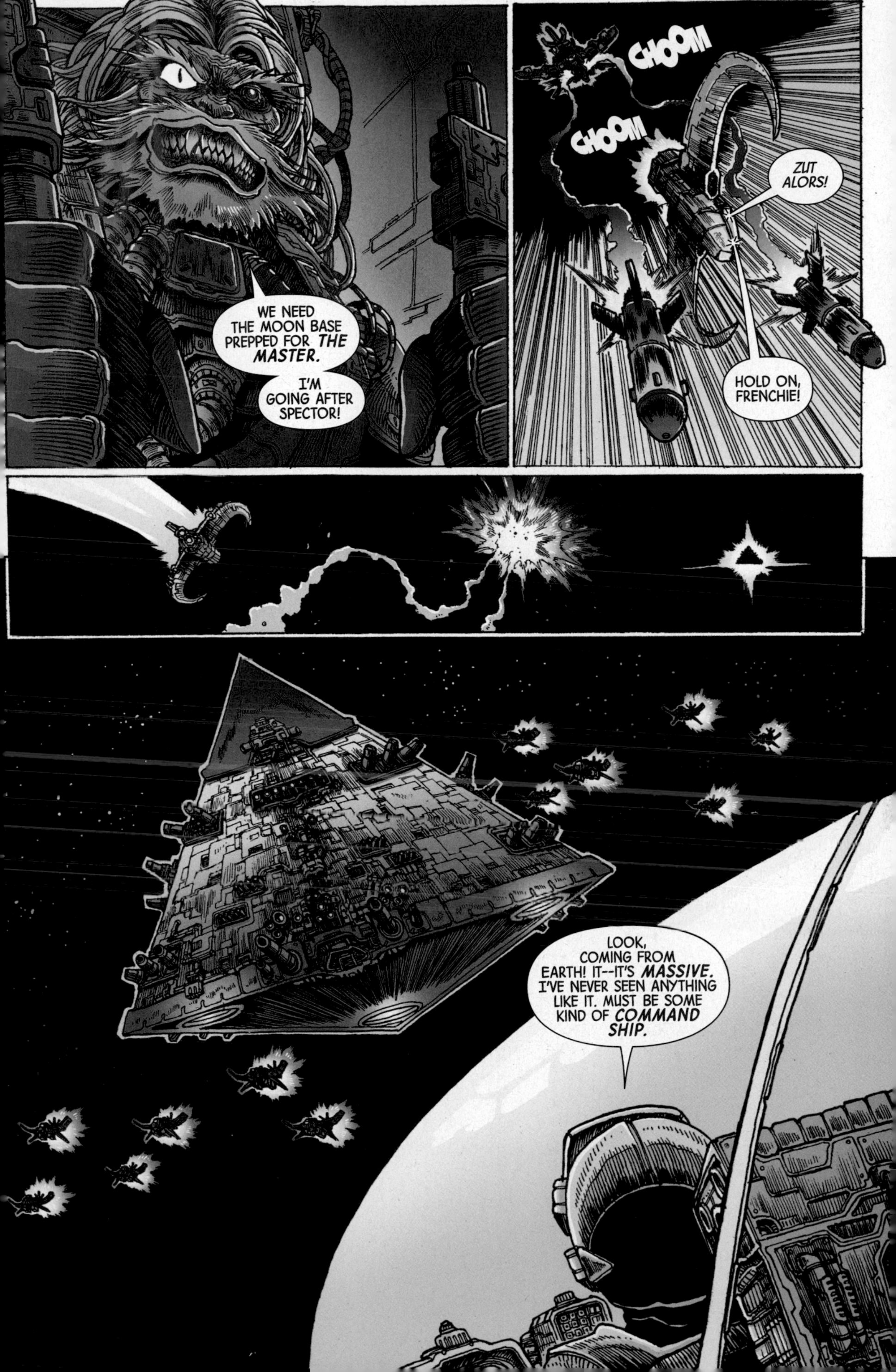
WE NEED THE MOON BASE PREPPED FOR THE MASTER.
I'M GOING AFTER SPECTOR!
CHOOM
CHOOM
ZUT ALORS!
HOLD ON, FRENCHIE!
LOOK, COMING FROM EARTH! IT--IT'S MASSIVE. I'VE NEVER SEEN ANYTHING LIKE IT. MUST BE SOME KIND OF COMMAND SHIP.

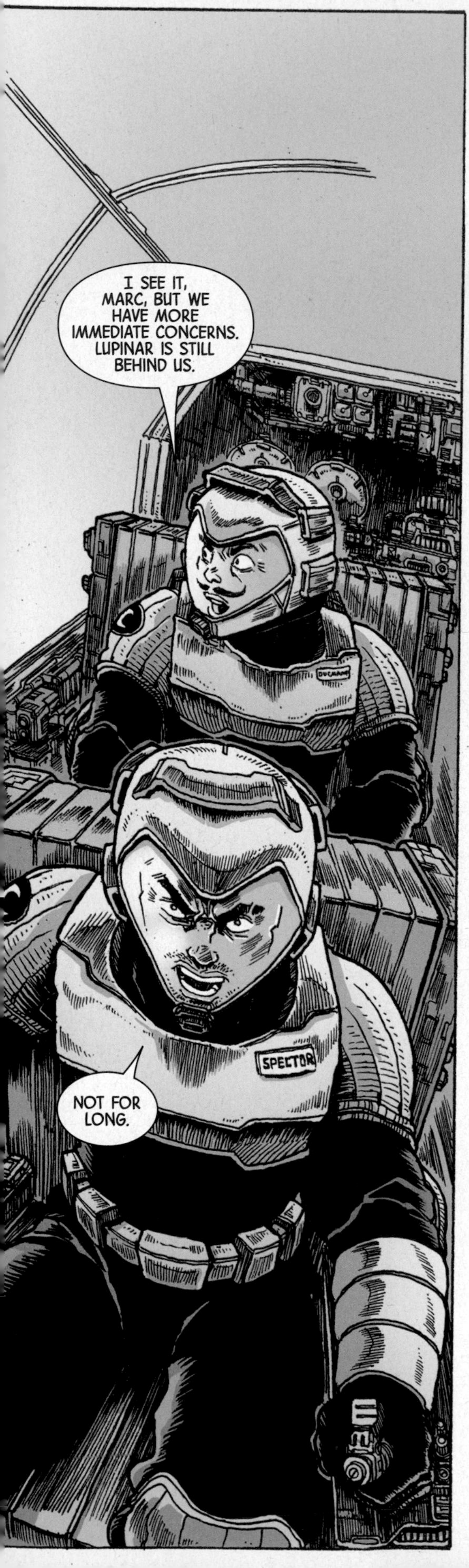
I SEE IT, MARC, BUT WE HAVE MORE IMMEDIATE CONCERNS. LUPINAR IS STILL BEHIND US.
DUCHAMP
SPECTOR
NOT FOR LONG.

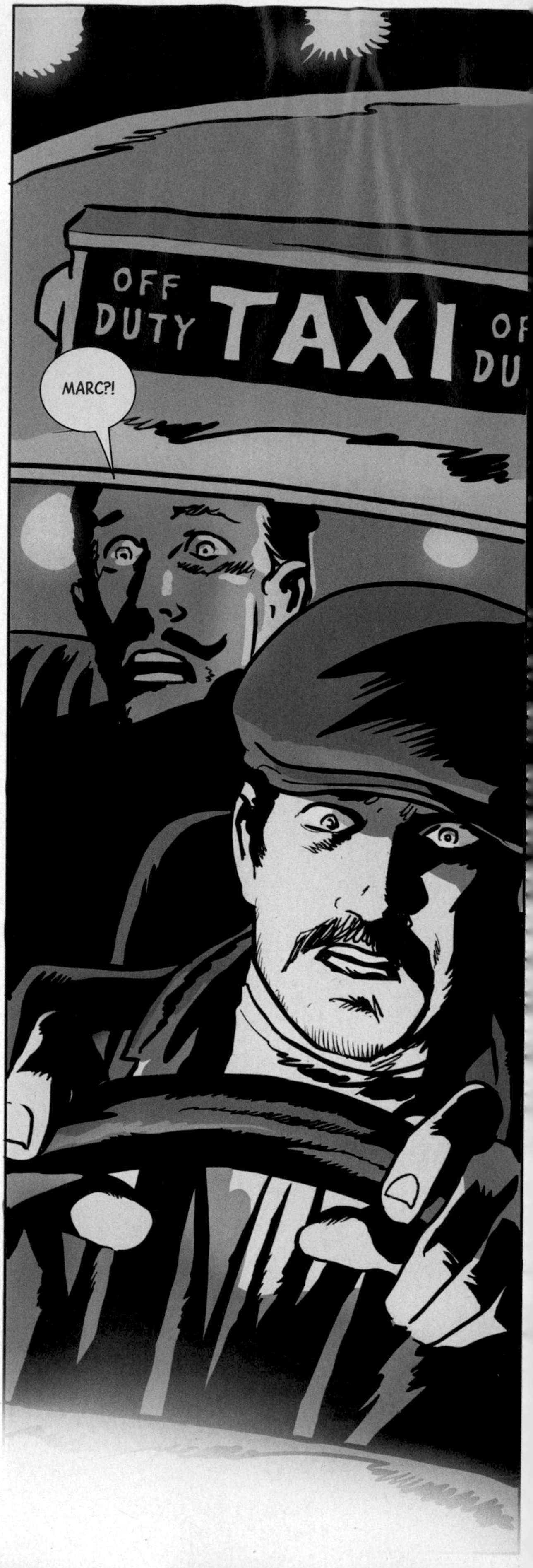
OFF DUTY TAXI
MARC?!

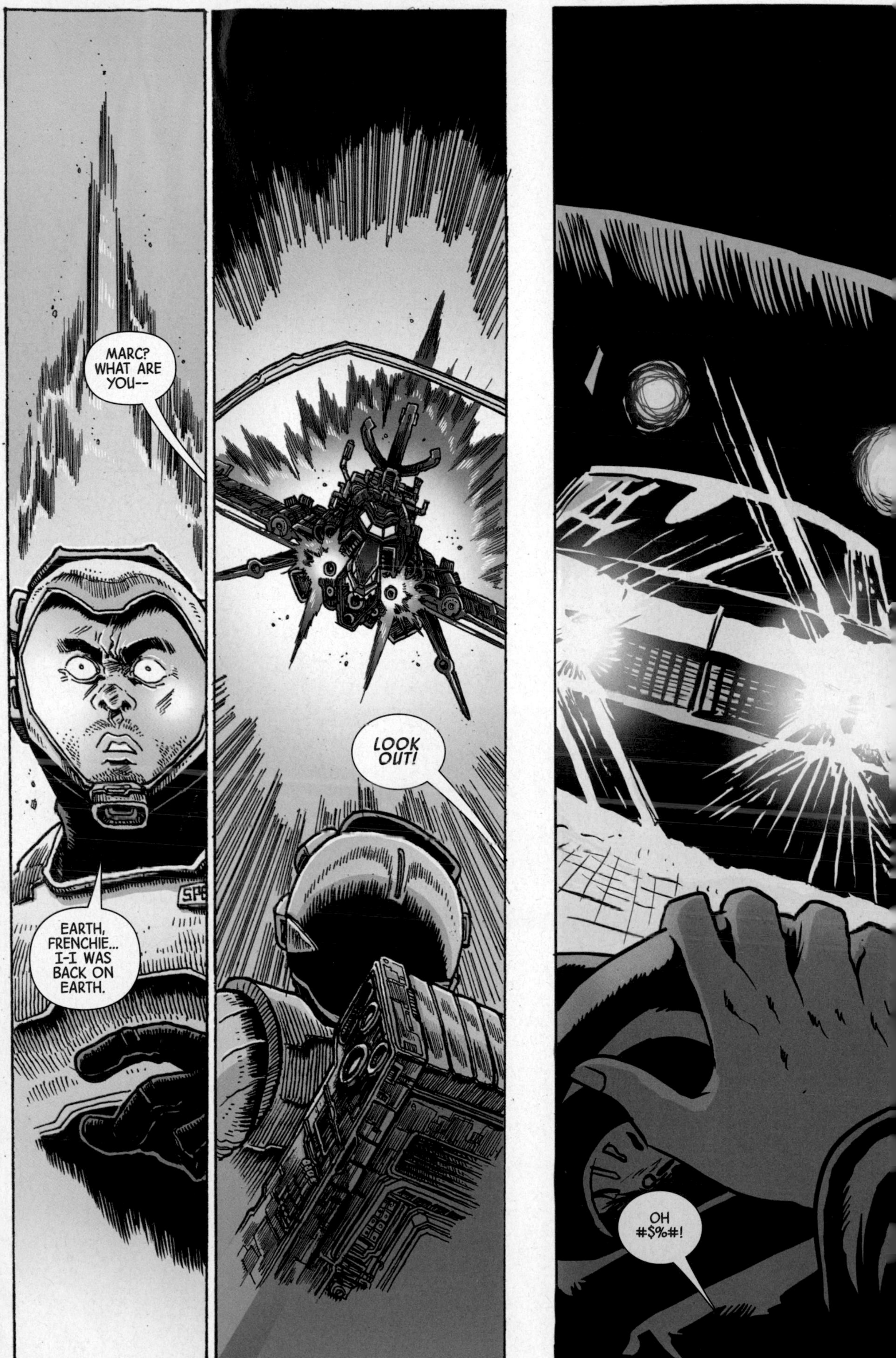
MARC? WHAT ARE YOU--
EARTH, FRENCHIE... I-I WAS BACK ON EARTH.
LOOK OUT!
OH #$%#!

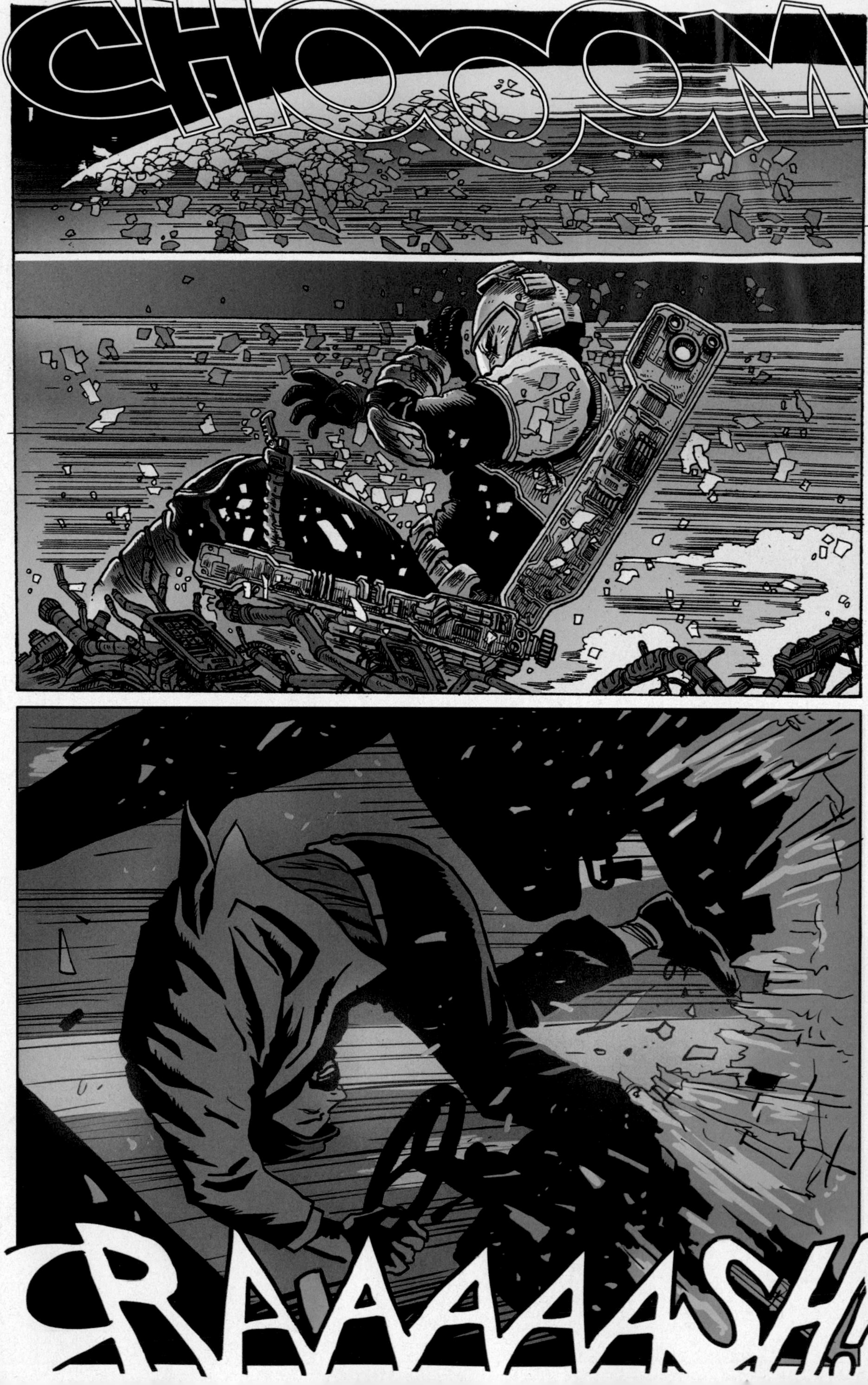
CHOOOM
CRAAAASH

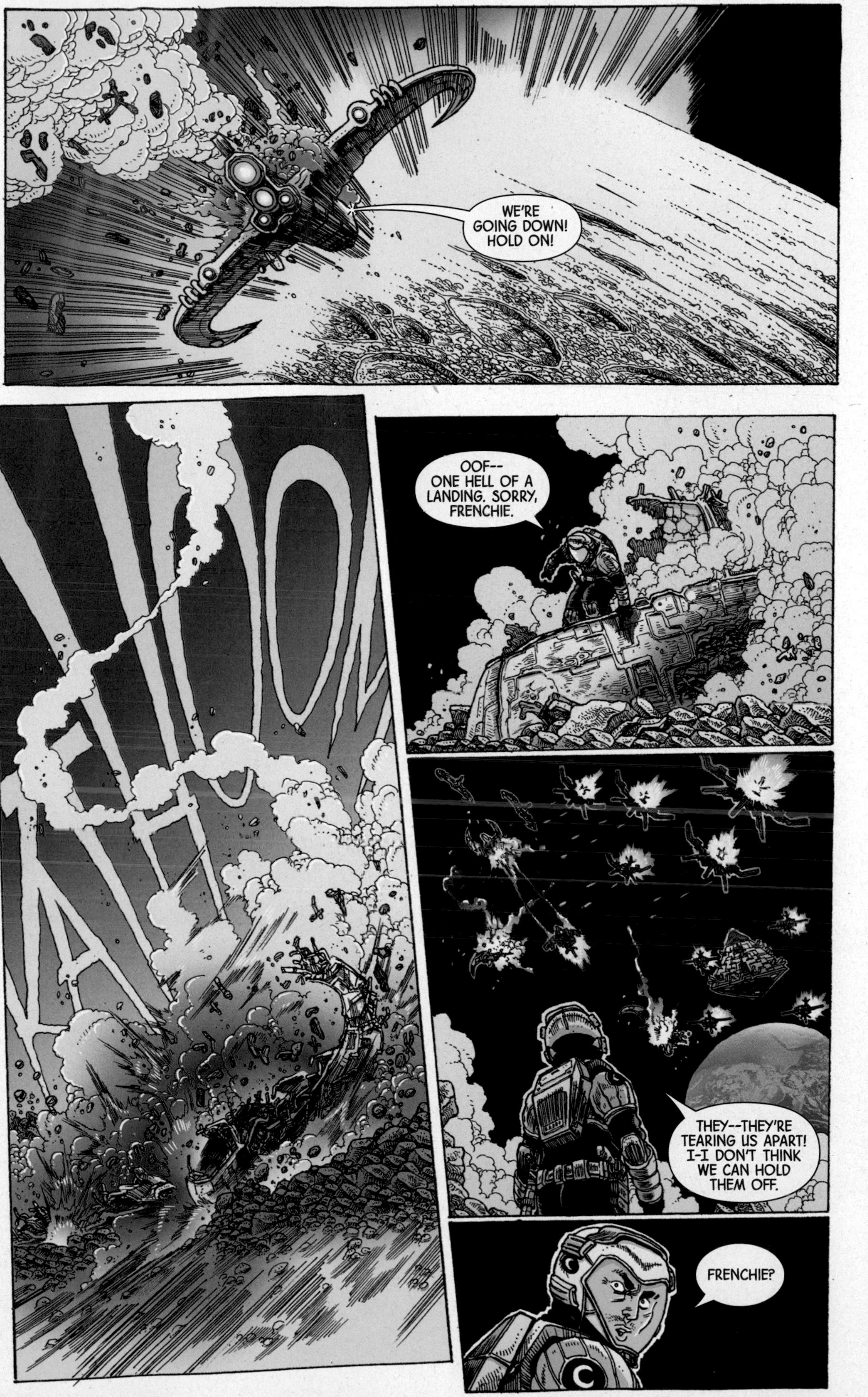
WE'RE GOING DOWN! HOLD ON!
KRAKOOM
OOF-- ONE HELL OF A LANDING. SORRY, FRENCHIE.
THEY--THEY'RE TEARING US APART! I-I DON'T THINK WE CAN HOLD THEM OFF.
FRENCHIE?

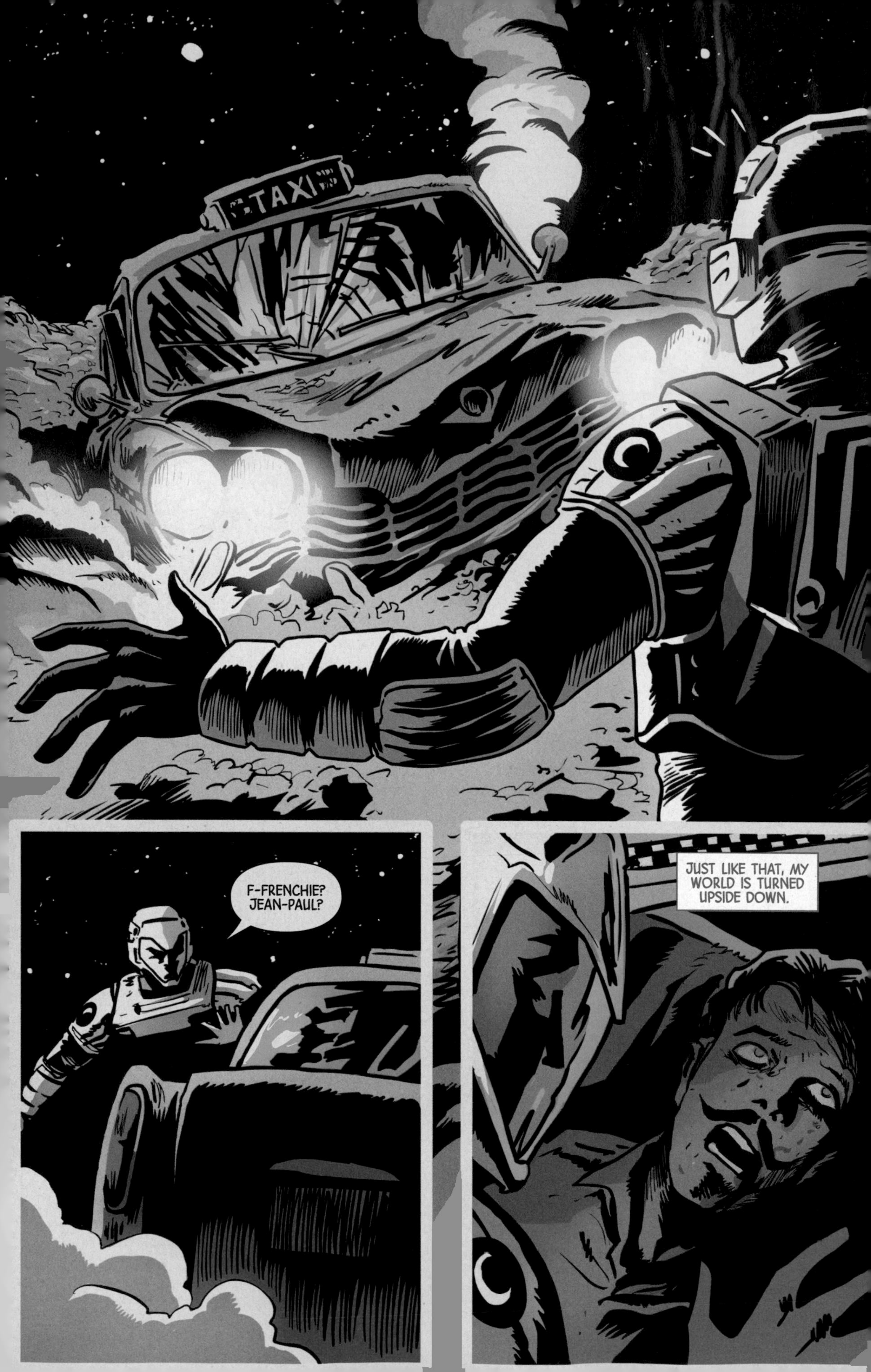
TAXI
F-FRENCHIE? JEAN-PAUL?
JUST LIKE THAT, MY WORLD IS TURNED UPSIDE DOWN.

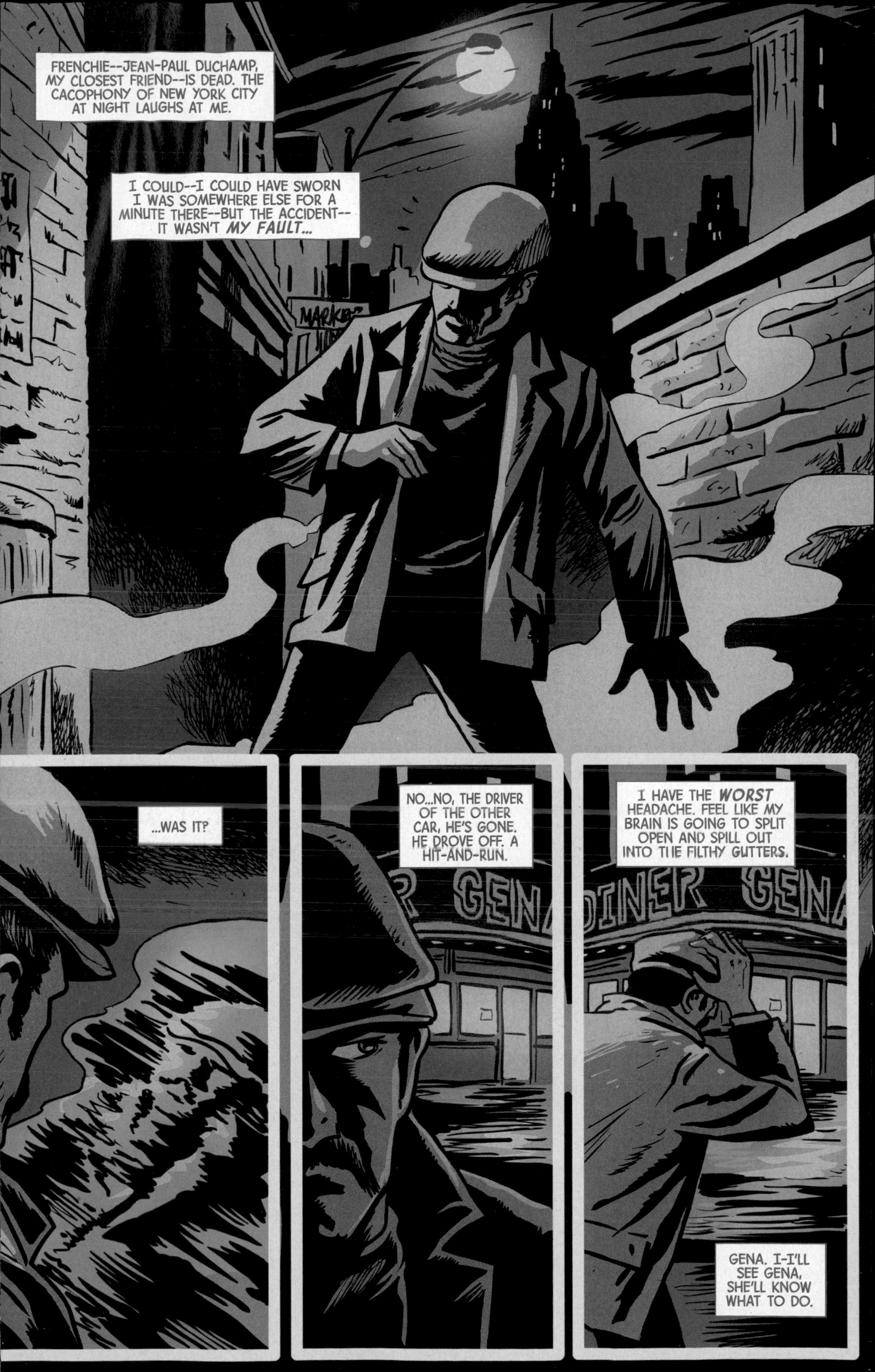
FRENCHIE--JEAN-PAUL DUCHAMP, MY CLOSEST FRIEND--IS DEAD. THE CACOPHONY OF NEW YORK CITY AT NIGHT LAUGHS AT ME.
I COULD--I COULD HAVE SWORN I WAS SOMEWHERE ELSE FOR A MINUTE THERE--BUT THE ACCIDENT--IT WASN'T *MY FAULT*...
...WAS IT?
NO...NO, THE DRIVER OF THE OTHER CAR, HE'S GONE. HE DROVE OFF. A HIT-AND-RUN.
I HAVE THE *WORST* HEADACHE. FEEL LIKE MY BRAIN IS GOING TO SPLIT OPEN AND SPILL OUT INTO THE FILTHY GUTTERS.
DINER GENA
GENA. I-I'LL SEE GENA, SHE'LL KNOW WHAT TO DO.

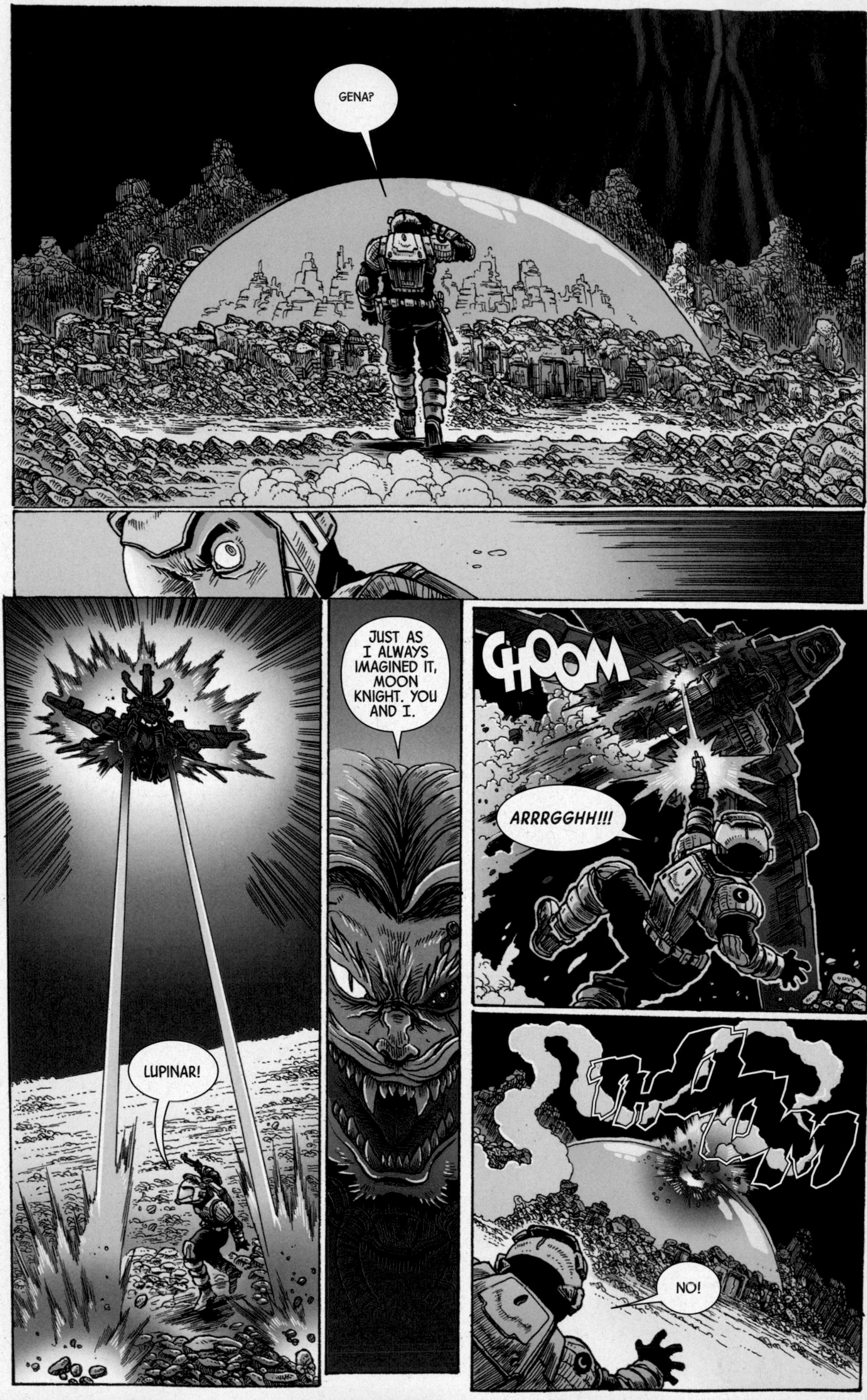
GENA?
LUPINAR!
JUST AS I ALWAYS IMAGINED IT, MOON KNIGHT. YOU AND I.
CHOOM
ARRRGGHH!!!
NO!

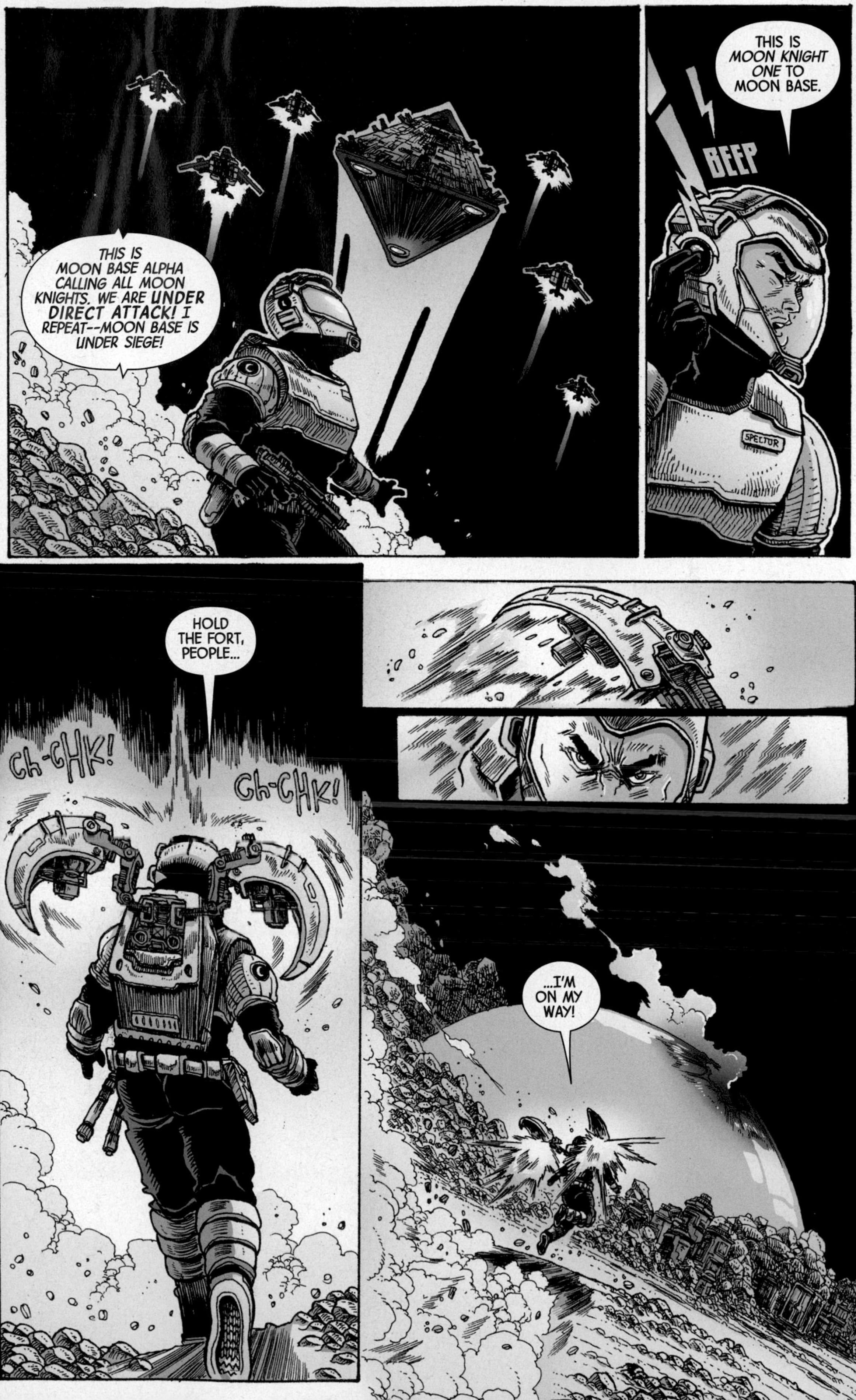
THIS IS MOON BASE ALPHA CALLING ALL MOON KNIGHTS. WE ARE UNDER DIRECT ATTACK! I REPEAT--MOON BASE IS UNDER SIEGE!
BEEP
THIS IS MOON KNIGHT ONE TO MOON BASE.
SPECTOR
HOLD THE FORT, PEOPLE...
Ch-CHK!
Ch-CHK!
...I'M ON MY WAY!

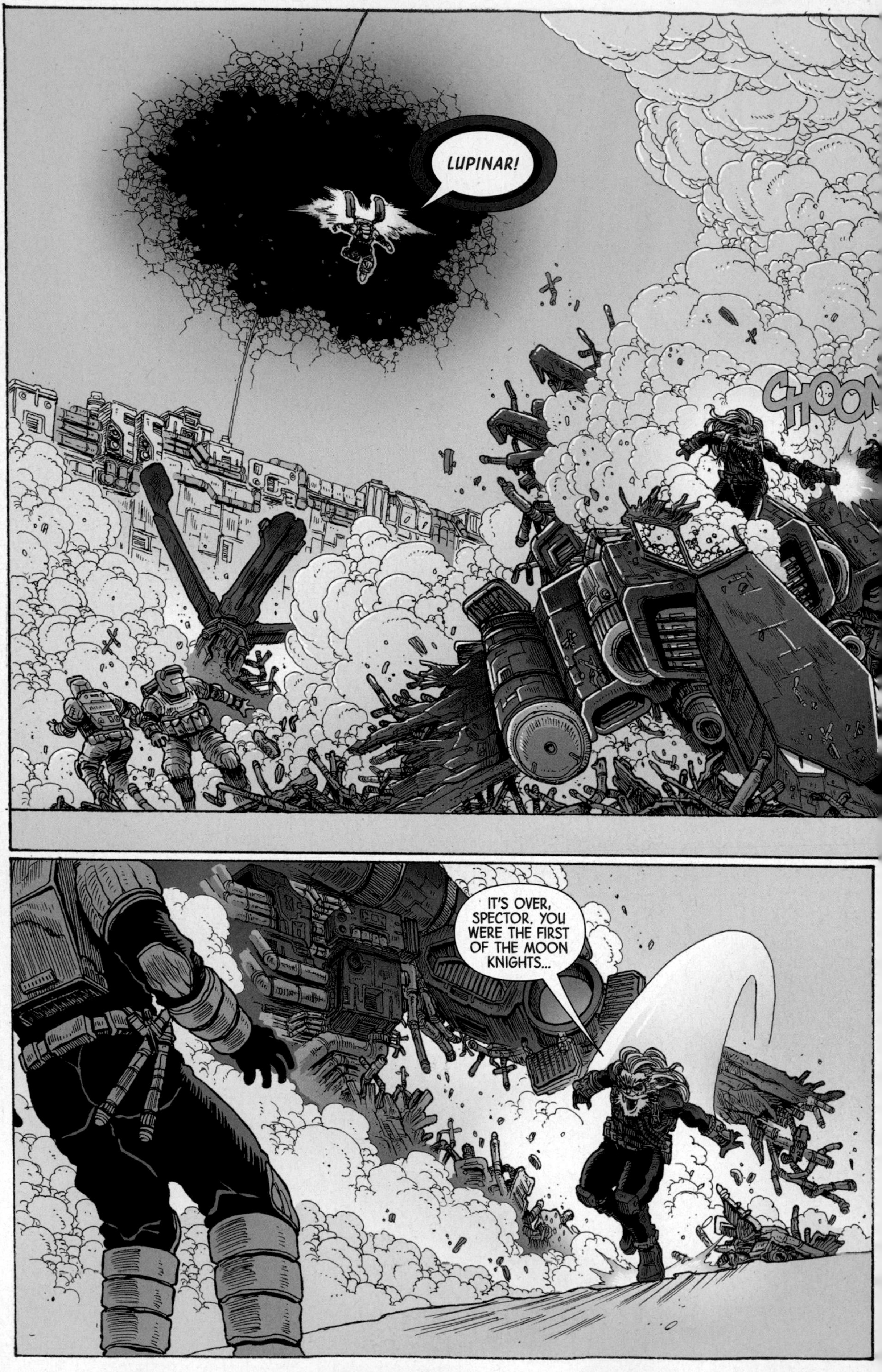
LUPINAR!
CHOOM
IT'S OVER, SPECTOR. YOU WERE THE FIRST OF THE MOON KNIGHTS...

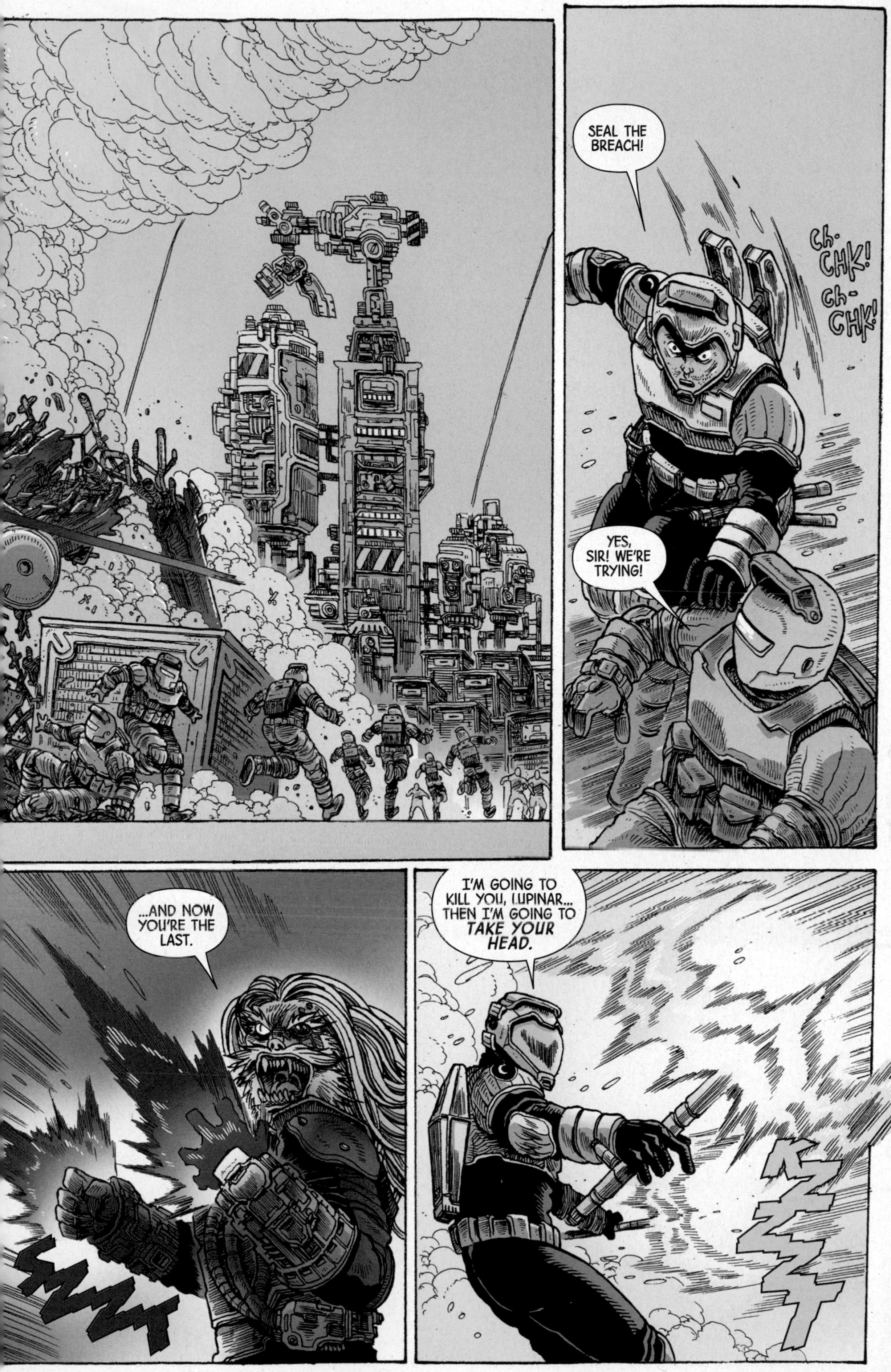
SEAL THE BREACH!
Ch-CHK! Ch-CHK!
YES, SIR! WE'RE TRYING!
...AND NOW YOU'RE THE LAST.
I'M GOING TO KILL YOU, LUPINAR... THEN I'M GOING TO *TAKE YOUR HEAD.*

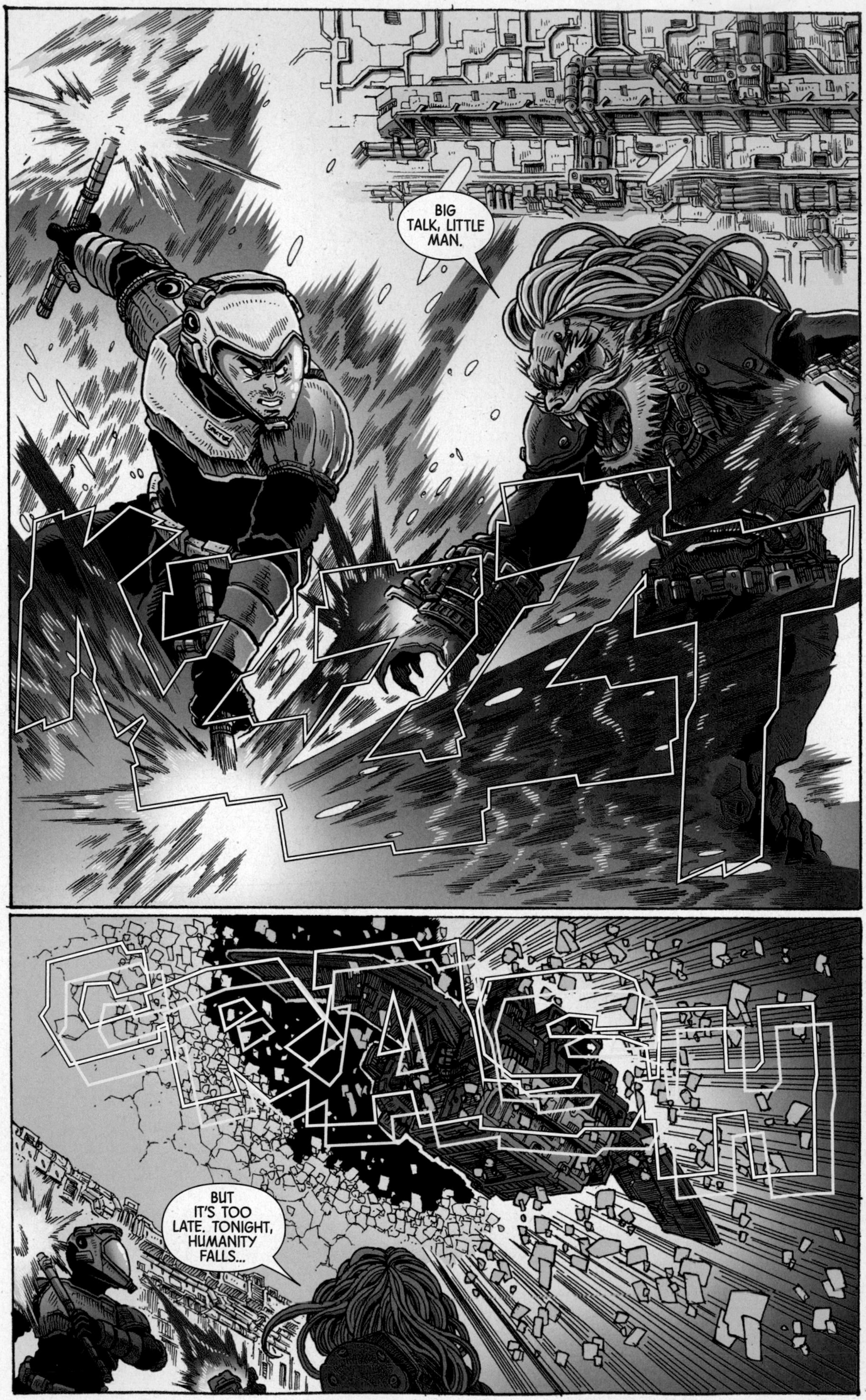
BIG TALK, LITTLE MAN.
BUT IT'S TOO LATE. TONIGHT, HUMANITY FALLS...

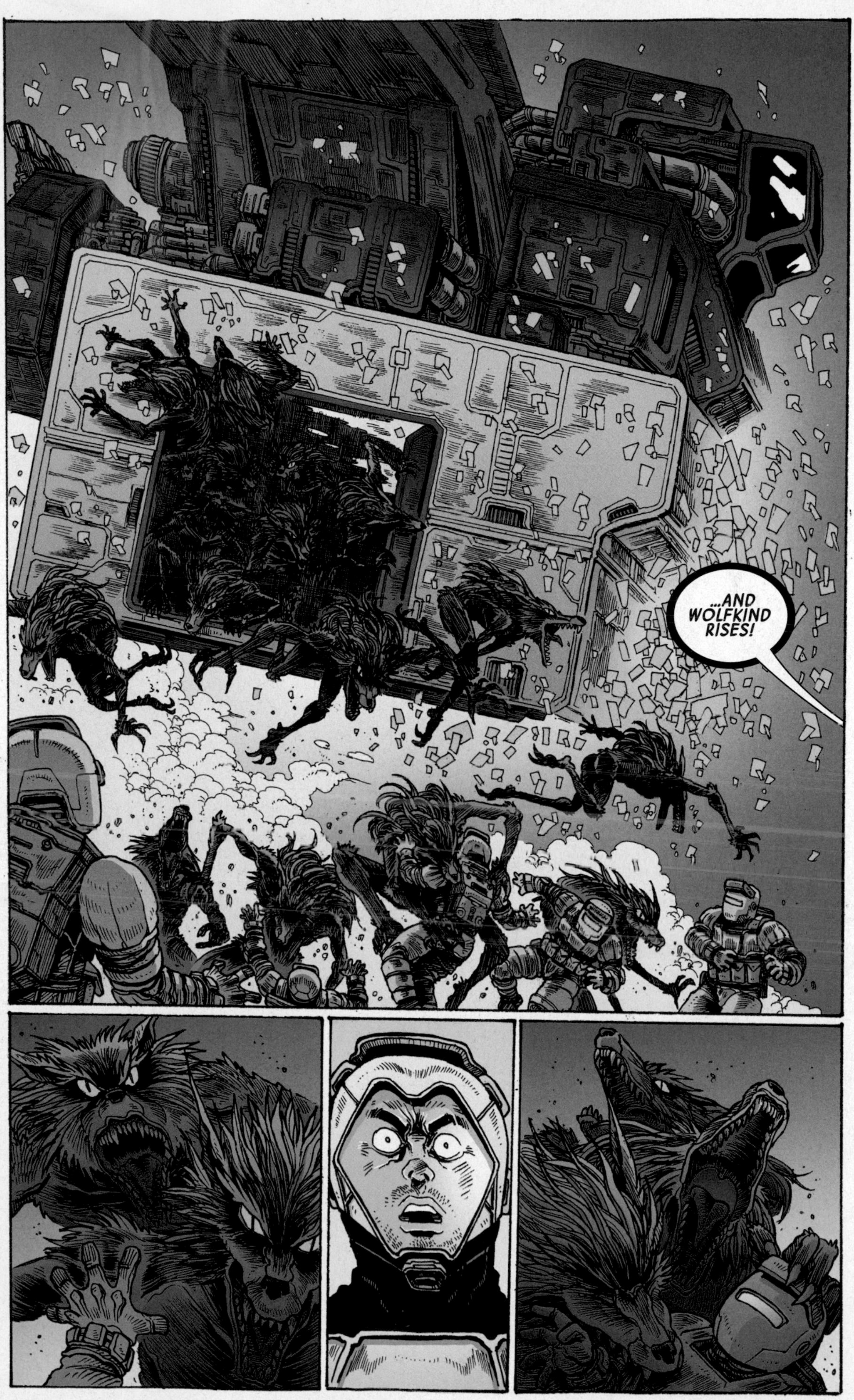
...AND WOLFKIND RISES!

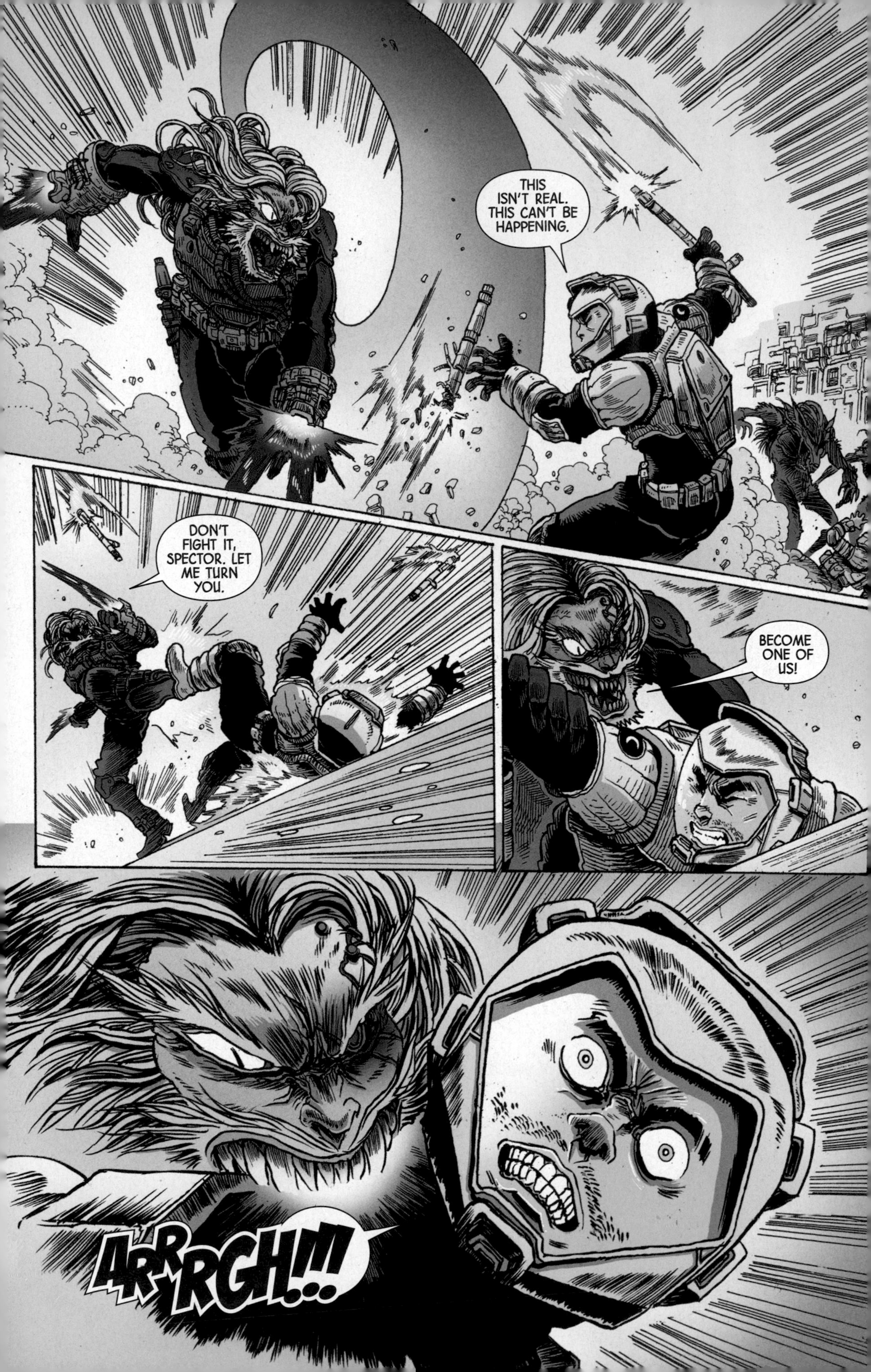
THIS ISN'T REAL. THIS CAN'T BE HAPPENING.
DON'T FIGHT IT, SPECTOR. LET ME TURN YOU.
BECOME ONE OF US!
ARRRGH!!!

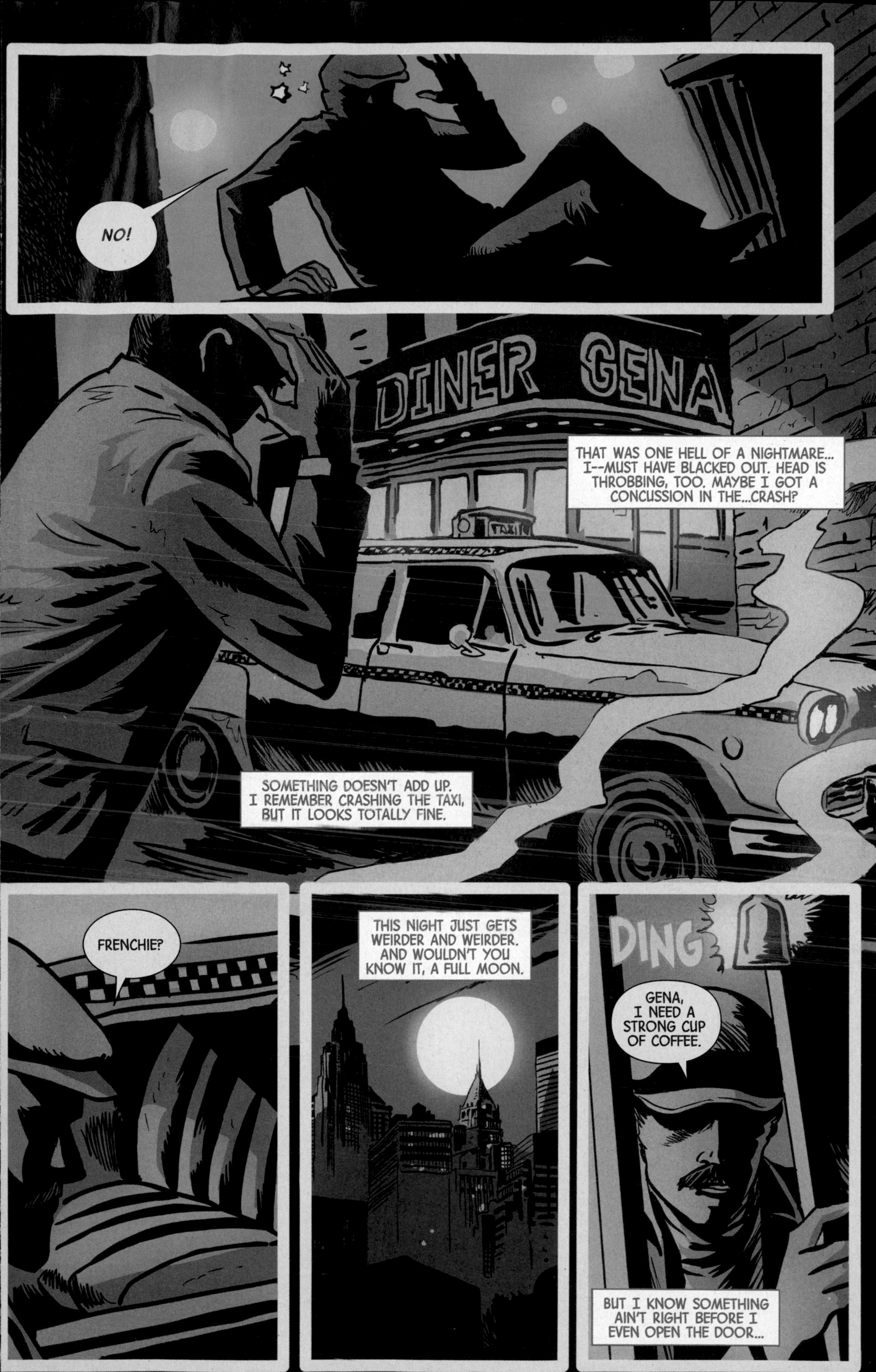
NO!
DINER GENA
THAT WAS ONE HELL OF A NIGHTMARE... I--MUST HAVE BLACKED OUT. HEAD IS THROBBING, TOO. MAYBE I GOT A CONCUSSION IN THE...CRASH?
SOMETHING DOESN'T ADD UP. I REMEMBER CRASHING THE TAXI, BUT IT LOOKS TOTALLY FINE.
FRENCHIE?
THIS NIGHT JUST GETS WEIRDER AND WEIRDER. AND WOULDN'T YOU KNOW IT, A FULL MOON.
DING
GENA, I NEED A STRONG CUP OF COFFEE.
BUT I KNOW SOMETHING AIN'T RIGHT BEFORE I EVEN OPEN THE DOOR...

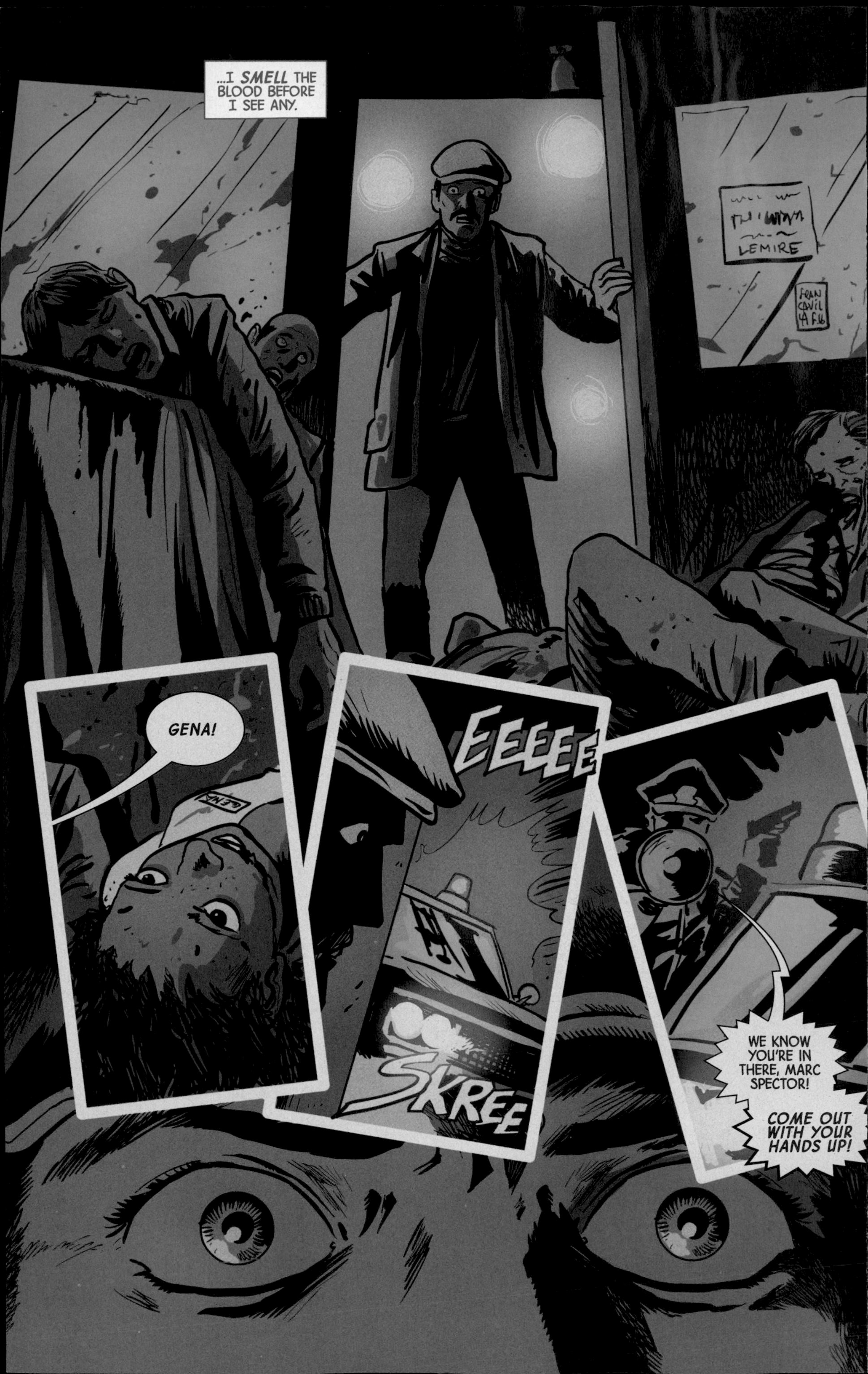
...I SMELL THE BLOOD BEFORE I SEE ANY.
LEMIRE
FRAN CAVIL
GENA!
EEEEE
SKREE
WE KNOW YOU'RE IN THERE, MARC SPECTOR!
COME OUT WITH YOUR HANDS UP!

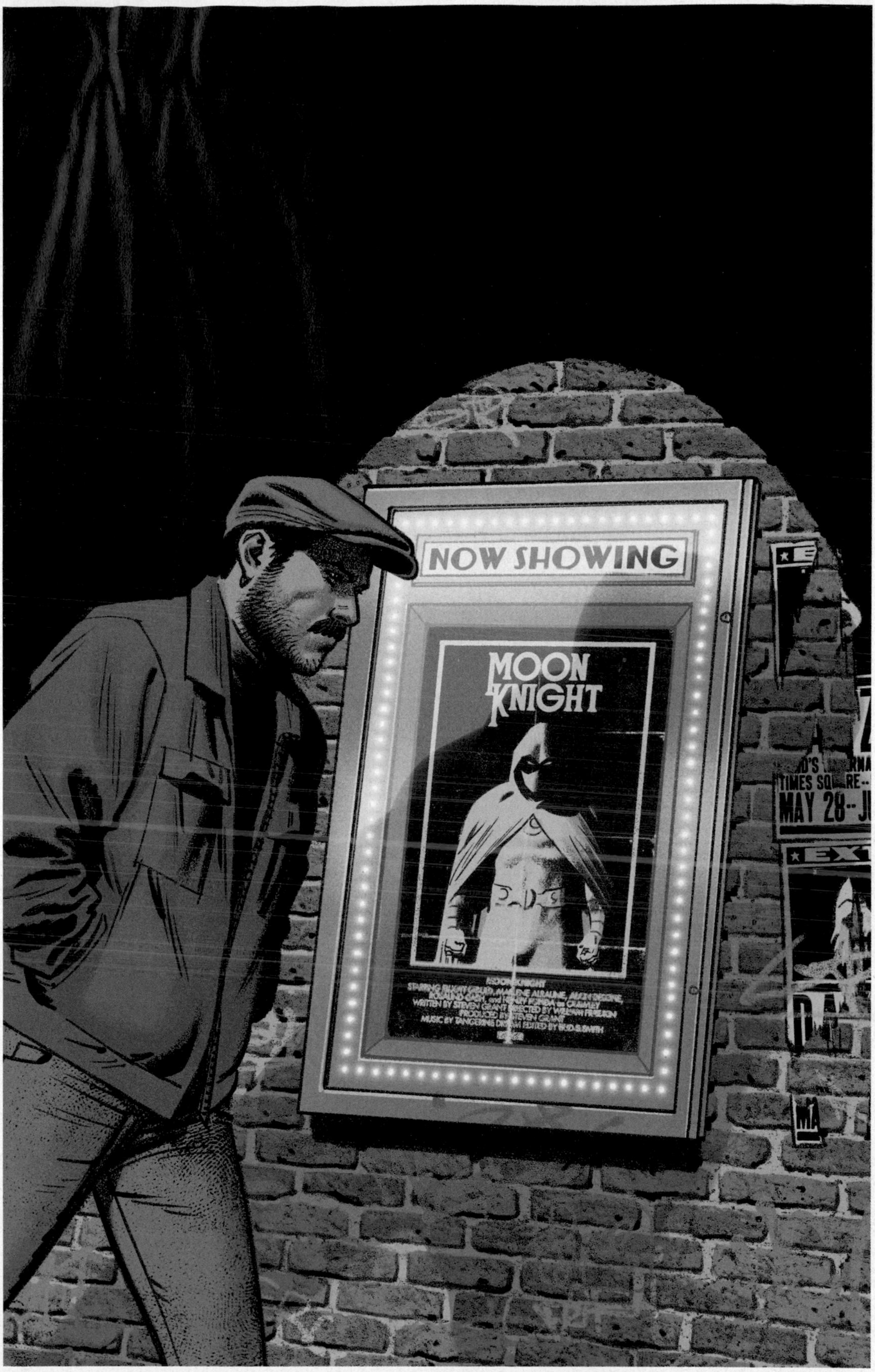
NOW SHOWING
MOON KNIGHT
TIMES SQUARE
MAY 28

INCARNATIONS
PART THREE
8

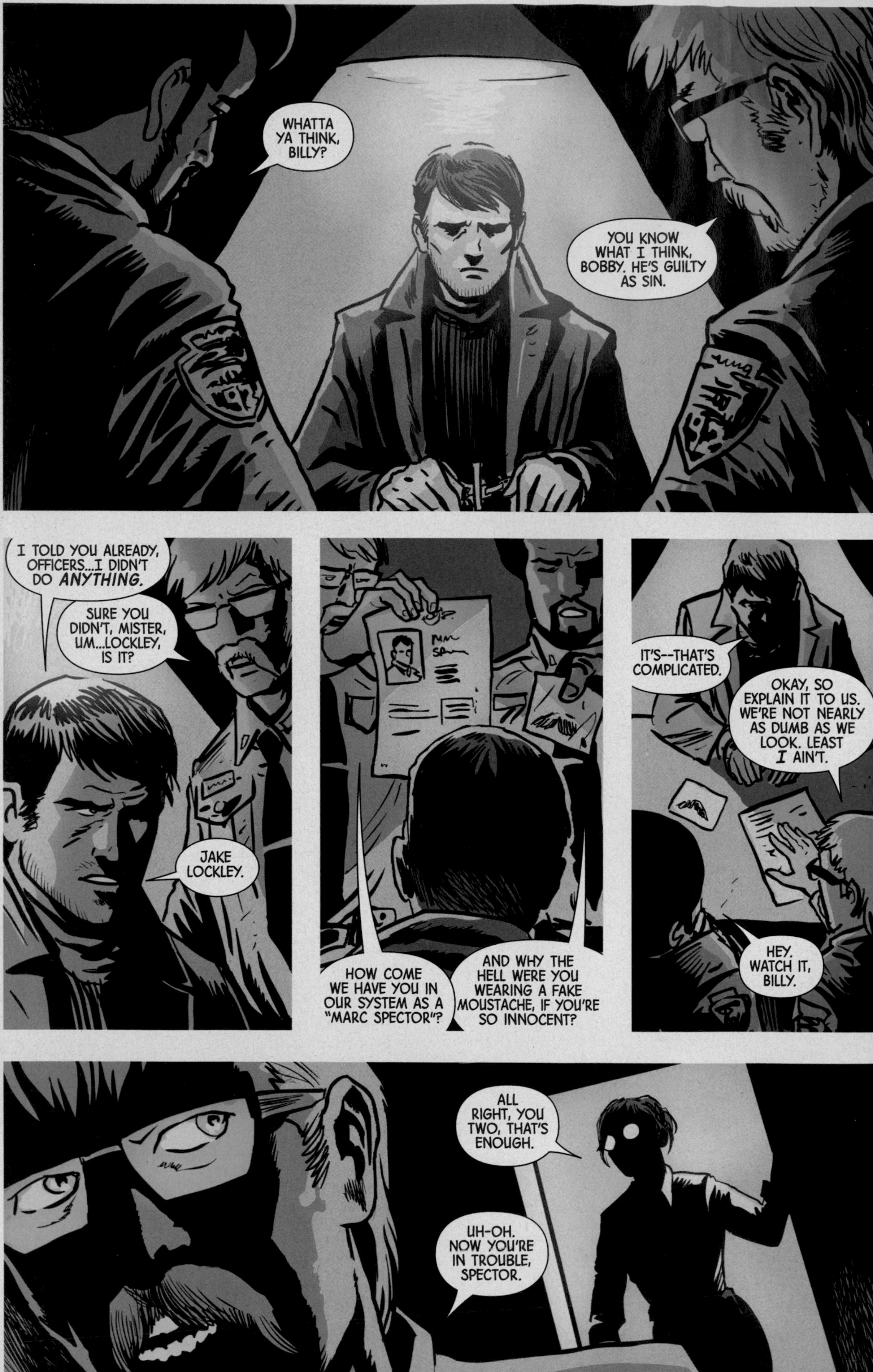
WHATTA YA THINK, BILLY?
YOU KNOW WHAT I THINK, BOBBY. HE'S GUILTY AS SIN.
I TOLD YOU ALREADY, OFFICERS...I DIDN'T DO *ANYTHING.*
SURE YOU DIDN'T, MISTER, UM...LOCKLEY, IS IT?
JAKE LOCKLEY.
HOW COME WE HAVE YOU IN OUR SYSTEM AS A "MARC SPECTOR"?
AND WHY THE HELL WERE YOU WEARING A FAKE MOUSTACHE, IF YOU'RE SO INNOCENT?
IT'S--THAT'S COMPLICATED.
OKAY, SO EXPLAIN IT TO US. WE'RE NOT NEARLY AS DUMB AS WE LOOK. LEAST *I* AIN'T.
HEY. WATCH IT, BILLY.
ALL RIGHT, YOU TWO, THAT'S ENOUGH.
UH-OH. NOW YOU'RE IN TROUBLE, SPECTOR.

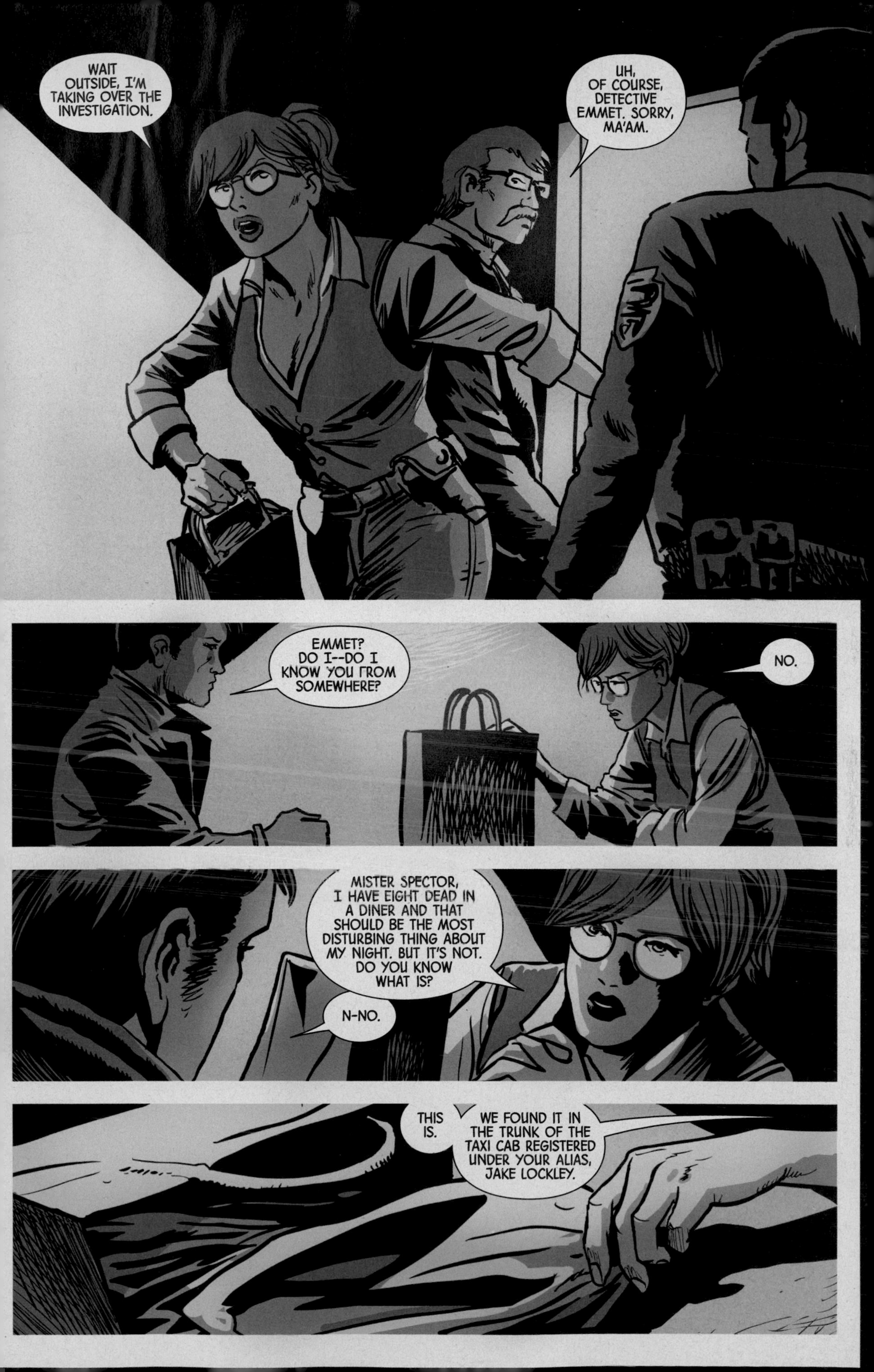
WAIT OUTSIDE, I'M TAKING OVER THE INVESTIGATION.
UH, OF COURSE, DETECTIVE EMMET. SORRY, MA'AM.
EMMET? DO I--DO I KNOW YOU FROM SOMEWHERE?
NO.
MISTER SPECTOR, I HAVE EIGHT DEAD IN A DINER AND THAT SHOULD BE THE MOST DISTURBING THING ABOUT MY NIGHT. BUT IT'S NOT. DO YOU KNOW WHAT IS?
N-NO.
THIS IS.
WE FOUND IT IN THE TRUNK OF THE TAXI CAB REGISTERED UNDER YOUR ALIAS, JAKE LOCKLEY.

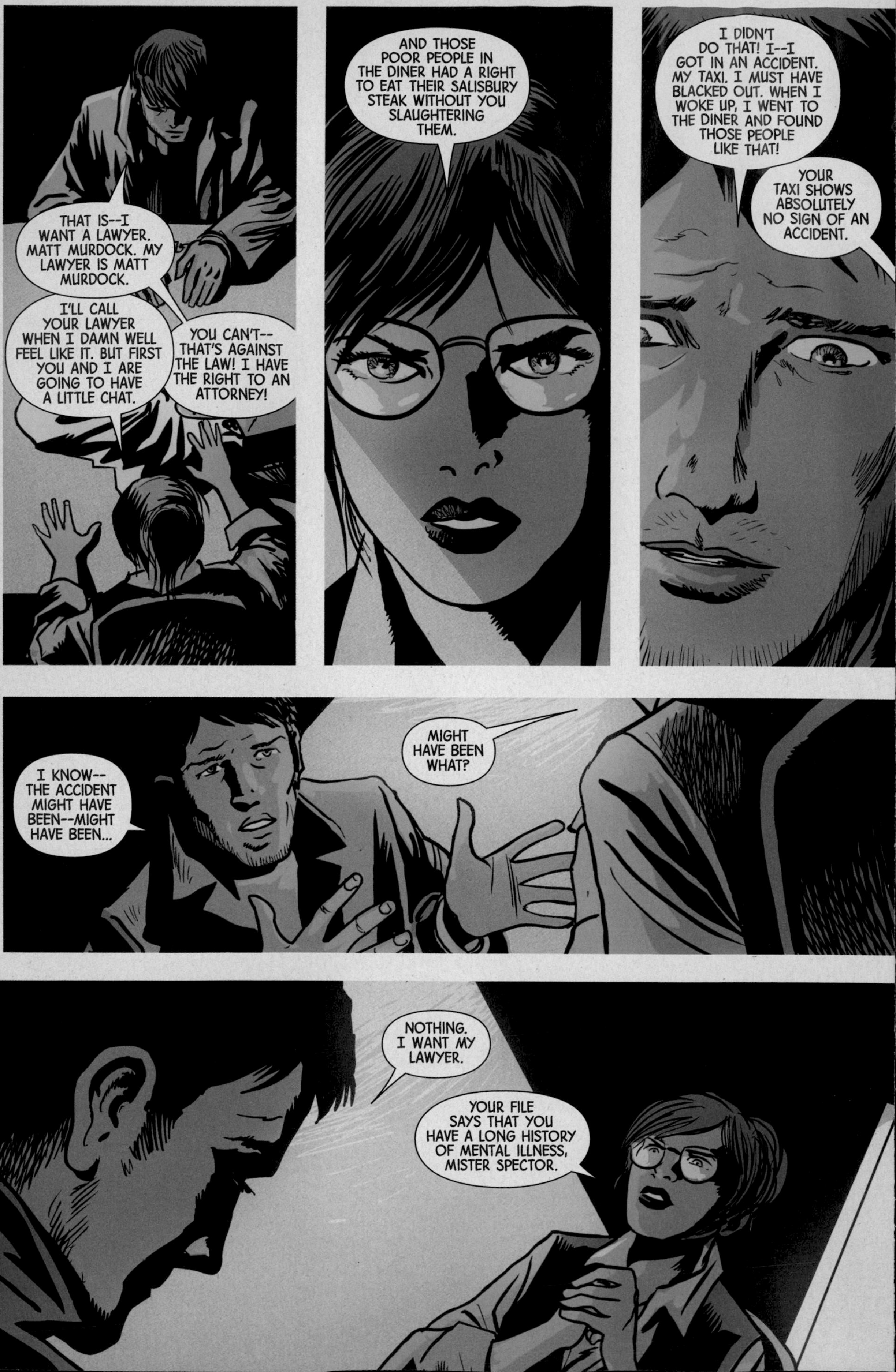
THAT IS--I WANT A LAWYER. MATT MURDOCK. MY LAWYER IS MATT MURDOCK.
I'LL CALL YOUR LAWYER WHEN I DAMN WELL FEEL LIKE IT. BUT FIRST YOU AND I ARE GOING TO HAVE A LITTLE CHAT.
YOU CAN'T--THAT'S AGAINST THE LAW! I HAVE THE RIGHT TO AN ATTORNEY!
AND THOSE POOR PEOPLE IN THE DINER HAD A RIGHT TO EAT THEIR SALISBURY STEAK WITHOUT YOU SLAUGHTERING THEM.
I DIDN'T DO THAT! I--I GOT IN AN ACCIDENT. MY TAXI. I MUST HAVE BLACKED OUT. WHEN I WOKE UP, I WENT TO THE DINER AND FOUND THOSE PEOPLE LIKE THAT!
YOUR TAXI SHOWS ABSOLUTELY NO SIGN OF AN ACCIDENT.
I KNOW--THE ACCIDENT MIGHT HAVE BEEN--MIGHT HAVE BEEN...
MIGHT HAVE BEEN WHAT?
NOTHING. I WANT MY LAWYER.
YOUR FILE SAYS THAT YOU HAVE A LONG HISTORY OF MENTAL ILLNESS, MISTER SPECTOR.

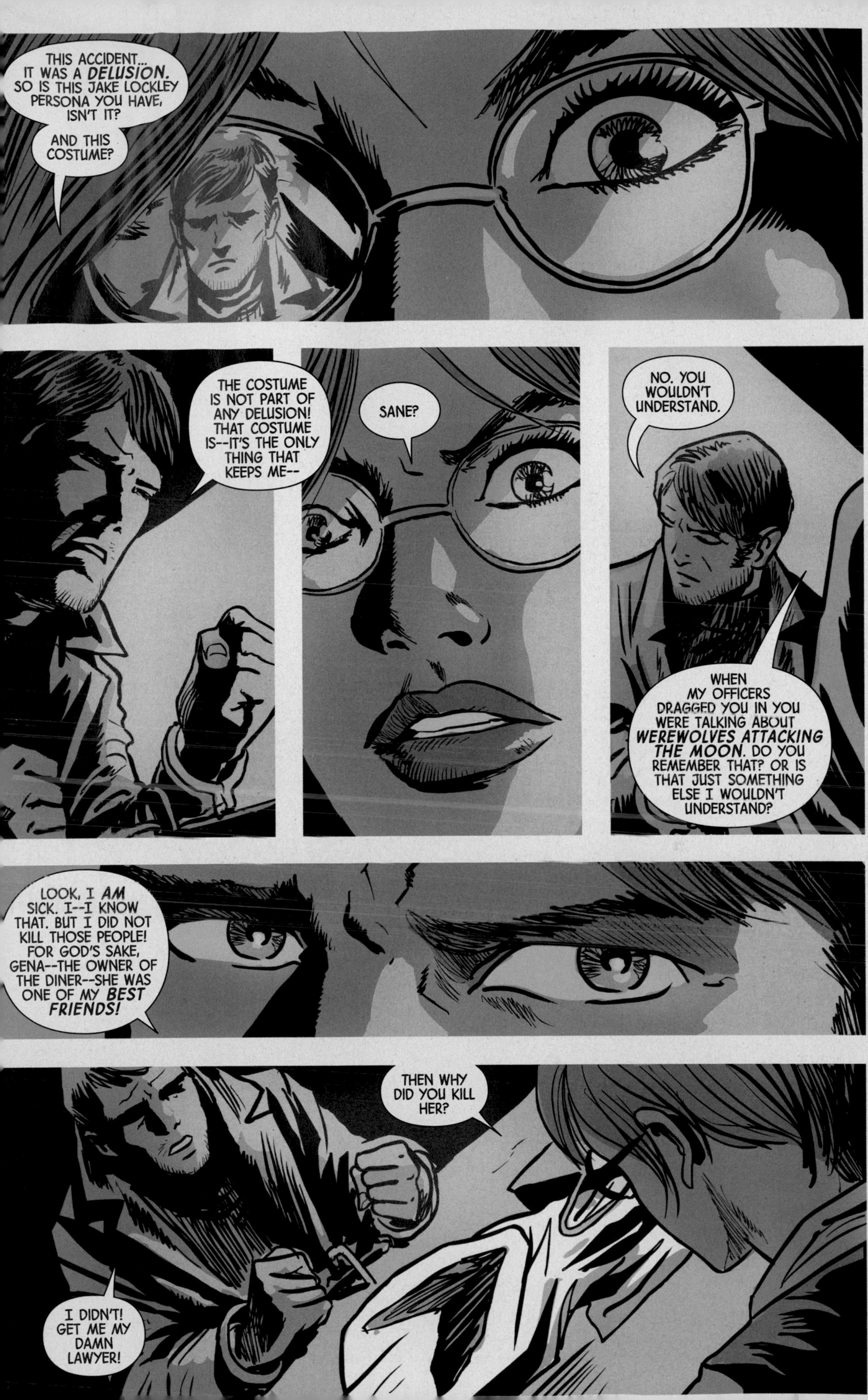
THIS ACCIDENT... IT WAS A DELUSION. SO IS THIS JAKE LOCKLEY PERSONA YOU HAVE, ISN'T IT?
AND THIS COSTUME?
THE COSTUME IS NOT PART OF ANY DELUSION! THAT COSTUME IS--IT'S THE ONLY THING THAT KEEPS ME--
SANE?
NO. YOU WOULDN'T UNDERSTAND.
WHEN MY OFFICERS DRAGGED YOU IN YOU WERE TALKING ABOUT WEREWOLVES ATTACKING THE MOON. DO YOU REMEMBER THAT? OR IS THAT JUST SOMETHING ELSE I WOULDN'T UNDERSTAND?
LOOK, I AM SICK. I--I KNOW THAT. BUT I DID NOT KILL THOSE PEOPLE! FOR GOD'S SAKE, GENA--THE OWNER OF THE DINER--SHE WAS ONE OF MY BEST FRIENDS!
THEN WHY DID YOU KILL HER?
I DIDN'T! GET ME MY DAMN LAWYER!

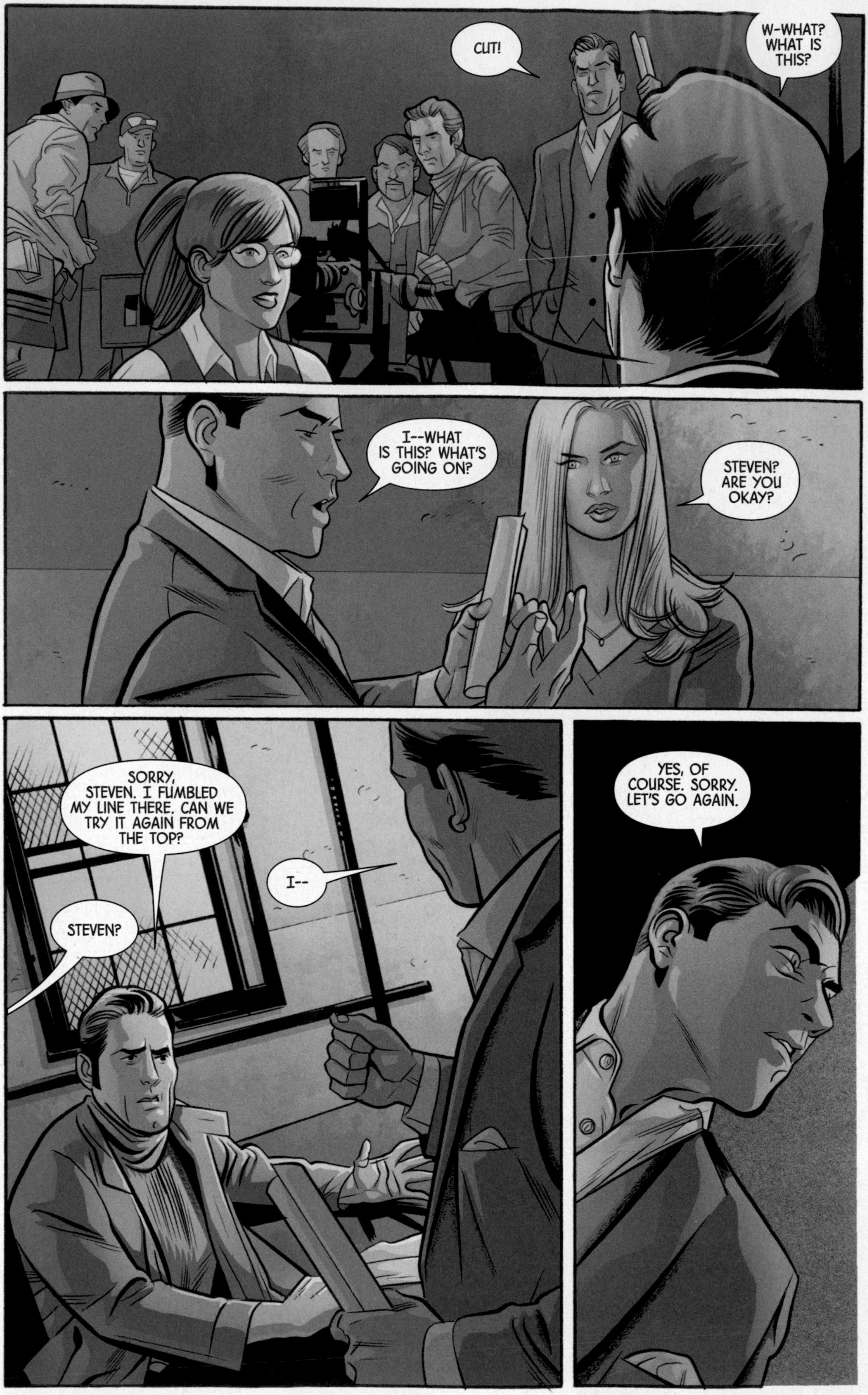
CUT!
W-WHAT? WHAT IS THIS?
I--WHAT IS THIS? WHAT'S GOING ON?
STEVEN? ARE YOU OKAY?
SORRY, STEVEN. I FUMBLED MY LINE THERE. CAN WE TRY IT AGAIN FROM THE TOP?
I--
STEVEN?
YES, OF COURSE. SORRY. LET'S GO AGAIN.

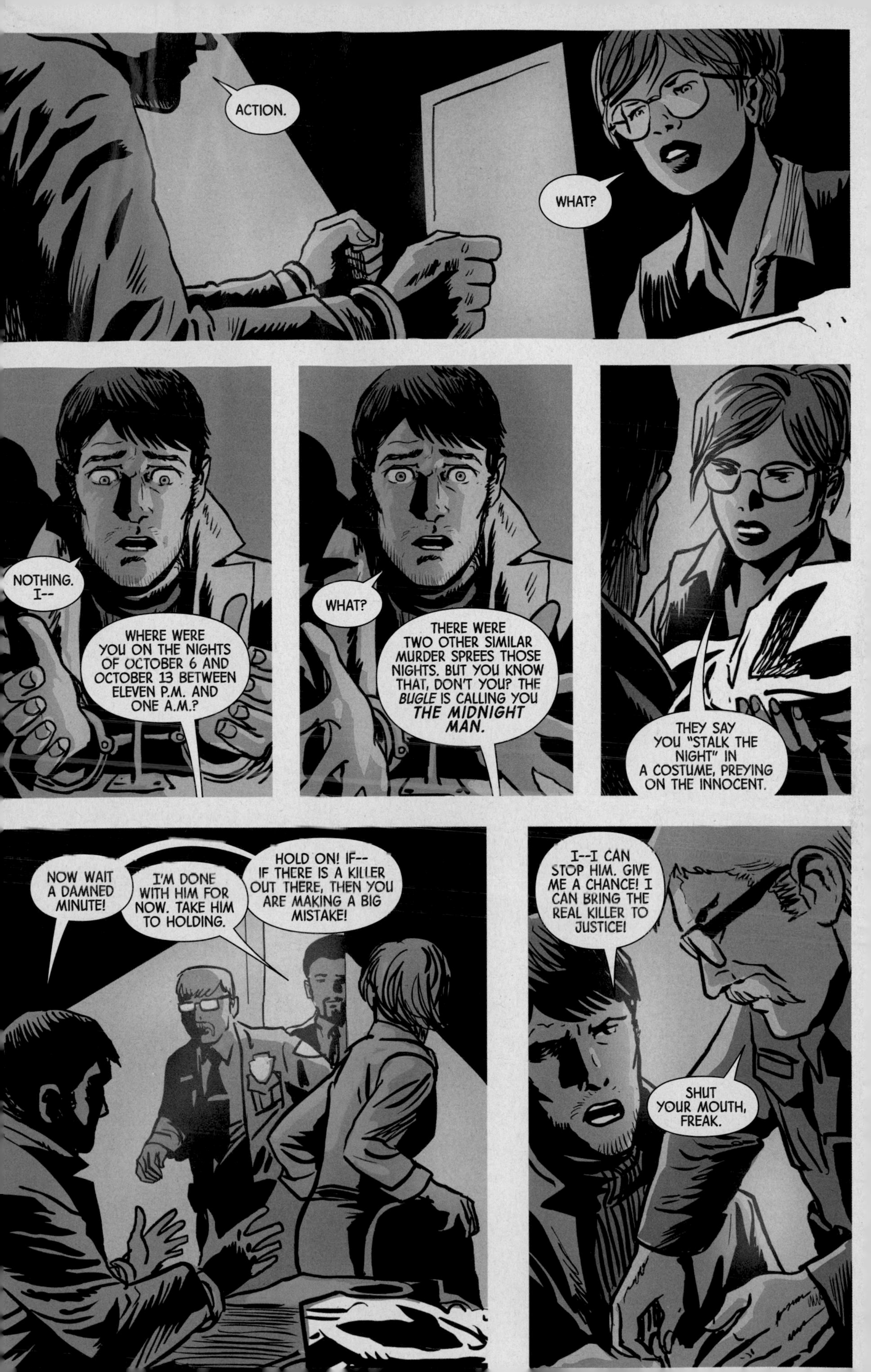
ACTION.
WHAT?
NOTHING. I--
WHERE WERE YOU ON THE NIGHTS OF OCTOBER 6 AND OCTOBER 13 BETWEEN ELEVEN P.M. AND ONE A.M.?
WHAT?
THERE WERE TWO OTHER SIMILAR MURDER SPREES THOSE NIGHTS. BUT YOU KNOW THAT, DON'T YOU? THE *BUGLE* IS CALLING YOU ***THE MIDNIGHT MAN.***
THEY SAY YOU "STALK THE NIGHT" IN A COSTUME, PREYING ON THE INNOCENT.
NOW WAIT A DAMNED MINUTE!
I'M DONE WITH HIM FOR NOW. TAKE HIM TO HOLDING.
HOLD ON! IF-- IF THERE IS A KILLER OUT THERE, THEN YOU ARE MAKING A BIG MISTAKE!
I--I CAN STOP HIM. GIVE ME A CHANCE! I CAN BRING THE REAL KILLER TO JUSTICE!
SHUT YOUR MOUTH, FREAK.

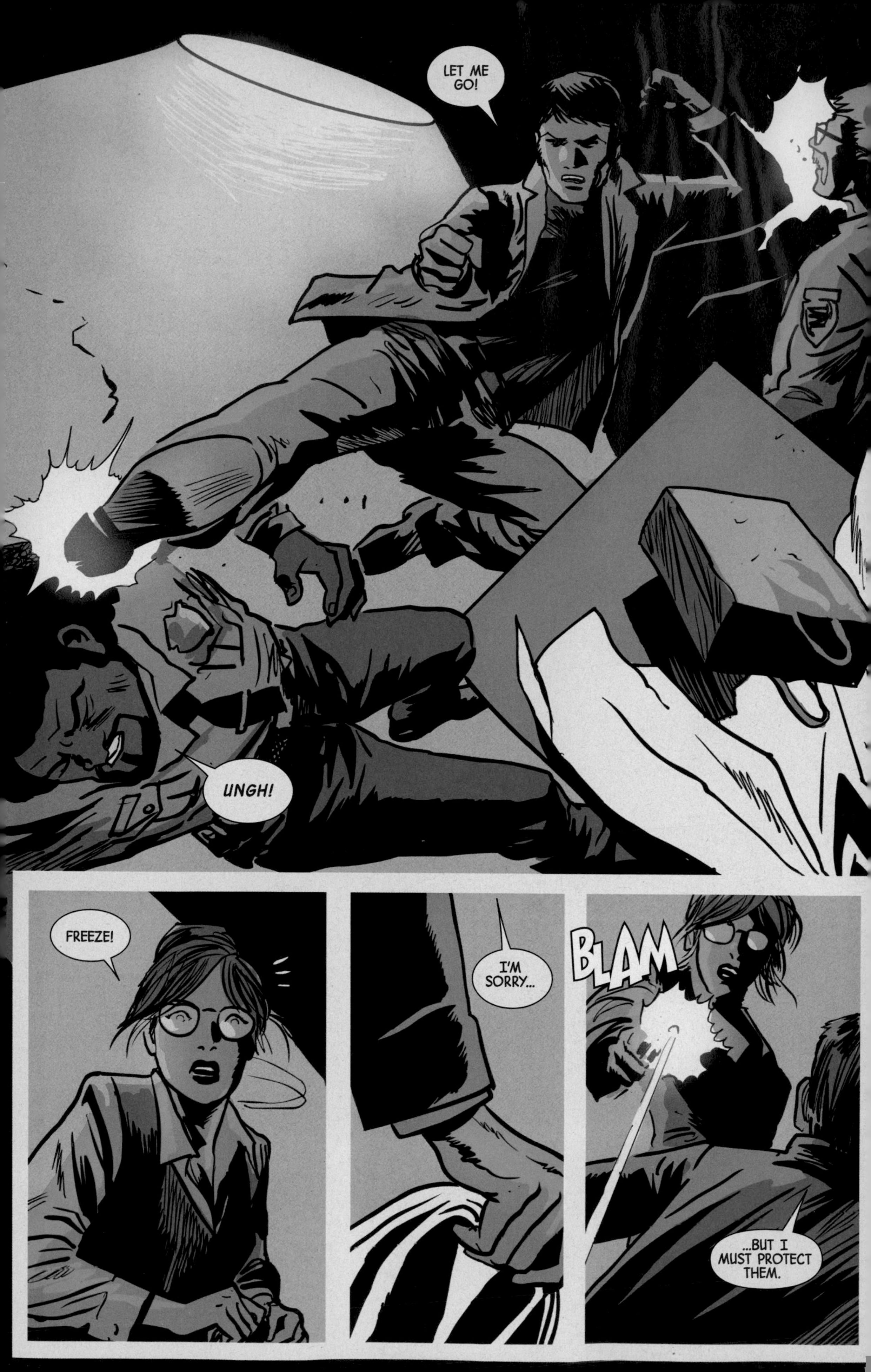
LET ME GO!
UNGH!
FREEZE!
I'M SORRY...
BLAM
...BUT I MUST PROTECT THEM.

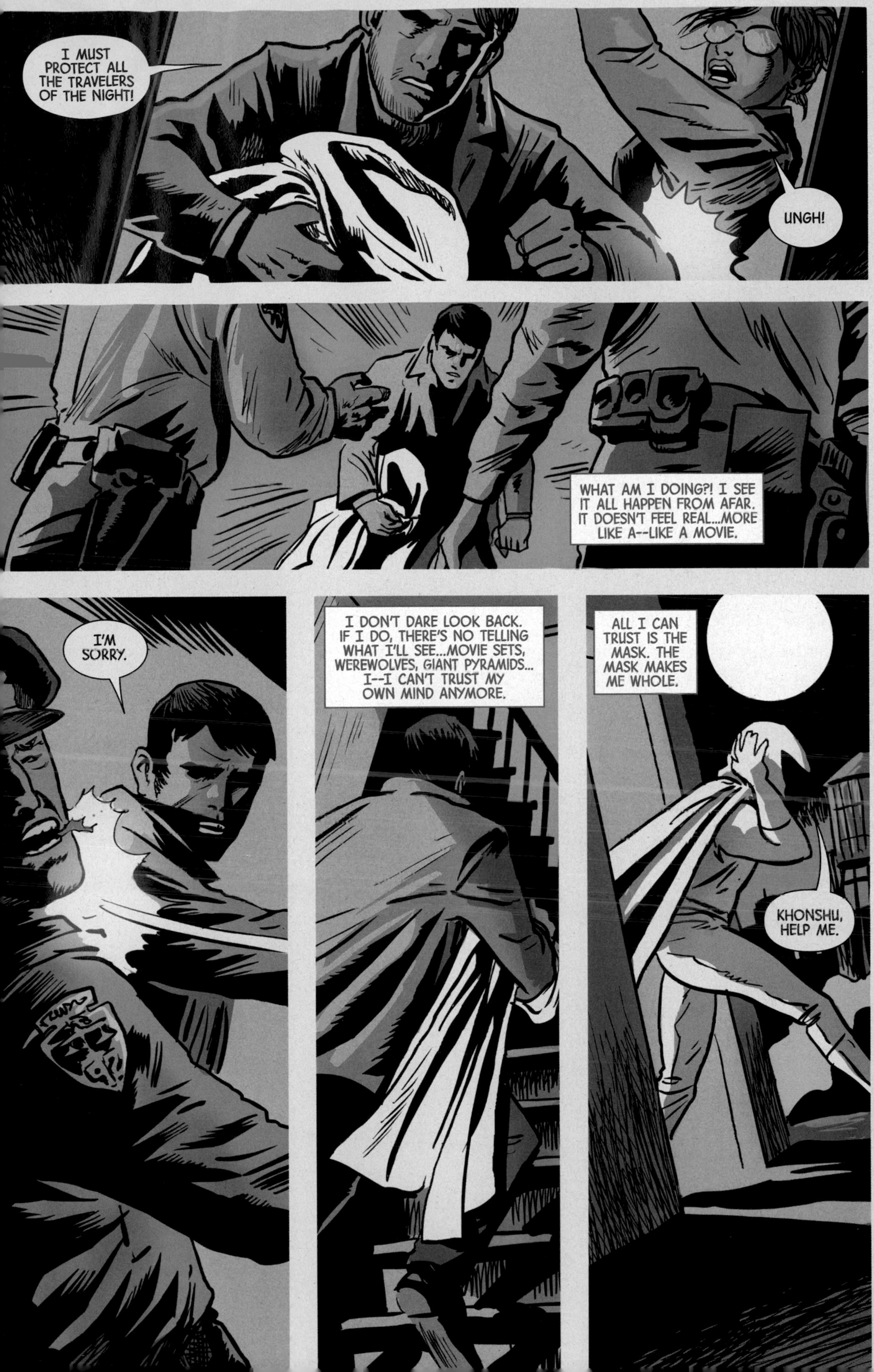
I MUST PROTECT ALL THE TRAVELERS OF THE NIGHT!
UNGH!
WHAT AM I DOING?! I SEE IT ALL HAPPEN FROM AFAR. IT DOESN'T FEEL REAL...MORE LIKE A--LIKE A MOVIE.
I'M SORRY.
I DON'T DARE LOOK BACK. IF I DO, THERE'S NO TELLING WHAT I'LL SEE...MOVIE SETS, WEREWOLVES, GIANT PYRAMIDS... I--I CAN'T TRUST MY OWN MIND ANYMORE.
ALL I CAN TRUST IS THE MASK. THE MASK MAKES ME WHOLE.
KHONSHU, HELP ME.

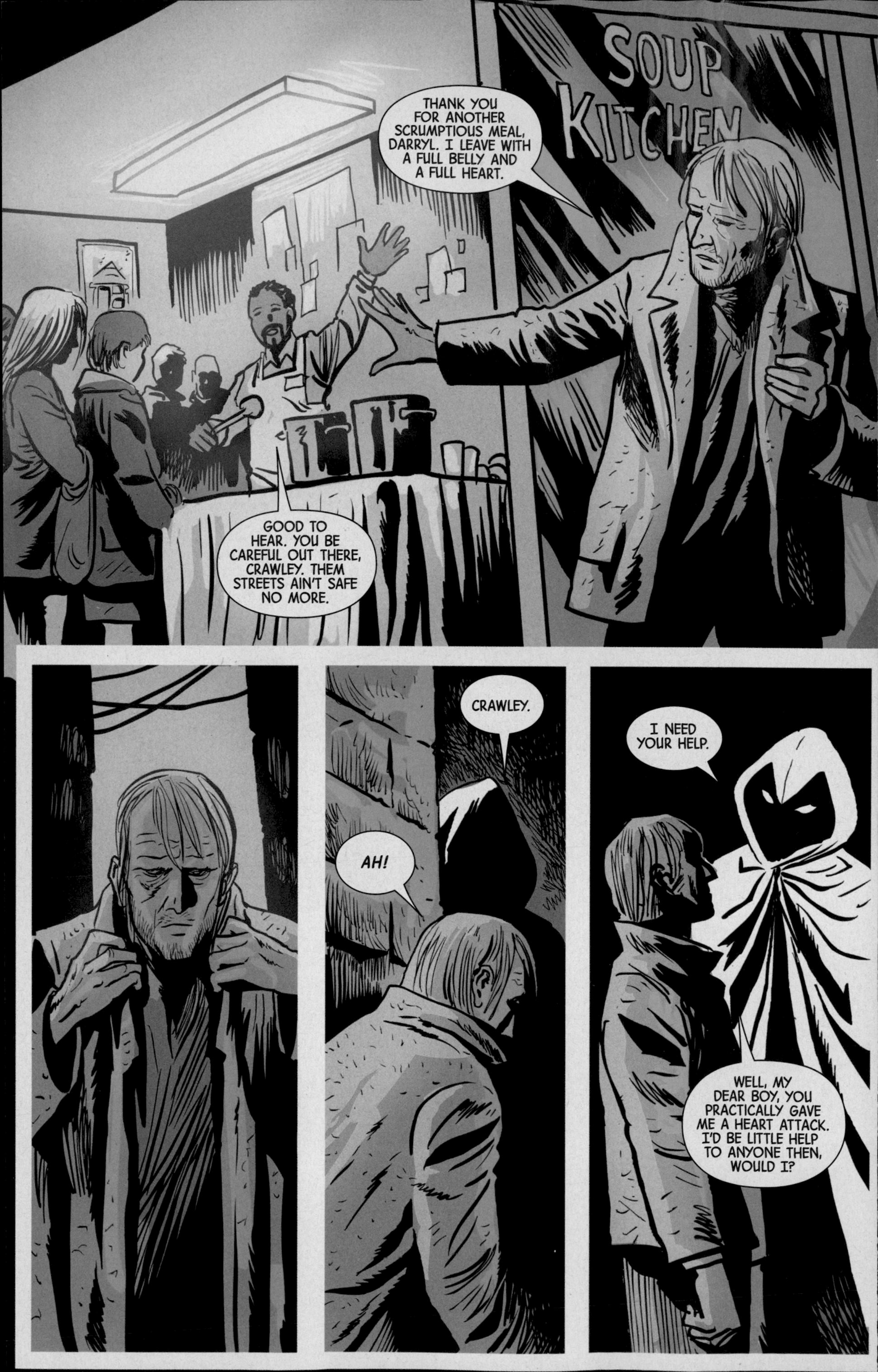
SOUP KITCHEN
THANK YOU FOR ANOTHER SCRUMPTIOUS MEAL, DARRYL. I LEAVE WITH A FULL BELLY AND A FULL HEART.
GOOD TO HEAR. YOU BE CAREFUL OUT THERE, CRAWLEY. THEM STREETS AIN'T SAFE NO MORE.
CRAWLEY.
AH!
I NEED YOUR HELP.
WELL, MY DEAR BOY, YOU PRACTICALLY GAVE ME A HEART ATTACK. I'D BE LITTLE HELP TO ANYONE THEN, WOULD I?

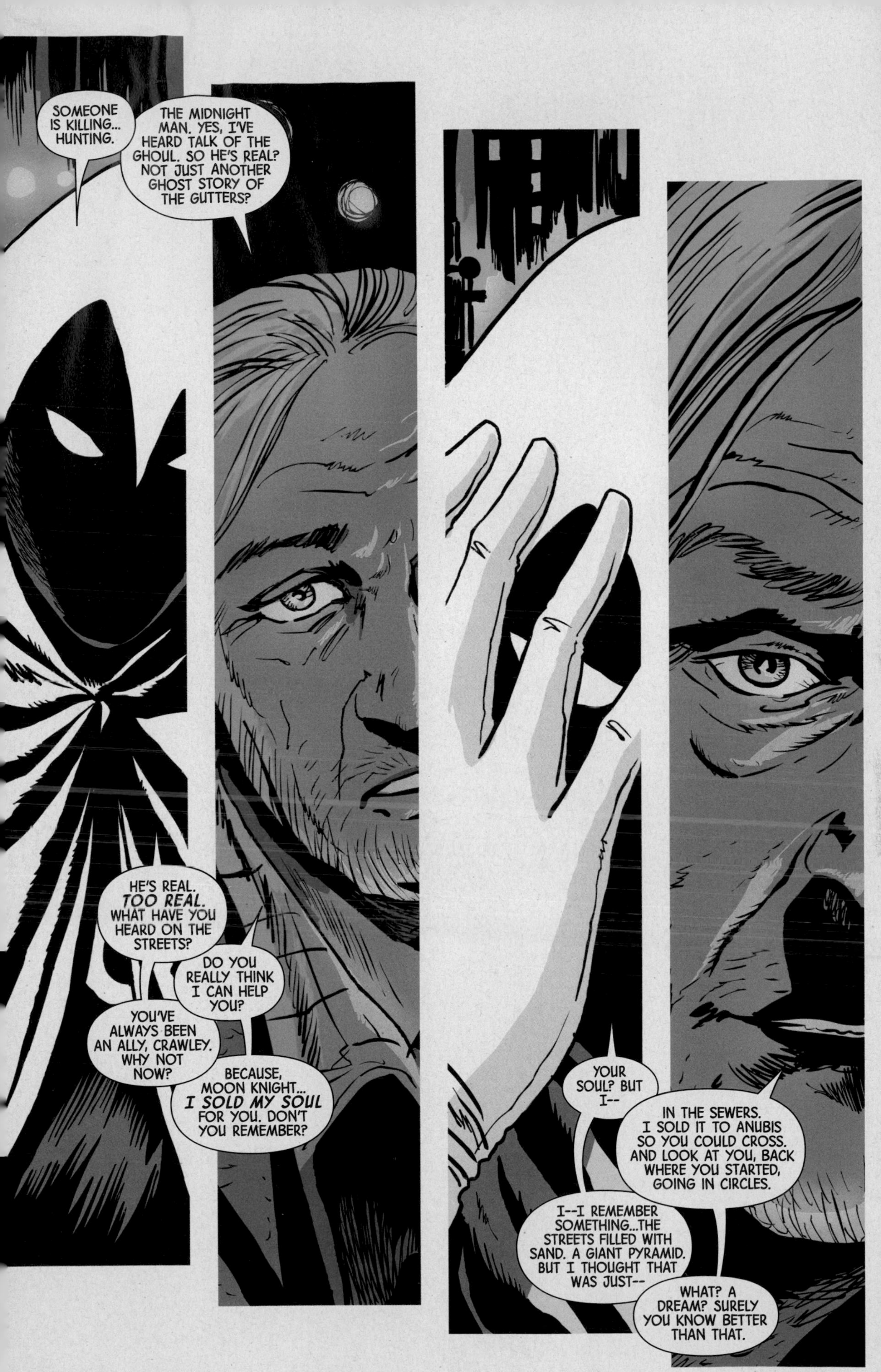
SOMEONE IS KILLING... HUNTING.
THE MIDNIGHT MAN. YES, I'VE HEARD TALK OF THE GHOUL. SO HE'S REAL? NOT JUST ANOTHER GHOST STORY OF THE GUTTERS?
HE'S REAL. *TOO REAL.* WHAT HAVE YOU HEARD ON THE STREETS?
DO YOU REALLY THINK I CAN HELP YOU?
YOU'VE ALWAYS BEEN AN ALLY, CRAWLEY. WHY NOT NOW?
BECAUSE, MOON KNIGHT... *I SOLD MY SOUL* FOR YOU. DON'T YOU REMEMBER?
YOUR SOUL? BUT I--
IN THE SEWERS. I SOLD IT TO ANUBIS SO YOU COULD CROSS. AND LOOK AT YOU, BACK WHERE YOU STARTED, GOING IN CIRCLES.
I--I REMEMBER SOMETHING...THE STREETS FILLED WITH SAND. A GIANT PYRAMID. BUT I THOUGHT THAT WAS JUST--
WHAT? A DREAM? SURELY YOU KNOW BETTER THAN THAT.

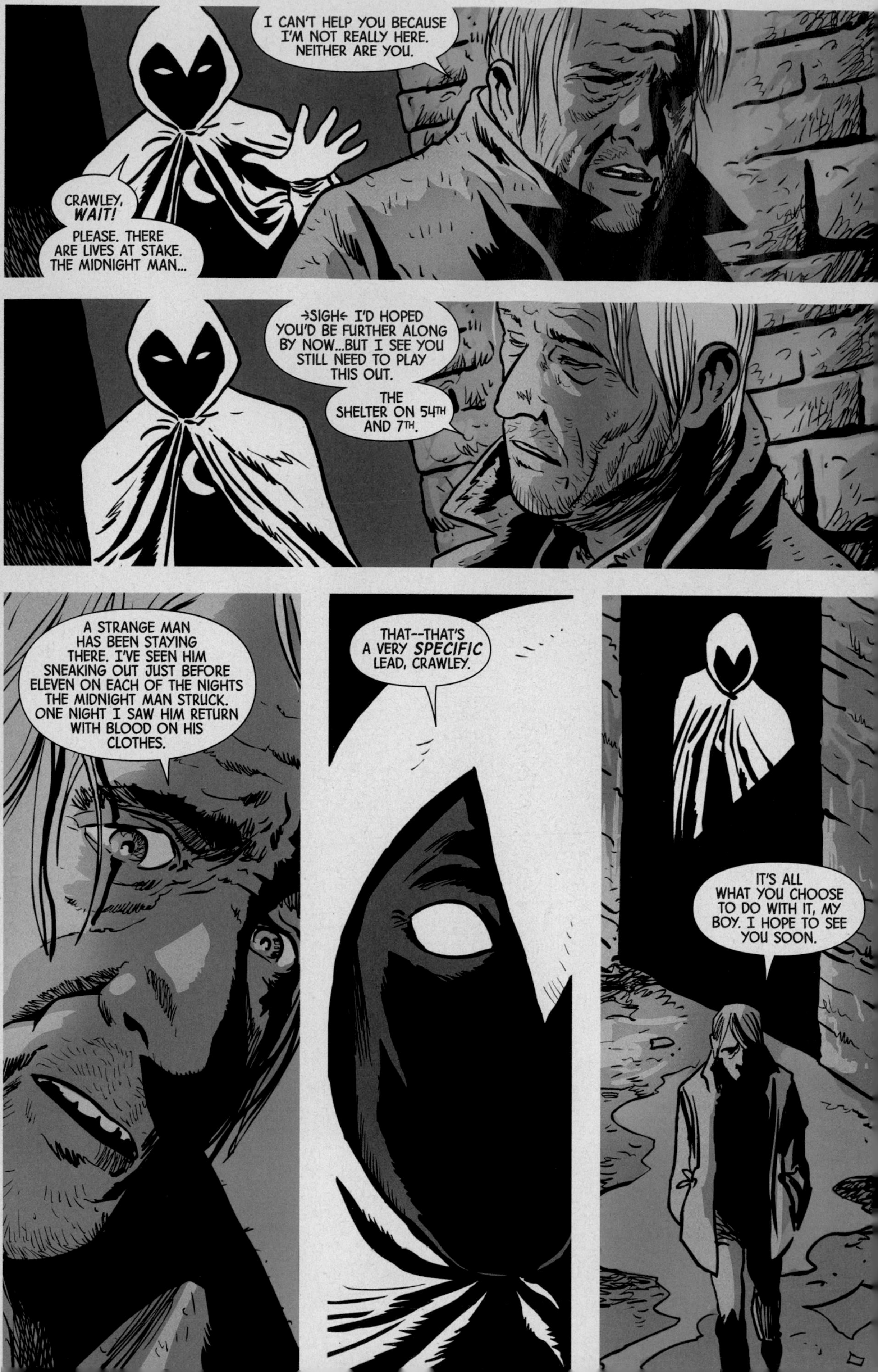
I CAN'T HELP YOU BECAUSE I'M NOT REALLY HERE. NEITHER ARE YOU.
CRAWLEY, WAIT!
PLEASE. THERE ARE LIVES AT STAKE. THE MIDNIGHT MAN...
>SIGH< I'D HOPED YOU'D BE FURTHER ALONG BY NOW...BUT I SEE YOU STILL NEED TO PLAY THIS OUT.
THE SHELTER ON 54TH AND 7TH.
A STRANGE MAN HAS BEEN STAYING THERE. I'VE SEEN HIM SNEAKING OUT JUST BEFORE ELEVEN ON EACH OF THE NIGHTS THE MIDNIGHT MAN STRUCK. ONE NIGHT I SAW HIM RETURN WITH BLOOD ON HIS CLOTHES.
THAT--THAT'S A VERY SPECIFIC LEAD, CRAWLEY.
IT'S ALL WHAT YOU CHOOSE TO DO WITH IT, MY BOY. I HOPE TO SEE YOU SOON.

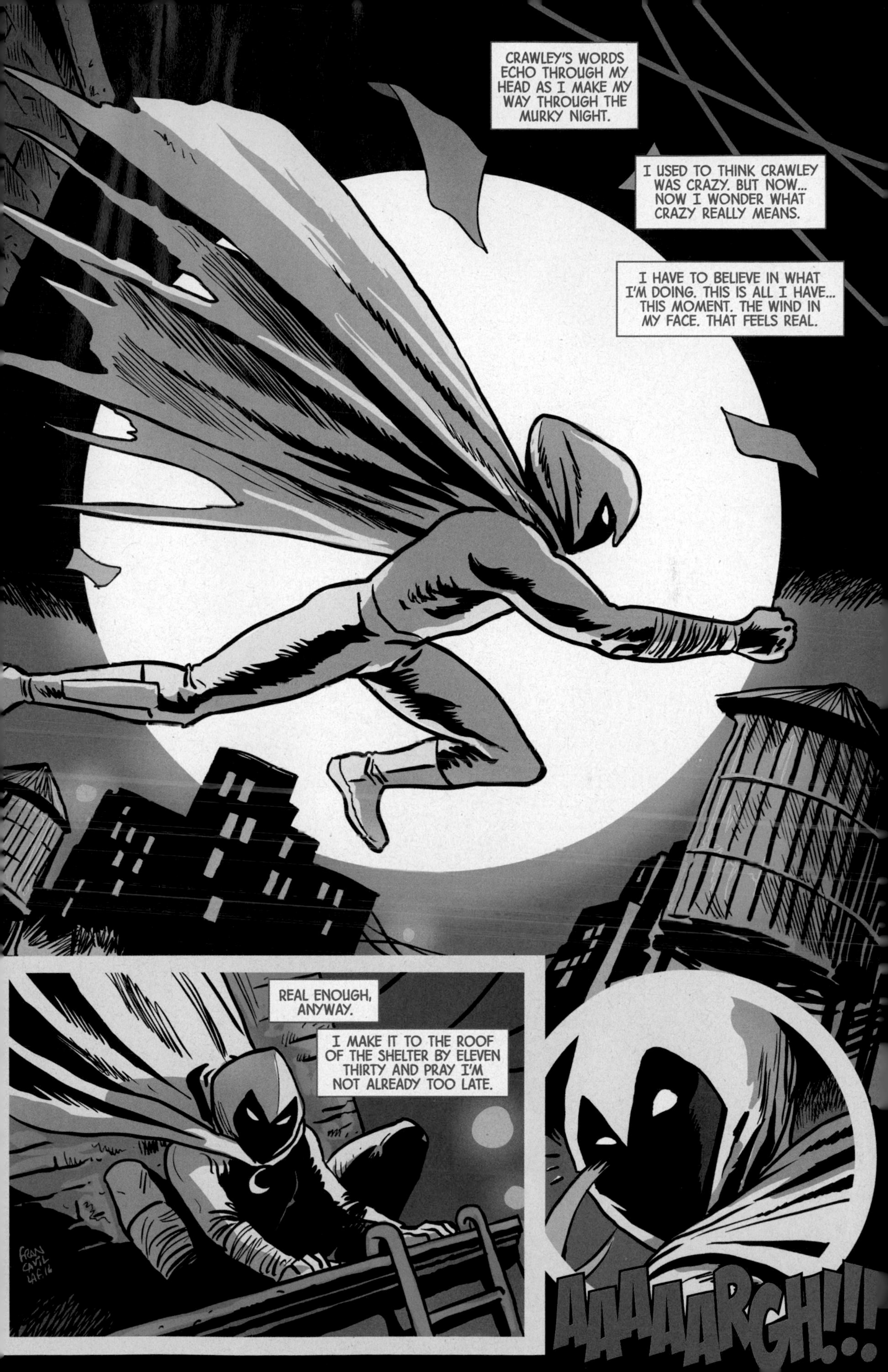
CRAWLEY'S WORDS ECHO THROUGH MY HEAD AS I MAKE MY WAY THROUGH THE MURKY NIGHT.
I USED TO THINK CRAWLEY WAS CRAZY. BUT NOW... NOW I WONDER WHAT CRAZY REALLY MEANS.
I HAVE TO BELIEVE IN WHAT I'M DOING. THIS IS ALL I HAVE... THIS MOMENT. THE WIND IN MY FACE. THAT FEELS REAL.
REAL ENOUGH, ANYWAY.
I MAKE IT TO THE ROOF OF THE SHELTER BY ELEVEN THIRTY AND PRAY I'M NOT ALREADY TOO LATE.
FRAN CAVIL LAF. '16
AAAAAARGH!!!

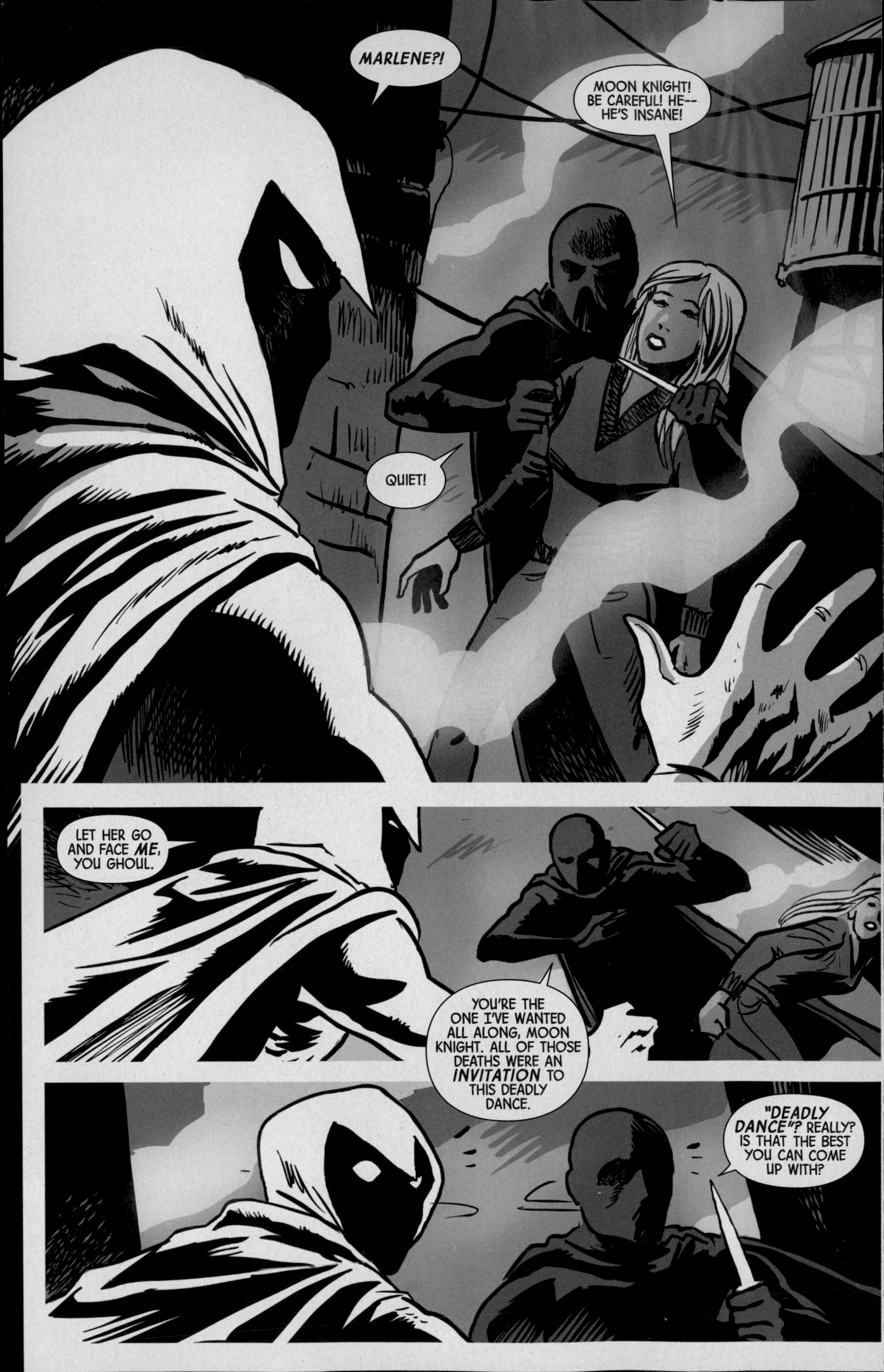
MARLENE?!
MOON KNIGHT! BE CAREFUL! HE-- HE'S INSANE!
QUIET!
LET HER GO AND FACE *ME*, YOU GHOUL.
YOU'RE THE ONE I'VE WANTED ALL ALONG, MOON KNIGHT. ALL OF THOSE DEATHS WERE AN *INVITATION* TO THIS DEADLY DANCE.
"DEADLY DANCE"? REALLY? IS THAT THE BEST YOU CAN COME UP WITH?

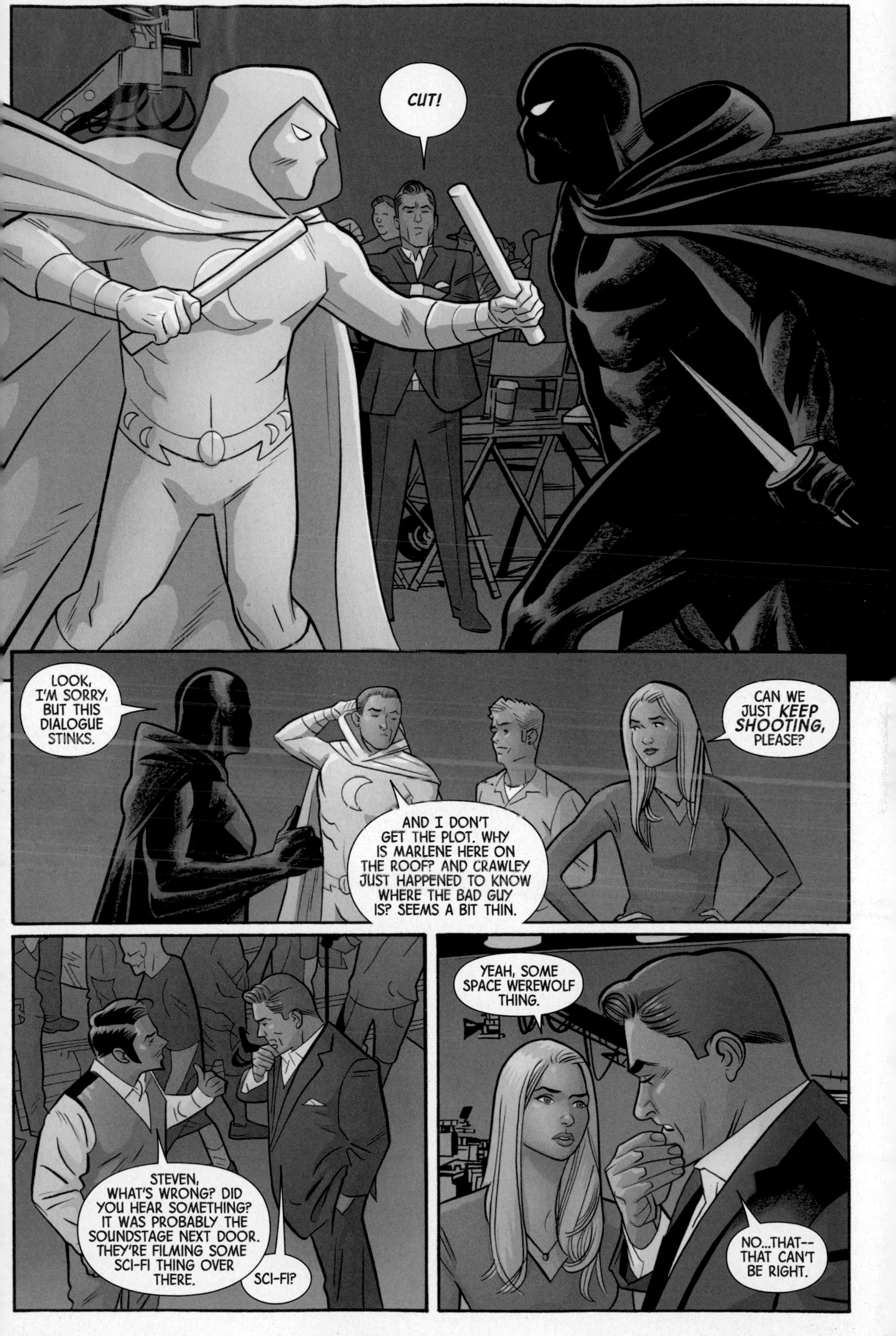
CUT!
LOOK, I'M SORRY, BUT THIS DIALOGUE STINKS.
CAN WE JUST KEEP SHOOTING, PLEASE?
AND I DON'T GET THE PLOT. WHY IS MARLENE HERE ON THE ROOF? AND CRAWLEY JUST HAPPENED TO KNOW WHERE THE BAD GUY IS? SEEMS A BIT THIN.
STEVEN, WHAT'S WRONG? DID YOU HEAR SOMETHING? IT WAS PROBABLY THE SOUNDSTAGE NEXT DOOR. THEY'RE FILMING SOME SCI-FI THING OVER THERE.
SCI-FI?
YEAH, SOME SPACE WEREWOLF THING.
NO...THAT-- THAT CAN'T BE RIGHT.

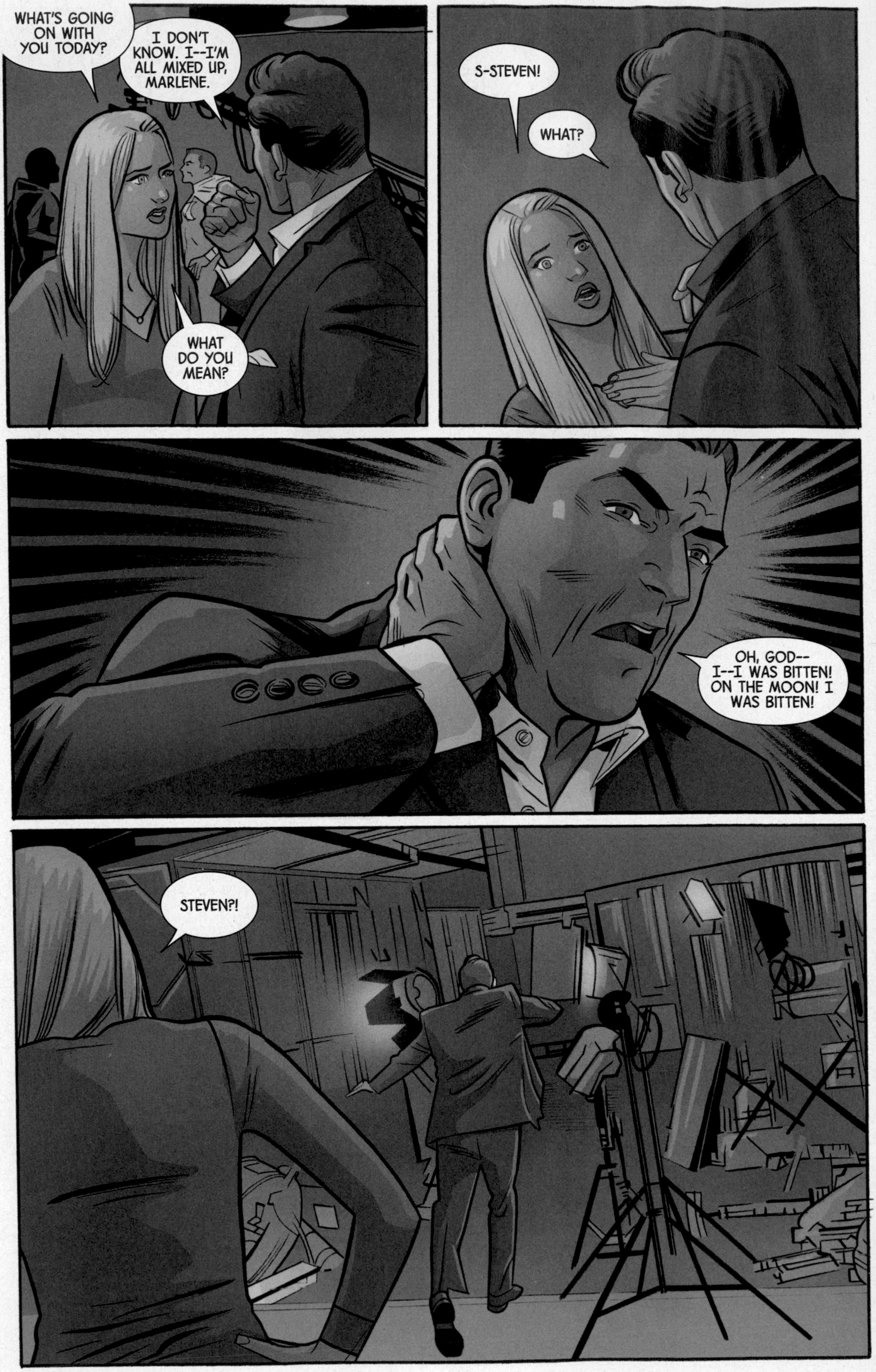
WHAT'S GOING ON WITH YOU TODAY?
I DON'T KNOW. I--I'M ALL MIXED UP, MARLENE.
WHAT DO YOU MEAN?
S-STEVEN!
WHAT?
OH, GOD-- I--I WAS BITTEN! ON THE MOON! I WAS BITTEN!
STEVEN?!

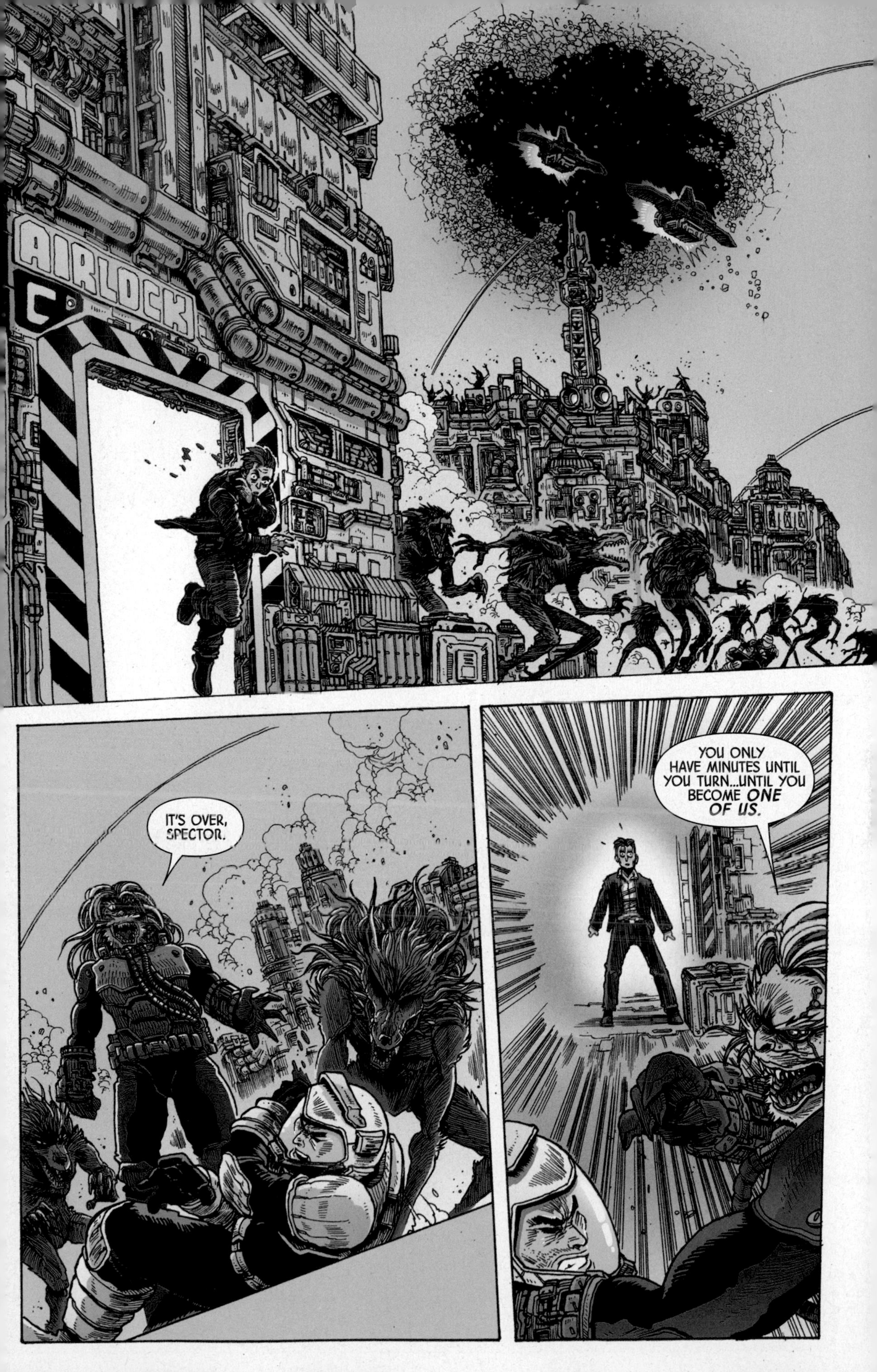
AIRLOCK
C
IT'S OVER, SPECTOR.
YOU ONLY HAVE MINUTES UNTIL YOU TURN...UNTIL YOU BECOME *ONE OF US.*

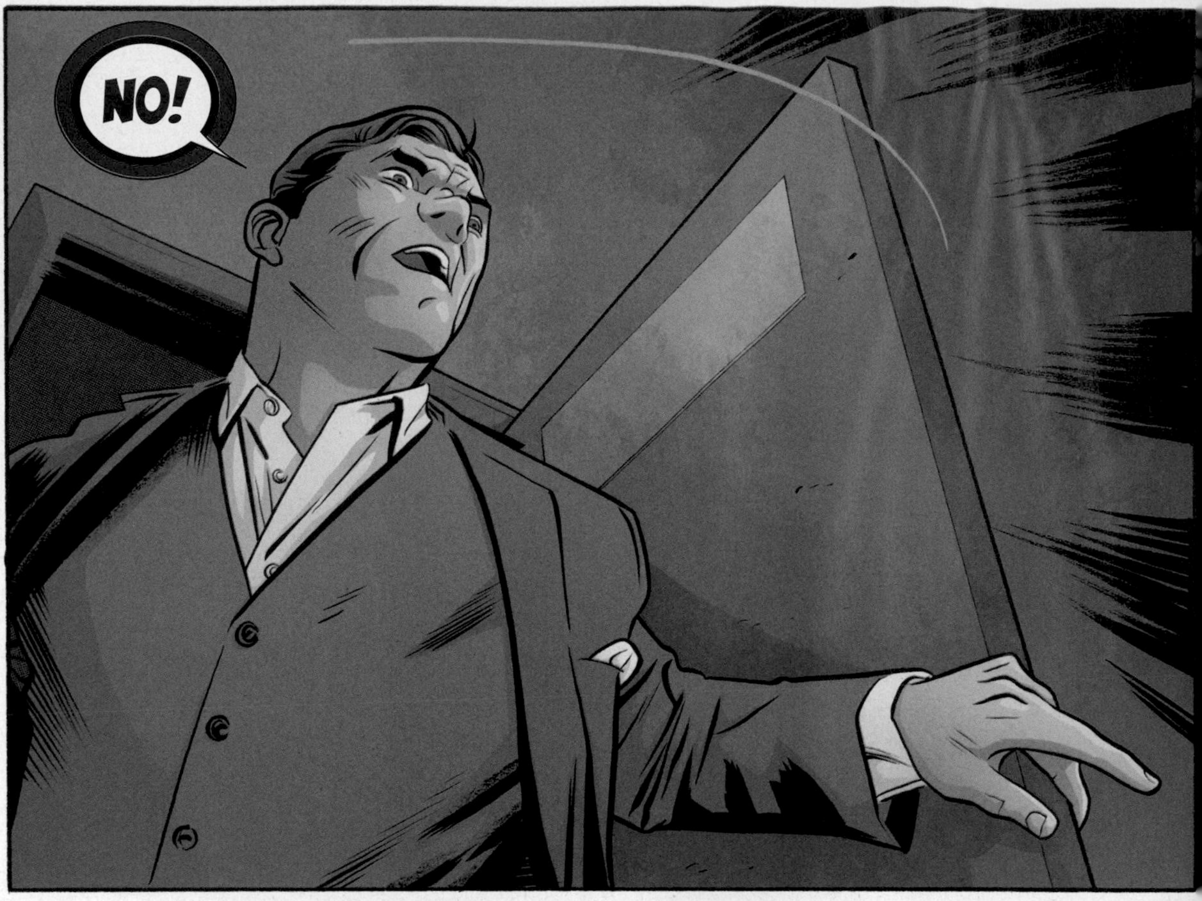
NO!

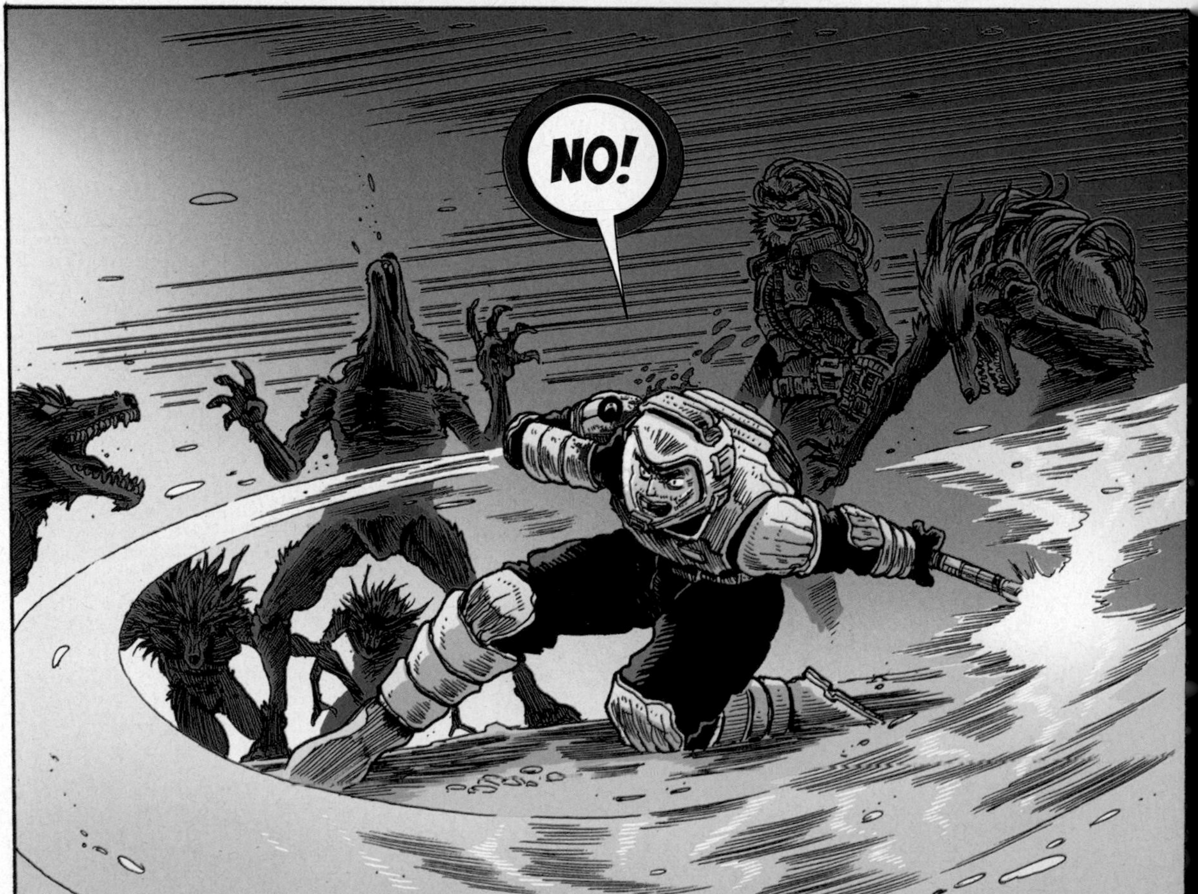
NO!

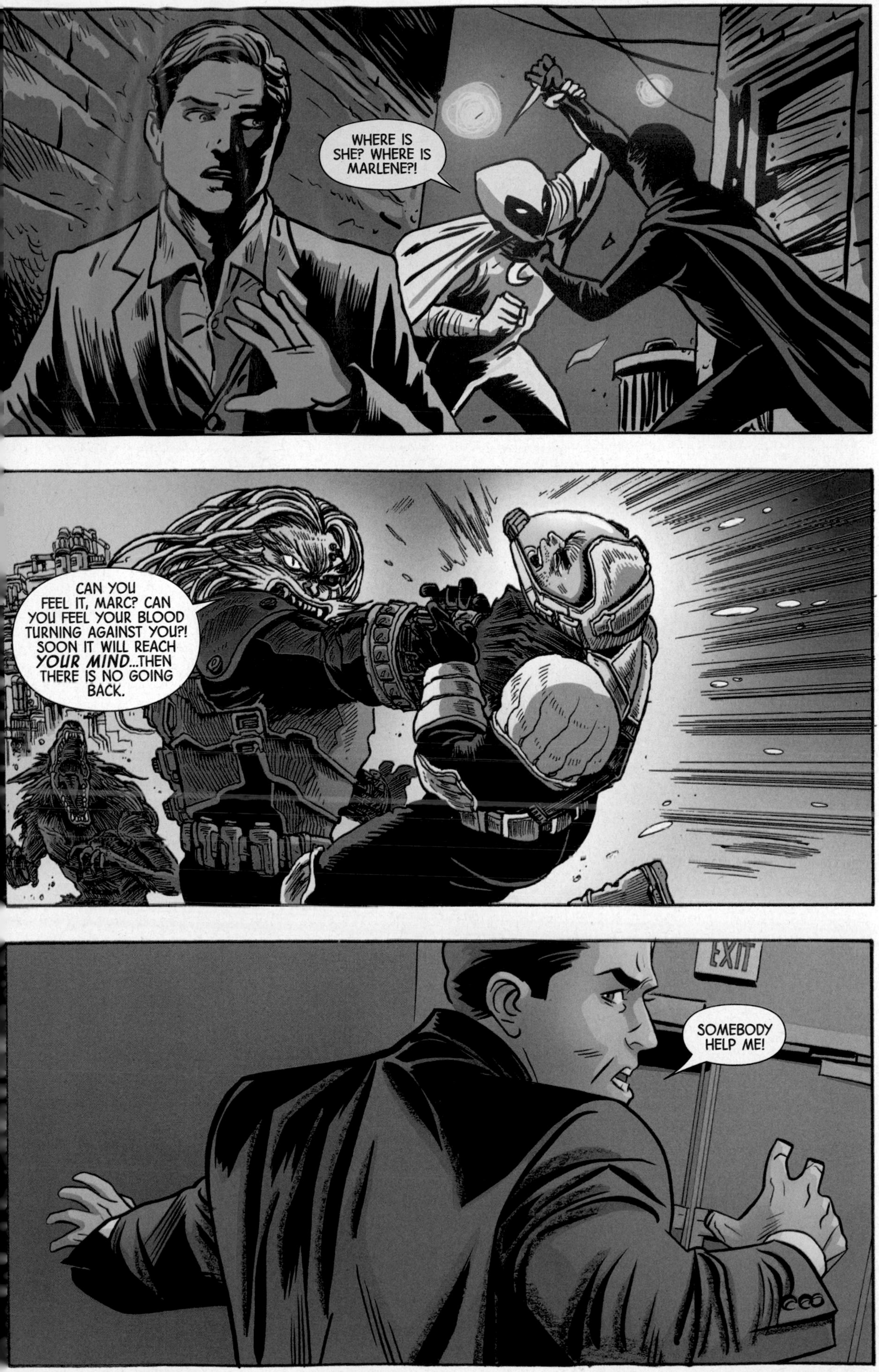
WHERE IS SHE? WHERE IS MARLENE?!
CAN YOU FEEL IT, MARC? CAN YOU FEEL YOUR BLOOD TURNING AGAINST YOU?! SOON IT WILL REACH *YOUR MIND*...THEN THERE IS NO GOING BACK.
EXIT
SOMEBODY HELP ME!

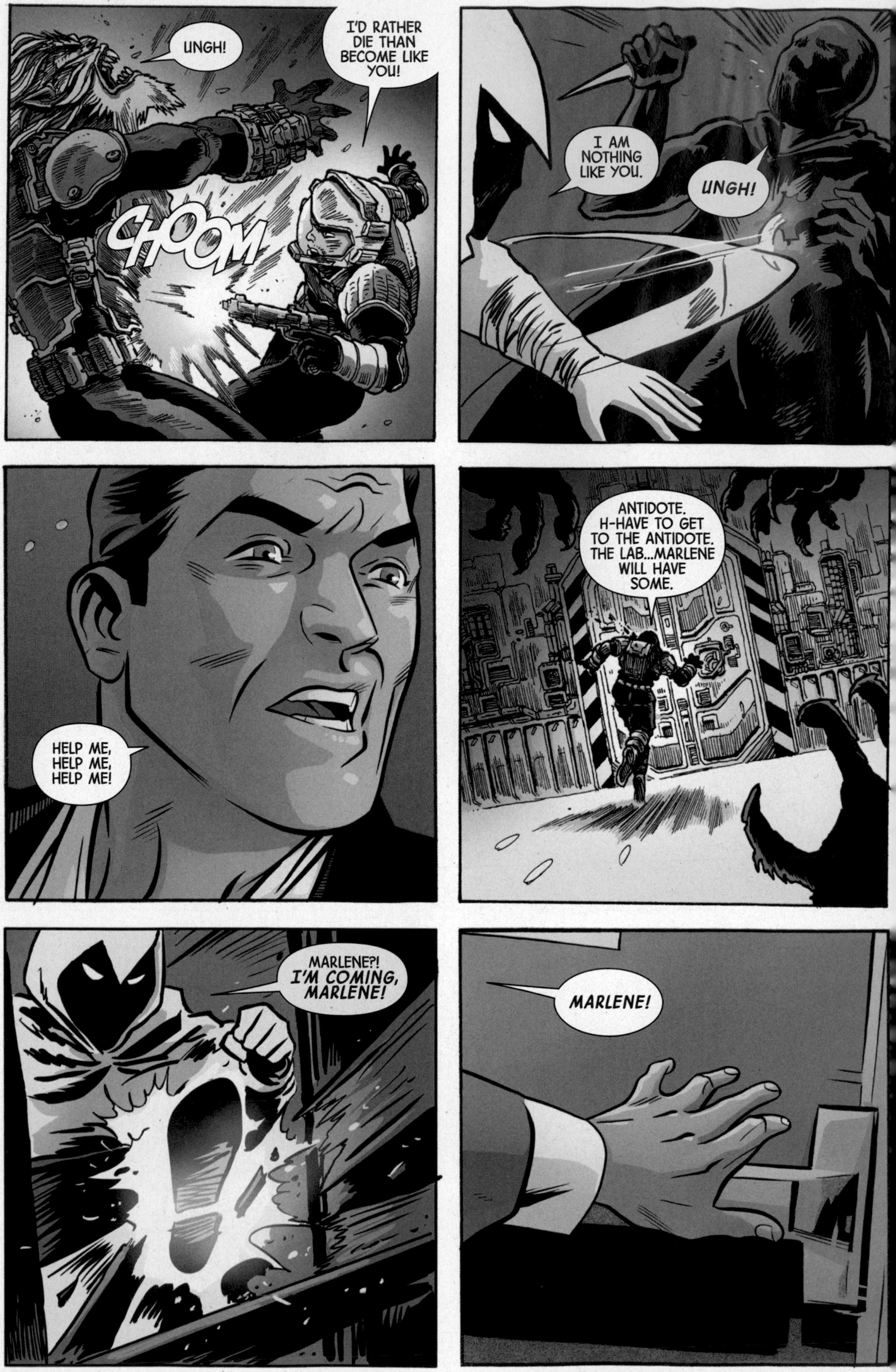
UNGH!
I'D RATHER DIE THAN BECOME LIKE YOU!
CHOOM
I AM NOTHING LIKE YOU.
UNGH!
HELP ME, HELP ME, HELP ME!
ANTIDOTE. H-HAVE TO GET TO THE ANTIDOTE. THE LAB...MARLENE WILL HAVE SOME.
MARLENE?! I'M COMING, MARLENE!
MARLENE!

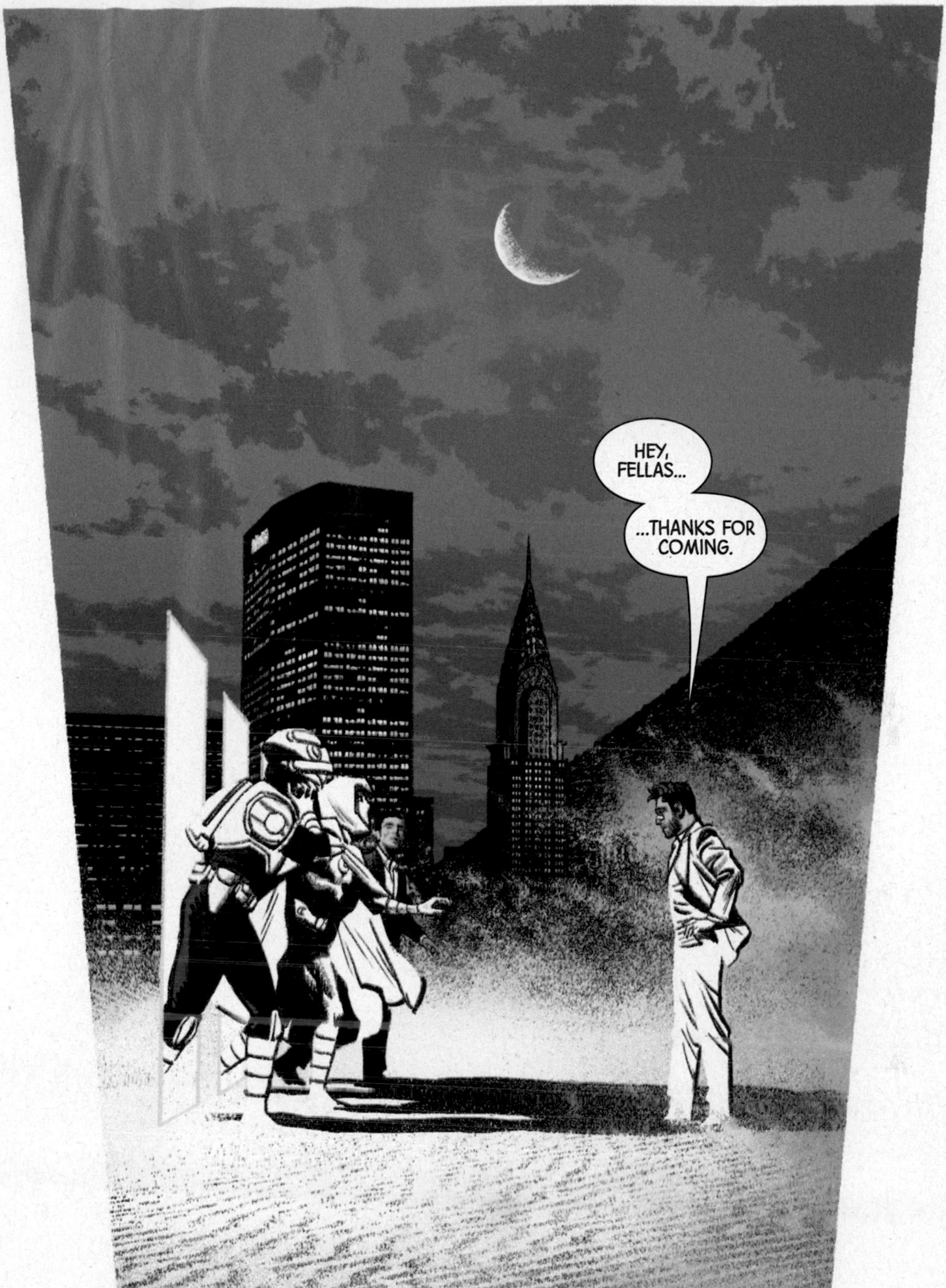
HEY, FELLAS...
...THANKS FOR COMING.
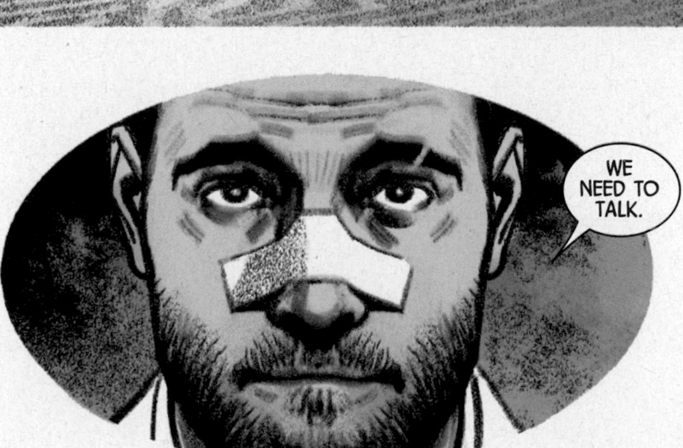
WE NEED TO TALK.

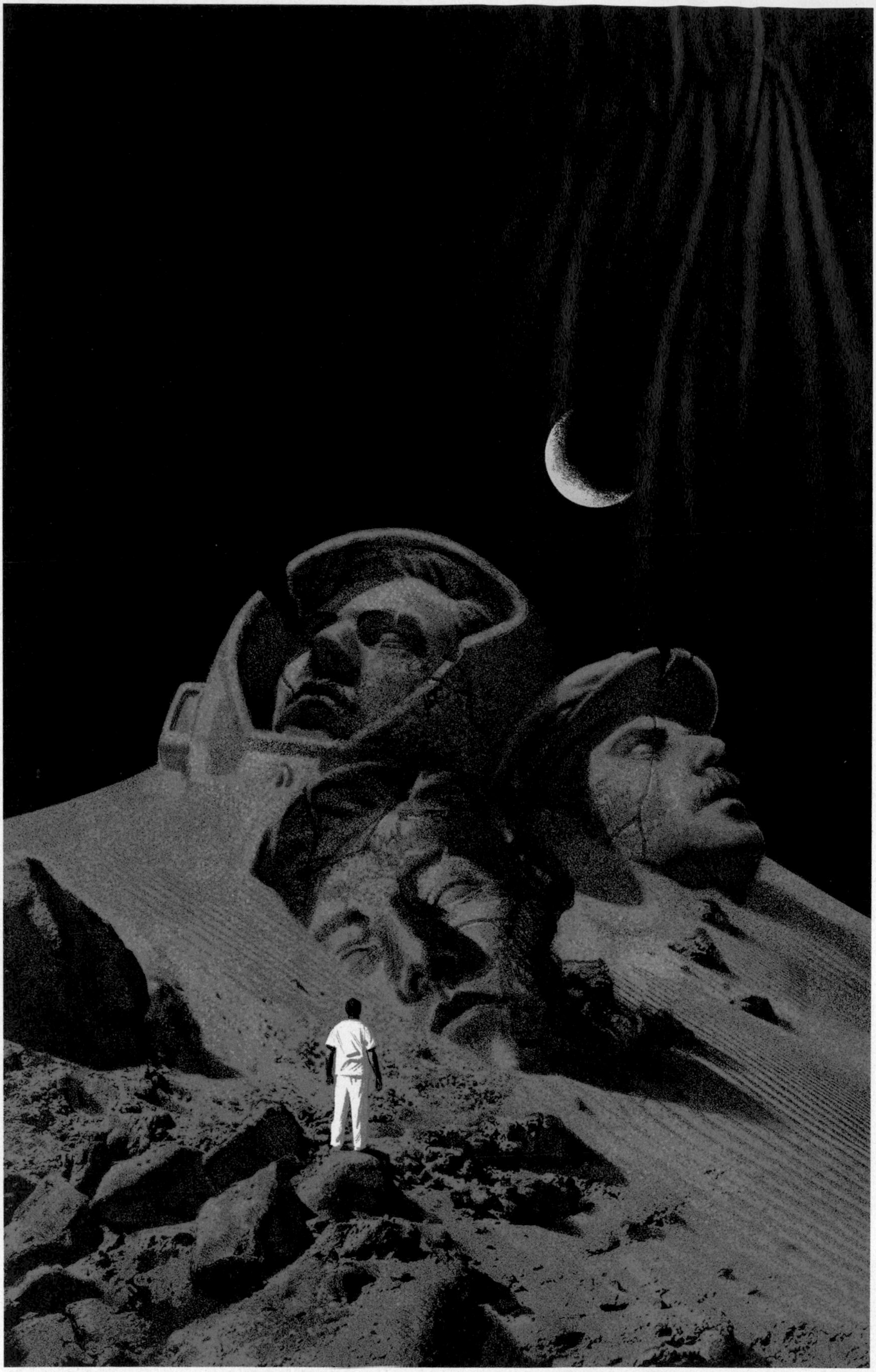

INCARNATIONS
PART FOUR

9

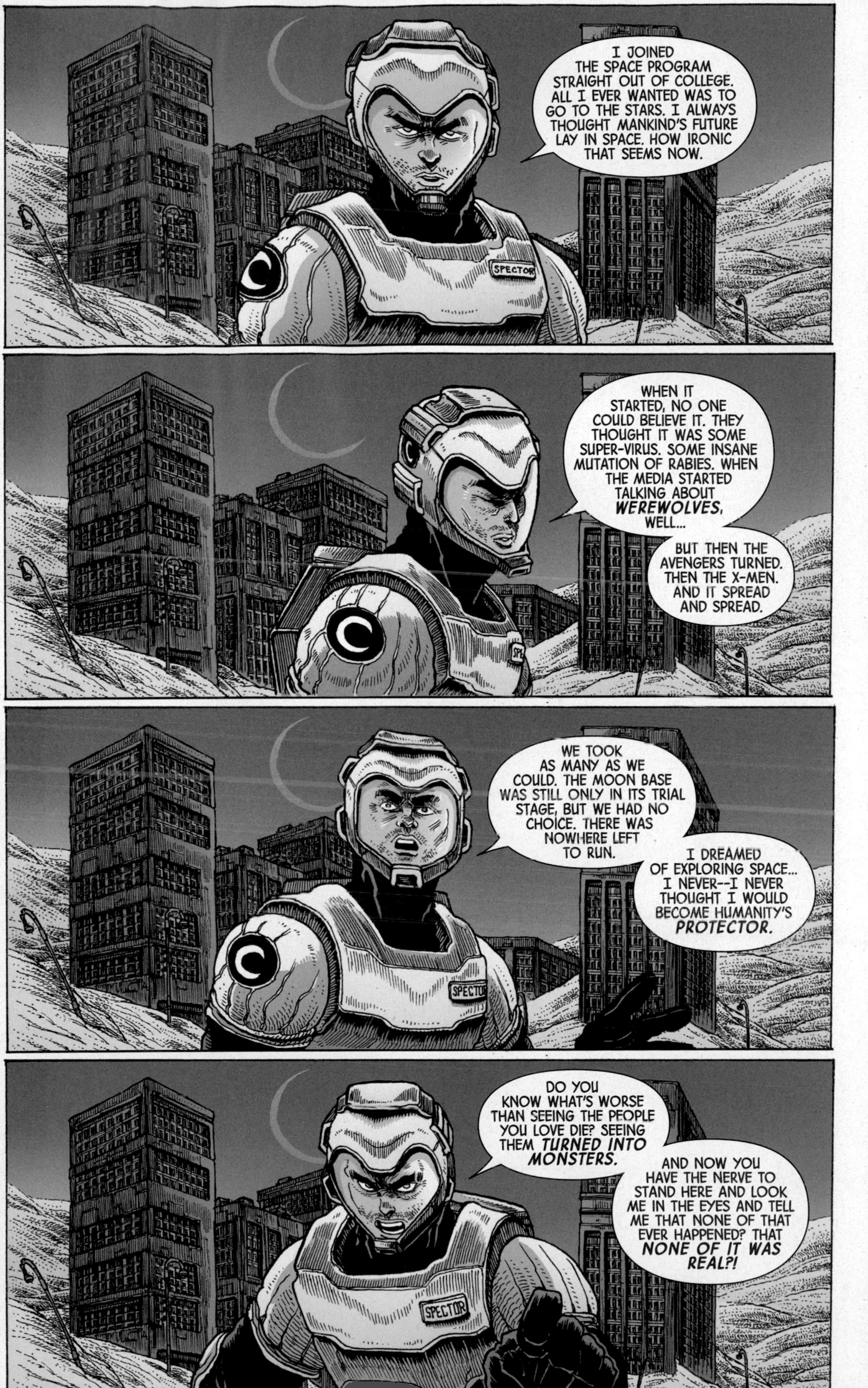
I JOINED THE SPACE PROGRAM STRAIGHT OUT OF COLLEGE. ALL I EVER WANTED WAS TO GO TO THE STARS. I ALWAYS THOUGHT MANKIND'S FUTURE LAY IN SPACE. HOW IRONIC THAT SEEMS NOW.
SPECTOR
WHEN IT STARTED, NO ONE COULD BELIEVE IT. THEY THOUGHT IT WAS SOME SUPER-VIRUS. SOME INSANE MUTATION OF RABIES. WHEN THE MEDIA STARTED TALKING ABOUT WEREWOLVES, WELL...
BUT THEN THE AVENGERS TURNED. THEN THE X-MEN. AND IT SPREAD AND SPREAD.
WE TOOK AS MANY AS WE COULD. THE MOON BASE WAS STILL ONLY IN ITS TRIAL STAGE, BUT WE HAD NO CHOICE. THERE WAS NOWHERE LEFT TO RUN.
I DREAMED OF EXPLORING SPACE... I NEVER--I NEVER THOUGHT I WOULD BECOME HUMANITY'S PROTECTOR.
SPECTOR
DO YOU KNOW WHAT'S WORSE THAN SEEING THE PEOPLE YOU LOVE DIE? SEEING THEM TURNED INTO MONSTERS.
AND NOW YOU HAVE THE NERVE TO STAND HERE AND LOOK ME IN THE EYES AND TELL ME THAT NONE OF THAT EVER HAPPENED? THAT NONE OF IT WAS REAL?!
SPECTOR

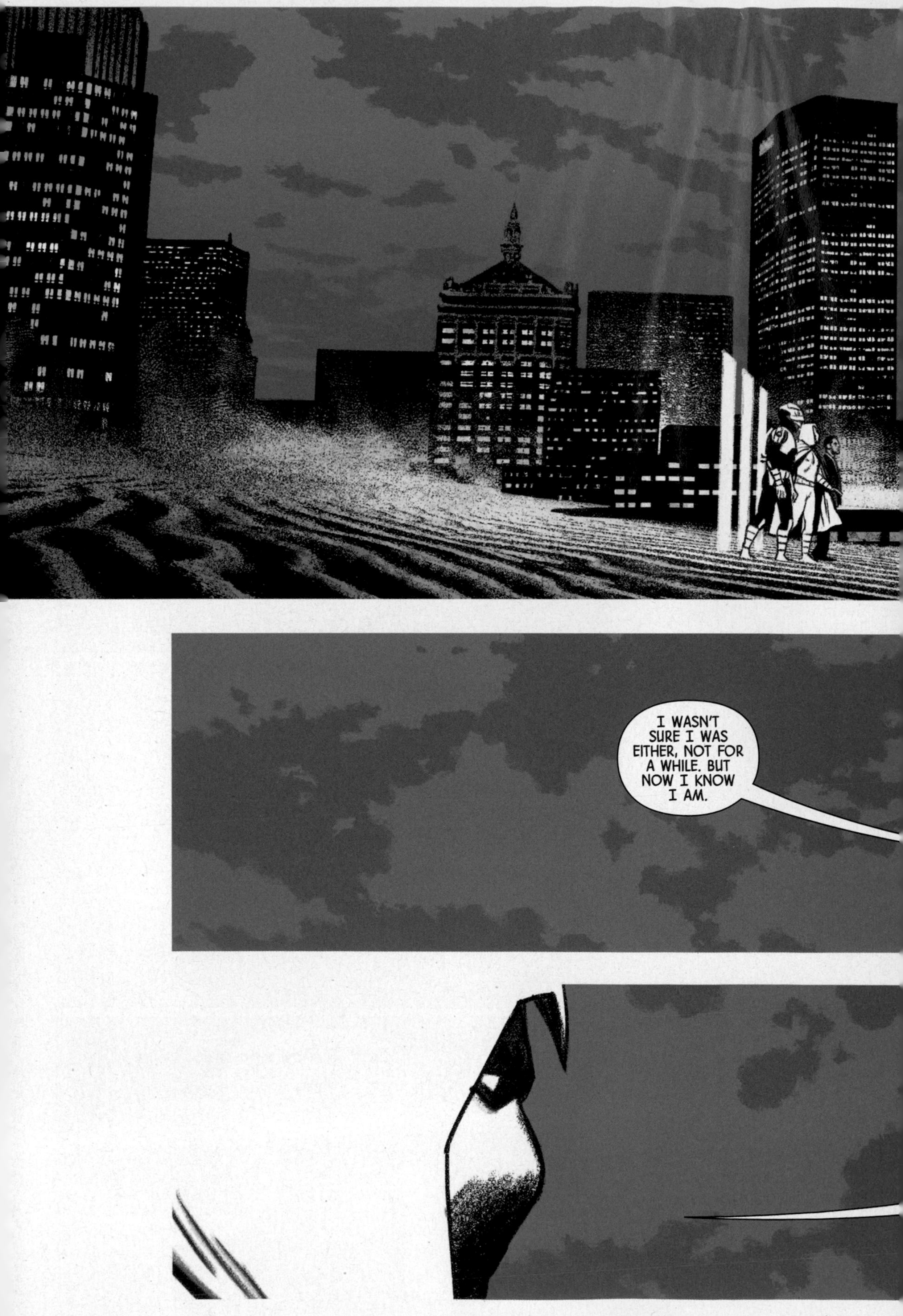
I WASN'T SURE I WAS EITHER, NOT FOR A WHILE. BUT NOW I KNOW I AM.

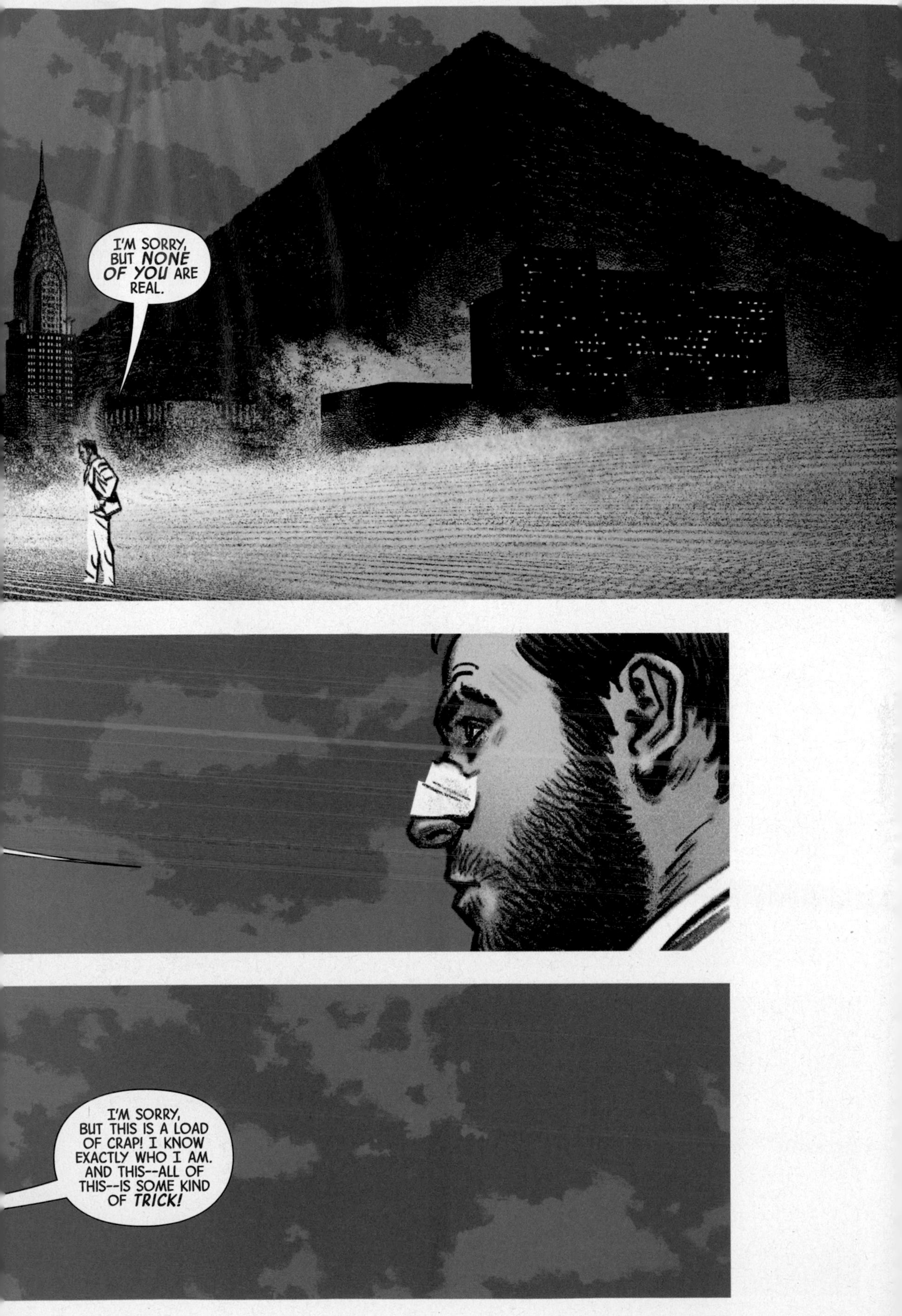
I'M SORRY, BUT NONE OF YOU ARE REAL.
I'M SORRY, BUT THIS IS A LOAD OF CRAP! I KNOW EXACTLY WHO I AM. AND THIS--ALL OF THIS--IS SOME KIND OF TRICK!

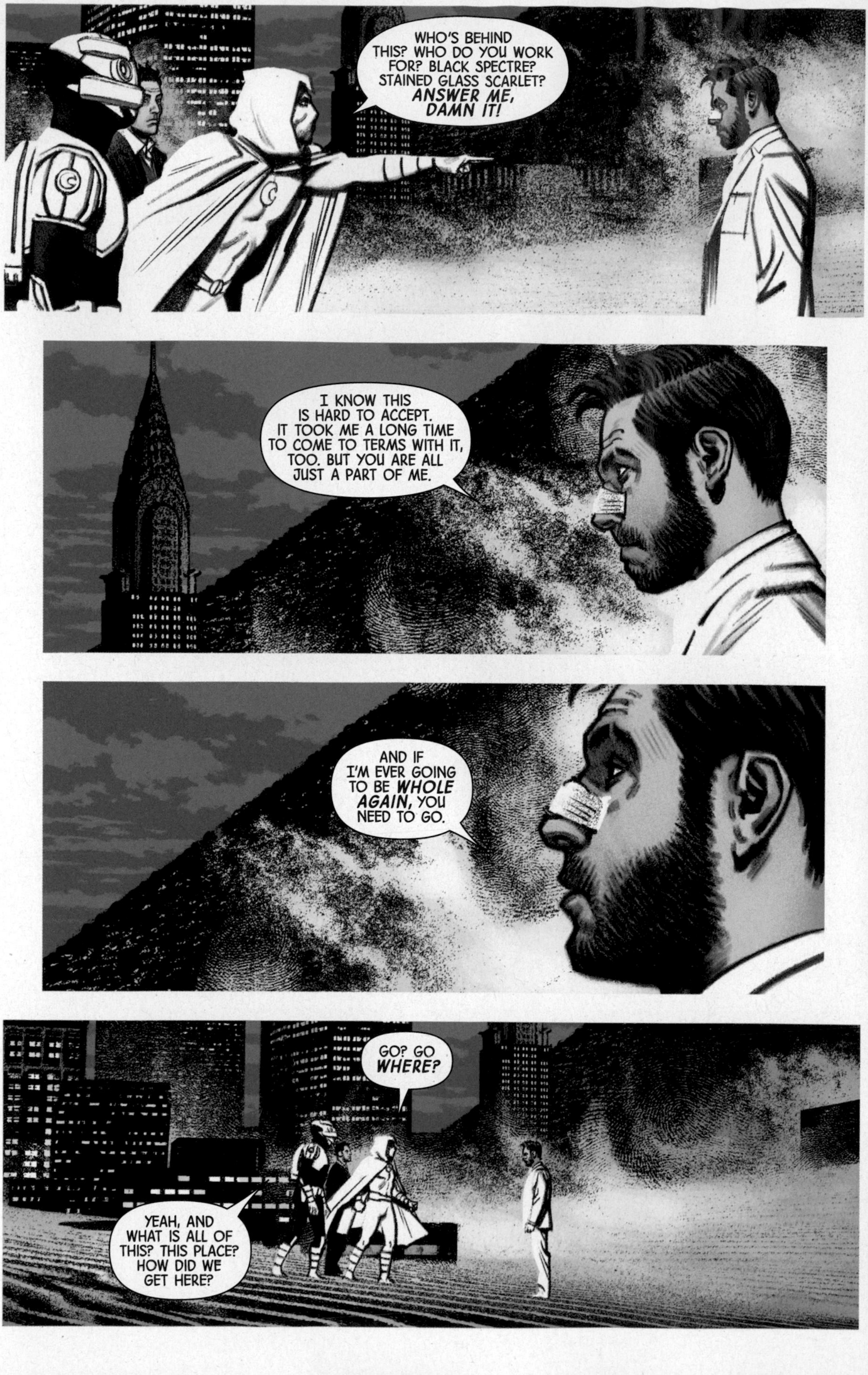
WHO'S BEHIND THIS? WHO DO YOU WORK FOR? BLACK SPECTRE? STAINED GLASS SCARLET? ANSWER ME, DAMN IT!
I KNOW THIS IS HARD TO ACCEPT. IT TOOK ME A LONG TIME TO COME TO TERMS WITH IT, TOO. BUT YOU ARE ALL JUST A PART OF ME.
AND IF I'M EVER GOING TO BE WHOLE AGAIN, YOU NEED TO GO.
GO? GO WHERE?
YEAH, AND WHAT IS ALL OF THIS? THIS PLACE? HOW DID WE GET HERE?

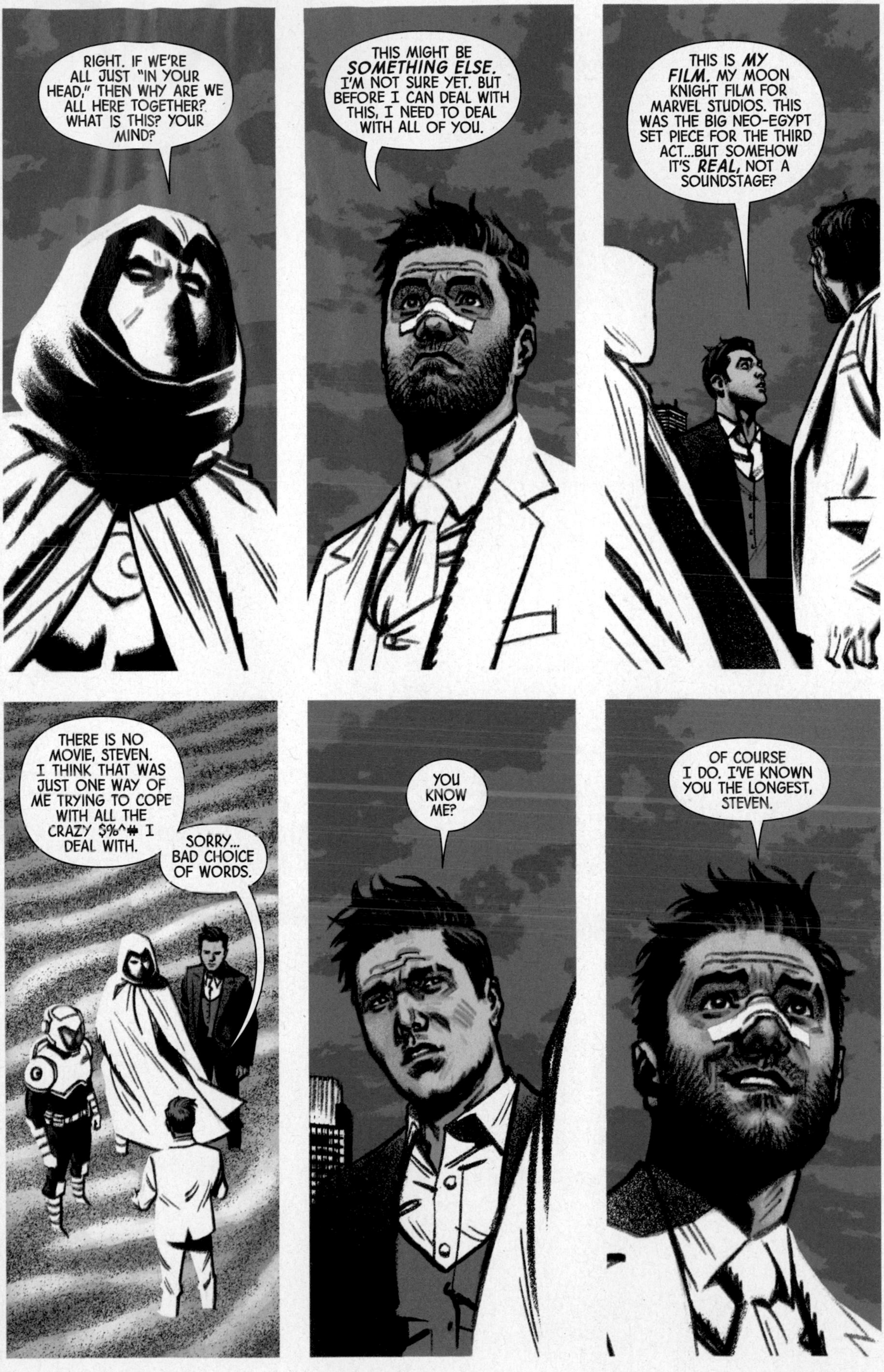
RIGHT. IF WE'RE ALL JUST "IN YOUR HEAD," THEN WHY ARE WE ALL HERE TOGETHER? WHAT IS THIS? YOUR MIND?
THIS MIGHT BE SOMETHING ELSE. I'M NOT SURE YET. BUT BEFORE I CAN DEAL WITH THIS, I NEED TO DEAL WITH ALL OF YOU.
THIS IS MY FILM. MY MOON KNIGHT FILM FOR MARVEL STUDIOS. THIS WAS THE BIG NEO-EGYPT SET PIECE FOR THE THIRD ACT...BUT SOMEHOW IT'S REAL, NOT A SOUNDSTAGE?
THERE IS NO MOVIE, STEVEN. I THINK THAT WAS JUST ONE WAY OF ME TRYING TO COPE WITH ALL THE CRAZY $%^# I DEAL WITH.
SORRY... BAD CHOICE OF WORDS.
YOU KNOW ME?
OF COURSE I DO. I'VE KNOWN YOU THE LONGEST, STEVEN.

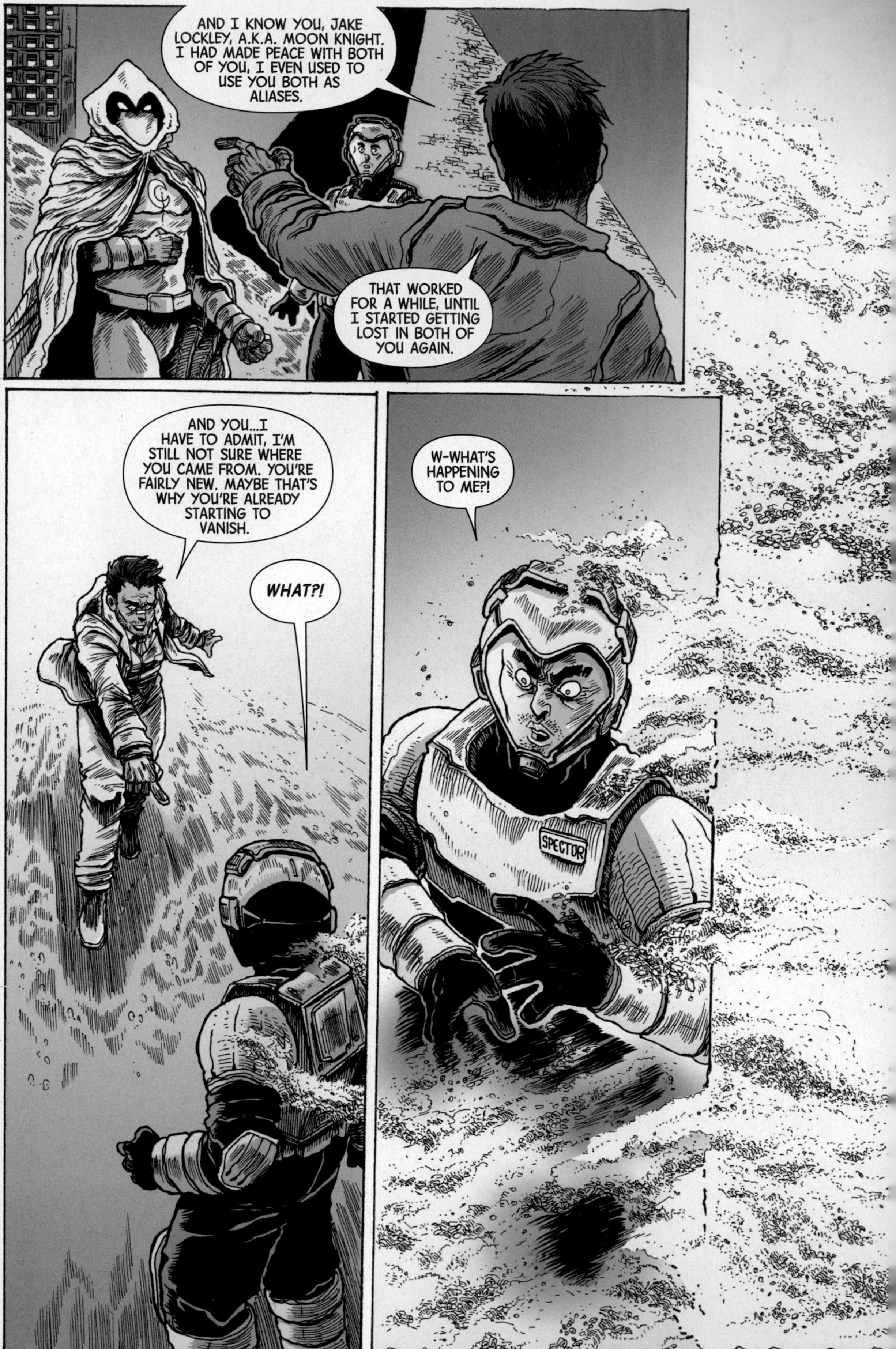
AND I KNOW YOU, JAKE LOCKLEY, A.K.A. MOON KNIGHT. I HAD MADE PEACE WITH BOTH OF YOU, I EVEN USED TO USE YOU BOTH AS ALIASES.
THAT WORKED FOR A WHILE, UNTIL I STARTED GETTING LOST IN BOTH OF YOU AGAIN.
AND YOU...I HAVE TO ADMIT, I'M STILL NOT SURE WHERE YOU CAME FROM. YOU'RE FAIRLY NEW. MAYBE THAT'S WHY YOU'RE ALREADY STARTING TO VANISH.
WHAT?!
W-WHAT'S HAPPENING TO ME?!
SPECTOR

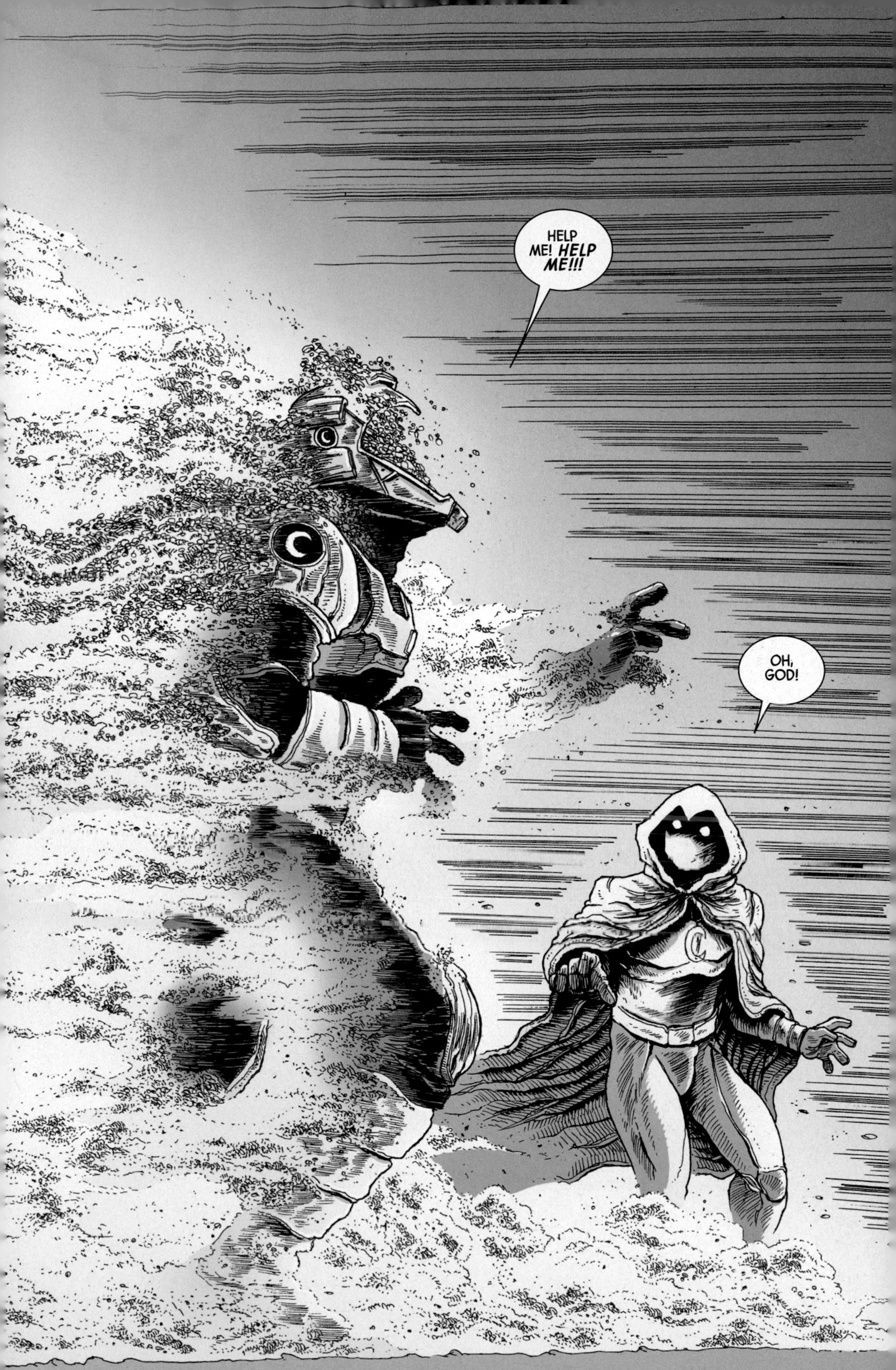
HELP ME! HELP ME!!!
OH, GOD!

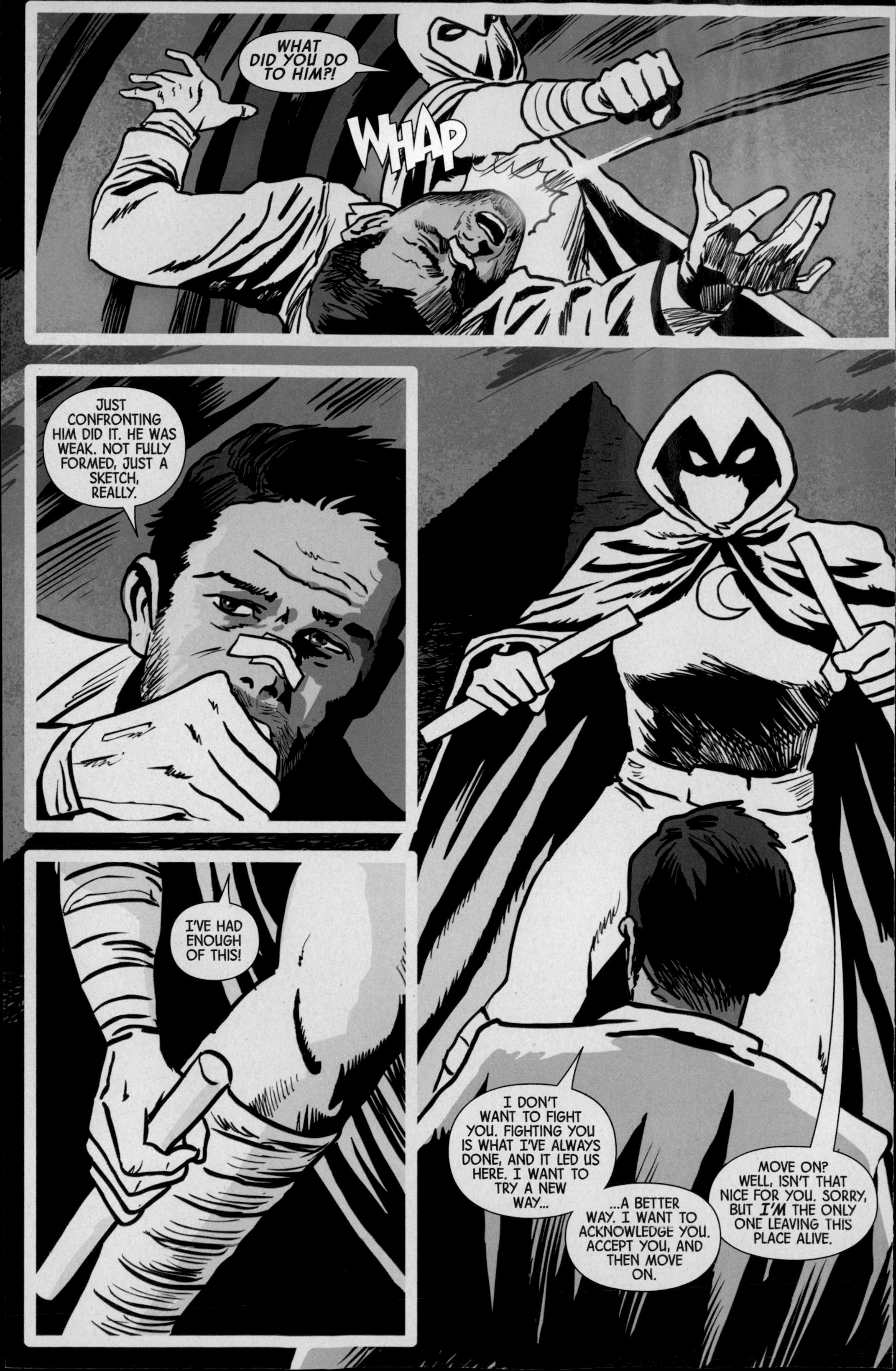
WHAT DID YOU DO TO HIM?!
WHAP
JUST CONFRONTING HIM DID IT. HE WAS WEAK. NOT FULLY FORMED, JUST A SKETCH, REALLY.
I'VE HAD ENOUGH OF THIS!
I DON'T WANT TO FIGHT YOU. FIGHTING YOU IS WHAT I'VE ALWAYS DONE, AND IT LED US HERE. I WANT TO TRY A NEW WAY...
...A BETTER WAY. I WANT TO ACKNOWLEDGE YOU. ACCEPT YOU, AND THEN MOVE ON.
MOVE ON? WELL, ISN'T THAT NICE FOR YOU. SORRY, BUT I'M THE ONLY ONE LEAVING THIS PLACE ALIVE.

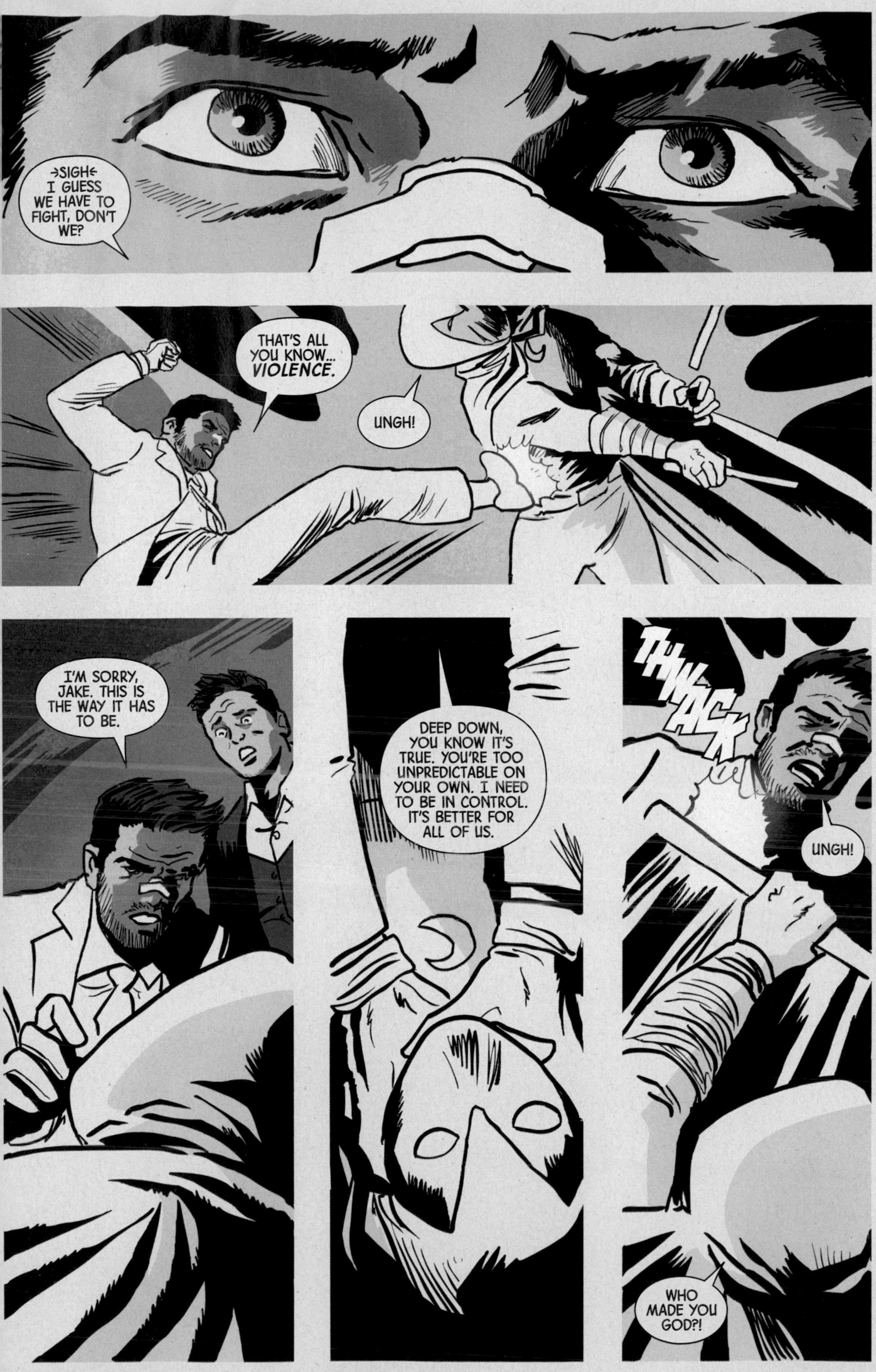

→SIGH← I GUESS WE HAVE TO FIGHT, DON'T WE?
THAT'S ALL YOU KNOW... *VIOLENCE.*
UNGH!
I'M SORRY, JAKE. THIS IS THE WAY IT HAS TO BE.
DEEP DOWN, YOU KNOW IT'S TRUE. YOU'RE TOO UNPREDICTABLE ON YOUR OWN. I NEED TO BE IN CONTROL. IT'S BETTER FOR ALL OF US.
THWACK
UNGH!
WHO MADE YOU GOD?!

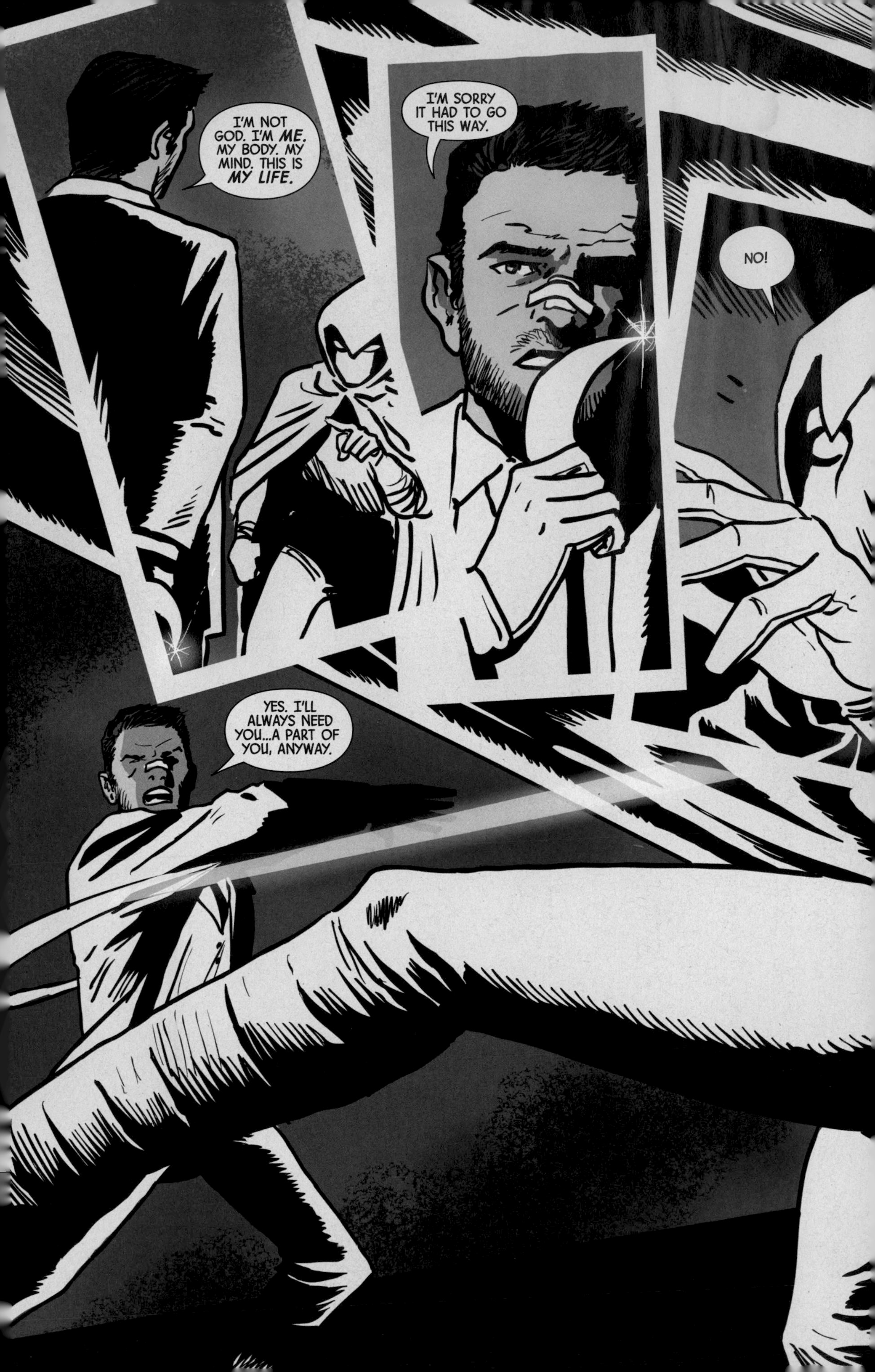
I'M NOT GOD. I'M ME. MY BODY. MY MIND. THIS IS MY LIFE.
I'M SORRY IT HAD TO GO THIS WAY.
NO!
YES. I'LL ALWAYS NEED YOU...A PART OF YOU, ANYWAY.

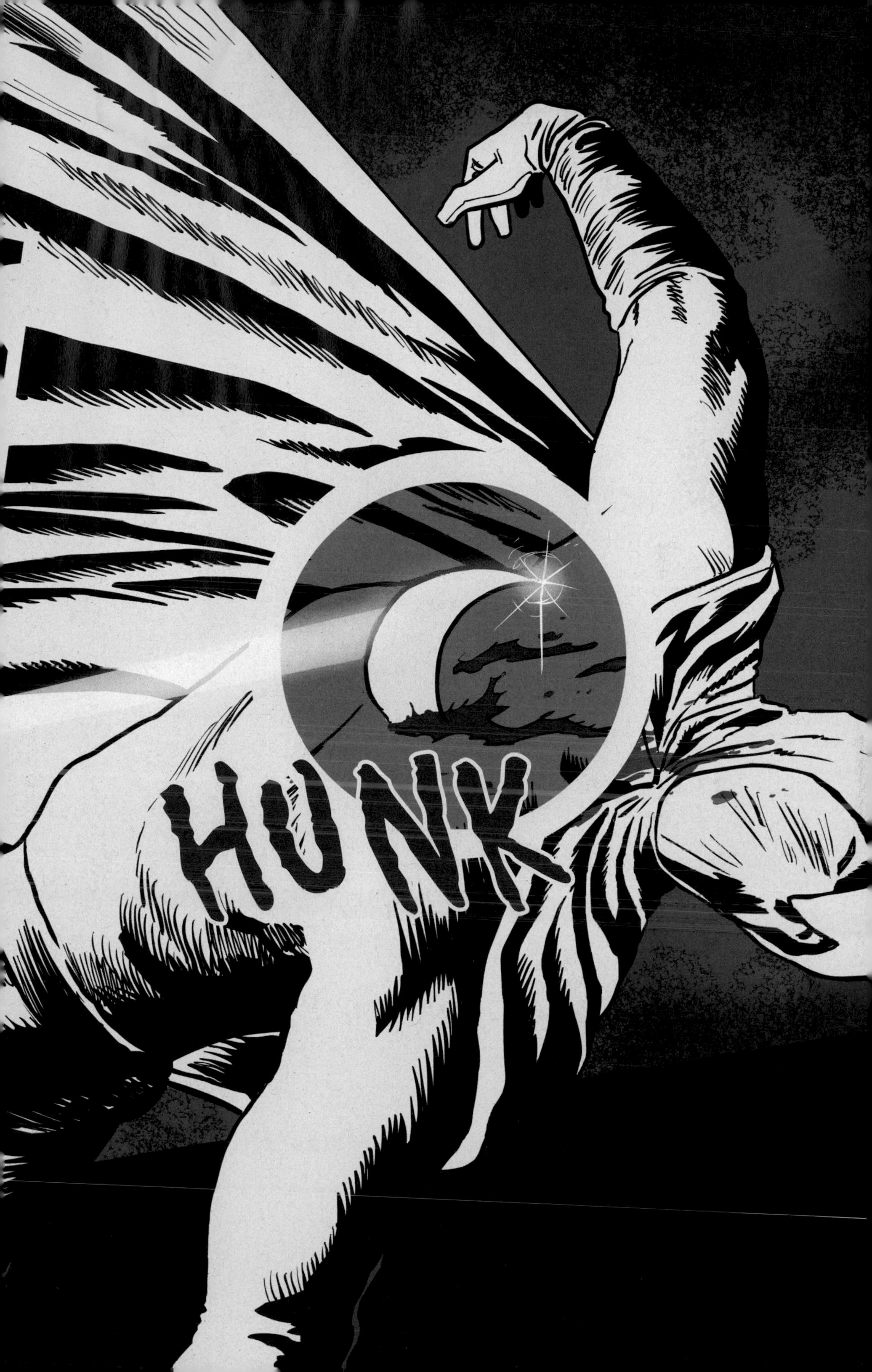
HUNK

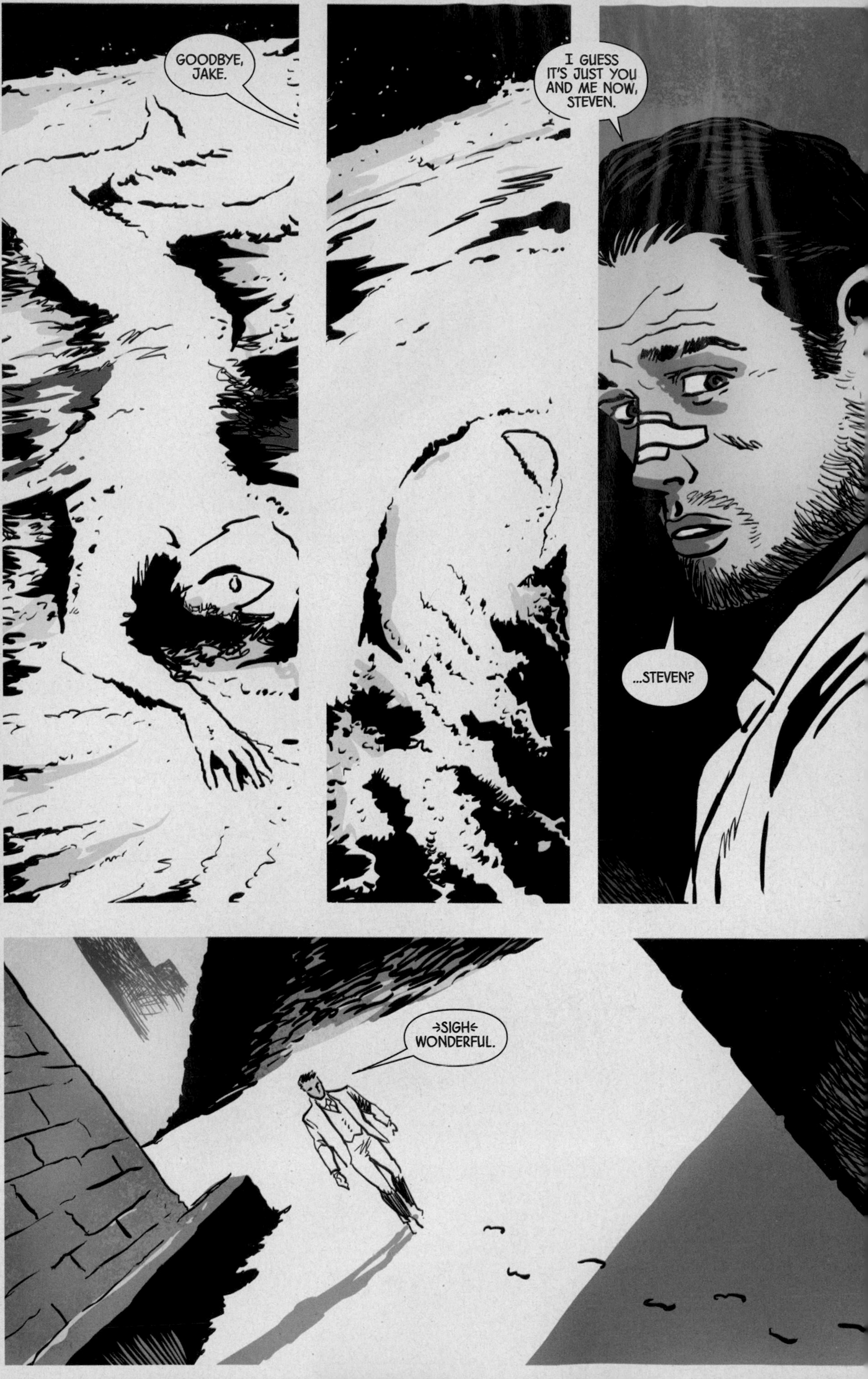
GOODBYE, JAKE.
I GUESS IT'S JUST YOU AND ME NOW, STEVEN.
...STEVEN?
SIGH
WONDERFUL.

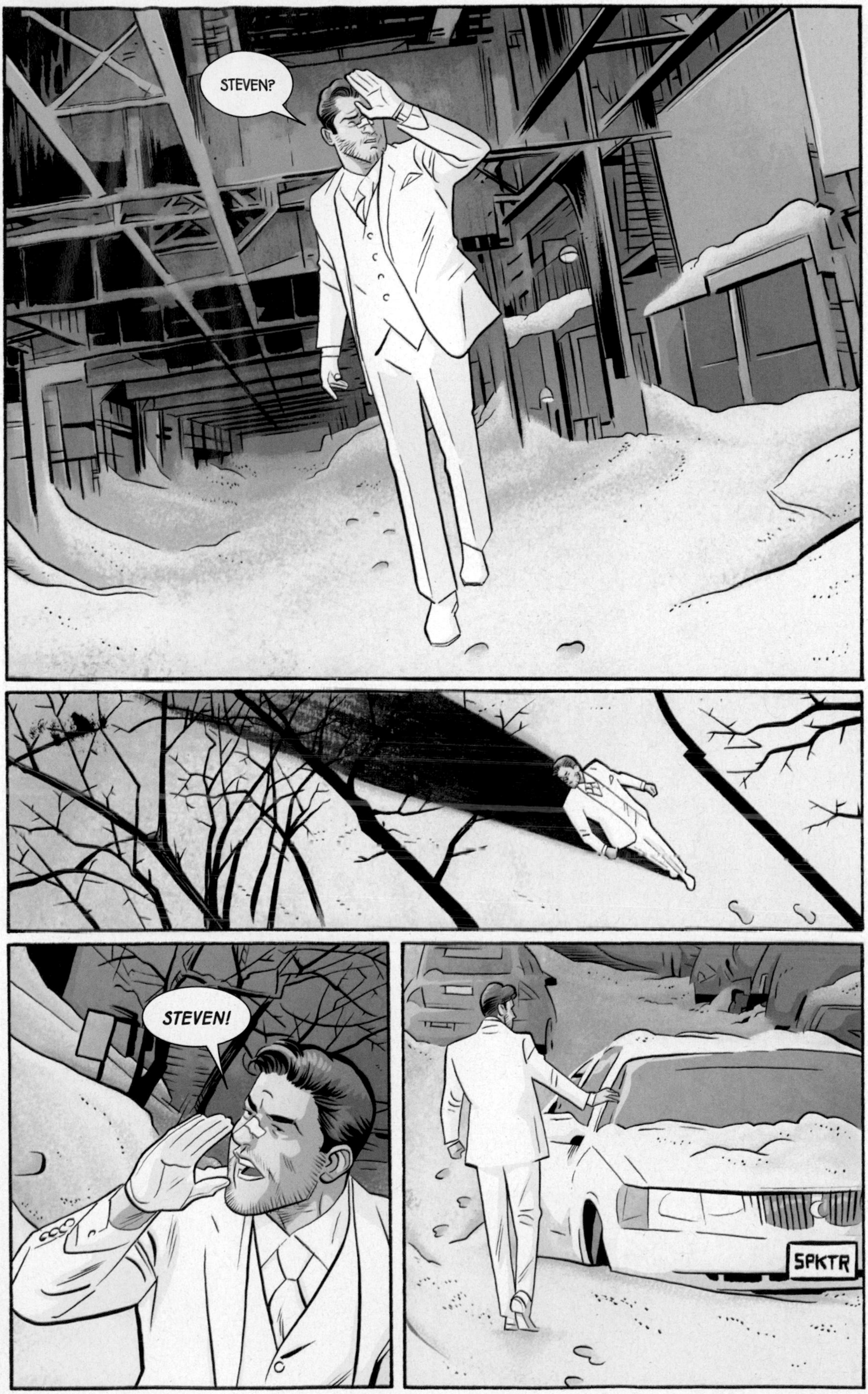
STEVEN?
STEVEN!
SPKTR

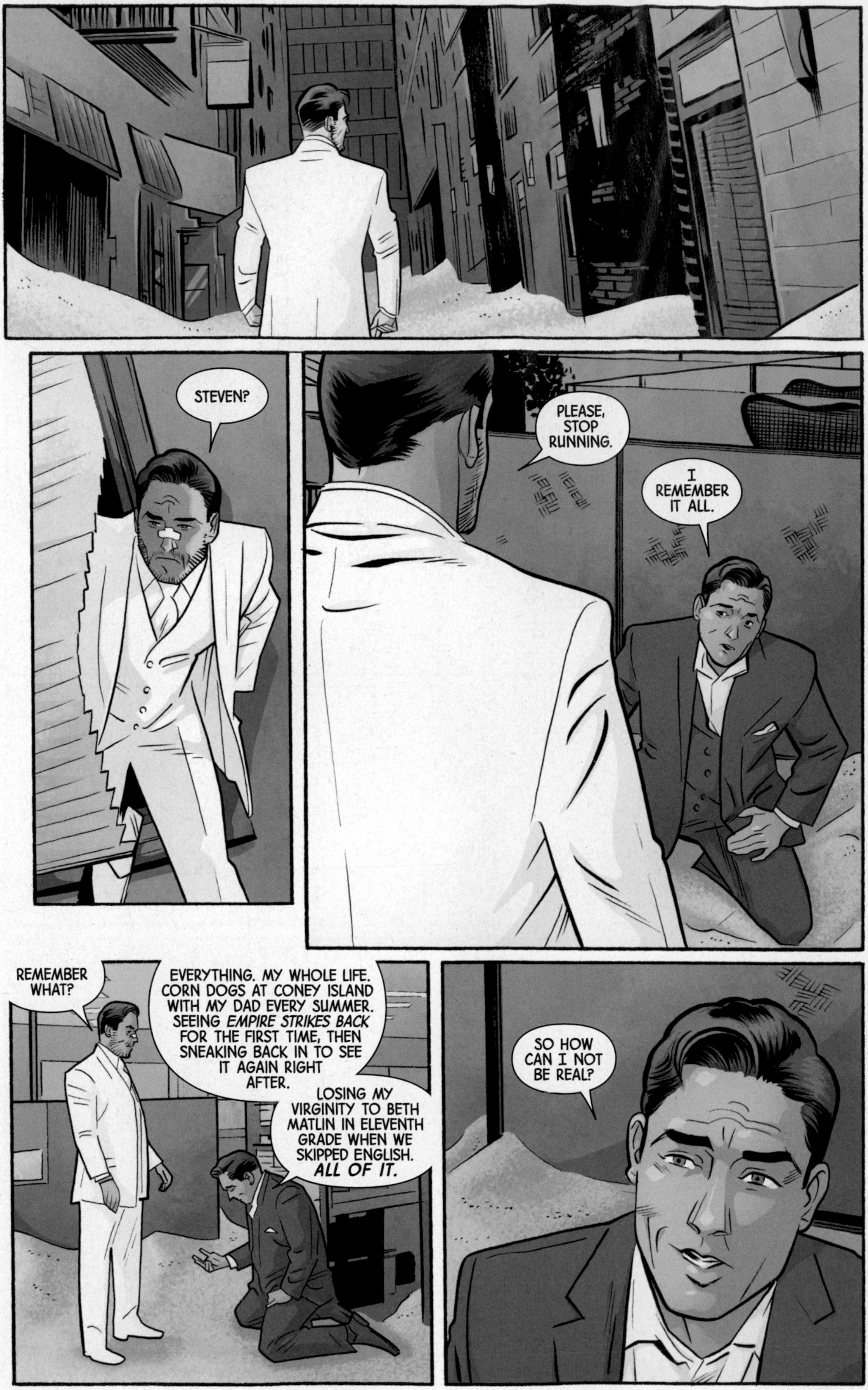
STEVEN?
PLEASE, STOP RUNNING.
I REMEMBER IT ALL.
REMEMBER WHAT?
EVERYTHING. MY WHOLE LIFE. CORN DOGS AT CONEY ISLAND WITH MY DAD EVERY SUMMER. SEEING *EMPIRE STRIKES BACK* FOR THE FIRST TIME, THEN SNEAKING BACK IN TO SEE IT AGAIN RIGHT AFTER.
LOSING MY VIRGINITY TO BETH MATLIN IN ELEVENTH GRADE WHEN WE SKIPPED ENGLISH. ***ALL OF IT.***
SO HOW CAN I NOT BE REAL?

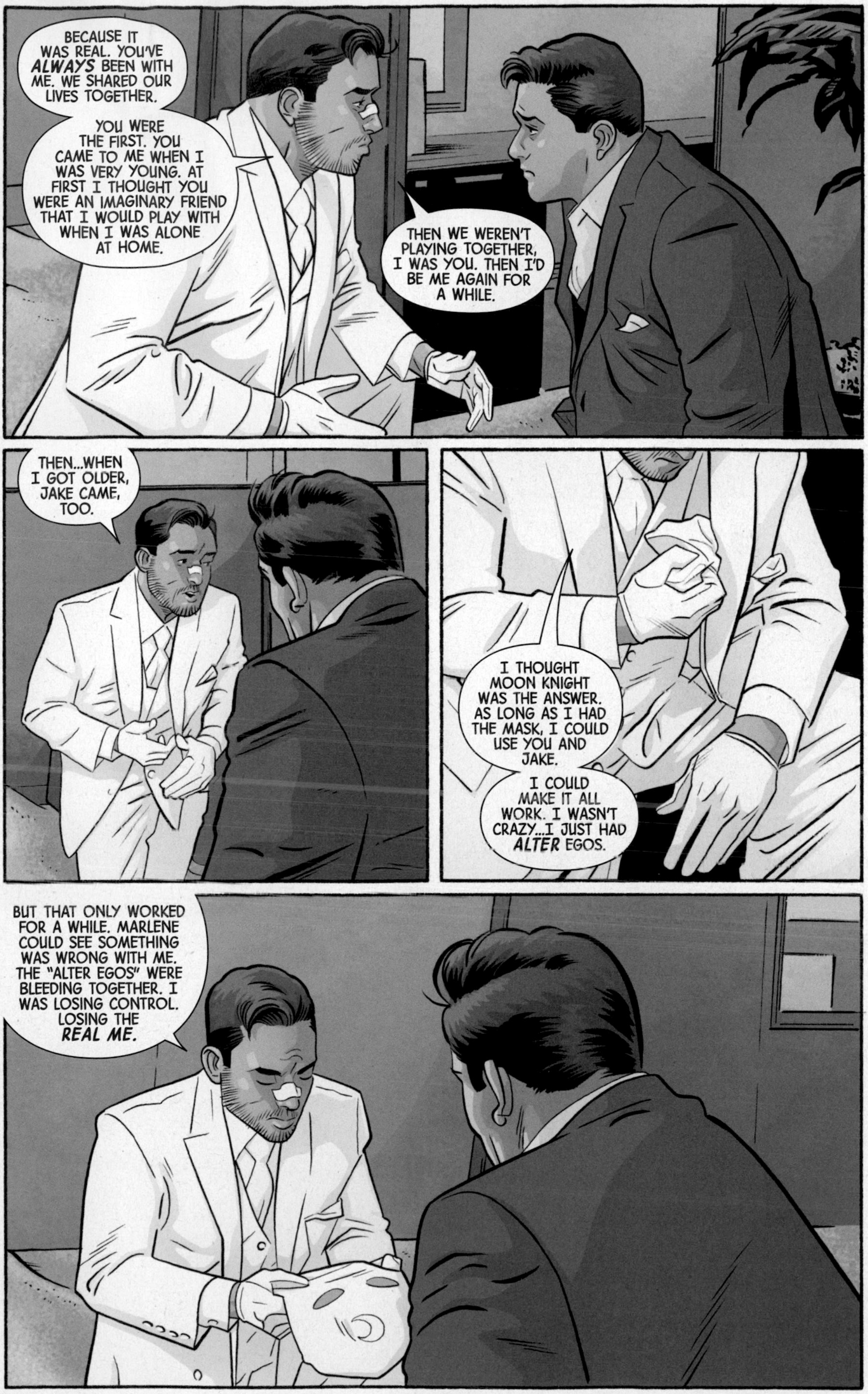
BECAUSE IT WAS REAL. YOU'VE ALWAYS BEEN WITH ME. WE SHARED OUR LIVES TOGETHER.
YOU WERE THE FIRST. YOU CAME TO ME WHEN I WAS VERY YOUNG. AT FIRST I THOUGHT YOU WERE AN IMAGINARY FRIEND THAT I WOULD PLAY WITH WHEN I WAS ALONE AT HOME.
THEN WE WEREN'T PLAYING TOGETHER, I WAS YOU. THEN I'D BE ME AGAIN FOR A WHILE.
THEN...WHEN I GOT OLDER, JAKE CAME, TOO.
I THOUGHT MOON KNIGHT WAS THE ANSWER. AS LONG AS I HAD THE MASK, I COULD USE YOU AND JAKE.
I COULD MAKE IT ALL WORK. I WASN'T CRAZY...I JUST HAD ALTER EGOS.
BUT THAT ONLY WORKED FOR A WHILE. MARLENE COULD SEE SOMETHING WAS WRONG WITH ME. THE "ALTER EGOS" WERE BLEEDING TOGETHER. I WAS LOSING CONTROL. LOSING THE REAL ME.

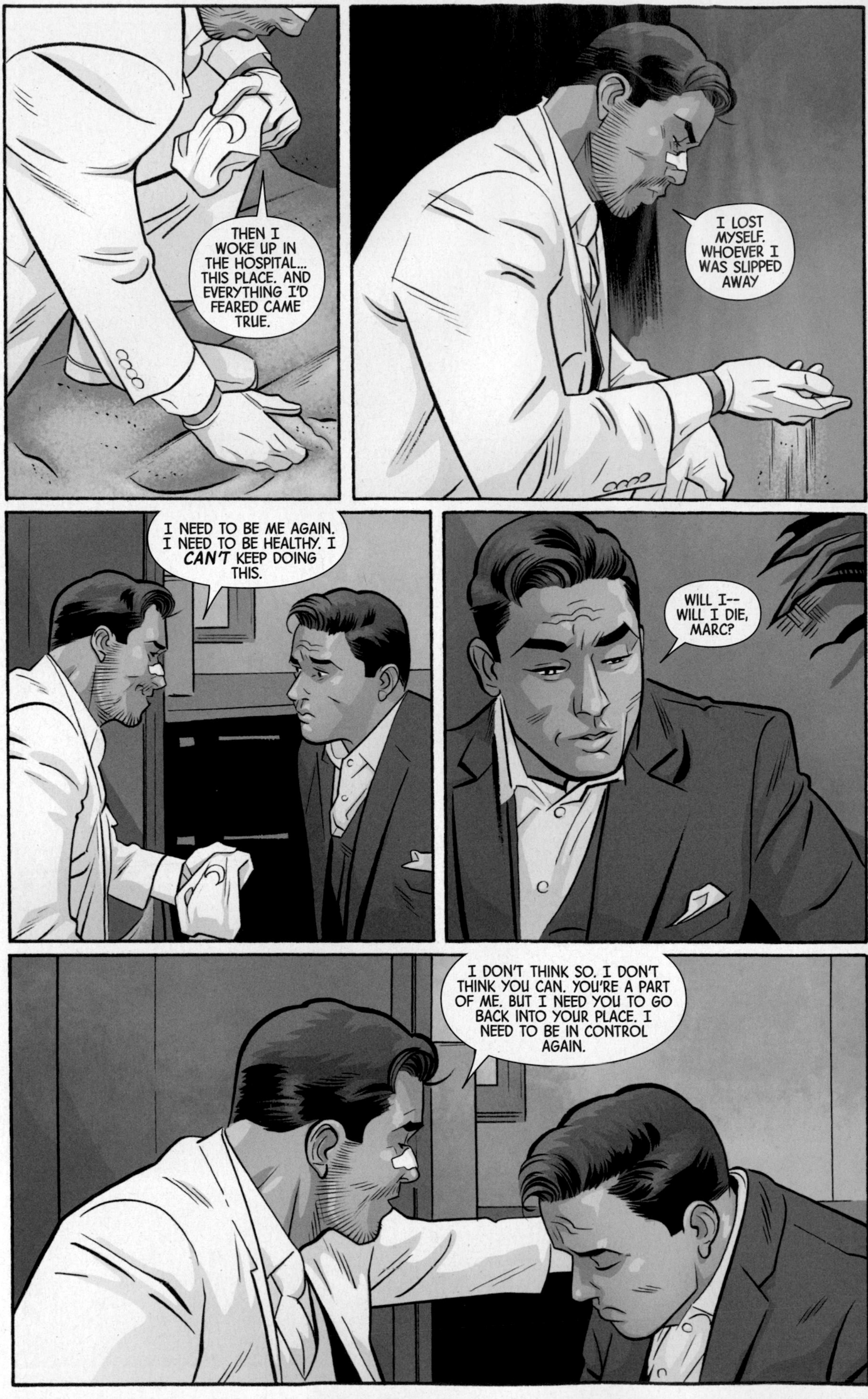
THEN I WOKE UP IN THE HOSPITAL... THIS PLACE. AND EVERYTHING I'D FEARED CAME TRUE.
I LOST MYSELF. WHOEVER I WAS SLIPPED AWAY
I NEED TO BE ME AGAIN. I NEED TO BE HEALTHY. I *CAN'T* KEEP DOING THIS.
WILL I-- WILL I DIE, MARC?
I DON'T THINK SO. I DON'T THINK YOU CAN. YOU'RE A PART OF ME. BUT I NEED YOU TO GO BACK INTO YOUR PLACE. I NEED TO BE IN CONTROL AGAIN.

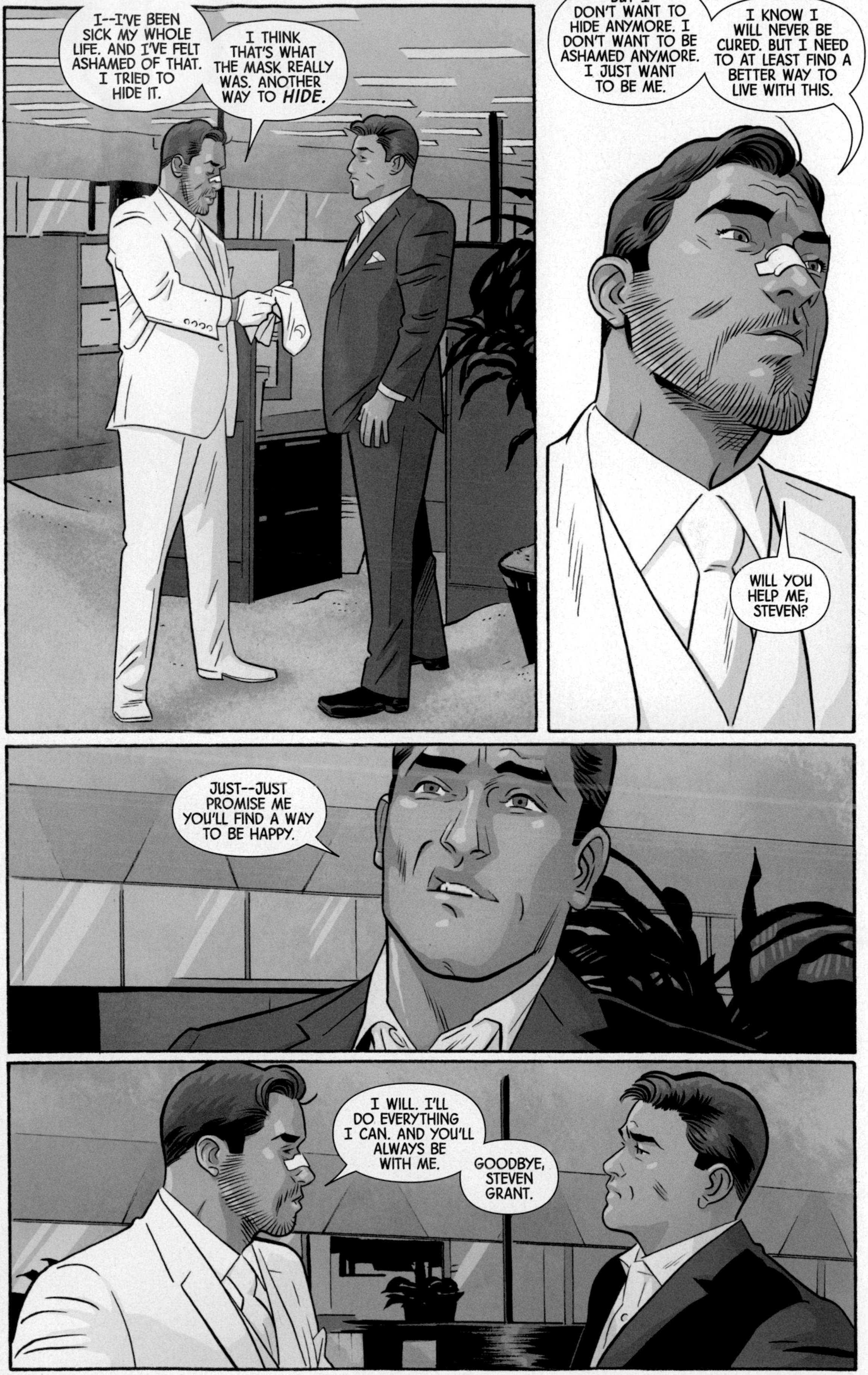
I--I'VE BEEN SICK MY WHOLE LIFE. AND I'VE FELT ASHAMED OF THAT. I TRIED TO HIDE IT.
I THINK THAT'S WHAT THE MASK REALLY WAS. ANOTHER WAY TO HIDE.
BUT I DON'T WANT TO HIDE ANYMORE. I DON'T WANT TO BE ASHAMED ANYMORE. I JUST WANT TO BE ME.
I KNOW I WILL NEVER BE CURED. BUT I NEED TO AT LEAST FIND A BETTER WAY TO LIVE WITH THIS.
WILL YOU HELP ME, STEVEN?
JUST--JUST PROMISE ME YOU'LL FIND A WAY TO BE HAPPY.
I WILL. I'LL DO EVERYTHING I CAN. AND YOU'LL ALWAYS BE WITH ME.
GOODBYE, STEVEN GRANT.

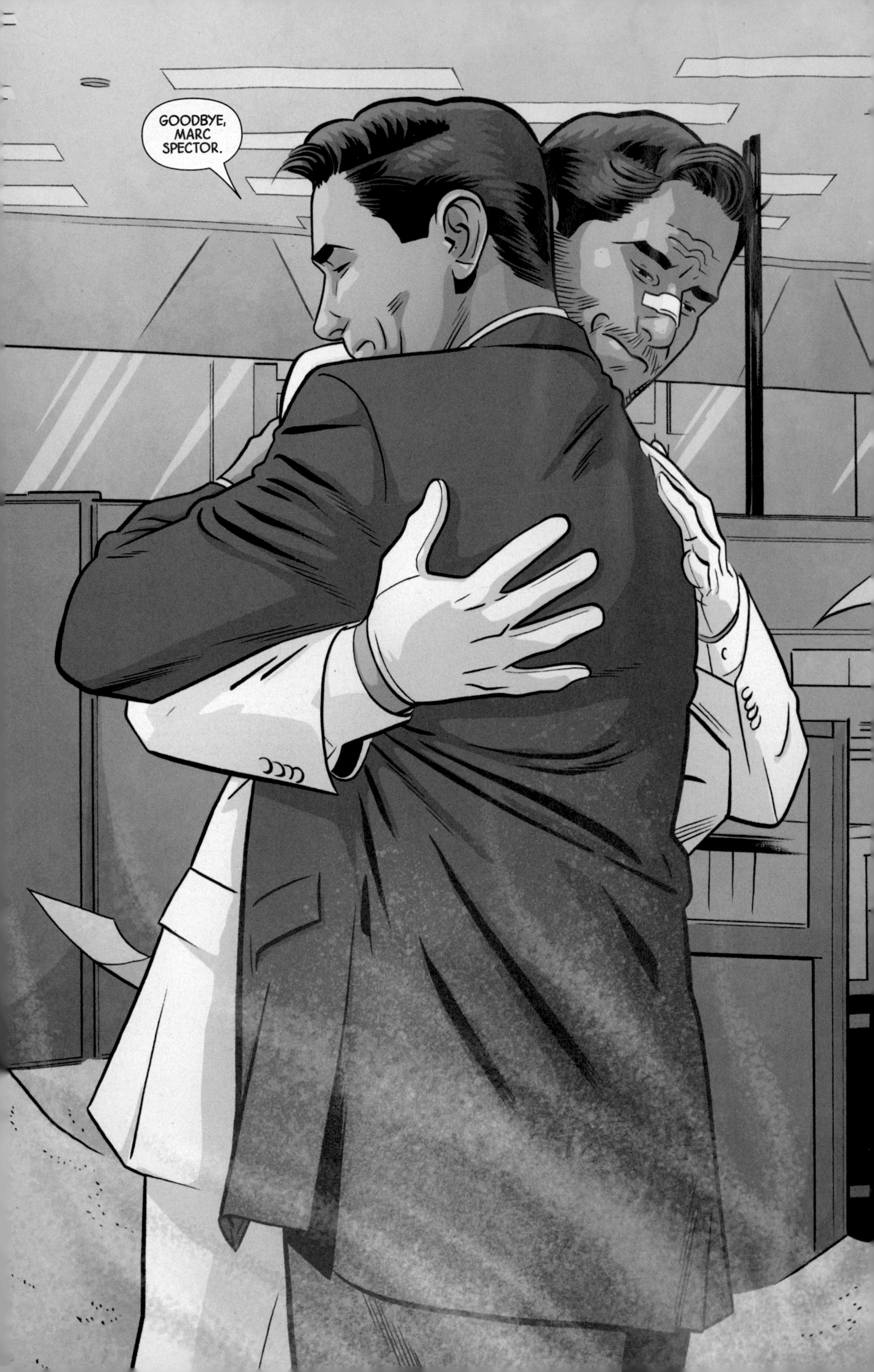
GOODBYE, MARC SPECTOR.

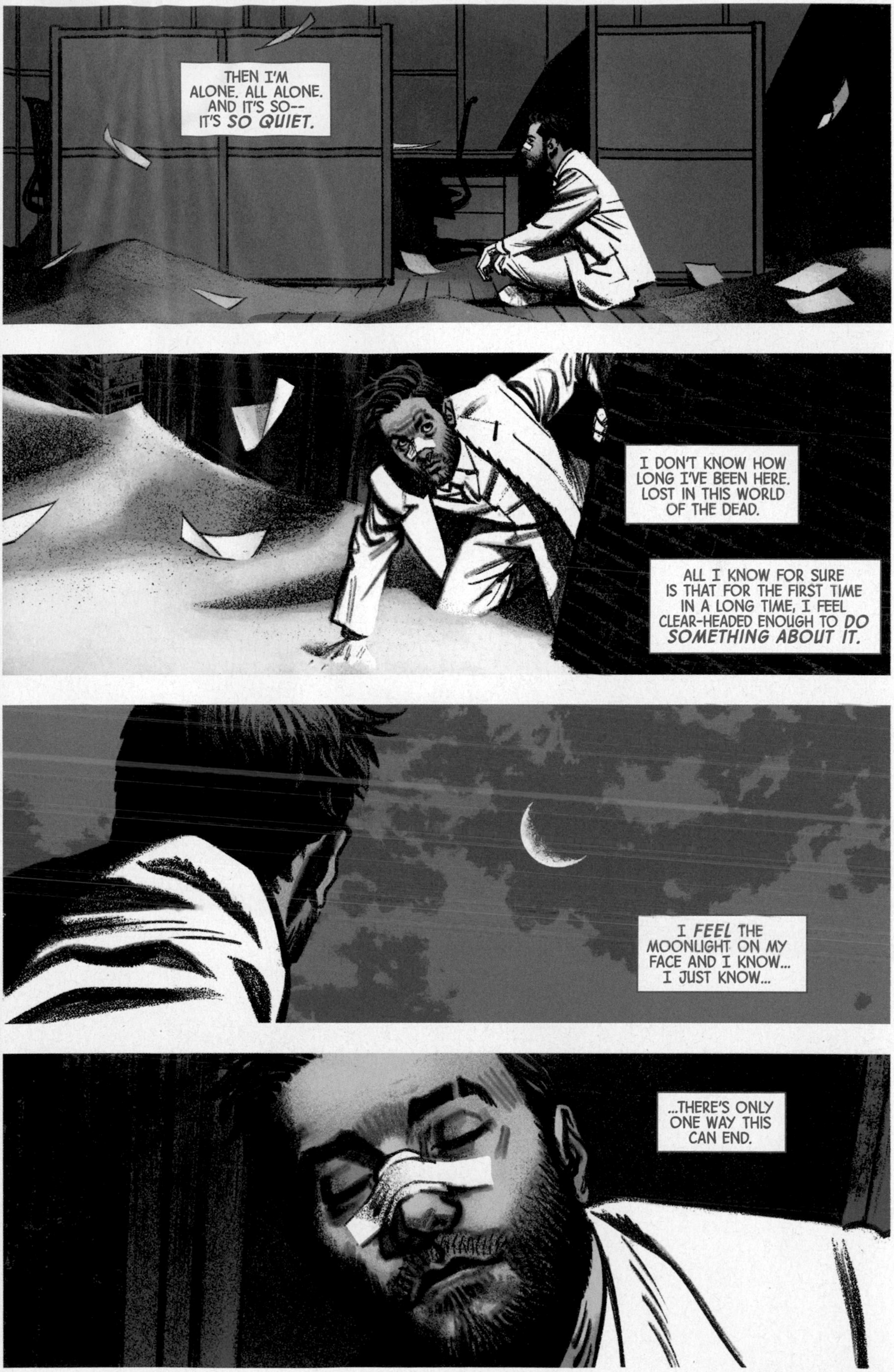
THEN I'M ALONE. ALL ALONE. AND IT'S SO-- IT'S SO QUIET.
I DON'T KNOW HOW LONG I'VE BEEN HERE. LOST IN THIS WORLD OF THE DEAD.
ALL I KNOW FOR SURE IS THAT FOR THE FIRST TIME IN A LONG TIME, I FEEL CLEAR-HEADED ENOUGH TO DO SOMETHING ABOUT IT.
I FEEL THE MOONLIGHT ON MY FACE AND I KNOW... I JUST KNOW...
...THERE'S ONLY ONE WAY THIS CAN END.

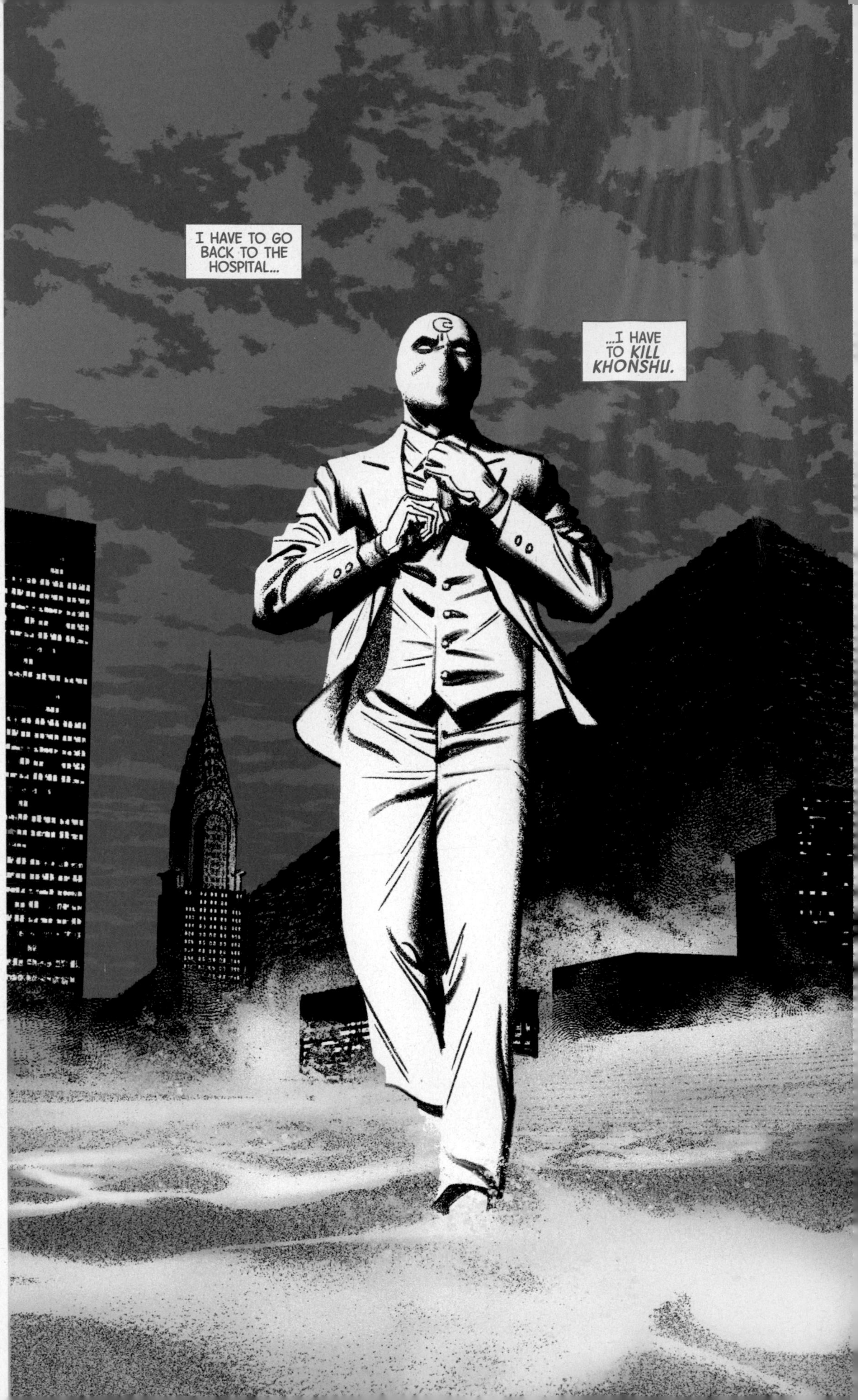
I HAVE TO GO BACK TO THE HOSPITAL...
...I HAVE TO KILL KHONSHU.

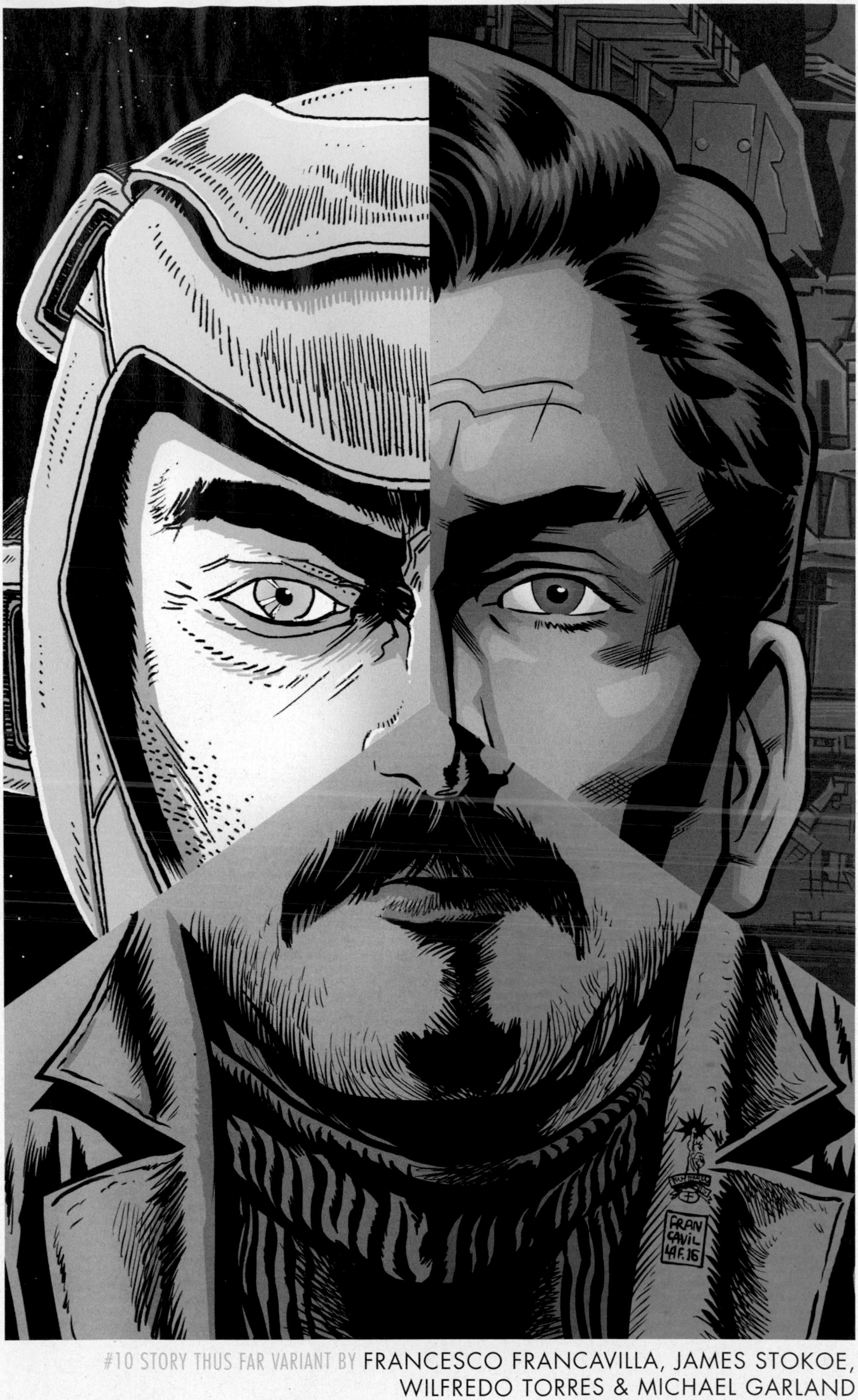
FRAN
CAVIL
LA F. 16

#10 STORY THUS FAR VARIANT BY FRANCESCO FRANCAVILLA, JAMES STOKOE, WILFREDO TORRES & MICHAEL GARLAND

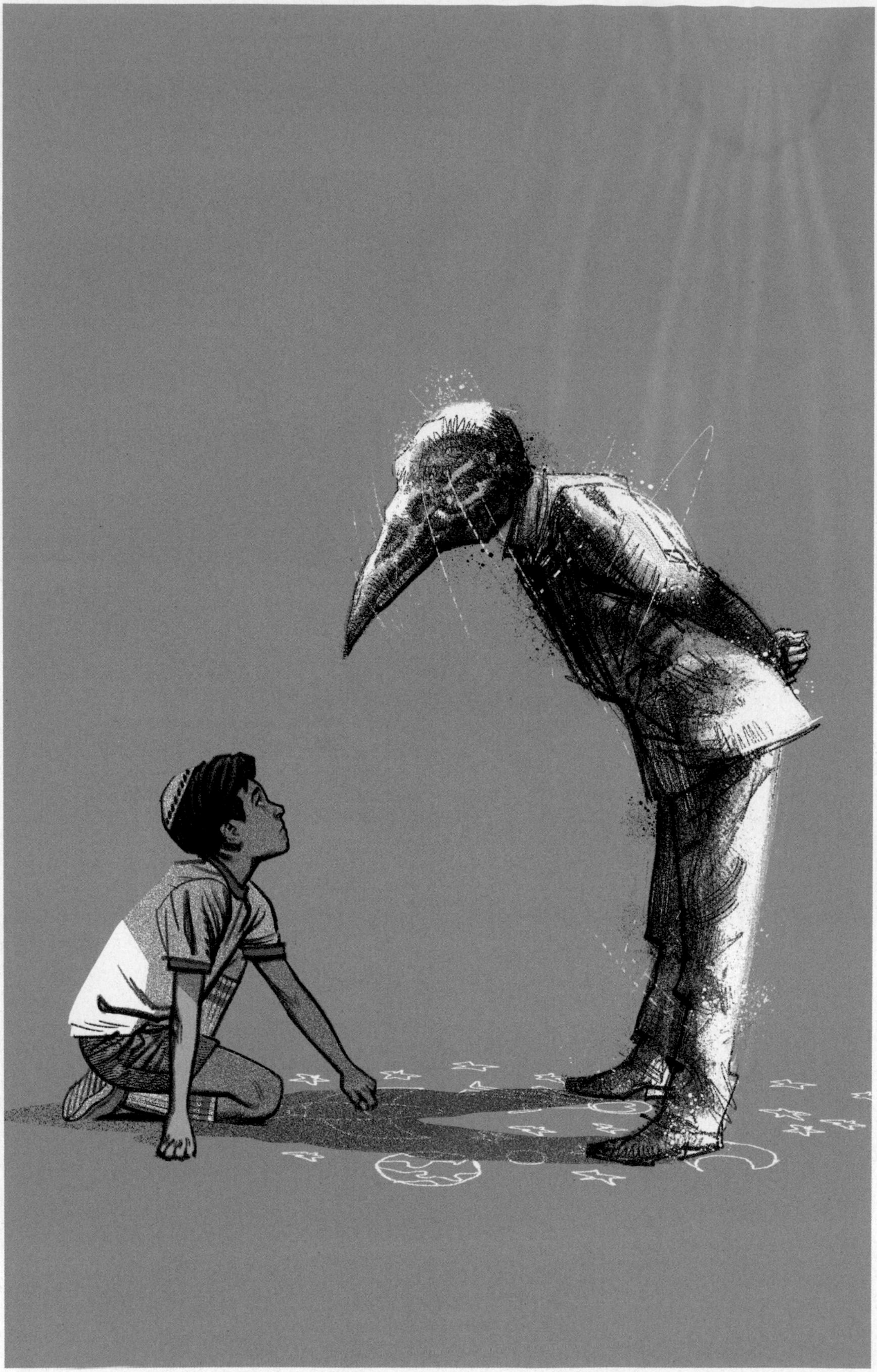

BIRTH AND DEATH
PART ONE

10

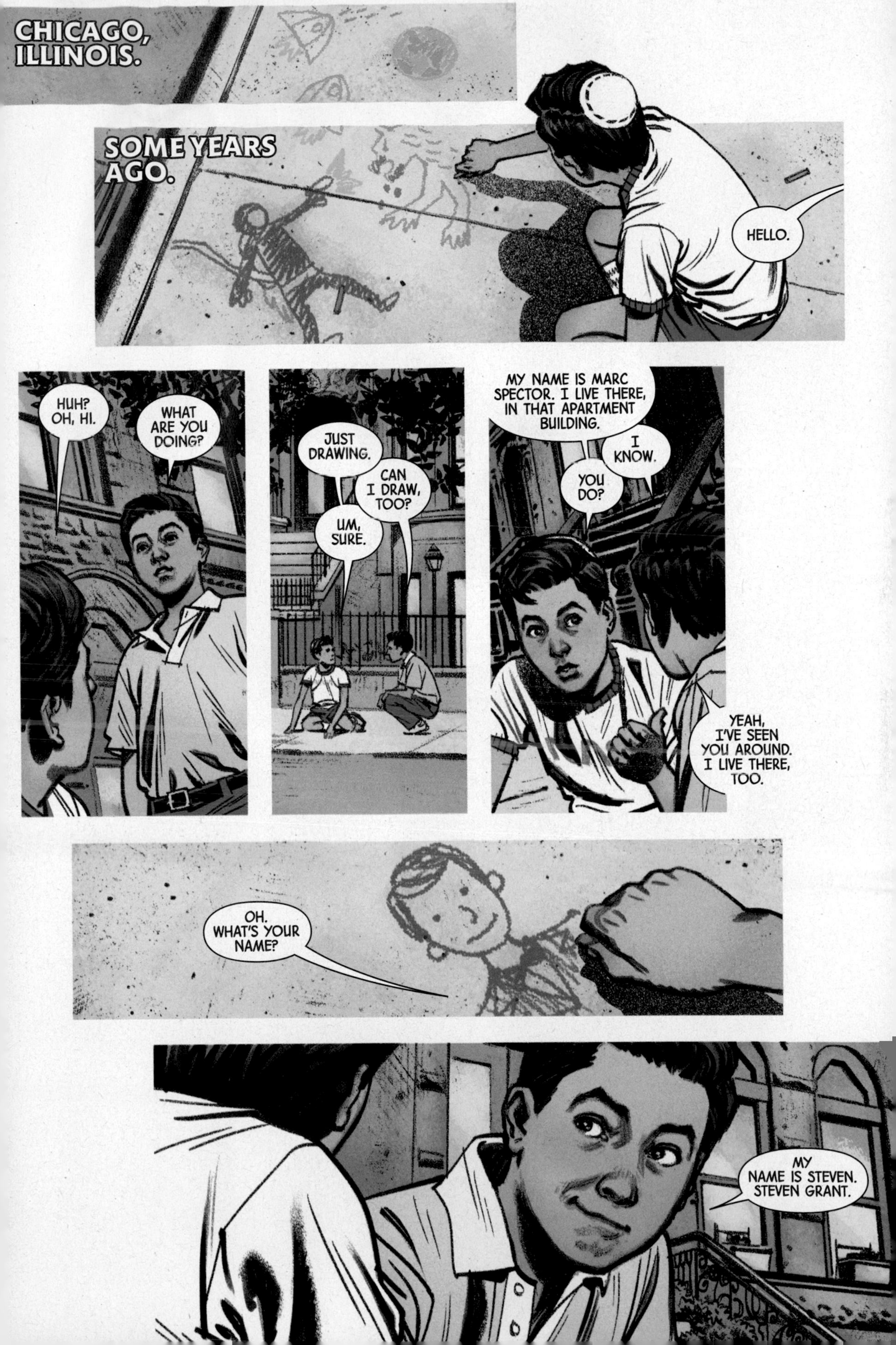
CHICAGO, ILLINOIS.
SOME YEARS AGO.
HELLO.
HUH? OH, HI.
WHAT ARE YOU DOING?
JUST DRAWING.
CAN I DRAW, TOO?
UM, SURE.
MY NAME IS MARC SPECTOR. I LIVE THERE, IN THAT APARTMENT BUILDING.
YOU DO?
I KNOW.
YEAH, I'VE SEEN YOU AROUND. I LIVE THERE, TOO.
OH. WHAT'S YOUR NAME?
MY NAME IS STEVEN. STEVEN GRANT.

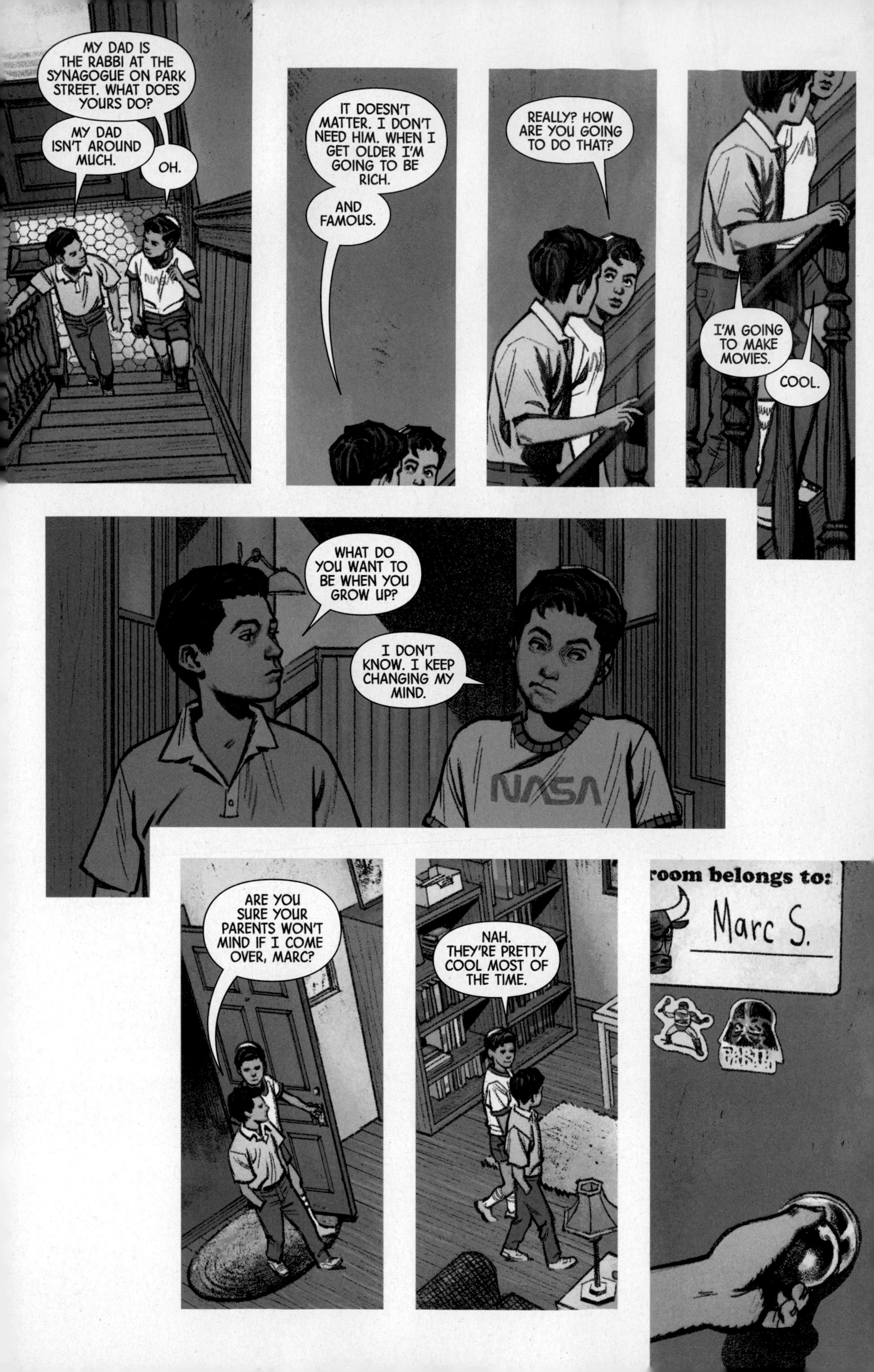
MY DAD IS THE RABBI AT THE SYNAGOGUE ON PARK STREET. WHAT DOES YOURS DO?
MY DAD ISN'T AROUND MUCH.
OH.
IT DOESN'T MATTER. I DON'T NEED HIM. WHEN I GET OLDER I'M GOING TO BE RICH.
AND FAMOUS.
REALLY? HOW ARE YOU GOING TO DO THAT?
I'M GOING TO MAKE MOVIES.
COOL.
WHAT DO YOU WANT TO BE WHEN YOU GROW UP?
I DON'T KNOW. I KEEP CHANGING MY MIND.
NASA
ARE YOU SURE YOUR PARENTS WON'T MIND IF I COME OVER, MARC?
NAH. THEY'RE PRETTY COOL MOST OF THE TIME.
room belongs to:
Marc S.

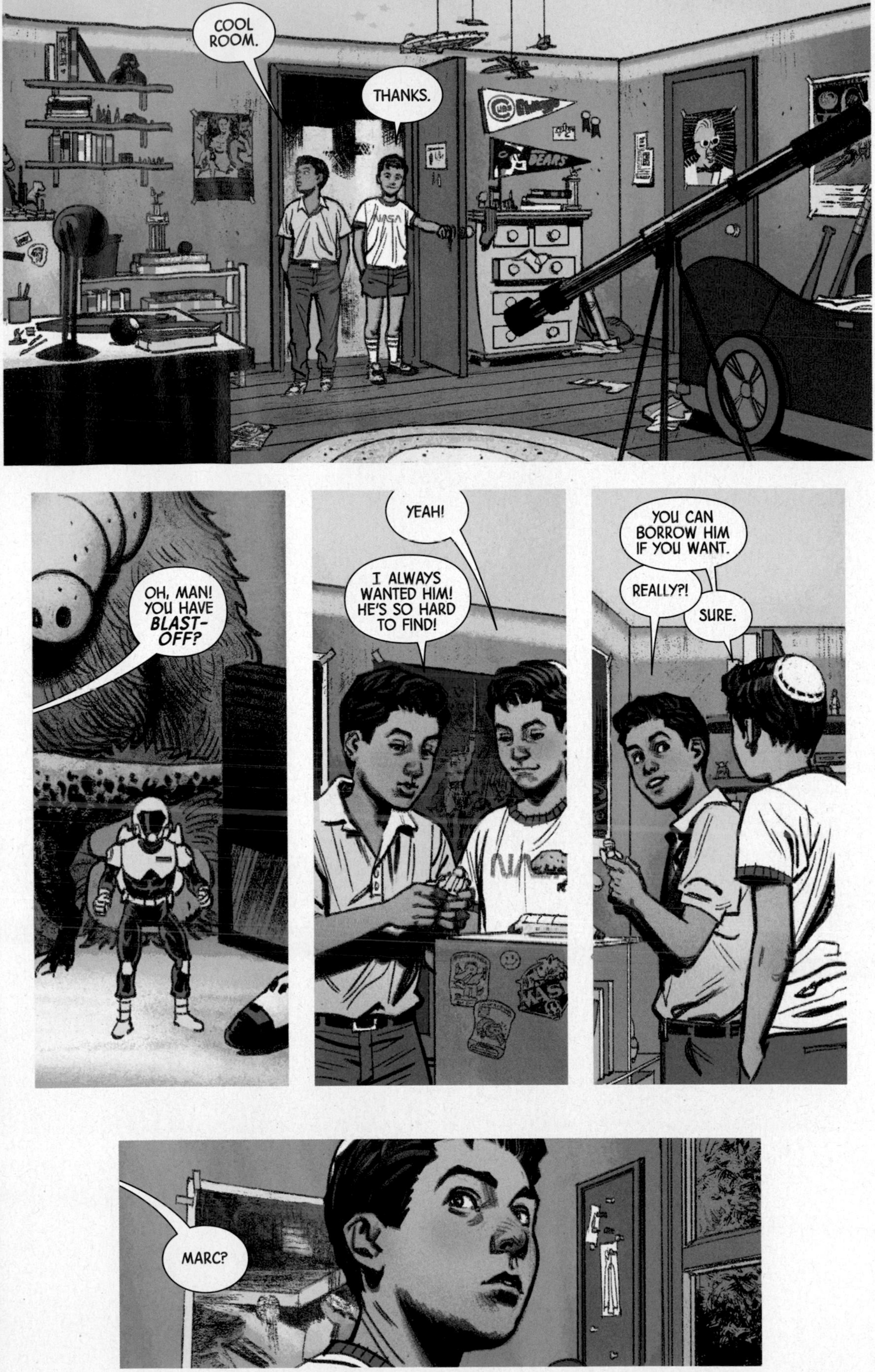
COOL ROOM.
THANKS.
OH, MAN! YOU HAVE *BLAST-OFF?*
YEAH!
I ALWAYS WANTED HIM! HE'S SO HARD TO FIND!
YOU CAN BORROW HIM IF YOU WANT.
REALLY?!
SURE.
MARC?

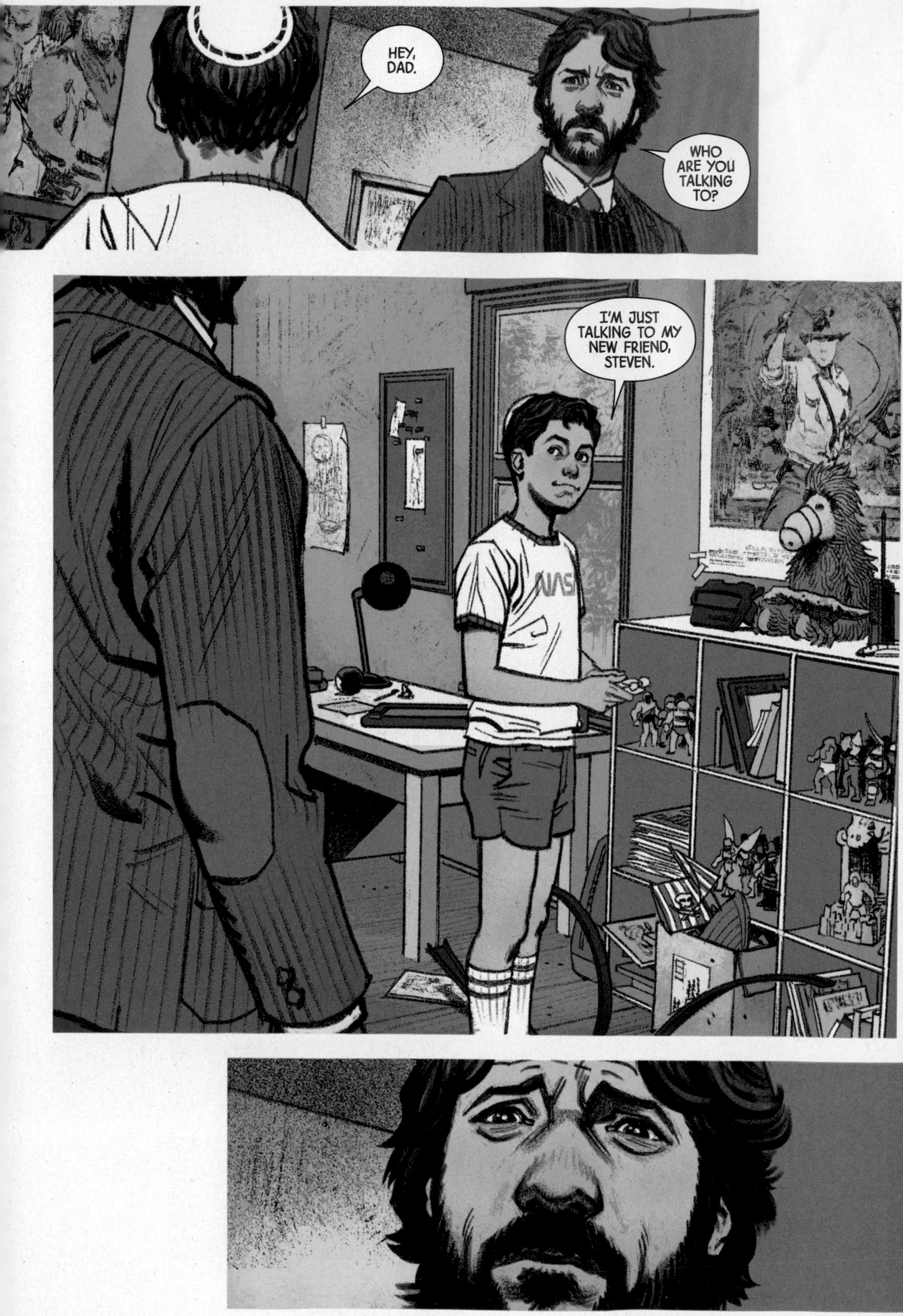
HEY, DAD.
WHO ARE YOU TALKING TO?
I'M JUST TALKING TO MY NEW FRIEND, STEVEN.

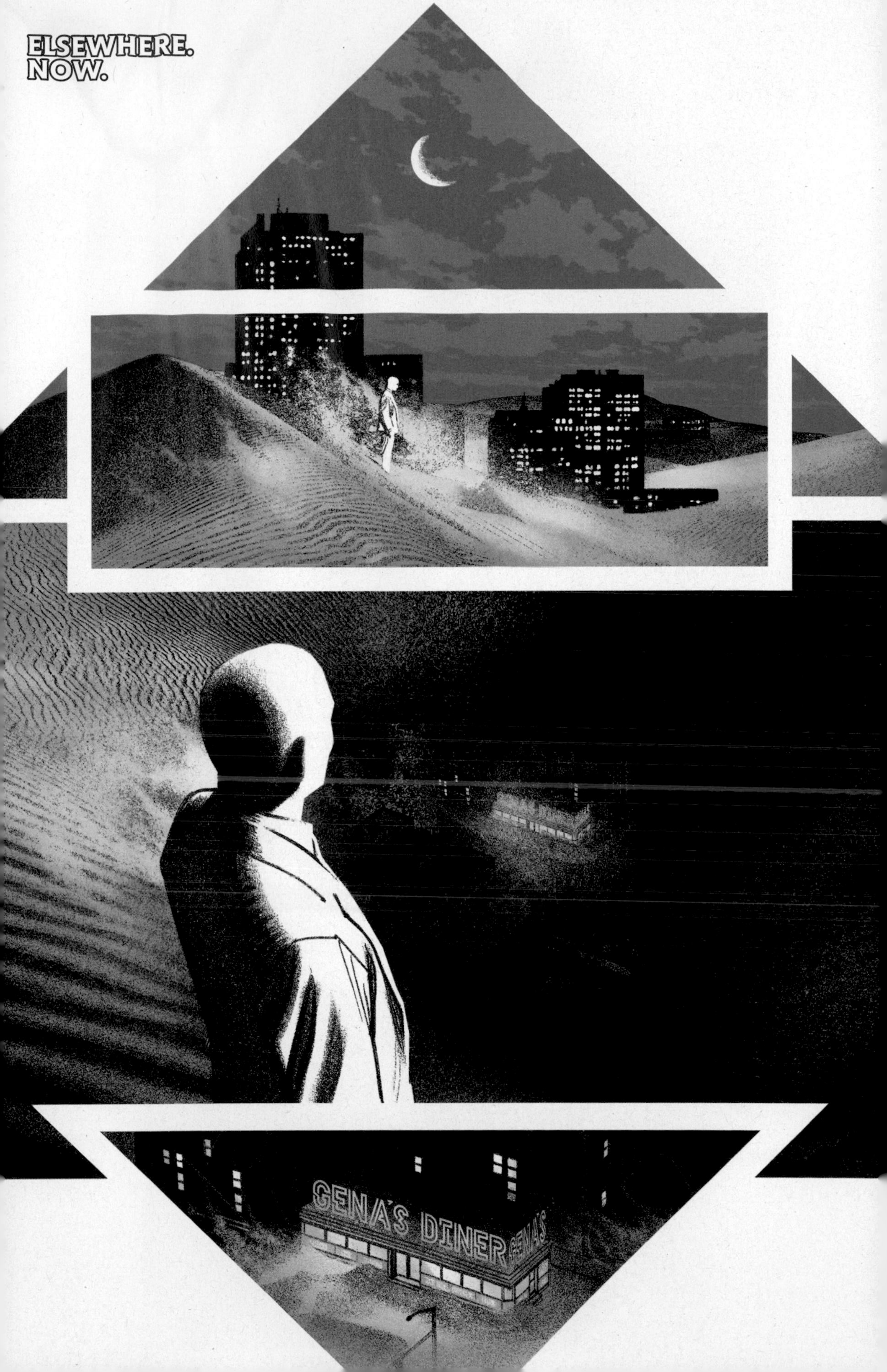
ELSEWHERE.
NOW.
GENA'S DINER
GENA'S

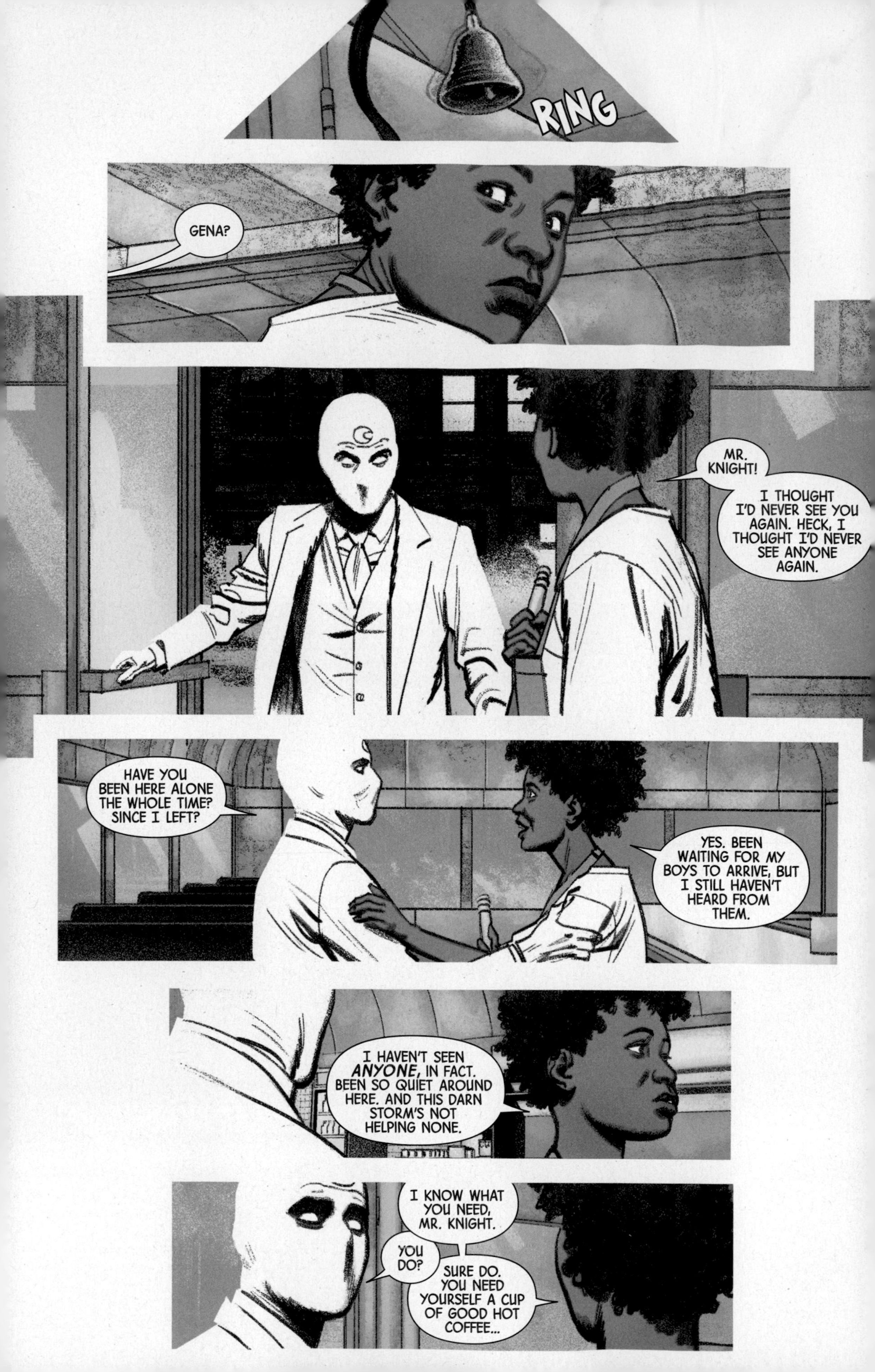
RING
GENA?
MR. KNIGHT!
I THOUGHT I'D NEVER SEE YOU AGAIN. HECK, I THOUGHT I'D NEVER SEE ANYONE AGAIN.
HAVE YOU BEEN HERE ALONE THE WHOLE TIME? SINCE I LEFT?
YES. BEEN WAITING FOR MY BOYS TO ARRIVE, BUT I STILL HAVEN'T HEARD FROM THEM.
I HAVEN'T SEEN *ANYONE*, IN FACT. BEEN SO QUIET AROUND HERE. AND THIS DARN STORM'S NOT HELPING NONE.
I KNOW WHAT YOU NEED, MR. KNIGHT.
YOU DO?
SURE DO. YOU NEED YOURSELF A CUP OF GOOD HOT COFFEE...

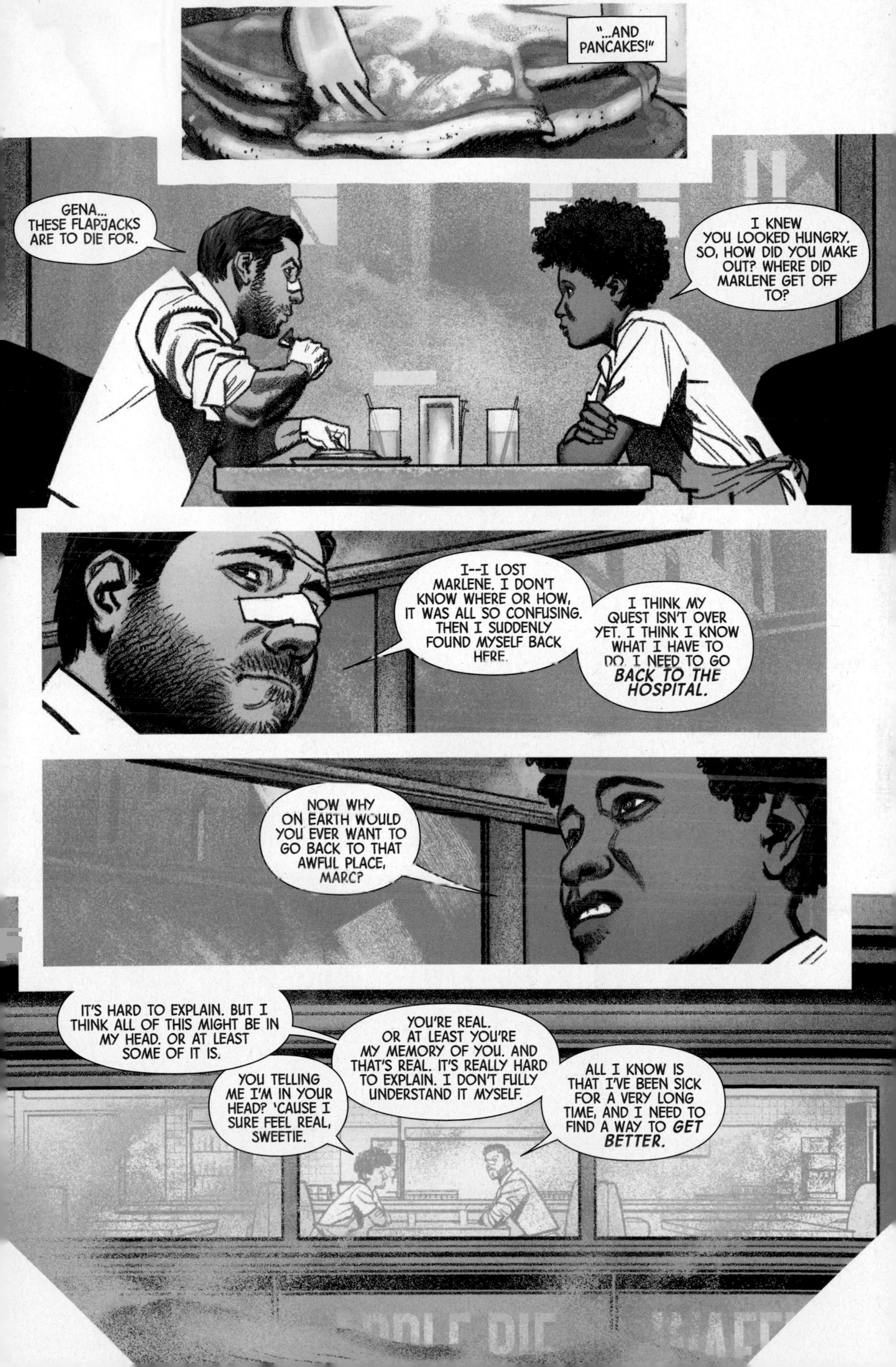
"...AND PANCAKES!"
GENA... THESE FLAPJACKS ARE TO DIE FOR.
I KNEW YOU LOOKED HUNGRY. SO, HOW DID YOU MAKE OUT? WHERE DID MARLENE GET OFF TO?
I--I LOST MARLENE. I DON'T KNOW WHERE OR HOW, IT WAS ALL SO CONFUSING. THEN I SUDDENLY FOUND MYSELF BACK HERE.
I THINK MY QUEST ISN'T OVER YET. I THINK I KNOW WHAT I HAVE TO DO. I NEED TO GO *BACK TO THE HOSPITAL.*
NOW WHY ON EARTH WOULD YOU EVER WANT TO GO BACK TO THAT AWFUL PLACE, MARC?
IT'S HARD TO EXPLAIN. BUT I THINK ALL OF THIS MIGHT BE IN MY HEAD. OR AT LEAST SOME OF IT IS.
YOU TELLING ME I'M IN YOUR HEAD? 'CAUSE I SURE FEEL REAL, SWEETIE.
YOU'RE REAL. OR AT LEAST YOU'RE MY MEMORY OF YOU. AND THAT'S REAL. IT'S REALLY HARD TO EXPLAIN. I DON'T FULLY UNDERSTAND IT MYSELF.
ALL I KNOW IS THAT I'VE BEEN SICK FOR A VERY LONG TIME, AND I NEED TO FIND A WAY TO *GET BETTER.*

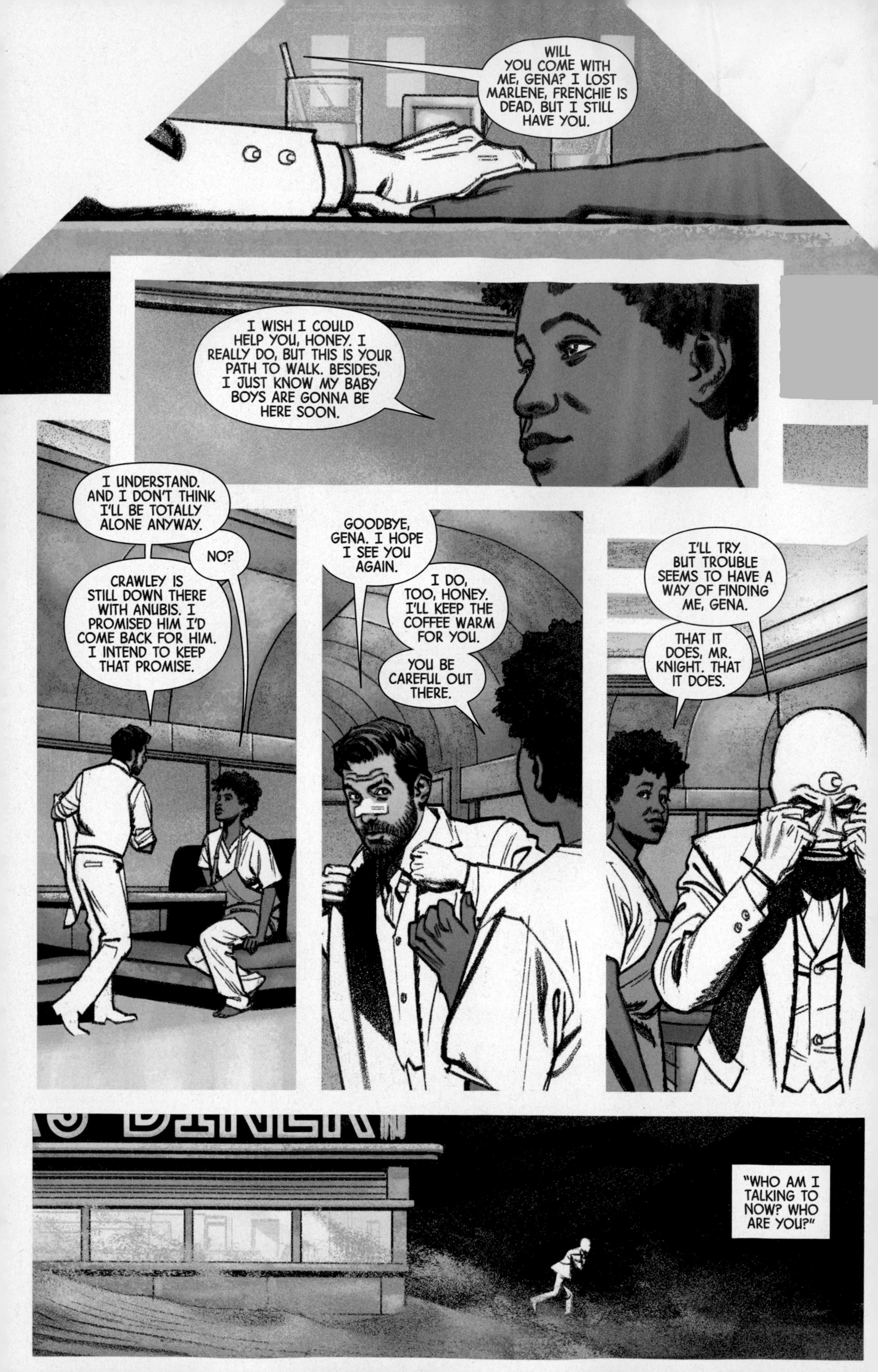
WILL YOU COME WITH ME, GENA? I LOST MARLENE, FRENCHIE IS DEAD, BUT I STILL HAVE YOU.
I WISH I COULD HELP YOU, HONEY. I REALLY DO, BUT THIS IS YOUR PATH TO WALK. BESIDES, I JUST KNOW MY BABY BOYS ARE GONNA BE HERE SOON.
I UNDERSTAND. AND I DON'T THINK I'LL BE TOTALLY ALONE ANYWAY.
NO?
CRAWLEY IS STILL DOWN THERE WITH ANUBIS. I PROMISED HIM I'D COME BACK FOR HIM. I INTEND TO KEEP THAT PROMISE.
GOODBYE, GENA. I HOPE I SEE YOU AGAIN.
I DO, TOO, HONEY. I'LL KEEP THE COFFEE WARM FOR YOU.
YOU BE CAREFUL OUT THERE.
I'LL TRY. BUT TROUBLE SEEMS TO HAVE A WAY OF FINDING ME, GENA.
THAT IT DOES, MR. KNIGHT. THAT IT DOES.
"WHO AM I TALKING TO NOW? WHO ARE YOU?"

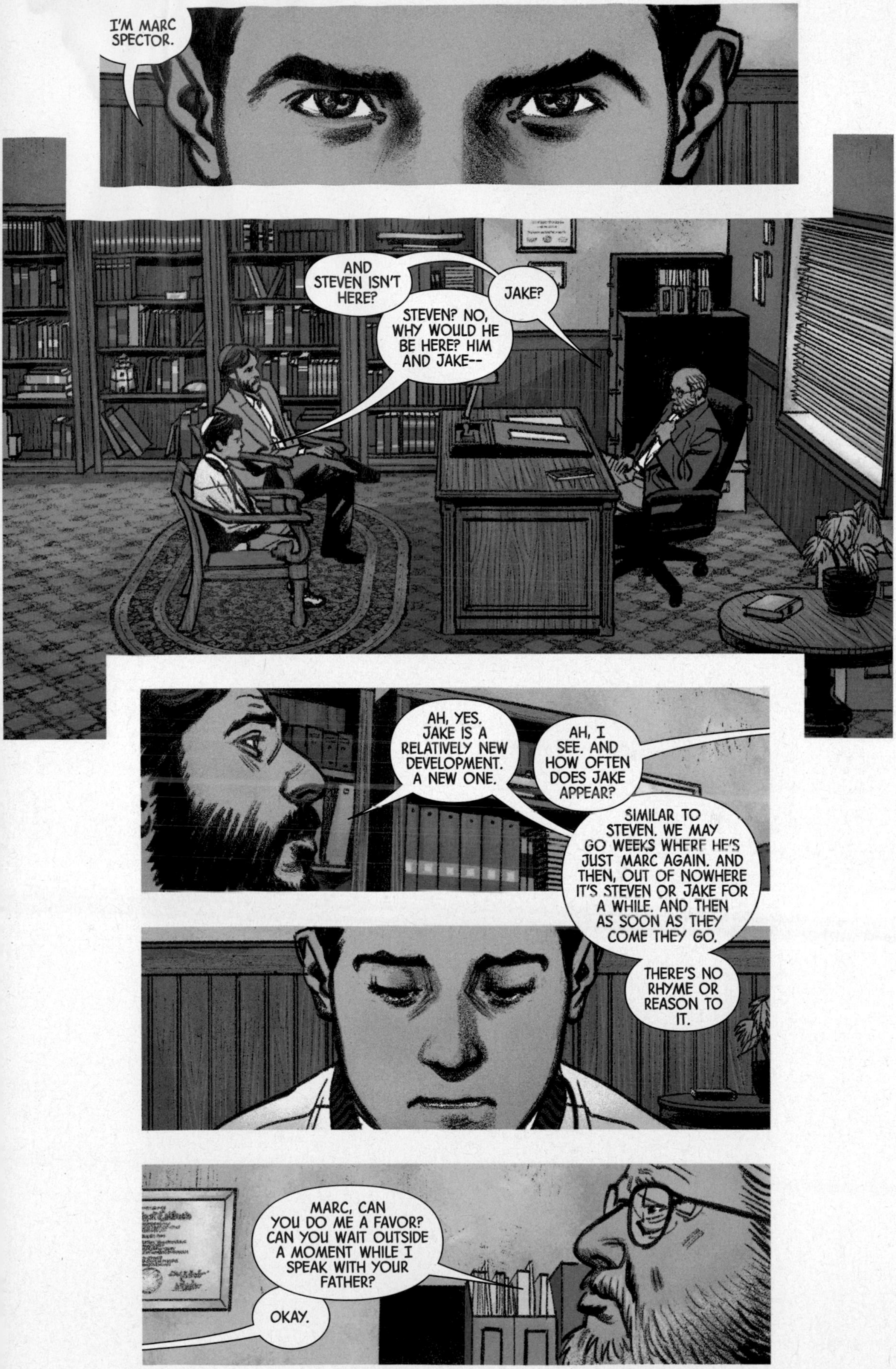

I'M MARC SPECTOR.
AND STEVEN ISN'T HERE?
JAKE?
STEVEN? NO, WHY WOULD HE BE HERE? HIM AND JAKE--
AH, YES. JAKE IS A RELATIVELY NEW DEVELOPMENT. A NEW ONE.
AH, I SEE. AND HOW OFTEN DOES JAKE APPEAR?
SIMILAR TO STEVEN. WE MAY GO WEEKS WHERE HE'S JUST MARC AGAIN. AND THEN, OUT OF NOWHERE IT'S STEVEN OR JAKE FOR A WHILE. AND THEN AS SOON AS THEY COME THEY GO.
THERE'S NO RHYME OR REASON TO IT.
MARC, CAN YOU DO ME A FAVOR? CAN YOU WAIT OUTSIDE A MOMENT WHILE I SPEAK WITH YOUR FATHER?
OKAY.

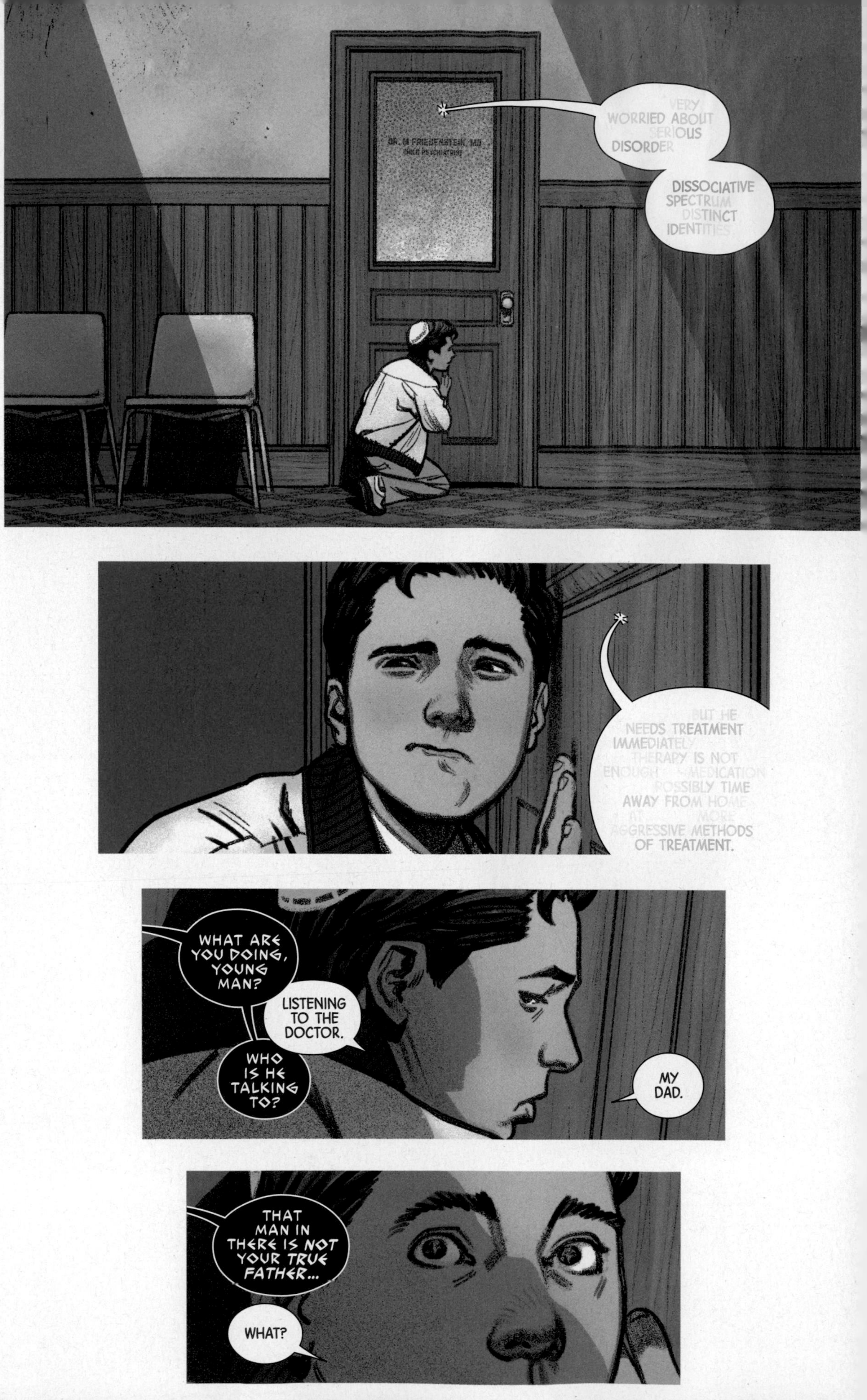

VERY WORRIED ABOUT SERIOUS DISORDER
DISSOCIATIVE SPECTRUM DISTINCT IDENTITIES
BUT HE NEEDS TREATMENT IMMEDIATELY THERAPY IS NOT ENOUGH MEDICATION POSSIBLY TIME AWAY FROM HOME AT MORE AGGRESSIVE METHODS OF TREATMENT.
WHAT ARE YOU DOING, YOUNG MAN?
LISTENING TO THE DOCTOR.
WHO IS HE TALKING TO?
MY DAD.
THAT MAN IN THERE IS *NOT* YOUR *TRUE FATHER*...
WHAT?

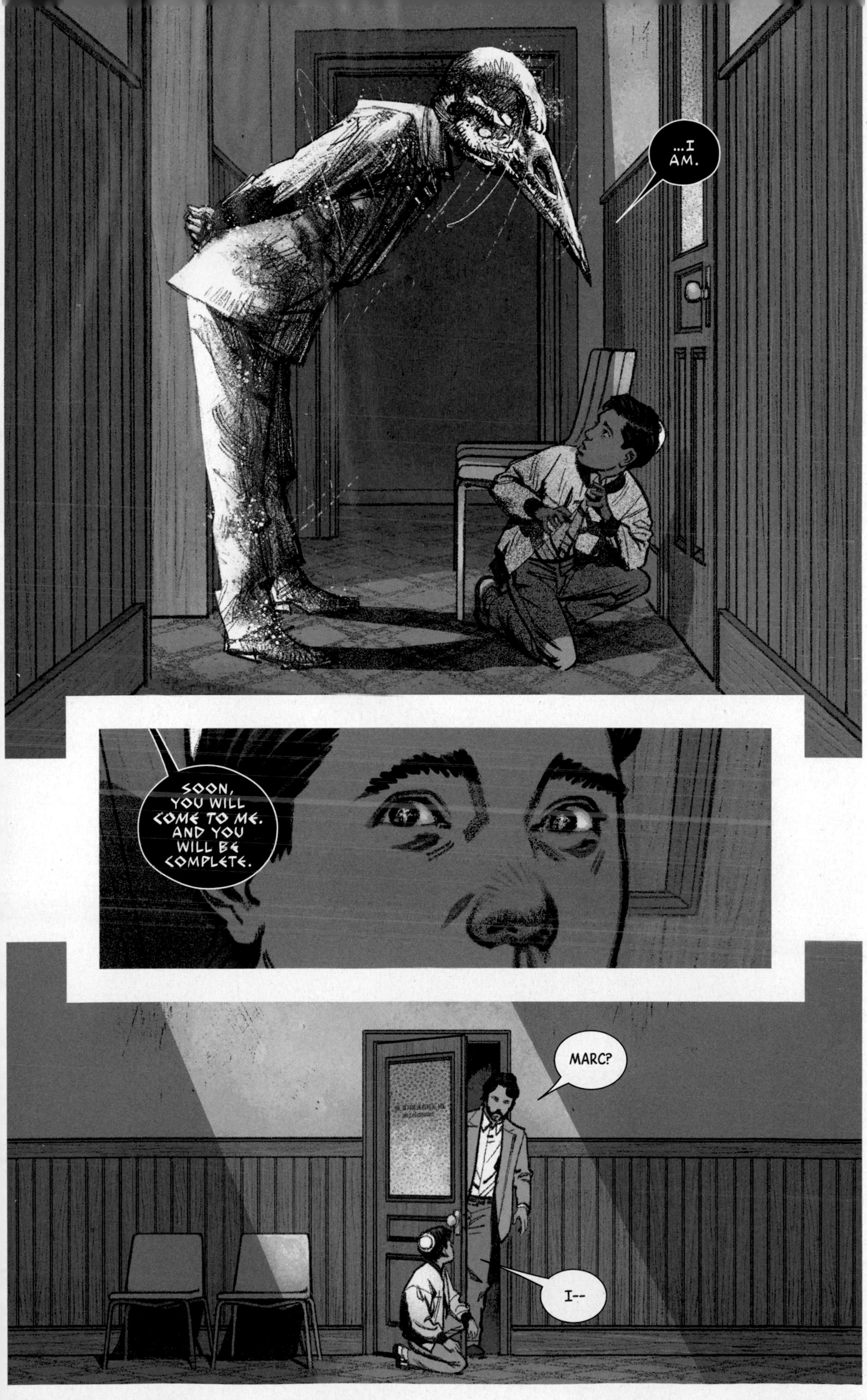
...I AM.
SOON, YOU WILL COME TO ME. AND YOU WILL BE COMPLETE.
MARC?
I--

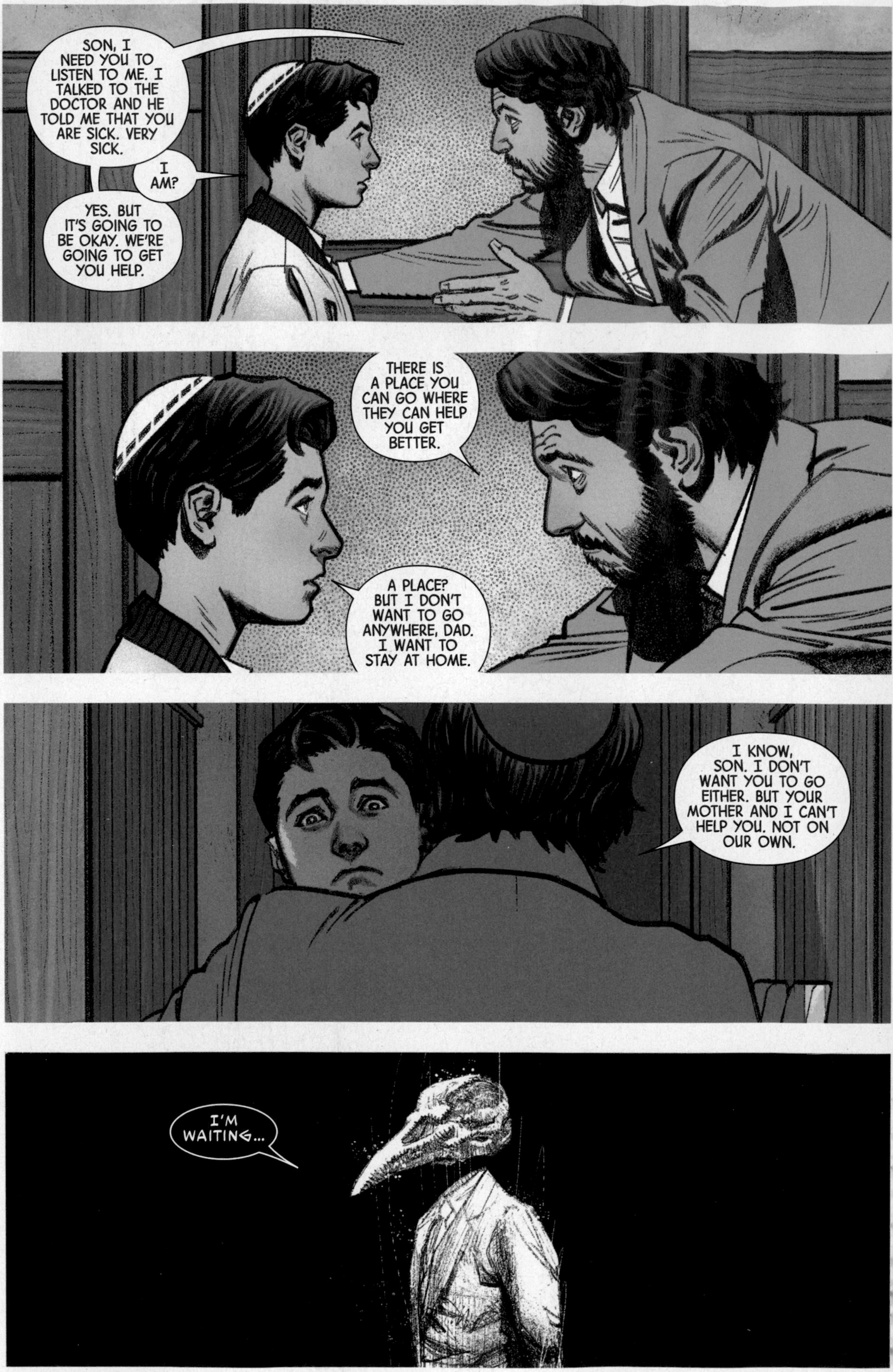
SON, I NEED YOU TO LISTEN TO ME. I TALKED TO THE DOCTOR AND HE TOLD ME THAT YOU ARE SICK. VERY SICK.
I AM?
YES. BUT IT'S GOING TO BE OKAY. WE'RE GOING TO GET YOU HELP.
THERE IS A PLACE YOU CAN GO WHERE THEY CAN HELP YOU GET BETTER.
A PLACE? BUT I DON'T WANT TO GO ANYWHERE, DAD. I WANT TO STAY AT HOME.
I KNOW, SON. I DON'T WANT YOU TO GO EITHER. BUT YOUR MOTHER AND I CAN'T HELP YOU. NOT ON OUR OWN.
I'M WAITING...

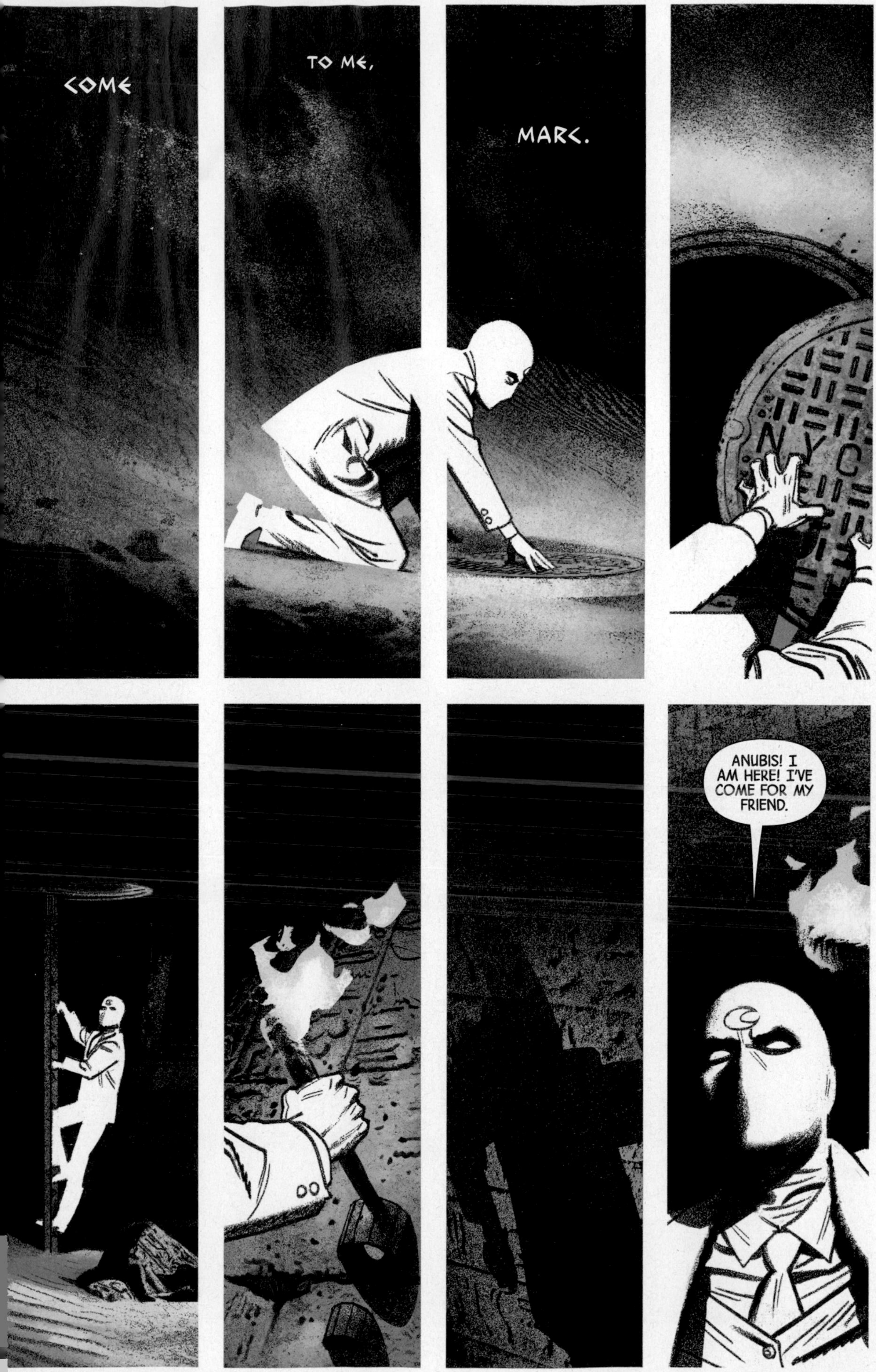
COME
TO ME,
MARC.
NYC
ANUBIS! I AM HERE! I'VE COME FOR MY FRIEND.

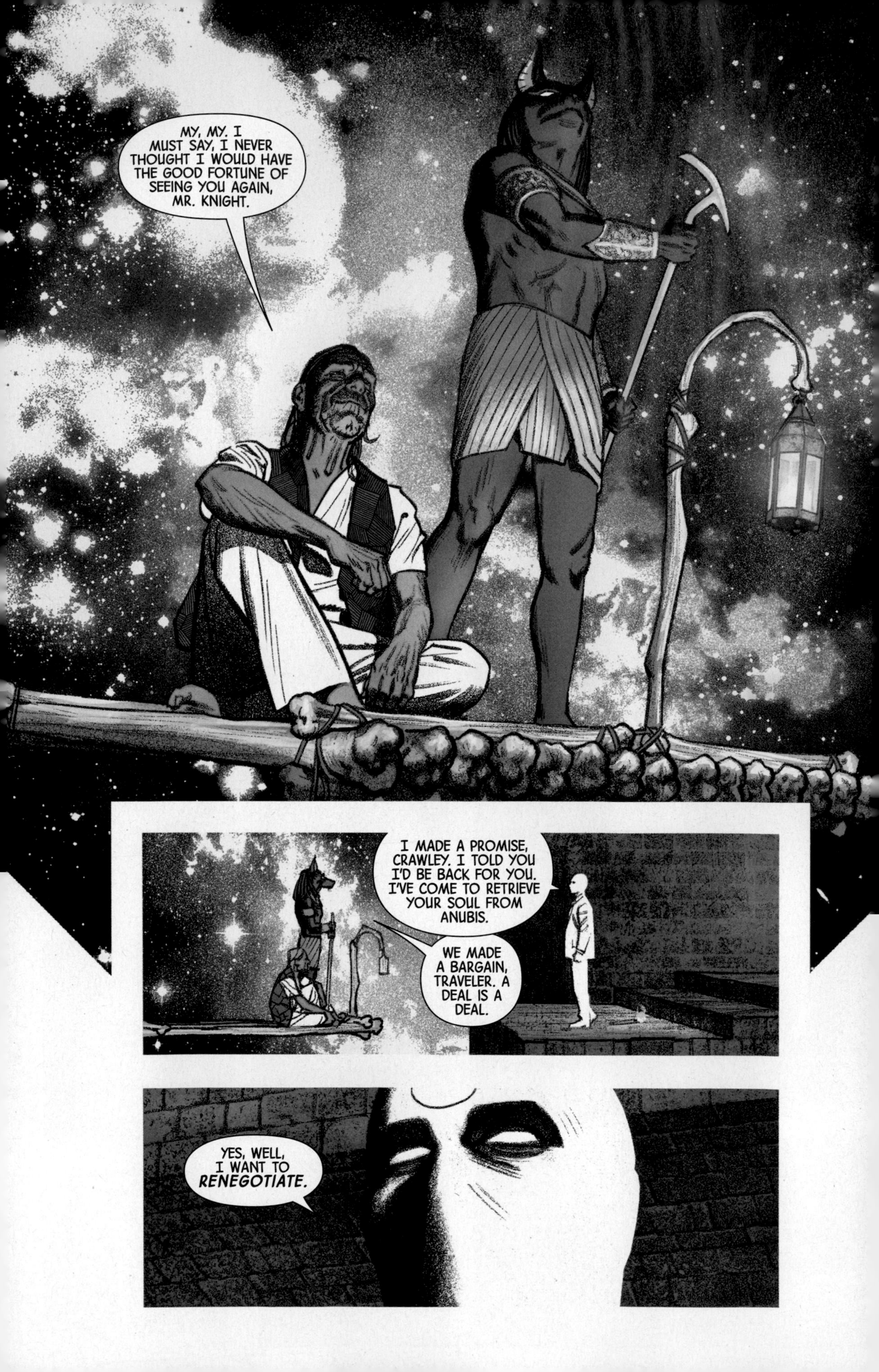
MY, MY. I MUST SAY, I NEVER THOUGHT I WOULD HAVE THE GOOD FORTUNE OF SEEING YOU AGAIN, MR. KNIGHT.
I MADE A PROMISE, CRAWLEY. I TOLD YOU I'D BE BACK FOR YOU. I'VE COME TO RETRIEVE YOUR SOUL FROM ANUBIS.
WE MADE A BARGAIN, TRAVELER. A DEAL IS A DEAL.
YES, WELL, I WANT TO *RENEGOTIATE.*

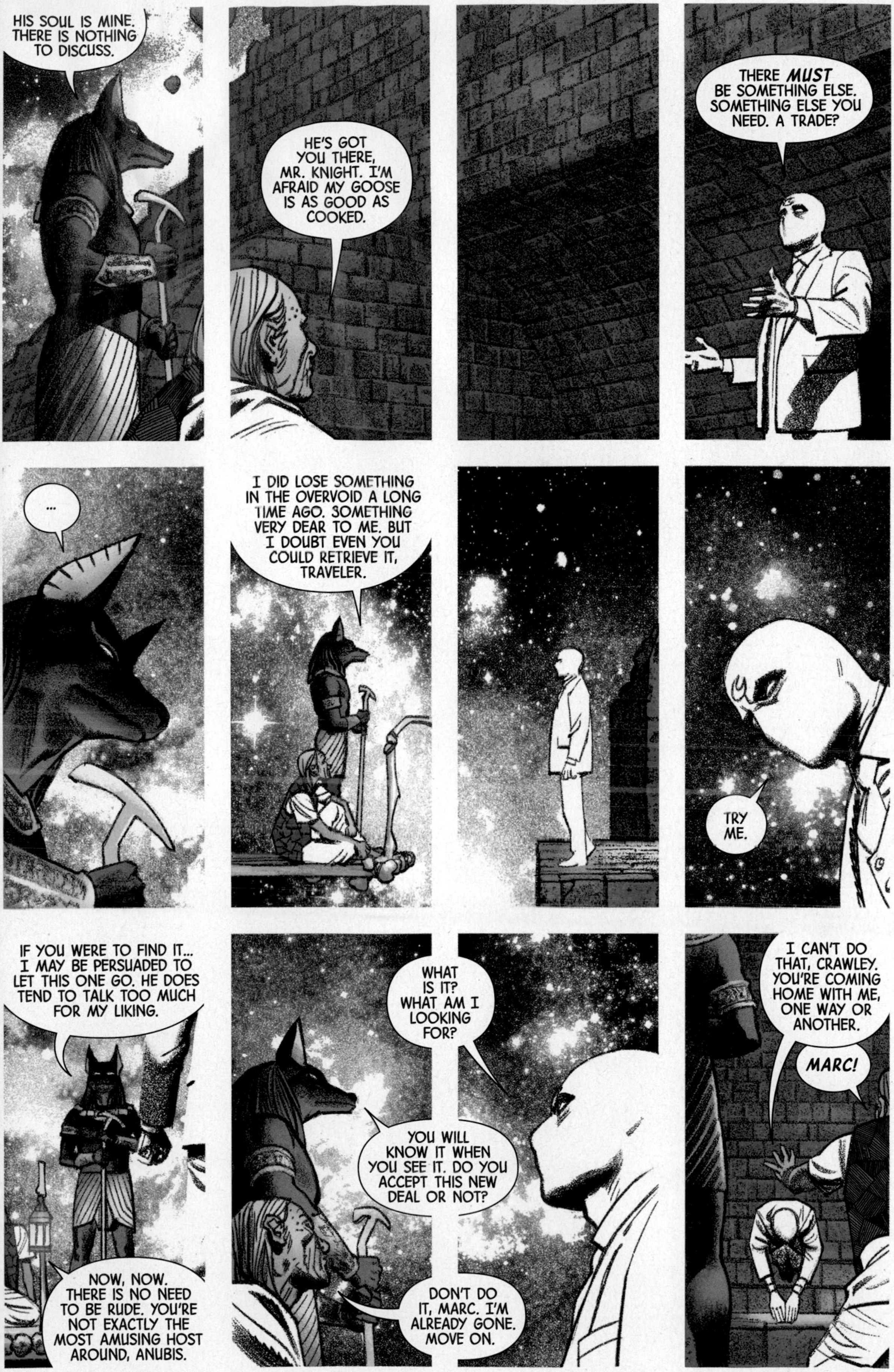
HIS SOUL IS MINE. THERE IS NOTHING TO DISCUSS.
HE'S GOT YOU THERE, MR. KNIGHT. I'M AFRAID MY GOOSE IS AS GOOD AS COOKED.
THERE MUST BE SOMETHING ELSE. SOMETHING ELSE YOU NEED. A TRADE?
...
I DID LOSE SOMETHING IN THE OVERVOID A LONG TIME AGO. SOMETHING VERY DEAR TO ME. BUT I DOUBT EVEN YOU COULD RETRIEVE IT, TRAVELER.
TRY ME.
IF YOU WERE TO FIND IT... I MAY BE PERSUADED TO LET THIS ONE GO. HE DOES TEND TO TALK TOO MUCH FOR MY LIKING.
NOW, NOW. THERE IS NO NEED TO BE RUDE. YOU'RE NOT EXACTLY THE MOST AMUSING HOST AROUND, ANUBIS.
WHAT IS IT? WHAT AM I LOOKING FOR?
YOU WILL KNOW IT WHEN YOU SEE IT. DO YOU ACCEPT THIS NEW DEAL OR NOT?
DON'T DO IT, MARC. I'M ALREADY GONE. MOVE ON.
I CAN'T DO THAT, CRAWLEY. YOU'RE COMING HOME WITH ME, ONE WAY OR ANOTHER.
MARC!

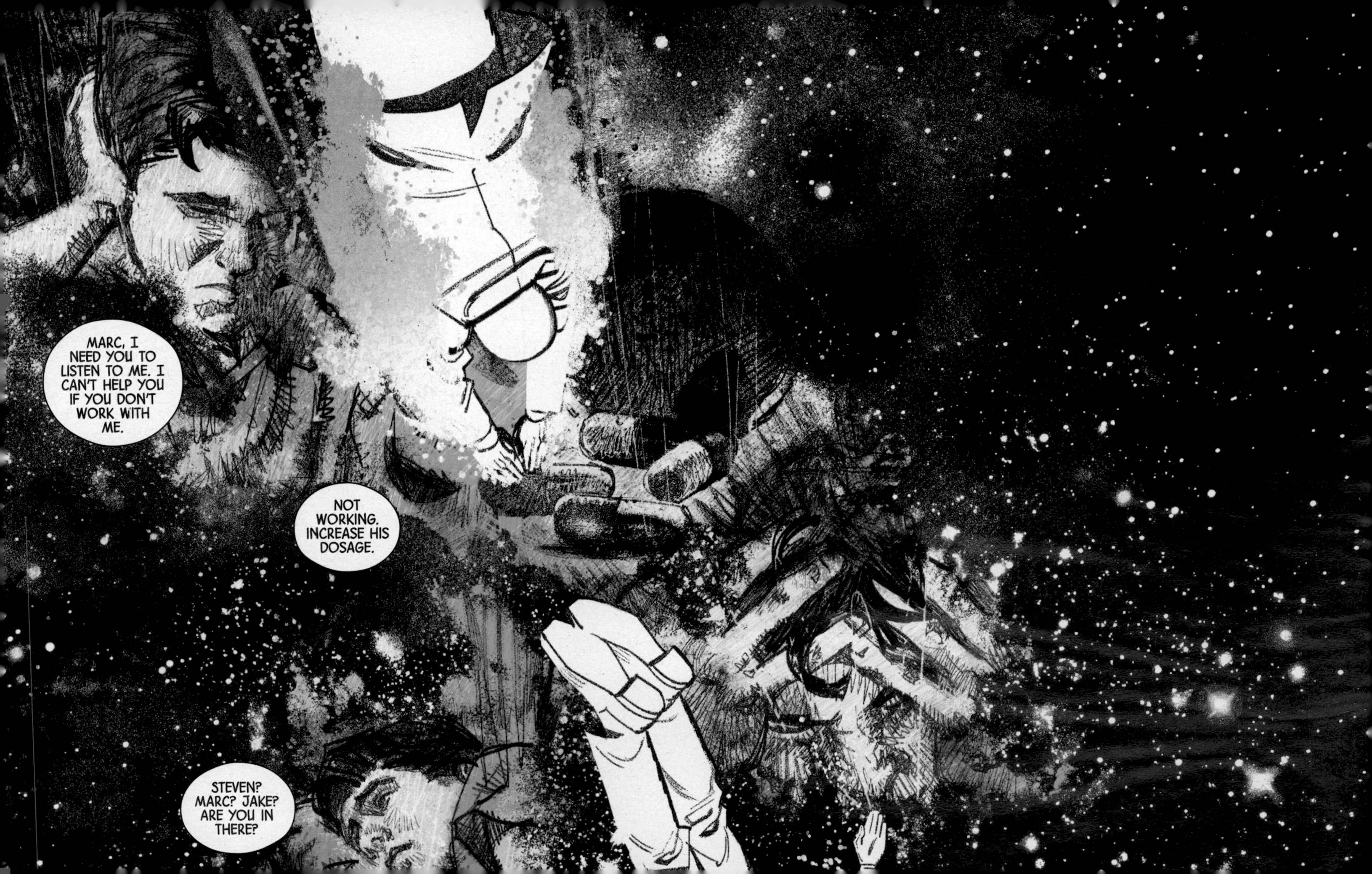
MARC, I NEED YOU TO LISTEN TO ME. I CAN'T HELP YOU IF YOU DON'T WORK WITH ME.
NOT WORKING. INCREASE HIS DOSAGE.
STEVEN? MARC? JAKE? ARE YOU IN THERE?

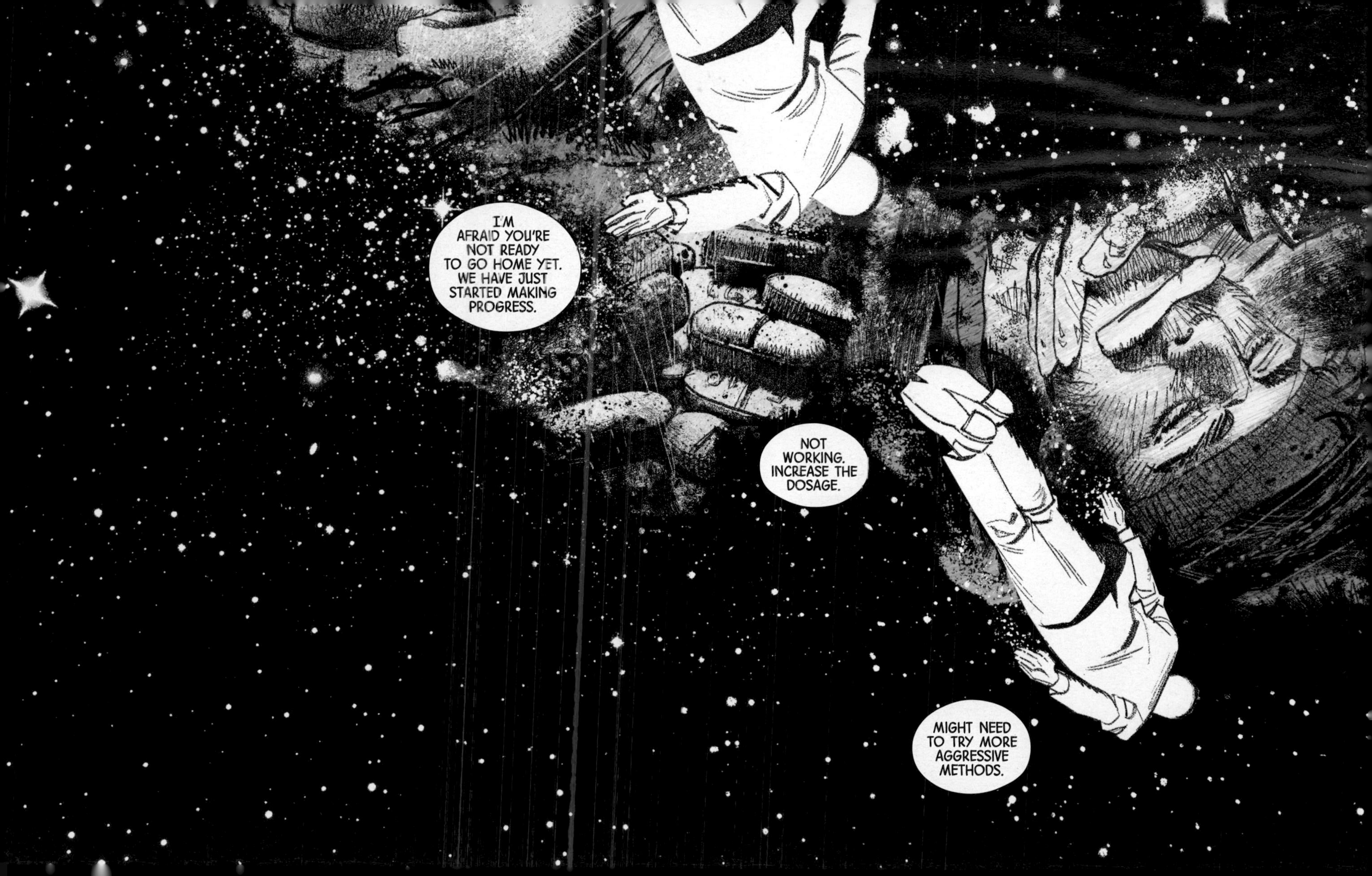
I'M AFRAID YOU'RE NOT READY TO GO HOME YET. WE HAVE JUST STARTED MAKING PROGRESS.
NOT WORKING. INCREASE THE DOSAGE.
MIGHT NEED TO TRY MORE AGGRESSIVE METHODS.

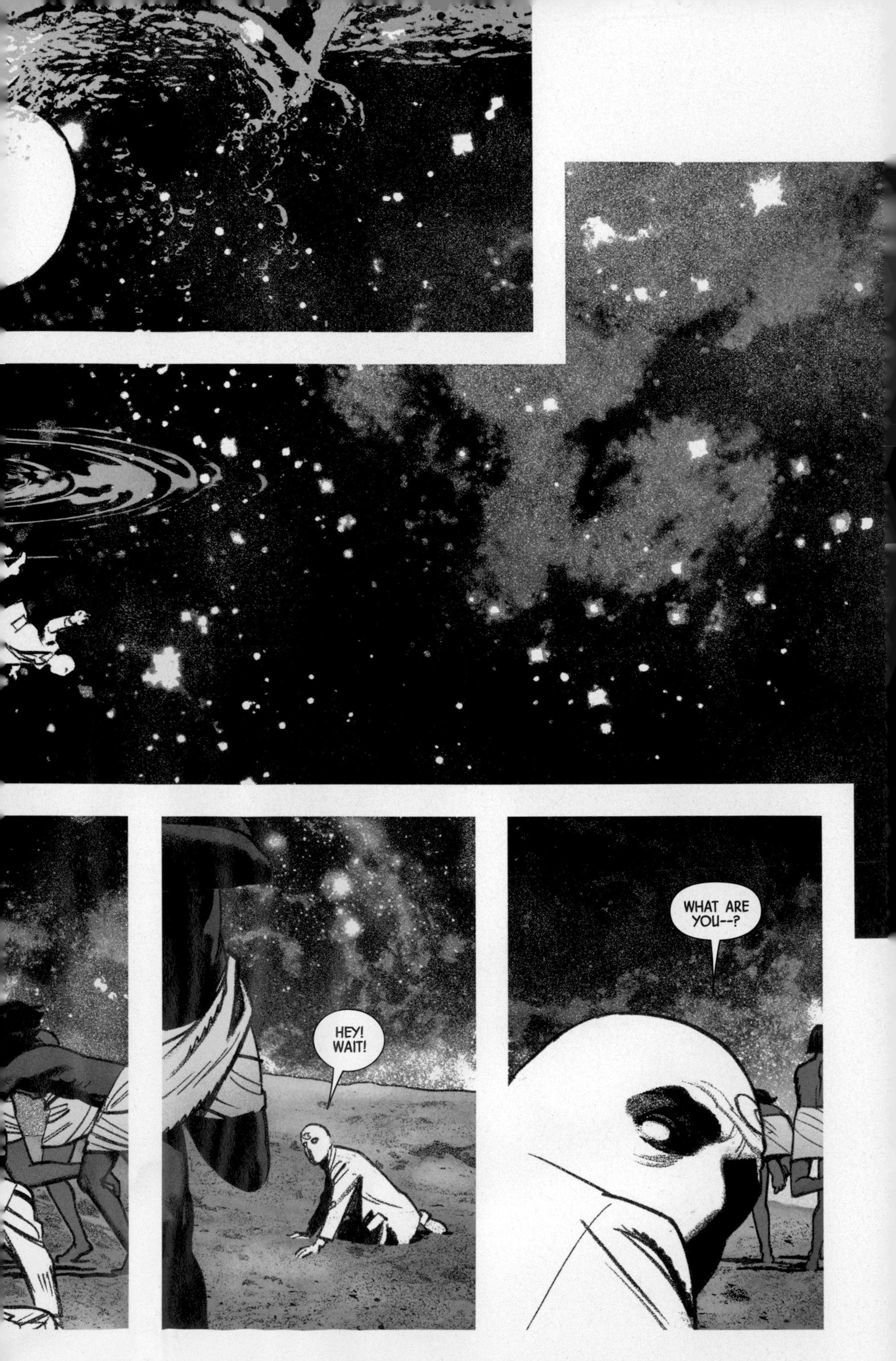
HEY! WAIT!
WHAT ARE YOU--?

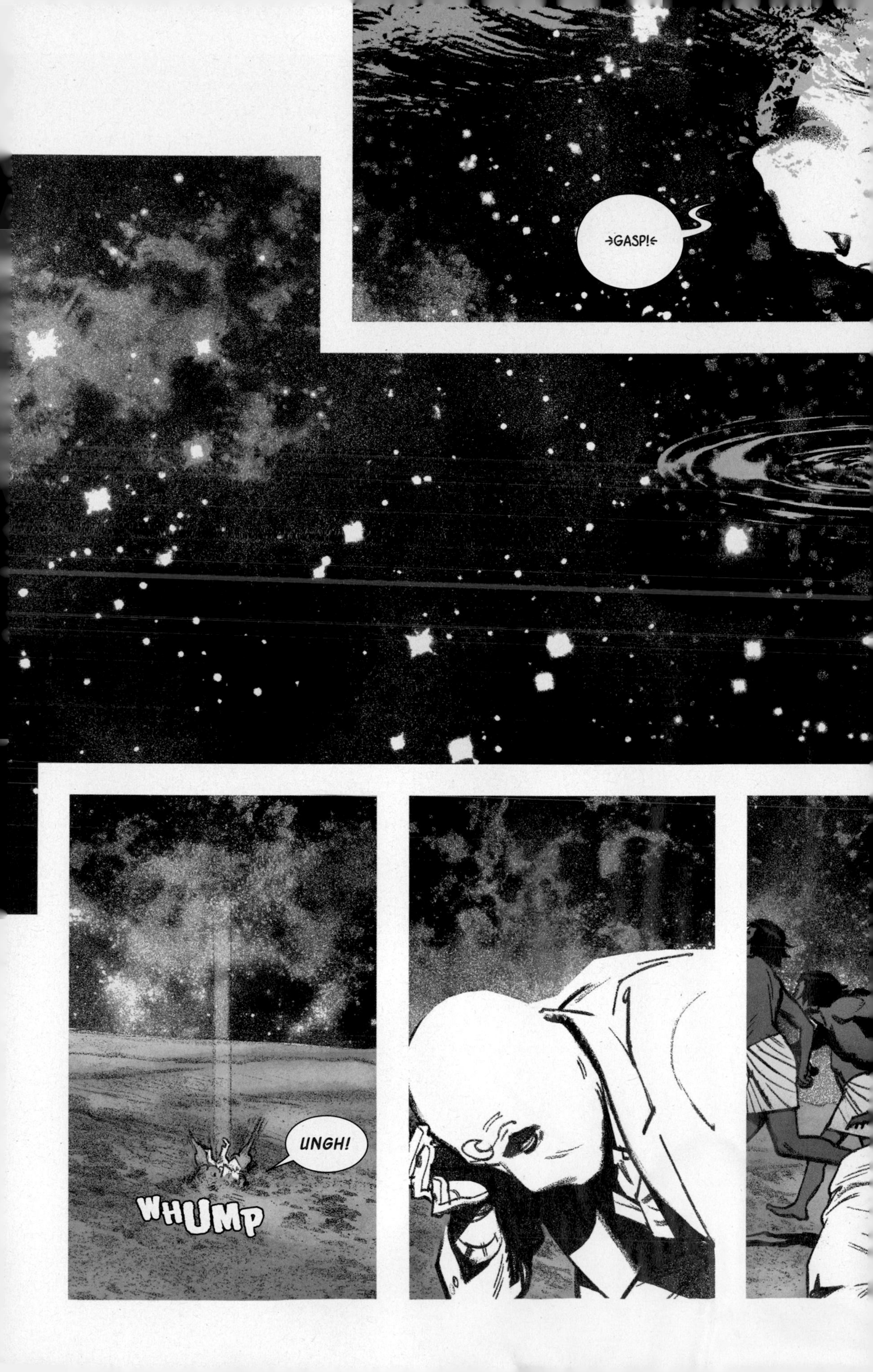
→GASP!←
UNGH!
WHUMP

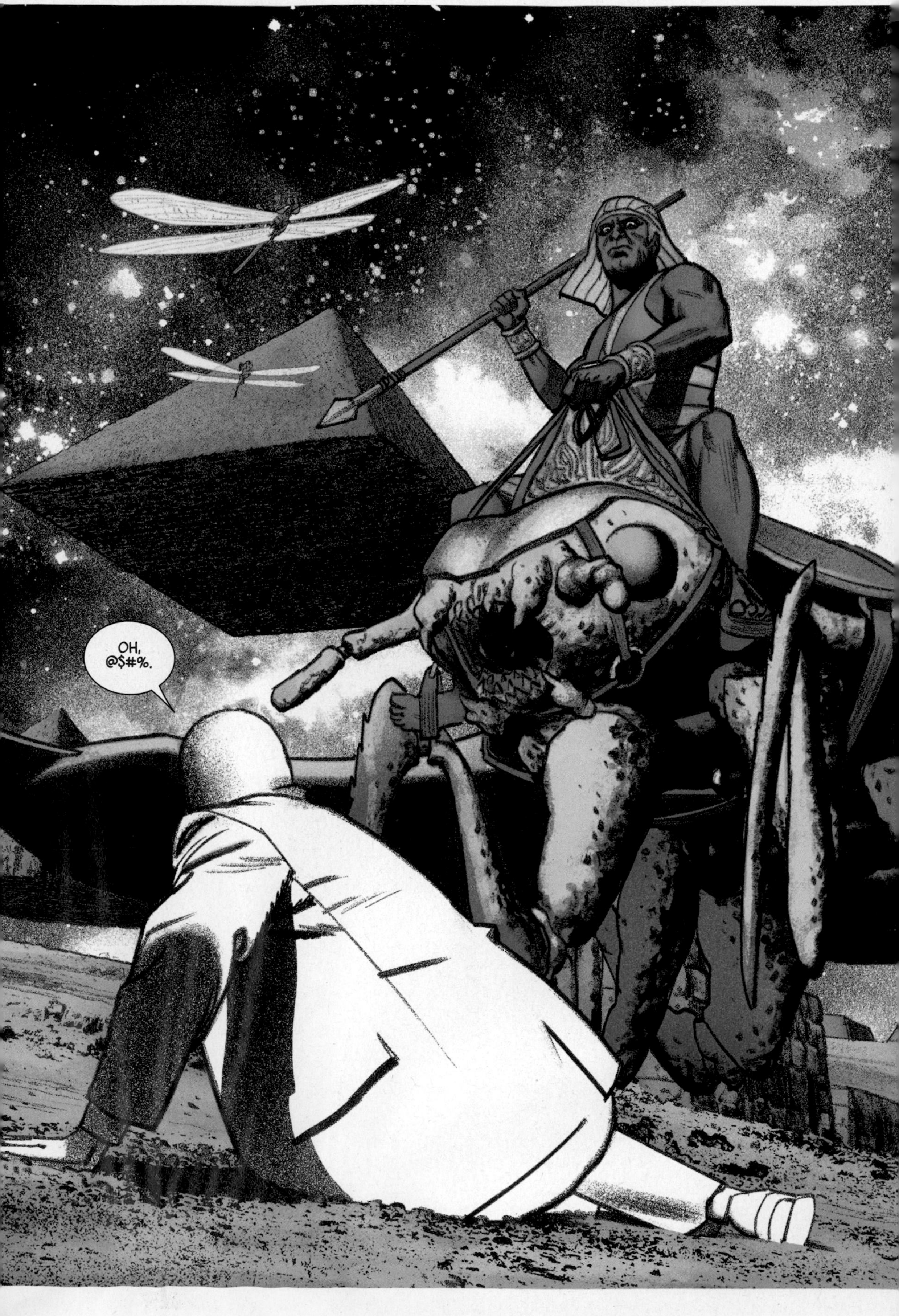
OH, @$#%.

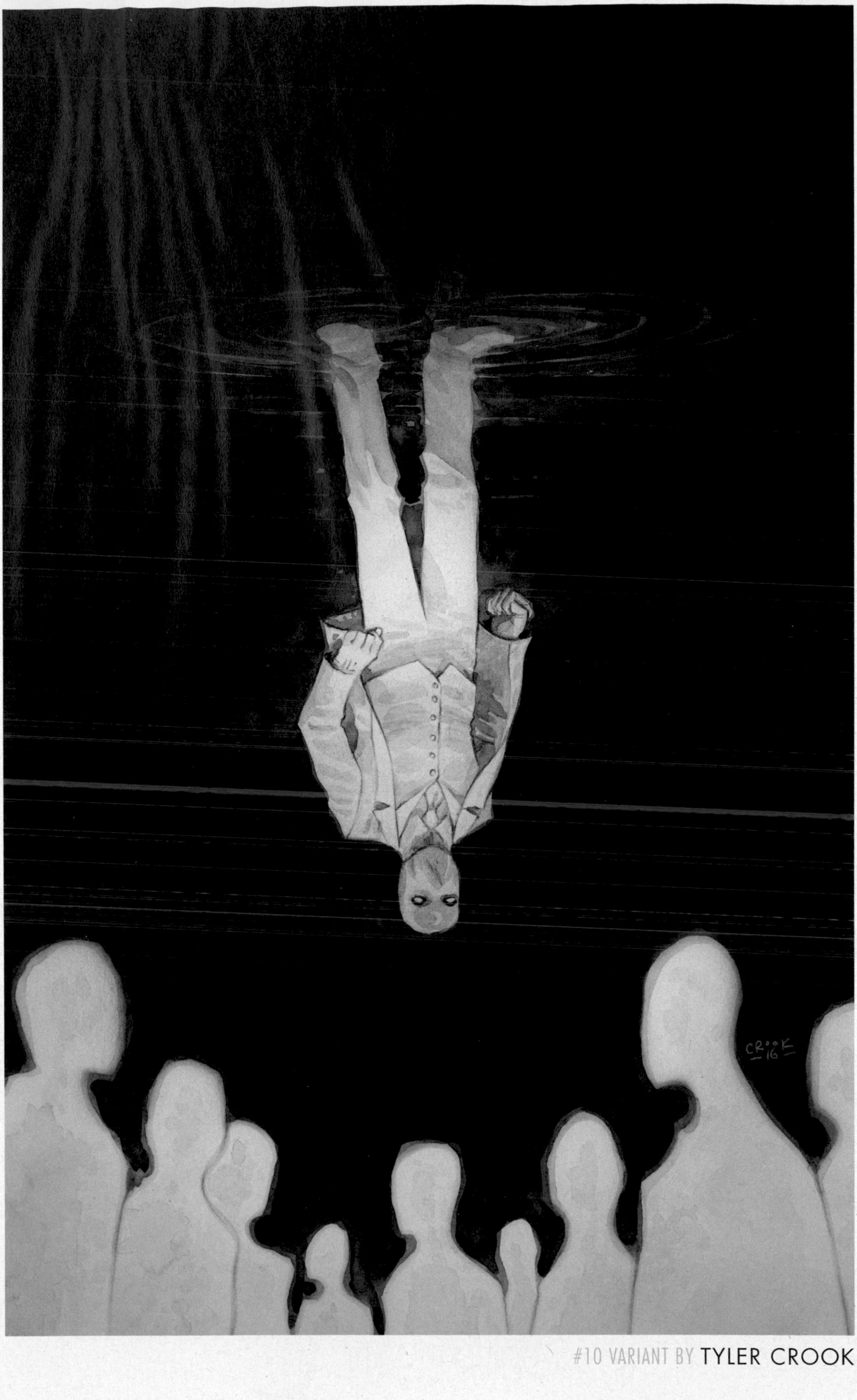
CROOK
16

#10 VARIANT BY TYLER CROOK

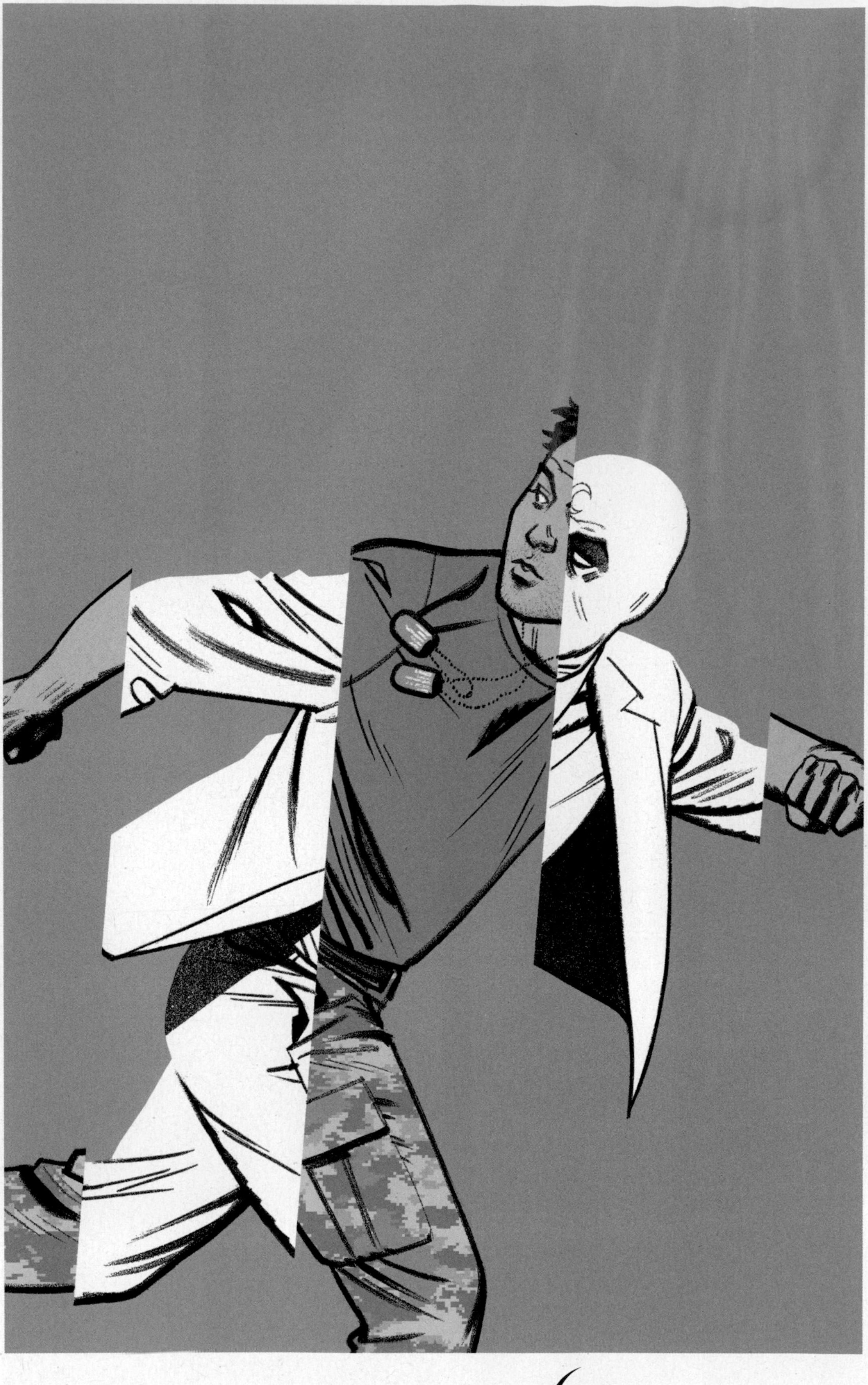

BIRTH AND DEATH
PART TWO

11

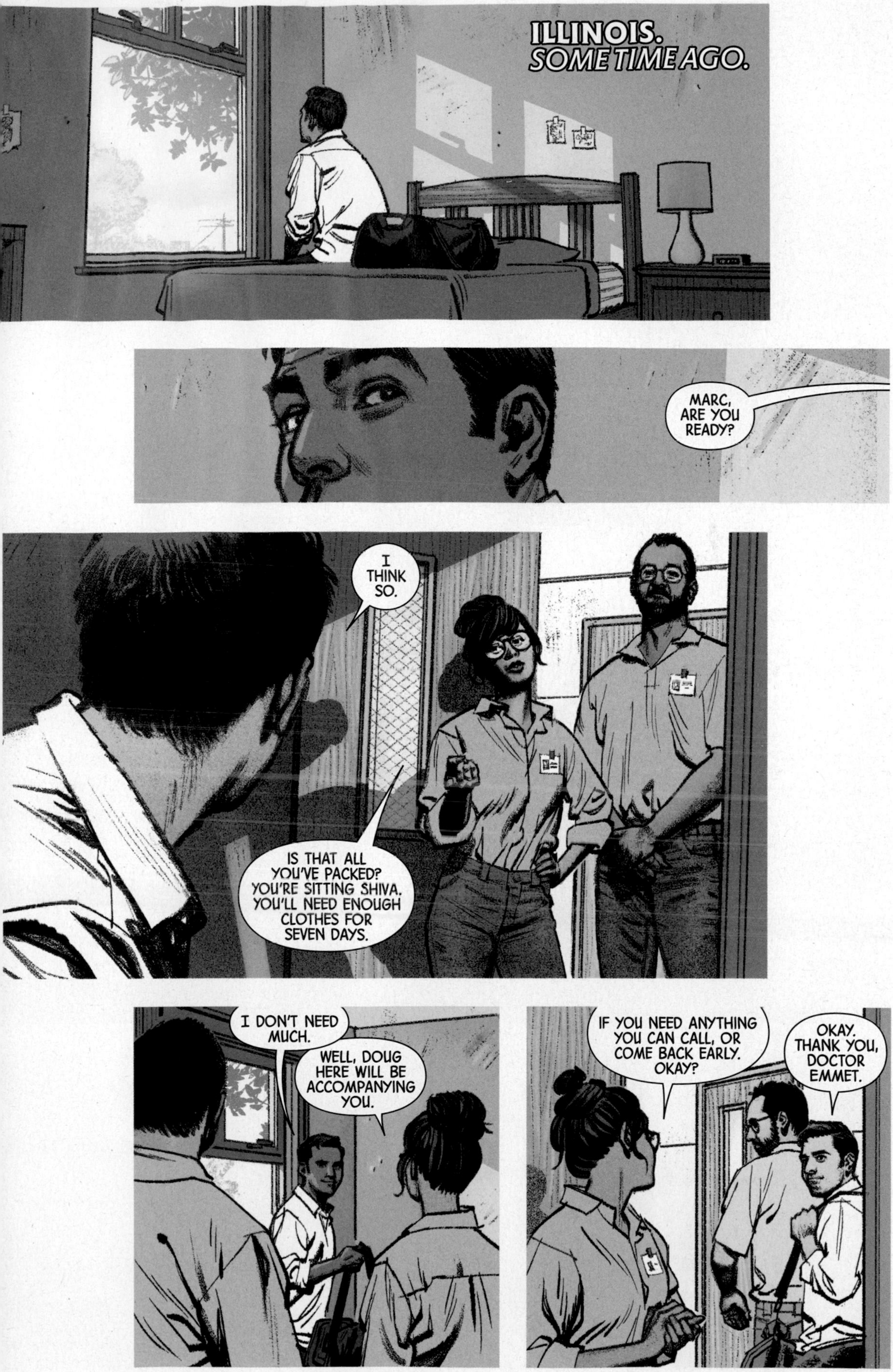
ILLINOIS.
SOME TIME AGO.
MARC, ARE YOU READY?
I THINK SO.
IS THAT ALL YOU'VE PACKED? YOU'RE SITTING SHIVA. YOU'LL NEED ENOUGH CLOTHES FOR SEVEN DAYS.
I DON'T NEED MUCH.
WELL, DOUG HERE WILL BE ACCOMPANYING YOU.
IF YOU NEED ANYTHING YOU CAN CALL, OR COME BACK EARLY. OKAY?
OKAY. THANK YOU, DOCTOR EMMET.

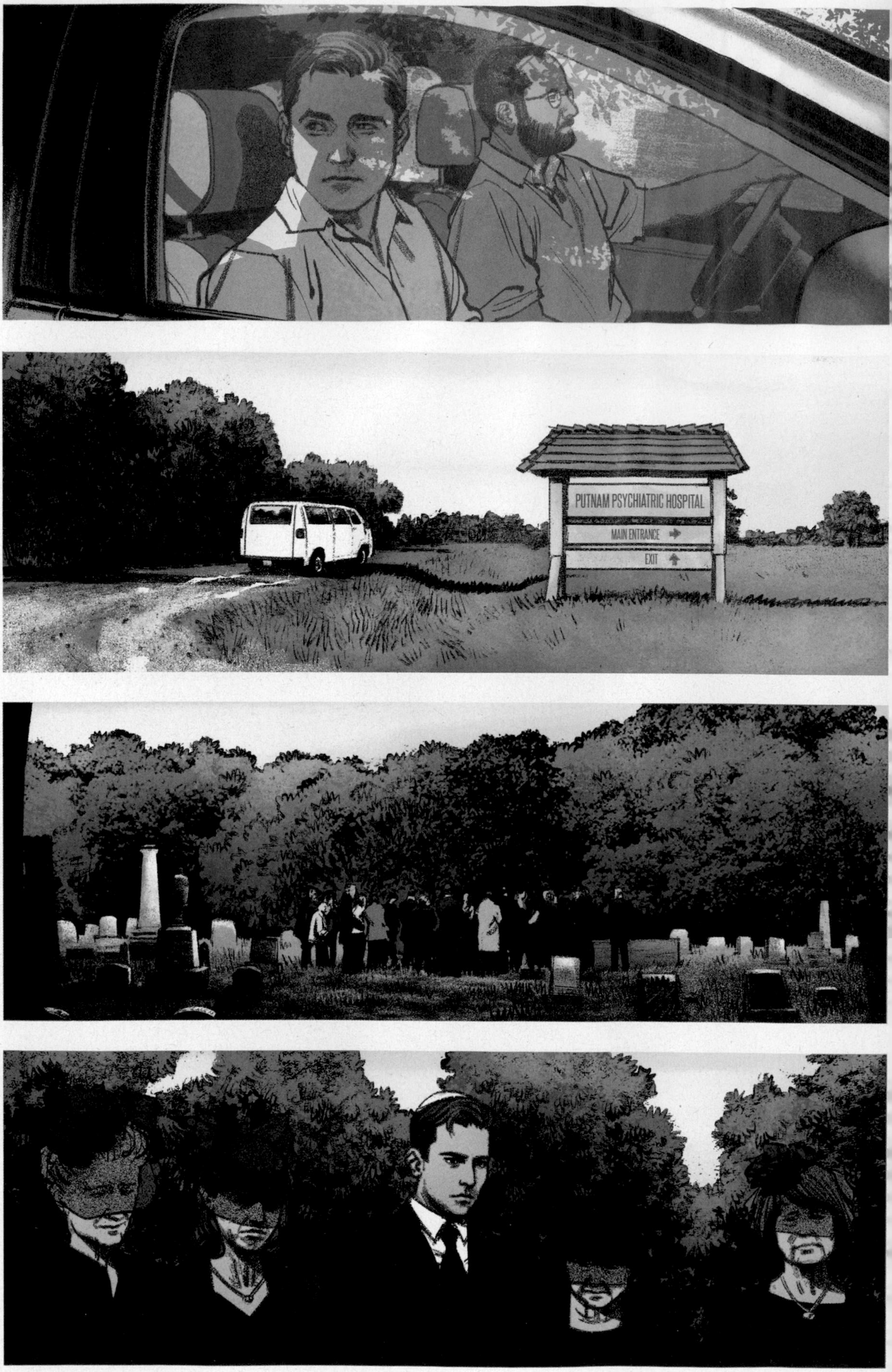
PUTNAM PSYCHIATRIC HOSPITAL
MAIN ENTRANCE
EXIT

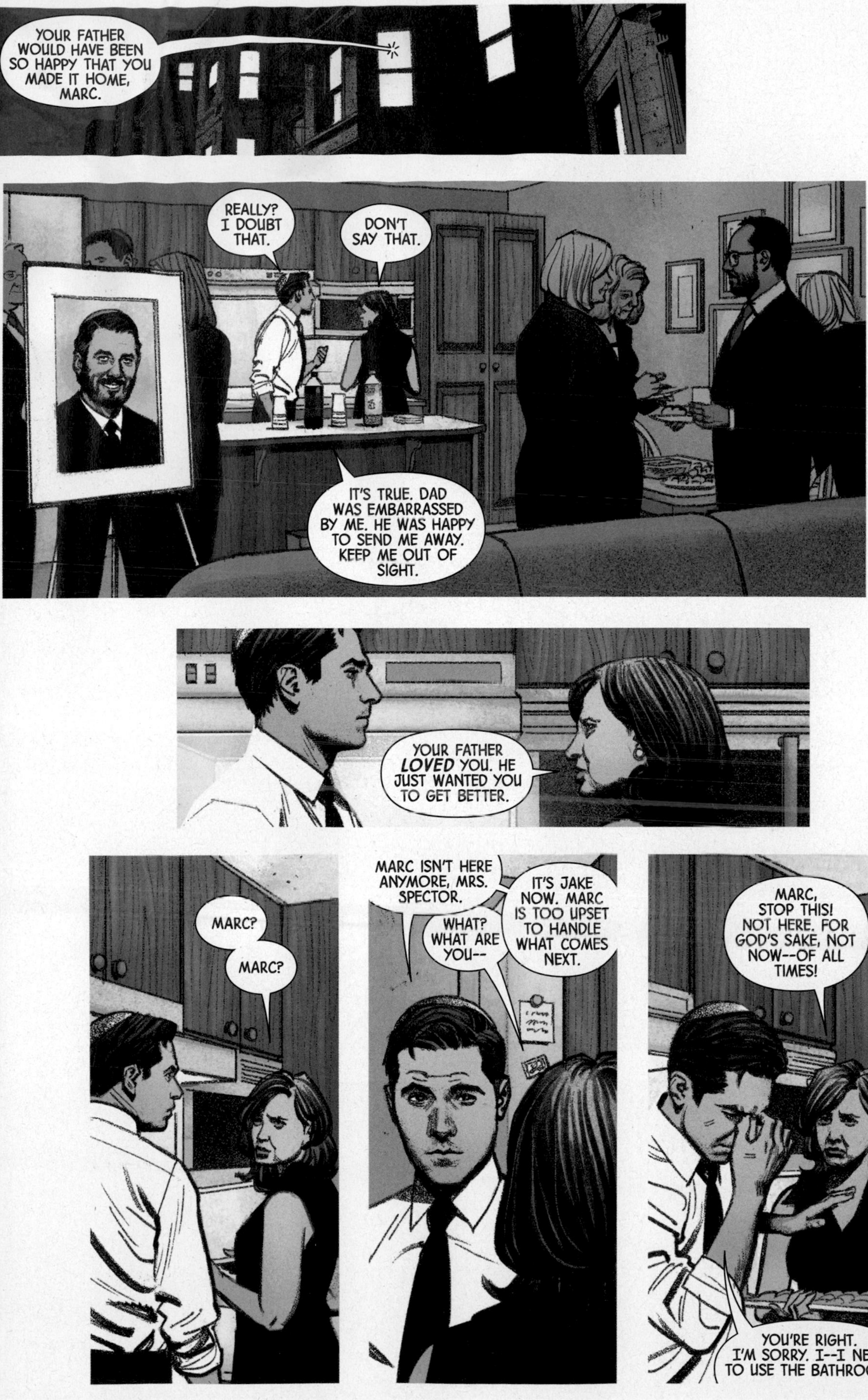
YOUR FATHER WOULD HAVE BEEN SO HAPPY THAT YOU MADE IT HOME, MARC.
REALLY? I DOUBT THAT.
DON'T SAY THAT.
IT'S TRUE. DAD WAS EMBARRASSED BY ME. HE WAS HAPPY TO SEND ME AWAY. KEEP ME OUT OF SIGHT.
YOUR FATHER LOVED YOU. HE JUST WANTED YOU TO GET BETTER.
MARC?
MARC?
MARC ISN'T HERE ANYMORE, MRS. SPECTOR.
WHAT? WHAT ARE YOU--
IT'S JAKE NOW. MARC IS TOO UPSET TO HANDLE WHAT COMES NEXT.
MARC, STOP THIS! NOT HERE. FOR GOD'S SAKE, NOT NOW--OF ALL TIMES!
YOU'RE RIGHT. I'M SORRY. I--I NEED TO USE THE BATHROOM.

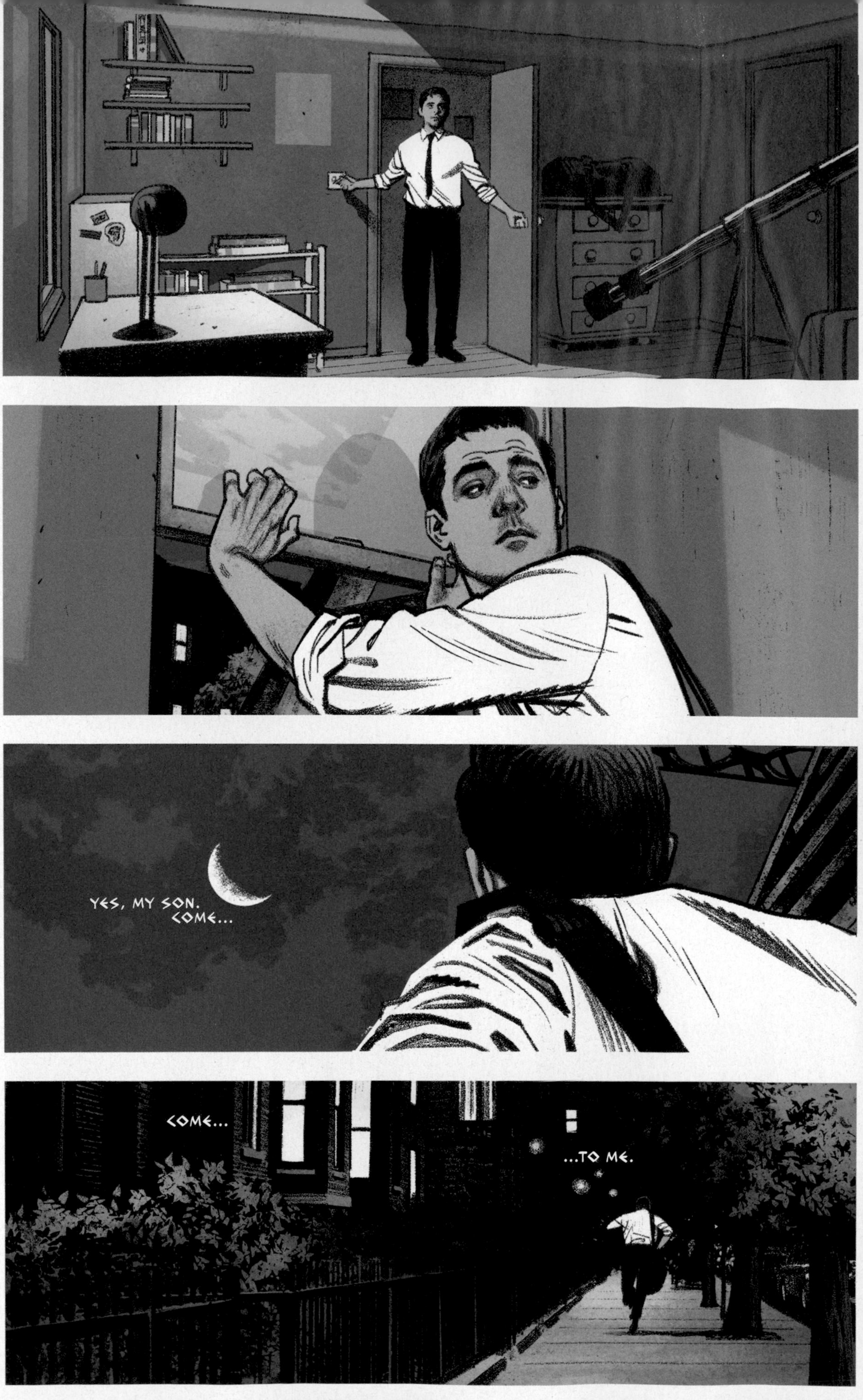
YES, MY SON.
COME...
COME...
...TO ME.

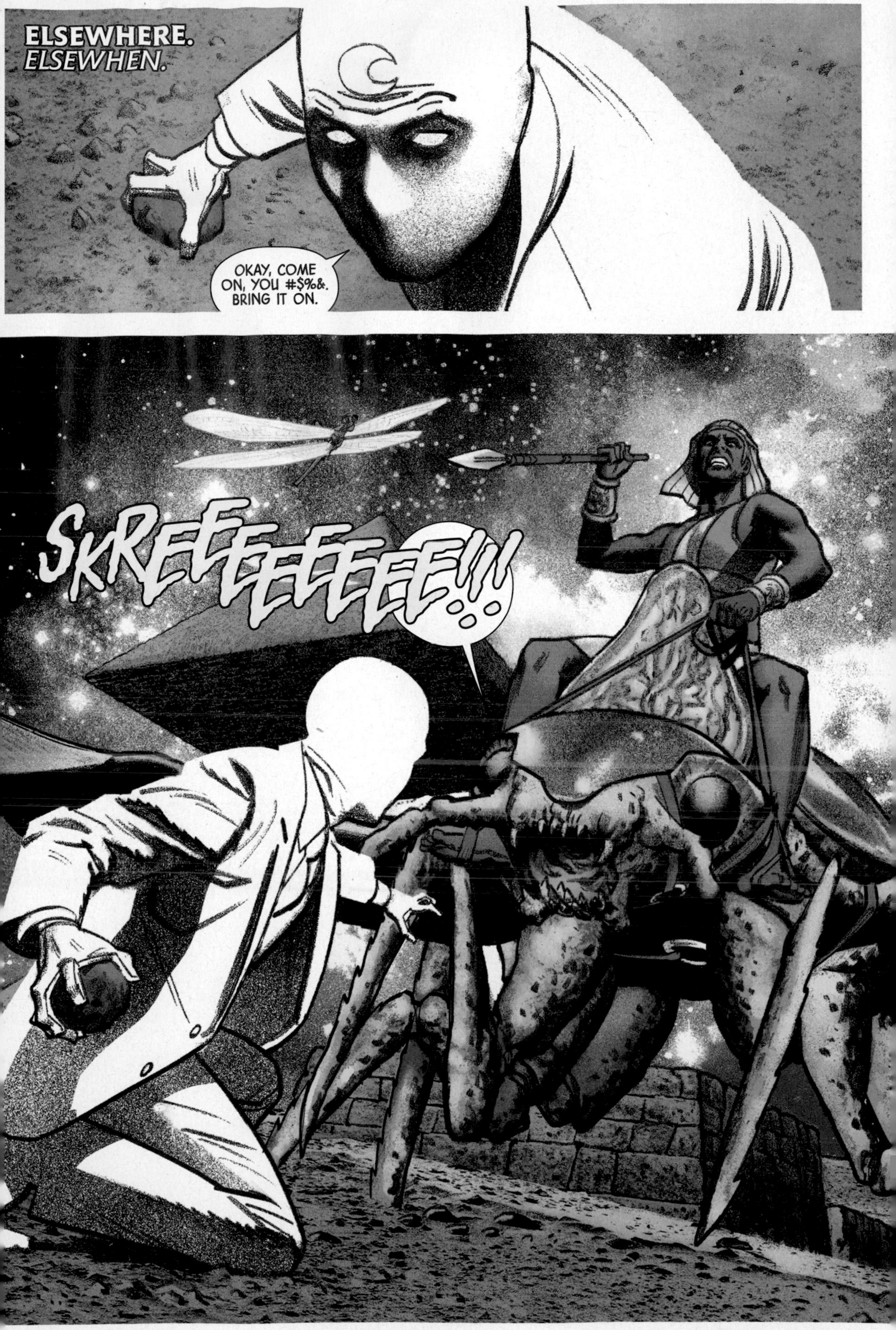
ELSEWHERE.
ELSEWHEN.
OKAY, COME ON, YOU #$%&. BRING IT ON.
SKREEEEEEEEEE!!!

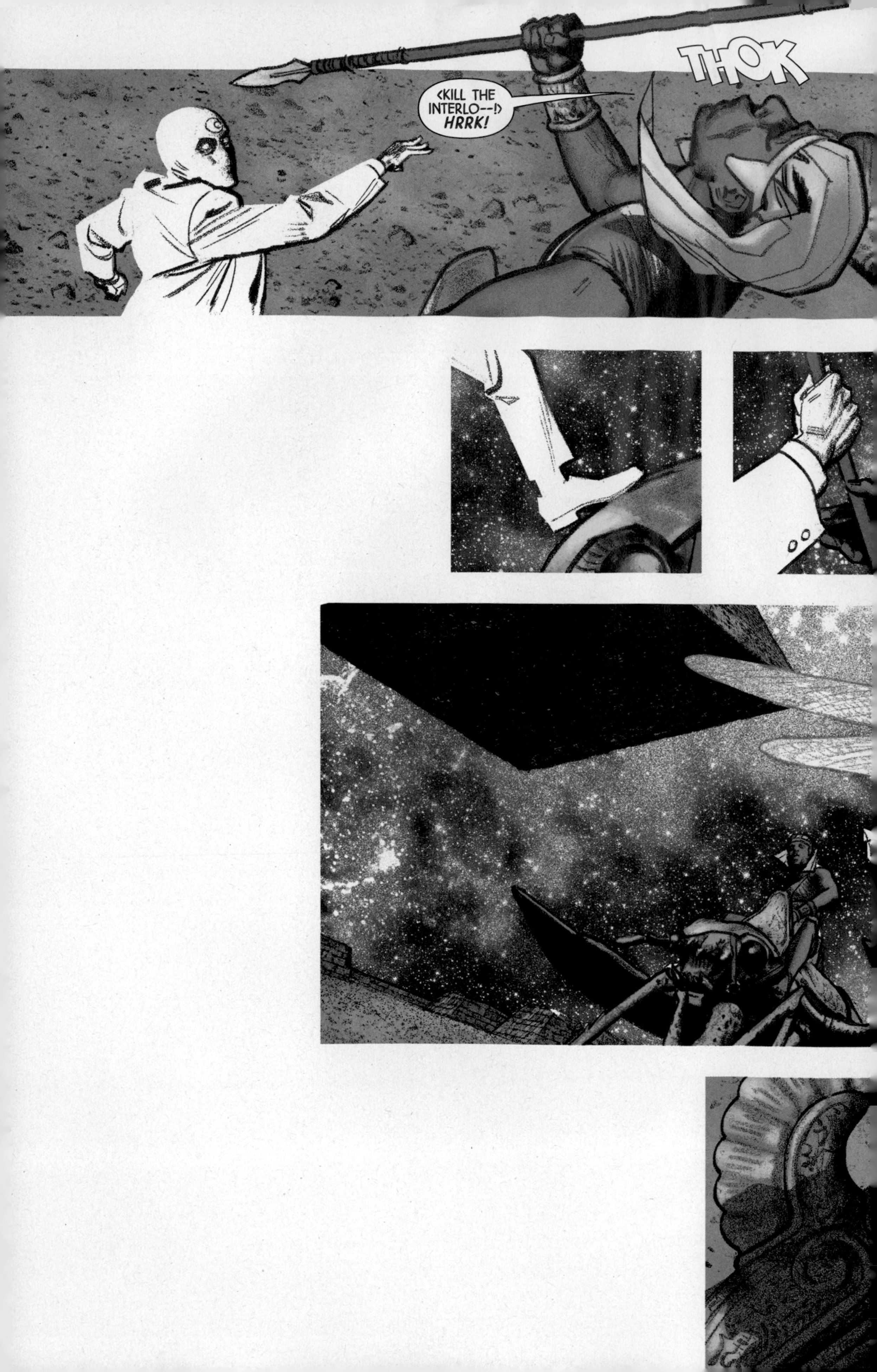

THOK
<KILL THE INTERLO--!> HRRK!

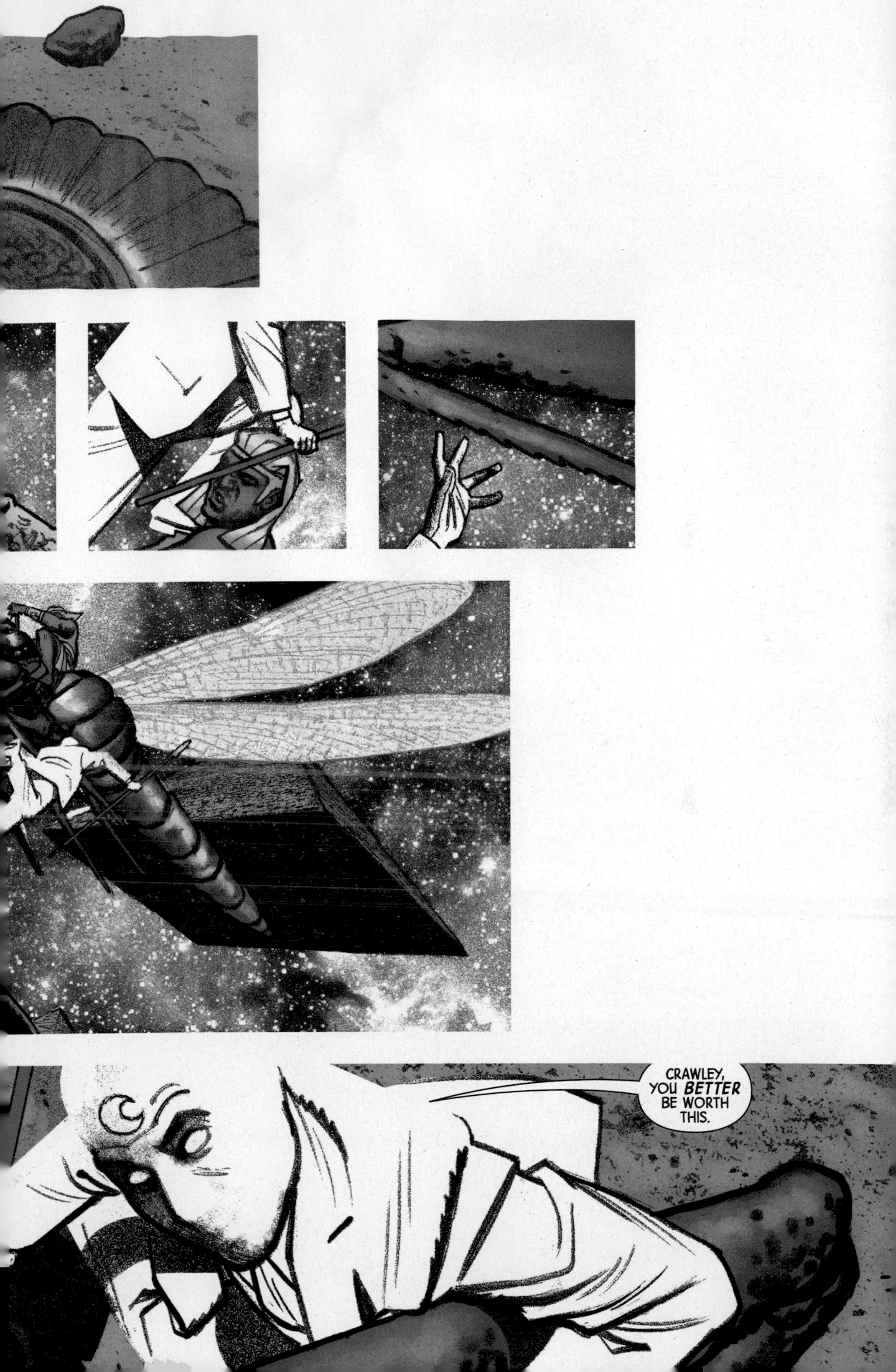
CRAWLEY, YOU BETTER BE WORTH THIS.

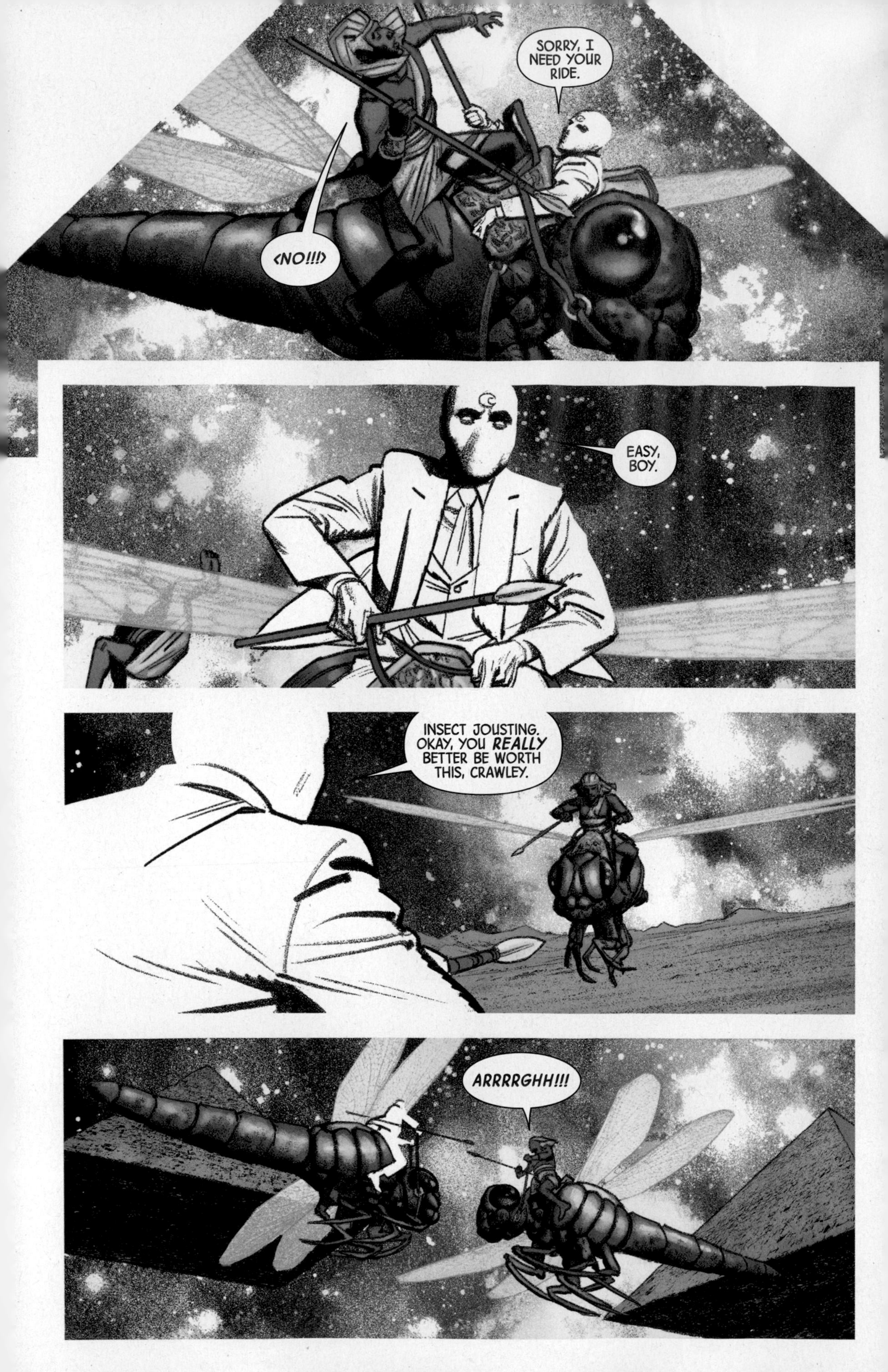
SORRY, I NEED YOUR RIDE.
<NO!!!>
EASY, BOY.
INSECT JOUSTING. OKAY, YOU *REALLY* BETTER BE WORTH THIS, CRAWLEY.
ARRRRGHH!!!

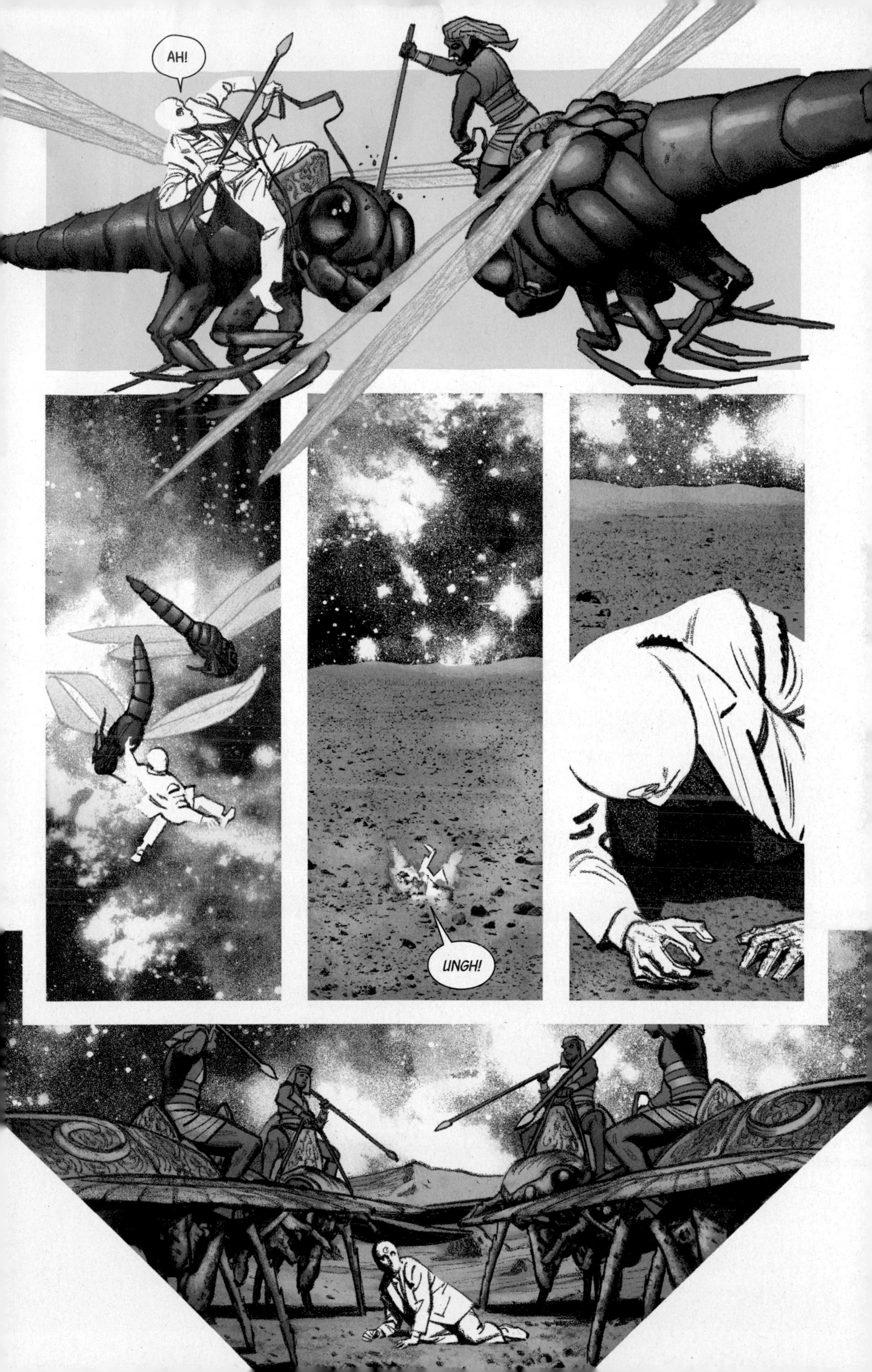
AH!
UNGH!

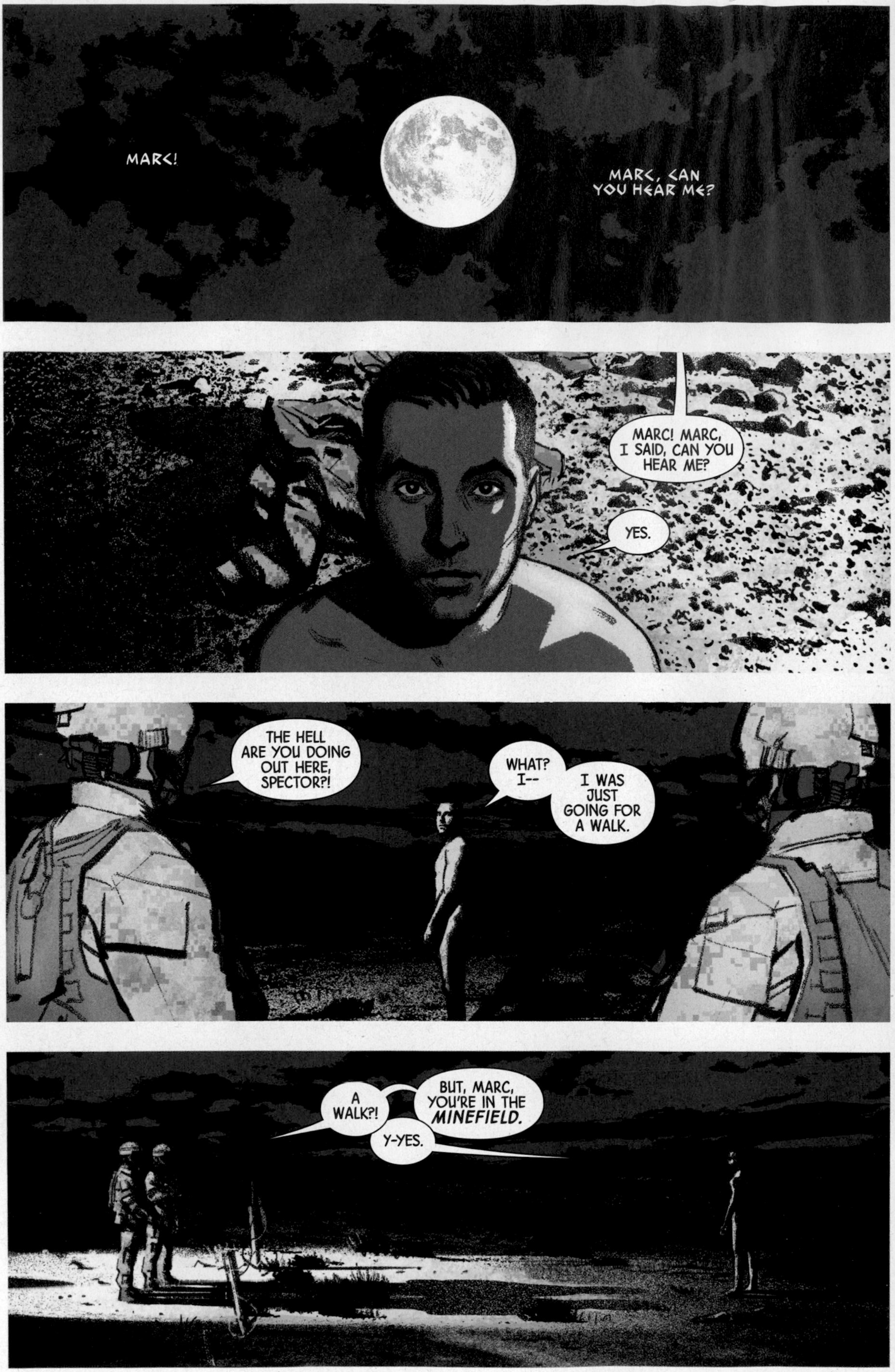
MARC!
MARC, CAN YOU HEAR ME?
MARC! MARC, I SAID, CAN YOU HEAR ME?
YES.
THE HELL ARE YOU DOING OUT HERE, SPECTOR?!
WHAT? I--
I WAS JUST GOING FOR A WALK.
A WALK?!
BUT, MARC, YOU'RE IN THE *MINEFIELD.*
Y-YES.

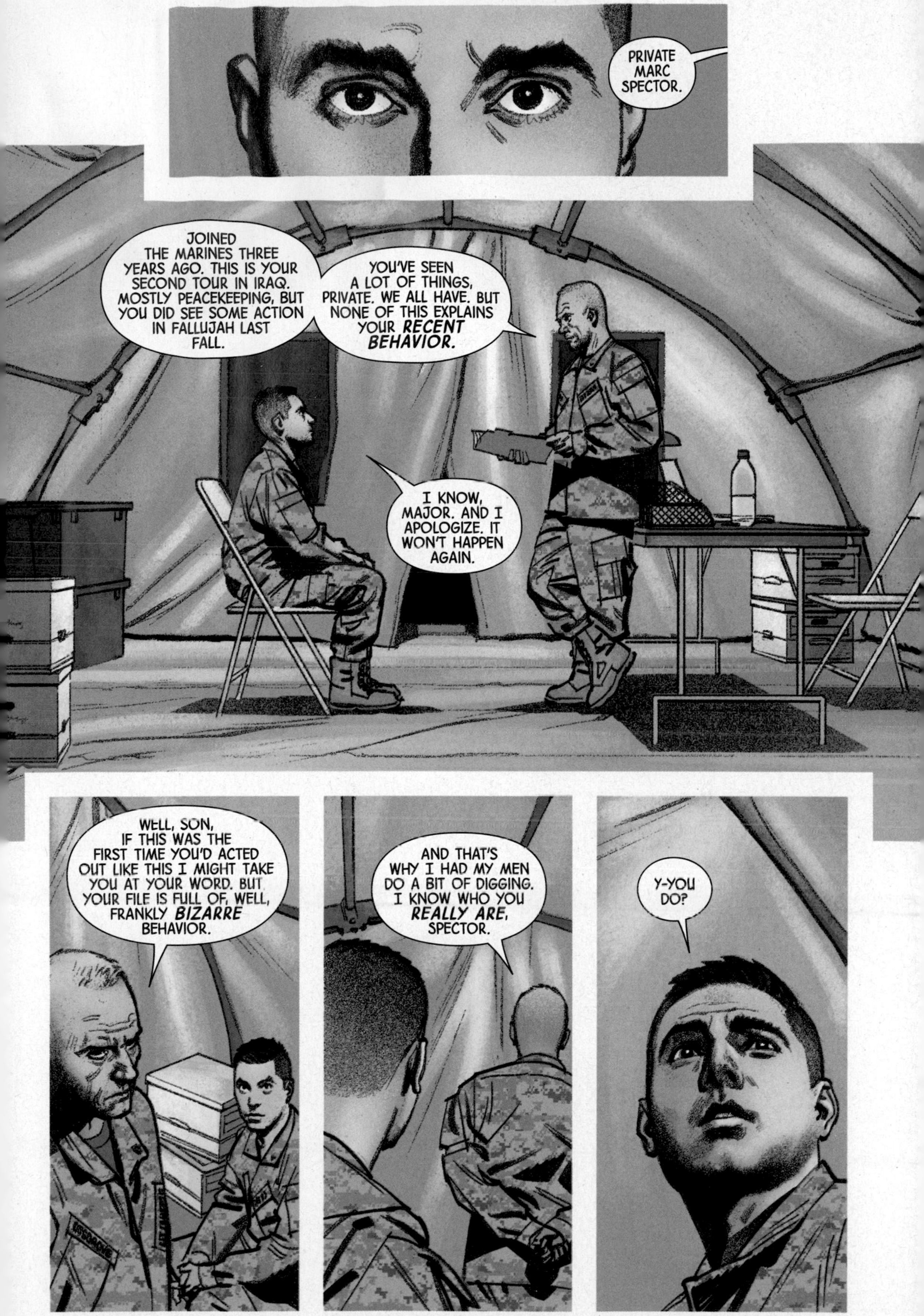
PRIVATE MARC SPECTOR.
JOINED THE MARINES THREE YEARS AGO. THIS IS YOUR SECOND TOUR IN IRAQ. MOSTLY PEACEKEEPING, BUT YOU DID SEE SOME ACTION IN FALLUJAH LAST FALL.
YOU'VE SEEN A LOT OF THINGS, PRIVATE. WE ALL HAVE. BUT NONE OF THIS EXPLAINS YOUR *RECENT BEHAVIOR.*
I KNOW, MAJOR. AND I APOLOGIZE. IT WON'T HAPPEN AGAIN.
WELL, SON, IF THIS WAS THE FIRST TIME YOU'D ACTED OUT LIKE THIS I MIGHT TAKE YOU AT YOUR WORD. BUT YOUR FILE IS FULL OF, WELL, FRANKLY *BIZARRE* BEHAVIOR.
AND THAT'S WHY I HAD MY MEN DO A BIT OF DIGGING. I KNOW WHO YOU *REALLY ARE*, SPECTOR.
Y-YOU DO?

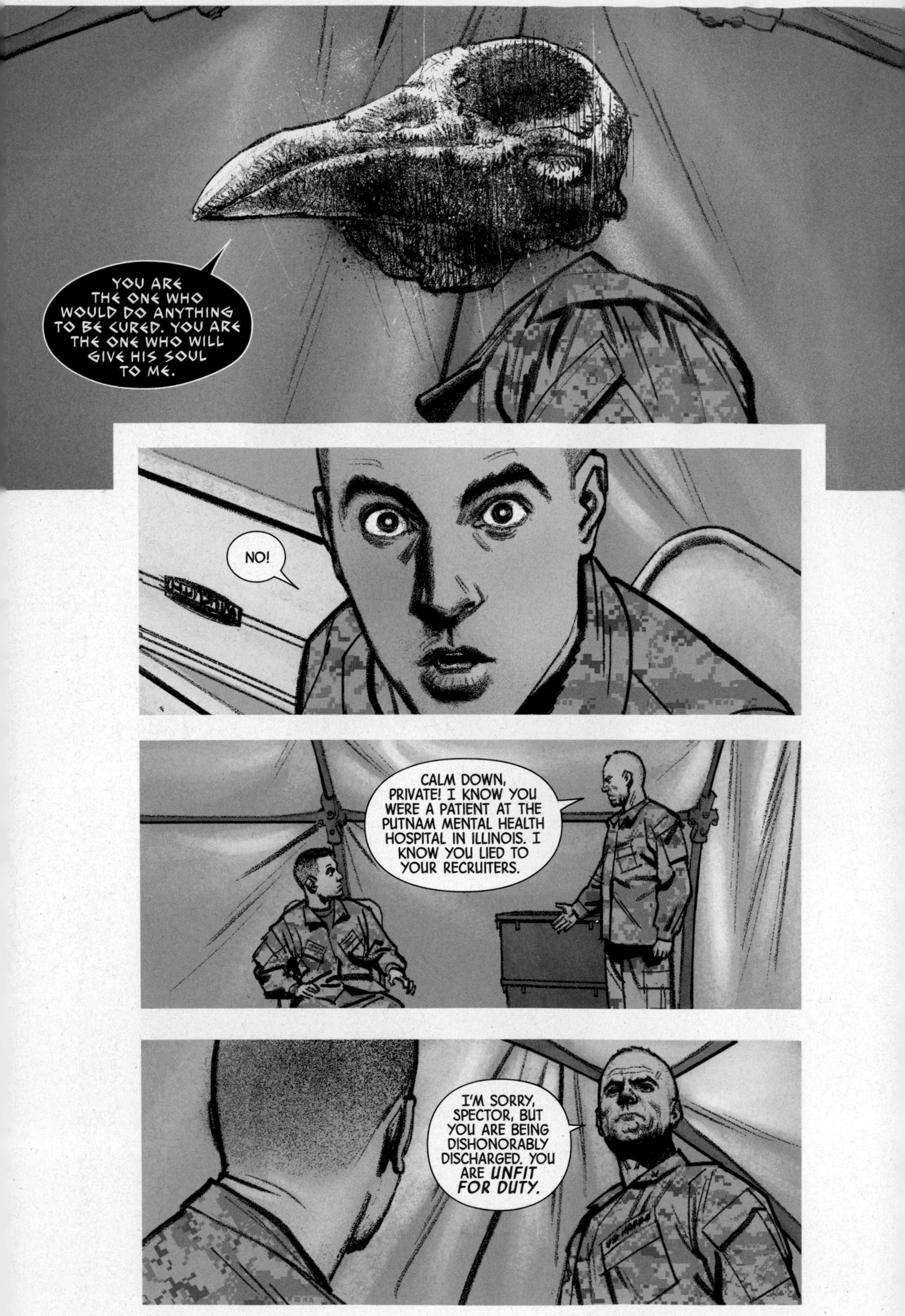
YOU ARE THE ONE WHO WOULD DO ANYTHING TO BE CURED. YOU ARE THE ONE WHO WILL GIVE HIS SOUL TO ME.
NO!
CALM DOWN, PRIVATE! I KNOW YOU WERE A PATIENT AT THE PUTNAM MENTAL HEALTH HOSPITAL IN ILLINOIS. I KNOW YOU LIED TO YOUR RECRUITERS.
I'M SORRY, SPECTOR, BUT YOU ARE BEING DISHONORABLY DISCHARGED. YOU ARE UNFIT FOR DUTY.

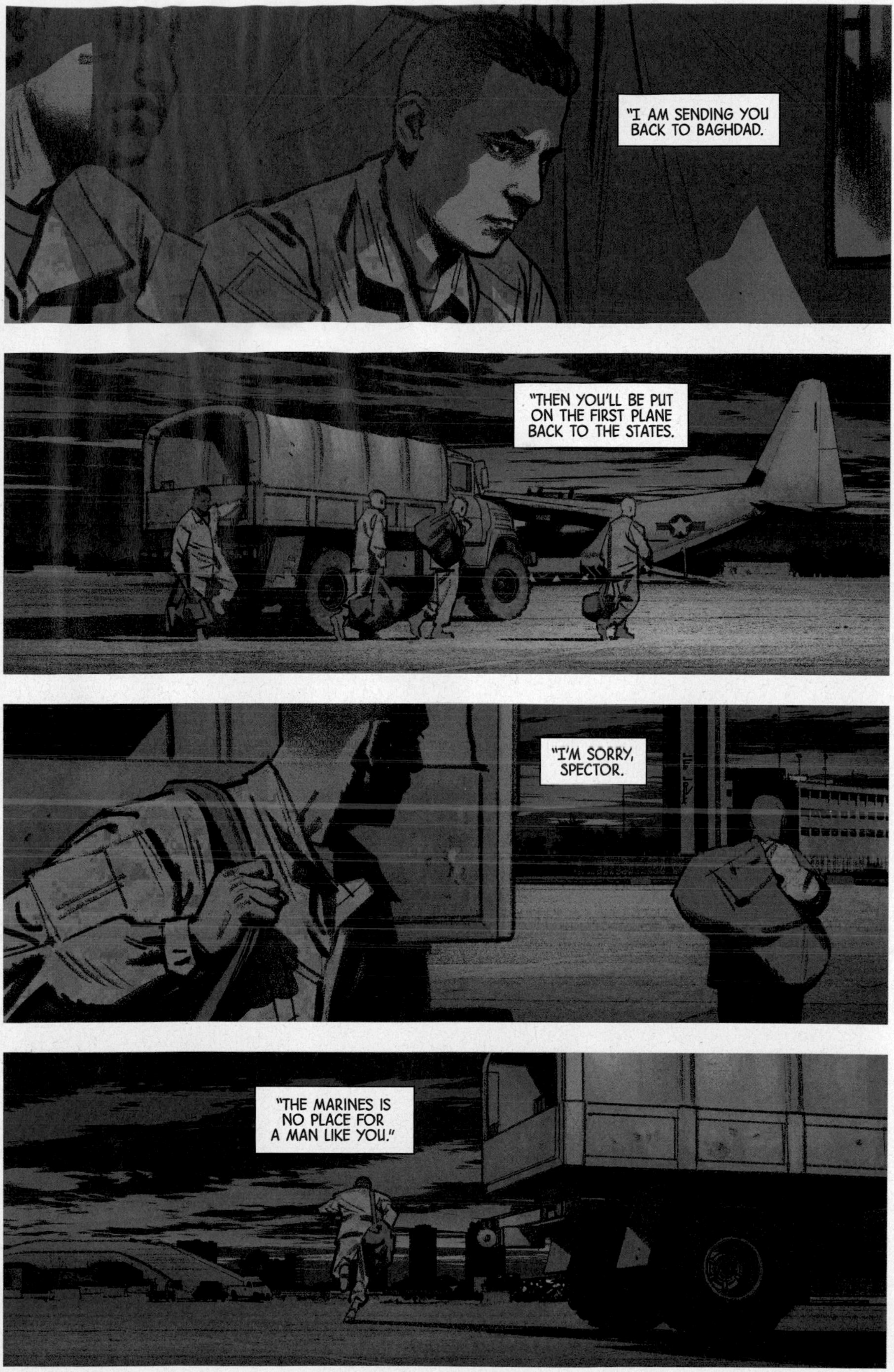
"I AM SENDING YOU BACK TO BAGHDAD.
"THEN YOU'LL BE PUT ON THE FIRST PLANE BACK TO THE STATES.
"I'M SORRY, SPECTOR.
"THE MARINES IS NO PLACE FOR A MAN LIKE YOU."

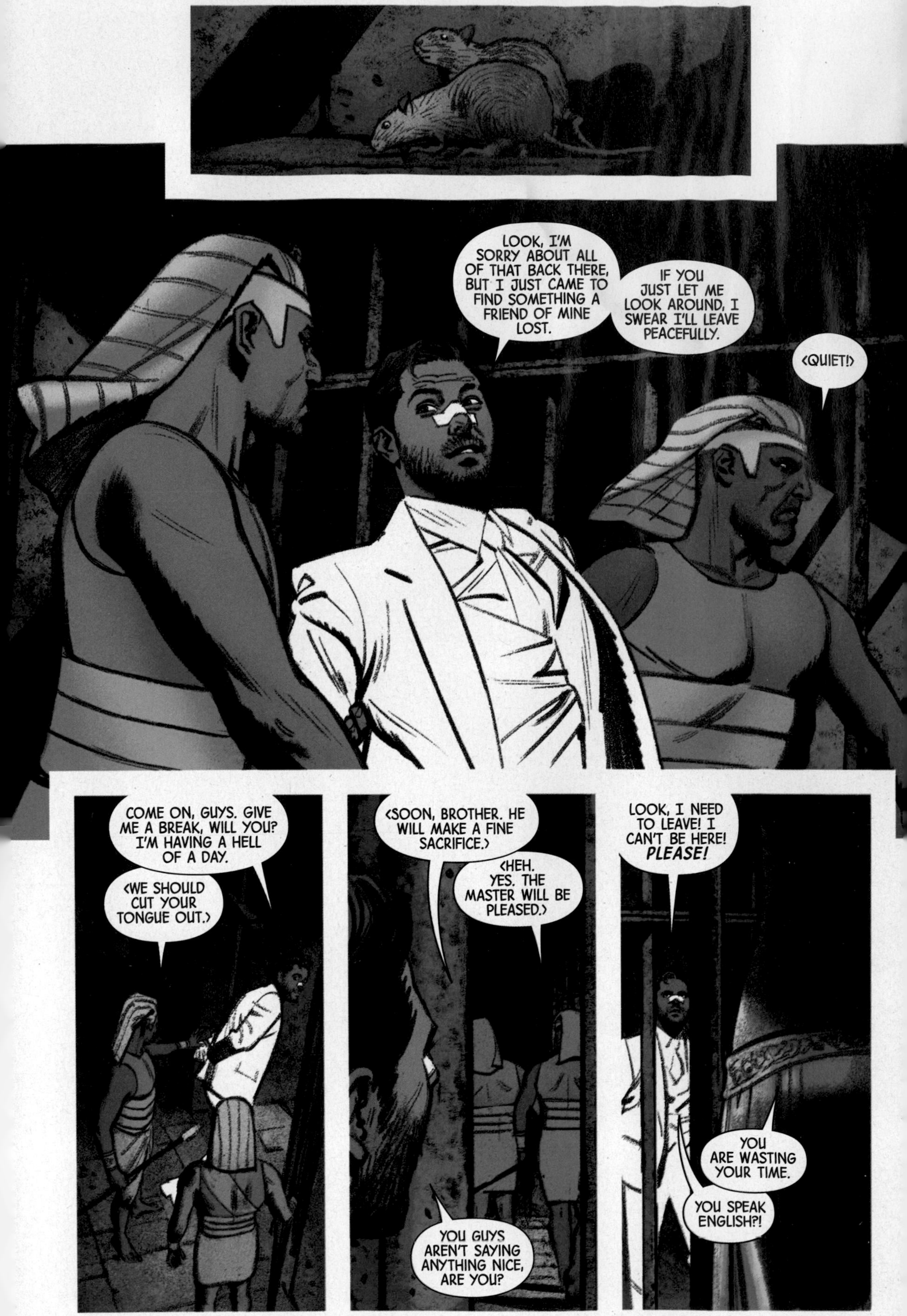
LOOK, I'M SORRY ABOUT ALL OF THAT BACK THERE, BUT I JUST CAME TO FIND SOMETHING A FRIEND OF MINE LOST.
IF YOU JUST LET ME LOOK AROUND, I SWEAR I'LL LEAVE PEACEFULLY.
<QUIET!>
COME ON, GUYS. GIVE ME A BREAK, WILL YOU? I'M HAVING A HELL OF A DAY.
<WE SHOULD CUT YOUR TONGUE OUT.>
<SOON, BROTHER. HE WILL MAKE A FINE SACRIFICE.>
<HEH. YES. THE MASTER WILL BE PLEASED.>
YOU GUYS AREN'T SAYING ANYTHING NICE, ARE YOU?
LOOK, I NEED TO LEAVE! I CAN'T BE HERE! *PLEASE!*
YOU ARE WASTING YOUR TIME.
YOU SPEAK ENGLISH?!

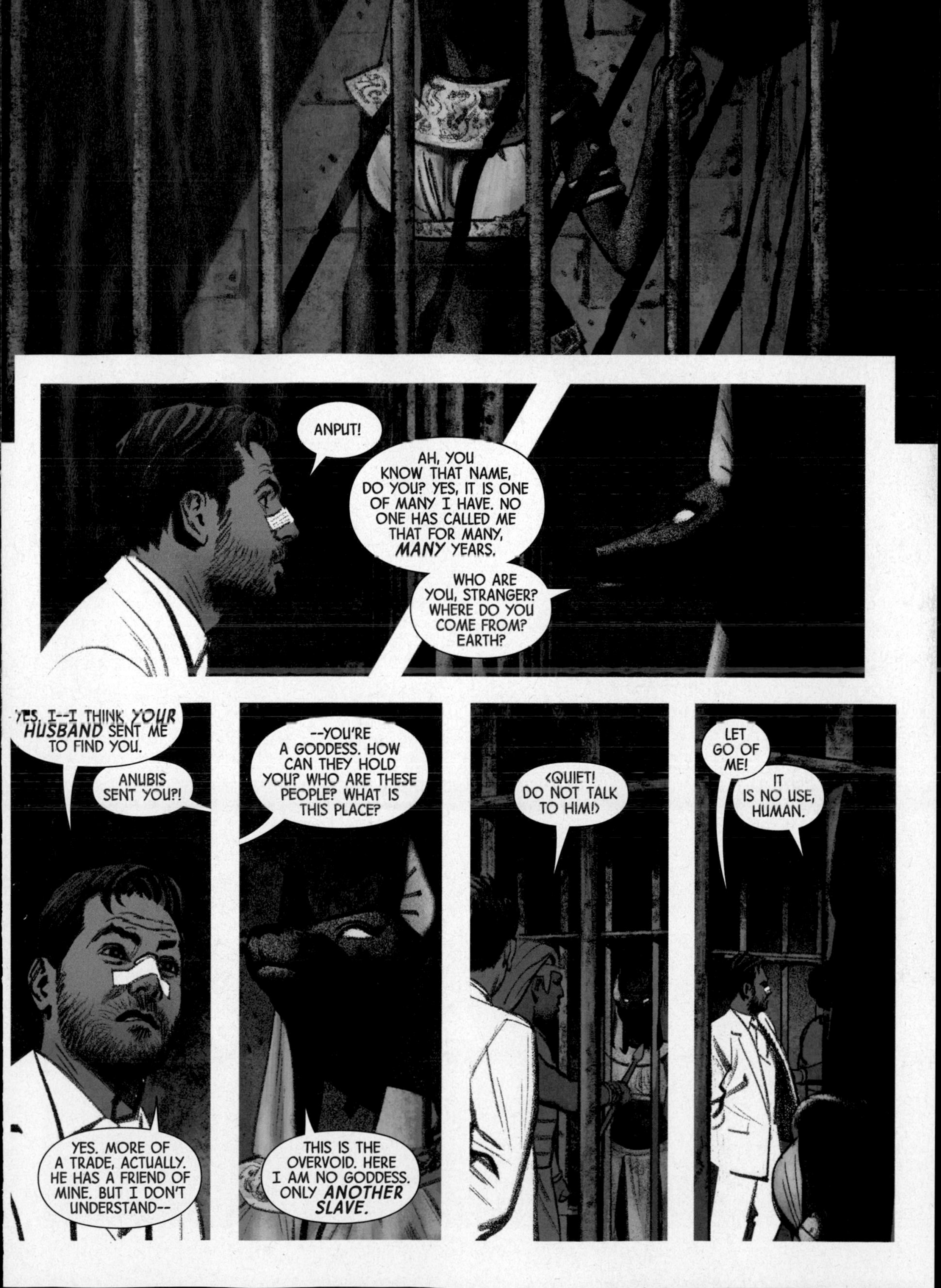

ANPUT!
AH, YOU KNOW THAT NAME, DO YOU? YES, IT IS ONE OF MANY I HAVE. NO ONE HAS CALLED ME THAT FOR MANY, *MANY* YEARS.
WHO ARE YOU, STRANGER? WHERE DO YOU COME FROM? EARTH?
YES. I--I THINK *YOUR HUSBAND* SENT ME TO FIND YOU.
ANUBIS SENT YOU?!
YES. MORE OF A TRADE, ACTUALLY. HE HAS A FRIEND OF MINE. BUT I DON'T UNDERSTAND--
--YOU'RE A GODDESS. HOW CAN THEY HOLD YOU? WHO ARE THESE PEOPLE? WHAT IS THIS PLACE?
THIS IS THE OVERVOID. HERE I AM NO GODDESS. ONLY *ANOTHER SLAVE.*
<QUIET! DO NOT TALK TO HIM!>
LET GO OF ME!
IT IS NO USE, HUMAN.

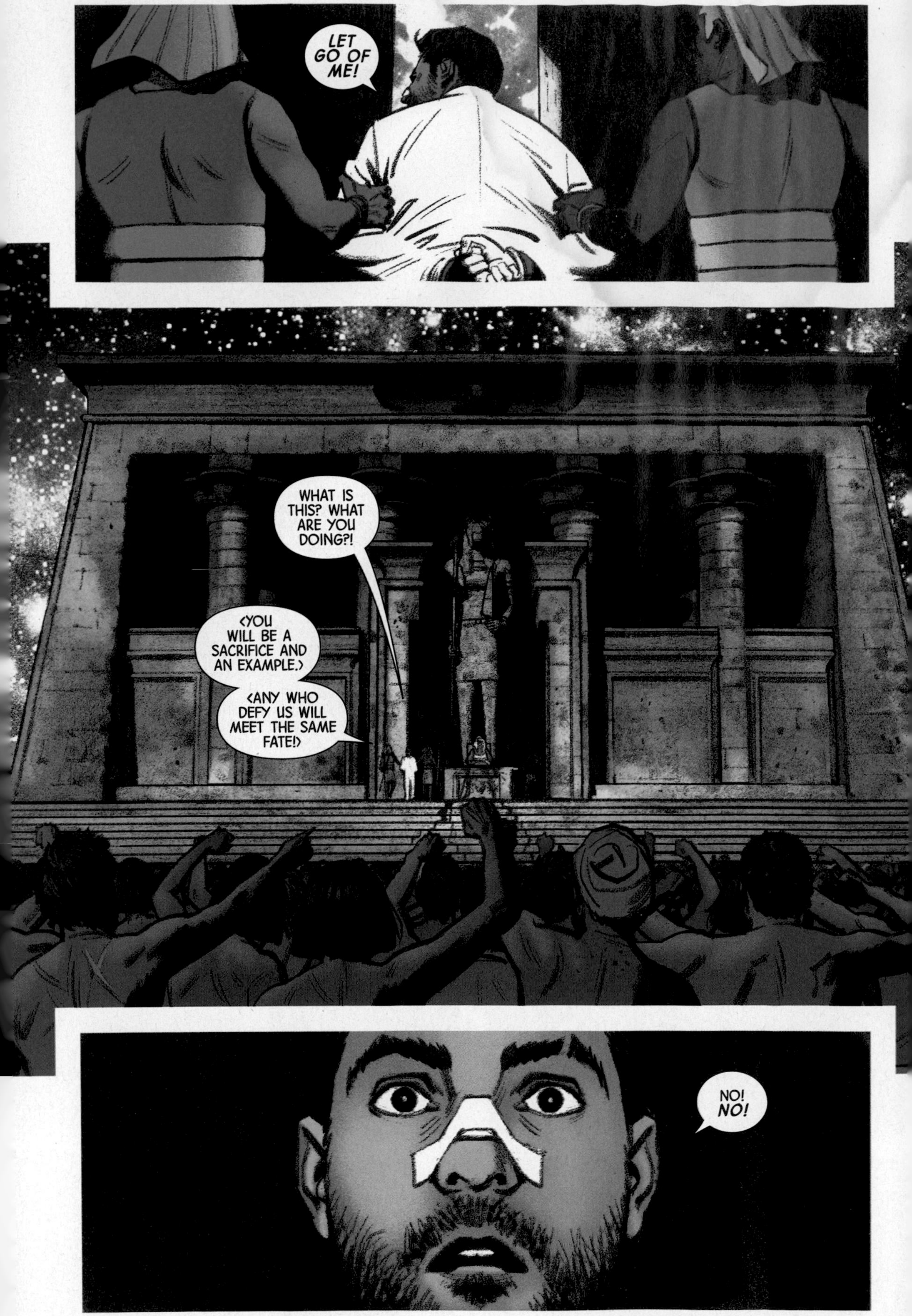
LET GO OF ME!
WHAT IS THIS? WHAT ARE YOU DOING?!
<YOU WILL BE A SACRIFICE AND AN EXAMPLE.>
<ANY WHO DEFY US WILL MEET THE SAME FATE!>
NO! NO!

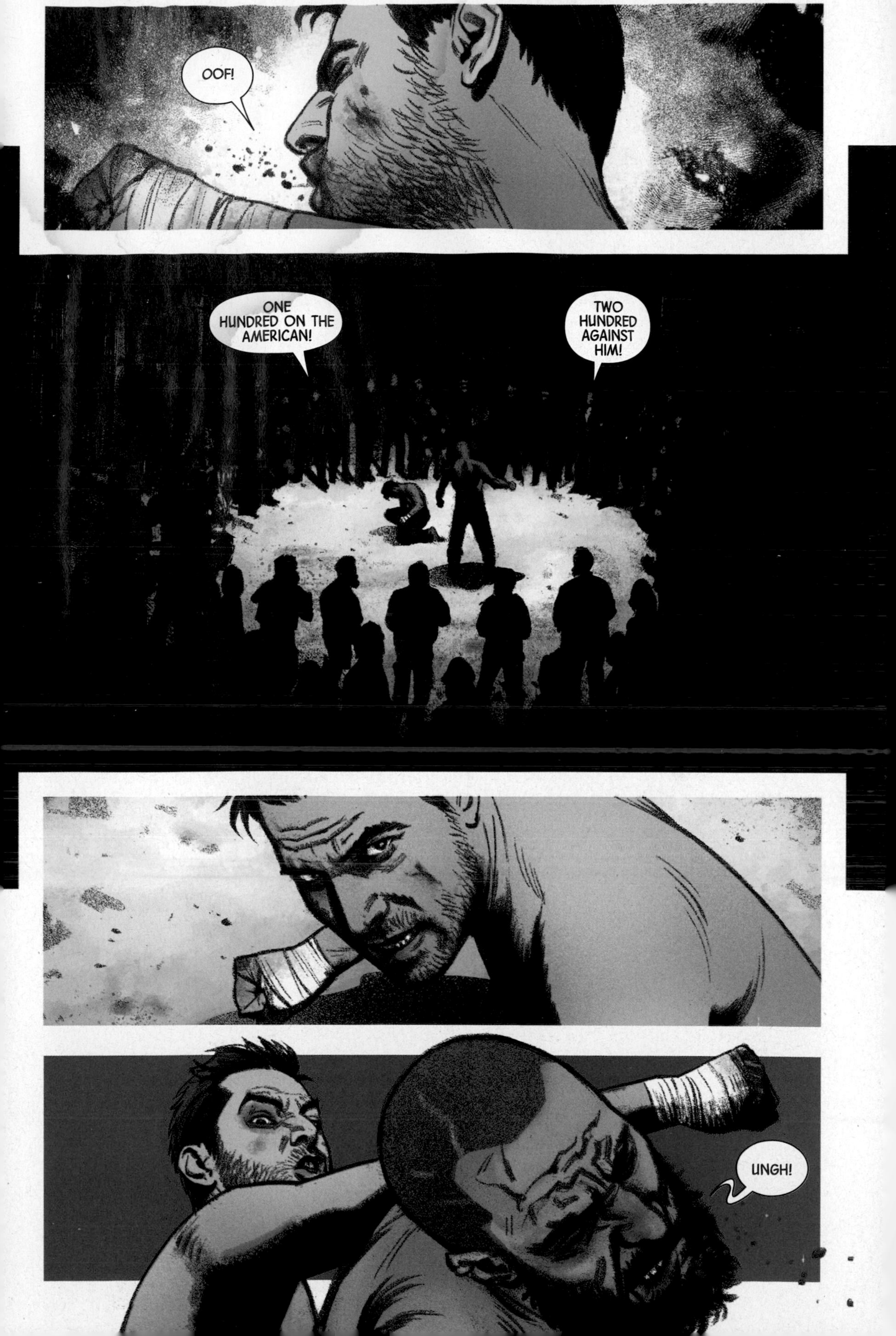
OOF!
ONE HUNDRED ON THE AMERICAN!
TWO HUNDRED AGAINST HIM!
UNGH!

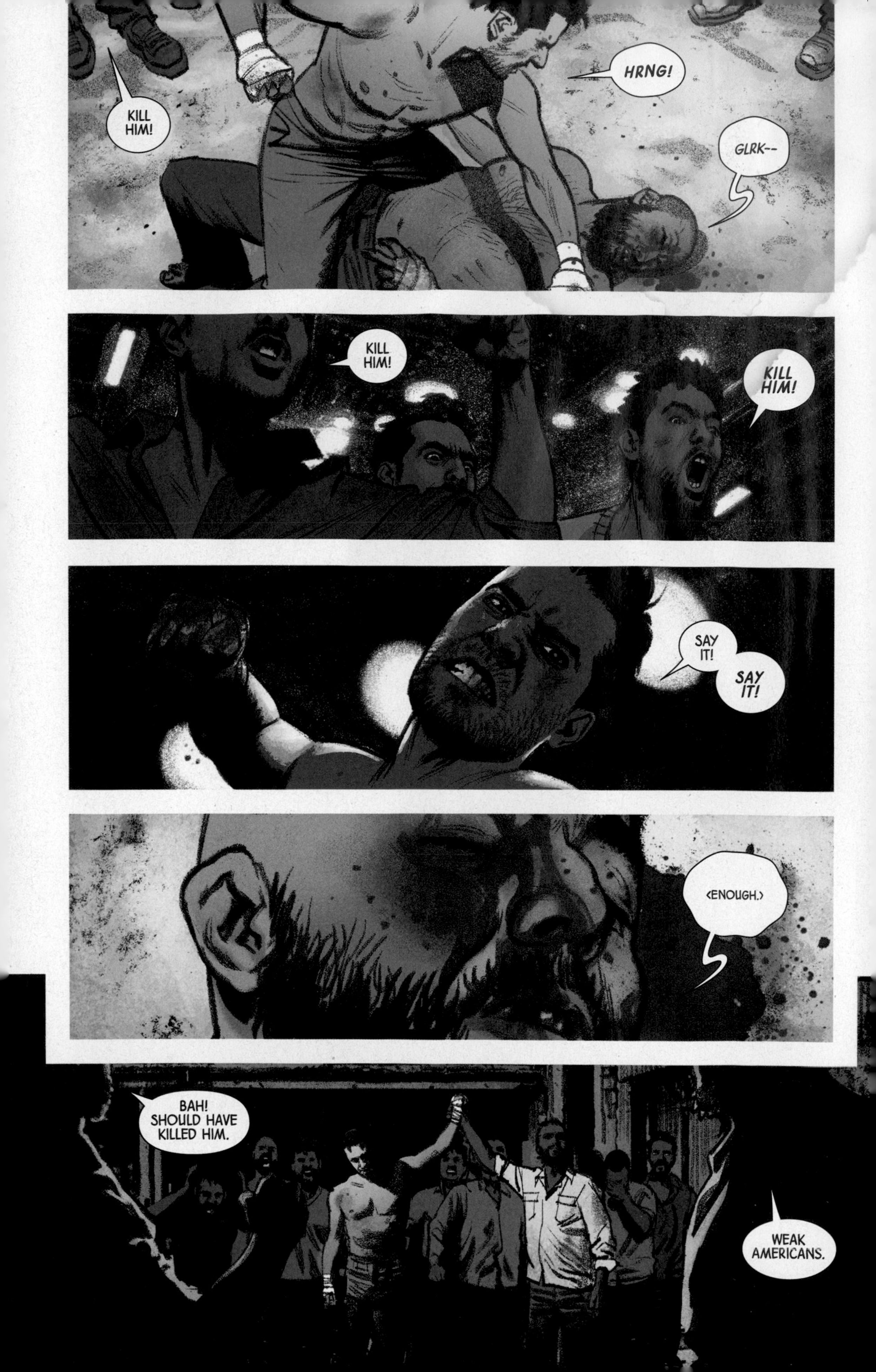
KILL HIM!
HRNG!
GLRK--
KILL HIM!
KILL HIM!
SAY IT!
SAY IT!
<ENOUGH.>
BAH! SHOULD HAVE KILLED HIM.
WEAK AMERICANS.

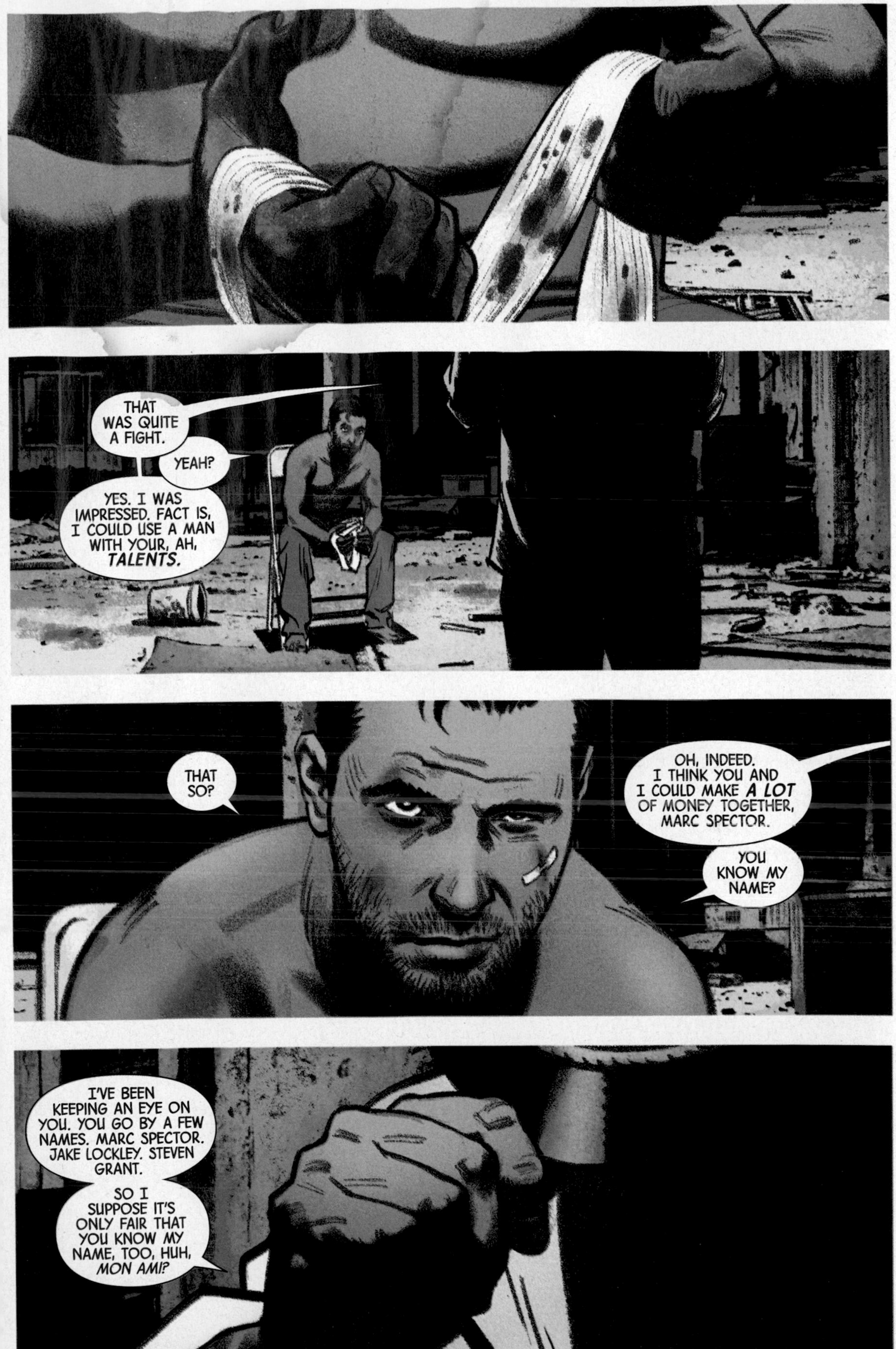

THAT WAS QUITE A FIGHT.
YEAH?
YES. I WAS IMPRESSED. FACT IS, I COULD USE A MAN WITH YOUR, AH, TALENTS.
THAT SO?
OH, INDEED. I THINK YOU AND I COULD MAKE A LOT OF MONEY TOGETHER, MARC SPECTOR.
YOU KNOW MY NAME?
I'VE BEEN KEEPING AN EYE ON YOU. YOU GO BY A FEW NAMES. MARC SPECTOR. JAKE LOCKLEY. STEVEN GRANT.
SO I SUPPOSE IT'S ONLY FAIR THAT YOU KNOW MY NAME, TOO, HUH, MON AMI?

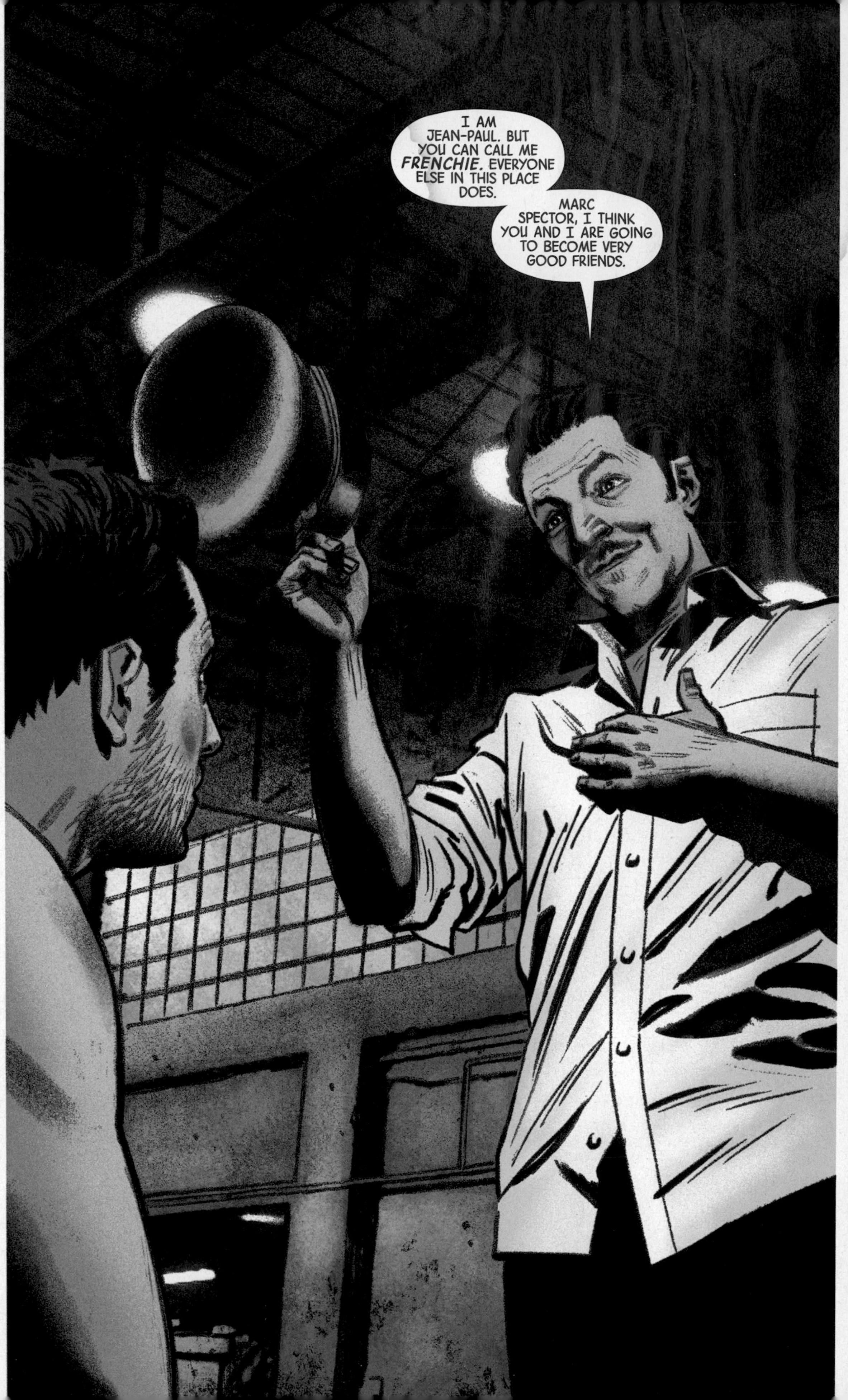
I AM JEAN-PAUL. BUT YOU CAN CALL ME FRENCHIE. EVERYONE ELSE IN THIS PLACE DOES.
MARC SPECTOR, I THINK YOU AND I ARE GOING TO BECOME VERY GOOD FRIENDS.

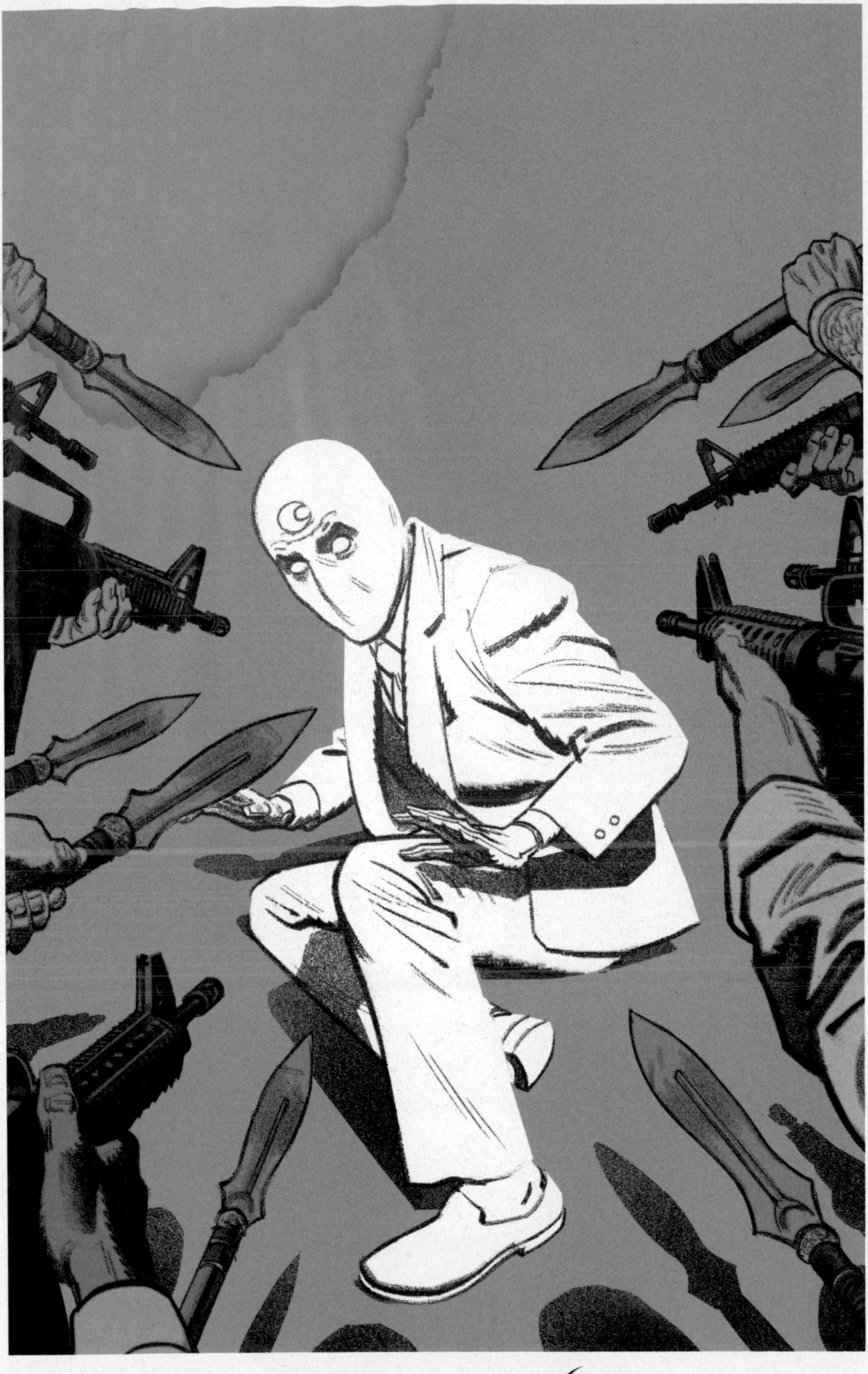

BIRTH AND DEATH
PART THREE

12

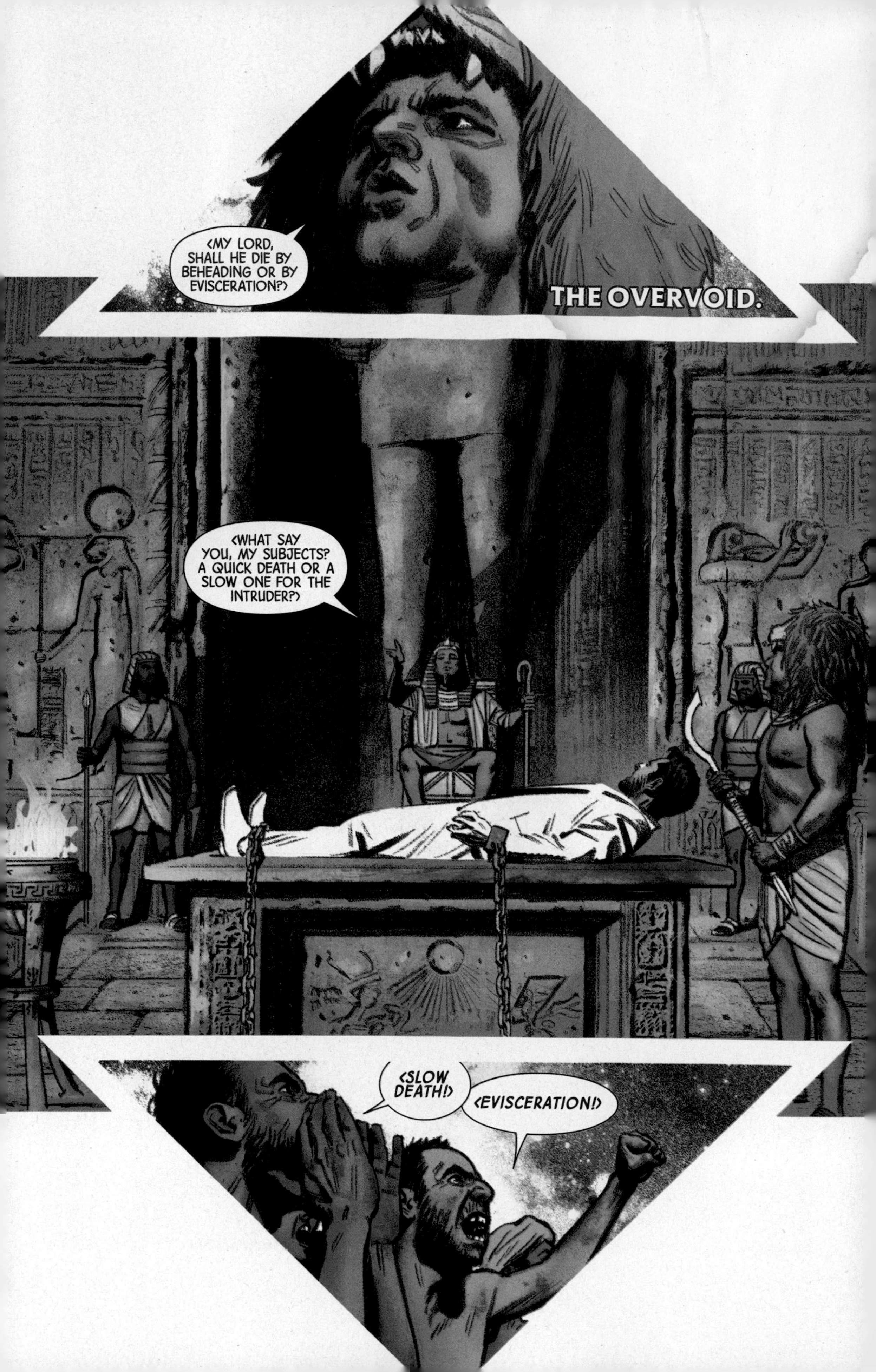

<MY LORD, SHALL HE DIE BY BEHEADING OR BY EVISCERATION?>
THE OVERVOID.
<WHAT SAY YOU, MY SUBJECTS? A QUICK DEATH OR A SLOW ONE FOR THE INTRUDER?>
<SLOW DEATH!>
<EVISCERATION!>

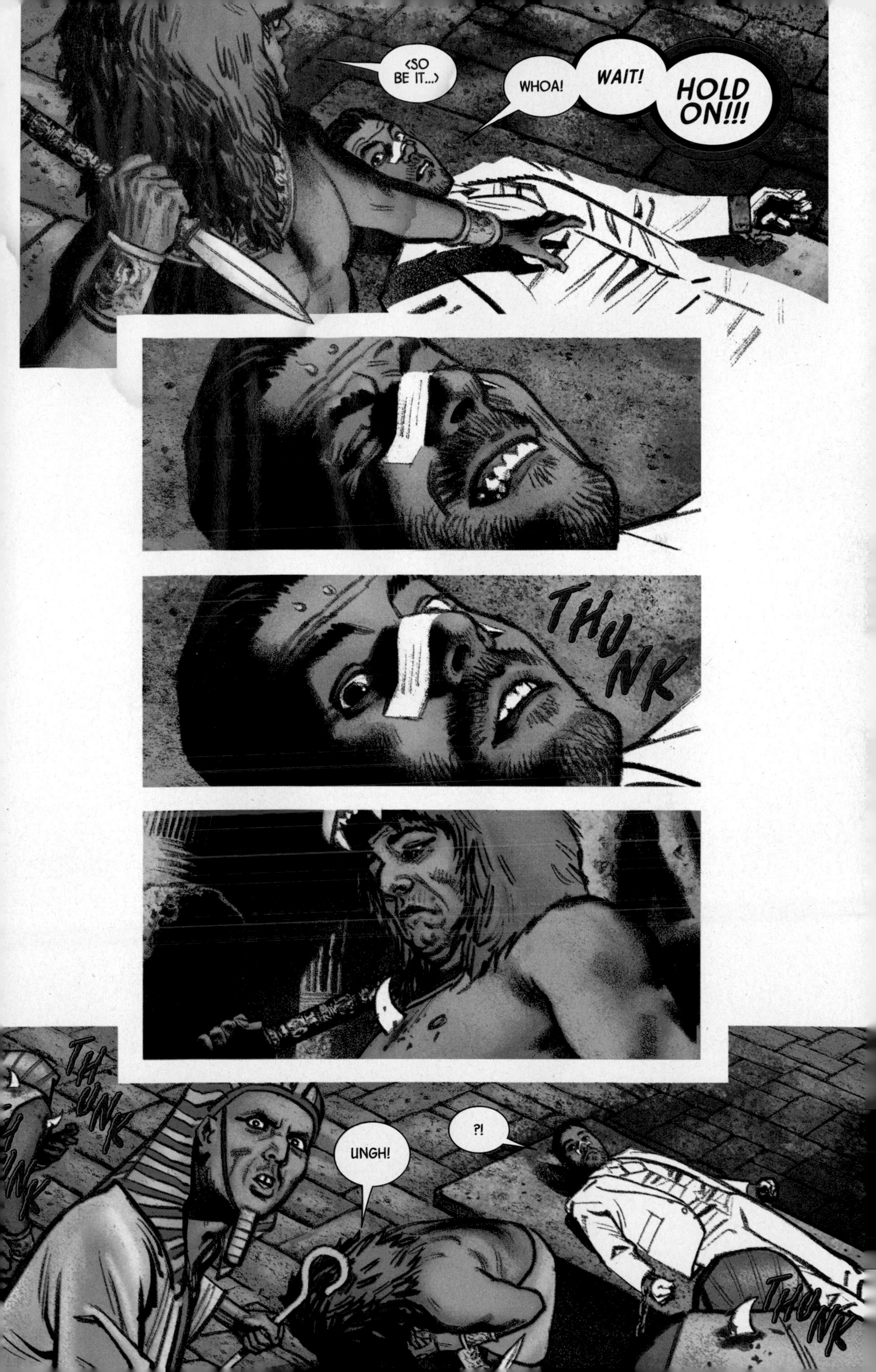

<SO BE IT...>
WHOA!
WAIT!
HOLD ON!!!
THUNK
THUNK
THUNK
UNGH!
?!
THUNK

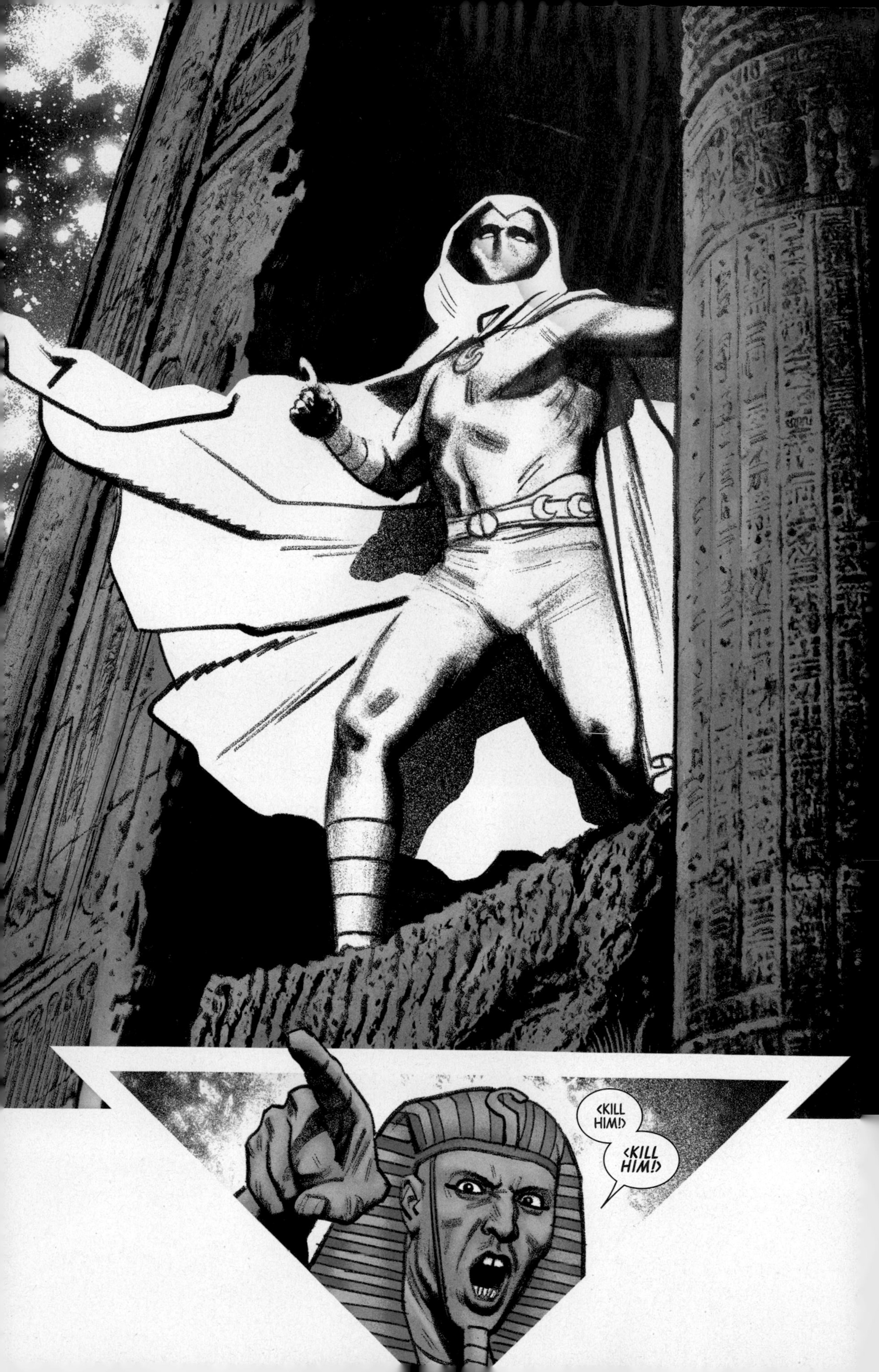
<KILL HIM!>
<KILL HIM!>

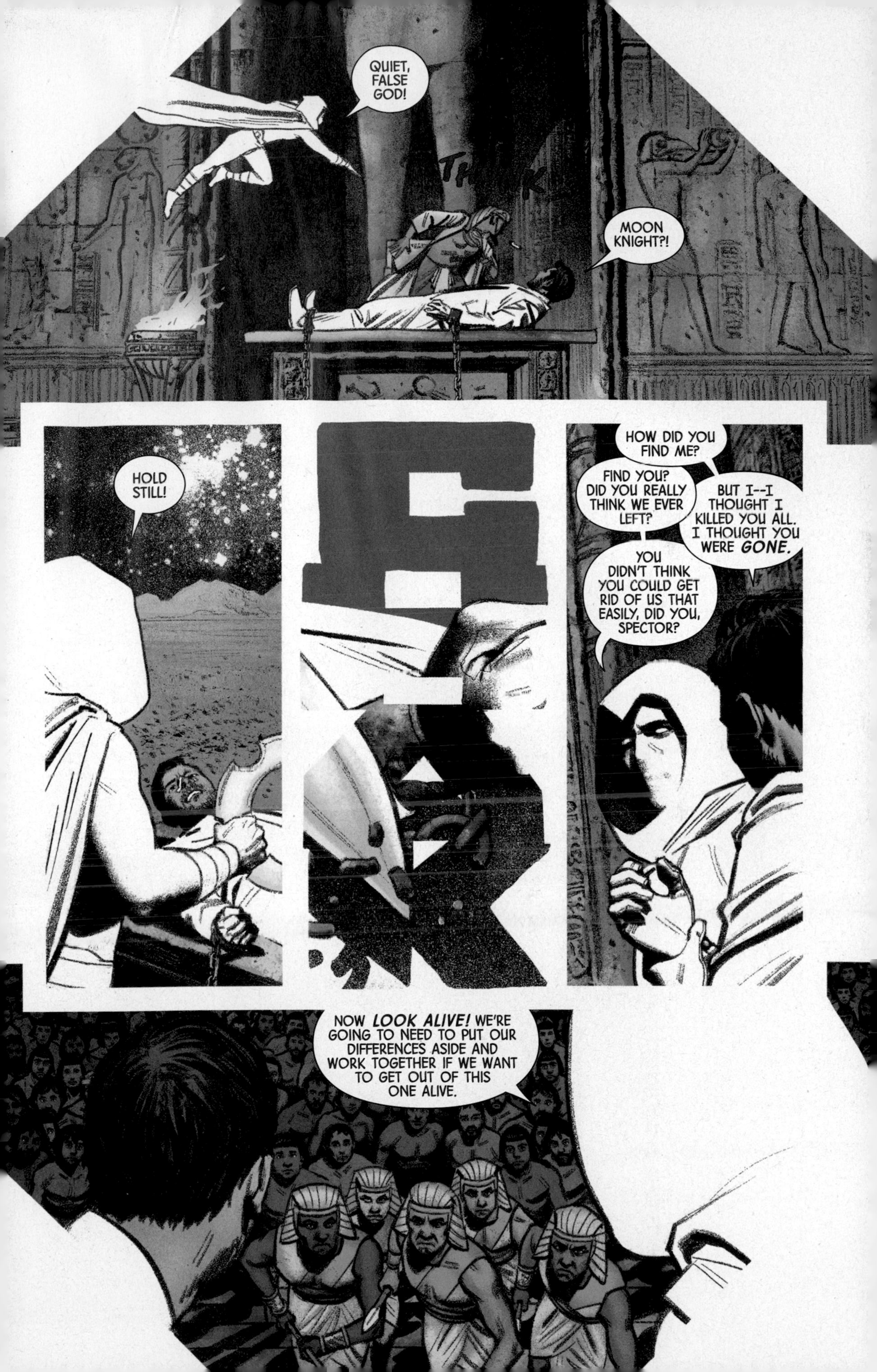
QUIET, FALSE GOD!
THUNK
MOON KNIGHT?!
HOLD STILL!
HOW DID YOU FIND ME?
FIND YOU? DID YOU REALLY THINK WE EVER LEFT?
BUT I--I THOUGHT I KILLED YOU ALL. I THOUGHT YOU WERE GONE.
YOU DIDN'T THINK YOU COULD GET RID OF US THAT EASILY, DID YOU, SPECTOR?
NOW LOOK ALIVE! WE'RE GOING TO NEED TO PUT OUR DIFFERENCES ASIDE AND WORK TOGETHER IF WE WANT TO GET OUT OF THIS ONE ALIVE.

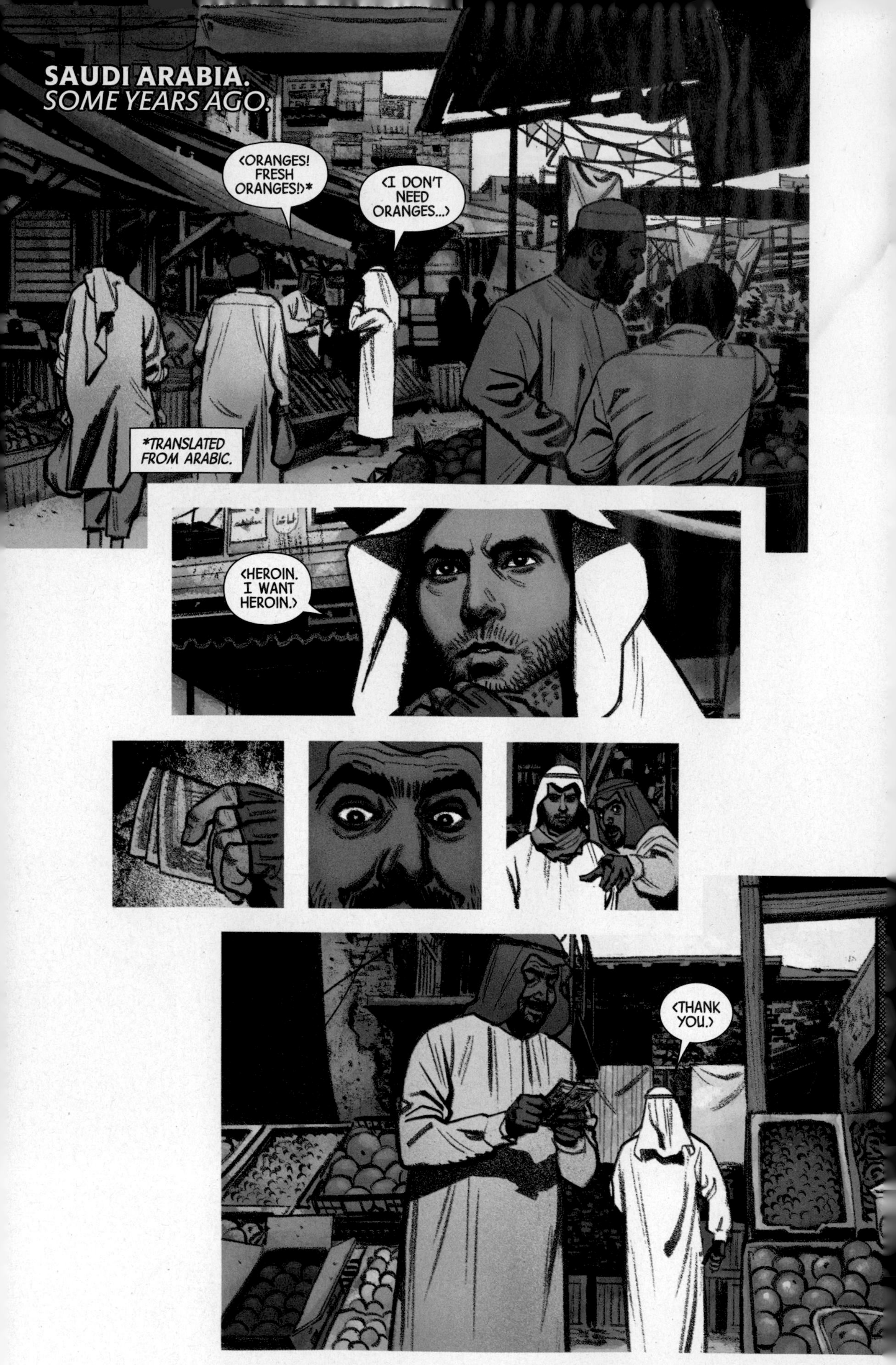
SAUDI ARABIA.
SOME YEARS AGO.
<ORANGES! FRESH ORANGES!>*
<I DON'T NEED ORANGES...>
*TRANSLATED FROM ARABIC.
<HEROIN. I WANT HEROIN.>
<THANK YOU.>

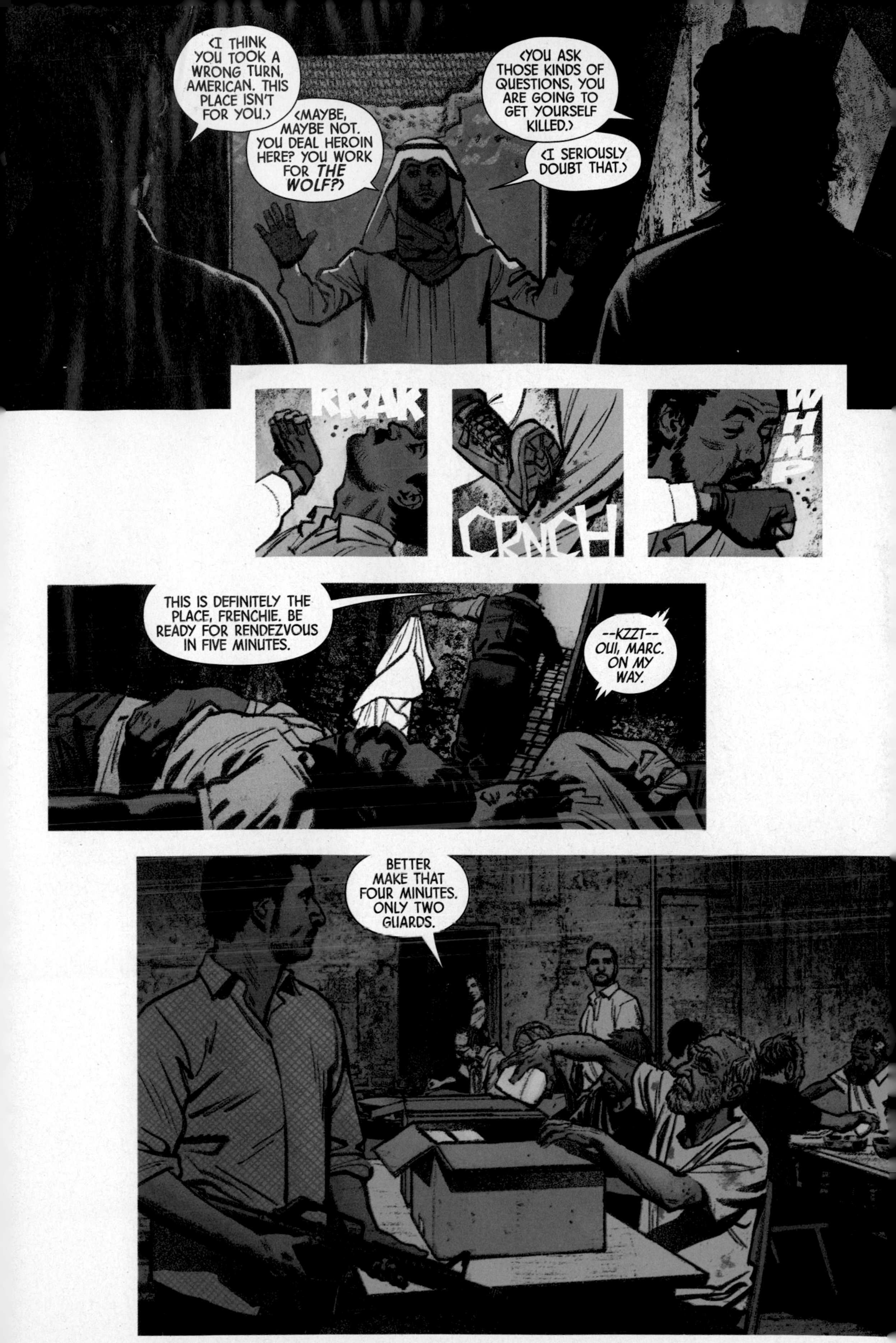
<I THINK YOU TOOK A WRONG TURN, AMERICAN. THIS PLACE ISN'T FOR YOU.>
<MAYBE, MAYBE NOT. YOU DEAL HEROIN HERE? YOU WORK FOR *THE WOLF?*>
<YOU ASK THOSE KINDS OF QUESTIONS, YOU ARE GOING TO GET YOURSELF KILLED.>
<I SERIOUSLY DOUBT THAT.>
KRAK
CRNCH
WHMP
THIS IS DEFINITELY THE PLACE, FRENCHIE. BE READY FOR RENDEZVOUS IN FIVE MINUTES.
--KZZT-- OUI, MARC. ON MY WAY.
BETTER MAKE THAT FOUR MINUTES. ONLY TWO GUARDS.

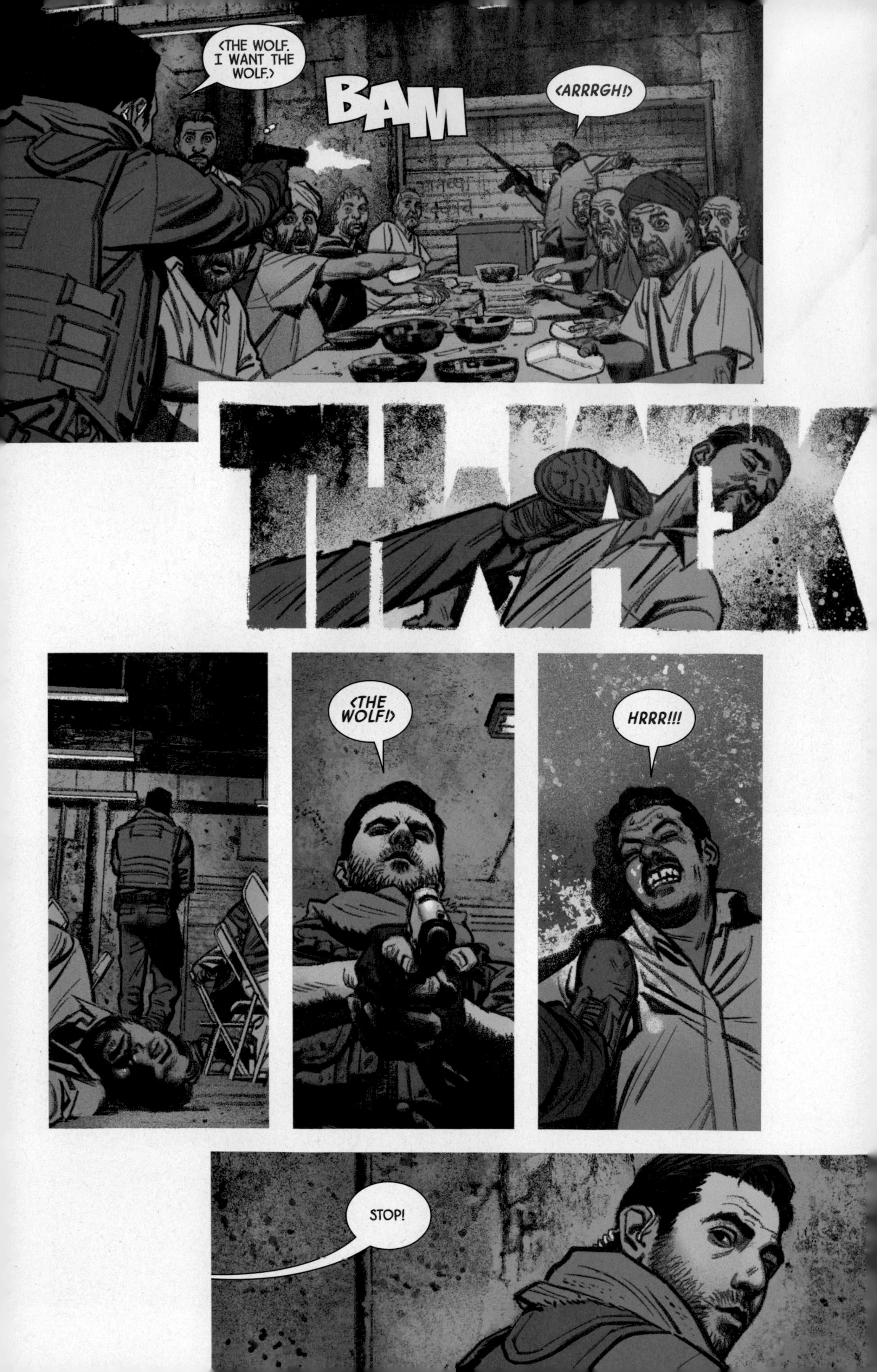
<THE WOLF. I WANT THE WOLF.>
BAM
<ARRRGH!>
THWACK
<THE WOLF!>
HRRR!!!
STOP!

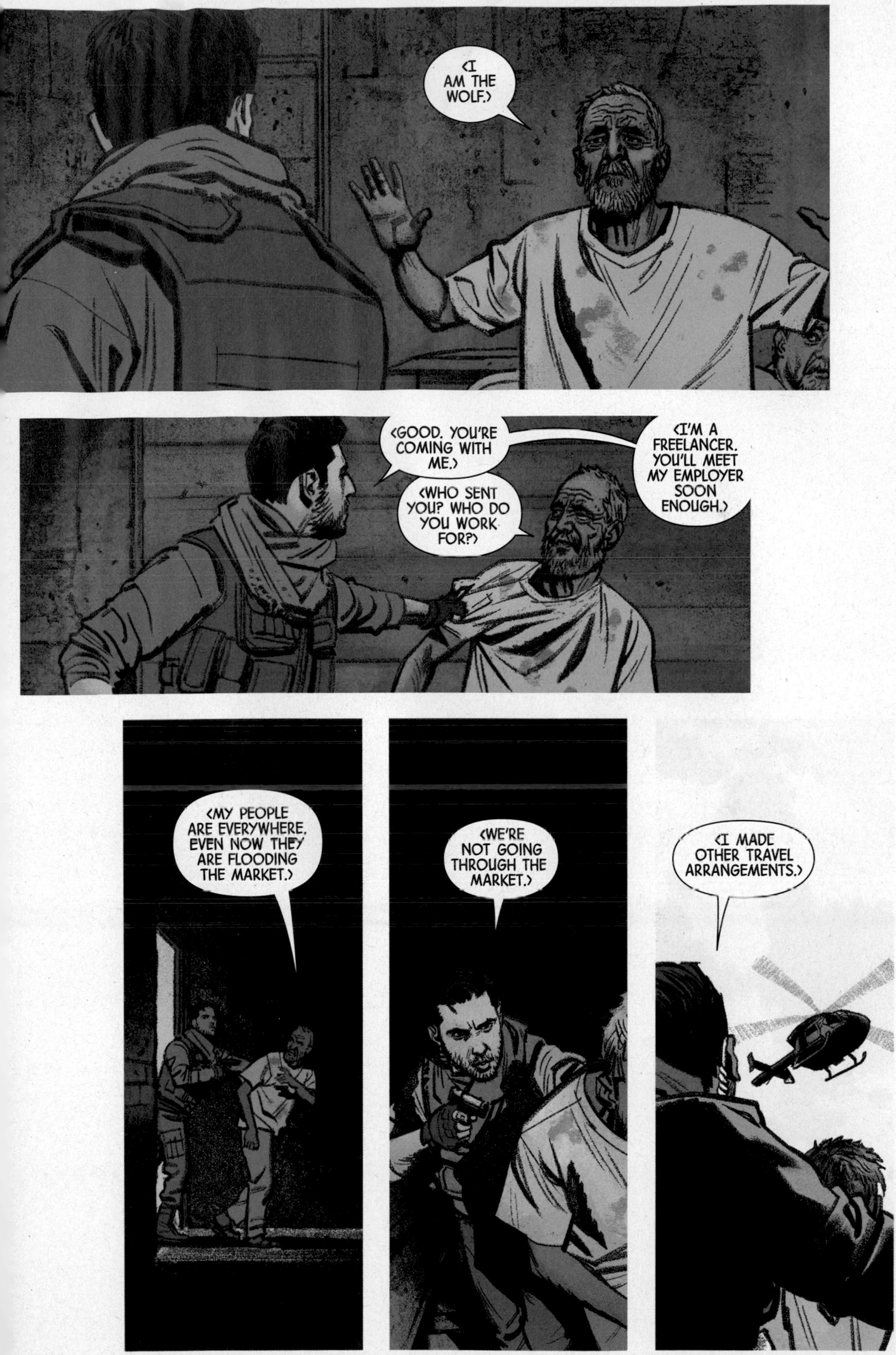
<I AM THE WOLF.>
<GOOD. YOU'RE COMING WITH ME.>
<WHO SENT YOU? WHO DO YOU WORK FOR?>
<I'M A FREELANCER. YOU'LL MEET MY EMPLOYER SOON ENOUGH.>
<MY PEOPLE ARE EVERYWHERE. EVEN NOW THEY ARE FLOODING THE MARKET.>
<WE'RE NOT GOING THROUGH THE MARKET.>
<I MADE OTHER TRAVEL ARRANGEMENTS.>

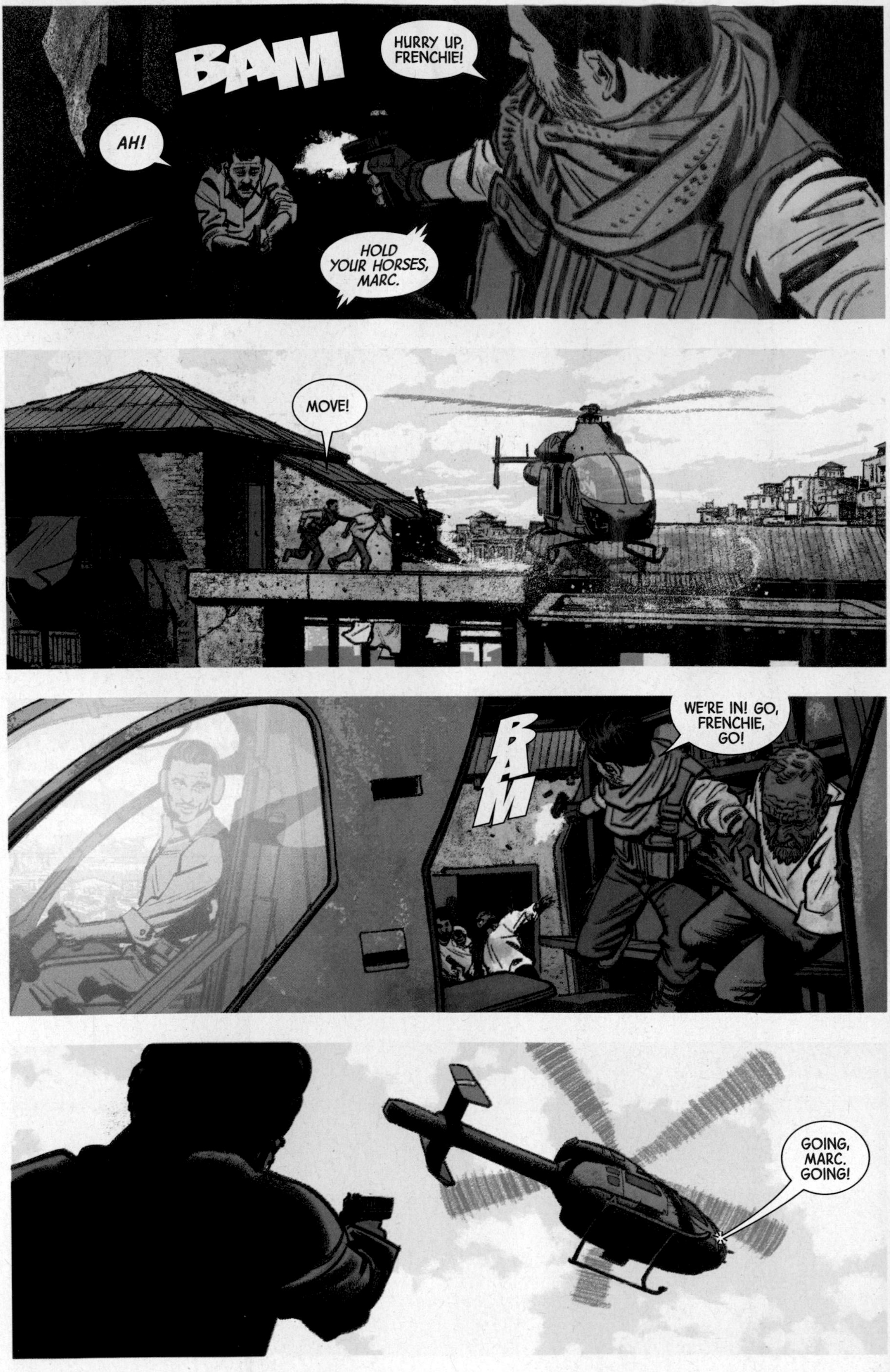
BAM
HURRY UP, FRENCHIE!
AH!
HOLD YOUR HORSES, MARC.
MOVE!
BAM
WE'RE IN! GO, FRENCHIE, GO!
GOING, MARC. GOING!

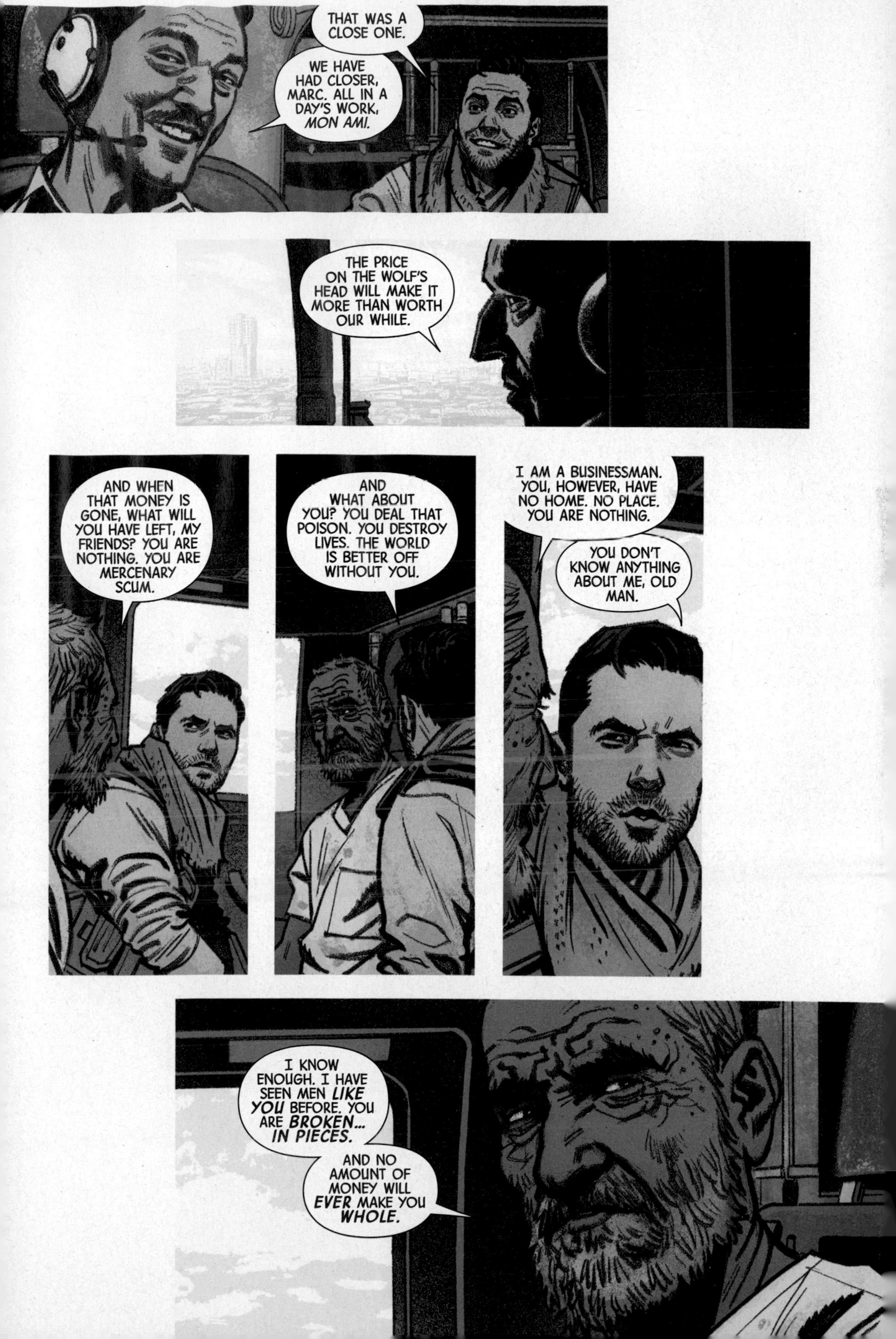

THAT WAS A CLOSE ONE.
WE HAVE HAD CLOSER, MARC. ALL IN A DAY'S WORK, *MON AMI.*
THE PRICE ON THE WOLF'S HEAD WILL MAKE IT MORE THAN WORTH OUR WHILE.
AND WHEN THAT MONEY IS GONE, WHAT WILL YOU HAVE LEFT, MY FRIENDS? YOU ARE NOTHING. YOU ARE MERCENARY SCUM.
AND WHAT ABOUT YOU? YOU DEAL THAT POISON. YOU DESTROY LIVES. THE WORLD IS BETTER OFF WITHOUT YOU.
I AM A BUSINESSMAN. YOU, HOWEVER, HAVE NO HOME. NO PLACE. YOU ARE NOTHING.
YOU DON'T KNOW ANYTHING ABOUT ME, OLD MAN.
I KNOW ENOUGH. I HAVE SEEN MEN ***LIKE YOU*** BEFORE. YOU ARE ***BROKEN... IN PIECES.***
AND NO AMOUNT OF MONEY WILL ***EVER*** MAKE YOU ***WHOLE.***

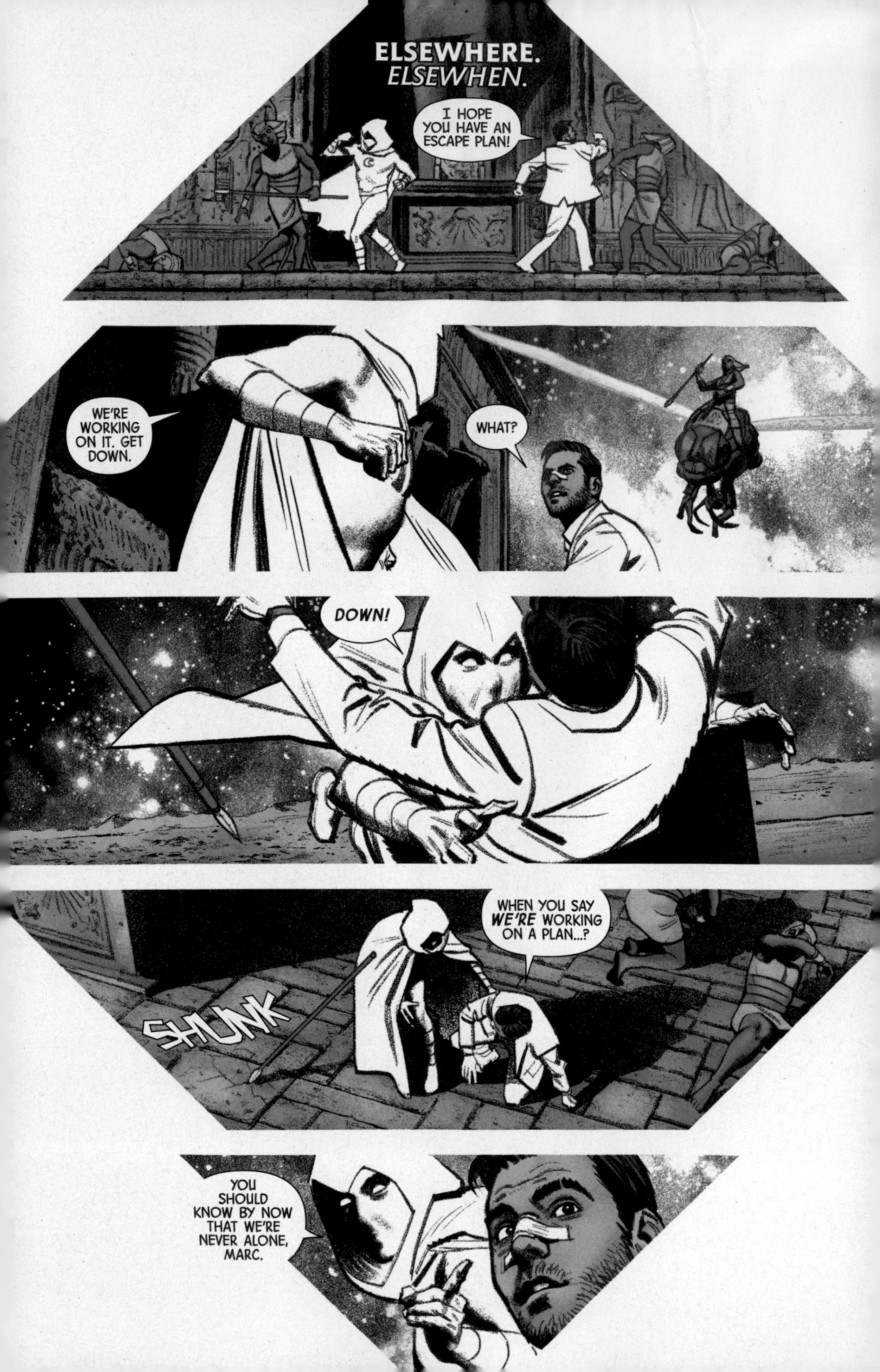
ELSEWHERE.
ELSEWHEN.
I HOPE YOU HAVE AN ESCAPE PLAN!
WE'RE WORKING ON IT. GET DOWN.
WHAT?
DOWN!
WHEN YOU SAY WE'RE WORKING ON A PLAN...?
SHUNK
YOU SHOULD KNOW BY NOW THAT WE'RE NEVER ALONE, MARC.

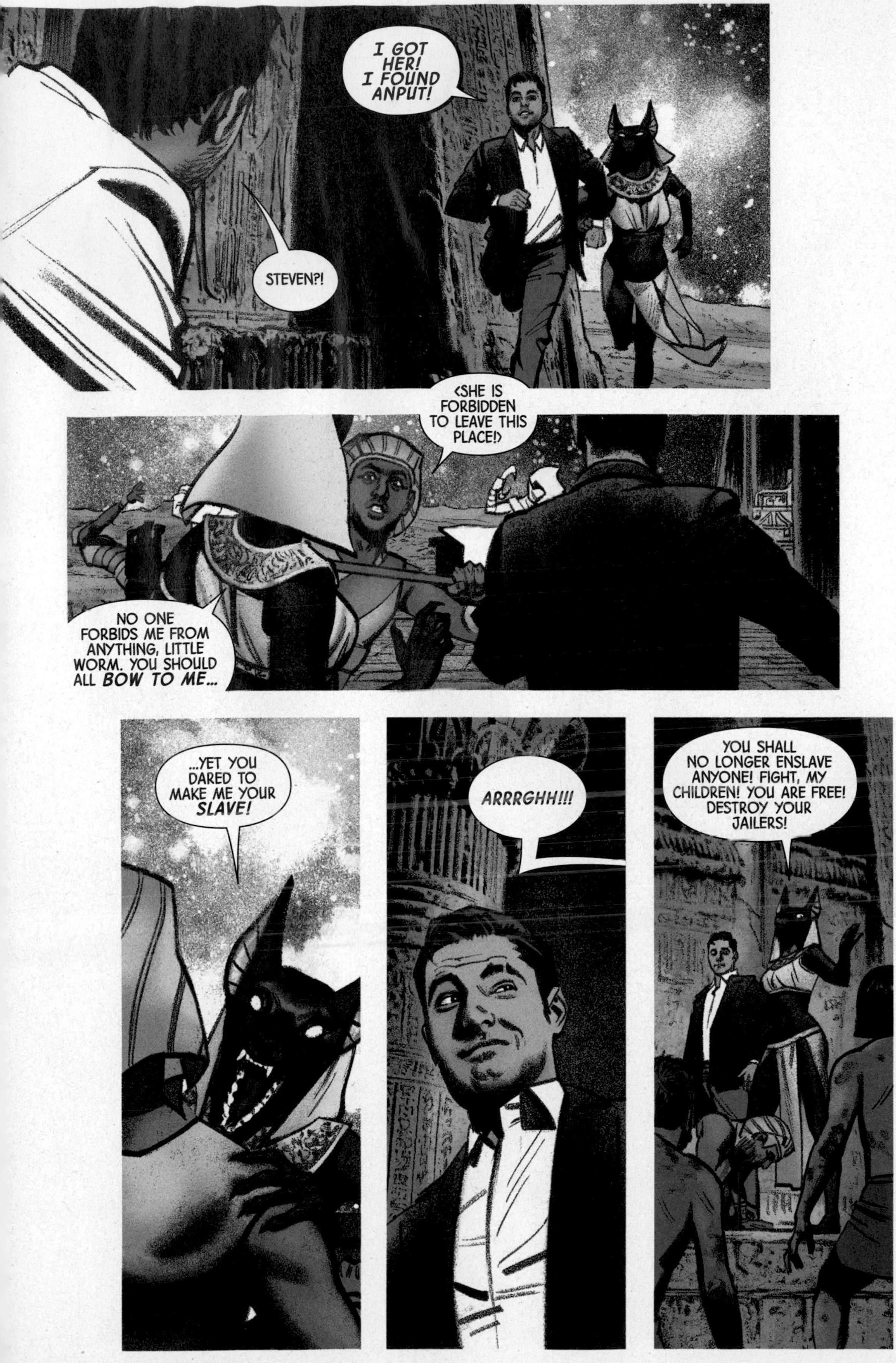
I GOT HER! I FOUND ANPUT!
STEVEN?!
<SHE IS FORBIDDEN TO LEAVE THIS PLACE!>
NO ONE FORBIDS ME FROM ANYTHING, LITTLE WORM. YOU SHOULD ALL BOW TO ME...
...YET YOU DARED TO MAKE ME YOUR SLAVE!
ARRRGHH!!!
YOU SHALL NO LONGER ENSLAVE ANYONE! FIGHT, MY CHILDREN! YOU ARE FREE! DESTROY YOUR JAILERS!

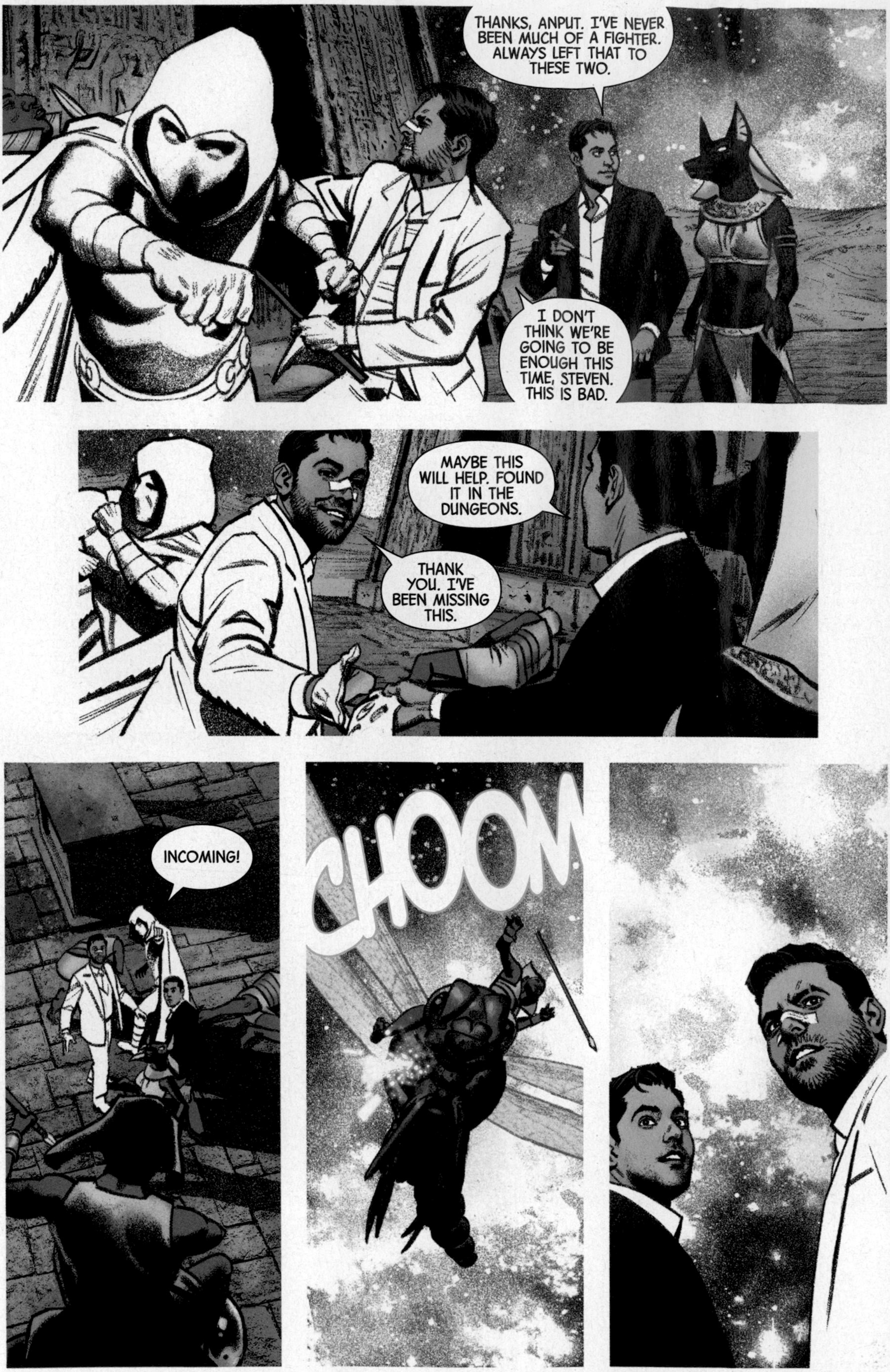

THANKS, ANPUT. I'VE NEVER BEEN MUCH OF A FIGHTER. ALWAYS LEFT THAT TO THESE TWO.
I DON'T THINK WE'RE GOING TO BE ENOUGH THIS TIME, STEVEN. THIS IS BAD.
MAYBE THIS WILL HELP. FOUND IT IN THE DUNGEONS.
THANK YOU. I'VE BEEN MISSING THIS.
INCOMING!
CHOOM

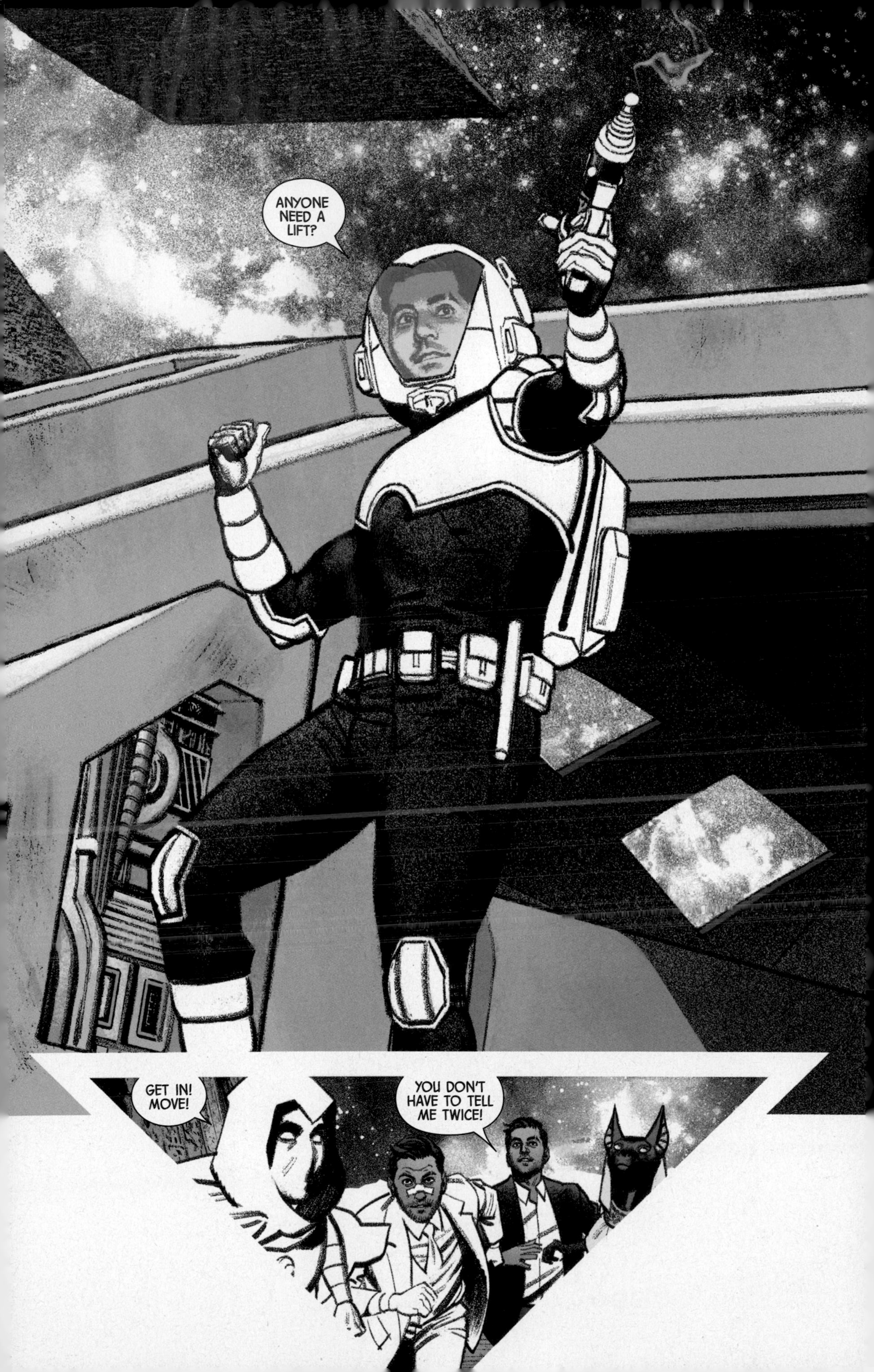
ANYONE NEED A LIFT?
GET IN! MOVE!
YOU DON'T HAVE TO TELL ME TWICE!

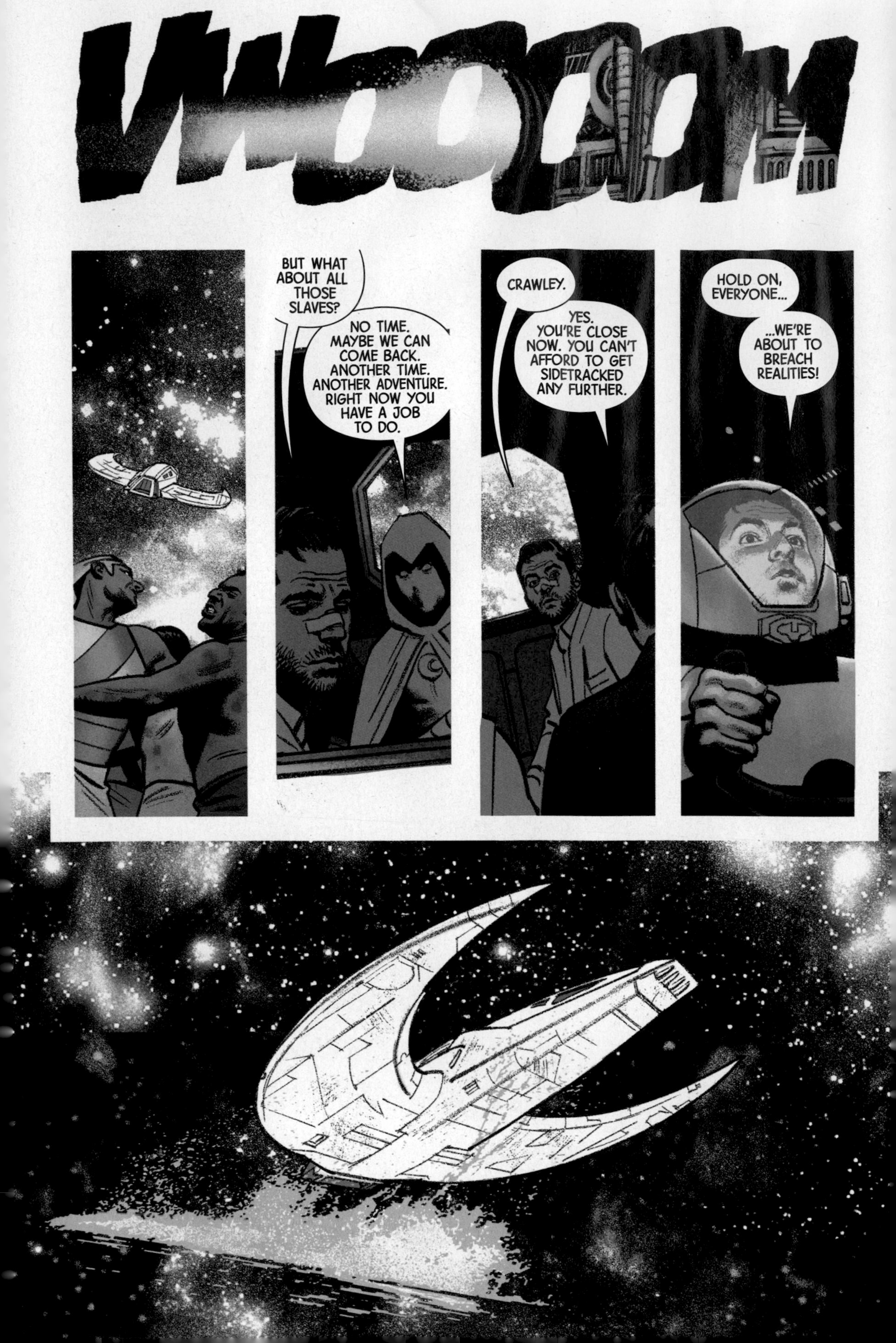
VWOOOOM!
BUT WHAT ABOUT ALL THOSE SLAVES?
NO TIME. MAYBE WE CAN COME BACK. ANOTHER TIME. ANOTHER ADVENTURE. RIGHT NOW YOU HAVE A JOB TO DO.
CRAWLEY.
YES. YOU'RE CLOSE NOW. YOU CAN'T AFFORD TO GET SIDETRACKED ANY FURTHER.
HOLD ON, EVERYONE...
...WE'RE ABOUT TO BREACH REALITIES!

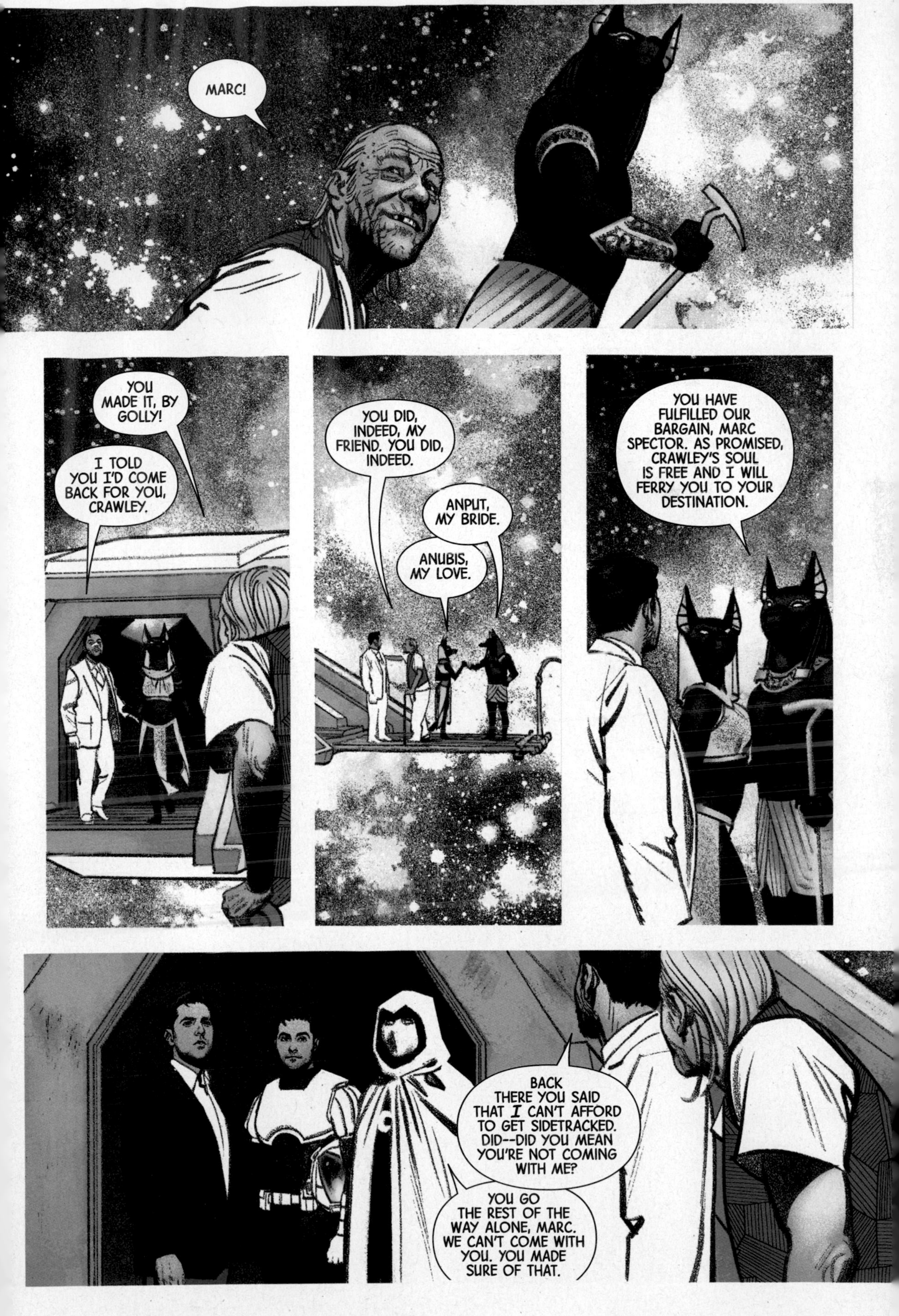
MARC!
YOU MADE IT, BY GOLLY!
I TOLD YOU I'D COME BACK FOR YOU, CRAWLEY.
YOU DID, INDEED, MY FRIEND. YOU DID, INDEED.
ANPUT, MY BRIDE.
ANUBIS, MY LOVE.
YOU HAVE FULFILLED OUR BARGAIN, MARC SPECTOR. AS PROMISED, CRAWLEY'S SOUL IS FREE AND I WILL FERRY YOU TO YOUR DESTINATION.
BACK THERE YOU SAID THAT I CAN'T AFFORD TO GET SIDETRACKED. DID--DID YOU MEAN YOU'RE NOT COMING WITH ME?
YOU GO THE REST OF THE WAY ALONE, MARC. WE CAN'T COME WITH YOU. YOU MADE SURE OF THAT.

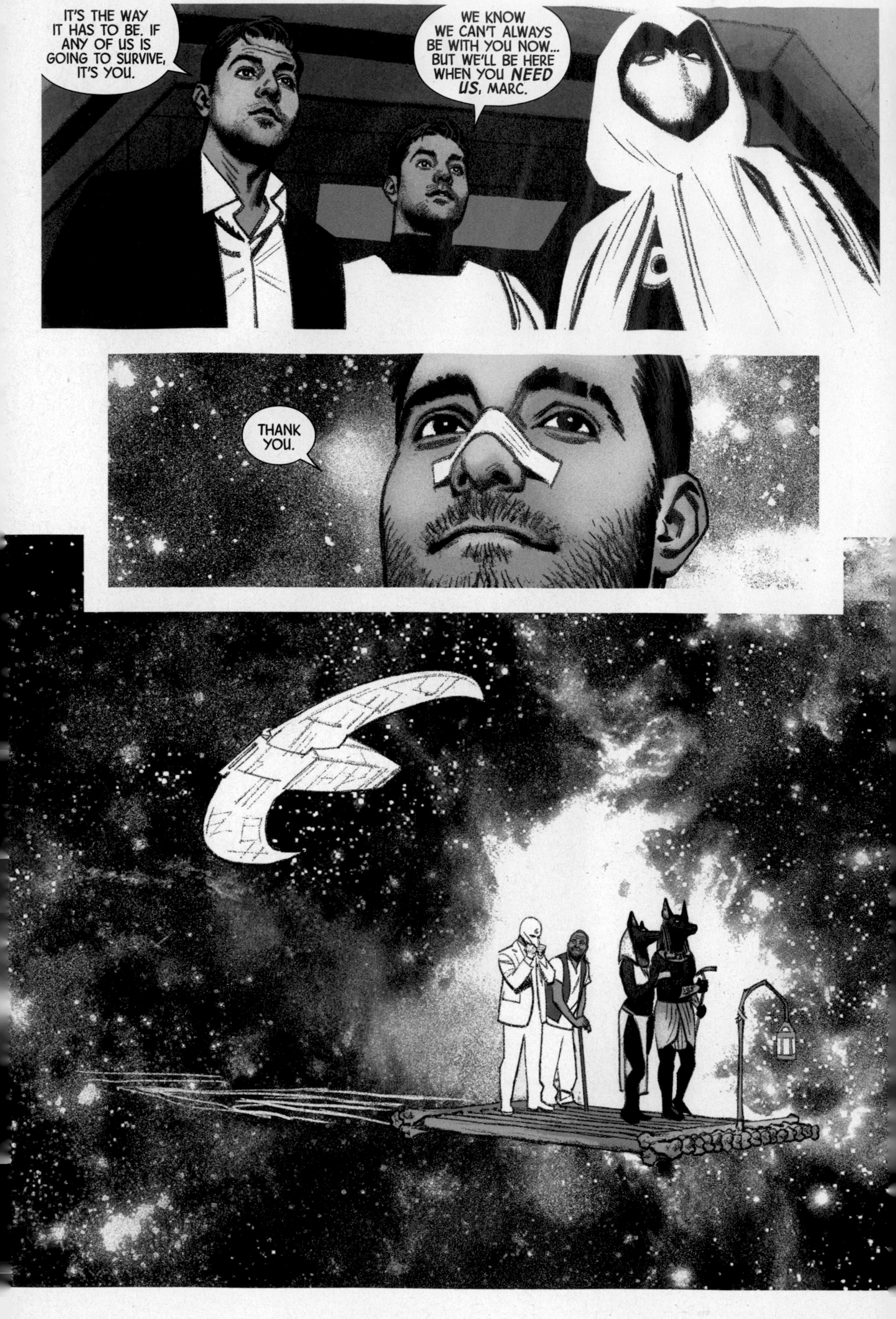
IT'S THE WAY IT HAS TO BE. IF ANY OF US IS GOING TO SURVIVE, IT'S YOU.
WE KNOW WE CAN'T ALWAYS BE WITH YOU NOW... BUT WE'LL BE HERE WHEN YOU NEED US, MARC.
THANK YOU.

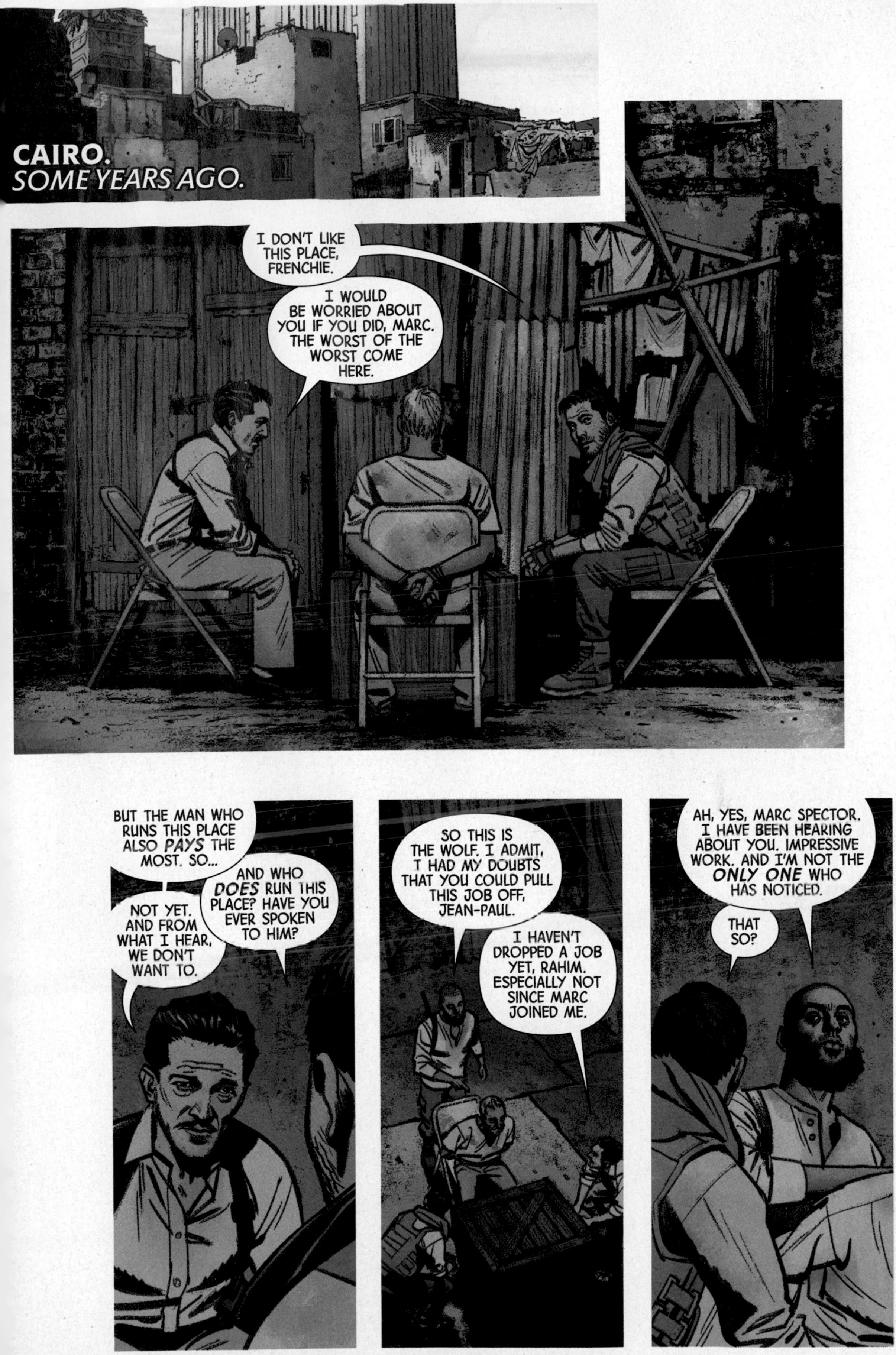
CAIRO.
SOME YEARS AGO.
I DON'T LIKE THIS PLACE, FRENCHIE.
I WOULD BE WORRIED ABOUT YOU IF YOU DID, MARC. THE WORST OF THE WORST COME HERE.
BUT THE MAN WHO RUNS THIS PLACE ALSO PAYS THE MOST. SO...
AND WHO DOES RUN THIS PLACE? HAVE YOU EVER SPOKEN TO HIM?
NOT YET. AND FROM WHAT I HEAR, WE DON'T WANT TO.
SO THIS IS THE WOLF. I ADMIT, I HAD MY DOUBTS THAT YOU COULD PULL THIS JOB OFF, JEAN-PAUL.
I HAVEN'T DROPPED A JOB YET, RAHIM. ESPECIALLY NOT SINCE MARC JOINED ME.
AH, YES, MARC SPECTOR. I HAVE BEEN HEARING ABOUT YOU. IMPRESSIVE WORK. AND I'M NOT THE ONLY ONE WHO HAS NOTICED.
THAT SO?

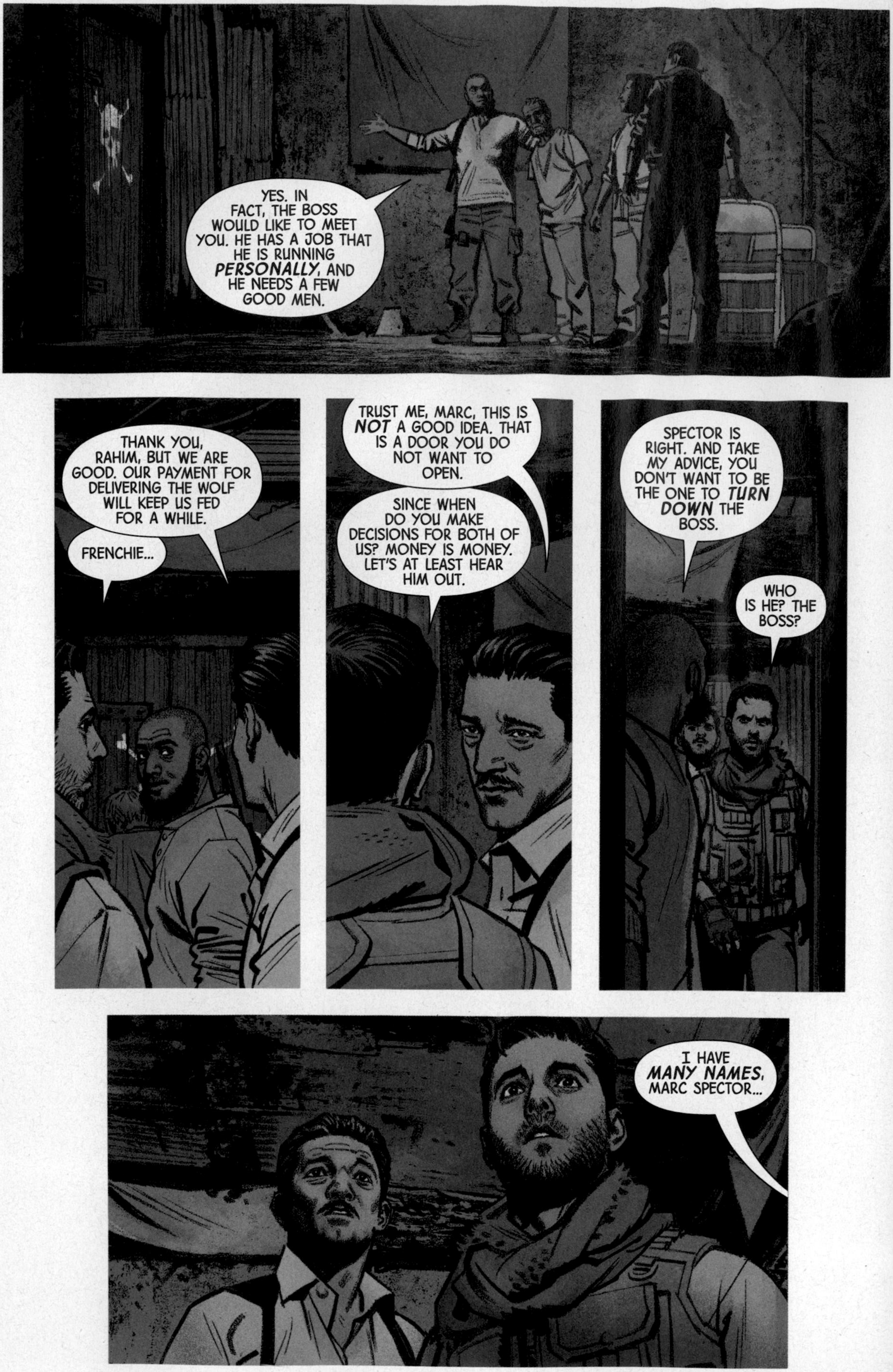
YES. IN FACT, THE BOSS WOULD LIKE TO MEET YOU. HE HAS A JOB THAT HE IS RUNNING PERSONALLY, AND HE NEEDS A FEW GOOD MEN.
THANK YOU, RAHIM, BUT WE ARE GOOD. OUR PAYMENT FOR DELIVERING THE WOLF WILL KEEP US FED FOR A WHILE.
FRENCHIE...
TRUST ME, MARC, THIS IS NOT A GOOD IDEA. THAT IS A DOOR YOU DO NOT WANT TO OPEN.
SINCE WHEN DO YOU MAKE DECISIONS FOR BOTH OF US? MONEY IS MONEY. LET'S AT LEAST HEAR HIM OUT.
SPECTOR IS RIGHT. AND TAKE MY ADVICE, YOU DON'T WANT TO BE THE ONE TO TURN DOWN THE BOSS.
WHO IS HE? THE BOSS?
I HAVE MANY NAMES, MARC SPECTOR...

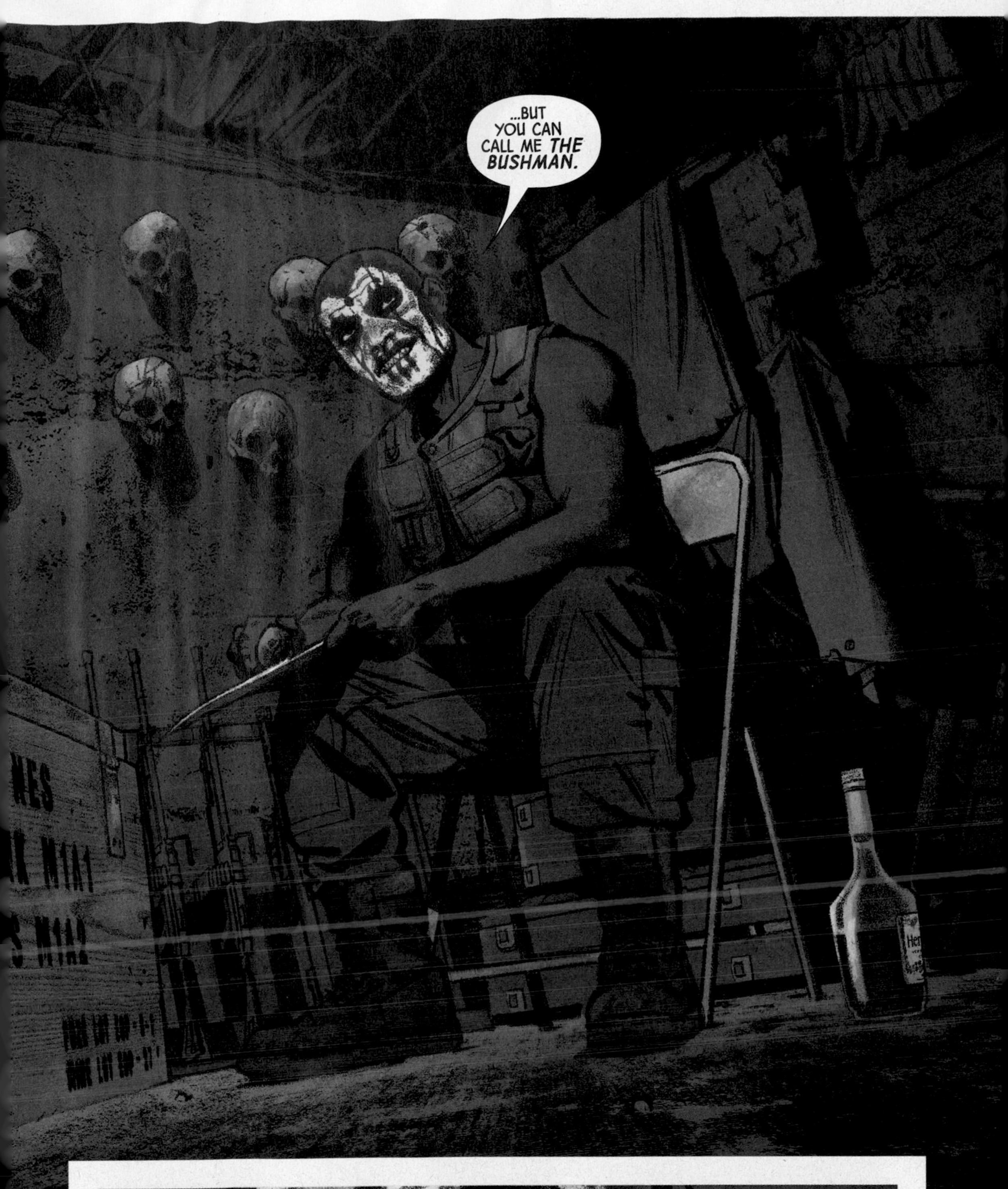
...BUT YOU CAN CALL ME THE BUSHMAN.

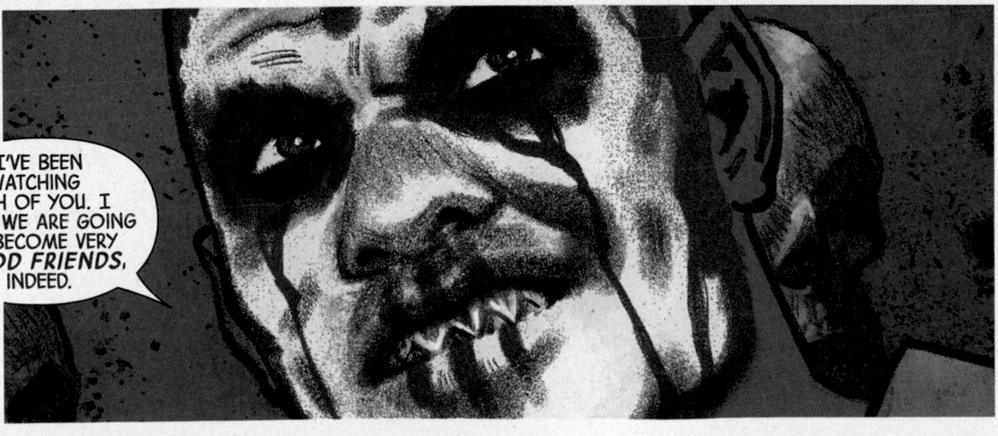
I'VE BEEN WATCHING BOTH OF YOU. I THINK WE ARE GOING TO BECOME VERY GOOD FRIENDS, INDEED.

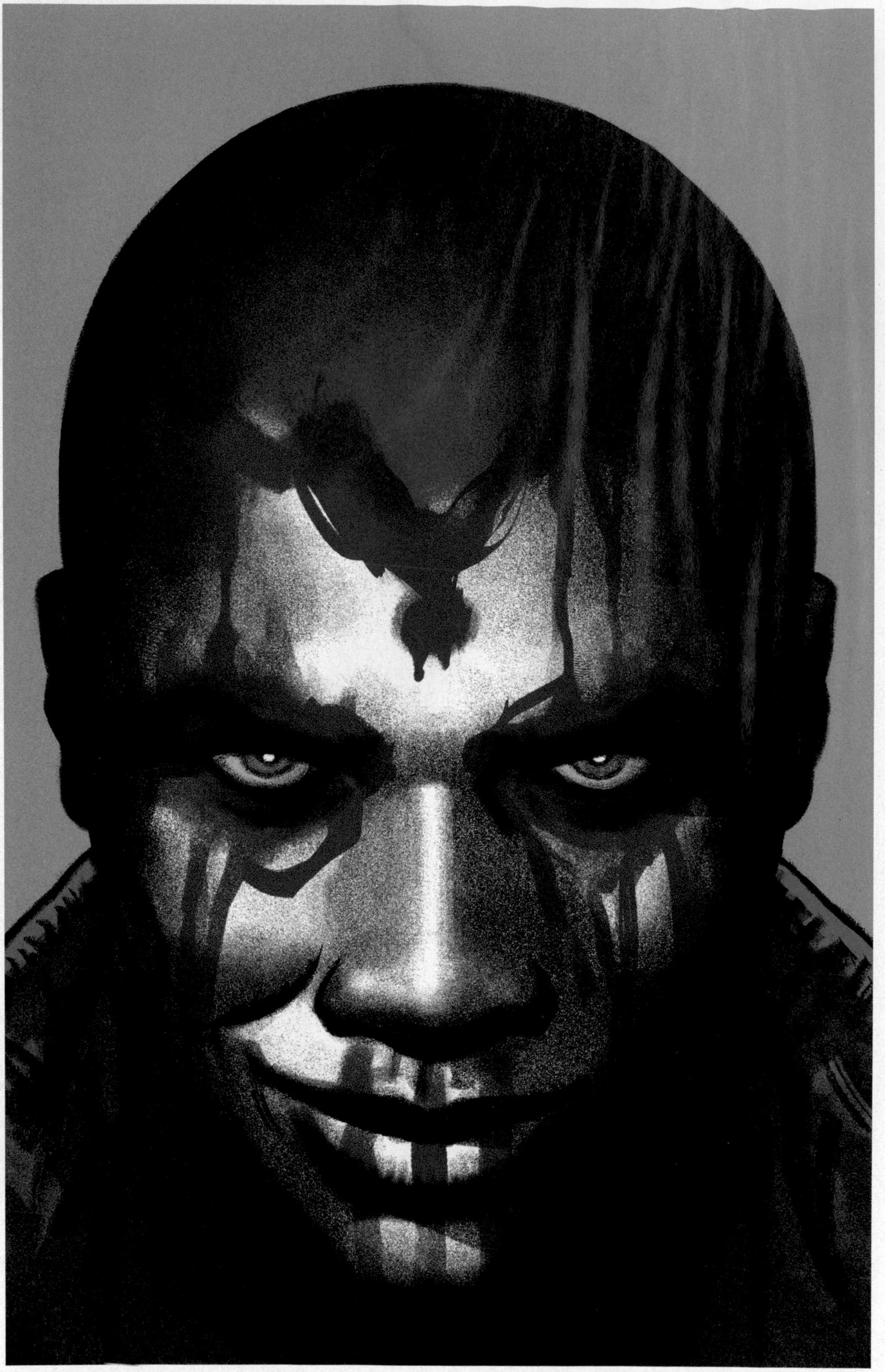

BIRTH AND DEATH
PART FOUR

13

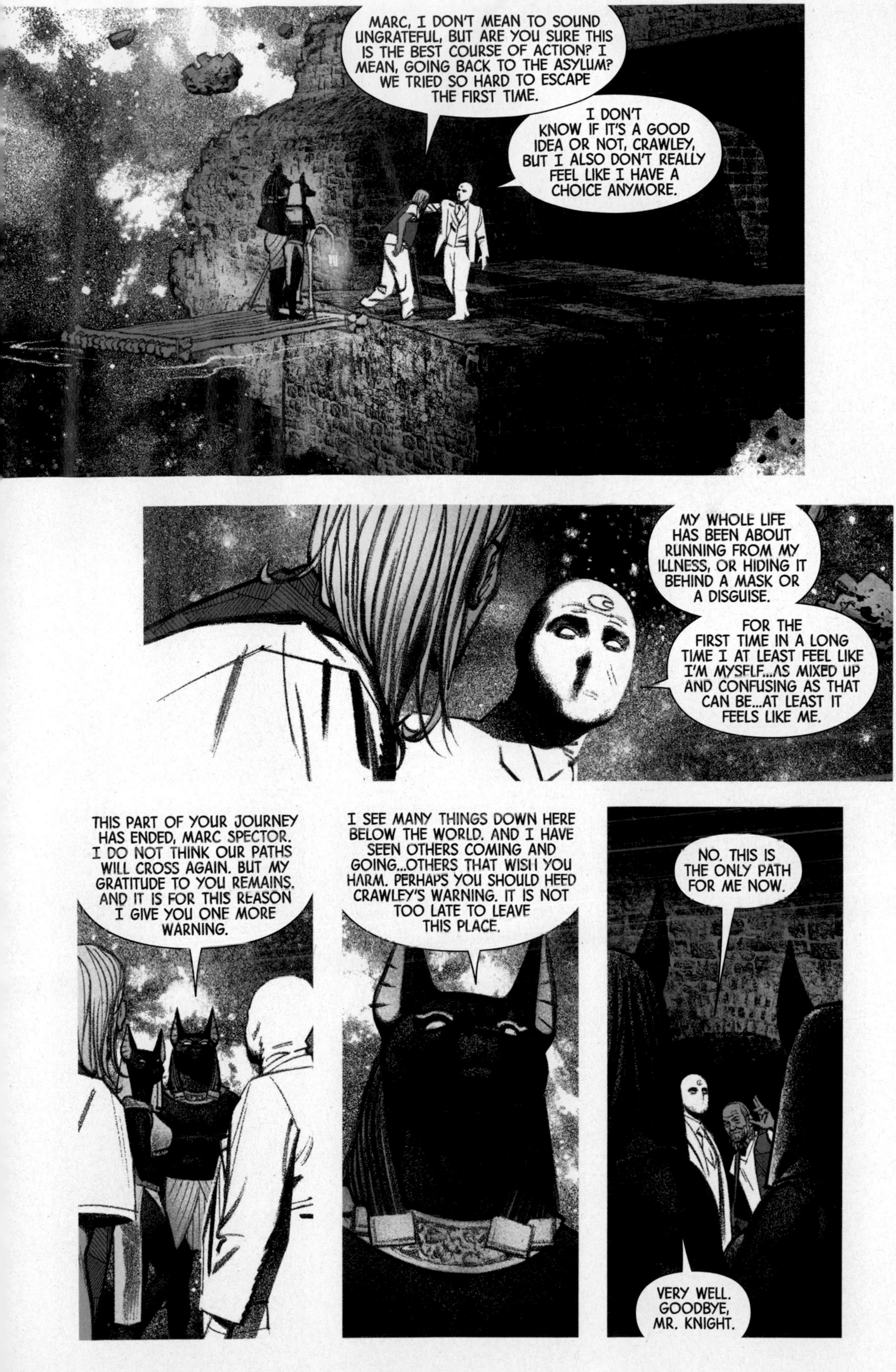
MARC, I DON'T MEAN TO SOUND UNGRATEFUL, BUT ARE YOU SURE THIS IS THE BEST COURSE OF ACTION? I MEAN, GOING BACK TO THE ASYLUM? WE TRIED SO HARD TO ESCAPE THE FIRST TIME.
I DON'T KNOW IF IT'S A GOOD IDEA OR NOT, CRAWLEY, BUT I ALSO DON'T REALLY FEEL LIKE I HAVE A CHOICE ANYMORE.
MY WHOLE LIFE HAS BEEN ABOUT RUNNING FROM MY ILLNESS, OR HIDING IT BEHIND A MASK OR A DISGUISE.
FOR THE FIRST TIME IN A LONG TIME I AT LEAST FEEL LIKE I'M MYSELF...AS MIXED UP AND CONFUSING AS THAT CAN BE...AT LEAST IT FEELS LIKE ME.
THIS PART OF YOUR JOURNEY HAS ENDED, MARC SPECTOR. I DO NOT THINK OUR PATHS WILL CROSS AGAIN. BUT MY GRATITUDE TO YOU REMAINS. AND IT IS FOR THIS REASON I GIVE YOU ONE MORE WARNING.
I SEE MANY THINGS DOWN HERE BELOW THE WORLD. AND I HAVE SEEN OTHERS COMING AND GOING...OTHERS THAT WISH YOU HARM. PERHAPS YOU SHOULD HEED CRAWLEY'S WARNING. IT IS NOT TOO LATE TO LEAVE THIS PLACE.
NO. THIS IS THE ONLY PATH FOR ME NOW.
VERY WELL. GOODBYE, MR. KNIGHT.

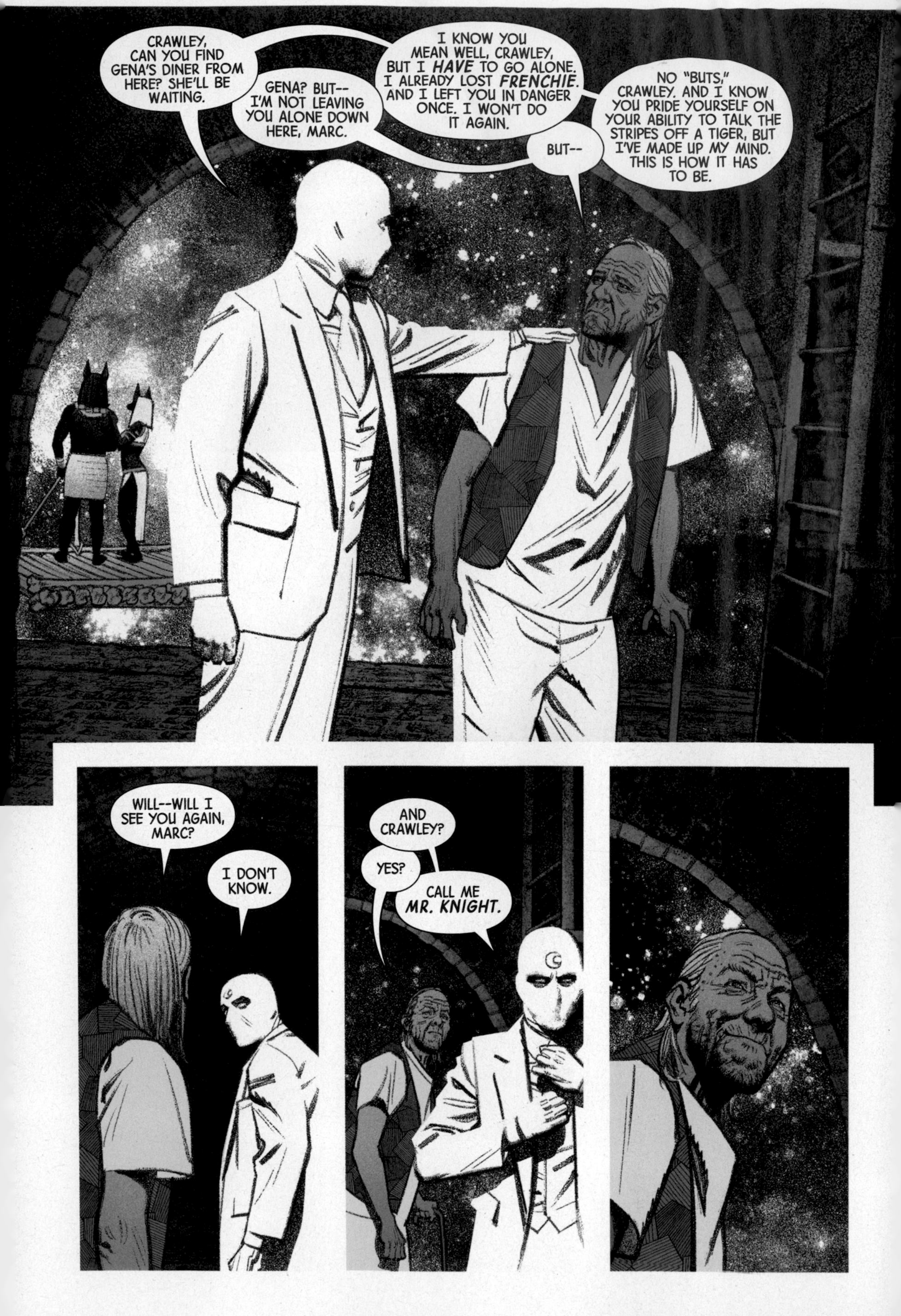
CRAWLEY, CAN YOU FIND GENA'S DINER FROM HERE? SHE'LL BE WAITING.
GENA? BUT-- I'M NOT LEAVING YOU ALONE DOWN HERE, MARC.
I KNOW YOU MEAN WELL, CRAWLEY, BUT I HAVE TO GO ALONE. I ALREADY LOST FRENCHIE. AND I LEFT YOU IN DANGER ONCE. I WON'T DO IT AGAIN.
BUT--
NO "BUTS," CRAWLEY. AND I KNOW YOU PRIDE YOURSELF ON YOUR ABILITY TO TALK THE STRIPES OFF A TIGER, BUT I'VE MADE UP MY MIND. THIS IS HOW IT HAS TO BE.
WILL--WILL I SEE YOU AGAIN, MARC?
I DON'T KNOW.
AND CRAWLEY?
YES?
CALL ME MR. KNIGHT.

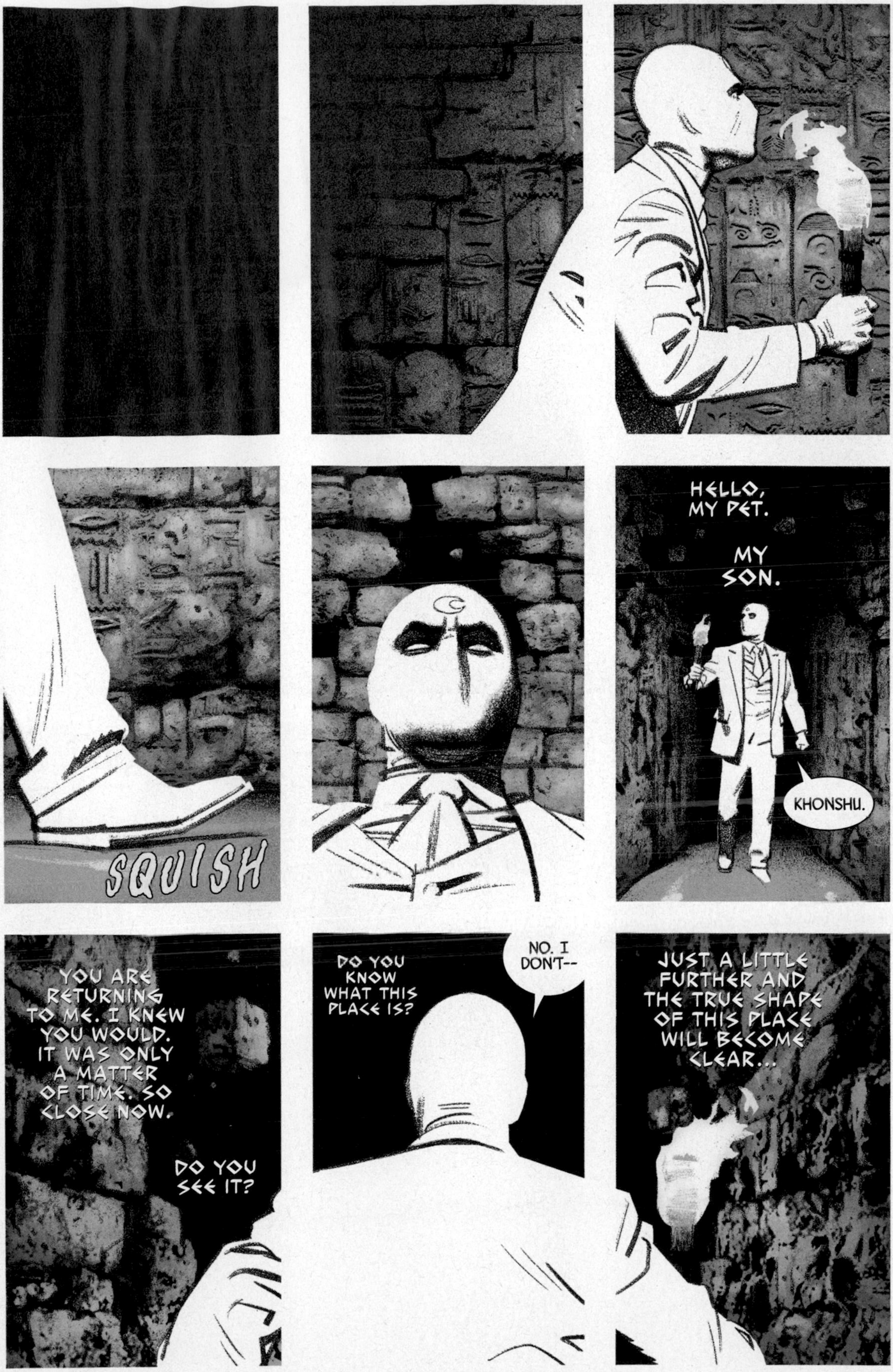
SQUISH
HELLO, MY PET.
MY SON.
KHONSHU.
YOU ARE RETURNING TO ME. I KNEW YOU WOULD. IT WAS ONLY A MATTER OF TIME. SO CLOSE NOW.
DO YOU SEE IT?
DO YOU KNOW WHAT THIS PLACE IS?
NO. I DON'T--
JUST A LITTLE FURTHER AND THE TRUE SHAPE OF THIS PLACE WILL BECOME CLEAR...

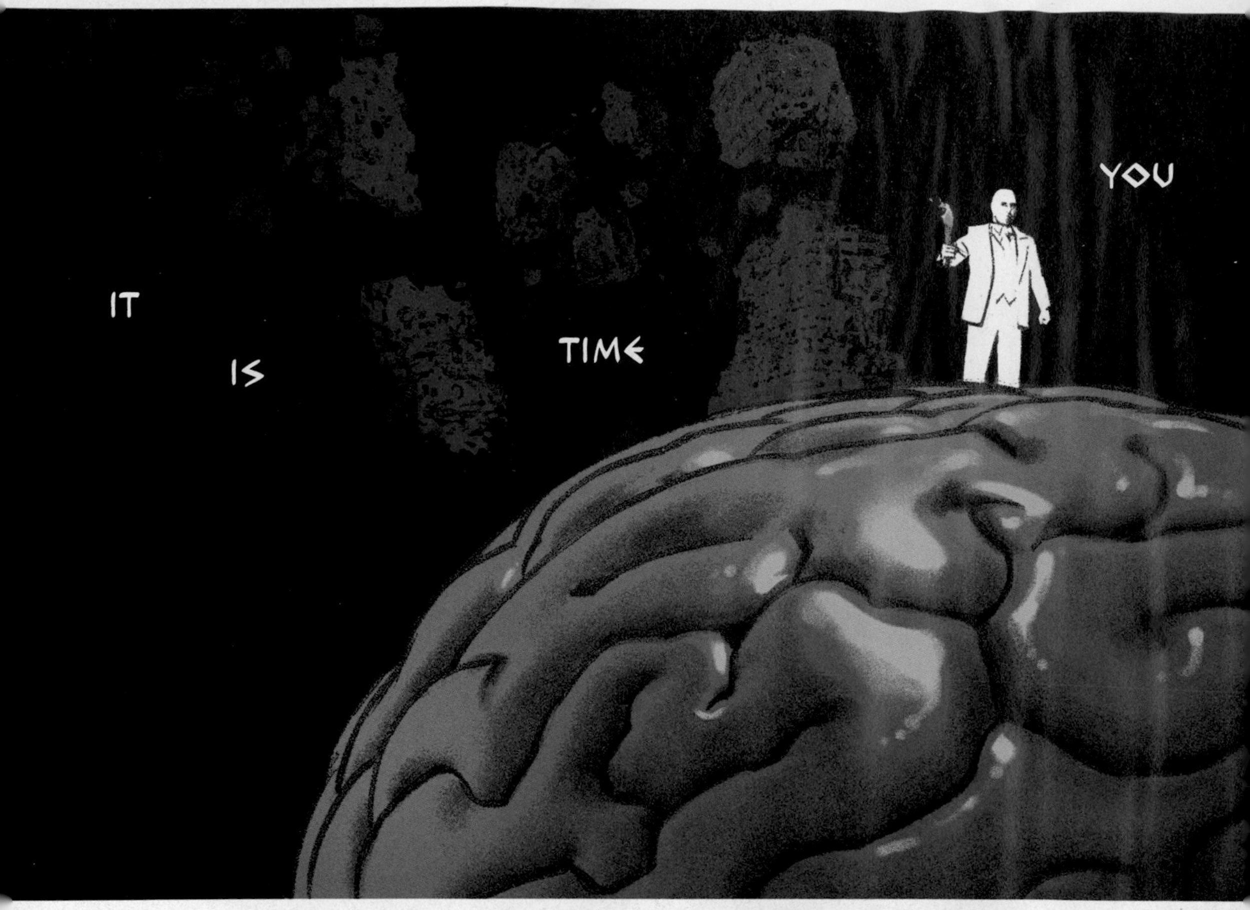
IT
IS
TIME
YOU

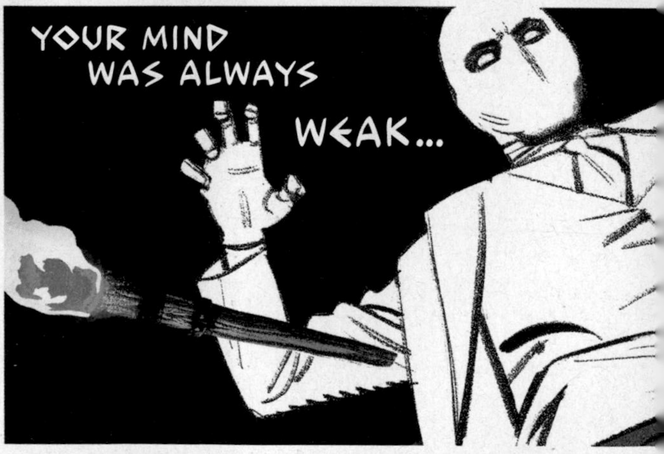
YOUR MIND WAS ALWAYS
WEAK...

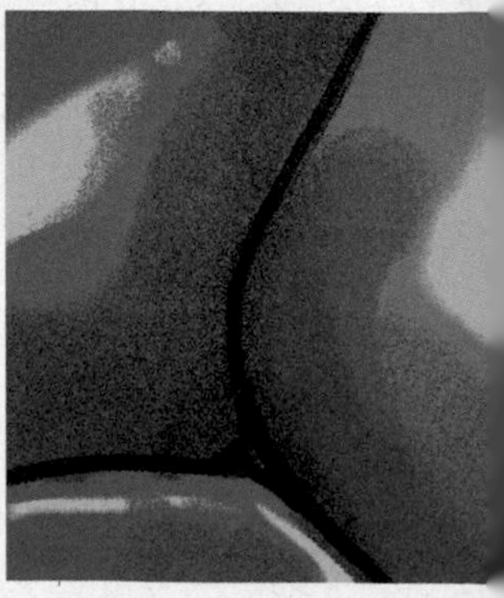

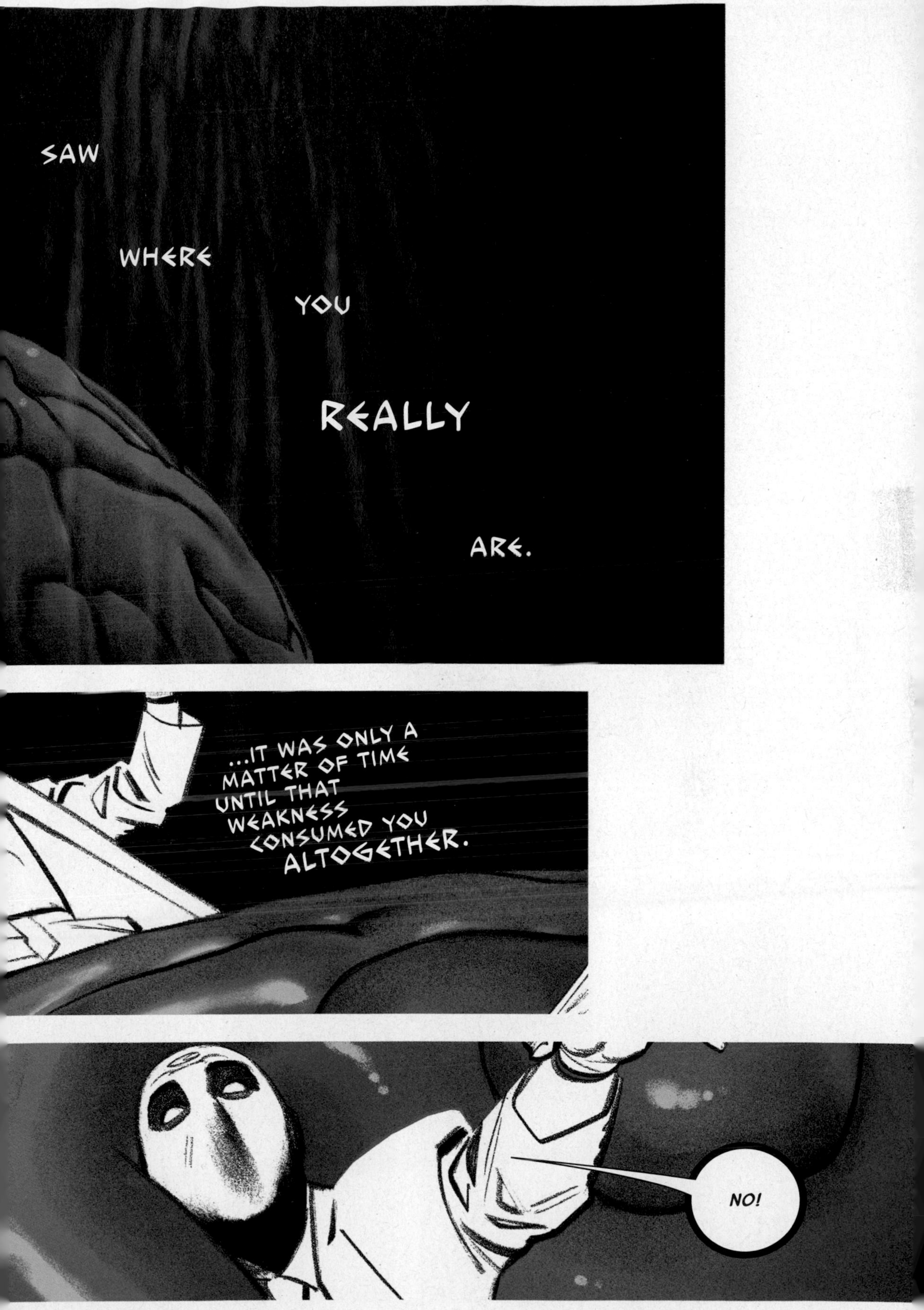
SAW
WHERE
YOU
REALLY
ARE.
...IT WAS ONLY A MATTER OF TIME UNTIL THAT WEAKNESS CONSUMED YOU ALTOGETHER.
NO!

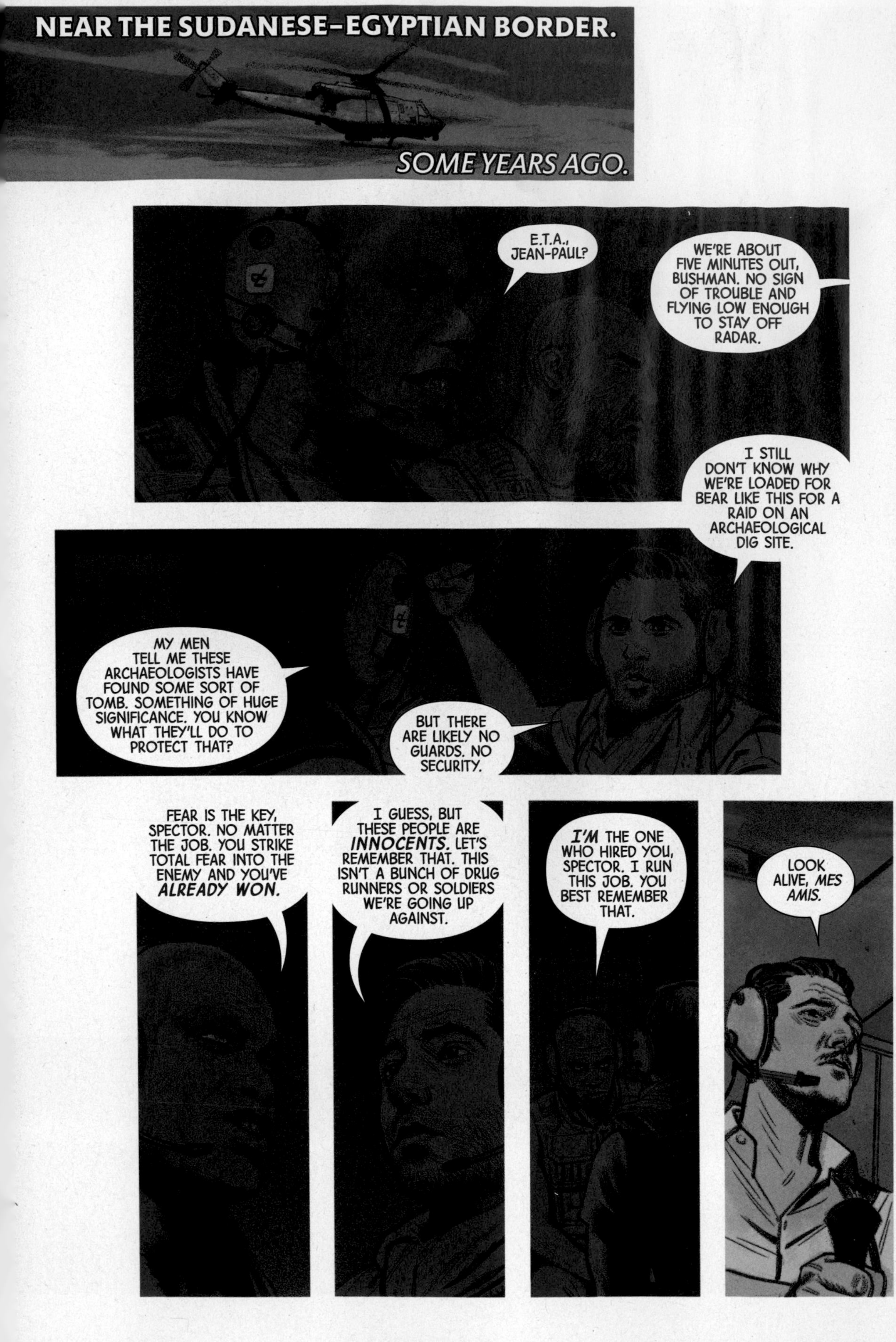
NEAR THE SUDANESE-EGYPTIAN BORDER.
SOME YEARS AGO.
E.T.A., JEAN-PAUL?
WE'RE ABOUT FIVE MINUTES OUT, BUSHMAN. NO SIGN OF TROUBLE AND FLYING LOW ENOUGH TO STAY OFF RADAR.
I STILL DON'T KNOW WHY WE'RE LOADED FOR BEAR LIKE THIS FOR A RAID ON AN ARCHAEOLOGICAL DIG SITE.
MY MEN TELL ME THESE ARCHAEOLOGISTS HAVE FOUND SOME SORT OF TOMB. SOMETHING OF HUGE SIGNIFICANCE. YOU KNOW WHAT THEY'LL DO TO PROTECT THAT?
BUT THERE ARE LIKELY NO GUARDS. NO SECURITY.
FEAR IS THE KEY, SPECTOR. NO MATTER THE JOB. YOU STRIKE TOTAL FEAR INTO THE ENEMY AND YOU'VE *ALREADY WON.*
I GUESS, BUT THESE PEOPLE ARE *INNOCENTS.* LET'S REMEMBER THAT. THIS ISN'T A BUNCH OF DRUG RUNNERS OR SOLDIERS WE'RE GOING UP AGAINST.
I'M THE ONE WHO HIRED YOU, SPECTOR. I RUN THIS JOB. YOU BEST REMEMBER THAT.
LOOK ALIVE, *MES AMIS.*

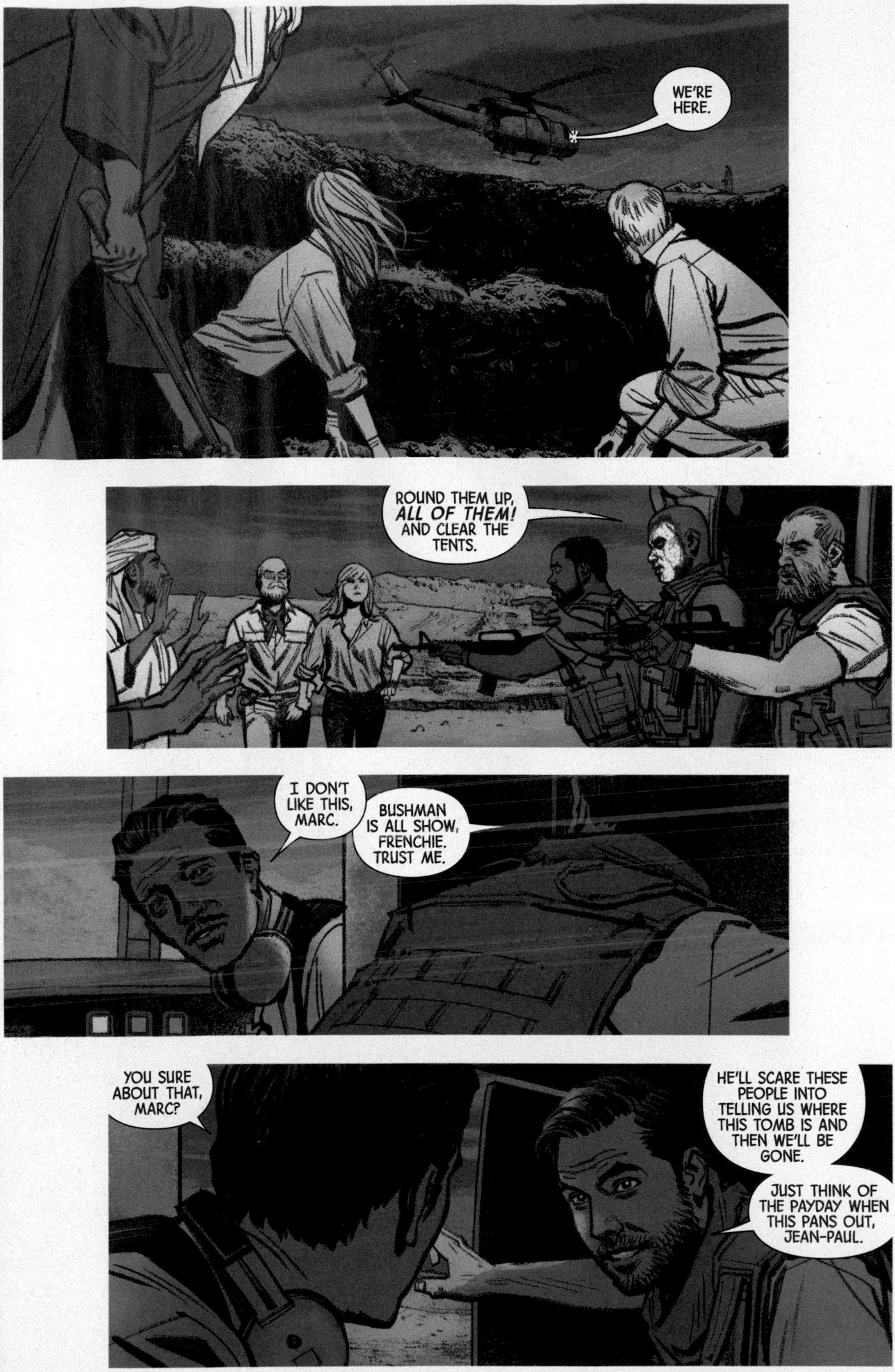
WE'RE HERE.
ROUND THEM UP, ALL OF THEM! AND CLEAR THE TENTS.
I DON'T LIKE THIS, MARC.
BUSHMAN IS ALL SHOW, FRENCHIE. TRUST ME.
YOU SURE ABOUT THAT, MARC?
HE'LL SCARE THESE PEOPLE INTO TELLING US WHERE THIS TOMB IS AND THEN WE'LL BE GONE.
JUST THINK OF THE PAYDAY WHEN THIS PANS OUT, JEAN-PAUL.

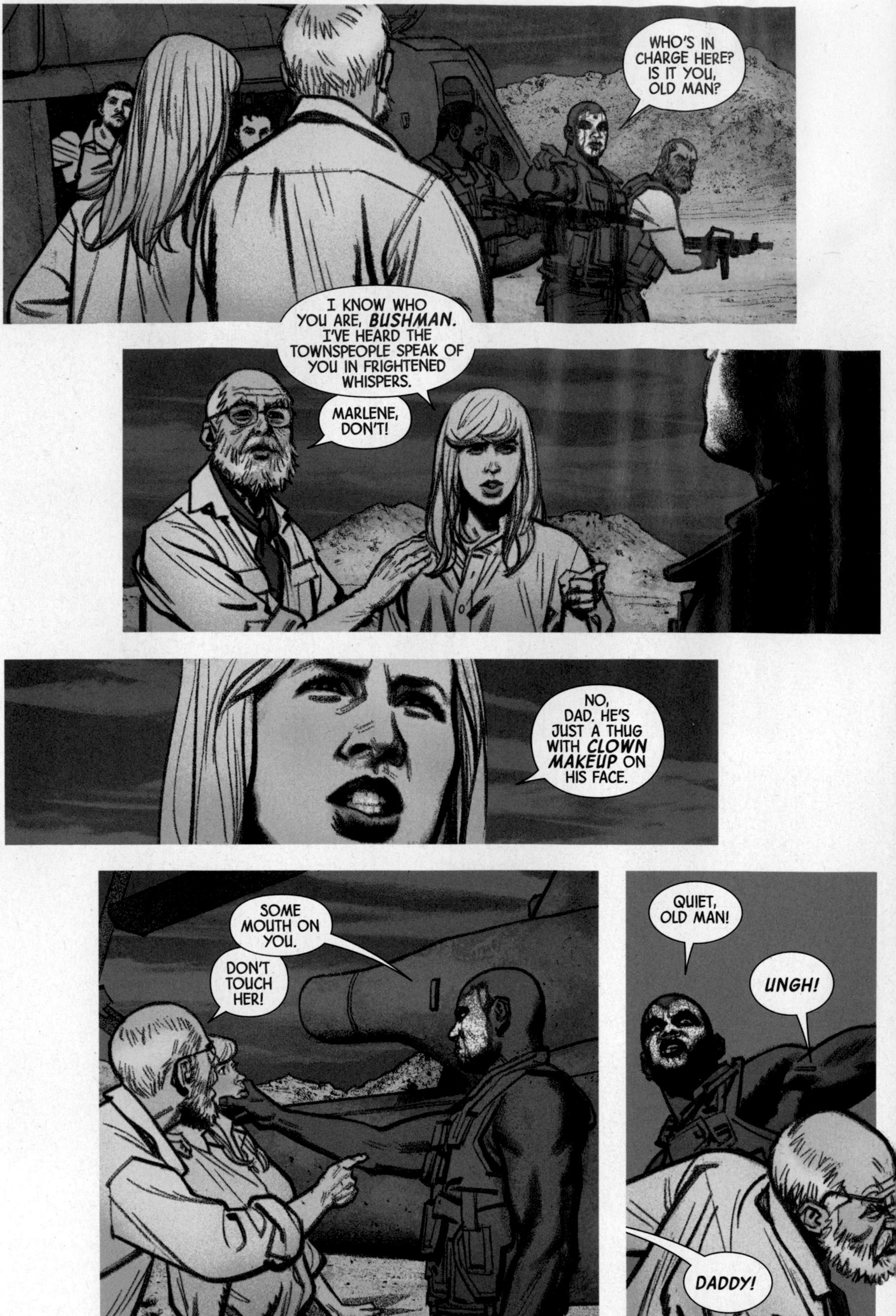
WHO'S IN CHARGE HERE? IS IT YOU, OLD MAN?
I KNOW WHO YOU ARE, BUSHMAN. I'VE HEARD THE TOWNSPEOPLE SPEAK OF YOU IN FRIGHTENED WHISPERS.
MARLENE, DON'T!
NO, DAD. HE'S JUST A THUG WITH CLOWN MAKEUP ON HIS FACE.
SOME MOUTH ON YOU.
DON'T TOUCH HER!
QUIET, OLD MAN!
UNGH!
DADDY!

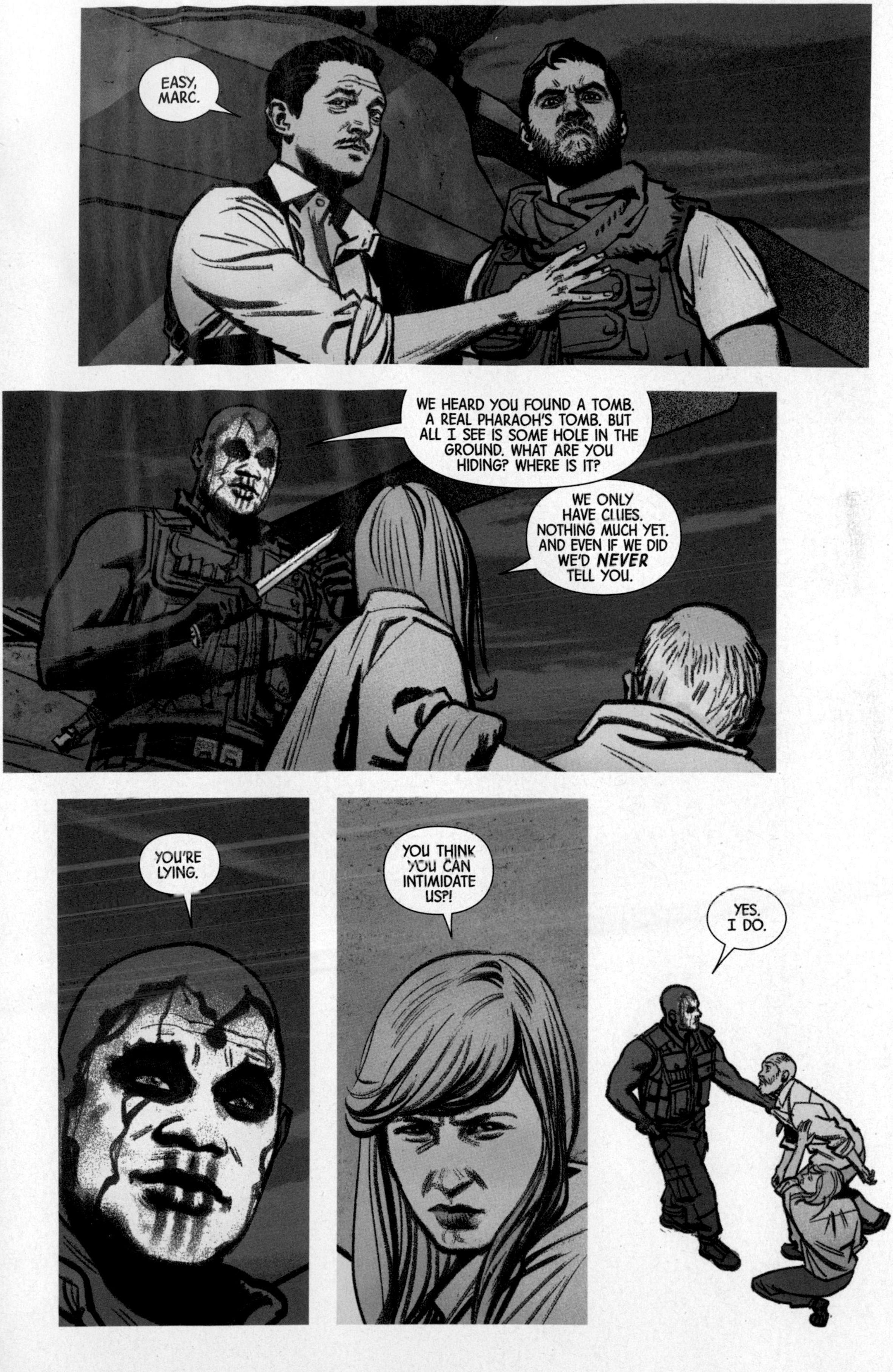
EASY, MARC.
WE HEARD YOU FOUND A TOMB. A REAL PHARAOH'S TOMB. BUT ALL I SEE IS SOME HOLE IN THE GROUND. WHAT ARE YOU HIDING? WHERE IS IT?
WE ONLY HAVE CLUES. NOTHING MUCH YET. AND EVEN IF WE DID WE'D NEVER TELL YOU.
YOU'RE LYING.
YOU THINK YOU CAN INTIMIDATE US?!
YES. I DO.

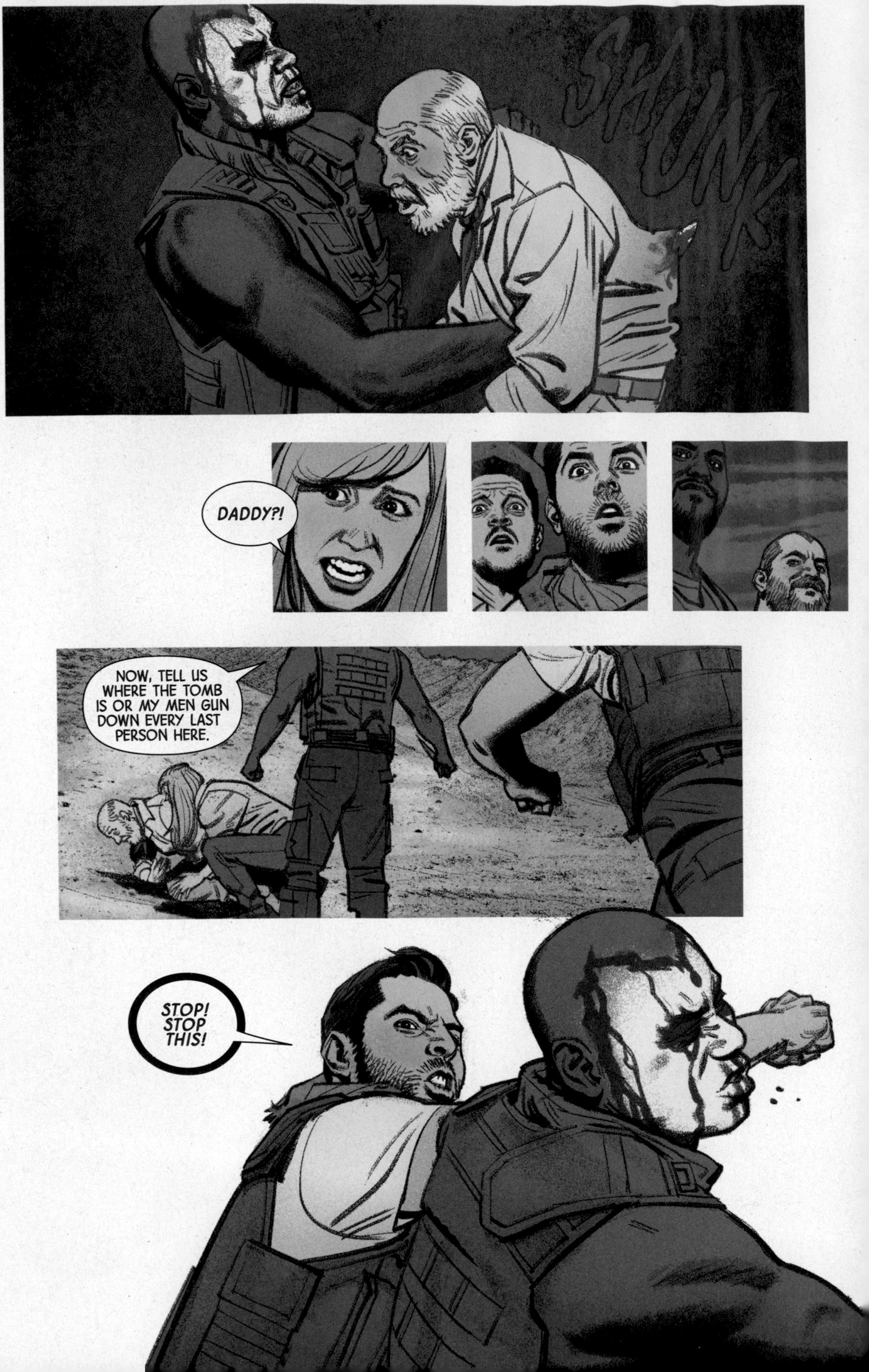
SHUNK
DADDY?!
NOW, TELL US WHERE THE TOMB IS OR MY MEN GUN DOWN EVERY LAST PERSON HERE.
STOP! STOP THIS!

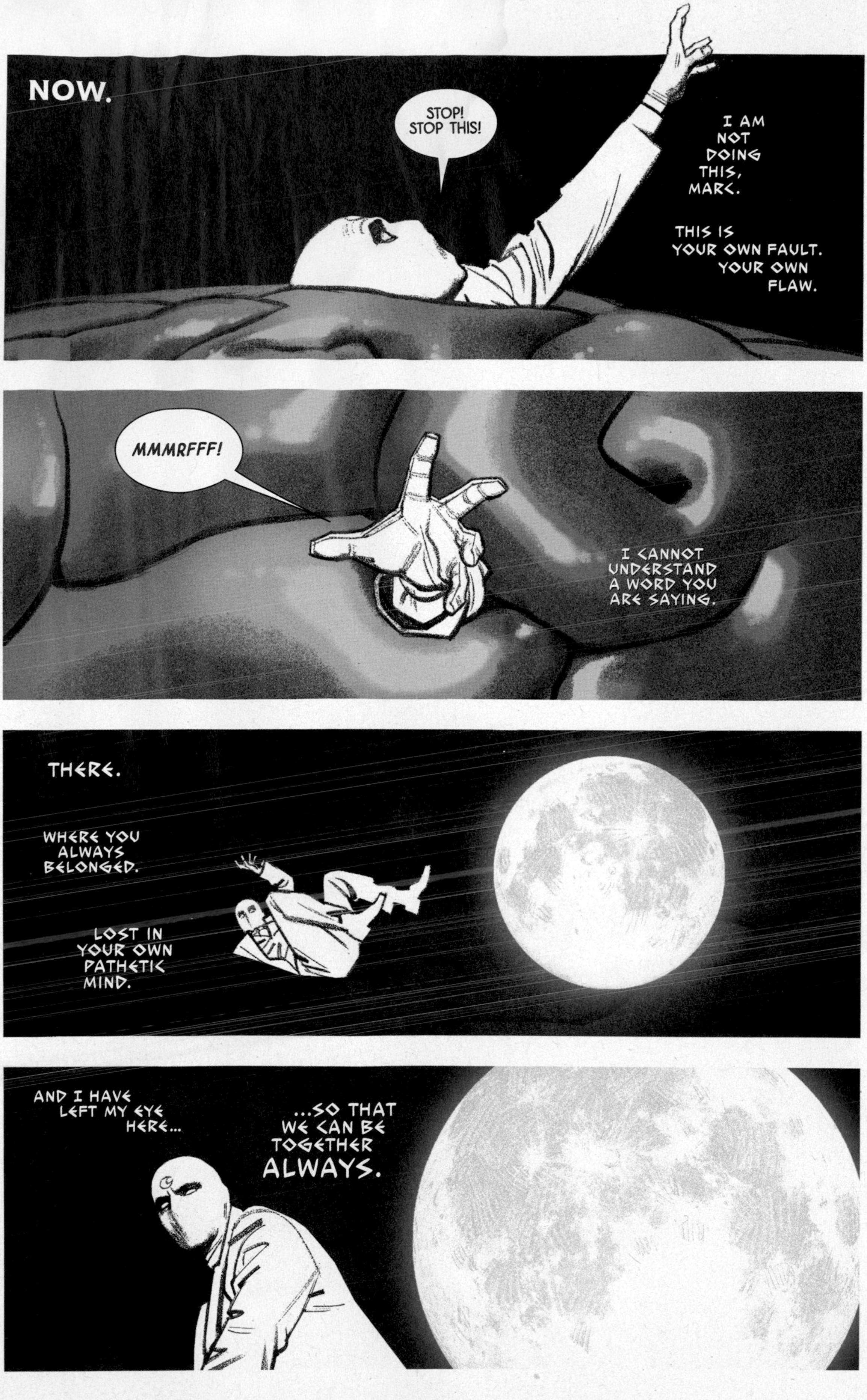
NOW.
STOP! STOP THIS!
I AM NOT DOING THIS, MARC.
THIS IS YOUR OWN FAULT. YOUR OWN FLAW.
MMMRFFF!
I CANNOT UNDERSTAND A WORD YOU ARE SAYING.
THERE.
WHERE YOU ALWAYS BELONGED.
LOST IN YOUR OWN PATHETIC MIND.
AND I HAVE LEFT MY EYE HERE...
...SO THAT WE CAN BE TOGETHER ALWAYS.

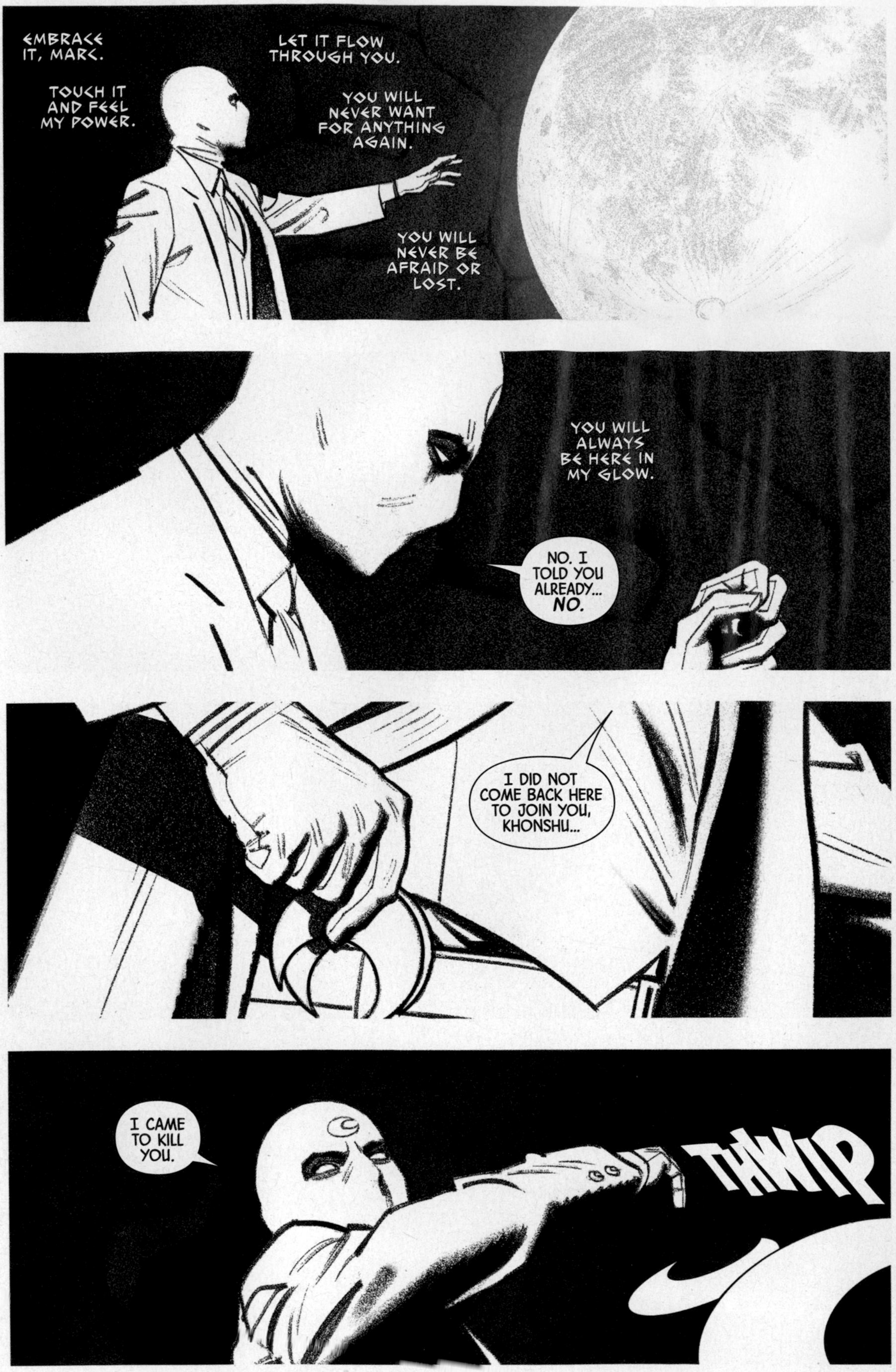
EMBRACE IT, MARC.
TOUCH IT AND FEEL MY POWER.
LET IT FLOW THROUGH YOU.
YOU WILL NEVER WANT FOR ANYTHING AGAIN.
YOU WILL NEVER BE AFRAID OR LOST.
YOU WILL ALWAYS BE HERE IN MY GLOW.
NO. I TOLD YOU ALREADY... NO.
I DID NOT COME BACK HERE TO JOIN YOU, KHONSHU...
I CAME TO KILL YOU.
THWIP

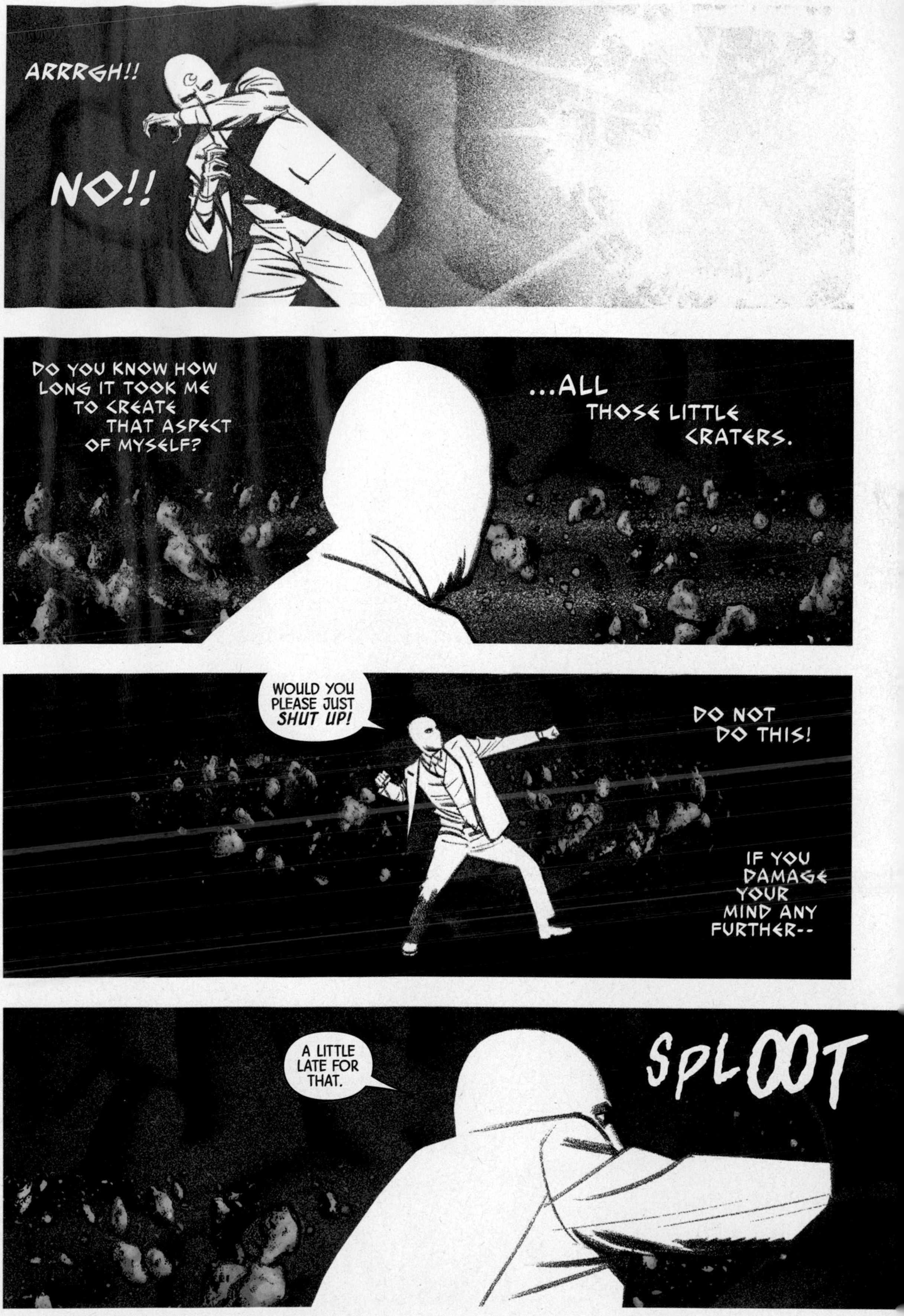

ARRRGH!!
NO!!
DO YOU KNOW HOW LONG IT TOOK ME TO CREATE THAT ASPECT OF MYSELF?
...ALL THOSE LITTLE CRATERS.
WOULD YOU PLEASE JUST SHUT UP!
DO NOT DO THIS!
IF YOU DAMAGE YOUR MIND ANY FURTHER--
A LITTLE LATE FOR THAT.
SPLOOT

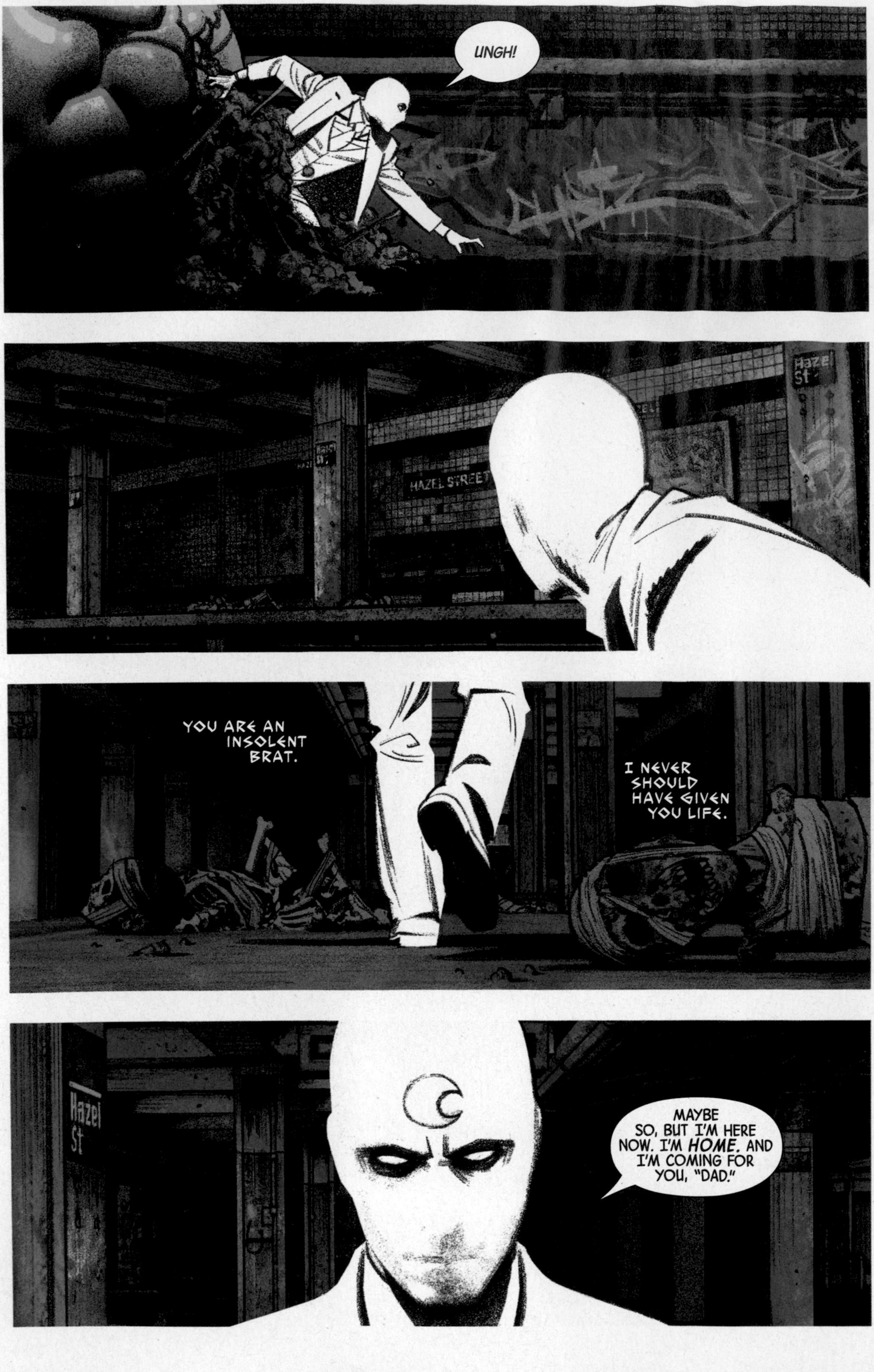
UNGH!
HAZEL STREET
Hazel St
YOU ARE AN INSOLENT BRAT.
I NEVER SHOULD HAVE GIVEN YOU LIFE.
Hazel St
MAYBE SO, BUT I'M HERE NOW. I'M HOME. AND I'M COMING FOR YOU, "DAD."

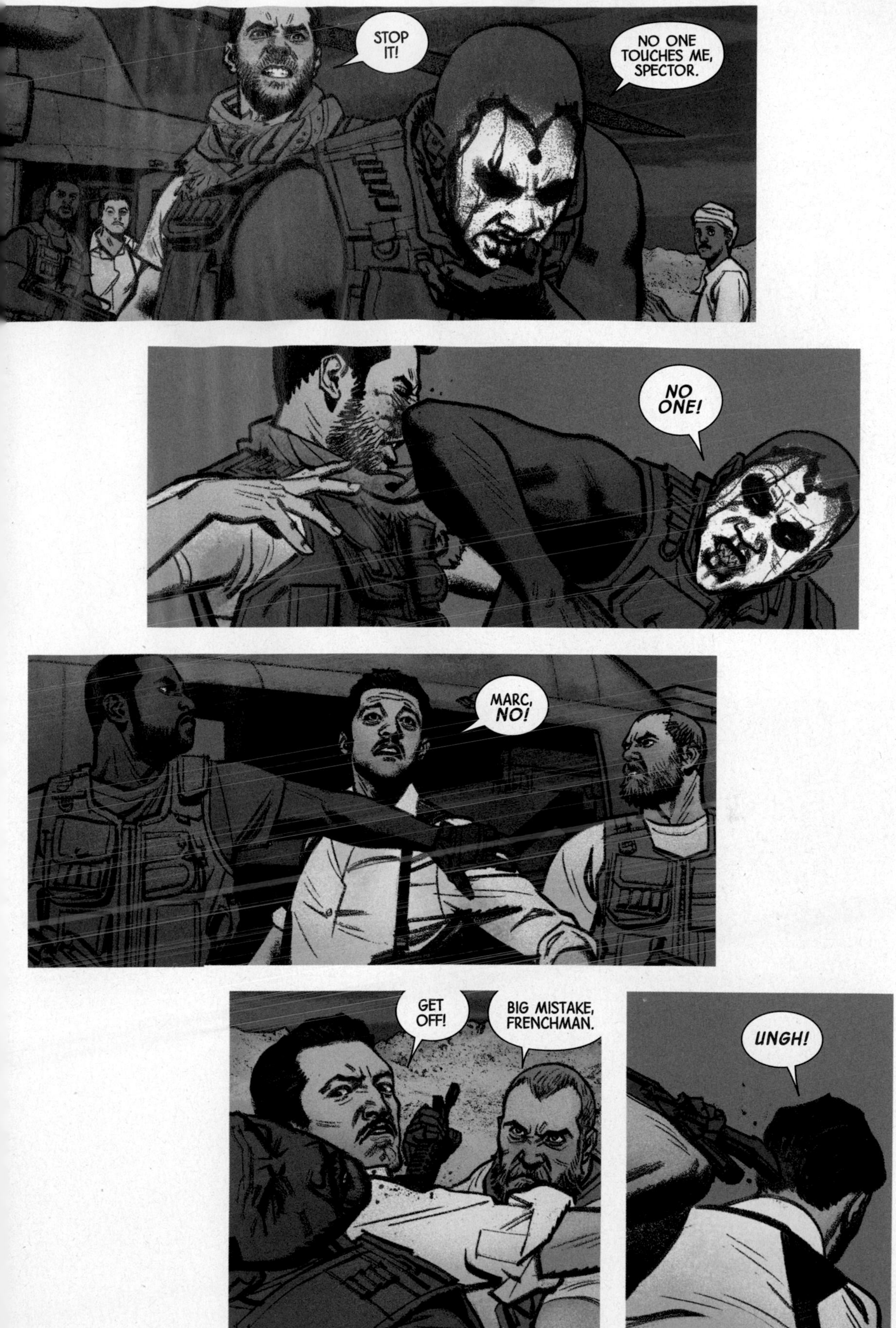
STOP IT!
NO ONE TOUCHES ME, SPECTOR.
NO ONE!
MARC, NO!
GET OFF!
BIG MISTAKE, FRENCHMAN.
UNGH!

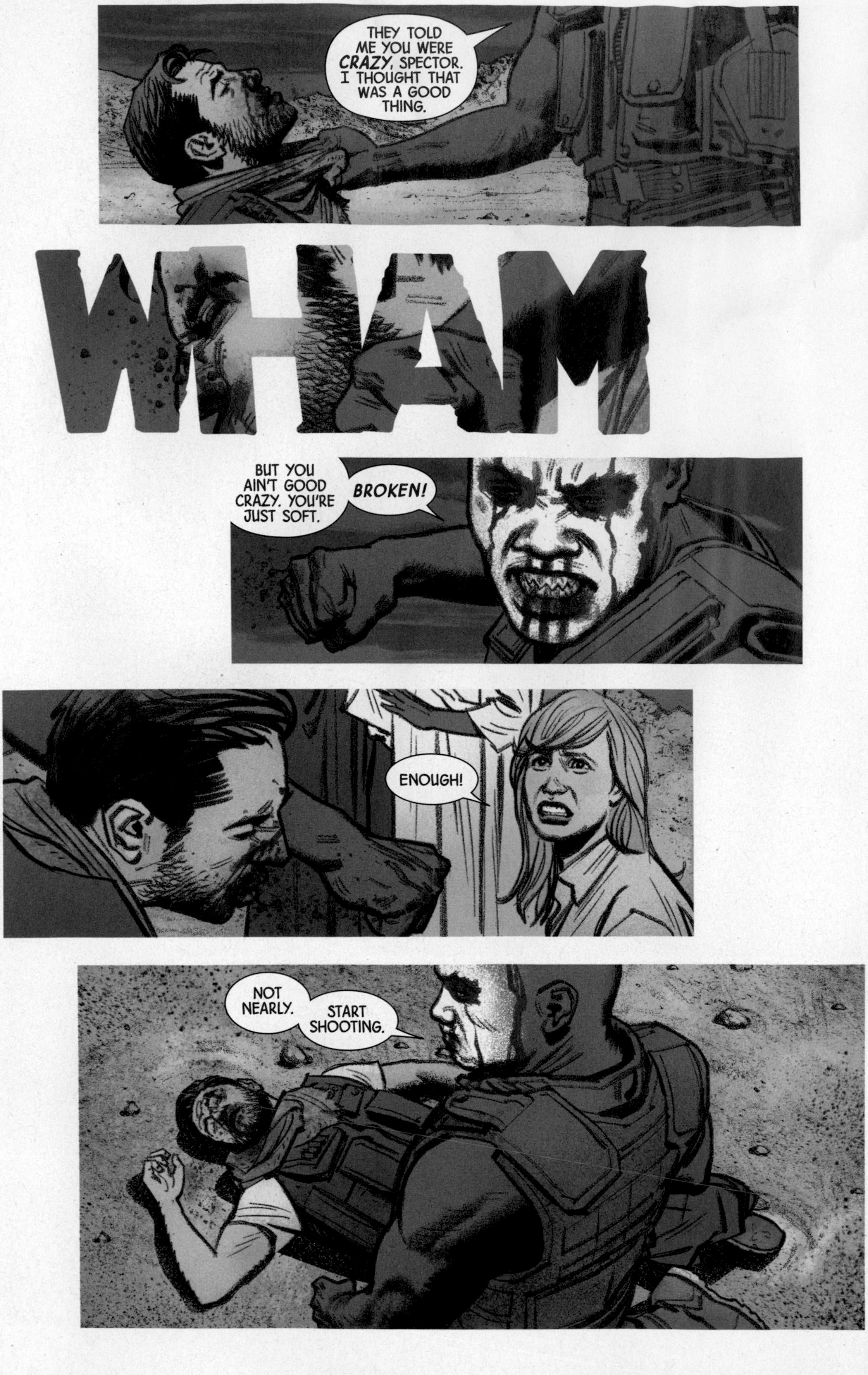
THEY TOLD ME YOU WERE *CRAZY*, SPECTOR. I THOUGHT THAT WAS A GOOD THING.
WHAM
BUT YOU AIN'T GOOD CRAZY. YOU'RE JUST SOFT.
BROKEN!
ENOUGH!
NOT NEARLY.
START SHOOTING.

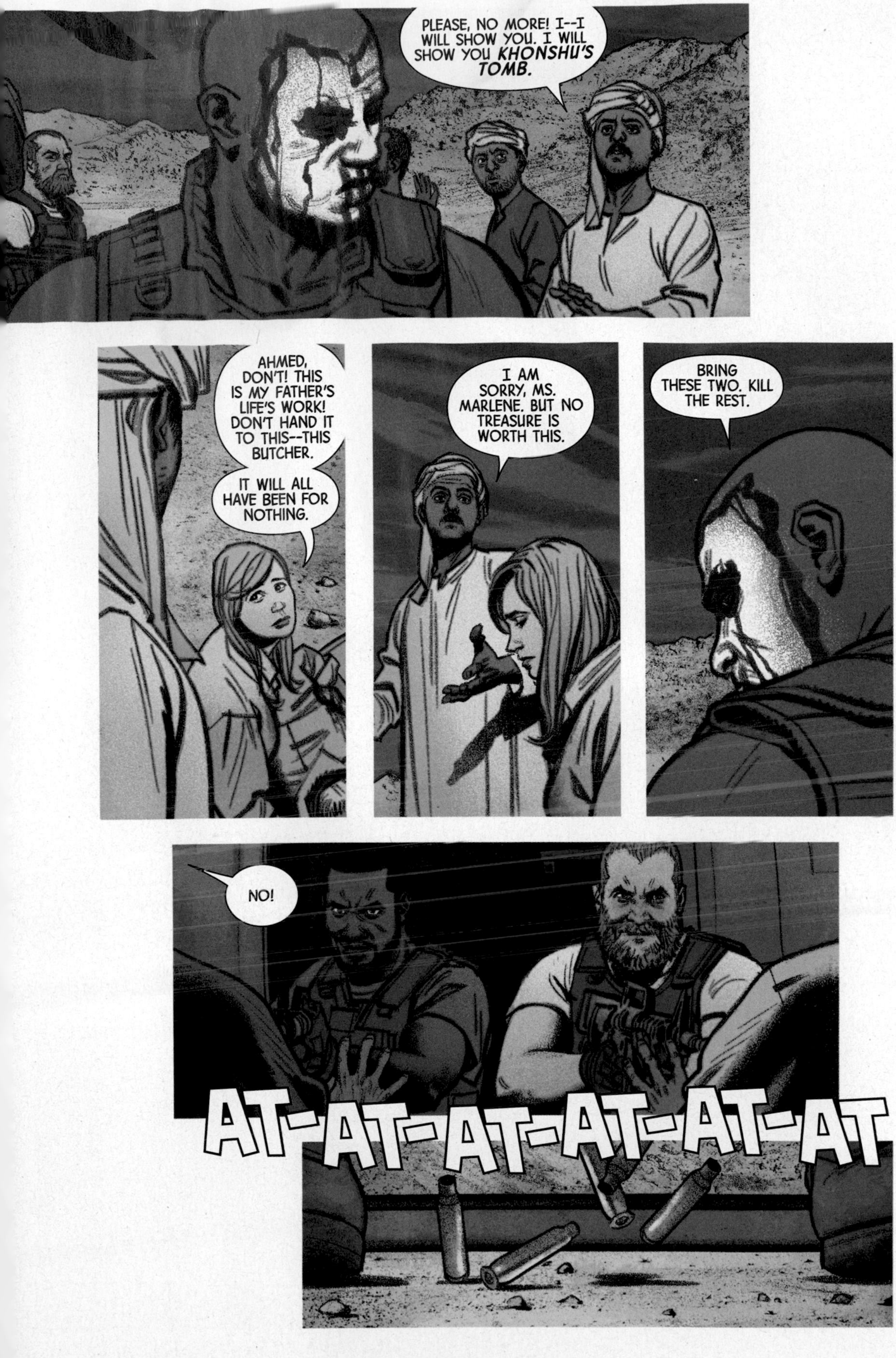
PLEASE, NO MORE! I--I WILL SHOW YOU. I WILL SHOW YOU KHONSHU'S TOMB.
AHMED, DON'T! THIS IS MY FATHER'S LIFE'S WORK! DON'T HAND IT TO THIS--THIS BUTCHER.
IT WILL ALL HAVE BEEN FOR NOTHING.
I AM SORRY, MS. MARLENE. BUT NO TREASURE IS WORTH THIS.
BRING THESE TWO. KILL THE REST.
NO!
AT-AT-AT-AT-AT-AT

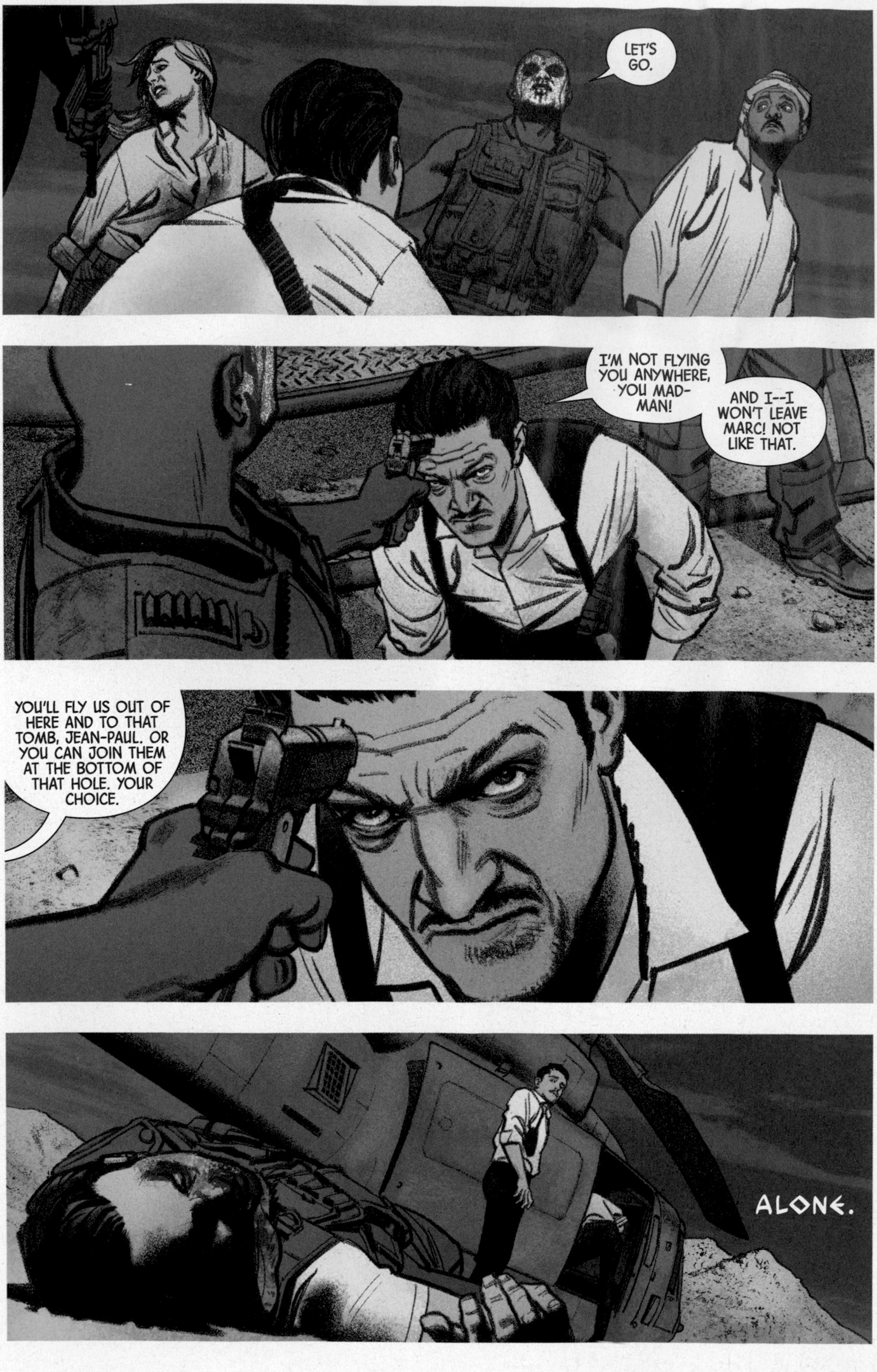
LET'S GO.
I'M NOT FLYING YOU ANYWHERE, YOU MAD-MAN!
AND I--I WON'T LEAVE MARC! NOT LIKE THAT.
YOU'LL FLY US OUT OF HERE AND TO THAT TOMB, JEAN-PAUL. OR YOU CAN JOIN THEM AT THE BOTTOM OF THAT HOLE. YOUR CHOICE.
ALONE.

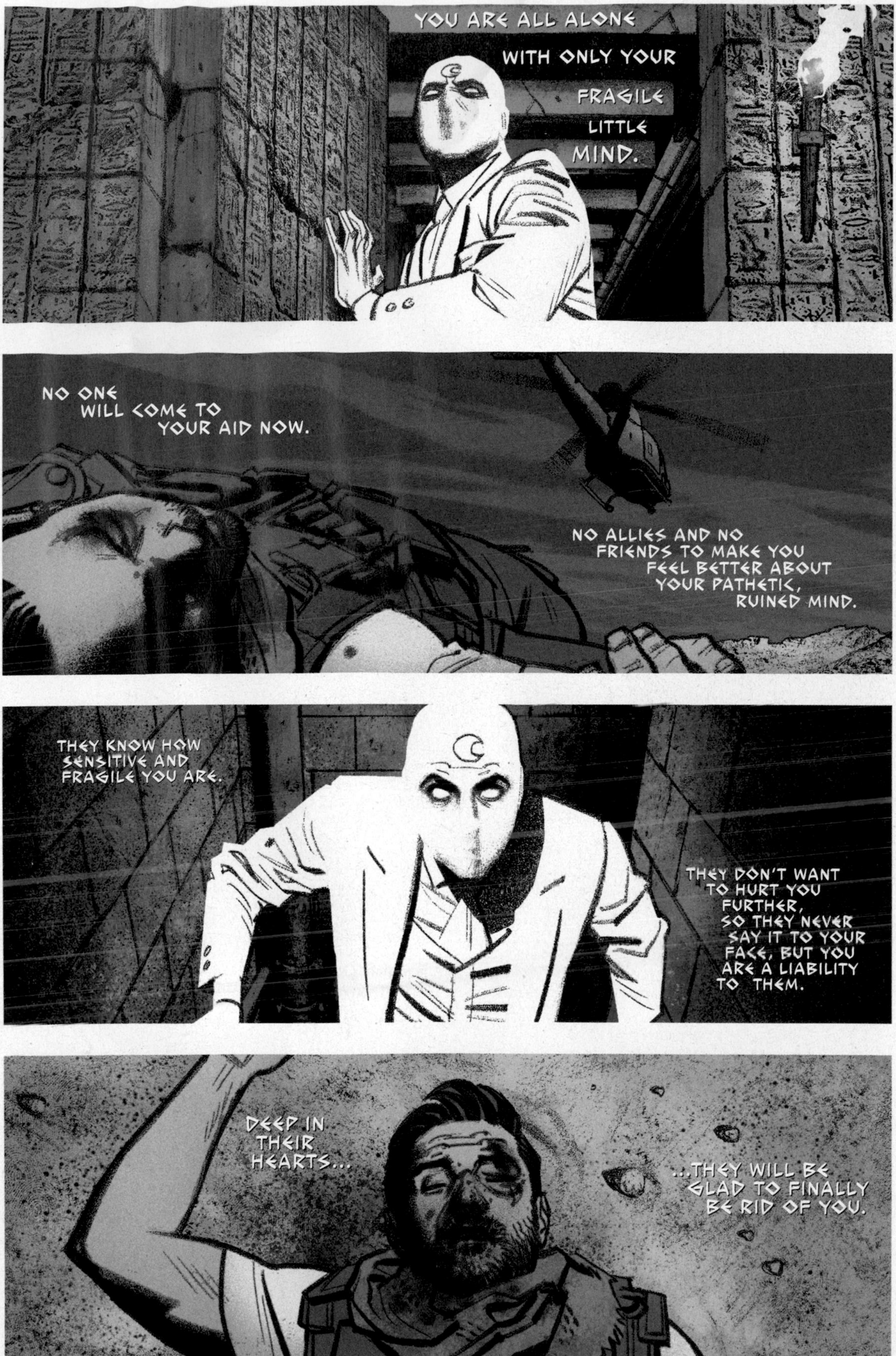
YOU ARE ALL ALONE
WITH ONLY YOUR
FRAGILE
LITTLE
MIND.
NO ONE WILL COME TO YOUR AID NOW.
NO ALLIES AND NO FRIENDS TO MAKE YOU FEEL BETTER ABOUT YOUR PATHETIC, RUINED MIND.
THEY KNOW HOW SENSITIVE AND FRAGILE YOU ARE.
THEY DON'T WANT TO HURT YOU FURTHER, SO THEY NEVER SAY IT TO YOUR FACE, BUT YOU ARE A LIABILITY TO THEM.
DEEP IN THEIR HEARTS...
...THEY WILL BE GLAD TO FINALLY BE RID OF YOU.

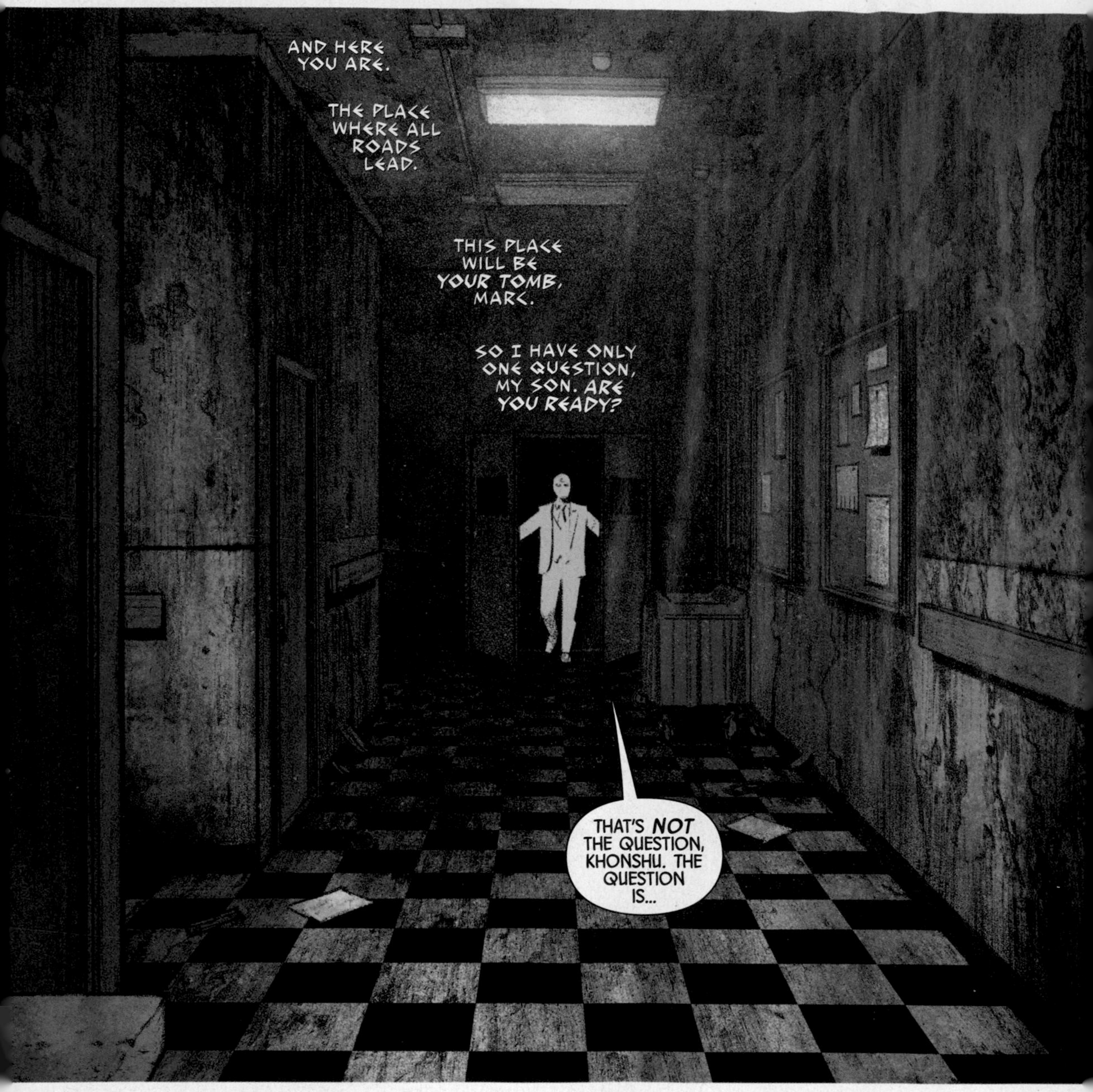
AND HERE YOU ARE.
THE PLACE WHERE ALL ROADS LEAD.
THIS PLACE WILL BE YOUR TOMB, MARC.
SO I HAVE ONLY ONE QUESTION, MY SON. ARE YOU READY?
THAT'S NOT THE QUESTION, KHONSHU. THE QUESTION IS...

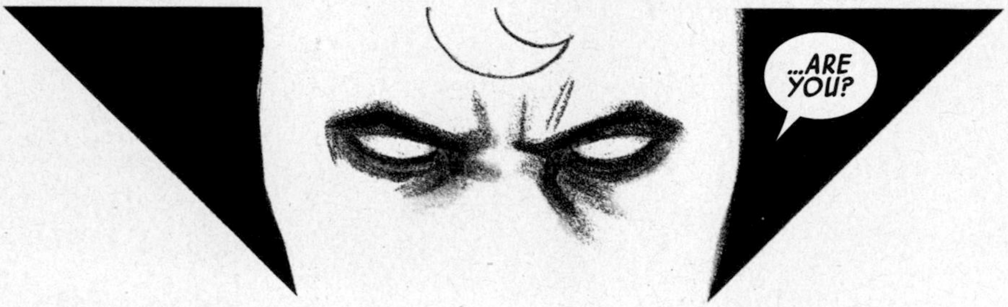
...ARE YOU?

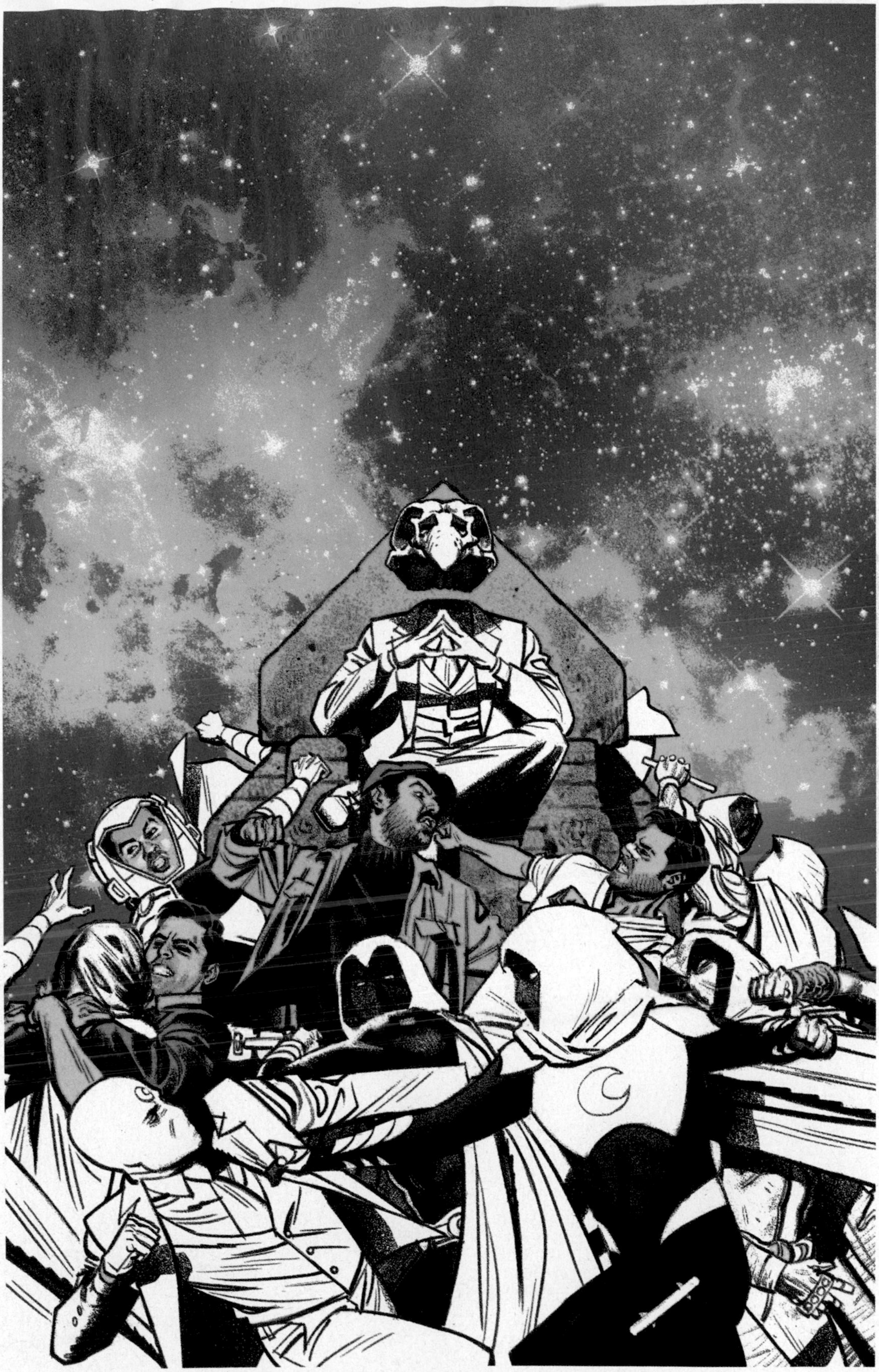

BIRTH AND DEATH
PART FIVE

14

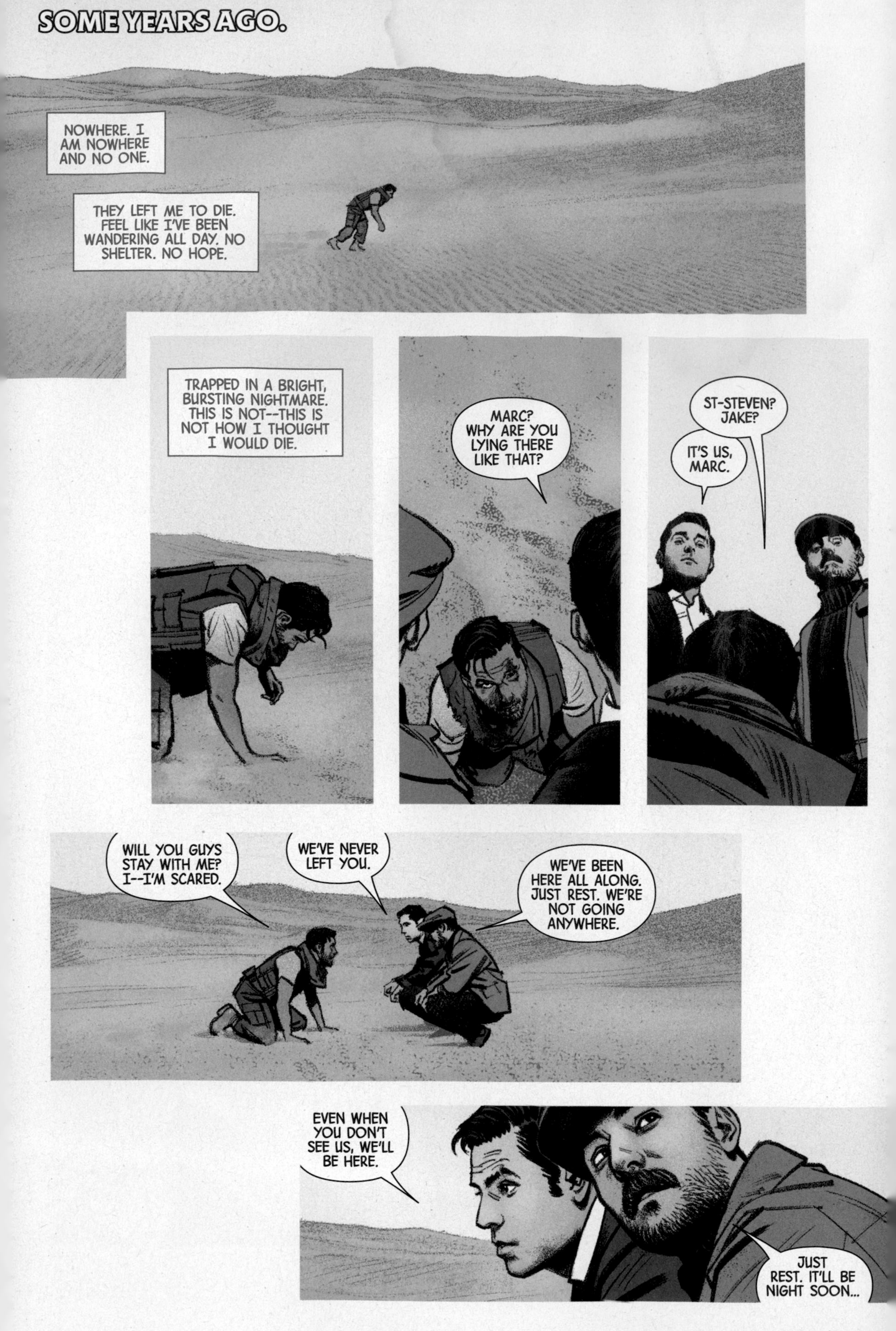
SOME YEARS AGO.
NOWHERE. I AM NOWHERE AND NO ONE.
THEY LEFT ME TO DIE. FEEL LIKE I'VE BEEN WANDERING ALL DAY. NO SHELTER. NO HOPE.
TRAPPED IN A BRIGHT, BURSTING NIGHTMARE. THIS IS NOT--THIS IS NOT HOW I THOUGHT I WOULD DIE.
MARC? WHY ARE YOU LYING THERE LIKE THAT?
ST-STEVEN? JAKE?
IT'S US, MARC.
WILL YOU GUYS STAY WITH ME? I--I'M SCARED.
WE'VE NEVER LEFT YOU.
WE'VE BEEN HERE ALL ALONG. JUST REST. WE'RE NOT GOING ANYWHERE.
EVEN WHEN YOU DON'T SEE US, WE'LL BE HERE.
JUST REST. IT'LL BE NIGHT SOON...

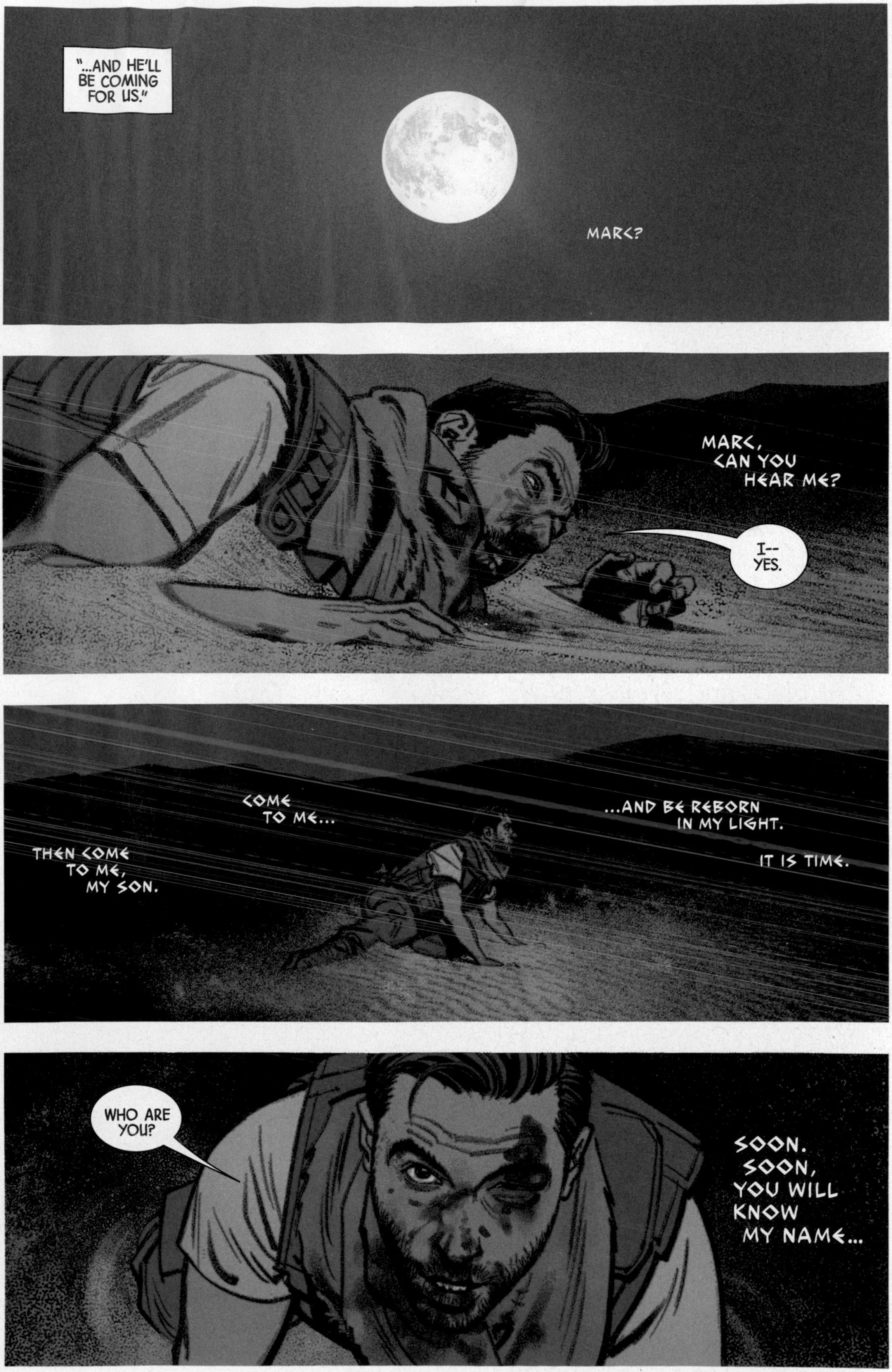
"...AND HE'LL BE COMING FOR US."
MARC?
MARC, CAN YOU HEAR ME?
I-- YES.
THEN COME TO ME, MY SON.
COME TO ME...
...AND BE REBORN IN MY LIGHT.
IT IS TIME.
WHO ARE YOU?
SOON. SOON, YOU WILL KNOW MY NAME...

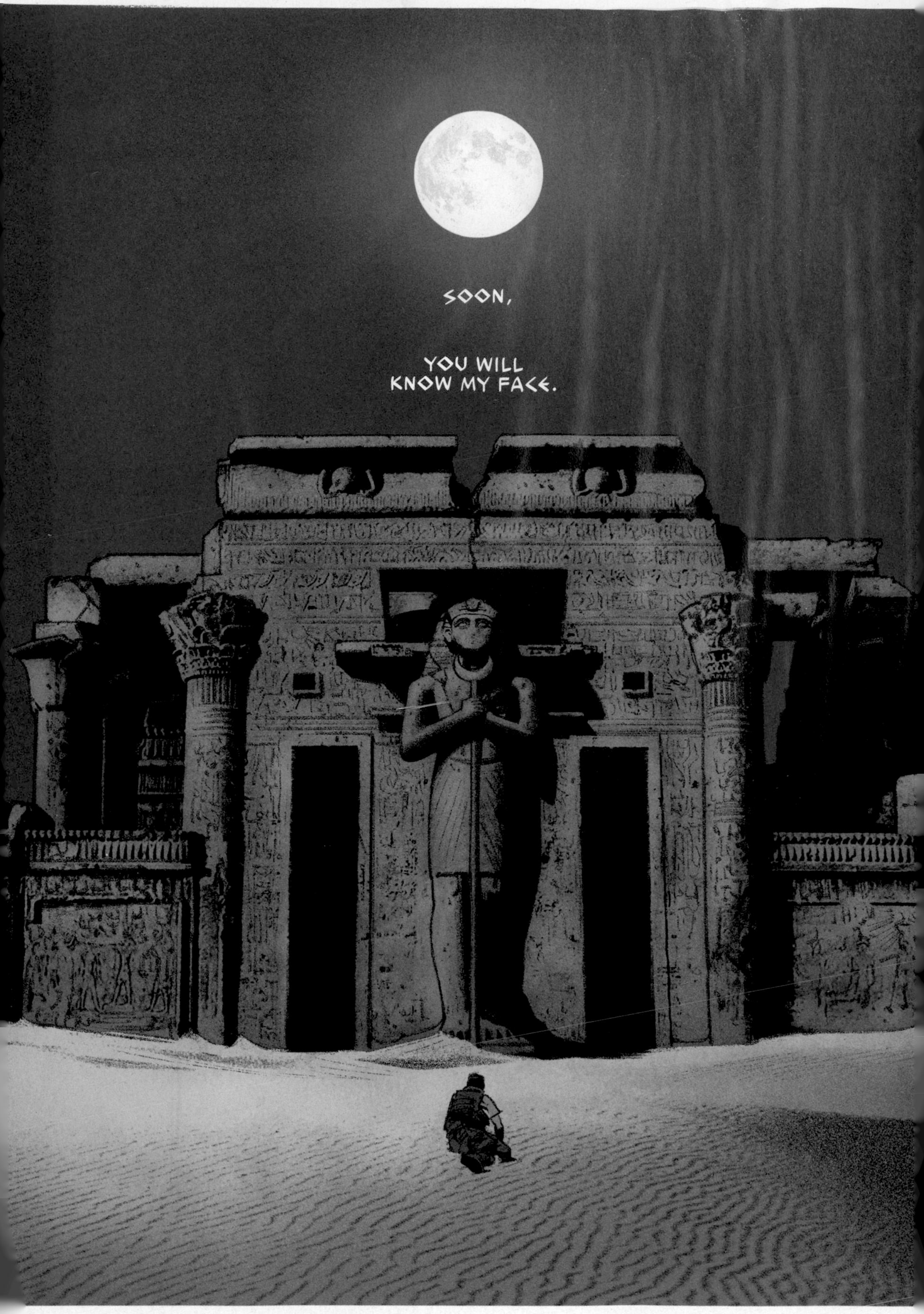
SOON,
YOU WILL KNOW MY FACE.

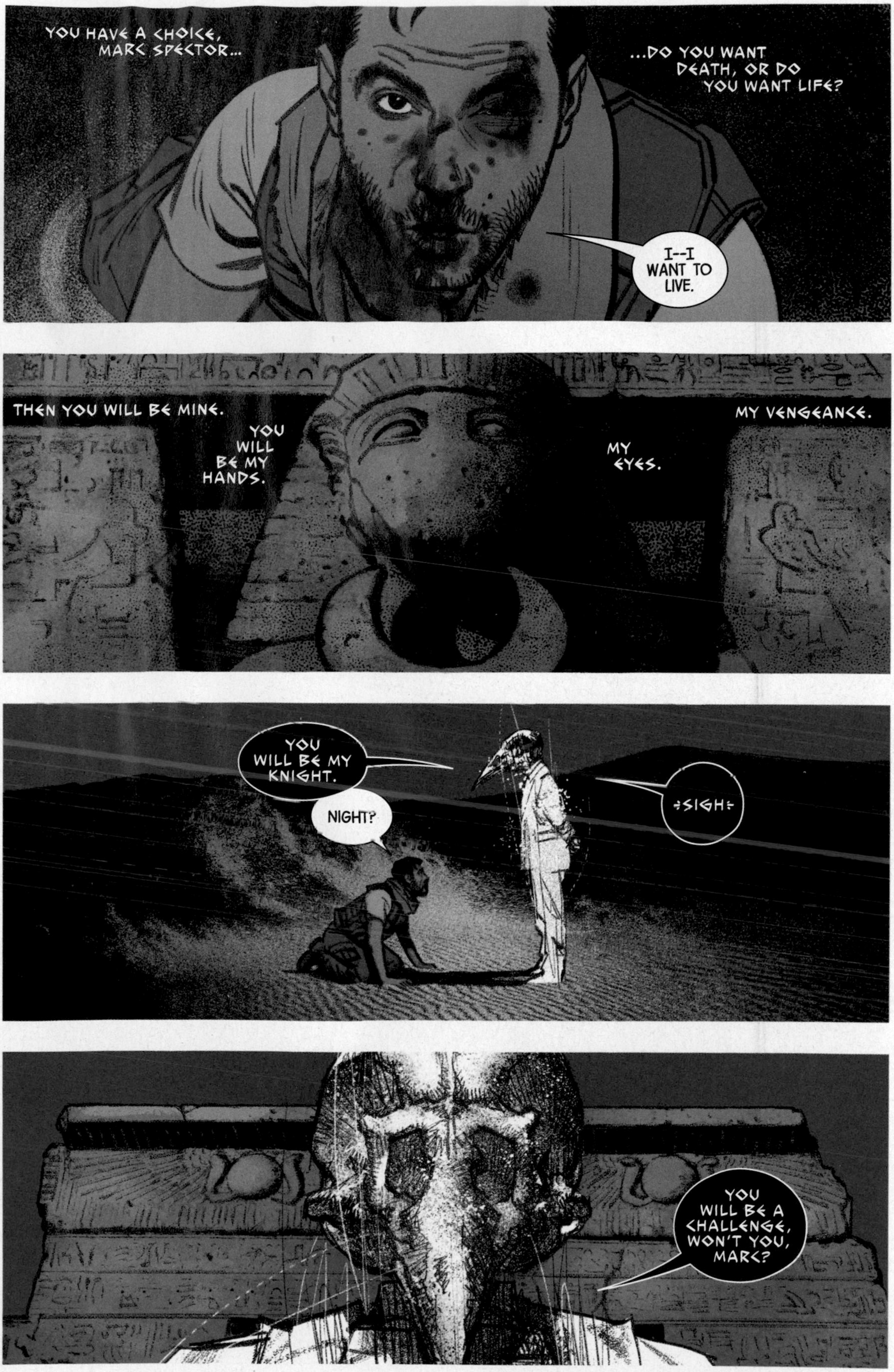
YOU HAVE A CHOICE, MARC SPECTOR...
...DO YOU WANT DEATH, OR DO YOU WANT LIFE?
I--I WANT TO LIVE.
THEN YOU WILL BE MINE.
YOU WILL BE MY HANDS.
MY EYES.
MY VENGEANCE.
YOU WILL BE MY KNIGHT.
NIGHT?
SIGH
YOU WILL BE A CHALLENGE, WON'T YOU, MARC?

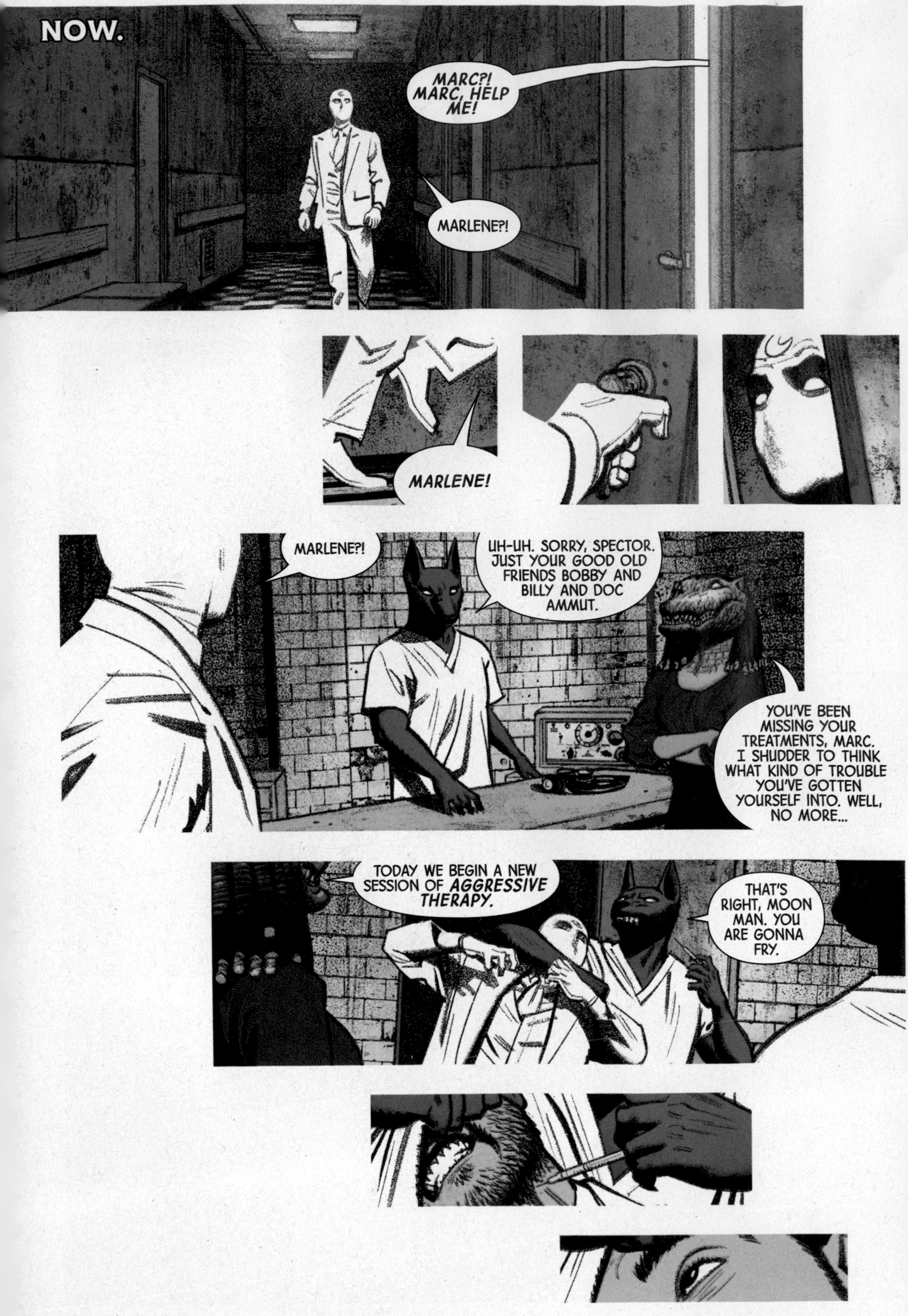
NOW.
MARC?! MARC, HELP ME!
MARLENE?!
MARLENE!
MARLENE?!
UH-UH. SORRY, SPECTOR. JUST YOUR GOOD OLD FRIENDS BOBBY AND BILLY AND DOC AMMUT.
YOU'VE BEEN MISSING YOUR TREATMENTS, MARC. I SHUDDER TO THINK WHAT KIND OF TROUBLE YOU'VE GOTTEN YOURSELF INTO. WELL, NO MORE...
TODAY WE BEGIN A NEW SESSION OF *AGGRESSIVE THERAPY.*
THAT'S RIGHT, MOON MAN. YOU ARE GONNA FRY.

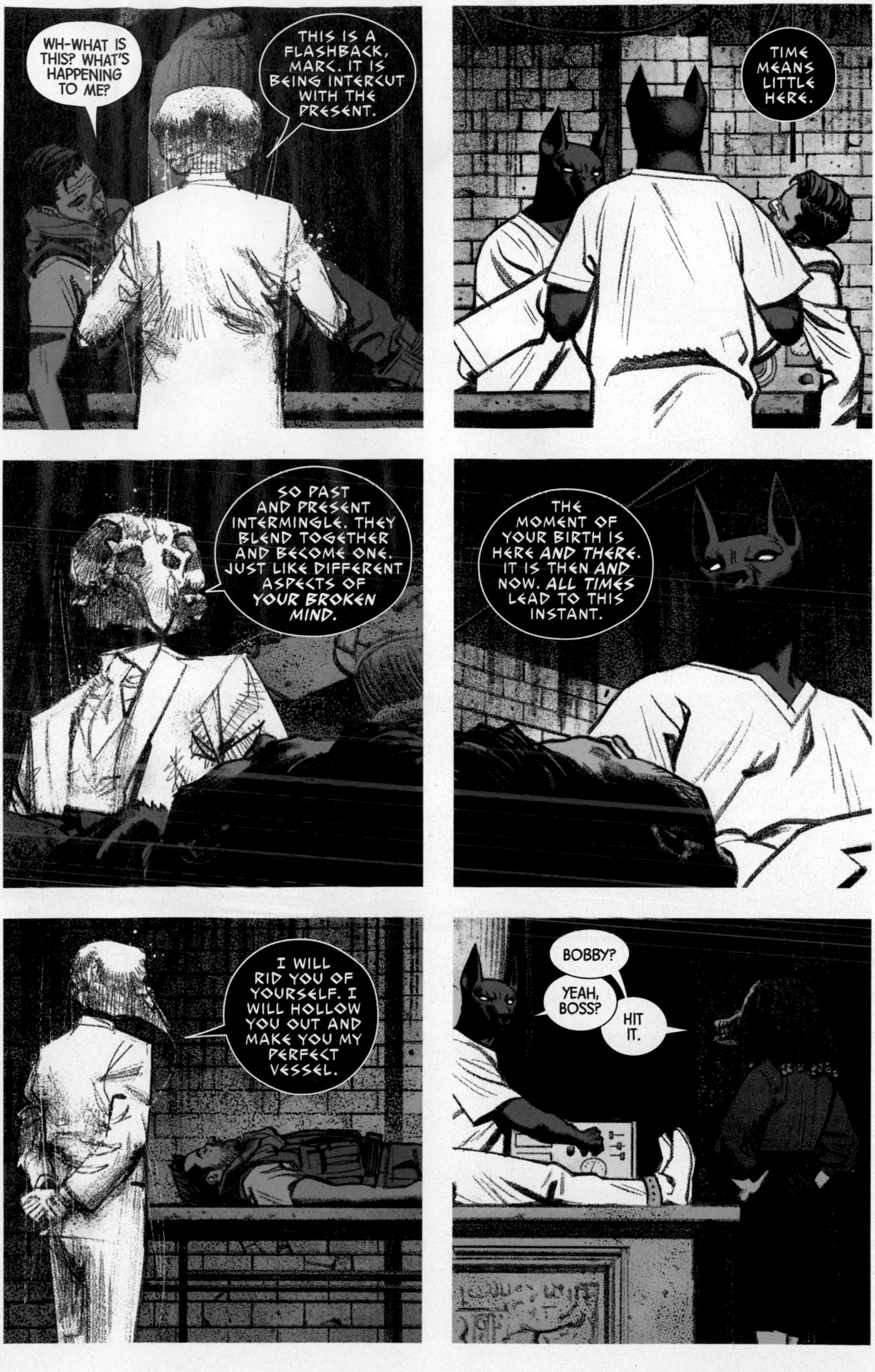
WH-WHAT IS THIS? WHAT'S HAPPENING TO ME?
THIS IS A FLASHBACK, MARC. IT IS BEING INTERCUT WITH THE PRESENT.
TIME MEANS LITTLE HERE.
SO PAST AND PRESENT INTERMINGLE. THEY BLEND TOGETHER AND BECOME ONE. JUST LIKE DIFFERENT ASPECTS OF YOUR BROKEN MIND.
THE MOMENT OF YOUR BIRTH IS HERE AND THERE. IT IS THEN AND NOW. ALL TIMES LEAD TO THIS INSTANT.
I WILL RID YOU OF YOURSELF. I WILL HOLLOW YOU OUT AND MAKE YOU MY PERFECT VESSEL.
BOBBY?
YEAH, BOSS?
HIT IT.

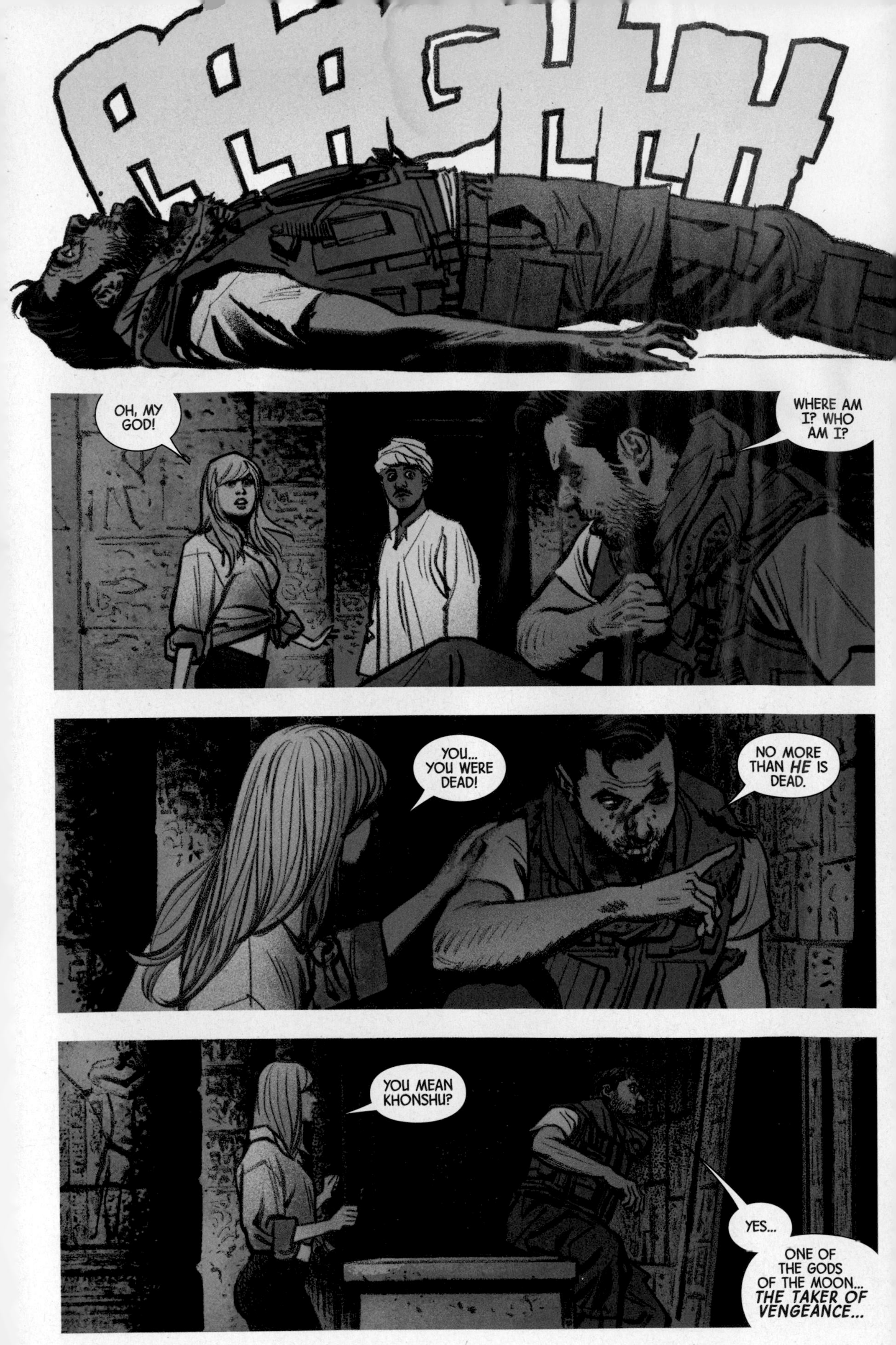
PPACHHH
OH, MY GOD!
WHERE AM I? WHO AM I?
YOU... YOU WERE DEAD!
NO MORE THAN HE IS DEAD.
YOU MEAN KHONSHU?
YES...
ONE OF THE GODS OF THE MOON... THE TAKER OF VENGEANCE...

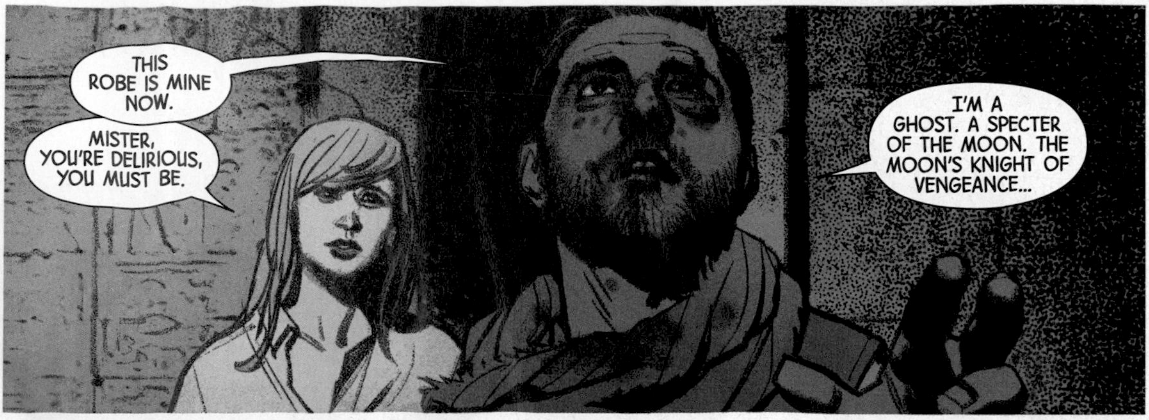
THIS ROBE IS MINE NOW.
MISTER, YOU'RE DELIRIOUS, YOU MUST BE.
I'M A GHOST. A SPECTER OF THE MOON. THE MOON'S KNIGHT OF VENGEANCE...

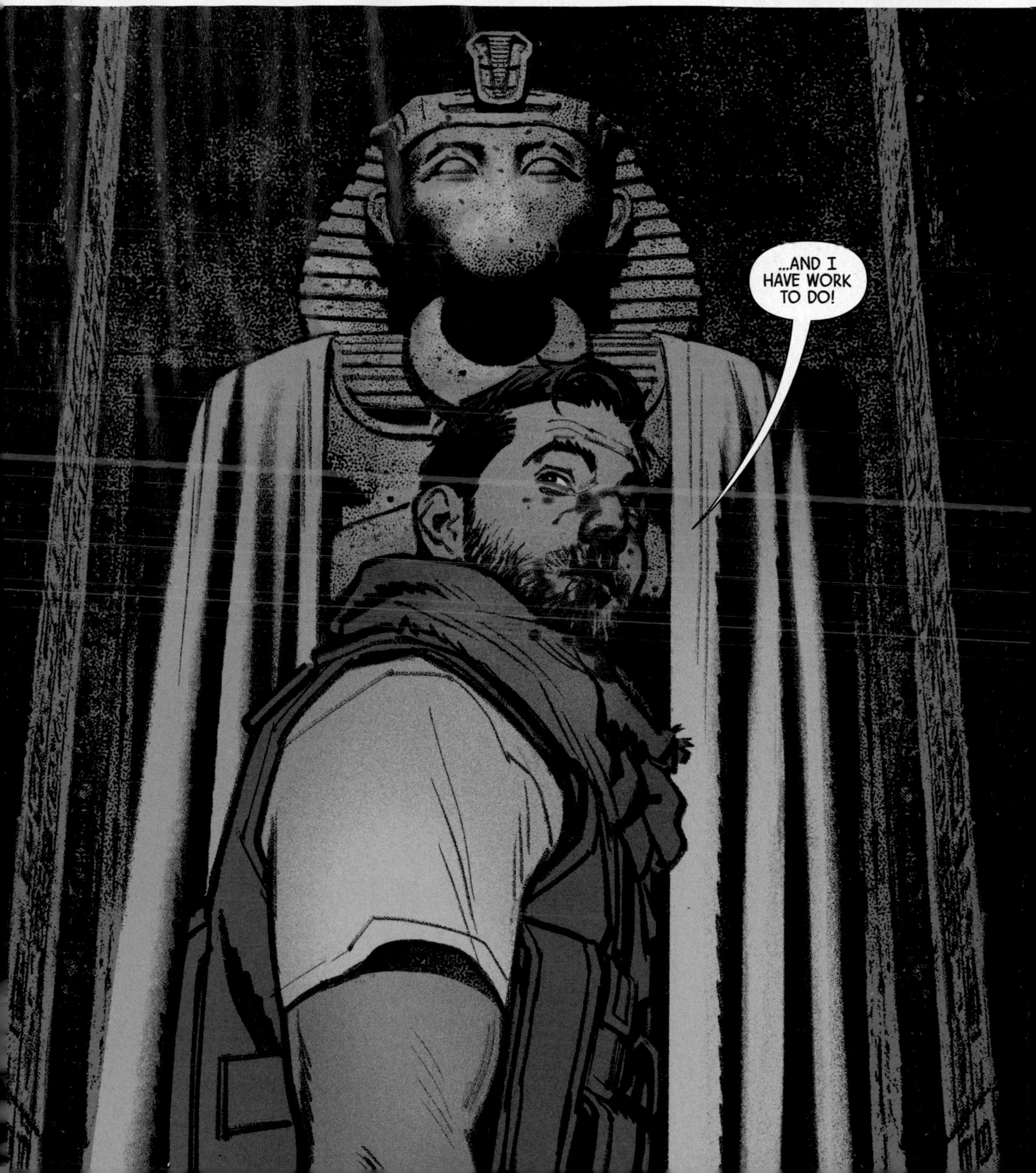
...AND I HAVE WORK TO DO!

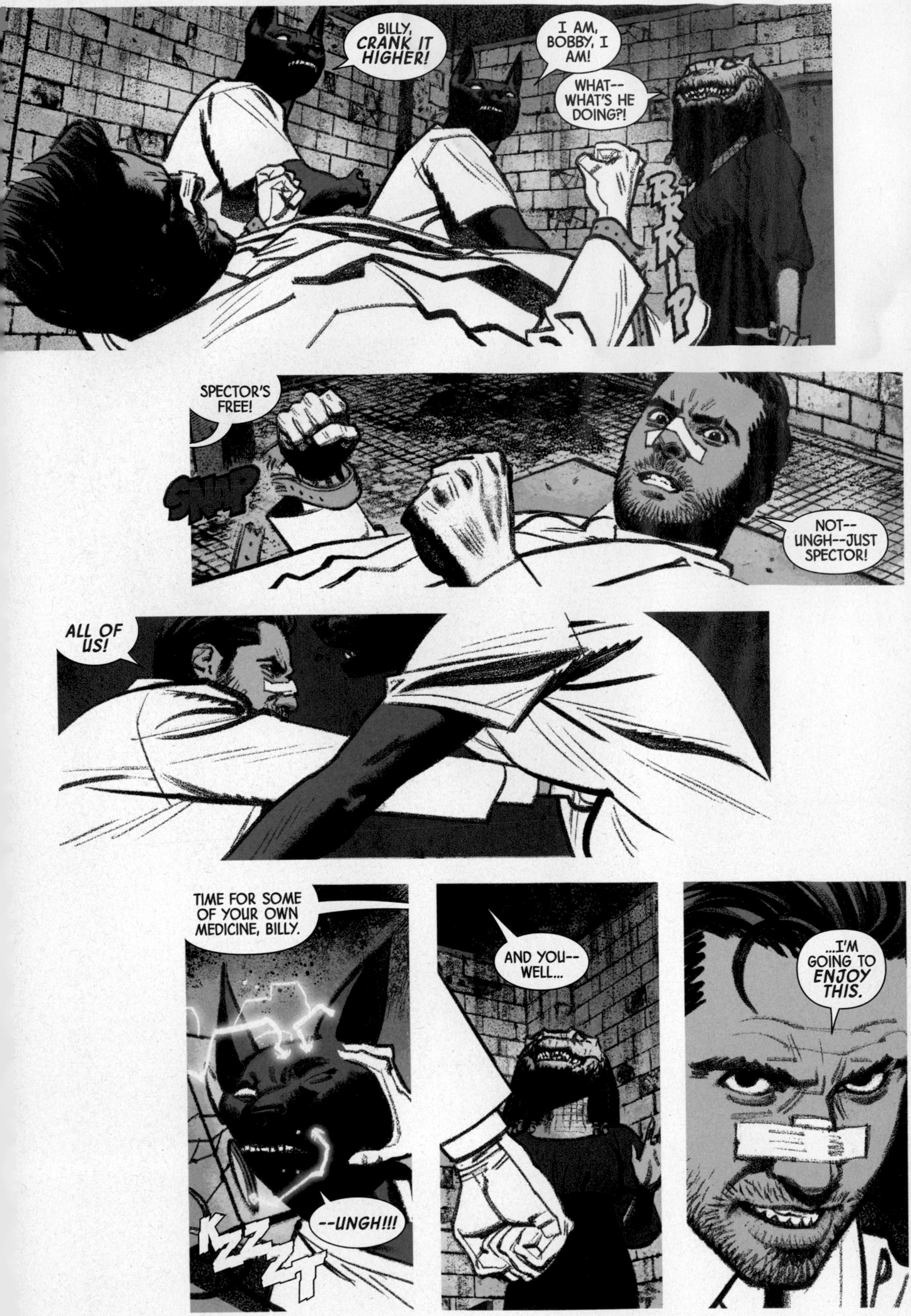
BILLY, CRANK IT HIGHER!
I AM, BOBBY, I AM!
WHAT-- WHAT'S HE DOING?!
R-R-RIP
SPECTOR'S FREE!
SNAP
NOT-- UNGH--JUST SPECTOR!
ALL OF US!
TIME FOR SOME OF YOUR OWN MEDICINE, BILLY.
KZZZT
--UNGH!!!
AND YOU-- WELL...
...I'M GOING TO ENJOY THIS.

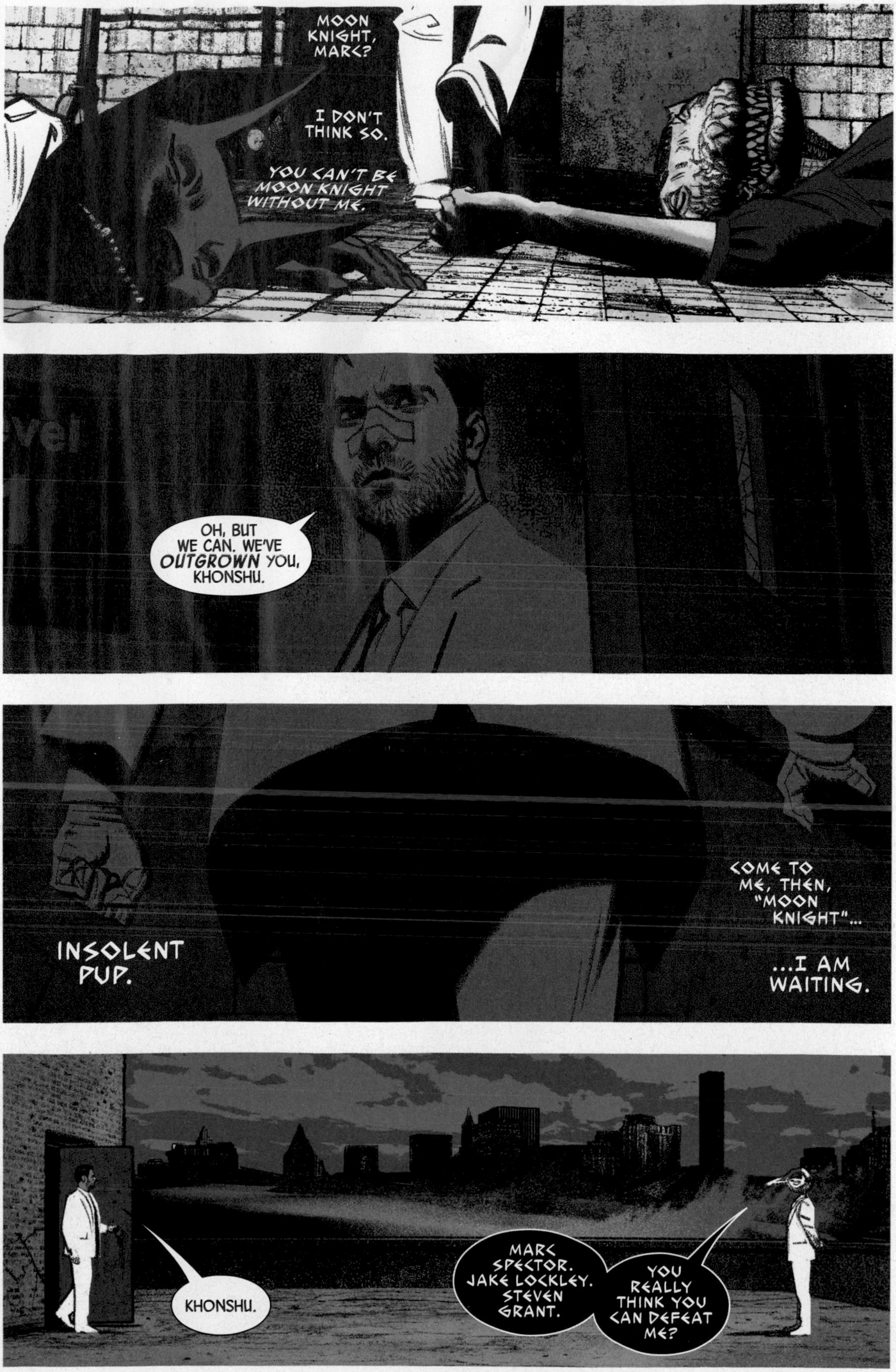
MOON KNIGHT, MARC?
I DON'T THINK SO.
YOU CAN'T BE MOON KNIGHT WITHOUT ME.
OH, BUT WE CAN. WE'VE OUTGROWN YOU, KHONSHU.
INSOLENT PUP.
COME TO ME, THEN, "MOON KNIGHT"...
...I AM WAITING.
KHONSHU.
MARC SPECTOR. JAKE LOCKLEY. STEVEN GRANT.
YOU REALLY THINK YOU CAN DEFEAT ME?

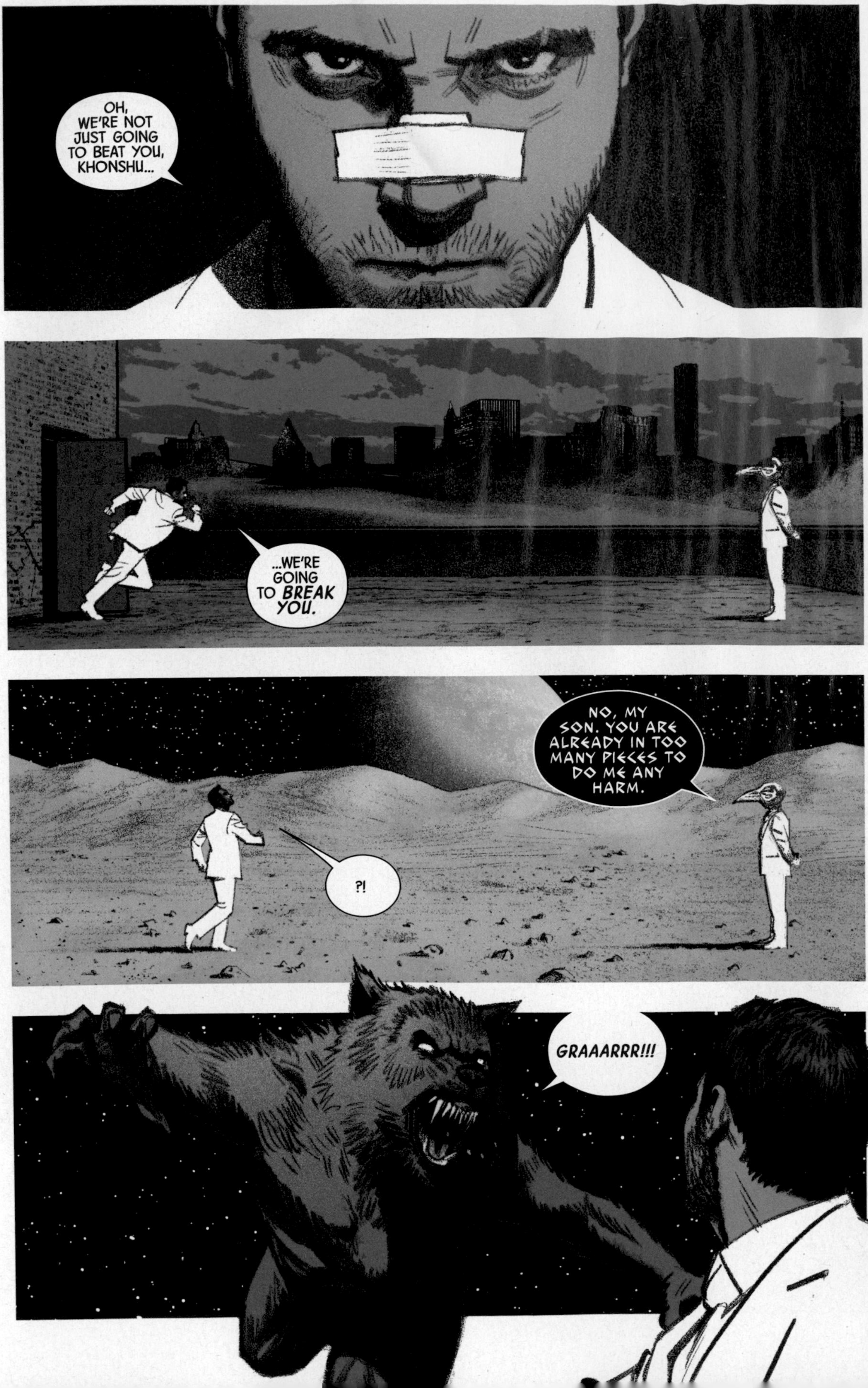
OH, WE'RE NOT JUST GOING TO BEAT YOU, KHONSHU...
...WE'RE GOING TO *BREAK YOU.*
NO, MY SON. YOU ARE ALREADY IN TOO MANY PIECES TO DO ME ANY HARM.
?!
GRAAARRR!!!

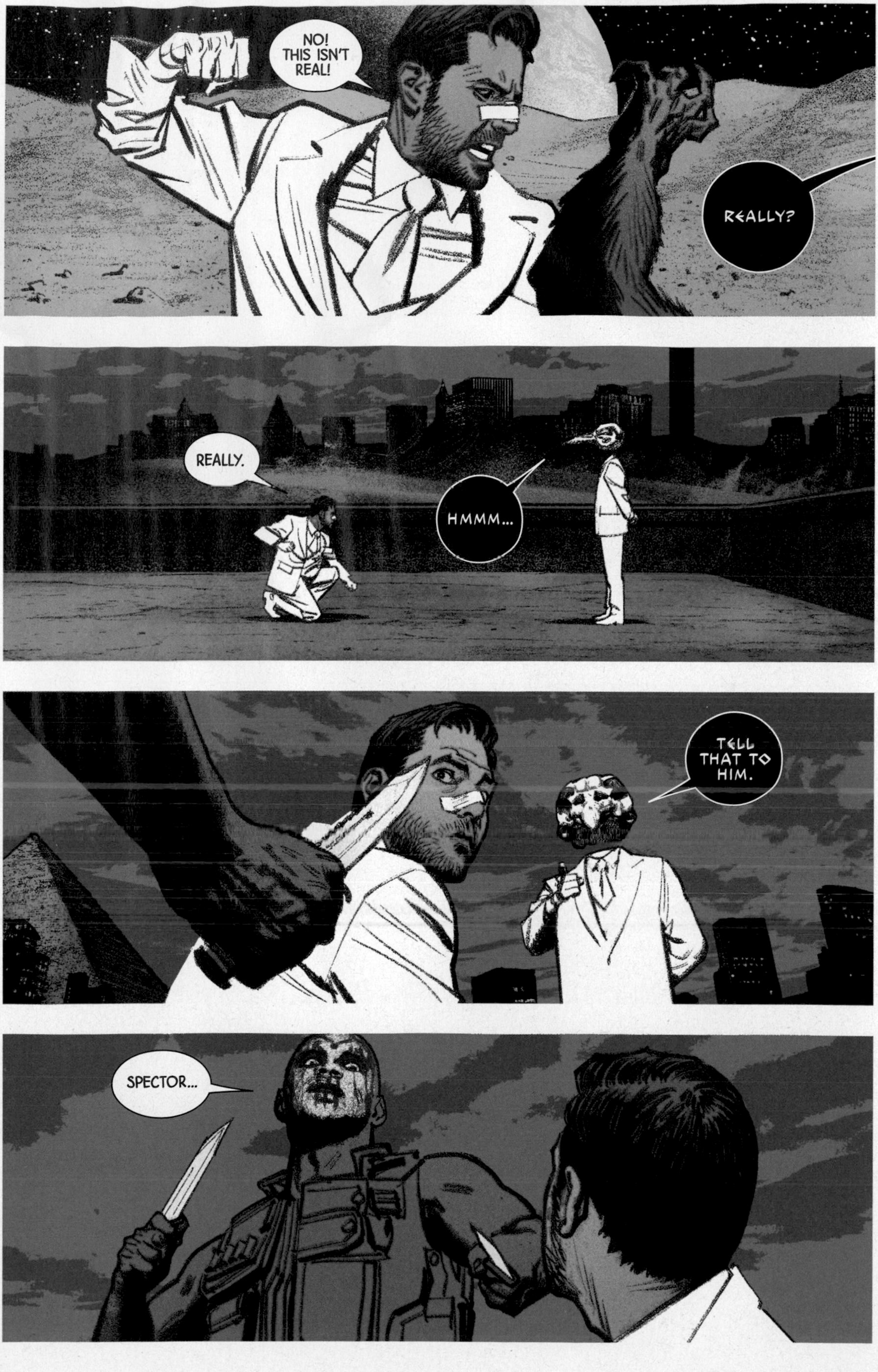
NO! THIS ISN'T REAL!
REALLY?
REALLY.
HMMM...
TELL THAT TO HIM.
SPECTOR...

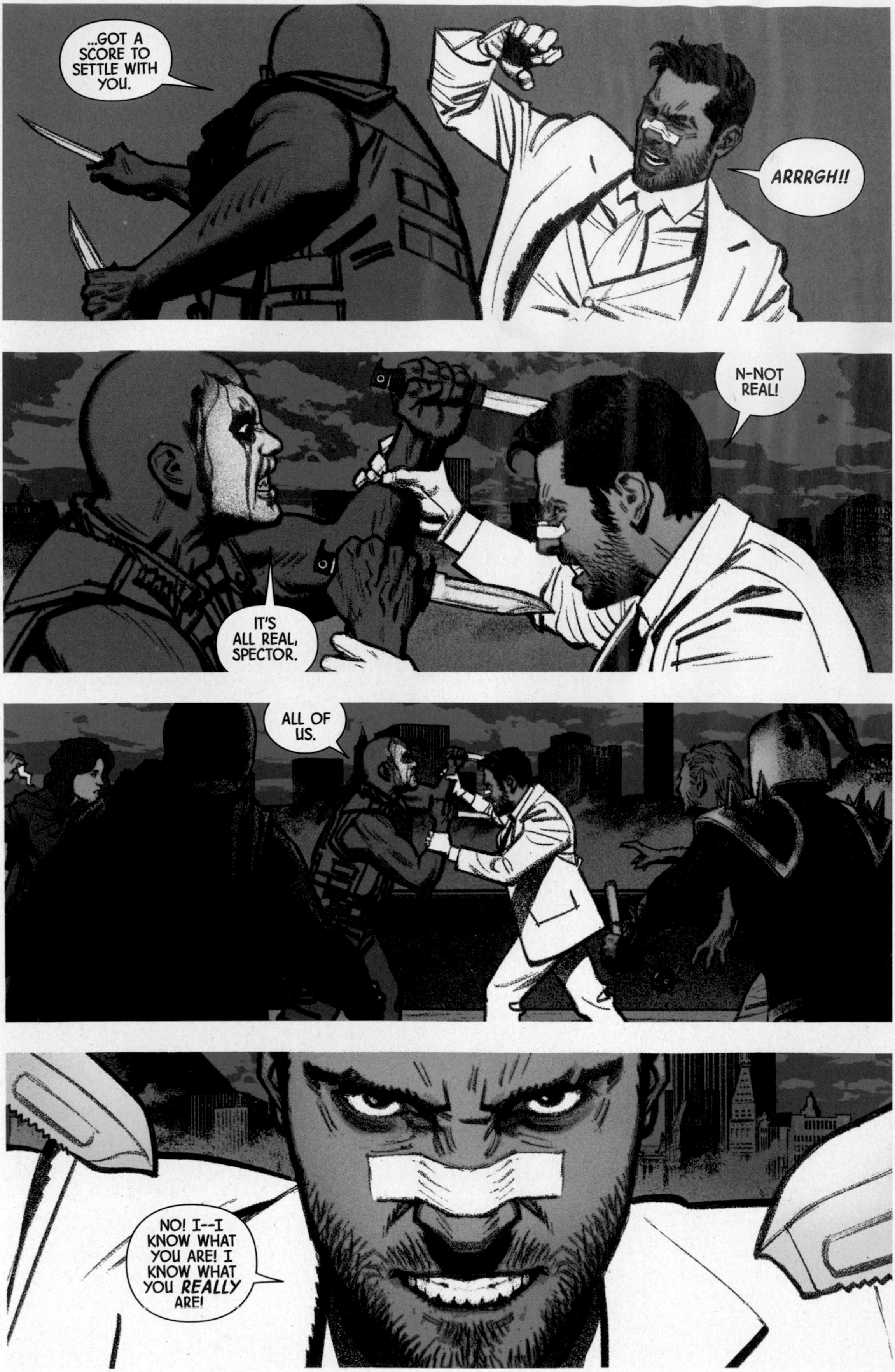
...GOT A SCORE TO SETTLE WITH YOU.
ARRRGH!!
N-NOT REAL!
IT'S ALL REAL, SPECTOR.
ALL OF US.
NO! I--I KNOW WHAT YOU ARE! I KNOW WHAT YOU *REALLY* ARE!

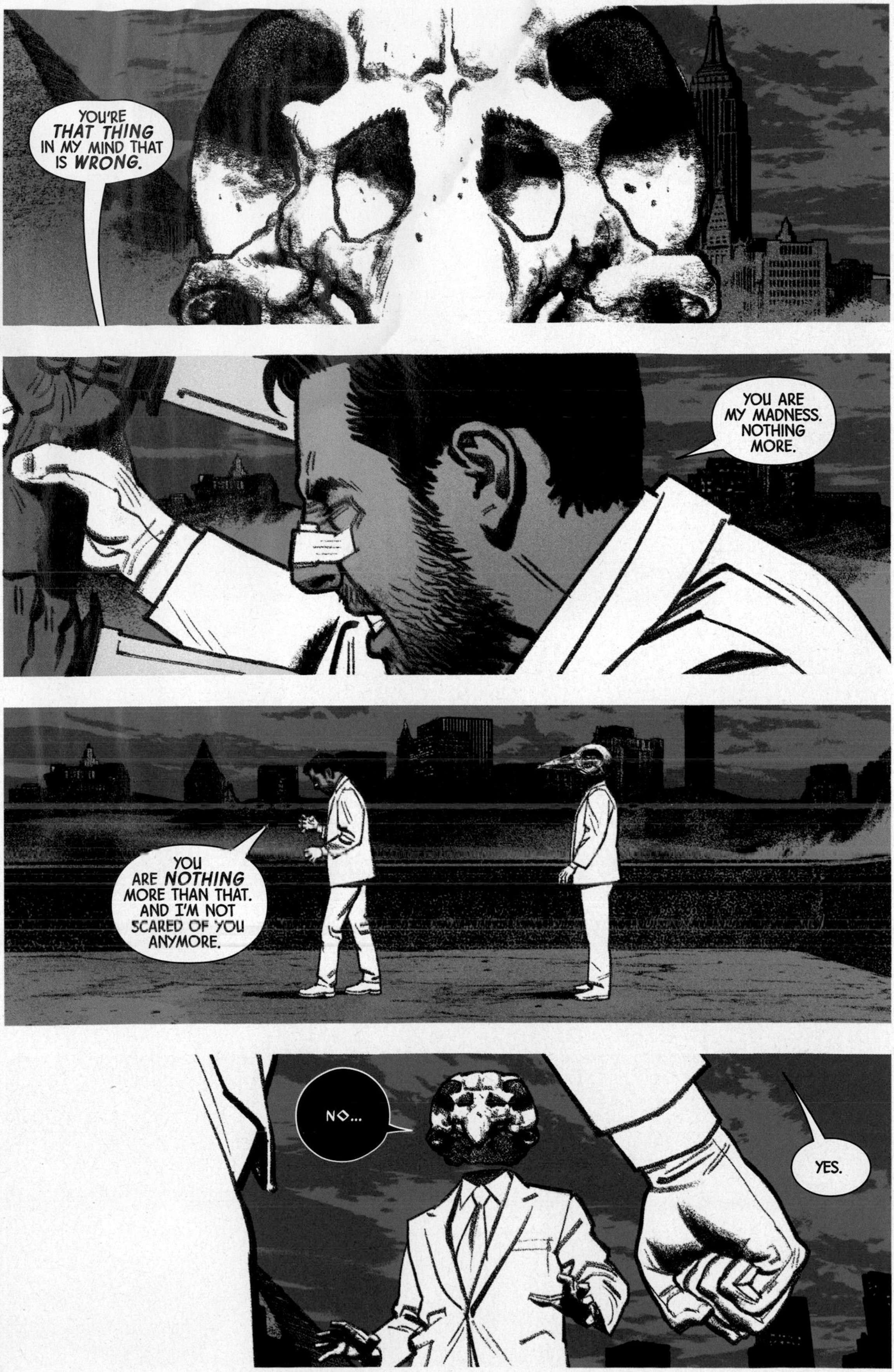
YOU'RE *THAT THING* IN MY MIND THAT IS *WRONG*.
YOU ARE MY MADNESS. NOTHING MORE.
YOU ARE *NOTHING* MORE THAN THAT. AND I'M NOT SCARED OF YOU ANYMORE.
NO...
YES.

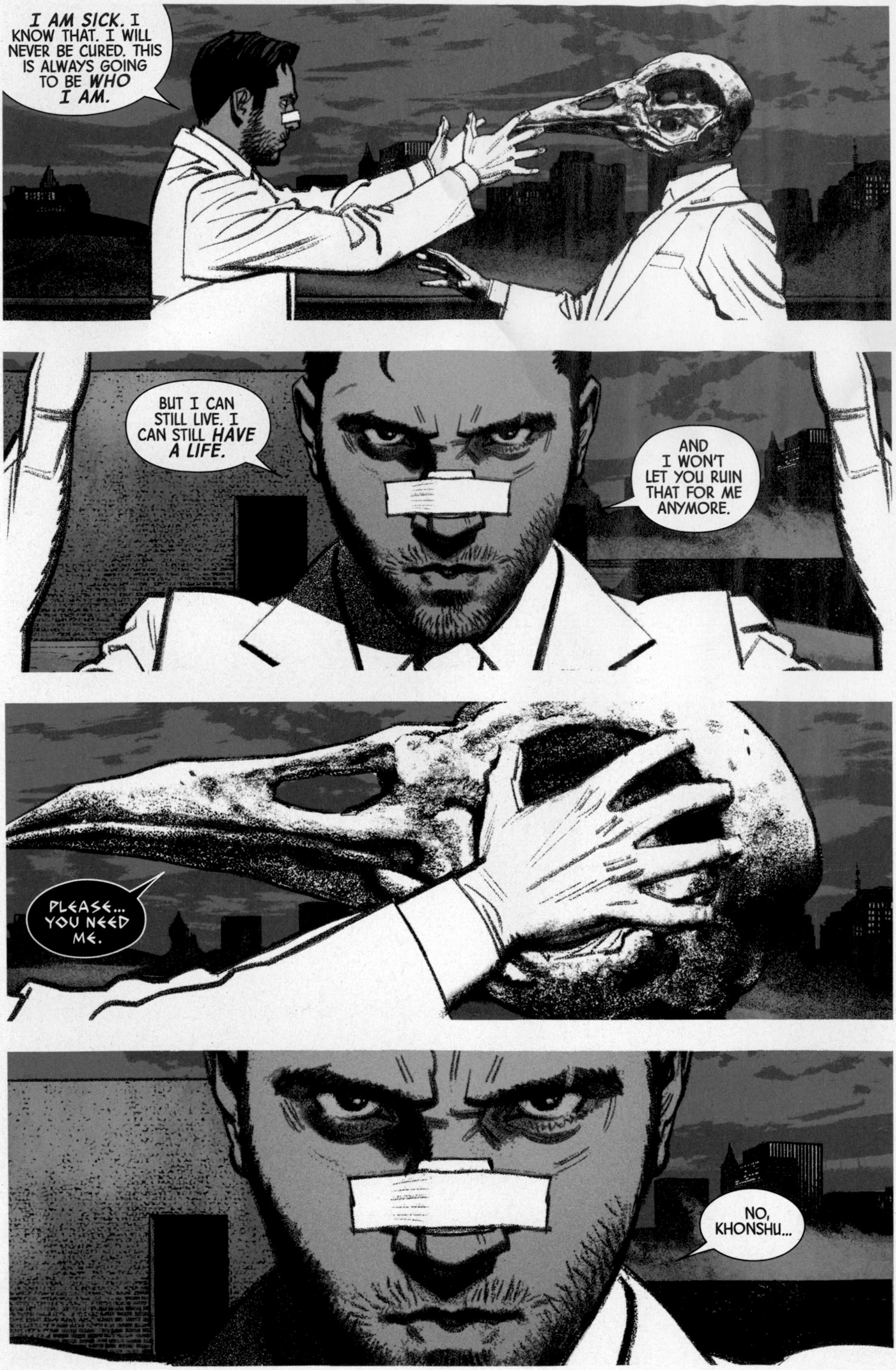
I AM SICK. I KNOW THAT. I WILL NEVER BE CURED. THIS IS ALWAYS GOING TO BE WHO I AM.
BUT I CAN STILL LIVE. I CAN STILL HAVE A LIFE.
AND I WON'T LET YOU RUIN THAT FOR ME ANYMORE.
PLEASE... YOU NEED ME.
NO, KHONSHU...

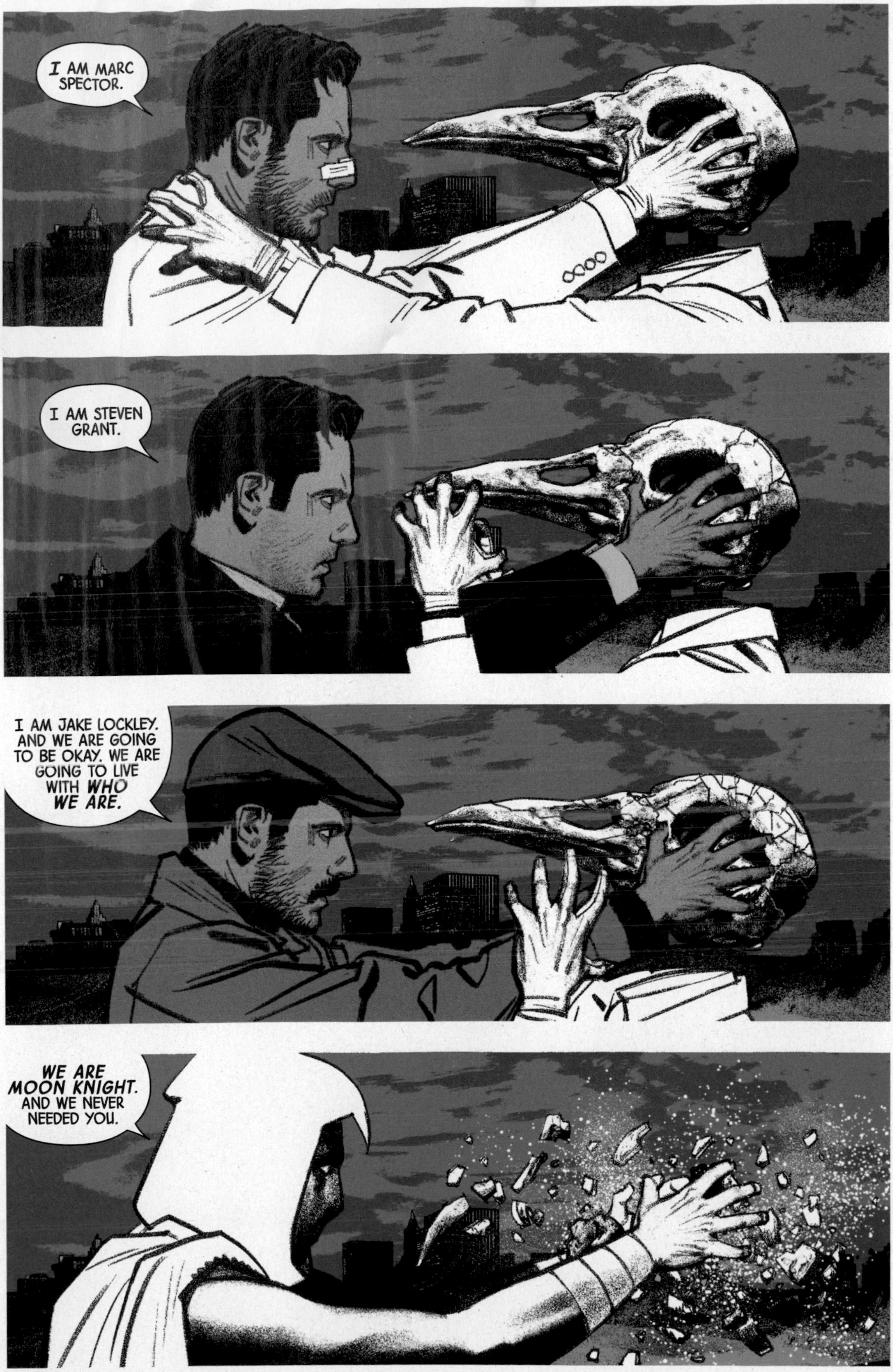
I AM MARC SPECTOR.
I AM STEVEN GRANT.
I AM JAKE LOCKLEY. AND WE ARE GOING TO BE OKAY. WE ARE GOING TO LIVE WITH WHO WE ARE.
WE ARE MOON KNIGHT. AND WE NEVER NEEDED YOU.

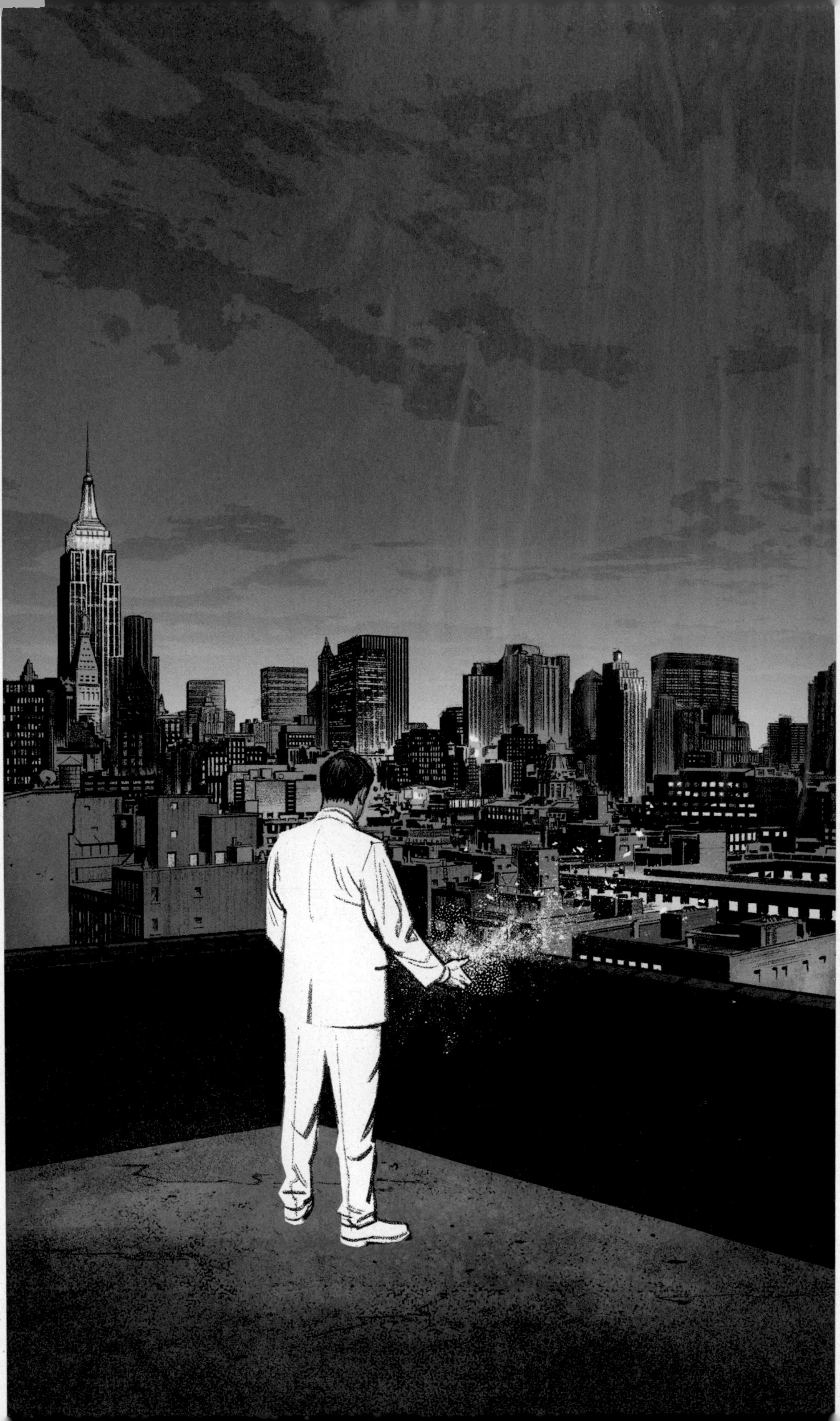

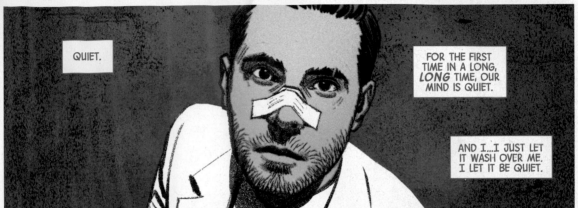

QUIET.

FOR THE FIRST TIME IN A LONG, *LONG* TIME, OUR MIND IS QUIET.

AND I...I JUST LET IT WASH OVER ME. I LET IT BE QUIET.

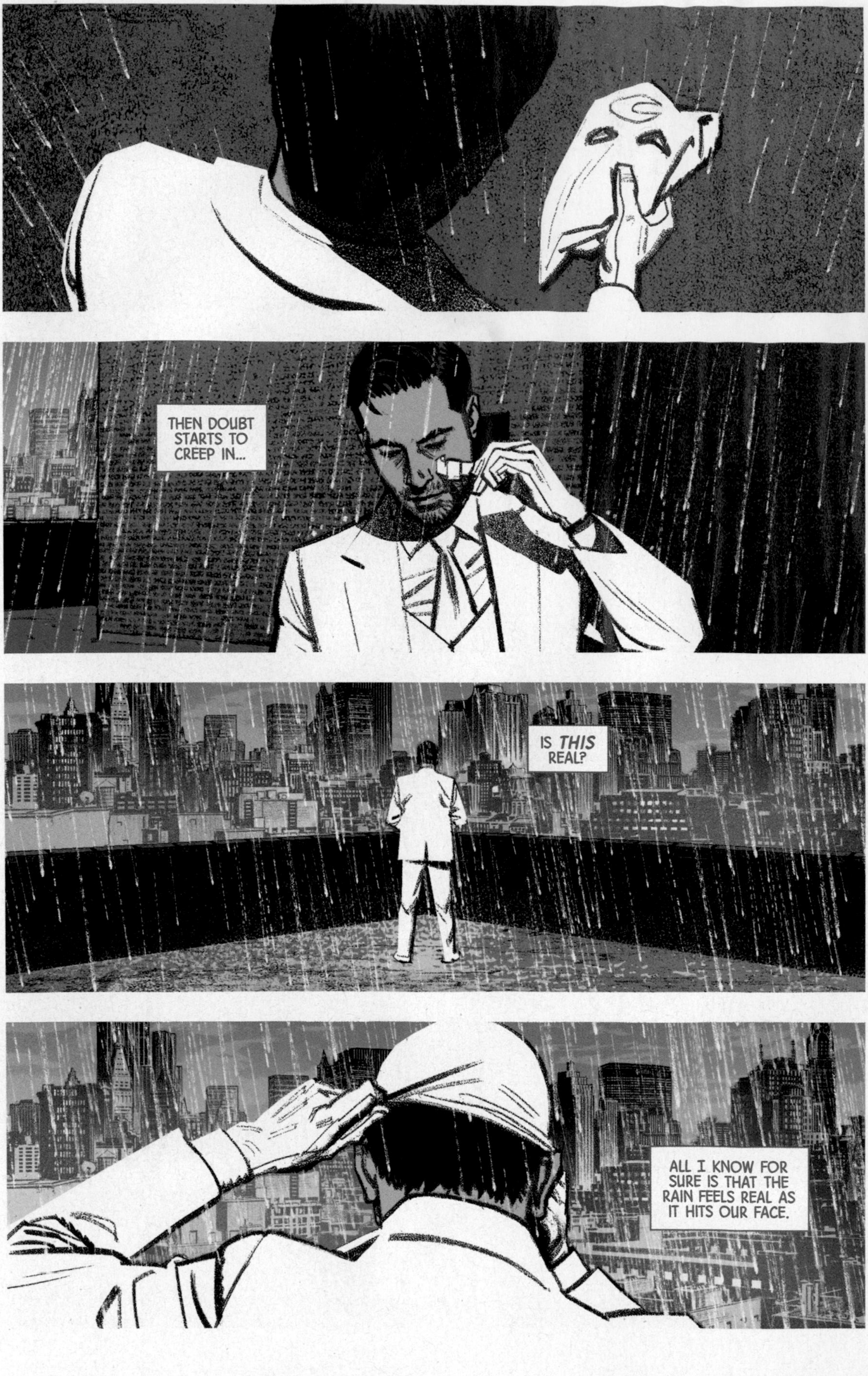
THEN DOUBT STARTS TO CREEP IN...
IS THIS REAL?
ALL I KNOW FOR SURE IS THAT THE RAIN FEELS REAL AS IT HITS OUR FACE.

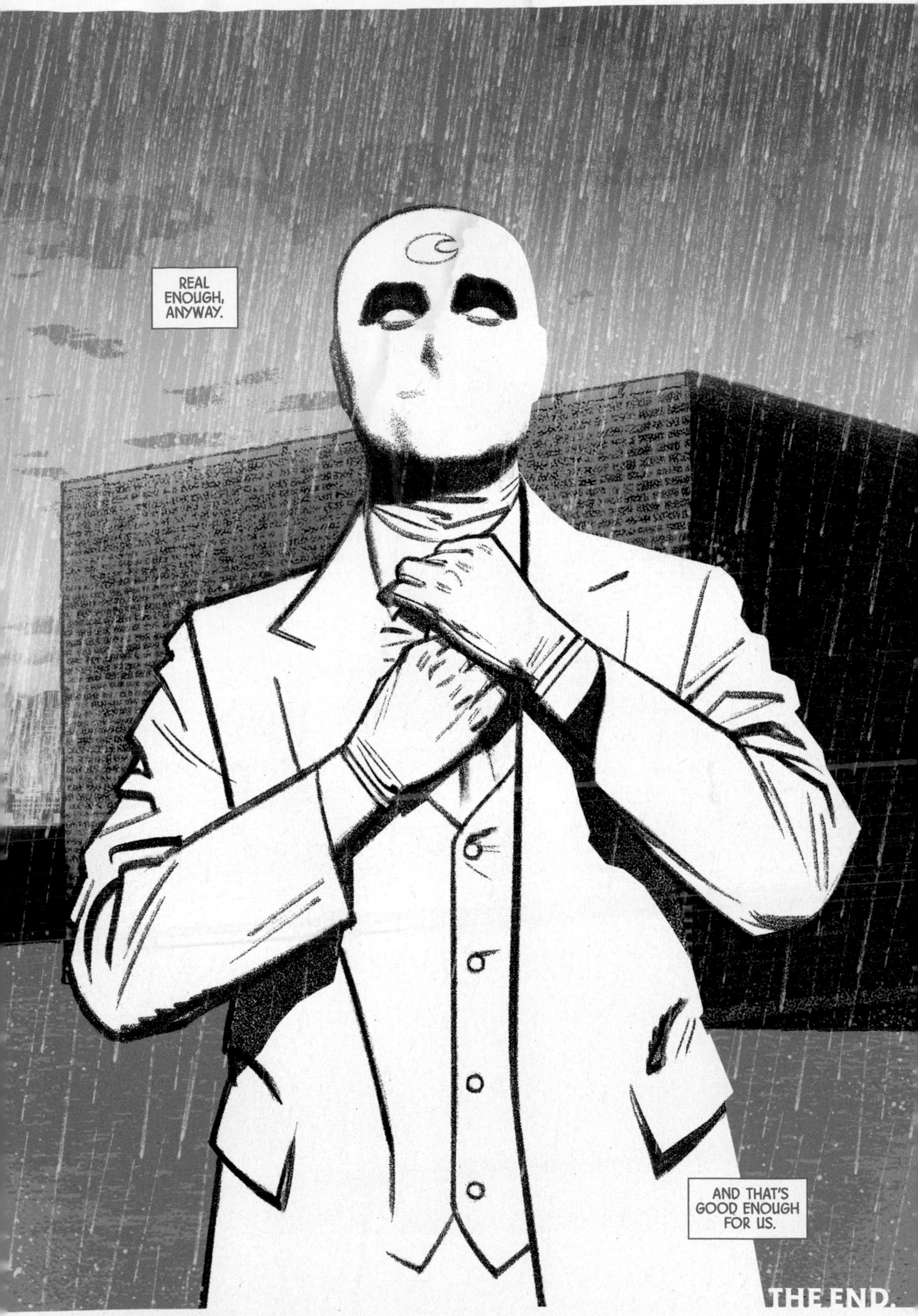
REAL ENOUGH, ANYWAY.
AND THAT'S GOOD ENOUGH FOR US.
THE END.

Working on MOON KNIGHT was a dream from start to finish. A weird, sometimes terrifying fever dream, but a dream nonetheless. This book would be nothing without the incredible work that Jordie and Greg did. Seeing the art and colors come in was so invigorating it inspired me to do better. In fact, my original pitch for MOON KNIGHT was only intended to last eleven or twelve issues, but Greg mentioned how he always wanted to do Marc Spector's origin, so I started expanding things to last another five issues. I loved working on this great character and drew so much inspiration from all the writers and artists who came before us, especially Doug Moench, Bill Sienkiewicz, Warren Ellis and Declan Shalvey. So, I hope this book read as a love letter to the character and to these great creators. Thanks for reading!

Jeff Lemire

I knew next to nothing about Moon Knight when I was first offered the book, but three years and two volumes later, I now count myself as one of the character's biggest fans. Readers like yourselves help keep MOON KNIGHT alive, and your enthusiasm for this series made its success possible. Thank you for joining us on this incredible and surreal journey through the mind of Marc Spector. I hope you enjoyed it as much as we did!

Many thanks to my fellow inmates — Jeff, Jordie, Cory, Francesco, James, Wilfredo and Michael — for raising the bar each and every step of the journey. And a very special thank you to the inmates running the asylum — Jake, Kathleen and Nick — for making sure I didn't get lost along the way.

Greg Smallwood

MOON KNIGHT has been an unexpected journey the past few years, and with Greg and Jeff, I've honestly shed some tears. The thing that has moved me the most is Jeff's absolute commitment to a story that will reward not only the readers but the characters as well. This book, in my opinion, has found its place at the top of Marvel titles dealing with mental illness. The brutality of losing one's self is heartbreaking, but Greg and Jeff found a way of telling this story without making it gimmicky or tired. It was honest, it was difficult, it was perfect. And through Marvel, it was available in such a mainstream way we were able to connect with so many people — that's the real honor. I'm so proud and happy to be part of this project and I pray to all ancient gods that we will unite another time — I hope the readers join us. Thanks to Nick, Jake and Kathleen for making this happen, and to Jeff, Greg and Cory for being the best crew a colorist could ask for. I love all of you.

Jordie Bellaire

What a wonderful ride this has been. I'd like to thank all the artists and the editorial team for making this book such a pleasure to work on! Unless, of course, I'm just a werewolf on the moon that is imagining that he is a letterer...

Cory Petit

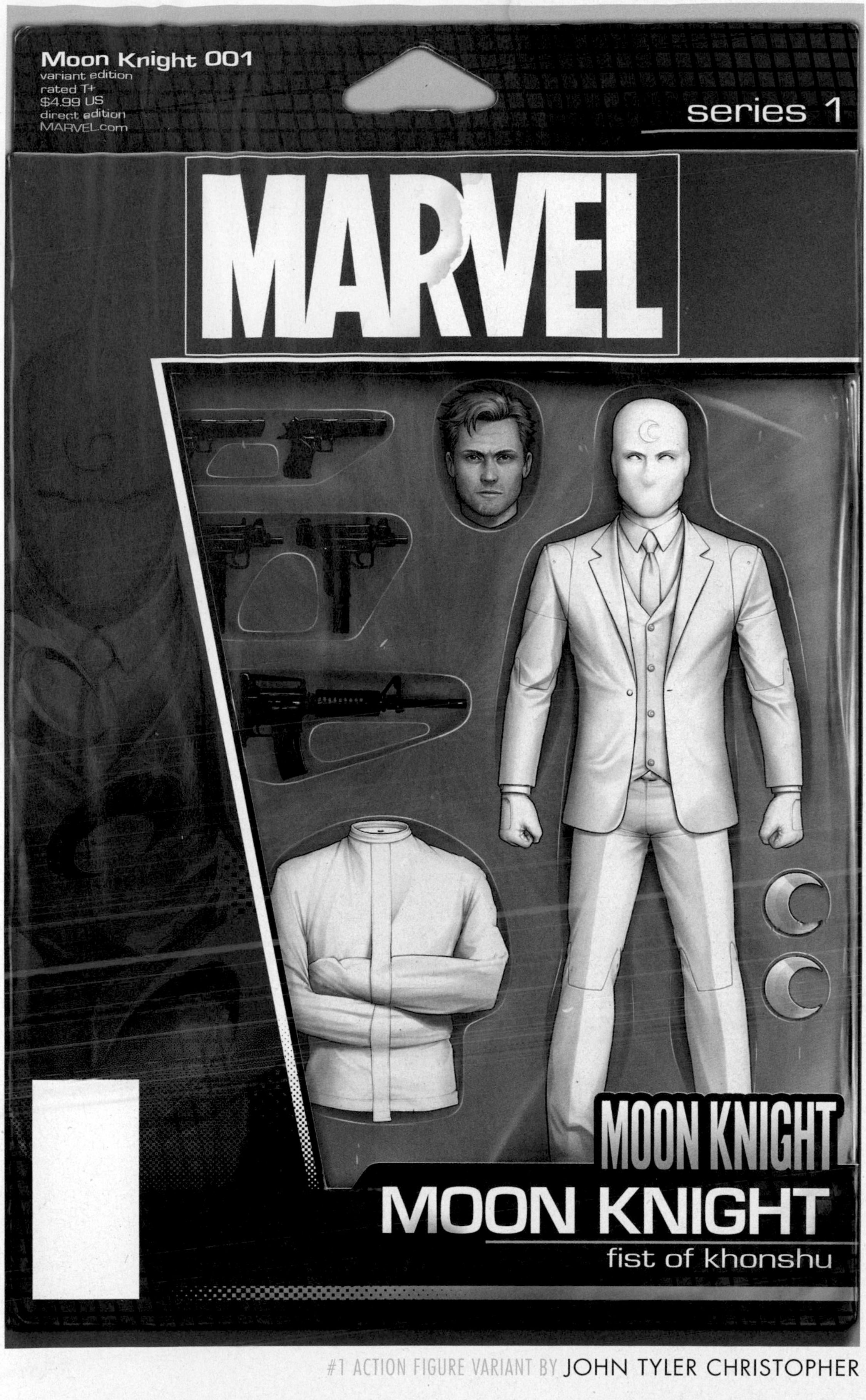
Moon Knight 001
variant edition
rated T+
$4.99 US
direct edition
MARVEL.com
series 1
MARVEL
MOON KNIGHT
MOON KNIGHT
fist of khonshu

#1 ACTION FIGURE VARIANT BY JOHN TYLER CHRISTOPHER

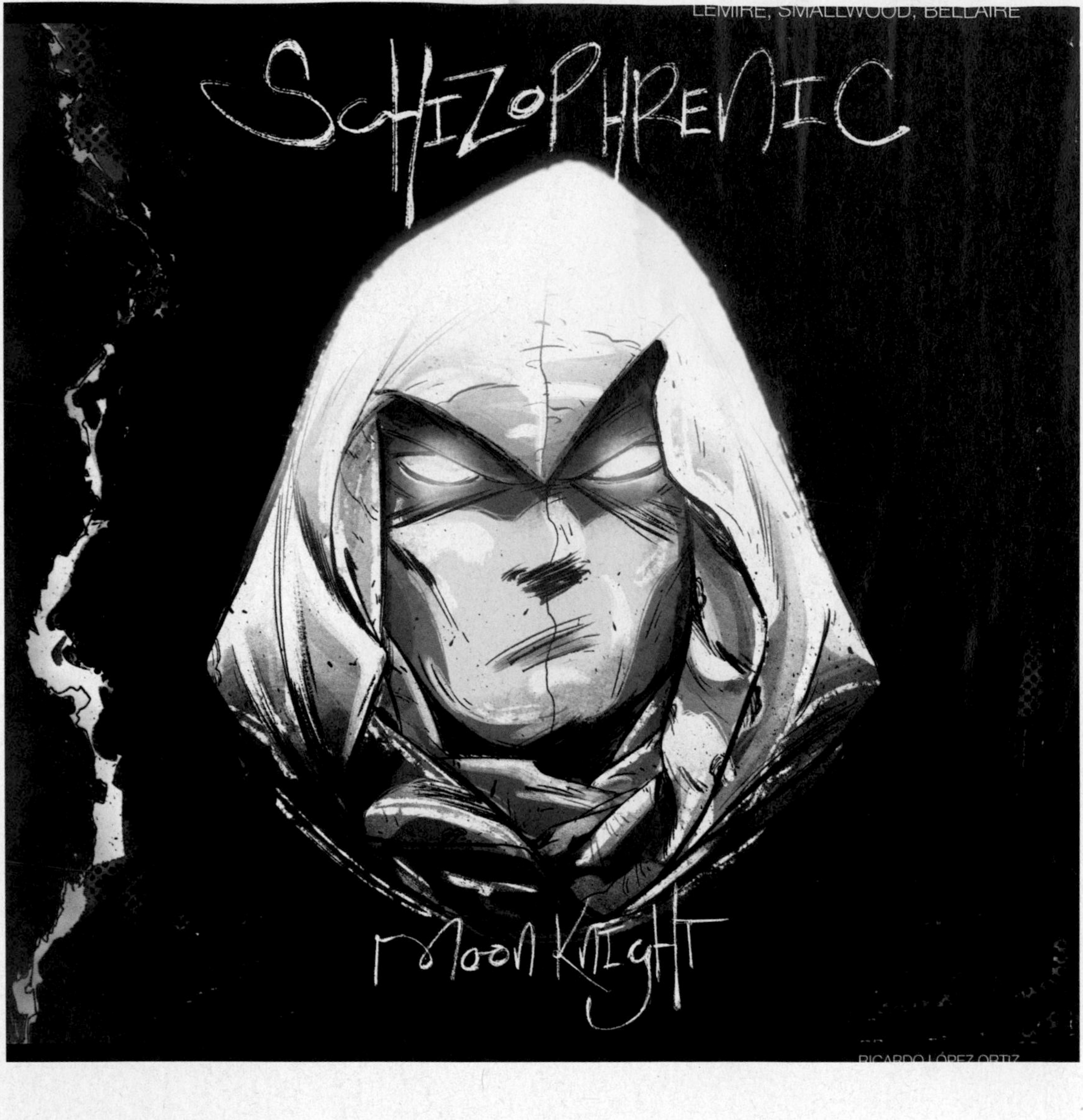
LEMIRE, SMALLWOOD, BELLAIRE
SCHIZOPHRENIC
MOON KNIGHT
RICARDO LÓPEZ ORTIZ

#1 HIP-HOP VARIANT BY RICARDO LÓPEZ ORTIZ

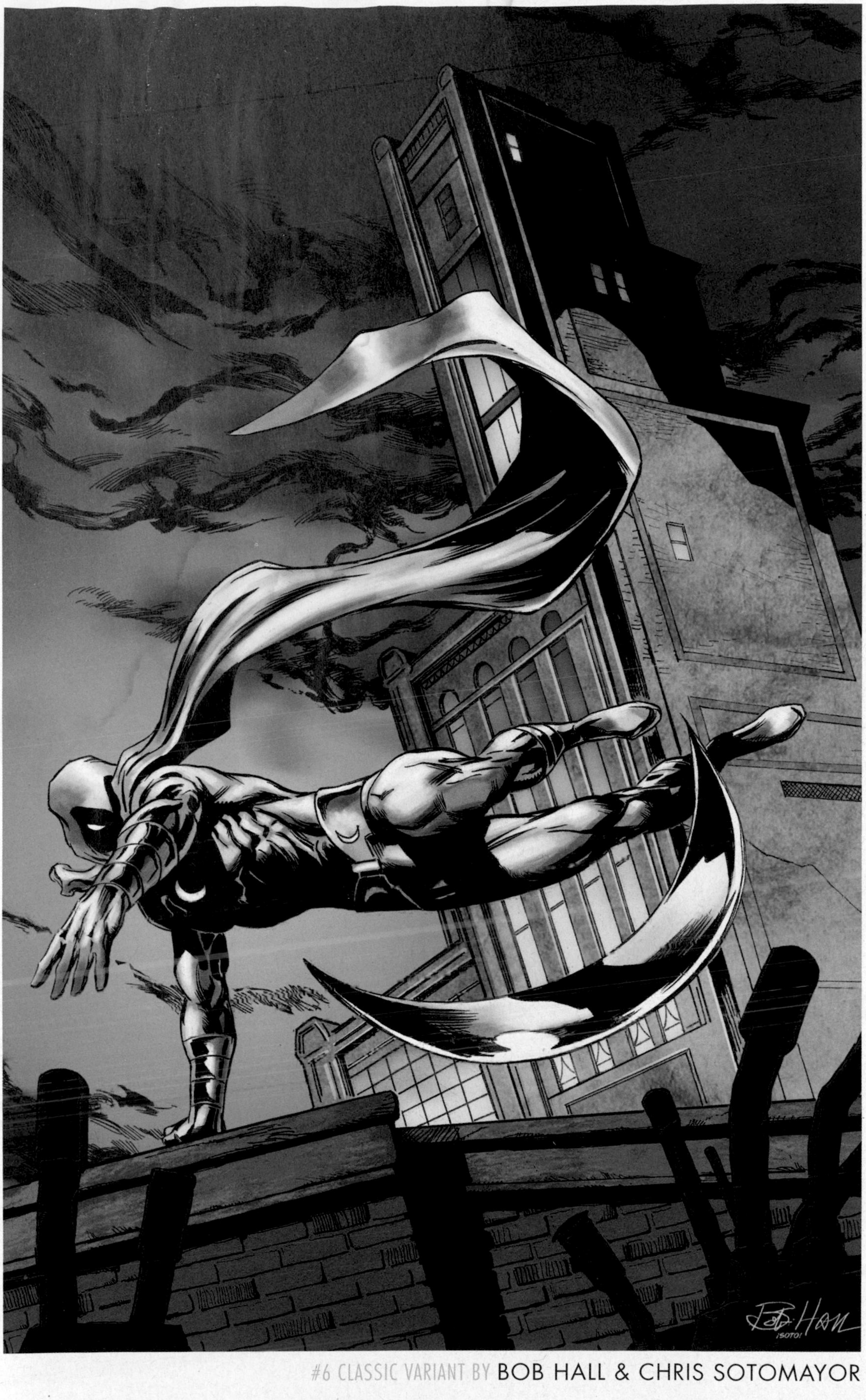

#6 CLASSIC VARIANT BY BOB HALL & CHRIS SOTOMAYOR

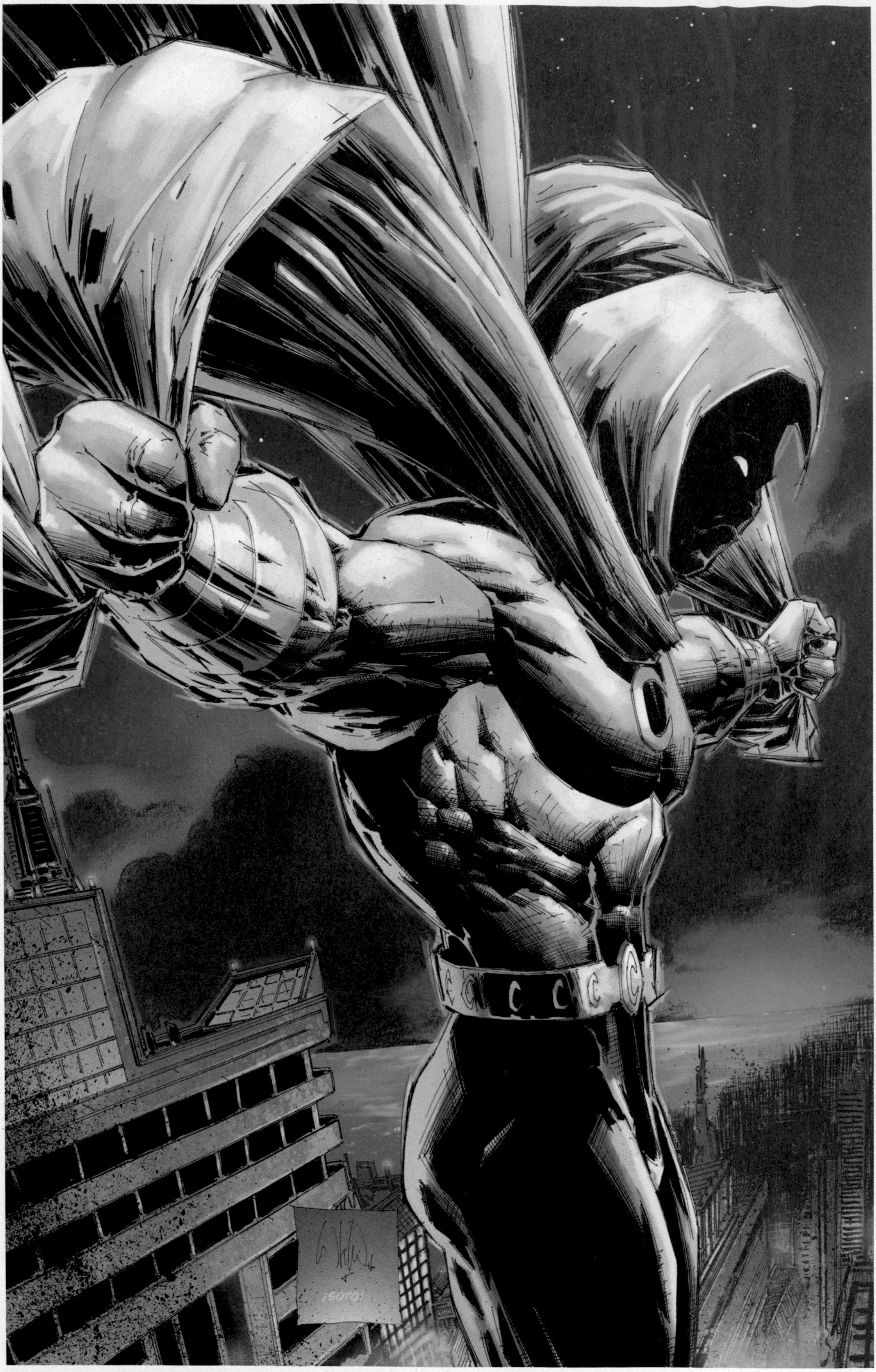

#10 VARIANT BY WHILCE PORTACIO & CHRIS SOTOMAYOR

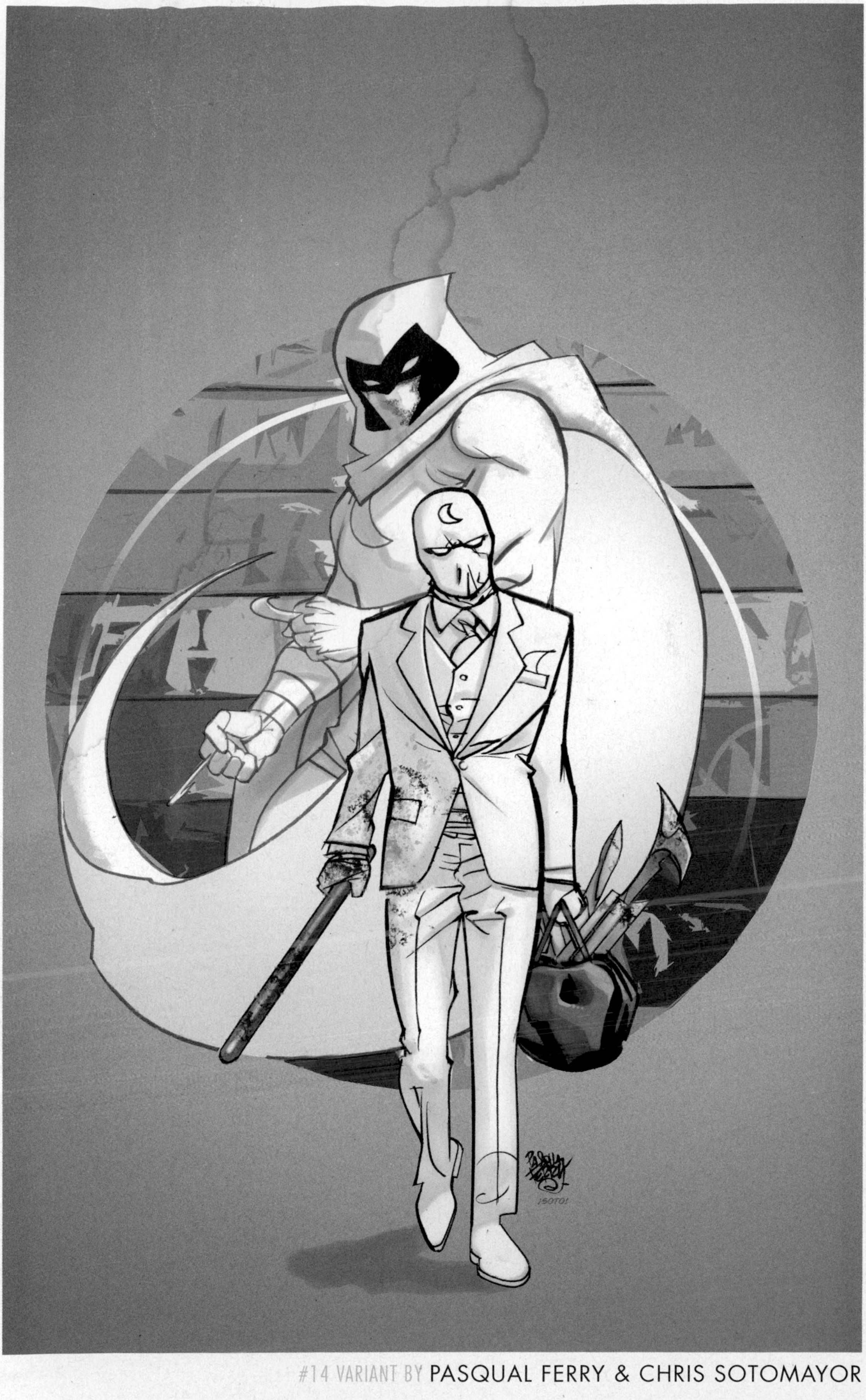

!SOTO!

#14 VARIANT BY PASQUAL FERRY & CHRIS SOTOMAYOR